Natural Science
in Western History

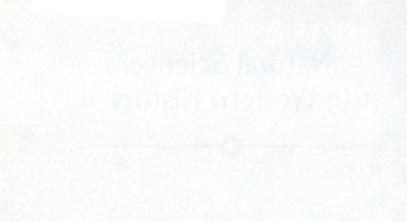

Natural Science in Western History

Frederick Gregory
UNIVERSITY OF FLORIDA

HOUGHTON MIFFLIN COMPANY   Boston   New York

Publisher: Suzanne Jeans
Senior Sponsoring Editor: Nancy Blaine
Senior Marketing Manager: Katherine Bates
Senior Development Editor: Lisa Kalner Williams
Senior Project Editor: Christina Horn
Art and Design Manager: Jill Haber
Cover Design Manager: Anne S. Katzeff
Senior Photo Editor: Jennifer Meyer Dare
Composition Buyer: Chuck Dutton
New Title Project Manager: Susan Peltier
Editorial Associate: Adrienne Zicht
Marketing Assistant: Lauren Bussard
Editorial Assistant: Carrie Parker

Cover image: Sir Isaac Newton dispersing sunlight through a prism, colored engraving. © The Granger Collection.

Printed in the U.S.A.

Library of Congress Control Number: 2007933468

ISBN-13: 978-0-618-22410-4
ISBN-10: 0-618-22410-6

23456789-VHO-11 10 09 08

◎

*for Kalée and Laura
and their wonderful families*

Brief Contents

Contents

————◎————

Preface

———◎———

Historians of science face the same challenges that confront any author who attempts to render an account of former times. As historians, we do our best to represent past events and achievements in the way that people experienced them rather than as we might imagine them. In the ancient world, for example, there was no such thing as "science" in anything like the twenty-first century meaning of the word. Although today we distinguish science from technology and science from religion, no clean separation of these endeavors existed in antiquity. To use present-day conceptions of natural science and other disciplines in our treatment of the past would surely distort the motivations, goals, and the practices of earlier peoples.

Having said that, we should not imagine that we can put ourselves wholly into the shoes of Babylonians or Greeks who lived so long ago, or even, for that matter, of those who lived in the last century. Try as we might not to bring the perspective of our own times to our investigation of the past, we will unwittingly smuggle some assumptions and perspectives of the culture in which we live into our portrait. When early in the twentieth century George Sarton, the founder of the discipline of history of science in the United States, chose the Egyptian goddess Isis to represent the challenge humans have faced in trying to discover how nature works, he did so because Isis said of herself that she was everything that ever existed and that "no mortal had ever disclosed her robe." His choice of Isis to stand for natural science was consistent with a long-standing Western tradition that has regarded nature as female and natural science as the process of uncovering her secrets. It reveals, as historian of science Carolyn Merchant has made clear, that our modern understanding of how to represent not only the ancient world, but also that of natural science itself, has been subtly informed by the sexual culture of the West.

How are we to handle a situation in which what we strive to do—to represent the past as it was experienced by those who lived it—must be acknowledged as impossible from the start? The first answer is that we should not conclude that nothing from the past is accessible to us. Just because we cannot give a completely unbiased account does not mean that we cannot do a reasonably decent job of representing the past on its own terms. In any event, borrowing from a common wish of the scientist to find the truth of nature, I adopt here the following procedure as an operating principle: I will aim at reaching the truth, even though I acknowledge that I cannot hope to achieve it. In claiming this maxim I shall not hesitate to make judgments about historical evidence at the same time that I register my hope to remain sensitive to my own fallibility.

All this means that what follows is a personal interpretation of the history of science that reflects the interests, abilities, and biases of the author. The title itself, *Natural Science in Western History*, already announces that it does not include developments in the East, nor does it include technology or the social sciences. As necessary and important as these subjects are, they exceed the scope of this endeavor. Every reader will no doubt discover that a topic he or she considers essential is not mentioned, while other matters regarded as spurious receive too much attention. Further, readers will have preferences that vary with the choices found here about how much the focus should be on the practice of science and on its social and cultural context as opposed to the scientific ideas themselves.

Undertaking a history of science textbook from antiquity to the present is a daunting task indeed. My introduction to the idea occurred in the 1980s, when the Department of History at the University of Florida sponsored a workshop that brought to Gainesville five historians of science—David Lindberg of the University of Wisconsin, William Ashworth of the Linda Hall Library in Kansas City, Sharon Kingsland of Johns Hopkins University, Thomas Hankins of the University of Washington, and the late Frederic Holms of Yale University—to explore the prospect of taking on such a project. That effort bore one important concrete product: David Lindberg's wonderful text on ancient and medieval science, an invaluable resource on which I have relied in this survey. Although Lindberg fulfilled his part of the projected whole, none of the rest of us did, and the collective endeavor foundered. David continued, however, to encourage me, even to the point of reading an early draft of the first chapter I attempted, on Newton. I owe him much.

Five or six years ago Nancy Blaine of Houghton Mifflin, who was visiting the University of Florida, asked during a conversation in my office why history of science was lacking a recent textbook. When I mentioned my previous flirtation with the idea of writing such a work, she persuaded me to submit a proposal. What interested her was my characterization of the type of text I would write, one that at the time was different from works in the field and one that, I am pleased to say, remains different from the textbooks that have since appeared. My text would be aimed at the average undergraduate and would attempt to do for history of science what U.S. history and Western Civilization texts have done for their respective fields. Having taught Western Civ for many years myself, I knew the value of an essentially chronological narrative of the subject matter, grouped under headings and subheadings, whose language and style were specifically designed to be accessible to university students. And so I began.

Acknowledgments

When a project lasts over several years, the number of people to thank increases rapidly. Locally, the Department of History has understood that a textbook project also serves the larger profession, as has the College of Liberal Arts and Sciences at the University of Florida. I have already made clear the great debt owed to Nancy Blaine of Houghton Mifflin. Not only did she provide the impetus to begin but she has also remained involved, always with words of encouragement and helpful advice. Numerous editors in various capacities at Houghton Mifflin have played constructive roles, including Stan Yarbro, Julie Swasey, Katie White, Adrienne Zicht, Christina Horn, Marilyn Rothenberger, Peggy Flanagan, and Bruce Carson.

To the many referees of the chapters, although unknown to me but listed by the publisher below, I owe a great deal. They have corrected errors and offered critiques on every aspect of the work. Many times I have heeded their advice, and at other times I have disagreed with their suggestions, but always I have appreciated and respected their views. The following individuals served as reviewers of the manuscript: David Boersema, Pacific University; Dan Burton, University of North Alabama; Jack Holl, Kansas State University; Florence Hsia, University of Wisconsin–Madison; Bruce Hunt, University of Texas; Michel Janssen, University of Minnesota; John Kemp, Truckee Meadows Community College; Dr. William C. Kimler, North Carolina State University; Kristie Macrakis, Michigan State University; Elizabeth Green Mussleman, Southwestern University (Texas); Timothy Moy, University of New Mexico; Warren Neal, Oklahoma City Community College; Anna Marie Roos, University of Minnesota; Andrea Rusnock, University of Rhode Island; David Sepkoski, Oberlin College; Warren Van Egmond, Arizona State University; Alice Walters, University of Massachusetts, Lowell; and G. J. Weisel, Penn State Altoona.

This project has demanded much more from my wife Patricia than does my regular scholarly research. Not only was it demanding and all consuming of my time and attention over a very long time, but it also produced far more frustration than does usual archival work. Organizing the material was by far the greatest challenge, eliciting constant complaints. I finally realized how this was impacting Tricia when she said to me one day, "You can only say how hard it is to organize your material *two more times,* so choose them wisely." As always, however, she has been there for me, ready to put things into perspective by taking me dancing.

Gainesville, Florida
July 2007

CHAPTER 1

———————◎———————

The Ancient Western Heritage

In the world of the ancient Near East there was no such thing as natural science as we understand it today, in the twenty-first century. The early civilizations of Egypt and Mesopotamia did, however, attempt to make sense of nature. They achieved a coherence in their understanding of nature through the development of a tradition of myths, and sometimes with the help of mathematical calculation. Natural processes, as we shall see, were directly linked to the presence of gods.

In ancient Greece, prior to the time of Plato, depictions of the natural world also revolved around the activities of divine beings. Then, at the end of the sixth century B.C., a distinctly Greek approach that emphasized the world's *rational* structure made its appearance. Scholars have referred to the unique perspective on nature that began to emerge in the Ionian region at this time as the Greek miracle. This ancient Ionian view of nature contained aspects that contrasted with the more personal understandings of the natural world that had been dominant previously in the West.

Two thinkers from ancient Greece whose ideas proved to be crucial for the development of systematic depictions of the natural world were the philosophers Plato (ca. 427–ca. 347 B.C.) and Aristotle (384–322 B.C.). As we shall see, they were responsible for defining fundamental issues that would occupy thinkers for centuries to come.

◎ Nature in Ancient Civilizations ◎

The Near East

In what one scholar has identified as a mythopoeic view of nature, ancient peoples of Egypt and Mesopotamia viewed nature itself as an expression of deities, and natural processes as the direct actions of these gods. For example, ancient Egyptians invoked the sky goddess, Nut, to account for the appearance of the heavens. As she

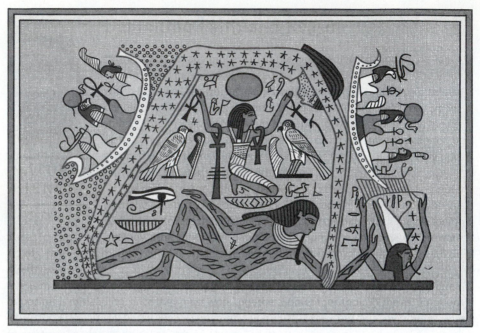

The Sky Goddess, Nut

bent over the Earth, touching it with her toes and fingers, her body was speckled with the stars. She was also the mother of the sun, which she swallowed every evening and gave birth to again each morning.

These mythological descriptions of nature did not prevent the Egyptians from devising means by which to use their knowledge of the movements of the heavens for religious, agricultural, and calendrical purposes. They marked the end of night, for example, not only by Nut giving birth to the sun, but also by the appearance of a pattern among the many stars that rose just before sunrise and marked where the sun would come up.

Over time they noticed, however, that the star pattern was appearing more and more in advance of the sun, so that after ten days it was rising in total darkness and a different pattern had to be chosen to mark the last hour of the night. As the process repeated, additional marker patterns were visible above the horizon in the darkness just before sunrise. They accumulated within a band, later called the band of the zodiac, which ran across the sky at the angle that the sun itself traversed once it rose and traveled across the sky.

The effect of these motions was that the sun, in lagging behind the stars, appeared to move through an entire series of marker patterns. (They were also aware that the moon lagged behind the stars, at a much greater rate than did the sun.) After using thirty-six different patterns, each lasting ten days, to denote the end of night, the Egyptians observed that the thirty-seventh served for only five days before the first pattern reappeared and began the series all over again. This clearly meant that a cycle of some sort was traversed in $(10 \times 36) + 5 = 365$ days. On the Egyptian calendar, which was established well before the Middle Kingdom (2040–1640 B.C.), the year took 360 plus 5 extra so-called epagomenal days that were observed at the end.

The Egyptians grouped three of the marker patterns together to form a month, so their year was twelve months plus five epagomenal days. We might expect that they would have divided the day and night into eighteen divisions each since it took thirty-six star patterns to go all around the sky. But they divided them unevenly into twenty-four periods—the night into twelve and the day into ten, with two more periods for the twilight of morning and evening. This meant that periods themselves lasted longer or shorter, depending on the seasonal fluctuation in the amount of daylight time. The Greeks later took over this division of the day-night cycle into twenty-four hours, making all the hours of equal length.

The ancient Babylonians devised a sexagesimal number system. Unlike the decimal system, which is based on 10, the Babylonians used 60 as a base. By repeating and spacing numerals, designated by a wedge-shaped mark, they were able to express very large numbers. Thus ▼▼▼ was 3, while ▼ ▼▼▼ was 63 $(1 \times 60 + 3)$ and, similarly, ▼ ▼ ▼▼▼ was 3663 $(1 \times 60^2 + 1 \times 60 + 3)$. From ancient tablets it is also clear that the Babylonians expressed fractions. To do this the spacings were interpreted from the context to indicate *division* by powers of 60 moving to the right instead of multiples of powers of 60 moving to the left. Hence, depending on the context, ▼ ▼▼▼ could also mean 63/3600 $(1/60 + 3/60^2)$. There are even tablets that indicate solutions to complex mathematical problems; for example, on one tablet the side of a square is determined through a series of steps that are equivalent to the solution of a quadratic equation.

By 400 B.C. the Babylonian astronomers were using twelve of their own marker patterns of stars to mark off the year. Each constellation took up 30° of the total of 360° that ran completely around the zodiac. Babylonian priests carefully prepared charts that recorded a great deal of astronomical data. They noted when eclipses occurred and they noted the positions of the sun and the moon in the zodiac over the course of the year. Within this huge amount of data they identified repeating numerical patterns that enabled them to predict important celestial events, such as the appearance of the new moon or even a lunar eclipse.

The priests also observed that the sun and moon were not the only objects in the zodiacal band that moved against the background of the remaining stars from night to night. There were five other stars that exhibited their own proper motion, although the motion was not confined to the "lagging behind" kind of motion the sun and moon underwent. These five stars—which we know as the planets Mercury, Venus, Mars, Jupiter, and Saturn—displayed various motions, sometimes lagging behind the rest of the stars and sometimes turning around and moving ahead of them. Not surprisingly, the priests associated these wandering stars with the gods, whose actions were responsible for these unusual motions.

Early Greek Conceptions of the Natural World

Some of these Egyptian and Babylonian conceptions made their way to the Greek world, which by the fifth century B.C. comprised the territory surrounding the Aegean Sea. The Greeks possessed their own rich mythology to explain the natural world. The sun's journey across the sky, for example, was due to the god Apollo, who daily rode his chariot across the sky. The Greek writers Homer and Hesiod had described the life of the gods in considerable detail by the end of the eighth century B.C. and the mythology they articulated continued to flourish for centuries.

The advent of Greek philosophy. In the sixth century, however, a new mode of thought, Greek philosophy, appeared alongside and sometimes mingled with these mythological accounts. The most distinguishing feature of this philosophy was that it explained natural phenomena not through a direct appeal to the actions of the gods, but as the course of nature itself. The philosophers lessened the role of personal agency in their explanations and increased the role of impersonal agency. For Anaximander, a philosopher who flourished during the mid-sixth century B.C. in the city of Miletus on the west coast of present-day Turkey, thunder and lightning had nothing to do with Zeus and his thunderbolts; rather, they were caused by wind breaking out of clouds.

Other thinkers from Miletus also removed personal agency from the explanations of nature and natural process. These early Milesians of the sixth century embraced the central conviction that the cosmos followed regular and necessary patterns of behavior, that it was not chaotic, that human existence was part of the natural world order. They went further. They were convinced that they could use their own powers of reason to uncover these patterns.

The Milesians asked new questions. They wanted to know what things were made of, how they moved or otherwise changed over time, why they had the shape and weight they did, and why they were located where they were. One of the most basic questions that sparked their curiosity had to do with the basic stuff from which everything else was made. Various Milesians answered this question with different substances. Thales, one of the earliest, said water was the basic stuff of things, while later in the century Anaximines said it was air. At the beginning of the fifth century B.C., Heraclitus, from nearby Ephesus, identified nature's most basic constituent as fire.

In posing the question about the basic stuff from which everything else was made, these early Greek philosophers introduced a crucial assumption that would continue to mark the Western tradition from this time forward. Behind the question lay the supposition that the diversity found in nature derived from a fundamental unity. If this was so, then it was possible to give reasons for this diversity in terms of the underlying unity. It was possible, in other words, to explain nature rationally.

Pythagoras and his followers. Another important Greek figure from the late sixth and early fifth centuries B.C. was Pythagoras, who is familiar to us from the famous mathematical theorem attributed to him. Much about the man is shrouded in mythology. According to various ancient sources he traveled to Egypt and then to Babylonia, where he became familiar with new mathematical techniques. On his return he set up a religious community among Greek colonists in southern Italy. Here, it is said, the group lived together communally and developed its own religious ritual practices of not eating meat or fish and not wearing wool or leather. The group also cultivated religious secrecy, especially about the propositions they uncovered in their mathematical school.

Pythagoras and his followers shared with the other late-sixth-century philosophers the need for a unified explanation of our experience of the senses, but they chose as their unifying entity not a material substance like water or air, but an abstract entity—*number*. An important illustration of what they meant by asserting that things were made of number was their investigation of the numerical ratios that corresponded to the harmonious pitches of musical tones. A string vibrates to produce a musical sound, as in a lyre. Shortening the vibrating portion of the string to half its length changes the pitch by an octave. Shortening it to a third, two-thirds, or three-fourths produces other pleasant harmonies.

Numerical relationships can present us with fascinating properties, some of them even bewildering. As the Pythagoreans uncovered new relationships, they invested them with greater and greater importance. That is, they became convinced that the mysterious relationships they uncovered were of divine origin. This belief separated them from other early Greek thinkers, who had completely removed divine agency from nature. The Pythagoreans embraced a religious outlook that invested the foundation of reality with number as its most basic constituent part.

Mathematical relationships are among the most rational we know. Therefore, the Pythagorean conviction that number governed nature meant that nature was describable in mathematical terms, which is to say that nature was rational. In other words, the Pythagoreans reinforced the new Greek assumption that nature was rationally explainable. They also demonstrated one manner in which strong religious belief and a firm commitment to rational explanation could go hand in hand.

When the Pythagoreans uncovered a mathematical relationship that was not rational, it challenged the very basis of their religion. From the famous theorem about the sides of a right triangle, they knew that the square built on the hypotenuse was equal in area to the sum of the squares erected on the other two sides. That led them to consider the case of an isosceles right triangle with sides equal to one unit of length. What is the length of the hypotenuse? They assumed that the answer to this question could be found, since reality was rational; that is, they assumed that they could find the common measure between the hypotenuse and one of the sides so that they could express both lengths as certain multiples of this common measure.

But, because they examined the question logically, they became convinced that there was no unit small enough that could measure the hypotenuse as an integral number of multiples of itself and at the same time measure a side with a different integral number of multiples of itself. The ratio of the side to the hypotenuse, in other words, could not be expressed as a ratio of integral numbers p/q where p and q had no common factors.

On realizing that there were some magnitudes that were not commensurate with each other it appeared to the Pythagoreans that they had discovered an instance where the world did not conform to number. Here reality was being *a logikos,* not rational. In today's mathematics the numbers assigned to such magnitudes are known as irrational numbers. In the previously mentioned triangle the irrational length of the hypotenuse is $\sqrt{2}$. But if there were such irrationalities, then perhaps even reality could not be guaranteed to be rational and to make sense.

This conclusion directly challenged the conviction of the early Greek philosophers that nature was in fact rational. If reality was ultimately chaotic, then what was the purpose of trying to explain it? Various legends cropped up about the dire consequences that followed for those who disclosed the knowledge that the hypotenuse bore an irrational ratio to the side of a right triangle.

◎ The Cosmos of Plato and Aristotle ◎

The capacity of reason to produce a contradiction was instrumental in the well-known paradoxes of the philosopher Zeno, who flourished during the middle of the fifth century B.C. Zeno was convinced that reason could be trusted, so much so that he was willing to discard obvious conclusions of experience when they differed from what reason said must be true. For example, our experience certainly tells us that things change, but Zeno trusted reason over experience and used it to argue that change was impossible.

Zeno set out to prove that change was an illusion of surface reality that we accept from our sense experience. That experience, however, does not draw directly on the basic unchanging reality accessible to reason. By using our reason we can convince ourselves that change is impossible, even the change of place so obvious to us in the experience of motion. Zeno's approach was to make an assumption based on experience, then to use reason to challenge the conclusions of experience. That, he felt, exposed the assumption of sense experience as erroneous.

Consider Achilles, who is pursuing a tortoise. We assume from observational experience that, because change of place is possible, Achilles will easily overtake the slow-moving tortoise. But the analysis of reason shows that this cannot be the case. In order for Achilles to catch the tortoise, he must first go to the point where the tortoise was when the pursuit commenced. But in that time the tortoise will have moved ahead. Now Achilles must go to the point where the tortoise is now. But when he reaches that point the tortoise will no longer be there either. It will always be so. The tortoise will always be ahead of Achilles, even if the distances between them keep shrinking. Rational analysis has shown the assumption that Achilles will pass the tortoise to be wrong. Since that assumption is based on the possibility of change, change has been shown to be impossible.

The development of Greek thought broadened in the fourth century B.C. to include a diversity of concerns, including political and ethical philosophy. The works of two men, Plato and Aristotle, proved to be exceptionally influential on

Western thought, so much so that it has been said that all Westerners are born as either Platonists or Aristotelians.

Plato and the Knowledge of the Cosmos

Plato was born in 427 B.C. in Athens, where he lived until after the turn of the fourth century. He then traveled to Italy, where he is reputed to have learned from the Pythagoreans there. Once back in Athens he established a school, which became known as the Academy. Here students could study and learn from the master himself.

The question of fundamental reality. Plato agreed with predecessors such as Zeno when they argued that our sense experience of the world did not put us directly in touch with the foundation that undergirds the reality of the world. But when he examined the objects of experience, he was struck by two things. First, they possessed similarities that permitted them to be placed into classes. Second, while objects like cups were all similar to each other, no two cups were *exactly* alike.

Plato believed that it was impossible to choose one material cup and say that it represented the reality of the class of cups, since to do so would ignore its differences from other cups. On the other hand, if he said that only individual cups were real, then he was ignoring the similarities that permitted them to be grouped into clearly identifiable classes.

Plato's solution to this problem was to declare that what was real was the *form* of cups—something we might call *cupness*. This was the basic reality underlying all individual cups, a reality in which they all participated and that they expressed in their own ways. What was true of cups was true of every other object of sense experience. Each object was an imperfect representation of the fundamental reality of the form in which it participated. So if we want to know fundamental reality, we must attempt to get to the forms—and not be content merely with the objects—of sense experience. Experience presents us with diversity and change, but the realm of the forms is eternal and changeless.

Reason is the tool that allows us to acquire knowledge of the forms. It alone enables us to recognize the sameness that all cups possess. Plato acknowledged that our experience of individual objects could assist reason in its task. But we must understand that what observation provides is not true knowledge. Observational knowledge derives from the realm of changing things, not that of eternal forms. In the last analysis, reason must operate on its own.

Plato's cosmogony. In a work entitled *Timaeus,* Plato set forth his cosmogony, that is, his account of the origin of the cosmos, the physical world known to the senses. He explained why even the world we experience was susceptible to rational explanation. He first made clear that the cosmos was not part of the eternal realm—it had not always existed, as did the eternal forms of reality. The cosmos had been created by an artificer, a divine workman.

Plato went on to say that when this divine workman created the world he looked to that which was eternal. At first the visible world was not at rest, but moved in an irregular and disorderly fashion. So the workman brought order out of disorder. Because the artificer was good, he framed the world "in the likeness of that which is apprehended by reason and mind and is unchangeable." The order undergirding the physical world, then, was unchangeable, even if the physical world itself underwent change in accordance with this order.

So in one important respect Plato disagreed with his predecessors. They had removed personal agency from explanations of nature's operations, arguing that nature's operations were simply the way things were, the inevitable and necessary natural course of things. For them the world's rationality derived from the underlying unity that tied all change together.

But for Plato the world could not be devoid of consciousness. It had been made in the likeness of *mind* and as a result it bore the qualities of mind. Mind, for example, was the source of intention and purpose; hence the cosmos bore the marks of purposefulness. In fact, for Plato the cosmos possessed a soul, which animated the world and caused it to move. Note that Plato did not wish to attribute every individual event in the world to the purposes of individual gods, as in the mythological accounts. In fact, the workman who had created the cosmos was not a ruler over it. He could not alter the arrangement or interfere with it. Like anyone else, he had to live in accordance with the plan he had imposed.

The structure of the cosmos.   Plato respected mathematical properties as expressions of divine reason, as had the Pythagoreans from whom he had learned. He therefore appealed to these properties when articulating the plan the divine workman had employed in creating the cosmos. He was aware, for example, that there were but five so-called regular solids, each of whose sides is an equilateral polygon. Plato associated four of these solids with the elements—earth, air, fire, and water— that had been identified by the philosopher Empedocles (ca. 492–ca. 432 B.C.) as the basic material constituents of the physical world. He associated the fifth regular solid with the overall cosmos.

Using this arrangement, Plato constructed a reasonable explanation for why and how elements combined to form the diverse substances we encounter in our experience of the world. For example, three of the five regular solids are made up of four, eight, and twenty equilateral triangles respectively. Plato could explain the formation of new substances by saying that triangles of the four elements were separated and recombined into new arrangements. Note that in this explanation substances are determined solely by the shapes that the combinations of triangles dictate. Thus, the nature we experience is determined by the properties of mathematics, and for Plato and his followers there was an expectation that descriptions of nature would utilize mathematics.

In Plato's description of the heavens the role of mathematics became very obvious. The outermost boundary of his cosmos—into which were fixed the myriad of stars of the heavens—was spherical. It turned around the central Earth, also a sphere, once every twenty-four hours, imparting to all heavenly bodies a twenty-four-hour, or diurnal, motion. In the *Timaeus,* Plato noted the existence of the seven stars that wandered against the background of the rest of the stars, each exhibiting its own so-called proper motion. Each wanderer, or "planetes," had a designated location, beginning with the moon and sun, which were closest to the Earth. He envisioned the planets as spherical and was aware that their proper motions occurred within the band of the zodiac, which was inclined at an angle to the axis of rotation of the celestial sphere.

Plato knew that each planet underwent its own kind of proper motion against the background of the stars. Some of these motions were quite complicated, involving changes of direction and speed. He also knew that these various motions could not be chaotic and unpredictable. If the heavens were rationally ordered, as he believed, then the planets had to be following a regular pattern of some sort. But which one? And how was it to be described?

It made sense to Plato and those who came after him that the accelerations some of the planets exhibited were apparent and not actual. Mars, for example, sometimes appeared to slow and reverse direction from night to night, only to soon resume its first direction. How to explain what was going on? To admit that Mars actually decelerated and accelerated seemed to Plato and the Greek astronomers to introduce a chaotic element into the heavens, something that ran completely against their philosophical assumptions. But if these motions were the resultant sum of individual uniform motions acting simultaneously, then the chaos of accelerated heavenly movements could be captured as a combination of these regular uniform motions.

According to historical tradition, Plato challenged the students of his academy to discover what combinations of regular uniform motions would result in the paths the planets were observed to follow. In coming up with solutions the students understood that they had to employ perfectly circular figures, the most rational of geometrical shapes. These two requirements—the use of circular paths for planets moving at uniform speeds—satisfied for them the conditions necessary to preserve nature's rationality. But could the right combination of circles be found that would result in the motions the planets were observed to undergo?

A student of Plato, Eudoxus of Cnidos (ca. 400–ca. 430 B.C.), offered the first solution to Plato's challenge. He assumed that the Earth was at the center of the cosmos and that the sphere of the stars lay at its outer extremity. This sphere, into which the stars were fixed, turned around the central Earth once every twenty-four hours and accounted for the observed daily motion of the heavens. To account for the motion of the planets Eudoxus created a set of interconnected spheres for each one, with the planet itself fixed onto the innermost sphere. For the sun and moon he used three spheres each, and for each of the remaining planets he employed four spheres. Including the sphere of the fixed stars, this amounted to a grand total of twenty-seven spheres.

Take for example the spheres used to explain the motion of the sun. The outermost of the three spheres rotated in a synchronized way with the sphere of the fixed stars and drove the other two in its wake. This outer sphere, then, explained why the sun shared the daily trip the stars took across the sky. The axes of rotation of the inner two spheres were positioned at the proper angles and rotated uniformly at the proper speeds so that, when combined with the motion of the first sphere, they permitted the sun to lag behind the stars along the zodiacal band as it was observed from Earth to do over the course of a year. Needless to say, Eudoxus was an excellent geometer to be able to combine the motions of the spheres in just the right way to obtain the desired resultant sum of the motions of the sun and the other planets as seen from Earth.

Aristotle's Worldview

One of the students who came to Athens to study with Plato was a young man of seventeen from Macedonia, a region that lay north of the Greek city-states. Aristotle (384–322 B.C.) became Plato's most famous pupil. He enjoyed an illustrious career, remaining with Plato for two decades before embarking on a period of travel and study after the master died. When his travels were over he came back to his native Macedonia, where he became tutor to the young Alexander, soon to become the great conqueror of foreign lands. He later established a school in Athens, where he spent most of his remaining days.

Aristotle's contrast to Plato.   It becomes clear that Aristotle had an independent mind when we examine how he differed from his teacher regarding the knowledge of nature. Plato influenced the development of Western natural science through his emphasis on the theoretical—the ideal order undergirding the natural world and the use of mathematics to describe it. Aristotle's contribution was different. He began with the individual existence of things and worked his way from the specific to the general.

Not surprisingly, Aristotle did not agree that Plato's eternal forms were somehow more real than the material world and existed apart from it. He refused to permit the separation of a sensible object's form from the substance of which it was made. For Aristotle, form and matter came together to constitute an object of sense. The iron in an iron ball supplied the matter, whereas the heaviness, spherical shape, hardness, and dark color were all attributes of form that gave the piece of iron its identity as a sensible object. Matter could not exist without form, nor could form exist without matter to serve as its subject.

Aristotle was no less convinced than his teacher that reality was ordered and could be rationally accounted for. But, except in certain areas that clearly lent themselves to mathematical representation (such as the mathematical description of the heavens), he did not want to begin at the level of the abstract. He preferred to begin with sense experience of actual things as they were and uncover from them whatever order there was to find. If Plato emphasized the theoretical approach to the investigation of nature, Aristotle represented its empirical side.

Aristotle agreed with Plato that the earliest Greek philosophers had erred when, in removing divine agency from their treatment of the cosmos, they ended up with a cosmos without purpose. But Aristotle's account of purpose in the cosmos was different from Plato's. Plato had traced the purpose that existed in the world to the mind of the divine workman. Aristotle located purpose in a thing's nature; that is, things change in a certain way because it is in their nature to do so. This explains why, for example, a baby grows or even why heavy objects fall. So, where natural objects are concerned, the cosmos is an inherently purposeful place, since all change comes about as the result of things acting according to their natures.

The world of living things. Aristotle paid more attention to the individual objects of sense experience than did Plato, so his interest in nature ranged much more widely than had that of his teacher. This was evident in Aristotle's investigation of the world of living things. Unlike many in his day, Aristotle did not think of the study of animals, for example, as repulsive. He wrote *The History of Animals,* in which he described hundreds of kinds of animals and even tried to group many into classes.

Aristotle's treatment of organisms, which drew on his understanding of the matter and form of natural things, greatly influenced those who came after him. While the matter of the body of organisms was obvious enough, the form, which involved the defining properties of a natural object, was very special in the case of living things. Aristotle appealed to the presence of *soul,* which he associated with the form of living organisms. For example, it was in the nature of things with soul to undergo reproduction and growth, activities that inanimate objects did not display.

Aristotle noted three kinds of soul, each one corresponding to a different type of organism: vegetable, animal, or human. Plants reproduced and grew because of their nutritive soul. Animals added to these activities the capacity to react to stimuli because of their sensitive soul. Humans had a rational soul, which added the capacity for reason. These distinctions would last well into the eighteenth century among physiologists struggling with the unique challenges of understanding living organisms.

Heaven versus Earth. Aristotle's treatment of the world of living things illustrates that he was an astute observer of the phenomena that he encountered on Earth. In the tradition of those who came before him, he also considered the heavens and what transpired there. But Aristotle insisted that the two realms, the terrestrial and the celestial, were qualitatively different places that should be kept separate. The dividing point between the two regions was the orbit of the moon. What occurred in the heavens had to be considered in isolation from the treatment of things below the moon.

The celestial realm for Aristotle was a place of perfection and eternity. What transpired there—for example, the movements of the stars and planets—followed eternally repeating patterns that never altered. As a result, nothing ever came to be or ceased to exist above the orb of the moon. To suggest that a new star could be born not only ran against what was observed, but it violated a principle that Aristotle had accepted from one of his early predecessors—the principle that something cannot come from nothing. This same principle was the basis for Aristotle's firm conviction that the cosmos itself could not have had a beginning. It must have always existed.

Because the heavens were completely different from the Earth, they were not made of the matter that was found on Earth. The matter constituting heavenly bodies did not consist of earth, air, fire, and water, but of a fifth kind of matter, a quintessence, found only in the celestial region. It did not make sense to Aristotle that there could be places where there was no matter at all, either in the heavens or on Earth.

Just as it was natural for the heavens to be as they were, so too was it with the region below the moon. Here, as we know well from experience, things do vary. This is the realm of change, the place of generation and corruption, where things come to be and go out of existence. Unlike the heavens, which exuded qualities of the divine, the terrestrial realm was anything but eternal and godlike.

When Aristotle examined the factors that gave rise to change he spoke of different kinds of causes that were necessary for change to occur. Each individual cause had to be present before change could take place, and knowing the individual causes was to understand why change occurred. From our discussion of both form and matter we can appreciate why he singled them out as two of the causes of change. For something to change it must take on new form, hence there was what Aristotle knew of as a *formal* cause of change. Since matter and form must exist together, the substance involved served as the *material* cause.

Aristotle noted two additional causes necessary for change. What he identified as the *efficient* cause was closest to what we consider a cause—the action that brought about the change. Finally, recall that Aristotle's cosmos was a very purposeful place. Natural purposes came from the nature of individual things. But agents, who supplied the actions that produced change, also acted with purpose. Whatever the source of the purpose, Aristotle regarded the end or goal of the change as its *final* cause.

We can illustrate the operation of the causes that produced change with the occurrence of a rain shower. The formal cause of the rain is the shape of the drops that water, the material cause, assumes. The efficient cause is the cooling of the warm air that has risen, which becomes water that falls as rain. The final cause here is the function rain serves to irrigate land so that things can grow. In the case of an artificially produced change, say the building of a birdhouse, the formal cause would be the shape of the house, the material cause the wood that takes on that shape, the efficient cause the person who constructs the house, and the final cause the builder's reason for making it—to give shelter to birds.

The constitution of natural objects.   Aristotle accepted the division of matter into four elements as set forth by Empedocles, but he did not regard these elements as the ultimate building blocks of natural objects. For that he chose qualities that we sense bodies to possess. Aristotle did not think of these qualities in the same way we might be tempted to. For example, it appears at first glance that he appealed to different degrees of temperature and moistness to explain the basis of the elements and different intensities of weight to determine where they naturally could be found. But when he spoke of hot versus cold, wet versus dry, and heavy versus light, he understood each member of a pair to be its own quality, the contrary quality of its opposite. It was not that something with the quality of coldness lacked heat. It had cold.

Each of the four elements resulted from a combination of the four qualities of cold, hot, wet, and dry. Cold combined with dry yielded earth; cold with wet gave water. Hot with wet produced air, and hot with dry resulted in fire. Nature, or for that matter humans, could alter existing combinations of the qualities to initiate transformations of one kind of matter into another. Take earth (cold and dry). If the dryness of earth could be displaced by wetness, earth could become water (cold and wet). This was what happened when a solid substance dissolved in a solution.

Aristotle, remember, did not think of hot and cold as degrees of one quality, temperature, but as individual qualities of their own. As such, however, these qualities *could* exist in various degrees. The great diversity of natural substances we observe in the terrestrial region resulted from various combinations of the four elements. The intensity of each individual quality making up an element also added to this diversity.

The qualities of heavy and light determined where a substance naturally was found. Consistent with his conception of the purposefulness of natural things, Aristotle believed that each natural object below the moon strove to be in its own place. This understanding is known as Aristotle's *doctrine of natural place*. It was the nature of objects with heaviness to strive toward the center of the cosmos, while those with lightness endeavored to recede from that center. Earth, the element with the greatest heaviness, displaced water, which possessed less heaviness. Likewise fire, with more lightness than air, displaced air as it receded from the center of the cosmos. Natural substances made of various combinations of elements assumed their location in the terrestrial realm according to the differing degrees of the fundamental qualities of heaviness or lightness they possessed.

How and why things move. From the preceding discussion we can understand one of the reasons why natural objects might move. If they were displaced for any reason from their natural place and not forcibly retained, they would endeavor to return to that natural place. Carry a rock to the edge of a cliff and throw it off. With only air to restrain it, the rock would fall toward the center of the cosmos, stopping only when it was hindered by the presence of a substance with greater heaviness.

It was an axiom of Aristotle's physics that "all motion requires a mover." That meant that no motion ever occurred by itself, without a mover to cause it. In the case of the rock falling from the cliff, the mover was the nature of the substance, which acted in concert with the external air. This doctrine provided one of the reasons why Aristotle and his many disciples believed that the Earth did not move. What could possibly be its mover? Another reason arose from the doctrine of natural place. The substance that made up the Earth—the element earth—strove to be at the center of the cosmos, where it naturally assembled in a stationary sphere.

What about the motion that did not result from substances moving toward their natural places? What of forced motion or the motion living things exhibited? Where in these circumstances was the mover Aristotle required?

In the case of living things that could initiate locomotion, the soul was the mover. In violent motion the application of force was necessary. This could happen naturally, when two things collided, or artificially, when a force was deliberately applied to move an object. When we throw a spear at an advancing enemy, our arm supplies the force that moves the spear. The action of the mover in this case is obvious.

But what mover is acting once the spear leaves our hand? The spear continues to move, but it is no longer in contact with a mover. In this case Aristotle claimed that the spear set up a current as it parted the air. This current of air rushed in behind the spear to communicate continuing motion to the spear. Of course this accounted only for the horizontal motion of the spear. It would also eventually fall to the ground as the result of its attempt to return to its natural place.

If this explanation of projectile motion was less than satisfactory, Aristotle's further analysis of how things moved was quite impressive. He concluded that there was a relationship between the speed of the motion produced and the force that was applied. In modern terminology the speed and force were directly proportional to each other; that is, the greater the force, the faster the speed produced. He also noted that there was an inverse relationship between the speed and any resistance that had to be overcome. Thus, the greater the resistance, the slower the speed. This beginning of a quantitative analysis of motion was impressive enough to serve as the basis for subsequent commentary until the time of Galileo, in the seventeenth century.

The structure of the heavens.   In his descriptions of the terrestrial realm Aristotle did not want to force the details and complexity of what he observed into the abstract relationships called for by mathematical description. To do so would, in his mind, have missed much of the richness of nature's intricacy. Aristotle felt that geometry lost much of its certainty when it was applied to the phenomena of the terrestrial region.

Where the heavens were concerned, however, Aristotle did not hesitate to utilize mathematical description. This was a territory of perfection, where the purity of abstract relationships demanded nothing less than the precision of mathematical expression. He considered the system of spheres put together by Eudoxus to account for the movements of the stars and planets and made an important correction to it. In so doing Aristotle demonstrated his sensitivity to the demands of reason.

Eudoxus utilized twenty-seven uniformly rotating spheres to answer Plato's challenge to find a rational explanation for what had to be the merely apparent confusion of planetary motions. By embedding a planet in the innermost sphere of the set assigned to it, and by connecting that sphere to others whose motion was communicated to the inner sphere, Eudoxus was able to explain why the planet underwent the unique motions that it did. Were we on the planet itself, we would experience only the uniform circular motion of the sphere in which it was embedded. But, as seen from the Earth, the planet appeared to move in an irregular pattern that was produced by the interconnected spheres.

Aristotle no doubt admired the solutions Eudoxus had come up with for the individual planets. But he then realized that there was something fundamentally wrong with them. As seen from the Earth, Eudoxus's system accounted for the motion of the nearest planet, the moon, well. But the motion of the next planet, the sun, would be affected by the moon's motion if the spheres were nested as Eudoxus asserted. Eudoxus treated each planet in isolation from the others, as if the motion of one planet would not be affected by the spheres of all of the other planets between it and the Earth.

Aristotle inserted a correction into the system to take care of the problem. He inserted new spheres for the moon just beyond the original set Eudoxus had created. These spheres undid what the three spheres had accomplished, so when the line of sight arrived at the sphere carrying the sun the distortion caused by the moon's spheres had been removed. He did the same beyond the sun and the other planets as well. In the end his system made use of over fifty spheres.

By insisting on this correction Aristotle revealed that he was concerned with a higher degree of rational explanation than his predecessors. He demanded that the depiction of the heavens be internally consistent. It was not enough to solve the mathematical challenge the complex motions of the planets raised. Aristotle took seriously the implication of using spheres. Their reality as objects in the heavens could not just be ignored. This is another example of the perceptibility of this remarkable Greek philosopher.

◎ The Greek Heritage in Natural ◎ Philosophy After Aristotle

The accomplishments represented by Plato and Aristotle set the tone in philosophy for years to come. The issues these great thinkers articulated continued to be debated for centuries; indeed, they are still discussed today. But as great as their philosophical achievement was, it did not go unchallenged in the intellectual world of the late fourth century B.C. A major rival emerged in the person of Epicurus (341–270 B.C.), who further developed the theme known as *atomism,* which had been introduced in the late fifth century B.C. According to Epicurus, everything in the world, including the gods, was made of atoms. As they moved through space, the atoms collided with each other in ways that accounted for all that happened. This was a deterministic system in which no divine mind or natural purposefulness existed. Everything that transpired resulted from purely mechanical interaction. By basing their explanation and understanding on mechanical causation, the atomists created an approach that would hold enormous appeal for many natural philosophers who came after them, including many today.

Epicurean atomism was not the only view of the time that opposed the idea of a purposeful cosmos as described by both Plato and Aristotle. But all who argued in favor of determinism faced the task of rendering a convincing account of the apparent purpose encountered in experience—for example, in the human capacity to exercise free will. In spite of this substantial challenge, atomism persisted. It remained viable among some in the ancient world and its revival much later in the early modern era would continue to serve as an alternative to Platonism and Aristotelianism.

The Continuing Development of Mathematics and Astronomy

Astronomy, as we have noted, was cultivated in ancient times in isolation from the world of change beneath the moon. Because it dealt with a realm of perfection, the heavens, it could be described by the abstract properties of mathematics. For this reason we should regard astronomy in this period and all the way to the early modern era as a branch of pure mathematics. Solving the problems of astronomy for Greek thinkers was a mathematical problem. In spite of Aristotle's concern with the disruption caused by interacting spheres, the physical constitution of the heavens played a less important role than their mathematical structure prior to the late sixteenth century.

There were some areas where mathematics was applied in the terrestrial realm, including optics and the law of the lever. The Greek mathematician Euclid (ca. 300 B.C.), author of the famous geometry book, *Elements,* also wrote a book entitled *Optics,* in which he used geometry to develop a theory of visual perspective. The most famous mathematician of the time, however, was Archimedes (ca. 287–212 B.C.)

Archimedes and the law of the lever.   Archimedes of Syracuse is best known for the legend that he exposed chicanery in the making of the king's crown by showing that the amount of water displaced by the crown was not the same as that displaced by an equal weight of gold. However improbable this event may be, Archimedes clearly was a man of genius. He is credited with numerous inventions and a wealth of mathematical insight. In his book *On the Equilibrium of Planes,* we can directly observe his application of mathematics to the lever.

Archimedes argued that geometrical symmetry can serve as the foundation for proving that when the weight times its distance from a fulcrum is equal on both sides of a fulcrum, a beam will be in equilibrium. He began by placing three equal weights on a beam, one directly over a fulcrum located at the middle of the beam, and the other two at the ends. Symmetry dictates that the beam will remain level. He then moved the weight that was above the fulcrum halfway to one end and compensated for this move by bringing the weight from that end to the same position. He now had a combined weight that was twice as heavy as the single weight at the other end, but located half as far from the fulcrum. Archimedes reasoned that these compensating moves left that side of the beam with the same capacity to balance the other side that it had before.

From this result Archimedes was able to generalize to the conclusion that equilibrium is achieved when force times distance to the fulcrum is equal on both sides of the fulcrum. Thus, a small force times a large distance can achieve the same effect as a large force over a small distance. It is possible, therefore, to move a very heavy object by placing a fulcrum close to it, inserting a lever over the fulcrum, and pushing down on the other end of the lever with a much smaller force. According to later testimony, Archimedes was reputed to have said: "Give me a place to stand and I will move the world."

Ptolemy's astronomy.   The greatest astronomer in the period after Aristotle was Claudius Ptolemy, whose contributions came in the second century A.D., some five hundred years after Aristotle's death. Ptolemy came from Alexandria in Northern Africa, although he had no relation to the Ptolemies who once ruled in Egypt.

When Ptolemy compiled his system of astronomy in a work later called the *Almagest,* he consulted and described the astronomical work done by those who had preceded him. He has thus become an important source of information about the work of some figures from between his time and that of Aristotle. Through him we have become acquainted with the new directions Greek astronomy was taking in the period before the birth of Christ. Ptolemy also added his own contribution to the solution of the main problem confronting the astronomer—how to devise a mathematical description of the movement of the heavens that best fit what careful observers saw happening there.

Ptolemy wrote, for example, about Apollonius of Perga, a Greek mathematician from the third century B.C. According to Ptolemy, Apollonius devised new mathematical techniques to describe planetary motion that improved the fit between what was described and what was observed. Even though observations were only as accurate as the naked eye permitted, astronomers became more and more demanding. They became less satisfied with the fit obtained using the techniques of interlocking homocentric spheres employed by Eudoxus and Aristotle. The new techniques Ptolemy described afforded much greater flexibility to the astronomer to adjust the mathematical depiction of the motion of the planets. One of these new techniques was the use of an eccentric point, a point positioned off-center.

The eccentric point permitted a ready depiction of the apparent slowing down and speeding up of a planet as it underwent its proper motion from night to night against the background of the stars. Consider the figure here, which shows the Earth (E) located at a vastly exaggerated eccentric position to the center (C) of the planet's orbit. As the planet travels in uniform motion around the circle, it will *appear* when viewed from Earth to go faster through the distance from A to B than through the longer distance from D to F. This is because an observer will note that the planet sweeps out angle AEB quicker than it does angle DEF (since the distance from A to B is less than that from D to F), even though the angles are the same size.

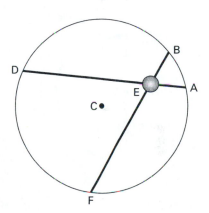

Eccentric Point

The introduction of another device, the epicycle (a circle on a circle), made greater sense of the apparent backward and forward movement over time of planets such as Mars. Here the assumption was that the planet (P) traveled uniformly around a smaller circle whose center (C) moved around the central Earth (E). The epicycle was a very flexible tool. It could be used to make minor adjustments in a planet's orbit, or to generate extremely complicated paths. Assume, for example, that in this figure the planet P moves uniformly around C faster than C moves around the Earth (E). Viewed from Earth, the speeds of P around C and C around E will add together when the planet is at P, giving the planet the appearance of an acceleration.

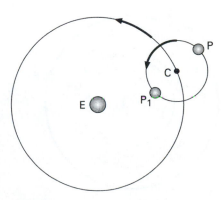

Epicycle

When the planet moves to the position P_1, however, its more rapid speed around C will dominate over the slower motion of C around E, so from Earth the planet will appear to be moving backward. Eudoxus had also been able to account for this retrograde motion of a planet, but the epicycle was a simpler explanation.

The epicycle was more useful than merely explaining the retrograde motion of planets. Depending on how big the epicycle was in comparison to the orbit of C around E, and depending on the relative speed assigned, extremely complicated paths could result. This provided the ancients with a tool of great flexibility when trying to simulate complex motions that were observed in the heavens.

From Ptolemy's viewpoint these devices had improved the fit, but they had not yet made it good enough. He wanted to do still better, so he introduced what would turn out to be a highly controversial new tool called the equant point. He employed this point in conjunction with the eccentric; that is, he located a second off-center point on the opposite side of the center from the first eccentric point, where the Earth was positioned. He then referred uniform motion around the circle to this second point, not to the center of the circle. This meant that as the planet traveled around the circle it passed through equal angles in equal amounts of time. However, the constant angular velocity was not referred to C, the center of the circle, but to the equant point. In this figure, for example, the planet passes through angle AQB in the same amount of time it takes to pass through angle AQF. But clearly it has farther to go from F to A than it does from A to B.

If it took the planet the same amount of time to go both distances, it must have been going faster from F to A than it was from A to B. This meant that its motion was no longer uniform throughout its path. By using an equant point, especially in combination with an eccentric point and epicycles, Ptolemy was able to improve the fit between the mathematical description of planetary motion and how the planets were observed to move.

More than others, Ptolemy did concern himself with how the physical constitution of the heavens might impact the theoretical explanations he had devised. He asked, for example, how the crystalline spheres in the heavens would have to be arranged in order to produce something like the epicycle. In this particular case he imagined a small sphere, in which the

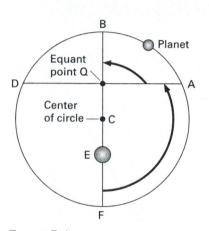

Equant Point

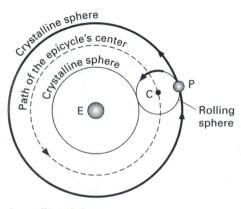

Crystalline Spheres

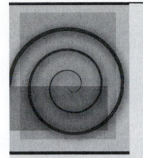

The NATURE of SCIENCE

The Problem with Ptolemy's Equant

Ptolemy's equant presented those who came after him with a dilemma that sometimes faces natural scientists today. By using the equant point he was able to depict and predict planetary motions more accurately. But is a new approach to a problem justified wholly by its usefulness? Is the natural philosopher free to choose *any* explanation as long as it enables him or her to give a more accurate rendering of observational data?

The problem for those who came after Ptolemy was that the equant implied that the planet actually accelerated and decelerated, and that ran directly against the Greek assumption that only uniform motion could exist in the heavens. Ptolemy, of course, could argue that he had retained uniform motion, that he had merely reinterpreted how it was to be understood. But, in the view of many who came later, permitting a planet to experience accelerated motion ruined the rationality of the explanation. To them, reinterpreting uniform motion to refer to the equant point was cheating.

In the sixteenth century one of the major motivations for Nicolaus Copernicus's new heliocentric system was to rid astronomy of the equant. He believed that the power driving the motion of the planets had to be constant. The prospect that it was fickle was one before which, he said, "the mind shudders." Actual acceleration might work better, but it eliminated the possibility of giving a rational explanation in the mind of Copernicus and those of his day. As we shall see in Chapter 5, Copernicus's greatest achievement was, in the eyes of the scholars of his time, to have removed the equant point from astronomy.

There are no easy answers to the questions posed here. The problem generated by Ptolemy's device has haunted natural philosophy throughout its history. On encountering a twentieth-century version of the challenge, a famous physicist once remarked that to grasp what nature is like we might have to change what we mean by *understanding*. To do that, however, is bound to generate opposition among those committed to a tried and true method. The investigation of nature, then, can present us with challenges that can lead to basic questions about what it is that we are actually doing.

planet was embedded, rolling around a channel between two larger crystalline spheres and carrying the planet with it as it went. As the outer large sphere rotated, its motion forced the small sphere to turn, generating the planet's proper motion and the epicyclic effect.

In spite of this attention to the physical spheres in the celestial realm, however, Ptolemy did not permit physical considerations to dictate or eliminate the mathematical descriptions. In the end he was content to have come up with a mathematical explanation that accurately depicted the motion of the planets. And this attitude persisted for centuries after him. While many variations of his system were created, consisting of different combinations of eccentrics, epicycles, and equant points, Ptolemy's basic approach lasted until the time of Galileo.

A Burgeoning Tradition in Medicine

The earliest Greek medicine shared a heritage similar to that of early Greek natural philosophy. Just as the first philosophers distinguished their explanations of nature from mythological understanding by removing divine agency from the world's operations, there were those who began to resist invoking the gods as the cause of individual disease. In both cases, however, the new tendency to appeal to natural process existed alongside a continuing tradition of mythology.

Medicine had its Pythagoras in the person of Hippocrates of Cos (ca. 450–370 B.C.), although he lived about a century later than the famous mathematician. Like Pythagoras, Hippocrates is a shadowy figure about whom we know very little. But— again like Pythagoras—his work gave rise to a group of like-minded followers and his name is widely known even today because of a development attributed to him, the famous Hippocratic oath. According to the original oath, medicine was to be practiced by those initiated into the holy mysteries, another similarity to the secrecy of the Pythagoreans.

For all that, there is a major difference between the Hippocratic writers and the Pythagoreans. While the latter incorporated the divine into their view of reality, the followers of Hippocrates presumed that bodily processes, health, and disease could be described as natural phenomena, without reference to arbitrary, supernatural involvement.

The authors of the Hippocratic writings commonly felt that health resulted from the proper balance among key bodily fluids, sometimes called humors. Initially three humors were identified: blood, phlegm, and bile. Disease resulted when the balance among the humors was disturbed as, for example, in winter, when the body excreted excess phlegm when sick with a cold. Excess bile was associated with summer vomiting, and too much blood was expelled in instances like nosebleeds or menstruation. The physician should imitate nature and remove excess blood to treat associated illnesses. Later physicians included a fourth humor—black bile (in contrast to bile, sometimes identified as yellow bile). Imbalance here produced melancholy.

The preferred treatment among the Hippocratic physicians, however, was to prescribe the right diet. Diet was not restricted to what patients put into their mouths, although proper food and drink was essential. It involved their entire lifestyle—how much sleep they had, how much exercise they did, how much fresh air they enjoyed. Keeping a proper diet, then, could prevent or cure illness by balancing what the body required.

Physicians attempted to learn about the body's internal parts by dissecting animals. Following the death of Alexander the Great, in the Hellenistic period, physicians in Alexandria were said by later writers to have shifted from dissecting animals to humans. This development revealed the internal structure of the body in a way that was unknown earlier. Herophilus of Chalcedon (ca. 330–260 B.C.) investigated male and female reproductive anatomy, distinguished between nerves, veins, and arteries, and described the basic structure of the brain. Others contributed as well to this new exploration of human anatomy.

At the time of Galen of Pergamum (ca. A.D.129–200), who was born in Asia Minor, human dissection was not permitted, as it had been earlier in Egypt. Forced to work from animal dissection, Galen nevertheless became the primary ancient authority whose influence dominated Western knowledge of medicine and anatomy for many centuries.

Galen is perhaps most well known for his anatomical and physiological work, even though he acknowledged that he had to infer the internal structure of human bodies from their counterparts in animals. He divided physiological functions into three parts. First, there was the brain, which governed the nerves. As the blood passed through the brain it received spirit, which the nerves carried to all parts of the body, enabling sensation and muscular stimulation. The other two parts had to do with the flow of blood. Galen concluded that there were two systems of blood flow. One began in the left side of the heart, carrying blood enlivened by the heat of the heart through the arteries to the rest of the body. The source of the other was the liver. From here nutrients were carried through the veins to other parts of the body, including the lungs, by way of the right side of the heart. Between the heart's right and left chambers was the septum wall, through whose invisible pores Galen claimed blood seeped.

From Plato's *Timaeus* Galen took the notion of a divine workman who made the cosmos according to the dictates of a rational order. Just as the heavens reflected this eternal order, so too, argued Galen, did the body of living organisms. He found the natural purposefulness of the world Plato endorsed in the adaptability of the animal and human body to the functions it performed. Although Galen himself was not a Christian, his celebration of the evidence of a wise creator that was to be found in the anatomy of living things made his work understandably appealing to Christian natural philosophers for a long time. This attraction provided another reason why Galen's authority grew to enormous stature in the West.

In the Roman Empire after the beginning of the Christian era Greek learning continued to set the tone. Rather than embark on their own intellectual pursuit of theoretical knowledge, the Romans took their cue from what Greeks had and were still accomplishing. As time passed and knowledge of the Greek language waned, some Roman scholars undertook translations of Greek works so that they would remain accessible. When Romans themselves delved into natural philosophy they did so as a leisure activity, not, as the Greeks had, out of an appreciation of the value of intellectual achievement for its own sake. As a result, the natural philosophy that marked the early Middle Ages made little pretence to being as original as what great Greek thinkers had done.

Early medieval natural philosophy has been characterized as popular and encyclopedic, meaning that it aspired to producing compendia of information that all educated people found fascinating. From handbooks of natural knowledge to compilations of information about natural history, mathematics, and geography, the Romans wished to keep their feet on the ground and not to become lost in abstruse thought that neither provoked their curiosity nor served some obviously useful purpose.

Where early Christian thought was concerned, the attitude of Augustine (A.D. 354–430), a bishop of the church who lived in North Africa, was mildly sympathetic to the merits of natural philosophy. While he emphasized the need to focus on spiritual matters, he did not want Christians to be dismissed because they were ignorant of knowledge about the material world. As a result he recommended that Christians study nature to the extent that natural knowledge promoted a hearing for the message of salvation. Augustine's view assigned natural philosophy the status of a handmaiden to religion—it remained in the service of something more important than itself.

The heritage of the Greek accomplishment moved from the Latin West to the Islamic world, where it underwent further development before it was retrieved again by Western scholars. But to a remarkable degree, what the ancients had achieved defined for the future the questions to be asked about nature, the problems to be solved, and the kinds of answers that would be permitted.

Suggestions for Reading

James Evans, *The History and Practice of Ancient Astronomy* (Oxford: Oxford University Press, 1998).

Alexander Jones, ed., *Ancient Science,* Volume I of *The Cambridge History of Science,* ed. David C. Lindberg and Ronald L. Numbers (New York: Cambridge University Press, 2007).

David C. Lindberg, *The Beginnings of Western Science* (Chicago: University of Chicago Press, 1992).

G. E. R. Lloyd, *Aristotle: The Growth and Structure of His Thought* (Cambridge: Cambridge University Press, 1968).

CHAPTER 2

———————◎———————

Learning in the Middle Ages

At the beginning of the fourth century of the Christian era, a Germanic people known as Visigoths, from the delta of the Danube River, began to invade northern Italy. By A.D. 410 they were successful in their attempt to take Rome. And this was not the only time Rome was sacked in the fifth century—it occurred again at mid-century. The lack of political and social stability that resulted from these wars meant that the pursuit of intellectual matters, and even the cultivation of education, took a back seat to more pressing concerns.

At the same time, the growth and development of Christianity as a religion brought with it a new institution—monasticism. Monasteries were places where those who wished to devote themselves to Christian holiness could focus on that task. To the extent that monasteries were self-supporting, they functioned as separate communities. This meant that in addition to requiring practical knowledge about such mundane matters as carpentry, food production, or the growing of herbs for medicines and spices, monks were responsible for whatever formal education was provided in the monastery.

For the most part, education was directed toward spiritual edification. There were exceptions, but in general the heritage of Greek natural philosophy did not hold great appeal in monasteries, where the primary goal was spiritual betterment. Monks consulted classical thought and sought new knowledge about nature only when it served a higher purpose, namely, the understanding of spiritual truth. But that is not to say that monasteries made no contribution at all to the intellectual development of the Latin West. Although monasteries differed about which secular works might be relevant to spiritual development, those with the broadest vision made sure that Greek works were translated into Latin. Through this activity, through the study of scripture, and eventually through the development of theology, the monasteries kept literacy and scholarship alive.

It must be said, however, that in the period from A.D. 400 to1000 there was no intellectual activity on a par with that of earlier Greek natural philosophy. We look in vain during this time for a Roman Ptolemy or Archimedes, figures distinguished by their grasp of earlier scholarly work and by their creative genius in developing new ideas about the natural world. Further, many Greek works on natural philosophy and mathematics were not translated and thus dropped from view.

◎ Transmission of Greek ◎ Learning to the Near East

The early development of Western Christianity drew its organization from the basic structure of the Roman Empire; that is, while local churches were self-governing, there emerged by the fourth century a structure that was modeled on the organization of the Empire itself. In this structure groups of churches were arranged into provinces, with preference given to churches of the large cities. By the fifth century there were five major patriarchies, the two most important being Rome, the oldest center of the Roman Empire, and Constantinople, to which the Emperor Constantine moved the seat of the Empire in 330.

In spite of their common religious origins, the development of the Eastern and Western churches reflected differences in language and outlook. For example, Latin became the universal language of liturgy in the West, while in the East the church

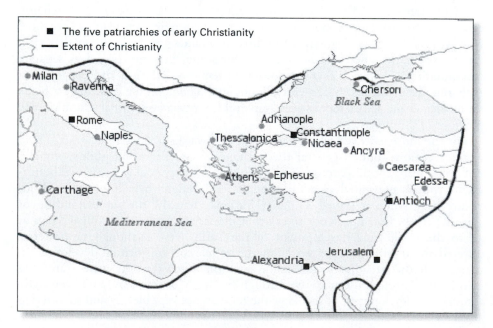

The Five Patriarchies of Early Christianity

tended not to require Greek, the major language of the Eastern church, but to defer to the vernacular language of its various ethnic regions. As a result, a so-called Orthodox Catholic tradition emerged in the East, under its patriarch, to counterbalance the emerging papal authority of Roman Catholicism in the West.

The Nestorians

The great diversity represented by the eastern patriarchies was bound to lead to internal dispute about Christian belief. In particular, disagreement arose about the nature of Jesus Christ himself. Did he have one nature that was wholly divine and wholly human at the same time, as some insisted, or did he have two separate natures, one human and one divine, that existed alongside each other? Nestorius (d. ca. 450), who was the Greek-speaking patriarch of Constantinople, supported the latter interpretation. When this view was formally condemned by a church council in 431, Nestorius retired to a monastery in Antioch and was subsequently banished to Egypt.

There were many who agreed with Nestorius's understanding of Christ's nature, however. When another church council condemned his teaching in the middle of the fifth century, his followers fled the Roman Empire and gathered first in Syria and then in Persia, where they were able to flourish. The Persian king was greatly interested in Greek culture and philosophy and over time the Nestorians, who supported the king's interest, rose to positions of importance.

Nestorian activity in Persia was responsible for the transmission of a great deal of Greek learning to the Near East. As was common in the Eastern church, the Nestorians deferred to the indigenous language in their liturgical practice; in this case it was Syriac, the language of Persian culture. As they continued to introduce Greek ideas and customs into the region, they translated Greek works into Syriac. This was the initial stage of the spread of Greek natural philosophy to the Near East.

Islam and Natural Philosophy

With the birth of Muhammad in Mecca in the late sixth century the destiny of Persia and many other lands of the Near East was substantially altered. Muhammad aggressively spread his new religion of Islam throughout the Arabian Peninsula and began to move to regions beyond. In Persia the new Muslim leaders granted protection to the Nestorians and they in turn continued to exert a significant cultural influence under their new rulers as the guardians of Greek learning. In the middle of the eighth century one of these rulers, al-Munsur (754–775), built a new capital in the city of Baghdad, which became known as a center of intellectual activity.

Beginning with the reign of al-Munsur and extending through his successors, Baghdad became a translation center where Syriac and Greek works were systematically brought into the Arabic language. Nestorian Christians were not the only people engaged in this massive translation effort. Muslims, Jews, and other Christians, known as Sabians, were also involved in what Islamic rulers regarded as an important task. By the turn of the first millennium of the Christian era there was very little of

Plato, Aristotle, Galen, and other authors of the Greek corpus that had not been made available in Arabic. Greek thought was cultivated to a sufficient degree to preserve a tradition that in many cases had been neglected in the West.

The attitude of Arab leaders toward Greek learning was in an important respect similar to that of the early Romans; that is, they were interested in foreign ideas primarily to the extent that they were useful. Mathematics and astronomy had obvious benefits, as did the knowledge gleaned from Greek medicine. The same could be said, perhaps to a lesser degree, about astrology and even natural history. Greek philosophical treatises proved relevant, and therefore useful, to Arabic theologians. As a result of this utilitarian outlook, the status of Greek learning always remained secondary to the heart of Islamic culture and religion.

The magnitude of the effort of translating so many Greek and Syriac sources into Arabic might suggest that translation defined the extent of the Islamic achievement. But Islamic thinkers did not simply take over Greek ideas without comment or question. While they acknowledged their debt to those who had come before them, Islamic authors sought to improve and correct the material they had inherited.

Islamic astronomers made lasting and innovative improvements to Ptolemy's system. They made new star charts, they introduced trigonometry into astronomical calculation, they corrected deficiencies in the Julian calendar, and they perfected the design of the astrolabe, an instrument used to measure the position of stars in the sky. In mathematics Islamic scholars introduced a system of numerals that they had inherited from India and then perfected. It included a zero as a placeholder, removing the sometimes misleading and ambiguous designations of numbers in existing numeration systems. They also made use of symbols for unknown quantities in an exceptional work from the ninth century with the Arabic words *al-Jabr* (from which we have *algebra*) in its title.

In the study of optics an Islamic scholar named Ibn al-Haytham, also known as Alhazen (ca. 965–ca. 1040), produced a new theory that was critical of the existing assumption that vision involved light streaming out from the eye. Alhazen argued that light entered the eye from the outside. He then brought together mathematical, physical, and medical ideas for the first time to explain how vision works.

Another area of knowledge that Arabic scholars developed was alchemy. Early Christians in Hellenistic Egypt pursued *chemia,* the practice of refining metals. Islamic thinkers were interested in the Greek texts on this subject, which they translated under the rubric *al-chemia.* They wanted to learn whatever they could about how material substances interacted because that could be useful in the production and purification of substances and in the coloring of alloys to look like gold and silver. As they pursued the subject on their own, Islamic thinkers improved practical techniques for distilling, crystallizing, and sublimating natural substances.

More than two thousand alchemical works are attributed to one Jabir ibn Hayyan, whose actual existence is in some doubt. Many of these writings originated from the long period between the middle of the ninth century to the end of the tenth. They contain the viewpoint that metals originated from combinations of two exhalations found underground. Because all metals shared a common origin, it was theoretically possible that one could be transmuted into another. To carry out this transmutation, the early Greeks attempted to prepare a substance called *xere,* which the Islamic authors translated as *al-iksir* and which later was known as the philosopher's stone. This very old process, then, became a focal point for the alchemical tradition that would later come to the West from Islam.

From the high point of translation activity, roughly between 900 and 1250, natural philosophy continued to flourish and develop in the Islamic world. By the thirteenth century internal strife and Mongol attacks from without led to instability and a decline of interest in natural philosophy. By the end of the fifteenth century, as those in the West were realizing the existence of unknown lands, little remained of the Islamic fascination with nature. However, the period of assimilation of Greek thought into Islam that began with al-Munsur at the end of the eighth century and started to decline in the thirteenth marked a span of over five hundred years during which the Islamic world remained the world's center of natural philosophy.

◎ Revitalization of Intellectual ◎ Pursuits in the West

In approximately 1000, priests and monks, or "those who pray," constituted one of three groups that made up the emerging political, economic, and social system known as feudalism. The other two were the knights who defended society, or "those who fought," and the almost 90 percent of the population known as "those who work." European society was agrarian—towns and cities were just beginning to emerge in the Northwest of the continent. For the most part farming was done communally in connection with a manor.

By the twelfth century change was evident. As they consolidated noble status for themselves knights began to define it in terms of lineage. For over two centuries powerful individuals had been emerging as kings, with lesser knights assembled around them at court. New agricultural techniques permitted the expansion of arable land and the growing of new crops. New villages and towns had sprung up, making possible the development of urban centers marked by trade and commercial activity. With these new urban centers came a new social group, the bourgeoisie, who provided the leadership for urban political institutions.

If these developments had been underway for some time, so had changes in attitudes toward intellectual pursuits and toward the role of education.

The Enlivening of Learning

In the early monasteries the cultivation of intellectual ideas was centered on religious and theological matters, so natural philosophy was virtually ignored. Occasionally a translation of a Greek work on philosophy appeared, but what interest it held stemmed from its relevance to theological study. With the emergence of a powerful leader in Europe in the latter half of the eighth century, however, education became a greater priority.

Flourishing of the schools.   Charlemagne (742–814) consolidated under his rule several areas of what is now continental Europe. By the time of his grandsons, virtually all of Europe, with the exception of contemporary Spain, had become part of the Carolingian Empire. Charlemagne concluded that as the leader of the state he himself would benefit from a broad education and he believed that educational reforms would strengthen the church as well. To head the school he wished to create he brought Alcuin of York (ca. 730–804) to his court at Aachen. Alcuin had been the head of the cathedral school in York in the British Isles. Together with his new teacher, Charlemagne proceeded to reform education throughout the realm, which, with the exception of Spain, included the greater part of the European continent.

It would be a long time before the literate monks outnumbered the illiterate monks. But through the establishment of new cathedral and monastery schools, education became a much more important enterprise than it had been before. As a result of broadening the content of education, some works on natural philosophy and mathematics began to reappear.

These changes were in part merely the flourishing of the venture begun under Charlemagne. Schools in the new urban centers naturally expanded the curriculum to match the new interests emerging around them. Even cathedral schools, which retained their religious focus, increased the subject matter investigated whenever it could be made relevant to their mission. A decisively greater willingness to rely on human reasoning marked the investigation of both traditional and new subject matter, especially in the urban schools. Of course scholars who sought to gain insight into religious truth by rationally examining the basis of Christian doctrine ran the risk of opposition from those who did not trust this method of philosophy.

The attraction of Platonic thought.   Another aspect of the enlivening of learning in the eleventh and twelfth centuries was a renewed appreciation of the classics. Charlemagne's grandson, Charles the Bald (823–877), supported the translation of several neo-Platonic Greek works into Latin. This attraction to Platonic thought marked the initial phase of translation activity in the West, and would increase significantly within a few hundred years. In the twelfth century Plato's *Timaeus*—which had been translated in the first half of the tenth century—and other Latin works whose neo-Platonic perspective could be reconciled with a Christian outlook, provided a framework in which ideas about the creation of the physical world through the work of a divine craftsman could be understood.

An important feature of this blending of Plato with Genesis was the introduction of what the historian of medieval natural philosophy David Lindberg has called "the new naturalism" of the twelfth century. By this Lindberg refers to the restriction of divine activity to the initial moment of creation. Scholars more and more assumed that from the time of creation on, things in nature, including human beings, followed a regular course dictated by natural causation. Humans represented a microcosm of what occurred in the cosmos writ large—the macrocosm. Both were tied together by the common structure they shared.

In the *Timaeus* the divine craftsman was bound by the order he created—he could not intervene to change it at will. In twelfth-century naturalism that claim was weaker. It was not that God *could not* intervene into nature's order, merely that God customarily did not do so. Nevertheless, by establishing the importance of nature's regular course, twelfth-century scholars opened themselves to new questions about how that course worked.

Translation of Works into Latin from Arabic and Greek

In the closing years of the eleventh century Europeans from all ranks of society joined together in response to a call from Pope Urban II to attack the Muslims who had besieged the Eastern church and who controlled Jerusalem. This and subsequent crusades provided contact between West and East, even if it did nothing to promote an appreciation of the achievements of Islamic thought and culture. But an awareness of the accomplishments of Islamic natural philosophy was not entirely absent. Men such as Gerbert (ca. 945–1003), who had traveled to northern Spain a century earlier to study Arabic mathematics and astronomy, enriched the Western perspective.

Christian forces began to be successful in driving Muslims from Spain during the eleventh century. Although it was not the only supply of information about Arabic natural philosophy and mathematics, Spain was, in fact, an important source. Not only was it close to other European countries, but there were also Christians in Spain who lived under Muslim rule. They proved to be of enormous value as Europeans sought to absorb Islamic thought.

Many Arabic works in the areas of medicine, natural philosophy, mathematics, alchemy, and astrology came into the Latin language in this fashion. Since Islamic scholars had taken Greek works as their original point of departure, classics from Ptolemy, Euclid, Aristotle, and Galen came into Latin through Arabic. At the same time, Latin scholars became aware of original Arabic works on subjects such as medicine and algebra.

Yet not all of the Greek classics came into Latin by way of this flood of translations from the Arabic that occurred in the twelfth century. Some were made directly from Greek texts that had been preserved in southern Italy. Once begun, the demand for translations continued to grow. By the end of the thirteenth century a great deal of the Greek and Arabic works on natural philosophy and mathematics had been recovered in the Latin West.

The Appearance of Universities

The existing educational establishments were not immune from the climate of social and intellectual change that was occurring in the eleventh and twelfth centuries. More and more young people wished to take advantage of the expansion of resources coming into the Latin West. In response to what was happening, a new institution—the university— made its appearance during this time. It differed from the urban school, which typically had one master and a dozen or two students, by bringing multiple masters together in one place.

The oldest university was founded in Bologna, Italy, around the middle of the twelfth century, followed by the University of Paris (1200), Oxford University (1220), and ten others over the course of the thirteenth century. By 1420 fifteen more had come into being, all but three of them during the fourteenth century. The explosion of the student population during this era called for a comparable expansion of the teaching force. Around the turn of the thirteenth century, for example, there were over seventy masters teaching at Oxford.

In the medieval university there were three higher areas of learning, or faculties, to deal with the advanced subjects of theology, medicine, and law. Before students could prepare themselves in one of these faculties, however, they had to study the arts. Traditionally, Roman education had consisted of seven liberal arts, which were divided into two groups known as the trivium and the quadrivium. Grammar, rhetoric, and logic formed the trivium, while arithmetic, geometry, astronomy, and music made up the quadrivium. The medieval university retained this basic division of the arts, although it placed more emphasis on logic than was common earlier.

The more technical subjects of the quadrivium were no more emphasized in the university than they had been in the urban schools. But it would be misleading to infer that concern with the natural world therefore received very little attention. On the contrary, the physical and metaphysical works of Aristotle, plus commentaries on these works, had come into Latin beginning in the second half of the twelfth century and in the thirteenth, exactly the time when the universities had come onto the scene. The great breadth of Aristotle's thought captured the attention of many scholars, and Aristotelian natural philosophy became a central feature, even a compulsory subject, of the university curriculum.

The early universities varied in size, from large centers such as Paris, which had over two thousand students, to small schools with a few hundred. There was considerable turnover among the students; many left after a short time for a variety of reasons. Students arrived at the age of thirteen or fourteen with a grammar school knowledge of Latin. Those who remained would take an examination for a bachelor's degree at age seventeen or eighteen from the master under whom they had studied. If they passed they could study for three more years to earn a master's degree, which gave them membership in the arts faculty with the right to teach. New masters were sometimes required to teach the arts for a certain period before they could opt to attend one of the higher faculties (theology, medicine, law) for another five or six years.

The medieval university was an important contributor to the development of Western scholarship in general and natural philosophy in particular. Medieval university scholars preserved and passed on to the West the Greek and Arabic wisdom that had accumulated for over a thousand years. They shared a dedication to systematically applying Aristotelian logic to the body of knowledge they had gained from both sacred and secular sources. They encountered new challenges when their investigations opened up new territory that had to be understood in light of received truth. In general they responded to these challenges, not by dismissing secular ideas

Medieval University Professors

whenever they ran counter to Christian revelation, but by creatively attempting to develop new perspectives that reconciled discrepancies. They undertook, in other words, a reasoned articulation of human meaning and in so doing they put in place an approach that would shape the Western mind for centuries to come.

◎ The Assimilation of Ancient ◎ Knowledge of Nature

Of the many different kinds of texts that were translated into Latin, those on more technical subjects such as mathematics and astronomy stood out as far superior to anything that was known previously. As a result, such works ran little risk of generating controversy. The same could not be said for Aristotle's thoughts about the cosmos because they involved claims that were different from received wisdom. And it was Aristotle's works that had become favorites of the scholars in the new universities.

Aristotelian Natural Philosophy and Christian Belief

Some of Aristotle's conclusions ran contrary to widely held religious beliefs. When this occurred it was necessary either to oppose them or to figure out a way to reconcile them with existing doctrine.

Problems raised by Aristotle's philosophy.   In Chapter 1 we learned that a fundamental principle of Aristotelian philosophy was that something could not come from nothing. For Aristotle that meant that the cosmos could not have had a beginning. Matter and the elements must have always existed. He also believed that matter would never go out of existence—the cosmos would not have an end.

This is just one example of an Aristotelian tenet that did not blend with traditional Christian thought. The Bible clearly indicated that God had created the world, although it was less clear whether the authors of the scriptures intended to convey the idea that God had created an ordered world out of preexisting chaos or that he had created it from nothing. By the medieval period, however, the principle of *creatio ex nihilo* (creation from nothing) was a commonly understood doctrine. Such a reading of the book of Genesis ran directly against Aristotle's belief that something cannot come from nothing.

God Creating the Universe

There were other points at which Aristotle's natural philosophy clashed with Christian doctrine. His understanding of nature's regularity highlighted the Greek tendency, evident in the earliest Greek philosophers, to remove or downplay the role of personal agency in explanations of natural processes. Not all Greek thinkers displayed this tendency. Plato's divine craftsman, for example, could be reconciled with the idea of a purposeful creator, even if the God of medieval Christian theologians could intervene in nature's workings and Plato's craftsman could not.

But, as we saw in Chapter 1, Aristotle agreed with Plato's criticism of the early Greek philosophers that, in removing personal agency from nature, they had also mistakenly removed purpose from the natural world. Like Plato, Aristotle insisted that there was purpose in nature, but he did not account for it by appealing to the role of a divine craftsman or any other external personal agent. Purpose for Aristotle came from the nature of things themselves. Effects followed causes in accordance with the natural purposes that reigned in nature. Aristotle appealed to the activity of the divine—in his notion of the unmoved mover—only to begin the chain of cause and effect.

As a result, Aristotle could sound very deterministic to Christian thinkers of the thirteenth century. The most blatant contradiction to Christian understanding was the denial of the possibility of miracle that was clearly implied in Aristotle's thought.

Aristotle's impersonal god was not responsible for the purpose in nature and certainly could not interfere with the cause and effect relationships it had set into motion. When believers prayed to God, they counted on his having the power to act on their requests. If Aristotle was right, their God was impotent, not omnipotent.

Aristotle's teaching about form and matter also supplied a problem for the university scholars who had turned to the translations of and commentaries on his works. According to Aristotle, form and matter could not exist apart from each other; there could be no form without matter and no matter without form. The form of the living body entailed more than its shape—it involved the organization necessary for life to exist. So for Aristotle the soul, which provided this organization, was the material body's form. Because form and matter existed together, when the body no longer continued to exist, neither did the soul. How could this viewpoint be reconciled to a belief in the immortality of the soul?

Reconciling Aristotle and Christian doctrine.   Aristotle's thought presented scholars of the thirteenth century with a real dilemma. In spite of these problems, they were very much attracted to the rich diversity of content of the Aristotelian corpus. Beginning with his treatment of logic, Aristotle enticed late-medieval thinkers to make use of their reasoning powers to undertake investigations of their own. Further, Aristotle had considered so many different subjects that the agenda he had set would keep scholars busy for generations to come. Nothing comparable to the wealth of information and analysis was available anywhere else. It was difficult to remain unimpressed.

There were therefore numerous attempts throughout the thirteenth century to explain how, in light of the obvious problems it created, Aristotle's thought was to be understood. One of the first university masters to lecture on Aristotelian natural philosophy was Roger Bacon (ca. 1220–1292) at the University of Paris. Bacon's approach was to emphasize the utility of the new philosophical texts, including Aristotle's, that were coming into the Latin West. In addition to the obvious ways in which, say, astronomical knowledge was helpful in making the church calendar accurate, Bacon declared that the new philosophical knowledge allowed a better understanding of scripture and was useful in confirming Christian doctrine.

Some were not as confident that potential problems could be ignored. They too enjoyed applying their rational abilities to understand God's word and God's world, especially with the new tools that had become available from pagan sources. But they showed an awareness that adopting the starting points of Aristotle—for example, that something could not come from nothing—might take their rational analysis to conclusions that challenged accepted belief.

Where Aristotle's system was concerned, they identified the eternity of the world, determinism, and the mortality of the soul as unacceptable conclusions that flowed from false starting points. They were not confident, as Bacon appeared to be, that the use of pagan philosophy was automatically beneficial. They trusted starting points that in their view had been divinely revealed to them, not those adopted by pagan Greeks.

The question therefore arose in the medieval university as to whether philosophy could be trusted. When philosophy was taken to mean Greek philosophy, it

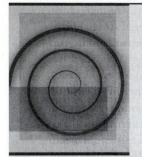

The NATURE of SCIENCE

Delimiting Faith and Reason

There was already precedent in the late medieval period for designating the different roles played by reason and faith. In a slogan for which he is well known, the early-twelfth-century archbishop, Anselm of Canterbury (1033–1109), declared, "I believe in order that I may understand." Anselm was aware that understanding, which depends on the use of reason to tease out the implications of an assumption, cannot be attained unless there is some assumption at the start. Reason only goes to work once that assumption is in place.

The role of reason here can be likened to the operation of a computer once the return key has been struck. The computer carries out an analysis based on software that dictates the contours within which the reasoning takes place. To carry the analogy a bit further, in natural philosophy the computer's hardware, including its read-only memory (ROM), might be likened to the physical universe with its "hard-wired" laws.

If there is merit in this analogy, it would suggest that the frequent positioning of faith and reason as opposites is misleading, since they must work together. Sometimes, though, the assumptions on which rational analysis is based are so commonly shared that they become invisible. In such cases—for example, when assumptions are widely shared in the scientific community—it may incorrectly appear that scientific analysis is devoid of any assumptions and that reasoning in science therefore stands in opposition to the embrace of assumption.

encountered substantial suspicion and criticism. But Thomas Aquinas (ca. 1224–1274), the doctor of theology at the University of Paris, argued that the problem did not lie with philosophy per se. He conceded that philosophy as a means of investigating God's truth could not justify its starting points on its own—it could not *by itself* make known the truths God had given by revelation. But, given those starting points, philosophy would never oppose them.

Why bother with philosophy at all, then? Aquinas argued that while philosophy would never contradict the truths of revelation (since it assumed them at the outset), it might nevertheless lead to new truths that had not yet been realized. Further, philosophy provided an excellent means of showing what was erroneous about critiques of Christian doctrine.

Thomas Aquinas constructed an elaborate synthesis of Aristotelian and Christian ideas, one that eventually became ensconced in medieval thought. To do this he had, of course, to explain where Aristotle was in error and where he was just misunderstood. The Thomistic synthesis, as it has been called, involved a great deal of subtle analysis, some of which became so involved that many readers did not follow it. In many cases Aquinas used philosophical speculation to uncover options most people had never realized were possible. For example, he disagreed with Aristotle's position that the world was eternal. But he suggested that eternal matter would be just as dependent on God for its existence as was matter that had come into existence at some point. Thus, Aristotle's position was wrong—but not absurd.

The Reception of the Thomistic Synthesis

Aquinas appears to have felt that it was a mistake to oppose reason to faith, philosophy to religion. Philosophy had mainly to do with reasoning from a set of starting points, not, as in religion, with the establishment of those starting points. The two should not be opposed because they functioned for different purposes. They could only be set in opposition if they were working to accomplish the same end.

Others, like Siger of Brabant (ca.1240–1284), took a narrower view of philosophy, focusing on the starting points themselves. Siger concluded that the two *should* be kept rigorously opposed to each other *because* their starting points were different. He was impressed not so much that philosophy and religion were doing different things, but that religion adopted assumptions of one kind, philosophy of a different kind. In religion the defining starting point involved a God above nature; in philosophy the starting point was nature itself.

Given this variation in the perception of the relationship between religion and philosophy, faith and reason, it is no wonder that church authorities grew suspicious of the role of philosophy. This was especially true because those who argued that philosophy was completely separate from religion felt free to engage in philosophical reasoning regardless of the conclusions that resulted. When their philosophical analysis produced outlandish conclusions that clashed with accepted doctrine, they simply declared their loyalty to church doctrine. Meanwhile the radical inferences of their philosophical reasoning circulated in their writings.

Church authorities felt that they could not stand idly by without taking a stand. Encouraged by Aquinas, the bishop of Paris condemned thirteen philosophical conclusions propagated by those who claimed that, because philosophy was separate from religion and subservient to it, they were free to draw whatever philosophical conclusions they wished. Aquinas died in 1274, but three years later 219 additional philosophical propositions were condemned, including many that Thomas himself had defended. Needless to say, his reputation suffered a blow.

Many of the condemned propositions had to do with what were regarded as limitations on God's power. For example, Aquinas had made it clear that he agreed with Aristotle that life as we know it did not exist elsewhere. But the bishop of Paris understood him to mean that there *could not* be life elsewhere—for the kind of philosophical reasons that Aristotle had given. Aquinas had in fact been careful to say that God could have created life elsewhere, but that he had not done so. Nevertheless, he was misunderstood. "That the First Cause cannot make other worlds" was one of the condemned propositions. With this condemnation the church put itself on the side of the possible existence of extraterrestrial life, reversing the judgment of earlier Christian theologians that such a pagan belief was unacceptable. It also opened up new questions for theologians and natural philosophers to ponder—whether, for instance, Christ's sacrifice covered beings that might live on other worlds or whether he would have to go to those worlds to die again. The consideration of such matters lasted well into the nineteenth century and forms a fascinating episode in the history of the interaction between astronomy and religion.

Aristotelian natural philosophy did not fare well in the condemnation of 1277. The bishop viewed Aristotle's assertion of the impossibility of some natural arrangements—his denial, for example, that a vacuum could exist—as a limitation of God's omnipotence and he condemned Aristotle's claim accordingly. But the ban on teaching any of the condemned propositions, on pain of excommunication, was less significant for what it prohibited than it was as an indication of the state of the intellectual world of the late thirteenth century. While it was clear that the recovery of ancient philosophical works had made their way into the minds of many university scholars, it was just as clear that not everyone agreed with this assimilation of ancient wisdom. In fact, the leaders of the church expressed the greatest opposition.

Aquinas's reputation and his blending of Aristotelian thought with Christianity soon recovered from the disrepute brought in 1277 by the bishop of Paris. But the relationship between philosophy and religion would remain a contentious issue for some time to come. As we will see in the next chapter, by the fourteenth and fifteenth centuries new objections were raised about the ability of philosophy to assist in the articulation of Christian truth.

◎ Late Medieval Natural Philosophy ◎

The natural world envisioned by medieval thinkers bore many resemblances to that of the ancient Greeks. By the same token, there were valuable new contributions made by university scholars that corrected and otherwise altered what had been received from the past. In many cases the new ideas about nature or mathematics emerged in the context of theological discussion, always a subject of primary concern at this time in Western history. There are important ways, then, in which medieval theology helped to shape the content and, even more significantly, the assumptions that would support the Western heritage in natural philosophy and, eventually, in natural science.

Change, Forms, and the Study of Motion

It seems curious to our modern minds that the early Greek philosophers spent so much effort discussing the question of whether change was possible. But the concept of change is profoundly fundamental to natural philosophy. Without some kind of change nothing would happen, and the universe could not be perceived to exist. How and why things change therefore became basic questions of Western natural philosophy. To answer these questions it was often less important to know what is changing than to focus on the *process* of change. For example, a medieval consideration of the problem of change might consider how grace or charity could be increased in a person. From the examination of such questions some remarkable conclusions about change emerged.

Medieval scholars followed Aristotle in acknowledging different kinds of change. In the heavens the only change was of place, as the stars and planets moved uniformly with their various spheres. Below the orb of the moon, in addition to change of place, things could exhibit changes in size or in the degree of the qualities they possessed. Finally, change occurred in the terrestrial realm when a thing came into or went out of existence.

The intension and remission of forms.   Medieval scholars were interested in an intriguing question about changes in form, specifically, when a change intensified or weakened. When a form or quality intensified—for example, a person's charity—did the increase occur in definite increments or did it do so continuously? One twelfth-century theologian suggested that charity was a gift of God; hence, when it increased, it did so in discrete amounts as the result of a specific act, not as a process. But in the next century another theologian asserted that charity could be *gradually* strengthened over time.

The theologians asked themselves how the form "flowed" from one state to the next. In the first case, when charity increased suddenly by a definite amount, the flow of change in the form occurred because the quality was first present in one degree and then in another. Here the flow is like that observed in the floor indicator lights of an elevator as they move from 1 to 2. The flow in this case is due to the light being first in one position and then in a completely different one. Even though it seems to, the light does not move from one location to the other; rather, it goes out at one point and reappears at the other. One state is replaced by a second state. When we see the light move from 1 to 2 we create the flow in our minds from our observation of one light going out and the other coming on. So a person whose charity increased in this way first had one amount, then, as the result of God's gift, a measurably greater amount. Any perception of flow in the increase of the charity was created by the observer.

In the second case, when the flow of change in the form is continuous, the flow is like the ascent of a person in a swing from a lower position to a higher one. Here the flow can be said to be real—it is inherent in the person who experiences the increase in height above the ground. If charity increased this way there would be no detectable difference from one moment to the next, but over time an augmentation would become evident.

With this admittedly esoteric discussion, medieval thinkers were treating a problem that would persist in natural philosophy—namely, the problem of continuous versus discontinuous change. The general subject behind the notion of flow in the intensification and remission of forms is the question of motion, which soon became an object of investigation. In the fourteenth century, for example, a remarkable group of scholars at Merton College of Oxford University came up with new concepts to characterize what was happening when things moved.

Because the Oxford professors were curious about the notion of the intensity of a form—the degree to which the form is present in a body—they asked what the intensity of *motion* might be. The ancients had talked about motion solely in terms of the distance traveled during a specific time. As a result of insisting that motion must have intensity, medieval scholars created a new parameter—velocity. This new quality was an abstraction to be sure, one of many such medieval concoctions. From it soon followed notions of uniform motion (constant velocity), nonuniform motion (acceleration), and even uniformly nonuniform motion (constant acceleration).

The Oxford scholars went beyond merely defining these new parameters. They developed propositions that employed the new concepts in their explorations of motion. They knew, for instance, that a body that was uniformly accelerated would cover a certain distance in a certain time. They established a proposition: The distance covered when a body is uniformly accelerated over a specified length of time is the same the body would cover if it moved at its average velocity for the same amount of time.

On the basis of the achievements of the Oxford scholars, others soon took an important new step—the mathematical representation of the new parameters. A professor named Nicole Oresme (ca. 1320–1382) at the University of Paris made major contributions in this area. Following the ancients, who had used lines of differing lengths to represent varying amounts of space and different durations of time, Oresme began by representing degrees of velocity by different lengths of a line. A line half as long as another represented a velocity half as great as the other.

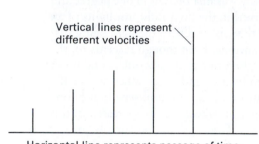

Vertical lines represent different velocities

Horizontal line represents passage of time

Use of Horizontal and Vertical Lines to Show Acceleration

His next step was to realize that he could also create a geometrical representation of acceleration. To do this he followed Aristotle in representing time by a horizontal line. He then placed vertical lines, which represented the increased velocities, at places along the horizontal line. In this way he was able to represent what the velocity was at the various points in time. He thus created a picture of what was happening in acceler- ated motion. If he drew a line connecting the tops of the vertical lines (not shown in the figure), it could be thought of as a repre- sentation of the acceleration.

Oresme could now use his new technique to prove the Oxford proposition con- cerning the distance covered by a uniformly accelerated object. Constant velocities were depicted by equal vertical lines along a horizontal time line, as indicated in the left-hand figure below. From the different velocities of the accelerated motion he chose the velocity at the halfway point, or the average velocity. Oresme conceived of the areas of the figures generated as a measure of the distance traveled. Since the two triangles emphasized in the right-hand figure below are equal, the area of the rectan- gle formed by the constant velocities is equal to the area of the triangle made by the accelerated motion. In other words, the distance traversed by a body moving for a

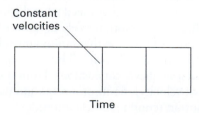

Constant velocities

Time

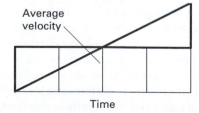

Average velocity

Time

certain time at uniformly accelerated motion is the same as that traversed by a body moving for the same time at the average velocity.

The cause of motion.   Apart from the descriptions of the various kinds of motion that exist, there is another basic question about motion that demanded the attention of ancients and medievals alike. It had to do with what causes motion. Aristotle had said that motion was caused by a mover; in fact, it was an axiom of his treatment of motion that all motion required a mover. Medieval scholars accepted Aristotle's axiom and they carefully considered his explanations of what the mover was in various cases of motion. They also responded to extensive Islamic commentaries on what the Greek master had set down.

A perceived problem almost since the time of Aristotle was his identification of the mover in cases of the unnatural motion of a projectile. In Aristotle's view such motion required the presence of an external mover because the projectile possessed neither a soul nor was its motion initiated by acting to seek its natural place. He had said that whatever supplied the power to launch the projectile was its mover, as long as that mover was in contact with the projectile. Once released, the projectile was moved by the medium through which it traveled. This was because the original propelling power moved not only the projectile, but also the air around it, imparting to the air the capacity to act as the mover from the point of release on.

Objection to Aristotle's requirement of an external mover for projectile motion had been raised as early as the sixth century. It was proposed then that the so-called violent motion of a projectile resulted from a motive power that was impressed on the projectile by the launching power and was afterwards *internal* to the projectile. This revision of Aristotle's teaching on motion came down through Islam to the Latin West, where it was initially rejected, later to be developed by the Parisian professor Jean Buridan (ca. 1300–ca. 1360).

Buridan suggested that when an arrow is shot from a bow, the bowstring impressed a power on the arrow. He called the impressed power *impetus,* which, he said, continued to act as long as it was not corrupted by resistance. In the case of projectiles the impetus moved the body, but as the motion was resisted, for example, by whatever medium it was moving through, the impetus was diminished until finally the projectile stopped.

Buridan's modification of Aristotle's explanation of projectile motion is but one example of the aggressive program of medieval natural philosophy. The professors of the medieval university did not simply accept whatever Aristotle had said; they actively sought to correct the master when they encountered what they regarded as insufficient or erroneous explanations.

The Heavens and the Earth

Medieval thinkers took care to respect any specific reference in the Bible to the Earth and its place in the cosmos. That did not prevent them, however, from considering possibilities not explicitly covered in Holy Writ.

The structure of the cosmos.   For the most part, a simplified view of Aristotle's understanding of the structure of the heavens became the dominant view of the medieval thinkers. That is, the cosmos was centered on the Earth and was surrounded by eight concentric spheres that carried the seven planets and the fixed stars. Clearly such a depiction of the heavens paid no regard to the proper motions the planets displayed, even though Aristotle himself had taken pains to account for planetary movement. He had, as we learned in Chapter 1, been aware of the combinations of spherical motions used by his predecessors and had inserted extra spheres to provide an internal consistency that the earlier systems had lacked.

If, in the common understanding of the structure of the heavens, medieval scholars ignored complicated motions, they also created new questions about that structure that were based on their Christian outlook. For example, the Genesis account of creation distinguished between the origin of the heavens, which occurred on the first day, and the firmament, which came into being on the second. In addition there was a reference to waters that existed above the firmament. To account for the various regions indicated in these passages, some medieval commentators inserted two extra spheres beyond the firmament or eighth sphere of the fixed stars—the first to provide a place for the waters above the firmament, and the second to designate a habitat for God and the angels.

Possible motion of the Earth.   The state of astronomy during the late medieval period did not rival the achievement of Ptolemy or the Arabic astronomers who came after him, but that is not to suggest that there were none who knew of Ptolemy's work or that there were no creative ideas at all. Both Jean Buridan and Nicole Oresme at the University of Paris revived the ancient question of whether a rotating Earth might produce the motions we observe the heavens undergoing. Buridan argued that if the Earth rotated on an axis it would not affect astronomical calculations, since astronomers dealt only with relative motions anyway. He concluded that it was impossible to decide the question on astronomical grounds alone, although it could be determined on physical grounds. Shoot an arrow into the sky. The arrow is not left behind by the Earth rotating under it, so the Earth must not be turning.

Buridan's younger colleague Oresme did not accept the argument about the arrow. He reasoned that if we look at the various motions that take place when sailors move on a ship, they all occur at the same time that the ship is moving through the water. He drew a parallel between this movement of the ship and that of the atmosphere above the Earth into which the arrow was shot. The motion of the arrow up and down could occur at the same time that the atmosphere turned with the Earth around an axis. Although Oresme appreciated the advantages of permitting the Earth to rotate, there were scriptural passages that seemed to rule it out. He explained away some of these passages as accommodations on the part of the writers of scripture, but in the end he deferred to the Psalmist, who declared that God had established the world, "which shall not be moved" (Psalm 92:1).

Heavenly influences on Earth and its inhabitants.   Everyone knew that the sun exercised a physical influence on the Earth. From this obvious knowledge it was but a small step to the more general assumption that the heavens and the Earth were physically linked to each other. The endorsement of a physical influence from the stars by ancient authorities like Ptolemy came down through Islam to the Latin West and remained unquestioned by medieval scholars and by their successors in the early modern era. To deny astrological influence would have seemed as ridiculous as denying that the seasons were linked to the annual motion of the sun or that the tides had something to do with the motion of the moon.

Astrological influence on human behavior was another matter. It was not that there were no defenders of such a link between the macrocosm and the microcosm. From the objections that were raised to this kind of influence it is clear that many believed in it. The opposition, present since the early Middle Ages, insisted that nothing impaired human free will. If astrology was seen as determining human affairs, it could not be accepted. This attitude remained well ensconced throughout the late medieval period and into the fifteenth and sixteenth centuries.

A modified position emerged during the twelfth and thirteenth centuries with the acquisition of ancient and Islamic works that discussed astrological influence. Although the stars did not affect the human exercise of free will, they could influence certain natural aspects of the lives of humans. For example, comparable to the kind of physical influence that seemed obvious where the seasons were concerned, there were likely arrangements in the heavens that affected a person's health and temperament. If the influence disrupted the health of whole communities, plague could result. It is therefore easy to understand why the study of astrology became a recognized part of the practice of medieval medicine.

Alchemy

The subject of alchemy came to the Latin West from Islam. The medieval theologian Robert of Ketton, who brought the Koran into Latin, translated an Arabic work on alchemy under the title *De compositione alchemiae* (*On Alchemical Composition*) in 1134. Although this was the first such work, many would follow. Within 250 years an enormous number of alchemical materials were accessible. In spite of this substantial growth of interest, alchemy was never part of the curriculum in the medieval university. This was because there developed, especially in the fourteenth century, a reaction against the subject among many theologians and philosophers, forcing those who pursued it to do so mainly on the margins of medieval intellectual society.

Late medieval opposition to alchemy was also dependent on Arabic thought, although medieval scholars believed that these criticisms had come from Aristotle. Around 1200 a section from a book by the early-eleventh-century Persian philosopher Avicenna (980–1037) was translated and inserted into an existing translation of one of Aristotle's works. Avicenna's critique of the transmutation of metals was thereafter routinely assumed to be by Aristotle himself, lending great credibility to its worth.

Avicenna's objection to claims that metals could be transmuted revolved around the difference between a natural and an artificial substance. In his view art was regarded as inferior to nature; hence those who attempted to transmute an inferior metal into a nobler one through an artificial process were doomed to failure. Further, according to Avicenna, the defining characteristics that made a metal unique were not accessible to the senses; rather, they existed deep in the nature of the metal. An alchemist could not get at them since he did not know what they were.

In response to this kind of criticism, which was frequently adopted in the universities, there were those who favored alchemy and disagreed with the limitations placed on art and on the human ability to transform the world. They also rejected the claim that humans could not know the defining characteristics of metals. In 1266 Roger Bacon argued that alchemy investigated matters of which Aristotle was ignorant, such as the way the elements gave rise to precious stones, minerals, and humors. Therefore, alchemy was a more fundamental subject than natural philosophy because it dealt with the elements as generators of new substances, whereas philosophy merely combined the four elements.

In the late thirteenth century the most significant alchemical work of the Middle Ages appeared, the *Summa perfectionis (Sum of Perfection)*, most likely written by an Italian named Paul of Taranto. He took the name Geber in a clear attempt to identify with the well-known alchemical figure in Arabic lore, Jabir ibn Hayyan. Geber provided extensive information about minerals and metals, how to work with them, and how to transmute one into another. To account for the properties of things Geber appealed to the smallest parts of their substance, which, incidentally, he did not think of as indivisible atoms. He explained, for example, that particles of a substance that were smaller than those of another could be packed tighter; hence such substances resisted the action of acids better than those that were packed together more loosely.

Alchemical practice was always vulnerable to exploitation by those with less than perfect integrity. Fake demonstrations of the transmutation of lead into gold convinced more than one investor to trust swindlers. With the development of legal restrictions placed on alchemical practice, the study of alchemy moved to the fringe of society during the course of the fourteenth century.

But interest in the subject did not wane; in fact, the official hostility to alchemy did not prevent its spread into the practice of medicine. Besides the transmutation of metals, another major goal of alchemists was to find healing medicines, even a substance that could prolong life. These two hopes, transmuting base metals into nobler ones and finding an elixir of life, would remain lasting and powerful goals of the Western alchemical tradition until well into the eighteenth century.

Medicine

Many of the general attitudes regarding medicine and its practice from the early years of Christianity were still in place in the late medieval period. The Christian West by and large had resolved early on the opposition between religious and secular understandings of medicine. For most Christians there was no contradiction between the perception of sickness as divine punishment or a vehicle of spiritual growth, and the view that illness was due to natural causes and should therefore be treated by natural means. God could, after all, work through natural means and the discoveries of effective treatments could be seen as divine gifts. While some still decried reliance on medical knowledge, most accepted it as useful.

Ancient works on medicine, however, suffered the same general fate in the early Middle Ages as other classical works of learning; that is, only a limited number of translations into Latin were available. To the extent that cultivation of medicine as a practice occurred at all, it took place largely in the monasteries, where care of the sick was seen as an expression of religious concern.

Because the writings of the Hippocratic and Galenic traditions were part of the vast corpus of Greek works that were translated into Arabic beginning in the eighth century, they and other Greek medical sources were preserved. Islamic medicine built on this Greek inheritance of medical wisdom by assimilating it into an existing indigenous tradition. Since almost all of the Greek medical texts were translated into Arabic, the materials that came down to the late Middle Ages from Islam represented a rich and diverse storehouse of medical knowledge.

The flourishing of urban schools provided the first context in which a Western medical tradition really began to take shape. Urban society produced elites who demanded people skilled in medicine to balance the proliferation of practitioners of all kinds that graced the landscape. From the wise woman who knew how to cure warts to the lithotomist who could "cut for the stone," the choices of a healer to treat a wide variety of medical ailments were legion. As the urban school gave way to the university, a process of differentiation developed that enabled recognized social distinctions to be made among healers.

Unlike alchemy, the study of medicine did find an institutional home in the university curriculum. This was an important development in Western medicine because it became an academic discipline, shaped by the Aristotelian natural philosophy to which it was exposed. Eventually an arts degree, which required the mastery of Aristotelian natural philosophy, became a prerequisite to medical study and medicine assumed a place among the higher faculties with theology and law.

But not all medical practice received the benefit of institutionalization among the intellectual elites. More than most aspects of intellectual culture, medical knowledge could not be confined to one social class. Virtually everyone in society was interested in the causes and remedies of disease, where relatively few expressed any interest at all in, for example, knowledge about the motions of the heavens. Because of this widespread interest in sickness and its treatment, there was not a radical difference between the medical ideas that circulated in society at large and those that were taught in medieval universities.

The central conceptions, widely shared, were that health depended on balance and that disease resulted from imbalance. The Greek understanding of the body's humors, or fluids, was easily grasped by anyone; hence, there was a basic conviction that a disturbance of the balance among the body's humors was responsible for sickness. Clearly, then, restoring balance was the fundamental treatment to be undertaken. Most often the assumption was made that the balance had been disturbed by the presence of an excess of one of the humors. To restore balance the extra fluid had to be removed; hence bloodletting and purgatives were the most common forms of treatment. Medievals also appreciated the information about the use of plants and herbs that came down to them from ancient authorities such as Dioscorides (fl. 50–70), especially those that induced vomiting or an evacuation of the bowel.

A variety of healers also stood ready to answer the call when a medical situation called for surgery. Depending on the procedure undertaken, the patient could be treated by an executioner or barber and even in some cases by a university-trained practitioner. In general, however, physicians with university degrees did not practice surgery because it was most often viewed as a craft that required technical expertise, not the mastery of medical theory.

We will consider the state of anatomical knowledge in the medieval university in Chapter 4, when we compare it to the important new developments that took place in the early modern period. Suffice it to say here that the anatomical work of Galen that first became known in translation from the Arabic during the late medieval period was not particularly helpful for instructing students. Only later, when more complete writings of Galen became available, did the study of anatomy take on greater importance.

The Bequest of the Middle Ages

More than any other single thing, the recovery of the writings of Aristotle shaped the content of late medieval natural philosophy. This fact should not overshadow the criticisms, revisions, and extensions of Aristotle's thought that took place first in the Islamic world and then in the Latin West. What eventually resulted was, of course, a Christianized version of Aristotelian natural philosophy. But at its foundation the categories in which nature was conceptualized—form, matter, and formal, efficient, material, and final cause—remained thoroughly Aristotelian. Because purposeful activity was exhibited throughout the natural world, the metaphor for nature was organism.

As they refined the description and treatment of the natural world, always integrating the results into their deeply religious outlook, medieval scholars set an agenda that lasted well beyond them. Many of the questions they asked, and to a surprising extent the kind of answers they permitted, persisted into the era that succeeded them.

Just as the growth of urban centers profoundly altered regional society in the Middle Ages, so too would the expansion of the known world that followed the late medieval period require new ways of envisioning nature and its inhabitants. Once again the writings of the ancients, including non-Aristotelian works, would play a part. The watchword of the coming era would be innovation.

Suggestions for Reading

Edward Grant, *The Foundations of Modern Science in the Middle Ages* (Cambridge: Cambridge University Press, 1996).

Edward Grant, *God and Reason in the Middle Ages* (Cambridge: Cambridge University Press, 2001).

David C. Lindberg, *The Beginnings of Western Science* (Chicago: University of Chicago Press, 1992).

David C. Lindberg, ed., *Science in the Middle Ages* (Chicago: University of Chicago Press, 1980).

CHAPTER 3

Early Modern Innovations

Dynamic changes began to emerge in the fourteenth and fifteenth centuries in the Latin West. On the intellectual level the recovery of ancient texts captured the attention of scholars, making them rethink the synthesis of Christianity and Aristotelian thought Thomas Aquinas had crafted. The invention of printing, which increased the dispersion of new ideas, contributed to the growing awareness of newness. And with explorers penetrating farther and farther into unknown waters, knowledge of the Earth itself expanded in unanticipated ways, opening up whole new worlds to the European imagination.

By this time the landscape of power was changing as well. The most obvious difference from earlier times was the erosion of the power of the papacy. In earlier years the pope, as the leader of a unified Western Christianity, exercised considerable political power. But with the growth of the power of kings, whose interests were regional and secular, respect for papal authority weakened.

The disruption of the Vatican's power became openly transparent during the 1300s and 1400s. Philip IV of France actually captured Pope Boniface VIII at the beginning of the fourteenth century in the course of a dispute over the king's right to imprison a bishop. As the result of Philip's action, the papacy moved from Rome to Avignon in France in 1309. From then until 1377 the popes, all French, were located in Avignon during what is known as the Babylonian Captivity. No sooner had the papacy been relocated to Rome near the end of the century when another crisis arose. In hostile reaction to decisions of the new pope, Urban VI, cardinals fled Rome and declared the papal election invalid. They then proceeded to elect a second pope, who simultaneously ruled from Avignon and produced a schism in church leadership that lasted until 1417. At one point during this so-called Great Schism there were three popes, none of whom recognized the legitimacy of the others!

◎   Recasting the Medieval Intellectual Heritage   ◎

The recovery of manuscripts from the past did not result in a permanent resolution of the differences between pagan and Christian notions about the cosmos or about nature's importance. Rather, it produced a continuing reexamination of existing ideas, a growing intrigue with the past, and even a reformation of faith.

Erosion of the Thomistic Synthesis

In a chaotic situation such as the Great Schism the appearance of new ideas was hardly surprising. One area of thought that felt the effect of intellectual change was the synthesis between faith and reason that Thomas Aquinas had forged in the thirteenth century. Especially in the fourteenth and fifteenth centuries, Aquinas's confidence that rational philosophical analysis was able to clarify and confirm the contents of revealed theological truth came under question. As we shall see, some of these new attitudes about the relationship between philosophy and theology had an impact on the manner in which mathematics and natural philosophy were viewed.

William of Ockham's new direction in philosophy.   Among those questioning the relationship between faith and reason was William of Ockham (1285–1349). Born in England, he received a degree from Oxford before earning his master's degree in Paris. A Franciscan, he chose a vow of strict poverty based on the claim that Christ and his apostles had owned no possessions. This brought him into dispute with Pope John XXII and, as a result, he spent some years in prison.

Ockham was skeptical of the ability of natural reason to prove Christian doctrines such as the immortality of the soul. It was not that he wanted to completely separate theology and philosophy; rather, he argued that philosophy could not demonstrate the conclusions of faith with certainty. Therefore, the tenets of revealed truth had to be accepted through faith alone.

These conclusions were consistent with Ockham's view of philosophy in general. He believed that, especially where nature was concerned, philosophy had to do with propositions, not with things. Philosophy dealt with what humans know and that is a product of the mind. He believed that it was a mistake to regard philosophy's objective as an examination of things that exist. If that were the case, then philosophy would never be able to deal with generalizations, or what he called universals. It would have to remain on the level of individual things. Philosophy did have to do with universals, he taught, but they exist in the mind and only in the mind.

The study of motion provided an example of the implications of Ockham's view for natural philosophy. For him the noun *motion* did not refer to a real thing. The only real thing was the moving body, which existed in successive places. When we create an idea of the body's existence in these successive places and call it motion, we have created a name that does not refer to a real thing. It is just a name. Ockham's view is therefore called nominalism. His wish to cut away what was not needed and to retain only the fewest assumptions necessary is known as Ockham's "razor."

Ockham represents an important new direction in natural philosophy. In his skeptical view of the traditional claims of philosophy he moved away from what is known as realism, which claims to deal with whether or not something exists, to epistemology, which inquires about what is known in the mind. The significance of this distinction is very important for understanding what is meant by natural scientific truth in later centuries.

Nicholas of Cusa and learned ignorance.   An example of the continuing skeptical tendency in theology from the fifteenth century is Nicholas of Cusa (1401–1464), a German theologian who eventually became a cardinal in the Roman Catholic Church and a legate for two different popes. In the late 1430s he composed his most well-known work, *On Learned Ignorance,* whose ostensible purpose was to clarify the relationship between God and humankind. In the course of making his case, Nicholas drew on the reader's knowledge of mathematics to illustrate his conclusions.

According to Nicholas, in acquiring new knowledge we compare what is unknown to what is certain. So in mathematics, for example, when we can trace a conclusion back to its origin in something we know to be true, we hope to establish the truth of our conclusion as well. This is obviously impossible, however, in all considerations of the infinite. The infinite has no comparison to anything we know, because human knowledge deals only in the realm of the finite. So clearly humans could have no knowledge about God, who is infinite in comparison to us.

But even when we compare finite things we run into difficulty. Nicholas agreed with Pythagoras that things are constituted and understood through number. He argued specifically that comparative relation could not be understood apart from number, or, as he put it, "number encompasses all things related comparatively." But when we compare two things we find degrees of equality. That is, it is always possible to find something that is more similar to or more different from an original thing than the thing we first used in our comparison, and so on, ad infinitum. Nicholas concluded that it was therefore "not the case that by means of likenesses a finite intellect can precisely attain the truth about things."

In Book II of his work Nicholas examined what conclusions our reason might lead to regarding the constitution of the cosmos. His results were surprising. Our world could not have a fixed center or a fixed outer boundary, for if it did it would have its own beginning and end. That would be false, because God is the center and the circumference of our world. Reason tells us, then, that the Earth must have motion, that it is a star. Nicholas concluded that the Earth's motion was circular and discussed a host of conclusions in order to demonstrate that humans simply cannot understand such things. The implication was that reason, even when used properly, leads to contradictions that are resolved only in God himself. "We recognize," wrote Nicholas, "through learned ignorance and in accordance with the preceding points, that we cannot know the rationale for any of God's works, but can only marvel."

The clear inference to be drawn from the work of both William of Ockham and Nicholas of Cusa was that the reasoning of philosophy did not lead to demonstrated and unambiguous truth about the world. Both believed that it was important to engage in philosophy in order to make clear its scope. Ockham wished to show that philosophy was not about the nature of real things but about the constructions of the mind. And Nicholas wanted to pursue learning in order to show that in the end it was ignorant. For both scholars, the lesson was that the tenets of revealed truth had to be accepted by faith alone, because reason could not deliver truth.

The Impact of Divine Omnipotence

Theologians and natural philosophers became preoccupied in the fourteenth century with the issue of God's power. This concern resulted less in a change of Aristotelian thought than it did in its reorientation. The increased focus on divine omnipotence affected the way in which scholars regarded the world of nature.

If nature was dependent solely on God's power, then nature could not be thought of as having its own necessary course as it appeared to have, for example, in ancient Greek astronomy. The cause and effect relationships we observe in nature have no necessary connection in themselves. They exist only because an all-powerful God decided that they should go together.

When a rock is thrown into the air, for example, it seeks to return to its natural place in the center of the cosmos, not because Aristotle had identified a necessary property of rocks, but because God had endowed it with that property. The implication was that God could have made rocks to seek a natural place away from the center of the Earth had he wished to. And occasionally, say when God chose to work a miracle, rocks might be made to seek a different natural place. The behavior of rocks was directly dependent on God's will.

Some historians have argued that such a conception undermined the development of natural philosophy because it did not presuppose the unchangeable natural order that had marked Aristotle's thought. But medieval natural philosophers did not believe that God frequently acted capriciously to change usual relationships among things in nature. In fact, they understood that God had created this world by his decree, which they had every expectation was an eternal decree. This understanding meant that God could retain absolute omnipotence and at the same time provide the kind of regularity in nature that would make natural philosophy possible. It was a Christian recasting of Aristotle's system.

Intrigue with Antiquity

Some thinkers began to see in the recovered writings from the past an opportunity to gain access to an ancient wisdom that had been lost. Attempts to restore this learning of old took several forms.

The beginnings of humanism.   Humanism, a major feature of which was the desire to recover and study the works of antiquity, first appeared in fourteenth-century Italy. Humanism's greatest influence on natural philosophy came in the sixteenth century, and will be dealt with in the next chapter. But its beginnings are found already in the fourteenth and fifteenth centuries.

Francesco Petrarca (1304–1374), an Italian known as Petrarch, is often called the father of humanism. Petrarch revived an appreciation for ancient poetry and condemned his own age for letting fall what he called "some of the richest and sweetest fruits that the tree of knowledge has yielded." He was, he said, tempted to regard this ancient learning as more valuable than anything else in the whole world. Petrarch was particularly enamored of the Roman orator Cicero, from whom he learned that communicating knowledge was as important as acquiring learning.

Historian of science Allen Debus has pointed out that Petrarch's love of natural things was instrumental in promoting a new observational study of nature. It also contributed to creating a distrust of medieval scholasticism, based as it was on a dogmatic acceptance of Aristotelian philosophy, which had come to dominate the intellectual atmosphere of the universities. Along with other early humanists, Petrarch made available an alternate outlook, one that would inspire individuals in succeeding generations to explore new intellectual possibilities.

Ancient magic restored. Among the writings of ancient wisdom that began to appear in the Latin West were texts attributed to one Hermes Trismegistus, whose works constitute what is known as the Hermetic corpus. They contained a different view of the relationship of humankind to nature from that common in Western Christianity, one in which nature played a more important role. Hermetic philosophy was a view of nature that held that the soul of the individual could unite with the cosmos. This alternate portrait of nature came into the early modern era largely—although certainly not exclusively—through the efforts of two men, Cosimo de' Medici (1389–1464) and Marsilio Ficino (1433–1499).

Cosimo de' Medici, the first effective ruler in Florence of the famous Medici dynasty that followed him, left as one of his many legacies the translation into Latin of a number of Greek manuscripts he had obtained from Constantinople. Cosimo surrounded himself with artists and scholars, whose company he enjoyed and whose efforts he supported. He was a great lover of books, investing large amounts of the family fortune in establishing a library of illuminated manuscripts and early printed volumes. He also established in Florence a new academy that would focus on bringing to Italy the works of the Greek philosopher Plato. It is believed that Cosimo's physician brought his son, Marsilio Ficino, to the academy, where the Florentine leader immediately recognized the boy's genius and his love of academic study. Cosimo instructed the father to make sure that the lad developed this natural disposition and he subsequently chose Ficino to head his new academy.

Having learned Greek, Ficino undertook Cosimo's mission to translate Plato's works into Latin. His many translations of Plato's works, and his role as head of the Florentine Academy, have solidified Ficino's reputation as one of the central figures in the early modern movement to establish a Platonistic academic tradition as an alternative to the dominant Aristotelianism of the universities.

Cosimo also charged Ficino with translating the works of Hermes Trismegistus, a somewhat mysterious figure thought to have lived at the time of Moses. Ficino was richly rewarded for bringing into Latin Hermes' work, *On Divine Wisdom and the Creation of the World.* His early biographer tells us that he was endowed by Cosimo with the most generous gift of a family estate at Careggi near the outskirts of Florence, as well as with a house in town, and even with beautifully written and costly Greek books by Plato and Plotinus.

The writings of Hermes were later determined to have come from the second or third century A.D., but Ficino believed they were part of a wisdom that predated Christianity. Many themes in the Hermetic writings were similar to those of Christian redemptive history. For example, in both visions it was humankind's main goal to become reunited with God after having fallen from grace. But the tone was different. In the Hermetic view, the fall from grace due to Adam's sin was not regarded as a punishment; rather, it was a necessary phase of the journey to spiritual growth and the ultimate union with the divine. The reunion with the divine did not simply represent a return to what humankind once had. In achieving union with the divine, humankind was transformed into something new that it had never yet been. Hermes drew on many sources outside those common to Christianity, including the religious perspectives of ancient Greece, Babylonia, and Egypt. As a result, Hermeticism embraced more diverse manifestations of the divine than could be found in the Christian understanding.

The place of nature played a much more central role in Hermetic religion than it did in Western Christianity. That was because for Hermes nature was a primary vehicle through which the divine could be known. Ficino accepted that individual souls were part of the world's soul, but that the link between the two had been impaired in the fall from grace. To reestablish the connection required the assistance of the magician—one who had gained an understanding of the secrets that revealed the presence of the divine in the physical world. Through the use of talismans, rituals, formulas, and procedures, the magician was able to get on God's wavelength, so to speak. In this way the magician could know God through nature.

Of course Ficino did not approve of the use of black magic, whose goal was far different from knowledge of the divine. In spite of this disclaimer, there were naturally those who opposed the Hermetic philosophy in the name of a more traditional understanding of God and nature. In fact, Hermeticism did tend to go its own way, producing followers who delighted in resisting the intellectual trends of the day.

Scholars have noted that the relationship of humankind to nature in this Renaissance magical tradition—which has flourished in various forms right down to our own day—carried with it a very different emphasis from that present in Christianity prior to its appearance. In the medieval perspective humans were helpless against nature. But in the Renaissance magical tradition, as a result of a general conviction that spiritual growth could not occur without human effort, the message was that humans should be active and aggressive. Nature was useful, and humans should try to manipulate it for the spiritual benefit it could provide. In this sense the magical tradition of the Renaissance served as a transition between the medieval period and a later era of natural philosophy in which nature's usefulness was exploited for yet different reasons.

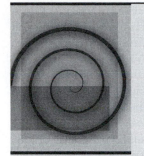

The NATURE of SCIENCE

Magic and Science

Using the tools of the magician may seem to be something quite different from the practice of natural science, and of course it is. In appealing to magic phrases and formulae the magician openly cuts short the search for regular causal relationships that link two events and even revels in the mystery connecting them. The fifteenth-century magician would maintain that trying to understand everything that God understood was being too presumptuous and arrogant. If we could merely discover ways to reproduce connections between things that only God was previously aware of, that would be sufficient.

Nevertheless, by striving to uncover these connections, the magician does resemble the natural scientist. The magician wishes to be in control of what happens, even if he or she does not want to know or disclose the connecting links. Just because a modern scientist insists on exposing as many of the intermediate phenomena as possible between two events, that does not mean that the ultimate question of why one event follows another has been accounted for once and for all.

Critics of the notion of causality later on in the early modern era pointed out that saying one thing is caused by another is really saying only that it always follows the other. Humans know how to initiate action to bring about a desired result—to cause the result. To cause something involves an intention to bring it about. We get so used to sequences of events that occur naturally in nature that we say one thing causes another, but in natural science we do not mean that the cause *intended* to produce the result, merely that the effect always follows the cause. A magician does not maintain anything more than that.

Paracelsus.   An example of the way the Hermetic philosophy could disrupt established trends in the early modern era can be seen in the work of Theophrastus Phillippus Aureolus Bombastus von Hohenheim, known commonly as Paracelsus (1493–1541). Paracelsus was aware that Hermeticism represented an alternative view to the teachings of the university, particularly in his chosen field of medicine. But he was the type of personality who enjoyed defying authority, especially where the treatment of the sick was concerned.

There is no evidence that Paracelsus ever took a medical degree, although he did attend several universities. He learned some alchemy and medicine from his physician father, who practiced in several mining towns during Paracelsus's youth. But he appears to have gathered the full range of his knowledge primarily from the treatment of patients, particularly as a surgeon accompanying the armies that were continually engaged in warfare.

Paracelsus openly denounced the growing reverence in university medicine for the Greek physician Galen. He rejected Galen's claim that health consisted in maintaining a balance among the body's four humors. He was motivated more by the Hermetic conviction that structural similarities ran through the natural world at all levels. For example, he discarded Galen's belief that opposites cure and replaced it with the principle that like cures like. If the body was affected by a poison, it should be treated by a similar poison. Much to the discontent of the physicians of his day he repeatedly appealed to analogies from chemistry and alchemy in his explanation of health and disease. For example, he believed that the body's organs separated the impure from the pure just as the alchemist did. Illness occurred when the organs failed in their function and impurities accumulated.

Paracelsus produced many followers who continued to champion his iconoclastic approach to medicine in opposition to the Galenists, who wished to restore ancient Greek medical practice. Not all of those who revered the Hermetic philosophy generated as much resistance as did Parcelsus. Still, because of its willingness to incorporate new ideas into its vision, many had regarded the main outlook of Hermeticism with suspicion from the beginning.

A Reformation of Faith

An enduring phase of the recasting of the medieval heritage occurred at the intersection of the intellectual sphere with that of practice. During this period of skepticism some registered their dissatisfaction with the interpretation of Christian doctrine and the way it was put into practice.

Along with the degeneration of the ecclesiastical hierarchy that accompanied the erosion of the authority of Rome came a marked decline in the moral life of the clergy. Such laxity was not entirely new. In different regions of Christendom various unorthodox practices had grown up over time until they were regarded as almost normal. Consequently the moral life that true Christian teaching required had been interpreted in a variety of ways for several centuries prior to the Protestant Reformation of the sixteenth century. As far back as the eleventh century Pope Gregory VII stood firm, at considerable cost, against clergy who had purchased their positions and against clergy who had married. His efforts resulted in his having to leave Rome, ending his days in self-imposed exile.

Not all subsequent popes were as concerned as Gregory VII was to, as he put it, "love justice and hate iniquity." But others in the church periodically felt obligated to denounce corruption, especially when it appeared to have become the order of the day. The efforts of these figures from the fourteenth and fifteenth century prepared the way for the great innovation of the early modern era known as the Protestant Reformation, which produced its own effect on the way in which God's relationship to nature was understood.

Early reformers.   The Oxford theologian John Wycliffe (1324–1384) was a key figure in the call for major reforms in the church. Wycliffe recognized that many church leaders had become indistinguishable from civil authorities in how they led their lives. So enamored were they of the power they wielded that they came to prize the enjoyment of life over their duties and their responsibilities to lead a holy life. Wycliffe's protest against clerics who accumulated considerable amounts of property, and his defense of monastic poverty, clearly put him at odds with many in the church hierarchy who regarded him as an extremist.

The issue that caused the greatest stir as the fourteenth century came to a close, however, was Wycliffe's denial of the doctrine of transubstantiation, the belief that in the sacrament of communion the bread and wine are transformed into the actual body and blood of Christ. Wycliffe did not believe that when Christ said "This is my body" to his disciples at the Last Supper he intended them to take him literally. To be so overly literal took attention away from the meaning of the sacrament, which was to hold in mind Christ's sacrifice and its central importance to a life of faith. Focusing on the material world meant that believers were dwelling on the letter, but not the spirit, of Christ's command to remember him. It promoted superficial, not deep and genuine, spirituality.

Wycliffe's attitude presaged the general view of reformers to come after him about the relative unimportance of the physical world in comparison to the spiritual. For these reformers natural philosophy would not be a major concern since there were much more vital matters. In calling for a return to a purer form of Christianity, Wycliffe was echoing the view of earlier theologians who insisted on subordinating the realm of the physical to that of the spiritual.

The church authorities could not stand idly by while Wycliffe attacked so central a doctrine as transubstantiation. He was condemned on several fronts, especially after he acquired a following among laymen, whom he sent forth to preach his reforms. No doubt he was able to escape personal harm because of the turmoil of the Great Schism that afflicted the papacy around this time.

One of his followers who lived in central Europe, however, was not so fortunate. Jan Hus (1369–1415) attended the University of Prague and was ordained a priest in 1400. Very impressed with the writings of Wycliffe, Hus translated one of them into Czech and made it known widely. He shared Wycliffe's anger at what he regarded as the immoral behavior of many clergy and soon became a thorn in the side of the established ecclesiastical authorities. As the result of a papal bull (decree), the archbishop of Prague decreed in 1410 that Wycliffe's works be burned, an action that Hus denounced from the pulpit. The pope excommunicated Hus in 1411, and in the following year ordered him placed under arrest. The Czech ruler, however, did not carry out the order, and Hus continued to support Wycliffe's views openly. He wrote a work, "Six Errors," which he posted on the walls of a church in Prague and in which authorities claimed to find heretical teachings. Called before the Council of Constance in 1415, Hus attempted to defend his calls for reform. The council, however, condemned him to the stake, and he was executed.

Hus continued to exert an influence on Bohemia after his death. Although different groups of Hussites formed over the course of the fifteenth century, the most lasting formed in 1457 as the Unity of the Brethren, a forerunner of the Moravian Church of the present day. Thus, well before Martin Luther nailed the famous ninety-five theses to the church door in Wittenberg in 1517, Protestants had already appeared in the early modern period.

Erasmus and Luther.   The story of the appearance of Protestantism in the sixteenth century is better known than that of the earlier reformers and it needs only a brief discussion here. Just prior to Luther's action in Wittenberg, Europe had been entertained by the writings of an irreverent scholar who took the name Desiderius Erasmus (1466–1536). Erasmus was born out of wedlock and was forced by guardians to attend a monastery. Although he became a priest, his heart and mind were far from those of a monk. He grew to revere the writers of antiquity, who taught him to bring to his work a secular tone that was detached from official religion. In fact, he delighted in using his eloquent, witty, and sarcastic style against the same kind of excesses and corruption that had motivated earlier reformers, and in favor of what he regarded as true religion.

By the end of the first decade of the century Erasmus's mockery of established religion won him great popularity in Europe. Theologians, he said in his *Praise of Folly* of 1509, are so conceited that they think they are already in heaven, from where they look down with pity on others as so many worms. They protect themselves with a wall of imposing definitions, conclusions, corollaries, and explicit and implicit propositions. Erasmus wished to expose this kind of attitude for what it was so that people could get beyond the letter to the spirit of real religion.

In 1517 Martin Luther challenged his contemporaries with his discontent, expressed in the language of theological argument. He stood in a long tradition of reformers who denounced hypocrisy and pleaded for a return to a more genuine Christian piety. The nineteenth-century Luther scholar Albrecht Ritschl noted that early in his career Luther believed that the issue of salvation was so central that it trumped all other concerns. In other words, both Wycliffe and the young Luther had little interest in claims made about the material world.

In Chapter 4 we shall see that later in life Luther permitted himself to be drawn into consideration of an assertion about the physical world, namely, about whether the cosmos was Earth-centered or sun-centered. Nevertheless, the view held by numerous reformers that the relationship between humankind and God had little or nothing to do with that between God and nature persisted. It would continue to be represented throughout the sixteenth century and beyond, threatening, as one scholar has put it, to sever the vertical dimension between God and nature as if the realm of nature could make no claims at all. Such a view would be invoked in the seventeenth century by those who opposed Galileo's attempt to demonstrate that knowledge of nature could not be ignored when trying to arrive at a true religion.

◎ The Impact of Printing ◎

An early modern innovation of a completely different kind was the invention of movable type in the middle of the fifteenth century. While technological in nature, this change had a profound impact on the development of Western civilization because it helped to spread ideas more rapidly and more extensively than ever before.

The Era of Scribes

From antiquity to the mid-fifteenth century books were produced by scribes, who laboriously copied manuscripts by hand. By the Middle Ages scribes worked independently or as part of a team in a scriptorium attached to a monastery or a records

A Medieval Scribe

office. After the rise of the universities in the Latin West, the so-called pecia system made its appearance in response to the increased pressure for books from university faculties. This system divided the labor so that a copyist worked only on selected portions of a text. Both male and female copyists then received payment for each completed piece from a lay stationer.

The most common material from which manuscripts were made was parchment, made from animal skin. Typically, monks would soak the skins of sheep or goats in a lime bath to remove the flesh, then, while the skins were still wet, they would stretch the skin and scrape it with a knife. Next they would rub it with pumice to raise the nap and with chalk to whiten it. The completion of each technique produced varying qualities of parchment. Once lay stationers instituted the commercial production of manuscripts, the making of parchment became a trade done by parchmenters, whose shops were located in the stationer's town near a supply of water.

Medieval and early modern scribes had to conform to strict rules when copying letters. Some manuscripts used letters of equal height confined between two lines; others used what might be thought of as "lower case" letters. By the Middle Ages copyists used both kinds of writing for most purposes. Sometimes illuminators were employed to add color or images to certain letters of the text. In general, copyists determined the formality of a work by what cut and thickness of pen they used and how slowly and carefully they wrote the letters. In the fourteenth century early humanists like Petrarch, who were very involved in producing books of the works of antiquity, introduced their own reforms into the kinds of scripts used.

Beginning in the thirteenth century paper began to be used for correspondence and around 1400 copyists used it for lower-grade books. Arab copyists had learned how to make paper from the Chinese and employed it as early as the ninth century. Its use spread into the Mediterranean region among merchants for notes and records and by the thirteenth century it was being produced in Italy. Paper made from cotton and linen rags was less expensive to produce, but it did not lessen copyists' time.

Once the pages had been completed, a binder undertook the final stages in the production of a book. Often the sheets of parchment were folded once to form two leaves, or *bifolia*. Writing on the front and back of each half sheet therefore produced four pages. Several of these bifolia were then gathered into *quires,* which were sewn together and attached to wooden covers that were sheathed with leather.

Although the production of books increased after the appearance of Western universities, it was still an extremely laborious process. The notion of identical copies of a book meant something quite different in the era of scribes, when individual differences could not help but exist from one copy to the next, from what it would mean after the advent of printing. Further, the total number of books circulating in society was nothing compared to what there would be once movable type was invented. It has been estimated that fewer books were put out between the early Middle Ages to the middle of the fifteenth century than those printed between then and the end of that century.

The Advent of Printing

The fifteenth century saw the appearance of printed books, a development that brought uniformity to bound volumes that scribes could not duplicate. The initial innovation of printing from blocks of wood was then quickly overtaken by the advent of movable type.

Block printing.   Printed books first began appearing in the fifteenth century using a technique that had been employed somewhat earlier to print fabrics and to produce playing cards and devotional images. In block printing a text or an image was carved into a block of wood in such a way that the raised portion of the block formed the letters or picture in mirror image. The block was then inked and paper was placed on the block. Rubbing or pressing the paper on the block transferred the image to the paper.

Initially, the text or image was transferred by printing one page at a time from a single block of wood. In this case printers used but one side of a page and pasted two sides back-to-back before binding. It was not long before presses that could print two sides came along. Woodcut prints, especially of images, could also be added to hand copied manuscripts or they could be printed first, with text added later by a copyist.

The obvious advantage of block printing over copying was that the printer could continue to put out identical copies of a book until the deterioration in the wood blocks affected the quality of the text. But there were disadvantages as well. Each page required its own wood block and preparing the blocks was slow and expensive work. Carving the letters into the wood so that they were well aligned and of even size was extremely difficult. A lot of effort went into the preparation of all the blocks needed for an entire book.

The earliest known European woodcut image dates from the third decade of the fifteenth century. Block-printed books flourished throughout the remainder of the century, but diminished after the invention of movable type. Their subject matter most frequently dealt with biblical stories that could be used by clergy for instructional purposes. For example, a prominent block book, *The Poor Man's Bible,* paralleled events in the life of Jesus to those of the Old Testament in order to portray him as the fulfillment of earlier history.

Movable type. The production of books changed again around the middle of the fifteenth century with the appearance of movable type. The major difference between this approach and that used in block printing was that there was a mold for each letter rather than one for each page. While that meant that the printer needed thousands of letter molds instead of just one mold per page, the molds could be assembled and reassembled to create a long running text much more easily than could be done in block printing. One additional innovation also made a huge difference. The letter molds were made from metal, not wood, so they could be used for a much longer time and they gave a cleaner image.

The story of the invention of movable type in the West is a familiar one. Most everyone has heard the name of Johann Gutenberg (ca. 1400–1468), although his original name was Johannes Gensfleisch. Gutenberg's father belonged to a line of wealthy and powerful merchants in Mainz, Germany. He adopted the name of his estate, Gutenberg, as his family name when Johannes was a young man.

Mainz was an important ecclesiastical principality, whose powerful archbishop had traditionally served as an elector of the Holy Roman Empire. Gutenberg's father and uncle were officials in the archbishop's mint. Knowledge of metalworking had been vital to the church since the early Middle Ages in the making of vessels and icons. It is presumed that Gutenberg learned about casting chambers, the casting of dies, and the stamping of gold coins from this connection to metalworking.

Specific details about Gutenberg's life are sparse. We do know that he moved to Strasbourg around the age of thirty and that he most likely made his living as a craftsman. In the late 1430s Gutenberg became involved in a legal dispute with associates in a business venture. In return for loans, Gutenberg taught his associates various skills, which included the art of printing. What becomes clear from the records is that Gutenberg had been experimenting with an idea he had, but needed outside support to develop it.

Gutenberg's specific idea was a way to cast individual letters from metal that could be used to form text. Others had tried to make metal type, and even to use individual wooden letters, but the problems of perfecting movable type were formidable. It would take an extremely inventive mind to solve the many facets of the problem sufficiently to make the process feasible. The first and one of the most challenging problems was how to cast molds for a typeface that would produce letters of the same height and also accommodate the spacing between such different letters as *i* and *m*. Gutenberg solved this by making two L-shaped pieces that slid into each other and by regulating the height and spacing.

But this was by no means the only problem Gutenberg needed to solve. He had to have a metal that was hard enough to use for printing, but was soft enough to cast. He had to have the right kind of ink. He could not use the water-based ink preferred by scribes and utilized in block printing. An oil-based ink was required. Finally, he had to devise a means for transferring the imprint from the type to the paper. Gutenberg was familiar with presses used in wine and cheese making, and adapted them to his own purpose.

By 1438 Gutenberg was back in Mainz. Having an idea was one thing, but realizing its potential was quite another. Thousand of letters had to be made, which necessitated hiring metalworkers to cast the molds and make the type. Materials had to be purchased, including metal, ink, and paper. He needed people to assemble text in braces, ready for the press. To make the production of a book worthwhile, several presses had to be built and people hired to run them. He made a deal in 1450 with a local businessman named Johann Fust that would enable him to move beyond perfecting his printing technique on small items such as tickets and flyers, and to undertake the huge task of printing the entire Bible.

In 1452 he secured another loan from Fust, on condition that if it was not repaid, he would forfeit the printing equipment. The Bible, once completed, contained two pages per sheet in double columns—some 641 sheets of text. It employed a black Gothic text common to manuscripts of the day and had red and blue leader letters that were added later by an illuminator. It is estimated that less than a few hundred copies were printed, some on vellum and some on paper. To accomplish such an enormous job Gutenberg produced several hundred thousand pieces of type. From a later account we learn that he supposedly used six presses and printed about three hundred sheets per day.

Unfortunately, Gutenberg was unable to repay the loan to Fust on time and he lost his equipment in a lawsuit in 1455, the year the Gutenberg Bible was completed. The sale of the Bible went well, although profits went to Fust, not Gutenberg. In 1465 Gutenberg obtained a pension from a wealthy citizen of Mainz, which supported him until his death three years later.

The impact of Gutenberg's work in perfecting the art of printing with movable type was immediate and profound. There were some who were suspicious of the new technique, assuming that any process that could put out such a magnificent product in so many identical copies came from the devil. But it was not long before printing presses were springing up everywhere. By 1481 they were present

The Gutenberg Bible

throughout the Holy Roman Empire and by 1500 they could be found in every important municipal center of Europe. The development obviously impacted scribes negatively. The Abbot of Sponheim, for example, exhorted monks not to stop copying just because printing had come along. It was good, he said, to keep idle hands busy, to encourage diligence and devotion, and to promote knowledge of the Scripture. But even he had seen the handwriting on the wall. He had his own works printed, including one entitled *Praise of Scribes.*

As we shall see in Chapter 4, the development of natural philosophy and mathematics benefited greatly from the invention of printing with movable type. Among the many works printed in the sixteenth century, those devoted to astronomy, natural history, anatomy, and other aspects of nature figured very prominently. Printing proved to be a great stimulant to the spread of new ideas about the natural world.

◎　Expanding Geographical Horizons　◎

The lure of travel was not new in the early modern period. The Venetian merchants Nicolo and Maffeo Polo, accompanied by Nicolo's son Marco, had journeyed to China in the thirteenth century, where Marco rose to a high status as a diplomat. In addition to traveling throughout China itself, he went as an envoy to Japan, India, Burma, and Tibet. On returning to Venice after a quarter century's absence, he wrote an account of his travels entitled *The Travels of Marco Polo.* The book became known in Europe and even played a key role in the story of Christopher Columbus.

In the fifteenth century the pace of exploration quickened substantially as travel was no longer left to curious individuals, but undertaken with government support. If the desire to see new and exotic lands was not new, the organization of specifically maritime exploration and the techniques used to carry it out were. What became clear to political leaders of the early modern period was that knowledge of new worlds brought with it an economic advantage. Here was an opportunity for investment that would increase trade with faraway lands that were already known. What happened, of course, was the discovery of lands not already known. This brought with it challenges no one had expected.

The Known World

For nearly everyone at the beginning of the early modern period the world contained four continents—Europe, Africa, Asia, and a vast unknown land in the Southern Hemisphere known as the Antipodes. Contemporary maps show little knowledge of the discoveries of the Norse sailors in the Northern Atlantic; in fact, they show the three known continents more or less crowded together with little space given to the oceans. The center of the world was Jerusalem, with Europe, Africa, and Asia positioned around it in a distortion of the more accurate maps that had been made by ancient Greek mapmakers.

Medieval people knew very little about Asia and Africa. Of course, Christians knew the story of the magi who had come to visit the newly born Christ child from Asia, and Africa was by tradition the land from which King Solomon's vast wealth derived. Africa was also supposedly the home of Prester John, who, according to many, was the apostle John himself. He had escaped death in fulfillment of John 21:22–23, which hinted that he would live until Jesus returned, and now ruled over a vast empire in which there was no crime. In addition to these links to religion, many stories about these regions had been passed down from classical times. Legends of fantasy about rivers of gold, giants, legless birds that never landed, and monsters of various sorts were common.

One of the ancient works that was translated into Latin in the early fifteenth century was Claudius Ptolemy's *Geography.* The translation of Ptolemy's text proved to be influential in important ways. For one thing, Europeans learned new mathematical means of representing three-dimensional surfaces on a two-dimensional plane. This played a role in the development of new techniques in mapmaking that were already underway. Europeans also learned how Ptolemy himself

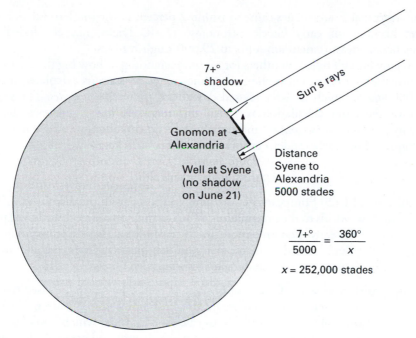

7+°
shadow

Sun's rays

Gnomon at
Alexandria

Well at Syene
(no shadow
on June 21)

Distance
Syene to
Alexandria
5000 stades

$$\frac{7+°}{5000} = \frac{360°}{x}$$

$x = 252,000$ stades

Determination of the Earth's Circumference

had depicted the world. Of course, his conception ran counter to the common view that centered the world on Jerusalem, so naturally it elicited opposition and criticism from many church leaders. But for those who regarded the ancient wisdom as authoritative, Ptolemy's understanding carried great weight. They accepted, for example, his depiction of the west coast of Africa at the edge of the map and his assumption that Asia extended a vast distance to the east. This implied that for a spherical Earth, the distance between Asia and Africa was not great.

The determination of the Earth's circumference went back a long time before Ptolemy. Aristotle had calculated its circumference to be about 1.8 times as great as the modern value of 24,901 miles. Eratosthenes in the third century B.C. employed an ingenious means of calculating how far it was around the Earth. He knew of a well, located at Syene (modern-day Aswan, Egypt), where on the summer solstice the sun cast no shadow on the walls at noon. This meant that the well was located near 23½° N latitude, which is the sun's altitude above the equator on June 21. On the same day, at the same time, some considerable distance almost due north in Alexandria, the sun did cast a shadow, the angle of which could be measured. Using the well at Syene as his base point, Eratosthenes determined that if the shadow's angle of a little more than 7° corresponded to the 5000 *stades* of distance along the Earth's surface between Syene and Alexandria, then all the way around the Earth should correspond to 360°. Simple proportionality revealed that distance to be 252,000 *stades*. Exactly how close that measurement is to the modern value depends on how big a *stade* is taken to be, and that is a controversial matter.

Some assert that Eratosthenes came to within 2 percent of the modern value, but an expert historian of early Greek astronomy, D. R. Dicks, has concluded that Eratosthenes' measurement amounts to 29,000 English miles.

Ptolemy himself relied on others for his understanding of how big the Earth was. A century after Eratosthenes, the Stoic philosopher Posidonius calculated it to be 240,000 *stades,* which he later revised downward to 180,000 *stades.* The significance of the latter calculation was that this relatively low figure was the one Ptolemy put into his *Geography,* and therefore the one that became authoritative for key figures of the early modern era.

An Era of Exploration

Starting around 1420 Europeans began taking to the sea in impressive fashion. They opened up new worlds to the imagination, which in their own way contributed to the innovations of the early modern period. To do this they had to rely on techniques of navigation they had learned from the past and they perfected new techniques that would enable them to face the new challenges ahead.

Finding position at sea.   Once out of sight of land on a sea that caused the ship to pitch and roll, determining accurate position was not a simple matter. The heavens provided the only means available to calculate latitude, which could be done with some accuracy. Determining longitude precisely required accurate timepieces. The common way to measure time on a ship was the hourglass, which made calculating longitude next to impossible.

To find latitude, or the position north of the equator, it was necessary to determine the altitude above the horizon of a known celestial object such as the Pole Star or the sun. In the case of the Pole Star, which is located above the North Pole, latitude is given directly by the Pole Star's altitude above the horizon. During the day sailors could measure the sun's altitude above the horizon and then find their latitude by consulting charts that showed at what latitude the sun had that altitude for that day of the year.

For both daytime and nighttime determinations of latitude, medieval mariners used a cross staff to measure altitude. The other instrument for measuring altitude available to astronomers, the astrolabe, was too difficult to hold steady enough at sea to give precise results. A cross staff consisted of two pieces of wood, a longer one with lengths calibrated on it, and a shorter one that was held perpendicularly to the first. A mariner would brace himself against the side of the ship, pointing the long stick about midway between the celestial object and the horizon. He would then position the cross piece at the precise spot on the long stick that permitted him to align the two ends of the cross piece in such a way that the sun, for example, was at one end at noon and the horizon was at the other. He could then read the altitude from the calibrations marked on the long stick.

If the latitude and longitude of a destination were known, then a captain could reach it by sailing to its latitude and running along that latitude until he reached his goal. More likely he would determine the course from his starting point and use a compass to reach it. The compass was the most trustworthy instrument at sea. By

A Mariner's Cross Staff

the end of the fourteenth century mariners were using a magnetized, north-pointing needle mounted on a card that had the four main directions marked on it. If the positions of two locations were known, then the compass bearing of one position from the other could be calculated and a ship could follow the course by constantly monitoring the direction traversed. Even when sailing into unknown waters the captain could still maintain knowledge of his direction so that he would be able to return. But determining how far along the bearing the ship had gone in a day was more difficult to estimate, especially when the presence of ocean currents and contrary winds were involved.

Early explorers faced an ominous challenge. Their ships and sails were built such that there was no real hope of maintaining a course in the middle of a major storm. Captains had to lower their sails and allow the storm to carry the ship where it would. More than one discovery of new lands resulted from ships being blown off course. Europeans discovered the Cape Verde islands in the middle of the fifteenth century, for example, while fleeing a storm. Despite the difficulties, mariners became bolder and bolder in their search for precious metals and spices and in their determination to win new converts to Christianity and to bring greater glory to their homelands.

Expanding knowledge of Africa.   Africa's west coast provided the first of the continent's shores to be explored. Prince Henry, the third son of the Portuguese king, had distinguished himself in battles on the north coast of Morocco. From traders in the captured region he learned about a gold trade that inspired him to extend Portugal's interest to the south. There was another goal as well. If it was possible to locate a southern entrance into Africa, the Portuguese might be able to find

Prester John and enlist him in the task of removing the Muslims from northern Africa and the Holy Land.

But Prince Henry was not a sailor himself. To send an expedition in this direction along Africa's west coast meant finding a captain who would not be deterred by claims about sea monsters and increasing heat that boiled the ocean. People believed that no one who had ventured beyond the cape at latitude 29° N had ever returned, so they named it Cape Nun. And if Africa were joined to the unknown land of the Antipodes, then it surely could not be circumnavigated.

Much later, in 1625, the claim surfaced that Prince Henry had established a center at Sagres on Portugal's coast in the third decade of the fifteenth century. Soon it became widely accepted that Henry had brought together experts in astronomy, mapmaking, and ship design, and in building nautical instruments that made possible major geographical discoveries. Recent scholarship, however, has discredited this well-established and commonly believed tradition, concluding that no such school ever existed and casting doubt on Prince Henry's own abilities in these areas of expertise.

What is clear is that Henry certainly encouraged geographical exploration and that during his lifetime Portugal established bases on islands off Africa's coast. These served as stopping points and supply stations for ships that were departing on or returning from voyages to the south. By 1434 Portuguese captains had ventured some 350 miles beyond Cape Nun. Not long thereafter other voyages returned with African slaves, a cargo that soon opened up a thriving market demand. Just before midcentury Portuguese sailors discovered that the African coast curved to the east, giving them hope that Africa could indeed be circumnavigated. They also gave the lie to the many tales of horror that had kept Europeans out of southern waters prior to Henry's time.

Although the Portuguese were secretive about the details of these voyages, Spain too began to take an interest in the African coast. As a result Portugal persuaded the pope in 1455 to grant them exclusive rights to the regions they had explored so successfully. This agreement did not prevent the Spanish and even the English from seeking their own agreements with the pope regarding various regions of the West African coast or from their engaging in the slave trade. When a new king came to the throne in 1481, the Portuguese determined that they must use their superior experience in the area to establish their claims to the African coast and to secure a short route to India by sailing around Africa.

On the first of several enterprises, the king commissioned a captain to take with him stone markers, which he was to set in place at various conspicuous points along his route. Inscribed in Latin, Arabic, and Portuguese, they laid claim for Portugal. A subsequent voyage in 1487 was to attempt to sail around Africa. The captain, Bartolomeu Dias, went as far south as anyone before him when, without knowing it, he was blown around the southern cape in a violent storm. He then traveled far enough north to convince himself that he had in fact found Africa's southernmost point. On his return home the king named the point the Cape of Good Hope, for a route to India now appeared more likely than it ever had.

The king also sent two overland missions east in 1487, one of which was to try to find Prester John, who was rumored to be near present-day Ethiopia. The other was to go to India via Arabia to find out the routes of Muslim ships that brought spices to the Persian gulf and eastern Africa. The traveler sent to find Prester John died in Cairo, and the other adventurer, Pero da Covilhã, also never made it home. But word of what Da Covilhã had discovered did reach the king. He had made it to the western coast of India and then traveled far enough down the eastern coast of Africa to suspect that the Indian Ocean did in fact join the Atlantic. This word, when it reached the Portuguese monarch, sustained him and his successor in their continuing quest to find a sea passage to India.

Having learned from the experience of others before him, Vasco da Gama (ca. 1469–1524) embarked in 1497 on a voyage supported by the Portuguese crown that was to succeed in reaching India. After rounding the Cape of Good Hope, he continued north to the port at Mozambique, where he encountered Arabs instead of the African chiefs that had usually greeted the ship. One of those on board who could speak Arabic learned that there were great ports to the north and also that Prester John held many cities along the coast, although John himself supposedly lived far inland from the shore. In one of these ports Da Gama found Hindus, whom he believed to be Christians, confirming in his mind that Prester John was close by.

With the help of a local pilot, Da Gama crossed the Indian Ocean to the west coast of India, where he was not well received. His fleet of ships represented a new threat—different from the occasional European traveler—to the established trade that Arabs and Persians conducted with India. But now that the sea route to India had been uncovered, the Europeans would not be turned back. News of Portugal's accomplishment spread far and wide in Europe after Da Gama's return in September of 1499. Although the Portuguese kept the details of the voyage secret, their success inspired other countries to set out on their own.

"Discovering" the new world. For Europeans, discovering a sea route to India confirmed a supposition that numerous scholars had harbored for some time. They knew that India existed even if they were uncertain that Africa could be circumnavigated. It was a matter of discovering whether or not a route could be found.

Christopher Columbus (1451–1506) had a similar goal. He wanted to find a sea route to China by sailing west. He had studied *The Travels of Marco Polo* and had consulted Ptolemy's *Geography*. From these sources he concluded that Asia extended extremely far to the east. If that was so, then the distance China's far eastern shore lay from the west coast of Africa, on an Earth of the small circumference Ptolemy reported it to be, could not be immense. The work of the Italian physician and geographer Paolo Toscanelli (1397–1482) confirmed that the distance was not great. Toscanelli had determined that the distance from Europe to China by sea was some 5,000 nautical miles. Using Toscanelli's computations selectively, Columbus was able to reduce the estimate to 3,500 miles, still an impressive distance to span, to be sure.

The novelty of Columbus's proposal, of course, was that he would sail west into the unknown. Hugging the coast of Africa was relatively easy in comparison. Other than the Azores, which were known to the Portuguese, there was no known land far out in the Atlantic. Columbus became more and more convinced of the feasibility of his plan, but persuading sponsors for the trip proved to be very difficult. As early as the 1480s he began trying to visit the courts of Portugal and Spain to present his case. The Portuguese eventually turned him down, and the Spanish throne only came around to his plan after long debate.

As is well known, Columbus left Spain for the Canary Islands in August of 1492. He intended to sail west along the latitude line of the Canaries because he knew there were favorable winds there at that time of year. But Columbus did not rely on celestial navigation to maintain his course. Born in Genoa, Italy, his earliest maritime experience had occurred in the Mediterranean, which is essentially all at the same latitude. To navigate there sailors had learned a technique known in English as "dead reckoning," a phrase derived from "deduced reckoning" and abbreviated as DED reckoning. It relied on the technique referred to earlier using a compass and determining the distance traversed. From a beginning point a navigator set the course with a compass and then measured the distance traveled each day, marking the new position with a pin on a chart.

Maintaining the direction by compass was one thing, but calculating the distance traveled was more difficult to do with precision. To accomplish it the navigator determined the ship's speed and then multiplied it by the time traveled at that speed. Speed and distance were measured every hour by throwing a piece of flotsam overboard and observing when it passed by a mark on the ship's rail. At that moment the pilot began a chant, stopping when the flotsam passed a second mark on the rail. After noting the syllable where the chant ended, the pilot converted the length of the chant into a measure of speed, thus permitting calculation of the distance made in that hour. In Columbus's case, he deliberately underreported the distances traversed in order not to alarm the crew more than necessary about how far they were from home. When he finally made landfall in the Bahamas in October, Columbus was convinced from the gold ornaments worn by the inhabitants that he had in fact reached his destination of Asia. On his return voyage he composed a letter to his Spanish royal sponsors announcing his success in reaching islands off the coast of Cathay that were rich in gold and spices and whose inhabitants could be converted to Christianity. Subsequent voyages to the region did not persuade Columbus that he was mistaken about having reached Asia, but there were others who became convinced that the lands reached were neither China nor Japan.

Among these was the Italian geographer Amerigo Vespucci (ca. 1450–1512), who visited what is now the north coast of Brazil in 1499. Two years later he followed up on a finding of the Portuguese explorer Pedro Alvares Cabral, who had reached the east coast of Brazil in 1500. Vespucci traveled south along the coast and became convinced that the land he saw comprised a continent not known before to Europeans. In 1504 he was quoted as saying that these lands across the ocean could rightfully be called a new world. When a German publisher put out a new map in 1507 in which these regions were depicted, he used Amerigo's name to label the new continent under the mistaken impression that he, not Columbus, had been the first to observe it.

By the beginning of the sixteenth century, then, the world was a different place from the one it had previously been for Europeans. In their self-centered and chauvinistic manner, they regarded the journeys of Da Gama, Columbus, and others as voyages of discovery, as though the people who lived in these regions represented something wholly new to existence. That the inhabitants of the so-called New World had their own history and civilization, which should be cherished for what it was, never occurred to them. Their goal for the future of the western lands was in one way similar to their goal for the East; they desired to make new converts to Christianity. But it was different as well. The task was not to engage the New World in trade, as it had been with China and India, but to conquer and exploit these previously unknown territories for the wealth they could bring to European monarchs.

There is a certain irony about the status of natural philosophy in particular and learning in general at the turn of the sixteenth century. In one sense the Western world was filled with the innovations of the early modern era that have been discussed in this chapter. New religious and intellectual ideas, a new technology of printing that permitted ideas to spread rapidly, and new realities about the Earth's geography captured the imagination of everyone but those in lowest classes, for whom the business of survival occupied all their attention. The world was turning out to be a different place from the one that most people had known. The future seemed to call for a new outlook.

On the other hand, especially where natural philosophers were concerned, scholars were increasingly looking backward, not forward. They strove to revive and regain a wisdom from the past. As we shall see, this striving to regain a lost wisdom was about to produce an even greater reorientation of humankind's view of itself and of its place in the cosmos than that produced by the innovations we have just examined.

Suggestions for Reading

Elizabeth Eisenstein, *The Printing Revolution in Early Modern Europe*, 2nd ed. (Cambridge: Cambridge University Press, 2005).

John R. Hale, *Age of Exploration* (New York: Time, Inc., 1975).

David C. Lindberg, *The Beginnings of Western Science* (Chicago: University of Chicago Press, 1992).

CHAPTER 4

---◎---

The Renaissance of Natural Knowledge

The meaning of *renaissance,* when applied to the early modern period, is "rebirth," or "beginning again." Evidence of a renaissance of European society in the period from the fifteenth through the seventeenth centuries consists of a number of developments. For example, commerce, industry, and cultural life expanded as the number and role of middle class burghers—residents of the town—increased and altered older feudal relations. Among the educated elites, new intellectual institutions emerged to offer an alternative to those predominant in the medieval world. And on the level of religious culture, there appeared a new secular outlook that challenged the dominance of the clergy's conception of learning.

These changes occurred first in Italy as the republican city-states began to give way to powerful leaders who wished to consolidate their authority in central governments. Everywhere in Italy the values of rebirth were evident. But they did not remain confined to Italy alone. Especially as the sixteenth century dawned, the notion of new beginnings spread to the countries of central and northern Europe.

◎ Humanism ◎

One particular expression of this rebirth of European society was named *humanism* by scholars in the nineteenth century. It is of interest to us as far as the natural sciences of anatomy, natural history, and astronomy are concerned. Humanism concerns the life of the mind, in particular, the acquisition of knowledge and the interpretation of its meaning. The fundamental assumption of this aspect of the Renaissance was that humans in the past had crafted a wisdom that had been lost, should be restored, and could serve as the foundation on which to build a new outlook. This ancient wisdom had been compiled by thinkers of old whose writings had

68

been lost or corrupted and whose original texts were just now beginning to be recovered. Because many of these texts were pre-Christian, humanists exhibited a secular interest that took its cue not from a transcendent Christian God, but from the human individual. The humanist scholars of the Renaissance integrated this secular outlook into their understanding of Christianity.

There were points where humanism and the Christian attitudes that had settled into the Latin West clashed. Humanists valued individual intellectual exploration of what the mind could discover. This presented a problem as humanists began to occupy chairs at universities, because the prevailing scholastic attitude was to defer to dogma, especially the established philosophical and theological interpretations that were based on the teachings of Aristotle. At Oxford University, for example, one statute decreed "that Bachelors and Masters who did not follow Aristotle faithfully were liable to a fine of five shillings for every point of divergence." If humanists valued individualism, the scholastics certainly did not.

Because they integrated Christianity into a wider perspective, humanists did not automatically regard the course of history as an unfolding of God's plan. That was too linear and deterministic for them. They believed that humans contributed to the formation of history, that God had given humans abilities to use in shaping history. Consequently, they believed that history could ebb and flow, so to speak; it did not proceed linearly, but was cyclic.

Humanists were impressed with knowledge that was useful and they often criticized the scholastics for using their rational gifts to pursue goals that were too esoteric to be practical. When it became clear that the ancients had possessed useful knowledge and wisdom that had been lost, it was important to humanists that the contents of ancient texts be recovered and mastered to learn what they contained. For them, to "begin again" meant to study ancient texts in order to regain a perspective that had been abandoned, or perhaps distorted, and to evaluate it using the reason of the present. This attitude of humanism, we shall find, became the predominant motive of some important sixteenth-century figures who turned their attention to the natural world.

◎ The Study of the Human Body ◎

Restoring what the ancients knew about the human body and using that knowledge as a basis for beginning the study of anatomy anew is a story that took a particular turn over the course of the first half of the sixteenth century. It involved breaking away from received tradition by returning to the anatomical knowledge of the ancient world as a starting point for a new anatomy.

The Heritage of Anatomical Knowledge

It is sometimes thought that the reason anatomical knowledge was in such an undeveloped state during the Middle Ages was that the church forbade the dissection of humans. The church did forbid boiling bodies to obtain skeletons, a practice crusaders sometimes employed in order to obtain bones that could be transported home for burial. But by the fourteenth century there was no prohibition against, for example, postmortem dissection for the purpose of investigating the cause of death. That did not mean, however, that anatomy was a subject eagerly pursued for its own sake. As a result, knowledge of the anatomy of the human body was not well developed at the beginning of the sixteenth century.

Mondino's *Anatomy*. One source that did exist had been written in 1316 by a professor at Bologna named Mondino dei Luzzi (ca. 1270–ca. 1326). He had read the only source that was available to him from the ancient Greek physician Galen. It was not the physiological treatise whose later recovery would exert a powerful effect on the study of anatomy; rather, it was a short version of Galen's work that had come into Latin from the Arabic. It was not helpful at all in setting a tone for how to study anatomy. In fact, it dealt simply with digestive organs and the limbs, but its use marked an early indication of interest in the Greek physician.

Mondino wrote up an outline of a procedure for dissectors that became something of a standard text in medical studies. Well into the fifteenth century most universities required medical students to observe one or two dissections a year, often prescribing Mondino's *Anatomy* as a text. By the late-fourteenth century Galen's work, *On the Use of the Parts*, did appear in translation, but it was relatively ignored. Mondino's work had become the standard text, especially after 1476, when the first printed version of Mondino made its appearance. It was reprinted several times on into the sixteenth century.

By 1400, then, anatomical dissections were conducted in medical courses of many universities, with others adding the practice over the course of the century. A professor would read from Mondino's *Anatomy* while a demonstrator, surrounded by student onlookers, pointed to the various organs and parts the professor described. Commentaries on Mondino's book also began to appear, written by professors who lectured on anatomy.

The recovery of Galen. By the beginning of the sixteenth century the study of anatomy was beginning to be regarded more highly than it had been. Now the enthusiastic examination of ancient texts brought new translations of Galen's works directly from the Greek. After 1500 Galen's *On the Use of Parts* was available and in 1523 a translation of his treatise on physiology, *On the Natural Faculties,* appeared. Then in 1531 a newly discovered text by Galen, *On Anatomical Procedures,* was translated into Latin with a commentary by a medical humanist at the University of Paris named Johannes Guinther (1487–1574).

With Guinther's textbook in 1536, *Anatomical Institutions According to the Opinions of Galen for Students of Medicine,* Galen's authority over Mondino and scholastic anatomy was established. With the recovery of Galen came changes from the way anatomy had been studied earlier. He began with the skeleton, not well known to Mondino, and then proceeded to the muscles, nerves, arteries, and veins of the arms, hands, and legs. Next came the internal organs, divided according to function. Such a systematic plan was something quite new and it soon generated enthusiasm to the point of hero worship.

Because of the general prohibition of human dissection at the time of Galen, he had carried out anatomical dissection on animals, trying to make reasonable inferences to human anatomy. This practice naturally resulted in some unavoidable errors, which were exposed by the practitioners of human dissection in the Renaissance. These two occurrences—the general enthusiasm for Galen's authority and the recognition of his mistakes—ran in opposite directions and created a challenge for the anatomists of the mid-sixteenth century.

Andreas Vesalius's On the Fabric of the Human Body

One of Guinther's students was Andreas Vesalius (1514–1564), a native of Brussels. He began his medical education at Louvain, then went to Paris, where he assisted Guinther in the preparation of the latter's textbook. From Paris he went to Padua, the site of the most famous medical school in Europe. After obtaining his doctoral degree in 1537, he conducted public human dissections for medical students and others at the university as a lecturer in anatomy and surgery.

During the years he lectured at Padua, Vesalius introduced a number of innovations into anatomical instruction. First, he did the dissections himself. He did not rely on a demonstrator to do them, as was the earlier practice. Further, he performed the dissections more often than had been done before and he even gave private dissections for more advanced students that went into greater detail than those done in public. He made charts to help the students master the complex detail they encountered as they watched him dissect, and he published six of them separately in 1538. Finally, he also dissected animals, not to make inferences to human anatomy, but to compare them to humans and show similarities and differences.

During these years Vesalius began work on his own anatomy textbook. While he appreciated his former teacher Guinther's devotion to ancient texts, Vesalius did not respect his abilities as a dissector. Further, Vesalius had worked out his own solution to the tension that existed between respect for Galen's authority and the results he himself uncovered as he dissected human cadavers. He retained his reverence for Galen, but at the same time he wished to make what he regarded as necessary corrections to Galen's work on anatomy.

In writing his book, *On the Fabric of the Human Body,* Vesalius made clear his humanist motivations. That is, he wished to restore the ancient wisdom and at the same time to build upon it. In his dedicatory preface to the Holy Roman Emperor, Vesalius noted that although anatomy in some universities was beginning to approach the importance it once had enjoyed in ancient times, the knowledge of medicine was still woefully inferior to that of long ago. Vesalius wished to change that, he said, by restoring the status of anatomy from the low level to which it had degenerated over time to the position it once held.

To do this, Vesalius set out to restore the kind of medicine Galen had practiced. He determined that he would honor Galen's excellence by holding him up as a model. In his book he followed the order now becoming popular among Galen enthusiasts—he began with the bones, not the soft internal organs of the body.

Vesalius also wanted to imitate Galen's conception of himself as a philosopher. He spoke of anatomy as a branch of natural philosophy, a branch that he wanted to recall from the dead. He did not propose to undertake a theoretical revision of Galen's philosophical stance; rather, he chose to expand upon it. As a result, his work not only provided a vastly greater amount of anatomical detail than had Mondino's brief descriptions, it even increased the coverage given by the master himself.

Wherever Vesalius's dissections uncovered errors in Galen, he did not hesitate to point them out. But Galen's errors in no way undermined Vesalius's goal of restoring ancient knowledge. He explained the errors by noting that Galen had had to rely on animal dissection. The mistakes had come about because Galen had not adopted the views of ancient physicians who predated him and who had based their conclusions on human dissection.

For all the emphasis on human dissection, that was not the only unusual aspect of Vesalius's book. More immediately striking was his use of anatomical illustration. Although some medieval manuscripts contained hand-painted pictures of the human body, illustrating the text was not commonly done. Mondino's *Anatomy*, for example, did not contain any anatomical illustrations. After the invention of printing a few anatomical texts contained woodcuts, but Vesalius's new work was by far the most heavily illustrated. He tied the illustrations so closely to the text that their use became indispensable.

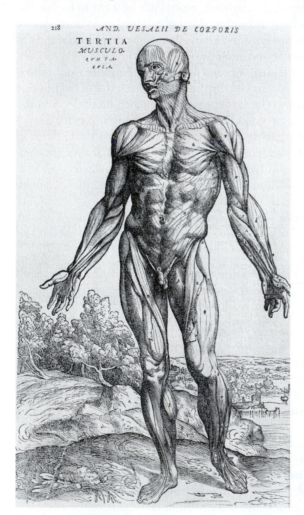

Vesalius's Anatomical Illustration

Vesalius never identified the authors of the illustrations even though their collaboration was essential to the purpose of the book. The images were works of art in their own right, revealing a depth and clarity of detail that was truly amazing. Many preserved a sense that it was a living individual who was being depicted. The illustrations were more impressive than those of any earlier anatomical text, and they were only outdone by the anatomical illustrations Leonardo da Vinci had completed at the end of the fifteenth century but never published.

On the Fabric of the Human Body was intended for practicing physicians, not medical students. It contained much more information than a medical student could use, nor could students generally afford to purchase such a large and well-illustrated volume. Vesalius published a shorter version for them in the same year the larger book appeared. Called the *Epitome,* it was an outline of the *Fabric* printed in a larger format with wall charts and oversize anatomical figures.

Among those who were highly impressed with what Vesalius had produced was the emperor to whom it was dedicated. Charles V of Austria, Holy Roman Emperor, quickly appointed Vesalius as physician to the imperial court. Vesalius did not hesitate to leave university life in order to accept a position of royal patronage. As we shall see again in other contexts, natural philosophers who valued freedom from the regimented duties of teaching were generally happy to accept the support of a patron.

Not everyone welcomed Vesalius's work, however. Strict Galenists, for example, reacted against his correcting the master so glibly. But many correctly recognized that here was one of those rare works that would endure. A second edition appeared in 1555, consistent with the enormous influence the book was to have on its time. The work stood as a testimony to the greatness of past works that had both inspired it and provided the model on which its innovations were based.

◎ Natural History: Animals, Vegetables, Minerals ◎

In 1555 there appeared in London a translation from the Latin of a book by Peter Martyr, entitled *The Decades of the Newe Worlde.* It was about the discoveries of the Spanish in the New World. "The diligent reader," Martyr observed, "may . . . learne many secreates touchynge the lande, the sea, and the starres." In the course of his narrative, Martyr referred to the ancient author Pliny, who, he reported, "hathe wrytten in xxxvii. bookes al that perteyneth to the naturall historie."

Martyr was using the phrase "natural history" in its original very broad sense, as information about the natural objects, plants, and animals of a certain place. Natural history, then, referred not just to the animal world, as it tends to in modern usage, but to all natural objects, animal, vegetable, and mineral. In their treatment of these subjects, Renaissance figures once again used ancient authorities as their point of departure.

The Kingdom of Animals

As is evident from Martyr's reference, the Renaissance took its cue from Pliny the Elder (ca. 23–79), who had written a massive work on natural history in the first century. Pliny was a Roman nobleman, who, after a military career, had become a prolific writer on a myriad of subjects.

Where animals were concerned, Pliny's descriptions formed the basis for so-called bestiaries in the Middle Ages, which were also available to humanist writers of the Renaissance. These were books on animals in which symbolic meanings were equally as important as defining characteristics. Following on Pliny's own practice, bestiaries included references to monsters and marvels, including fabulous creatures like dragons and unicorns. The Old Testament of the Bible, as well as ancient pagan sources, provided precedents for the use of animals as symbols of larger truths.

In the middle of the sixteenth century the Swiss humanist Conrad Gesner (1516–1565) composed a massive natural history. Gesner, who studied ancient languages and medicine in Paris, finished his doctorate in 1541 and lectured on natural philosophy in Zürich until he was appointed a municipal physician there in 1554. His five-volume *History of Animals* began appearing in 1551 and ran to some 4,500 pages!

Gesner did not hesitate to include information about monsters and imaginary animals, but his division of the animal kingdom in keeping with Aristotle showed his respect for ancient Greek sources. While he was dependent on the natural historians who preceded him, Gesner did on occasion add his own observations to the work. His *History of Animals* became well known, especially after notable artists provided illustrations to add to those Gesner had included from earlier authors.

Plants and Their Uses

The growth of humanism encouraged the study and depiction of plants, just as it had the study of animals. Latin and Greek translations of a work by the ancient Greek Theophrastus, called *History of Plants,* were available in the 1490s. Sixteenth-century

Illustration of a Sea Satyr from Gesner's *History of Animals*

humanists, however, were not as interested in this description of the parts and classification of plants as they were in the more practical use of plants and herbs as medicines.

Here the ancient authority was Dioscorides (fl. 50–70), a Greek physician who served in Nero's army. Dioscorides had a particular interest in medicines and in his travels he sought out pharmaceutical remedies of all sorts. He authored a five-volume medical work that was translated into Latin in the sixth century as *De Materia Medica.* Volume 1, on plant materials, contained descriptions of the store of plants familiar to the ancients, which Dioscorides claimed to have used in his own practice.

As was the case with both Galen and Vesalius, a shorter summary of Dioscorides became more popular than the longer work. Dioscorides' herbal, *Ex Herbis Femininis,* proved to be more useful to physicians of the Middle Ages. It contained but seventy-one plant medicines, none of which was unfamiliar to Europeans, as many of the ancient plants in the larger work were. Among the Latin encyclopedists there were those who added their own descriptions of plant medicines to the ancient literature. By the late fifteenth and early sixteenth centuries, then, there was a long tradition of interest in herbal medicines. Many of the books of herbals contained illustrations that had been copied from earlier manuscripts, some of which were based on ancient paintings of plants in Dioscorides.

When the humanist scholars of the Renaissance went back to Dioscorides, they tried to produce as accurate a text as they could. They brought to their work the assumption that also motivated Vesalius; namely, they wished to supplement the ancient wisdom with the knowledge they had from their own experience. In their first preparations of the early Greek texts, they simply left illustrations out. Further, in their quest for the pure text, they corrected errors from the original that had crept into later editions of Dioscorides. In 1544 Pietro Mattioli (1501–1577), famous in Italy for providing the first mention of the tomato, provided an edition with commentary on the *De Materia Medica* that was reproduced many times, guaranteeing that Dioscorides would remain the most popular authority on herbal medicine in the sixteenth century. Mattioli did include illustrations, including those of new plants unknown to Dioscorides.

The German school of botany. In the 1530s and 1540s several important botanists appeared in Germany who changed the way herbals appeared. Above all they inserted illustrations of plants—prepared by skilled artists—that were based on their own observation.

The first of these German botanists was Otto Brunfels (ca. 1488–1534), an early convert from Catholicism to Protestantism. After serving unsuccessfully as a pastor in two different German communities, he went to Strasburg in 1524. Here he established a school and turned to the study of natural science and medicine. His medical interests took him into botany, which Brunfels believed suffered greatly for want of adequate illustrations. His goal was to produce a work in which the illustrations were of plants as they actually appeared, not illustrations that resembled an ideal natural state. He took this so seriously that he directed an artist-illustrator to depict the plants just as they were—including broken leaves and whatever effects insect pests might have produced. His work, entitled *Living Portraits of Plants According to the Imitation of Nature,* appeared in three volumes between 1530 and 1536.

Leonhard Fuchs (1501–1566) continued the tradition of correcting the errors in earlier editions of Dioscorides. Like Brunfels, he was raised Catholic, but converted to Protestantism. He studied medicine at Tübingen, became a professor there, and in 1542 wrote *History of Plants.* Fuchs listed the plants in his book alphabetically by name. His illustrations were also his own, not those of Dioscorides on whom his work was based. They were done by artists, who tried to depict the plants realistically in some 516 pages of illustrations. While only the first illustration—of the *Anemone sylvestris*—was in full color, many were given in a single color other than black.

Finally, Hieronymus Bock (1498–1554), another early Protestant pastor who combined the study of medicine with his training in theology, served early in his career as garden inspector for the prince. In 1533 he met Brunfels, who, impressed with the work Bock shared with him, encouraged Bock to publish. In 1539 Bock's new herbal appeared in two parts, neither of which contained illustrations. This put Bock at a disadvantage, especially when compared to the massive work of Fuchs in 1542. Therefore, a second edition published in 1546 contained some 546 illustrations, followed in 1551 by a third edition with 70 more. These illustrations did not match the outstanding quality of those Fuchs had published, but Bock's work demonstrated the trend toward accurate illustration that had become the norm. What made Bock's work notable was its outstanding textual description of each plant's habitat and especially its medicinal effects, a feature lacking in Fuchs's work. Together these three German scholars—Brunfels, Fuchs, and Bock—helped to create a new era in herbal literature.

Herbaria and Botanical Gardens.   Other influences on the history of botany that proved to be of great importance were the invention of the herbarium and the establishment of botanical gardens. Herbaria were collections of plants that had been dried, and were preserved by pressing them between sheets of paper. The first known collection of this kind was created in Italy at the University of Bologna by Luca Ghini (1490–1556). Ghini was a member of the faculty of medicine there until 1544, when he was brought to the University of Pisa by the grand duke of Tuscany. By the time he died a dozen years later, herbaria were commonly found all over Europe. Because plants changed with the seasons and were not always available, herbaria provided a means of preserving them for teaching purposes or to serve as models for draftsmen to make illustrations for publication. Another indication of the flourishing of botany was the establishment of professorships of botany in medical schools of the time. The first such position was created at the venerable medical faculty of Padua in 1533 and then by at least five other universities over the course of the sixteenth century. At Padua the course of study initially involved mastering Dioscorides. With the passage of time, however, the new trend to supplement ancient wisdom with new information based on personal observation had an impact on medical education.

The new professors of botany soon found themselves responsible for an additional duty—the administration of botanical gardens. The presence of herb gardens in cloisters was an old tradition, going back at least to the late Middle Ages. The herbs supplied spices for the kitchen and medicines for common ailments. Now, the formal cultivation of herbs acquired a distinctly new status. Leonhard Fuchs had complained in 1542 that physicians were still ignorant of plants, but his work—along with that of the others we have discussed—changed that substantially. By the end of the century there were botanical gardens at Pisa, Florence, Bologna, Paris, and Montpellier. Not only did these gardens afford a means by which medical schools could further medical knowledge and education; they also demonstrated to the larger public that plants had acquired a significance that went well beyond their aesthetic value.

Understanding Fossils

The word *fossil* originally meant, simply, something that had been dug up out of the ground. When scholars wrote about fossils they included—besides what would be classified as fossils today—substances such as mineral ores, metals, crystals, and useful rocks. This wide array of objects, then, contained some items that looked like organisms and many that had no similarity whatever to living things. When there was a similarity it was certainly noted. Leonardo da Vinci (1452–1519), for example, held that the well-preserved fossil shells of northern Italy were so similar in general appearance to the mollusks living in his day in the Mediterranean Sea that they had to be organic in origin.

But this was the exception. Most scholars did not believe that even these fossils had once actually been alive. For one thing, often the fossils were of organisms that were extinct, so there was no existing living organisms with which to compare them. For another, depending on how they were preserved, many fossil remains of organic creatures were hard to interpret, and even remain so today for modern paleontologists.

Also, there were alternative explanations of fossils that made clear to humanist scholars why they were shaped as they were. When the shapes of forms resembled organisms or stars or some other object in the cosmos, the natural philosophers who were impressed with Plato's thought explained the similarity as a manifestation of the unity of the cosmos. A similarity born of the basic structure of reality linked the two objects, but it in no way required that one originated from the other. An Aristotelian natural philosopher, on the other hand, might say that just as simple organisms were formed by spontaneous generation from nonliving materials, a similar process might have occurred in the depths of the earth or in the sea to produce fossils that resembled simple organisms. In both Platonic and Aristotelian explanations fossils that resembled living things did not come from living things.

Agricola on fossils. Georg Bauer (1494–1555), better known as Agricola, wrote *On the Nature of Fossils* in 1546. He began his studies with the Latin and Greek classics before he decided to study medicine. After taking his degree at the University of Padua in 1526, he settled into a life that included medical practice, politics, and especially the study of mining and minerals. In the same year that he published his book on fossils, he was elected mayor of the Saxon town of Chemnitz, where mining was a local industry with a long tradition.

In his book, Agricola summed up what a long list of ancient authors had said about fossils. Again we see the typical attitude of the humanist—respect for the ancients, but a willingness to correct them when self-acquired knowledge contradicted them. Agricola changed the way knowledge about fossils was organized. Previously, they had been listed alphabetically by name, an approach Agricola found much too arbitrary. He proceeded to organize fossils by their physical properties. For example, gems were all put into one group, as were rocks, metals, hardened fluids (salt, amber), and stones (gypsum, mica).

Gesner's *On Fossil Objects.* In addition to the massive writing on the history of animals described earlier in this chapter, Conrad Gesner also studied objects that had been dug up from the earth. He knew and respected the work of Agricola, but he set out to produce a larger work on fossils. If the *History of Animals* is any indication, the anticipated project would have dwarfed everything that preceded it. The larger work never appeared, however, because of the author's untimely death in 1565. But he did publish a volume in that year that he intended as a preliminary book to the bigger project. Its full title was *A Book on Fossil Objects, chiefly Stones and Gems, their Shapes and Appearances.*

Reverence for classical antiquity was what motivated Gesner to give to his planned venture an encyclopedic scope. He gave the objects he was describing in his book their Latin and Greek names in addition to German labels. He wanted to restore as much as possible what the ancient authors had said and then add to that what he had learned in the present. This attitude was consistent with his sympathies, as a Swiss Protestant, for the Reformation's rejection of authority in favor of one's own experience. The reformers wished not to simply accept what church authorities said about the Bible, but to read it for themselves. Gesner learned Hebrew as well as Greek in order to read for himself the ancient texts of the Bible, rather than versions that had been corrupted as they were passed down.

As in his work on the history of animals, and in the works of Vesalius in anatomy, Gesner insisted on illustrating the text. A well-known historian of geology has noted that Gesner's work was the first in which illustrations were used systematically to supplement a text on fossils. This provided a means of checking that the names being used for fossils denoted the same objects that others meant when they used those names. In Agricola's work, for example, the absence of illustrations often left one in doubt about exactly which object the author was describing.

By using illustrations as he did, Gesner also confirmed how important firsthand experience was to him. He compiled his material as much as possible from his own observation. To prepare the illustrations, he employed experts who could do the job, but he insisted that they work under his supervision to guarantee a satisfactory degree of loyal representation.

Gesner's work on fossil objects was also important because it drew on another development of the sixteenth century—the formation of collections of specimens. As we saw earlier, botany led the way, through the new herbaria, in the deliberate

Gesner's Woodcut of a
Living Crab and Its Fossil

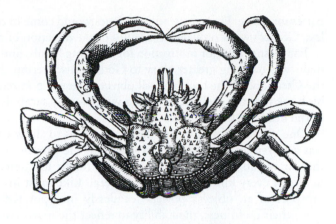

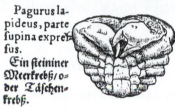

Pagurus la-
pideus, parte
ſupina expreſ-
ſus.
Ein ſteininer
Meerkrebß/o-
der Täſchen-
krebß.

formation and preservation of collections. Gesner helped to utilize collections for the study of fossils by referring to an existing collection. He had the catalog of the collection of a friend, the physician Johann Kentmann (1518–1574), bound together with his own book. On opening the work the reader encountered first Kentmann's catalog, whose frontispiece was an illustration depicting a cabinet with twenty-six numbered drawers. Alongside the cabinet was a key, entitled "The Ark of Fossil Objects of Johann Kentmann," that explained what was in each drawer. Of course, some of the drawers correlated with objects that would not be classified as fossils today. For example, drawer 10 referred to marbles and drawer 9 referred to gems. What moderns consider fossils were found in drawer 5 (stones) and drawer 12 (wood embodied in rocks).

In his work Gesner thanked his friend Kentmann for supplying him with specimens of objects he did not have. His endorsement of the catalog meant that other catalogs would soon appear, marking the increasing presence of museum collections of fossil objects. Historian Martin Rudwick has observed that "without the establishment of a tradition of museum preservation, it is difficult to imagine how a science of paleontology could have emerged."

Gesner's book was also the first to call for cooperative research on fossils. He explicitly stated that he had written the work to create interest in the field and to obtain from readers examples of stones that would enhance the collection depicted in his volume. Gesner knew that fossils varied a great deal from one region to the next, so that the study of fossil objects required cooperative efforts of many natural philosophers. Such a network formed a scholarly community, sustained by correspondence. Formal scientific societies would come in the next century; nevertheless, Gesner's work provided a stimulus in the direction of cooperative research.

For Gesner a major motivation for studying fossils, and in his other work on animals, was to bring greater glory to God by discovering the divine wisdom behind the Creation. In the case of fossil objects, Gesner pointed out in the dedication of his book that the gems he described were worthy symbols of the building materials of the heavenly City of God.

One way to bring glory to the Creator was to show nature's usefulness. Gesner was a physician by training and vocation. He promised in this preliminary book that he would, in the larger volume on fossils to come, describe the power and nature of every kind of stone and mineral. Like most investigators of his time, the prospect of an object's powers seamlessly incorporated several characteristics at once: their usefulness, their ability to reflect the macrocosm in the microcosm, and their general status as part of God's creation. Gesner helped to impart a greater significance to the study of fossils than it had had before.

◎ The World of Copernicus ◎

A new system of astronomy appeared in the middle of the sixteenth century that immediately caught the interest of European astronomers and eventually captured the attention of scholars in general. The cosmos was about to grow much, much larger.

The Humanist Background of Sixteenth-Century Astronomy

Like other disciplines, astronomy felt the effects of humanism. As we shall see, two important astronomers from central Europe—Regiomontanus and Copernicus—were steeped in the works of the ancients. Copernicus, the one from Poland, would leave the greater impact on Western natural philosophy.

Regiomontanus.   Astronomy and mathematics initially felt the impact of humanism most significantly in the work of Johann Müller (1436–1476), a fifteenth-century Bavarian scholar who was known as Regiomontanus. He was the son of a miller, but his keen intellect and his abilities in mathematics provided him with a means of rising above his low social origins. At 11 years of age he was already attending the University of Vienna, where he completed his bachelor's and master's degrees as rapidly as university regulations allowed.

The university was known for its cultivation of astronomy and cosmology and Regiomontanus quickly took to these subjects. Along with one of his professors at the university, he became involved in a project to make Ptolemy's *Almagest* more accessible than the original. Regiomontanus, who knew Greek, brought the project to completion in the early 1460s under the title *Epitome of the Almagest*. He supervised the various dimensions of the undertaking, updating Ptolemy's work through the addition of later astronomical observations and revised computations, and critical reflections on the text.

In the preface of *Epitome of the Almagest,* Regiomontanus openly exhibited his sympathies for humanism. His profound reverence for antiquity showed through clearly in his celebration of the marvelous achievements of the ancient Greek mathematicians. By contrast, he noted the woeful state of the study of mathematics in his own day. He took advantage of the newly invented technology of printing to produce multiple copies of numerous ancient mathematical, astronomical, and geographical texts. His *Epitome,* however, did not appear in print in Rome until 1496. In the fall of that year a young Polish scholar, also the product of a humanist education, traveled to Italy, where his studies would include astronomy.

Copernicus's education.   The budding Polish scholar was Nicolaus Copernicus (1473–1543), youngest child of a merchant in the town of Torun. Young Nicolaus must have shown promise in his early education because his uncle decided that he should follow in his own footsteps as a churchman and scholar. In 1491 Nicolaus went to Cracow to study at the university, although there is no evidence to suggest that he completed a degree there. Founded in the middle of the fourteenth century, Cracow was one of the universities in central Europe that was under the influence of humanism as it moved north from its birthplace in Italy. Here Copernicus mastered Latin and the classics and here he began the study of ancient mathematics and astronomy.

In 1496 his uncle, who had by this time become a bishop, sent Copernicus to Italy to study church law, as he had. In Bologna, where the oldest European university had been founded in 1088, humanism reigned supreme. Although Copernicus was there to master canon law, his interest in astronomy and mathematics continued unabated. He was able to learn from Domenico Maria da Novara, a professor of astronomy, who passed on to Copernicus his enthusiasm for ancient Greek astronomical works.

By his early thirties Copernicus had learned Greek, earned his degree in canon law, studied medicine, and returned to Poland, where he became an assistant and attending physician to his uncle, the bishop. His uncle had been successful in obtaining a position for him as canon in the cathedral at Frombork while Copernicus was still in Bologna. This provided a regular income, but did not require specific clerical duties of him.

Astronomy in Crisis

For several years Copernicus lived with his uncle in the bishop's residence in Lidzbark Palace, not far from Frombork. During these years Copernicus came up with the first version of his plan for improving Ptolemy's account of the heavens. Ptolemy's system needed improvement for at least two reasons, one theoretical and the other practical. First and foremost, Ptolemy had resorted to a technique that seemed to Copernicus to violate the most fundamental sense of a rational explanation of heavenly motions as required by the Platonic tradition, which Copernicus had embraced through his humanist education. An explanation of the heavens that lacked rationality was not the kind of world God had created. Copernicus was determined to replace that technique with an alternative that met the criteria of rational explanation. Second, Ptolemy's system was encountering practical difficulties when it was employed in the service of society.

Ptolemy's "irrational" system.   Among the assumptions of the ancient Greeks was that motion in the heavens shared the quality of perfection that characterized the entire realm above the orb of the moon. Heavenly bodies moved because they were carried on rotating celestial spheres, which, recall from Chapter 1, were assumed to be physically real. So the paths traced out by celestial bodies were perfect circles and the rotating movements of the spheres were uniform. To permit the path of a planet, for example, to deviate from the circle, or to speed up or slow down, introduced into the system an element of unpredictability, of imperfection, of irrationality.

But all observers of the heavens knew that the planets went faster and slower at different points in their orbits. How was this nonuniform motion to be explained? The Greek astronomers had constructed combinations of interlocked spheres, each one turning with uniform circular motion, which, when taken together, produced the observed irregularities. If we could be transported to the planet itself, we would not feel accelerated or decelerated motion; rather, we would experience only the uniform circular motion of the sphere carrying the planet itself. So the irregularities that were perceived in the heavenly motions from the vantage point of Earth were merely apparent. It was impossible, as Copernicus put it later, "that a heavenly body should be moved irregularly by a single sphere." Irregular motion could only result from combinations of uniformly rotating spheres.

The problem was that the predominant system of astronomy of the day, that of Ptolemy, did permit actual irregular motion in planets as they moved around the Earth. In order to improve the fit between what was observed and what the system depicted, Ptolemy had introduced a device, called the equant, which resulted in an actual acceleration and deceleration of planets as they moved at different points in their orbits (see Chapter 1). To Copernicus that meant that the moving power driving the system was not constant, but fickle, and that was a prospect before which "the mind shudders." To Copernicus and other humanist astronomers of his day who venerated the divine rationality of the ancient world, Ptolemy's equant was an inconsistency of the most fundamental kind. It represented the most glaring deficiency of astronomy and it had to be removed. For this reason, scholars have emphasized that Copernicus viewed his work in astronomy as a *restoration* of pure ancient astronomy.

Practical problems.   A theoretical challenge of this kind was not the only thing wrong with astronomy in Copernicus's day. There were practical problems as well. These practical problems stemmed from the increasing discrepancy between the predicted position of celestial objects and the positions where they were observed to be. The basic reason for this increasing lack of fit was that the passage of time had magnified any original discrepancy present in the system at the time of Ptolemy into much more glaring discrepancies by the late-fifteenth and early-sixteenth centuries. Ptolemy had accounted for the naked-eye observations of his era as best he could. But the fit had not been perfect and in the intervening millennium, as the heavens had continued to turn, this original tolerable lack of fit had grown to intolerable dimensions.

As a result there were—besides the *Almagest* itself—numerous systems that were based on Ptolemy's work but that had tried to improve it by altering the specific devices it contained. There was not just one Ptolemaic system, devised by the master himself; on the contrary, there were numerous "Ptolemaic" systems. For example, one system might try an epicycle where Ptolemy had used an eccentric circle, another altered the rates at which the interlocked spheres turned, and some had even returned to the older system of Aristotle, which used only homocentric spheres.

But none of this revision of Ptolemy, or return to Aristotle, worked to solve the crisis in astronomy. None of these "Ptolemaic" systems gave results that accurately matched up with the naked-eye observations of the day. This was especially obvious because the scholars of Copernicus's day had accumulated many more observations than those that had come down from antiquity. That made the errors more glaring than ever. There was no longer any denying that Ptolemy's system needed improvement.

One area in particular felt the practical effect of astronomy's increasing inability to depict the heavens accurately. For some time, the papacy had been aware of a growing problem with the calendar. It was important for the church because the holy day of Easter was determined by a formula that involved the annual motion of the sun and the monthly motion of the moon. (Easter is the first Sunday following the first full moon after the spring equinox.) The problem was that there were no common units with which to measure the length of a day and the time of the sun's complete trip through the zodiac.

Julius Caesar had decreed that a year was 365¼ days long, meaning that every fourth year there would be an extra day added to the normal 365. But the solar year is a bit more than eleven minutes longer than this, meaning that over time the accumulating minutes of the solar year were being overlooked. Keeping to the formula meant simply ignoring the extra time as the months of the year passed, so that by the end of the 365 days the accumulated extra time still remained. To just continue in this way had the effect of backing the calendar up because the new calendar year began before the solar year was over.

By Copernicus's time some ten extra days had accumulated. That meant that New Year's Day was celebrated ten days prior to when it should have occurred. This became particularly noticeable when the spring equinox, when every place on Earth has twelve hours of daylight and twelve of darkness, came on March 11 instead of on March 21, when it was supposed to occur. Because the celebration of Easter was determined by the spring equinox, the church was rightly concerned.

Regiomontanus was consulted on calendar reform by Pope Sixtus IV in 1475. A few decades later Pope Julius II sought the advice of astronomers and scholars on the same issue. One of those he consulted was Nicolaus Copernicus, who by 1514 had gained a reputation as an astronomer. This reputation was in part due to a work he had completed and circulated privately. It was his first attempt to improve the state into which Ptolemaic astronomy had fallen.

The Achievement of Copernicus

We have only a few works from the pen of Copernicus, and not all of them are on astronomy. Here we will consider two works that he wrote about the movements of the heavens. We will also look at another work written by a disciple who attempted to summarize the achievement of his master. Taken together, these three works gave Western civilization materials that literally changed the world.

Early effort.   Sometime before 1514 Copernicus completed a small work that has come to be known as the *Commentariolus,* or *Little Commentary*. It contains the basic ideas of his later, more developed, and more famous book. In the very first paragraph he makes clear what his major motive was—to follow the ancient astronomers in the wisdom of their assumption about the principle of regularity. Copernicus was exhibiting a conservative, as opposed to revolutionary, tendency when he agreed with the ancient Greeks, who thought that a heavenly body always moved with uniform velocity in a perfect circle and that by combining such regular motions in various ways they could account for the apparent nonuniform motion of the planets.

Copernicus noted that the earliest astronomers introduced eccentric circles and epicycles when simple concentric circles would not give a good enough account of the heavens. When Ptolemy came along, however, his account was not adequate without the introduction of certain equant points. That meant that the planets moved with nonuniform motion. For this reason Copernicus wrote that Ptolemy's system "seemed neither sufficiently absolute not sufficiently pleasing to the mind."

In listing the assumptions of his new system, Copernicus quickly served notice to the reader that his purification of ancient astronomy would be creative indeed. Among his unconventional assumptions he included the following:

a. The Earth is the center of heaviness for objects and it is the center of the moon's orbit, but it is not the center of the cosmos.
b. The sphere of the fixed stars is so enormously far away from the Earth that the distance from the Earth to the sun is imperceptible by comparison.
c. The daily revolution of the stars around the Earth is caused by the Earth's turning on its axis.
d. The annual motion of the sun is caused by the Earth's motion of revolution around the sun, which it shares with the other planets.

The *Little Commentary* proceeded to provide a few details about the apparent motions of the sun; the moon's motion; the motions of the superior planets Saturn, Jupiter, and Mars; and the movements of the inferior planets Venus and Mercury. Copernicus explained how he could replace the equant point by using a circle that was concentric around the sun with two small epicycles. By this means he duplicated the improved accuracy of the equant without making the planet actually move irregularly. Thirteenth- and fourteenth-century Islamic astronomers had used the exact same device, although they had not used it in conjunction with a heliocentric cosmos. So removing the equant was not an improvement that automatically entailed putting the Earth in motion. This would prove to be important to later astronomers as they studied Copernicus's new system.

Since the *Little Commentary* was not printed, it circulated only among a limited number of scholars. Not long after it was written, the pope requested Copernicus's advice on calendar reform. Copernicus declined, saying that until the motions of the sun and the moon were better understood, the problem could not be solved. Clearly he wanted to finish the larger work to which he alluded in his short introductory piece. He would spend the next two decades perfecting the longer work.

Georg Joachim Rheticus's summary. Four years before Copernicus's death a young lecturer from Wittenberg, Germany, came to Frombork. He had earned his master's degree in 1536 and was recruited to teach lower mathematics and astronomy. The young man's father, a physician, had been convicted of swindling and was beheaded when Georg was a teenager. He felt it best to change his family name, Iserin, to dissociate himself from the shame this had brought on the family. He became known as Rheticus, derived from the region in which he lived.

In 1538, Rheticus (1514–1574) decided to take a leave from Wittenberg, probably because of his association with a radical poet who had been expelled from the community. He went to Nuremberg, where Regiomontanus had lived earlier. There he met a publisher of astrological and astronomical manuscripts who had heard about the ideas of Copernicus, most likely from those who had seen Copernicus's *Little Commentary.* Such radical notions appealed to Rheticus, and he determined that he would go to Frombork to learn from Copernicus himself. He took with him as gifts bound volumes of astronomical work from Nuremberg to demonstrate that these well-known German printers would be able to do a good job with anything Copernicus might want to send back for publication.

At this early stage in the Reformation, being a Protestant did not prevent Rheticus from remaining with Copernicus until 1541, when he returned to Wittenberg. In his isolated position at Frombork, Copernicus must have enjoyed having someone present with whom he could share the technical achievement of his study of the heavens. For his part, Rheticus urged Copernicus to have the longer work he had been preparing published. But Copernicus was unwilling because he wanted to incorporate into it some of the new information that was contained in the materials Rheticus had brought him. He did, however, give Rheticus permission to write a summary of his ideas, which Rheticus sent back to Nuremberg in the fall of 1539. Rheticus returned to Wittenberg in 1541 for a short time, before taking up duties at the University of Leipzig.

The summary Rheticus wrote was called *Narratio Prima,* or *First Report.* It contained a general account of what Copernicus had done, with sufficient detail that it whetted the appetites of the astronomers of his time. Rheticus began by identifying his teacher as an astronomer comparable to Ptolemy because he had completed an entire system of astronomy. He noted that because Ptolemy had relied on the observations of his own day, and because an unnoticed error at the foundation was greatly increased by the passage of time, Copernicus had had to build astronomy anew rather than merely correct it.

Rheticus delighted to point out that his teacher was able to liberate astronomers from the equant through an ingenious use of eccentrics and epicycles. He announced that Copernicus accounted for observations of the planets' proper motions by having the sun occupy the center of the cosmos while the Earth revolved, instead of the sun. He gave six reasons why the old assumptions of ancient astronomers had to be relinquished. Number six was that Ptolemy had not paid attention to the need for his system to be internally harmonious. There was no necessary agreement among the parts, as if a musician need only tune one string to produce harmony, without insisting that the others also be adjusted. This was not a problem for Copernicus because the sun governed the celestial motions, so their harmony was under its control.

This appeal to the Greek philosophical belief in the complete rationality of nature resonated with humanist astronomers everywhere. Rheticus's seventy-page account was printed in 1540. It aroused sufficient interest to produce a second printing in 1541.

Rheticus was moving beyond a simple critique of Ptolemy's compromise of nature's rationality with his equant, to a more general indictment: Ptolemy's system was internally inconsistent. He did not use one geometry of the heavens to explain the positions of the planets; rather, he had employed seven different arrangements of spheres to capture the motions of the seven planets of the ancient world. But the arrangement he had used for Venus, for example, had nothing to do with the one employed for Mars, nor was it linked to the arrangement used for any of the other planets. It was a theme that Rheticus had learned from Copernicus himself, one that was to be repeated in Copernicus's own masterwork.

On the Revolution of the Heavenly Orbs. Rheticus finally persuaded Copernicus to have his work published in Nuremberg and he carried a copy of the manuscript with him when he returned to Wittenberg in 1541. He took a leave from Wittenberg in the spring of 1542 to bring the manuscript to Nuremberg and see it through the printing process. In the fall he took up a new position in Leipzig, and the process of proofreading the text was turned over to Andreas Osiander, a Protestant clergyman who was interested in mathematics. The book, *On the Revolution of the Heavenly Orbs,* came out in 1543.

When he received a copy of the work in April, Rheticus was shocked to note that his role in producing the work was nowhere indicated. Worse than that, in the front of the work was an anonymous preface, later determined to have been inserted by Osiander, that purported to explain away the central idea of Copernicus's work— that the Earth moved whereas the sun was at rest in the center of the cosmos. The author of the preface explained that Copernicus had introduced this idea merely to make calculations and that he was not saying that the Earth actually moved. If this was not understood, the preface concluded, then the reader would "depart from this study a greater fool than when he entered it." Rheticus was incensed and, in three copies he gave others as gifts, he marked out the preface with red ink.

It is clear that Rheticus was angry because he knew, as the one astronomer closer to Copernicus than any other, that his teacher did believe that the Earth actually moved. In his own preface, written as a dedication to Pope Paul III, Copernicus acknowledged that the idea that the Earth experienced movement would seem absurd to astronomers. He then confessed that he had considered communicating his ideas, "written to prove the Earth's motion," only to a few people rather than

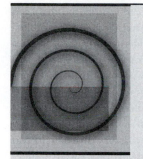

The NATURE of SCIENCE

Osiander and the Motion of the Earth

Osiander's position about the motion of the Earth has been cited as an early example of a philosophical position known as antirealism. In this view, scientific theories should be regarded as assumptions that are adopted because of their usefulness, not because they represent nature "as it really is." Theologians in the sixteenth century were familiar with the employment of hypotheses, particularly as a means of trying to ferret out heresies. That is, they would assume a particular proposition and then reason from it to see if any of the conclusions they came to through logical deduction turned out to be heretical. If so, then they could establish that the assumption was theologically problematic.

In adopting a proposition, then, they accepted it only provisionally. They in no way embraced the proposition's truth. Osiander adapted this use of hypotheses to the situation Copernicus faced. Suspecting that the assumption of the Earth's motion would in fact lead to heresy, he wanted to make sure that the reader did not embrace the proposition of the Earth's motion as true. In Osiander's eyes Copernicus had his own reason—mathematical, not theological—for adopting the assumption of the Earth's motion. Osiander acknowledged that mathematicians, too, could use hypotheses profitably, but his main concern was to remove all suspicion of heresy from the work of Copernicus.

publishing them. From this and other similar phrases it is clear that the Earth's motion was not just a hypothesis he had adopted to improve his calculations.

In sentiments similar to those Rheticus had signaled in his *First Report,* Copernicus complained to the pope about the many different systems that tried to render an account of the heavens. They used different assumptions and, referring to the equant, even permitted the fundamental principle of the uniformity of motion to be violated. In a famous passage, Copernicus recorded his distaste for the lack of harmony among the parts of the various Ptolemaic astronomical systems in use. "With them it is as though an artist were to gather the hands, feet, head, and other members for his images from diverse models, each part excellently drawn, but not related to a single body, and since they in no way match each other, the result would be a monster rather than man."

When he got down to business, Copernicus reviewed the reasons that the ancients had believed the Earth was at rest in the center of the cosmos and then argued why these reasons were insufficient. Anticipating the question, for example, of how the clouds could remain suspended in air if the Earth beneath them were moving at a tremendous speed, Copernicus argued that the air was associated with the Earth and would move with it.

Later in the work Copernicus explained how, by endowing the Earth with separate motions, he could account for what we see on a daily and annual basis. Allowing the Earth to turn once on its axis in a twenty-four-hour period produced the same visual effect of turning the entire heavens around a central Earth in the same period. Further, permitting the Earth to travel around the sun once a year accounted for other

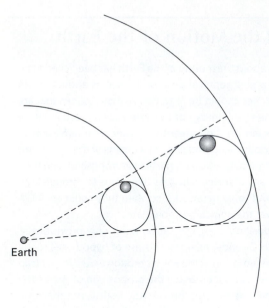

The Ptolemaic System

observations. As the Earth changed its position from month to month, the sun appeared against the background of the different constellations of the zodiac over the course of the year. And the Earth's annual motion also naturally explained why planets like Mars occasionally underwent retrograde motion. As the faster-moving Earth caught up with and passed its neighboring planet, Mars appeared to slow up, stop, go backward, stop again, and then resume its previous course.

Already in the *Little Commentary* Copernicus had realized that putting the Earth into motion around the sun meant that the size of the cosmos had to increase. Now, in *On the Revolution of the Heavenly Orbs,* the implications became even clearer. It now became possible to determine the order of the planets.

In Ptolemy's system a planet's distance from Earth could not be determined because the planet turned on an epicycle. Was the planet carried on a small epicylic sphere close to the Earth, or farther from the Earth on a larger epicycle? In both positions the observational lines of sight from Earth would be identical, so it was impossible to know how far away the planet was. That meant that the order of the planets could not be nailed down. Was Mars closer or farther away than Jupiter? Was Venus on this side of the sun or on the other side?

This was not the case in the new Copernican cosmos. There the order was determined by the geometry of the heliocentric, or sun-centered, cosmos; in fact, the relative sizes of the orbits could be calculated precisely. Consider, for example, the simple case of an inferior planet such as Venus, whose circle of orbit around the sun

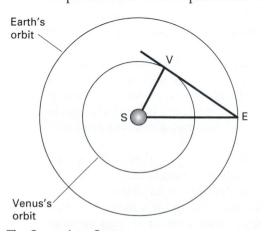

The Copernican System

is contained in the larger circle of the Earth's orbit. (The demonstration for superior planets is slightly more complicated.) The angle SEV is known from observation; it is the angle of Venus's maximum displacement from the sun. The angle SVE is also known; it is a right angle formed by a tangent drawn to a circle from an external point that intersects the radius of the circle at the point of tangency. And, if two angles of a right triangle are known, then all three are known. That means that we know the proportions of the sides of the triangle. So we know the proportion that SV is of SE;

that is, we know the proportion Venus's distance from the sun is of Earth's distance from the sun. This proof gives relative sizes of the orbit, not the absolute distances, but relative size is all that is needed to determine the order of the planets.

With the relative sizes of the orbits set, the general size of the cosmos had to increase. Copernicus pointed out that the farther a superior planet was to Earth, the smaller and less frequent was its retrograde motion as the Earth caught up to it and passed it. So Saturn underwent retrograde motion less frequently and to a lesser extent than did Jupiter, and Jupiter less than Mars. But the stars showed no shifting at all! So the gap between Saturn and the sphere of the fixed stars must be truly enormous. The Copernican cosmos was vastly larger than it had been in traditional cosmology.

Once he had chosen the sun as the center of the cosmos, these implications about the order of the planets and the size followed from observations and from the properties of mathematics. But why had he chosen the sun to be the center in the first place? Here Copernicus's humanism showed through clearly. After setting the order of all the planets, he justified placing the sun in their middle through an appeal to ideas he had absorbed while studying ancient texts. It was an appeal to ancient philosophical traditions whose wisdom carried religious overtones that were assigned to the sun itself: "In the middle of all sits the Sun enthroned. In this most beautiful temple could we place this luminary in any better position from which he can illuminate the whole at once? He is rightly called the Lamp, the Mind, the Ruler of the Universe; Hermes Trismegistus names him the Visible God, Sophocles' Electra calls him the All-seeing. So the Sun sits as upon a royal throne ruling his children the planets which circle round him."

Copernicus's book fell onto fertile ground. There were numerous astronomers who appreciated the magnitude of the crisis astronomy faced and who were as enamored of ancient philosophical perspectives as was Copernicus. An old and well-known claim that Copernicus had written a book nobody read has been shown to be wrong. Thanks to the persistent efforts of a few modern scholars in tracking down and examining copies of the first and second editions of the book, it has been possible to determine a great deal about the reception of the work. There was a rich tradition in the sixteenth century of writing in the margins of a work by those who read it and that has enabled scholars to fill in a great many of the gaps in our knowledge of the events the book set in motion. These events were as profound as any in the history of science.

Suggestions for Reading

Marie Boas-Hall, *The Scientific Renaissance, 1450–1630* (New York: Dover Publications, 1994).

Owen Gingerich, *The Book Nobody Read: Chasing the Revolutions of Nicolaus Copernicus* (New York: Walker and Co., 2004).

Thomas Kuhn, *The Copernican Revolution* (Cambridge: Harvard University Press, 1992).

Martin Rudwick, *The Meaning of Fossils: Episodes in the History of Paleontology* (Chicago: University of Chicago Press, 1985).

CHAPTER 5

———————◯———————

Heliocentrism Considered

In spite of the preface added to Copernicus's book that set aside any claim of the Earth's actual motion, Copernicus himself did believe that the Earth moved. It is abundantly clear that the person who had worked closest with Copernicus, Georg Joachim Rheticus, understood this. Rheticus was extremely unhappy with Andreas Osiander, who soon became known as the author of the anonymous prefatory comments.

By focusing on the issue of the Earth's actual motion, however, Osiander had struck a nerve. For most, this question was certainly incidental to the main task of the astronomer. That task was to depict the motions of the heavens in a mathematical description that was internally consistent and as accurate as possible. As Osiander put it, the astronomer "will adopt whatever suppositions enable the motions to be computed correctly from the principles of geometry for the future as well as for the past." It was a purely mathematical exercise that had only the most minimal concern with the physical state of the cosmos. In trying to make sure that the reader did not think Copernicus was overstepping the boundaries of mathematics into a consideration of physics, Osiander inadvertently drew particular attention to the Earth's motion.

But the question of how one took the hypothesis of the Earth's mobility continued to linger among astronomers in the sixteenth century. Most scholars initially dealt with it by trying to figure out a way to remove it from Copernicus's work, leaving the rest of his system intact. They had good reasons, both theological and physical, for dismissing the prospect of the Earth's actual motion as simply irresponsible and absurd. A few took the Earth's actual motion seriously, however. Copernicus's student, Rheticus, accepted it just as his master had done. And later, at the end of the century, Johannes Kepler incorporated the Earth's motion into his system. The consideration of heliocentrism in the sixteenth century, then, included most who rejected and a few who accepted the Earth's motion.

◎ The Immediate Reception ◎ of Copernican Heliocentrism

Among those who reacted to the publication of Copernicus's book, *On the Revolutions of the Heavenly Orbs,* the interest of scholars who taught astronomy was to be expected. Those in the university town of Wittenberg, heart of the Protestant Reformation, established a particular attitude toward what Copernicus had done. But the work also caught the eye of a foremost theologian of the day from Wittenberg, the Reformation leader Martin Luther, who also had definite views about the book.

The Response Within the Religious Community

Martin Luther nailed his ninety-five theses on the castle church door in the town of Wittenberg in the fall of 1517. He had been teaching at Wittenberg University since 1508 and he remained there as he continued to defy Pope Leo X. Students, faculty, and others in Wittenberg rallied around him, and by 1527 the new Lutheran doctrine had become permanently established there.

By 1539 Luther had heard about Copernicus, presumably from a faculty colleague. In that year, before either Copernicus's early manuscript or his book had been published, Luther made a general comment in the course of one of his "Table Talks" about a new astrologer who wanted to prove that the Earth, not the sky, moved. One of those present wrote down Luther's reaction. He had dismissed the notion, the writer noted, because it turned the whole of astronomy upside down. Luther attributed the idea's appearance to a trend in which everybody was just trying to be clever. For his part, Luther believed the scripture, in which Joshua had sought the Lord's help in making the sun, not the Earth, stand still.

But if the reformers provided no sustained measure of the impact of Copernicus (there is no evidence that the other major Reformation figure, John Calvin, had even heard of Copernicus), neither did the official Catholic Church. In 1545 Pope Paul III, to whom Copernicus had dedicated his book two years earlier, convened a council whose main purpose was to counter the spread of Protestantism. The Council of Trent would last until 1563 and its primary action was to undertake reforms to tighten up what had become lax behavior among clergy at all levels. Nowhere in the long time it existed did the Council consider the book by Copernicus.

We do know, however, that a theologian from the papal court criticized Copernicus in an unpublished analysis of the work that he wrote a year after Copernicus's book appeared. His criticism centered on Copernicus's ignorance of physics and theology; otherwise, the author contended, Copernicus would never have permitted himself to entertain a hypothesis that all philosophers and theologians knew to be contradictory to sound physics and scriptural interpretation. As was the case in the Protestant reaction, there was no attempt to evaluate the technical mathematical merits of the Copernican theory.

The Wittenberg Interpretation

Copernicus's book did receive heavy scrutiny from a group of faculty members at Wittenberg University. There emerged at this newly formed university a consensus on how to read Copernicus's book that has been called the Wittenberg interpretation. Among its features, two stand out. The first was its enthusiastic endorsement of Copernicus's removal of the equant, the off-center point Ptolemy had used that resulted in planets undergoing actual accelerations and decelerations. Like Copernicus, the Wittenberg astronomers felt that heavenly bodies could only undergo uniform circular motion. To them, permitting a planet to experience actual acceleration introduced into the heavens an element of irrationality and unreliability that the presence of uniformly moving circular orbits avoided. The heavens were perfectly rational and predictable; hence any perceived acceleration was merely apparent, the result of combinations of uniform circular motions.

A second feature of the Wittenberg interpretation was the wish to transplant the means Copernicus had used to remove the equant into a system that did not require a moving Earth. If for the Wittenberg scholars Copernicus's great achievement had been to show that it was possible to remove the horrid equant, then—given the unfortunate difficulties that were caused by hypothetically setting the Earth into motion—the obvious goal was to find a system in which they too removed the equant without adopting Copernicus's embarrassing hypothesis of a moving Earth.

Led by Philipp Melanchthon (1497–1560), Luther's articulate defender, these men all believed that the Creator had ordained the study of mathematics and astronomy, and that through such study they could gain unique insights into God's nature. Many of the numerous students of astronomy at Wittenberg later became astronomy professors in universities throughout Germany. Where Copernicus was concerned, Melanchthon appreciated the technical accomplishments of Copernican heliocentrism, but he himself did not focus on them. Rather, he emphasized the need to get back to a geocentric system so that there would be no contradiction between an alleged terrestrial motion and the scriptures. But his influence in supporting and encouraging others in Germany who were trying to preserve Copernicus's achievement while restoring geocentrism was truly remarkable.

Among those who did take up the technical challenge was a Wittenberg astronomer named Erasmus Reinhold (1511–1553). Reinhold openly stated that Copernicus stood as an equal to Ptolemy and that he had restored astronomy from the ruins into which it had fallen. Reinhold remained neutral on the question of the Earth's motion. The annotations he added to his copy of *On the Revolution of the Heavenly Orbs* came in the later technical sections of the book where individual planetary motions were described without using the equant. So convinced was he that these descriptions were more accurate than others that he constructed a new set of astronomical tables using them. These Prutenic Tables quickly became known as a compendium of more accurate data. One other person must be mentioned here, a scholar we met in Chapter 4. Georg Joachim Rheticus came to Wittenberg in 1532 from southwestern Austria. He caught Melanchthon's attention and, on finishing his master's degree in 1536, was appointed as a lecturer in lower mathematics. But he left Wittenberg in 1538 for Nuremberg, where he heard about Copernicus. His role in bringing Copernicus to the attention of the Wittenberg scholars and in getting Copernicus's work published was told in Chapter 4. His return to Wittenberg as a professor in 1541 was brief; the following year he moved on to Leipzig.

Rheticus is important here because he exhibited a different representation of the Wittenberg interpretation. Yes, he was convinced that one of Copernicus's great achievements was to have eliminated the equant from planetary astronomy. But he did not see the need to try to devise a means for transferring Copernicus's techniques for getting rid of the equant into a geocentric system. He was content, as was Copernicus himself, simply to accept a heliocentric system in which the Earth moved.

Rheticus even wrote up a tract, printed much later, to show how one was to understand passages in the Bible that seemed to run counter to Copernican theory, including the one in which the sun was made to stand still. However, the majority of the Wittenberg scholars wished to avoid having to reinterpret scripture by creating a geocentric system that was somehow equivalent to the system of Copernicus. That, in fact, is exactly what occurred in the work of a remarkable astronomer from Denmark, who himself visited Wittenberg as a young man.

◎ Tycho Brahe and the Copernican Theory ◎

Some natural philosophers who studied astronomy took up the challenge to keep the advantages Copernicus had introduced into astronomy while at the same time retaining an unmovable Earth. One of the most important was a Danish nobleman named Tycho Brahe (1546–1601). He made numerous contributions to the development of astronomy, not all of which emerged from his concern with the system of Copernicus.

The Denmark of Tycho's Day

For over a century prior to the sixteenth century the three lands of Denmark, Sweden, and Norway were joined together under the Danish king in order to resist the growing threat of German encroachment into the region. They especially needed to counter the influence of Germans from various cities who had joined together into what became known as the Hanseatic League. The intention of the members of this league was to promote a German monopoly in the lucrative fishing trade around the Baltic Sea.

By the 1520s, however, tensions had built up sufficiently between Denmark and Sweden that the union was no longer tenable. Although Norway remained united with Denmark, Sweden broke away and became an independent land in 1523. Still, the Danish state in the sixteenth century extended beyond the borders of present-day Denmark. It included parts of what is now southern Sweden and northern Germany.

One effect of the German involvement in Scandinavia was the spread of Protestantism. Christian III, who succeeded his father as king in 1534, had been a duke in Schleswig, a Danish province with many German inhabitants. His teachers included German Lutheran reformers and as a young man of eighteen he was present at the Diet of Worms, where Luther took his stand against the church authorities. He did his best to introduce Lutheran Protestantism into Schleswig and as duke made no secret of his wish that Denmark would become Lutheran. In 1536, as King Christian III, he declared Denmark Protestant, thereby bringing Lutheranism to Denmark as a whole.

Against this background of change the first of Denmark's famous natural philosophers, Tycho Brahe, made his name. His father and uncle were both members of the Rigsraad, which consisted of about twenty of the country's most influential nobles. Tycho (which he pronounced "Teeko") was thus born into wealth and privilege, much to the benefit of the natural science of his day and ever since.

Brahe's Unusual Youth

Tycho was born near the end of 1546, the third child of the eventual twelve his mother bore. His Danish name was Tyge (pronounced "Teeg"), which he changed to the Latin form Tycho when he was in the university. Four of the Brahe children did not survive, including Tycho's twin brother. Tycho's father, Otte Brahe, was himself the younger of two brothers, both of whom rose to prominent positions of power in the kingdom of Christian III. Tycho's future, however, lay with another family.

The benefit of being "kidnapped."   Unlike Otte, his brother Jorgen was childless. Jorgen waited until a younger nephew was born a year after Tycho's birth and then one day simply took Tycho home with him. Tycho was raised as the only child of Jorgen and his wife Inger. This caused no breach between Otte and his brother, surprisingly, as family ties extended more easily among nobility of the time than they do among families today.

Most of the time the sons of noblemen, once finished with formal education around the age of fifteen, acquired what more they needed to know as future leaders of Denmark by traveling to distant courts. There they learned foreign languages and new ways of thinking. They served as pages and squires to foreign lords, starting out at the bottom of the ladder as courtiers and working their way up to positions at court. Eventually they would be given administrative duties over a fief. This was the pattern that Tycho's four younger brothers followed.

Tycho took a different path, one followed by some of the men on his surrogate mother's side of the family. His new mother encouraged Tycho to continue developing his interest in academic subjects; hence, when he went abroad after his days at the University of Copenhagen, he attended foreign universities. Because he was raised in the house of his uncle, Tycho exercised an option that most likely would not have been open to him had he grown up with his biological father and mother.

Tycho studied various subjects, including astronomy and astrology, at several universities in Germany. While he was abroad the well-known incident involving Tycho's famous nose occurred. According to a much later account of the matter, Tycho had determined astrologically that an accidental incident was imminent, so he kept to his room all that day of December 29, 1566. But he came down to eat in the evening, and fell into an argument with a fellow Danish student that led to a duel. As a result of the swordplay Tycho suffered the loss of his nose. He later developed a prosthesis made of gold and silver to disguise his disfigurement.

Having followed a path different from that of most Danish noble youth, Tycho did not anticipate a life at court on his return to Denmark. Custom prohibited a nobleman from becoming a university professor, so that route was not open to him. One possibility for Tycho was to be made a canon of a Lutheran cathedral chapter, a position open to both nobles and commoners that carried a substantial income and permitted its holder to pursue a life of scholarship. Tycho was promised a canonry when he was twenty-two, although it was not actually bestowed on him until 1579, when he was thirty-three. In addition, Tycho inherited a share of his biological father's estate. He was therefore wealthy enough to follow whatever path he chose.

The empiricist emerges.   Around this time Tycho began to show how he would apply what he had learned from his teachers at the German universities. Just prior to his father's death, Tycho had been traveling abroad. He stayed primarily in Augsburg, where he revealed his concern that astronomy be based on careful and accurate observations. This conviction would later become associated with his name as an astronomer.

He did not go so far as Petrus Ramus (1515–1572), a radical thinker who came to Augsburg during the time of Tycho's visit and preached the overthrow of Aristotle. Ramus wanted to create a new astronomy based on observation and induction and in the process to eliminate all hypotheses. When he met Ramus, Tycho argued that astronomers could not dispense with all hypotheses; otherwise they would have to get rid of epicycles, uniform motion, and even the assumption that the cosmos was orderly. But he certainly agreed that new and accurate observations of the positions of the planets were indispensable to the future of astronomy.

To this end Tycho wished to improve the instruments available for identifying the location of heavenly objects. He had become convinced that existing devices were woefully inadequate. His first significant attempt to do better produced a pair of astronomical compasses that were large enough to measure reasonably small divisions of arc. Yet they were not so big and heavy that they could not be moved from one location to another.

His next try was on a grander scale, constructed for the mayor of the city. It was a giant quadrant, which was so large and heavy that it took forty men to install it on the mayor's country estate. A quadrant is a strip of metal or wood shaped into a quarter circle and mounted on a base. The quadrant strip is calibrated from 0 to 90 degrees, the sextant from 0 to 60 degrees. The degrees on both are further subdivided into 60 seconds of arc. Both are used to mark the altitude above the horizon of a heavenly object as it crosses the north/south meridian. The quadrant could be used to record the positions of stars, which do not move from night to night, or of planets and comets, which do change from one night to the next. While it was very difficult to use because of its size and weight, it represented Tycho's first step toward his goal to be able to produce measurements that were within a minute of arc of accuracy.

Marvelous Doings in the Heavens

After the death of his father, Tycho settled in for a few years on a property owned by an uncle on his mother's side—the monastery at Herrevad. This uncle, like Tycho, had spent years abroad attending universities in pursuit of an education. He had risen in the ranks of government before retiring to private life. Now he enjoyed being with others interested in matters of the intellect, especially alchemy. Tycho shared his interest in alchemy, cultivating it through experiments he conducted.

The new star of 1572.   By far the most significant event of this time occurred in the fall of 1572 when Tycho observed an object in the heavens that substantially challenged Aristotelian cosmology. Tycho wrote that after working on some alchemical experiments, he was on his way to supper when he noticed an unfamiliar star in the sky. Because he had studied the heavens since childhood, the appearance of a star never seen before, one brighter than Venus, was something that caught his eye.

Although the object became known as a new star, Tycho knew that it could not possibly be a star. Aristotle had taught that there was a fundamental difference between the heavenly and earthly realms. The heavens were eternal and changeless—stars did not suddenly appear. Nothing ever came to be or died away in the heavens. That kind of change, called generation and corruption, only occurred in the terrestrial region below the lunar orb. Therefore, anything in the heavens that appeared and then disappeared again was assumed to be located below the moon.

This view of Aristotle was still very much in vogue in Tycho's day. It had lasted so long because it was essentially correct. The only real challenge to such a view was the occasional appearance of a comet. Comets moved against the background of the stars as did planets, but to test whether the comet was beyond or below the moon was no easy task. As for the "new star" of 1572, anyone who was aware of its existence would assume that it was below the moon.

Because of its novelty Tycho gave this new star his full attention and soon determined that it did not move against the background of other stars from night to night. It did not, in other words, behave like comets or even like planets. This was a strange object indeed, especially if it was closer to us than the moon, as everyone assumed.

Although it was difficult to do with precision, there was a test he could try that might give him some information about the location of the object in comparison to the moon. The ancients knew that the heavens rotated around the Earth once each day, so two observations of the object made at different times of the night would very slightly change the relative position of the object against the background of the stars, as long as it was close to us. (The idea here can be simulated by holding a thumb in front of the face and noticing the shift in its position against a background when it is viewed first with one eye closed, then with the other. The shift in position is greater the closer the thumb is to the face.) For the moon this is called diurnal lunar parallax. It is constantly changing and even at its maximum it is around a degree for the moon. So any object closer than the moon would show an even greater parallax.

But this one did not. In fact, it showed no change whatever. It was possible that the object was moving very slowly in such a way that it just happened to cancel out a parallactic shift, so Tycho checked it over several nights. Still no change at all. That meant that it had to be farther away than the moon. When he continued to compare its position to other stars over several weeks and its position showed a complete lack of change, Tycho concluded that it was actually as far away as the stars themselves. That was a problem. Here was a star that was newly born. Apparently the heavens were not as changeless as Aristotle had thought.

The new star was bright, to be sure. To the trained eye it could even be seen during the day. But it was not something that was noticed by the casual observer. A few others in Europe had noted the appearance of the new star, although none had studied it as Tycho had. When Tycho went to Copenhagen early in 1573, no one there had heard about it. A physician on the faculty of medicine could not believe that his colleagues could have overlooked something this significant and originally concluded that Tycho was joking.

Going public as a scholar. This same professor, once convinced, urged Tycho to publish his findings. This was a major decision for Tycho because publication was not an approved activity for a person of Tycho's class and rank. He should not behave as a middle class scholar; rather, he should be pursuing the normal goals of a Danish nobleman. Tycho therefore merely wrote up a straightforward report of his findings. Then, after seeing what others were writing about the new star, he reworked his report into a book. In his book he criticized the others for describing the object as a comet and he made the revolutionary implications of his discovery unmistakably clear. He also confronted head on the issue of publishing as a nobleman. He wanted to achieve eternal glory, he said, not the passing fame brought by success in military combat. Indeed, the book made clear that he was an expert in astronomy.

These were technical matters, however. His book was not widely read and had relatively little impact. But Tycho continued to observe the new star. It began to fade by December of 1572 and continued to diminish until it finally disappeared in March of 1574. That summer Tycho moved to Copenhagen and soon was asked to give lectures on astronomy at the university. The same old problem arose—as a nobleman this was a request he could not meet. Noblemen were granted privileges, but in return they were expected to avoid intruding on the privileges of those in other stations. It was therefore not acceptable for him to give lectures at the university. So a group of noble students presented a petition to the king requesting that Tycho be allowed to lecture to them. The king added his own request to theirs, sanctioning the occasion as one requested by Tycho's peers.

Two subjects from the lectures are especially interesting. First, by basing his lectures on Copernicus as opposed to Ptolemy, it was clear that he regarded Copernicus as an astronomer with great ability who had contributed much to astronomy. But he also could not accept the Copernican system because it went against physical considerations. For one thing, it contradicted scripture, which contained several passages in which the immobility of the Earth and the mobility of the sun were clearly stated. Further, as a man skilled at detecting the parallactic shift caused by observations from two different locations, Tycho rejected the motion of the Earth because no parallax was detectable, even though the Earth radically changed its position in the course of its alleged travel around the sun. To Tycho it was only reasonable to assume that some indication of the enormous difference in the Earth's position in March from its position in September would crop up in the observations.

The other subject from the lectures was astrology. Tycho was convinced that God's vast celestial creation had a purpose beyond simple existence. That the heavens influenced events on Earth was obvious to him. However, many theologians of his day would not permit this influence to extend to the behavior of human beings. That would affect free will and thus could interfere with God's plan of salvation. For this reason they disapproved of astrology.

Once again, Tycho did not bend to official pressure. In his lectures Tycho defended astrology by taking the position that celestial influence was not the same thing as celestial determinism. People could be affected by the stars, but that did not mean that their response was determined by astral influence. By exercising free will humans could triumph over the stars and even become masters of them.

The comet of 1577.   The late-sixteenth century was unusually blessed with great astronomical events, certainly enough to reinforce the widespread astrological assumption that ominous events loomed ahead. In the late fall of 1577 Tycho was catching fish for dinner in a pond one evening at dusk when he noticed once again a bright star in the sky. Once darkness had set in, he could see that the object had a tail—it was a comet.

Given his experience with the new star of 1572, he naturally decided to see what he could determine about its position with respect to the moon. That was a much more difficult task than it had been for the new star five years earlier because the comet was near the sun and was therefore only visible for a short time after the sun had gone down. When he first saw the comet it was not visible long enough to permit the rotation of the heavens to produce much of a change in the relative position of an object against the background of the stars. A bit later, as the comet moved away from the sun in the sky, Tycho was able to attempt a measurement of diurnal parallax.

After taking various complicating factors into account, he could observe virtually no parallax. But he waited even longer so that he could check his results. His final conclusion was that, at best, the comet's parallax was not greater than fifteen minutes of arc, four times less than that of the moon. This meant that it had to be approximately four times farther away from the Earth than the moon. Tycho determined that the comet was going around the sun above the orb of the moon. Since it had suddenly appeared, here was another example of change in the celestial realm.

But this example had other implications as well, the most profound of which emerged for Tycho a decade later. It was a long time before he wrote up a Latin publication on the comet, and this work was much more detailed than the brief report he had given the king in 1578. In mid-January of 1587 he was nearing the end of his work, but the last chapter, in which he considered the writings of others on the comet, took the most time. For reasons we will examine shortly, Tycho either had not noticed or had not taken seriously a table in one of the works on the comet that he had obtained in 1579, a work by Michael Mästlin from the University of Tübingen.

Tycho must have noticed right away that Mästlin agreed with him about the supralunary position of the comet. But only in 1587 did one of the other implications in the report about the comet become clear to Tycho. Mästlin had plotted the comet's daily distances from the Earth as it traveled around the sun and found that they varied enormously. Mästlin's table had the comet at about three times the distance from the Earth to the moon at its closest point and some twenty-five times that distance before it disappeared. There was only one conclusion possible if Mästlin's table was correct: either the comet was crashing through the physically real crystalline spheres of the planets as it orbited the sun *or there were no crystalline spheres in the heavens.* For whatever reason, in 1579 Tycho did not draw this conclusion. He would come back to it in due time, after he had become a noteworthy figure in Danish society.

Tycho's Rise to Prominence

Two years prior to observing the comet, Tycho had once again been traveling in Europe. He visited old acquaintances, made new ones, and learned what others were thinking about issues in astronomy, medicine, and other topics. One of the people he met during this trip was Count Wilhelm of Hesse who, like Tycho, was an avid builder of astronomical instruments. They had much in common. Wilhelm was a man of considerable power who also made his own astronomical observations. He had found a very slight parallax for the new star of 1572, but had determined that it was so small the star must lie beyond the moon. He shared data with Tycho and Tycho helped him find an assistant to help with his work.

The fact that the two men got on so well turned out to be more than a mere curiosity. Wilhelm sent word to the Danish King Frederick that he had in his service a nobleman with outstanding abilities as an astronomer. Wilhelm recommended Tycho to the king and pointed out the advantages of supporting him in his work. The king responded by summoning Tycho once he was back in Denmark. In 1576 he offered Tycho the use of the island of Hven, with all the rents that came from the peasants who lived there. The king had decided that he wanted to capitalize on any fame that might come to Tycho, so he acted preemptively to keep him in Denmark. In so doing, the king was placing his stamp of approval on the non-traditional path Tycho had chosen to follow.

Uraniborg. Tycho set to work to build for himself a residence where he could carry out his studies of astronomy in peace and quiet, far from the political world of the court life that he so disliked. He called it Uraniborg, or fortress of Urania, after the Greek muse of astronomy. It would take some time to complete. As part of their obligation to him, the peasants of the island owed him two days of labor per week, and he made good use of it. Even so, the observatory he constructed was not completed until the fall of 1581.

Tycho filled his observatory with new instruments of all kinds. These instruments, most of which he designed himself, were constructed with an eye to providing him with the most accurate observational data possible. This was, as we have seen, a long-time goal of his. But the controversy over the new star had taught him anew how important precise data was. He determined that he would collect the most complete and precise information about the exact positions of heavenly objects possible.

To this end he either constructed or had built a series of instruments in his new observatory. They included sextants and quadrants of various sizes. The most well known, although not necessarily the most original, was Tycho's famous mural quadrant, which he mounted on a wall facing due north and south. Using this

Tycho's Mural Quadrant

instrument he could divide the calibration not only into minutes of arc (sixtieths of a degree), but into sixtieths of minutes! It was no wonder that Tycho's data became known as the most accurate available anywhere in the world.

The armillary sphere, which is a skeletal model of the celestial sphere with the Earth in the center, was especially helpful as Tycho instructed the various assistants that came to Uraniborg to learn from him. It helped them to envision the plane of rotation of the sun and the other planets around the Earth, whose equator was tilted to this plane. Tycho also had an elaborate celestial globe built, which he then improved himself into a showpiece. By 1595 Tycho claimed that he had marked on it the positions of a thousand stars.

Tycho was also interested in alchemy. He built sixteen alchemical furnaces in the basement of Uraniborg where, we must presume, he conducted experiments. Although he referred to his many findings about metals and minerals, he left no records of his alchemical work. We do know that his motives were not the making of gold; rather, he followed the Swiss alchemist Paracelsus in the quest to use alchemy to find new medicines.

The Tychonic system. When Tycho lectured on astronomy in Copenhagen during the fall of 1574, one of his goals was not to be held hostage to the assumptions of Ptolemy's equant but at the same time to try to convert the assumptions of Copernicus to the stability of the Earth. As we have seen, something of this had long been embraced as a hope among the Wittenberg astronomers. By 1577 Tycho was familiar with an arrangement of the planets first merely mentioned by Martianus Capella in the early Middle Ages. Capella's comment was in fact noted by Copernicus in Chapter 10, Book 1, of his book. It had the inferior planets Mercury and Venus orbit the sun as the sun orbited the Earth. So when in the summer of 1580 an unusual visitor who had actually tried to sketch out such a system appeared on the doorstep of Uraniborg, Tycho must have been very interested.

The visitor was the mathematician Paul Wittich, whom Tycho had first met fleetingly in Wittenberg. Tycho soon perceived that the mathematical techniques Wittich had devised would be greatly valuable to him in his astronomical work. For his part, Wittich had obtained Copernicus's book and had sketched in its margins how he would solve the problem of eliminating the equant, which was Copernicus's great achievement, while keeping the Earth at rest, which was Copernicus's great failing.

What Wittich did in the margins of his copy of Copernicus was to start with Copernicus's system and then modify it to accommodate a stable Earth. He sketched out a system with the Earth at the center, the moon and sun orbiting the Earth, Mercury and Venus orbiting the sun, and the superior planets Mars, Jupiter, and Saturn on epicycles that circled the Earth.

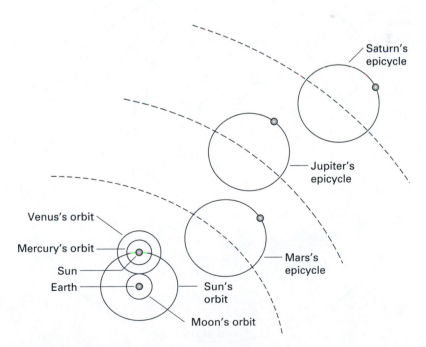

Wittich's Modification of the Copernican System

Tycho no doubt admired this achievement, but he quickly determined that it was an impossible arrangement. Tycho knew the Copernican system well. He knew that the relative distance each planet was from the sun in the Copernican system was set; for example, Saturn had to be roughly ten times as far from the sun as was the Earth. What Wittich had done, following tradition since Ptolemy, was to set the epicycles of the superior planets so that there was no wasted space. Each epicycle swung past the one above it such that it barely missed it. That gave a neatly compressed system in which the planetary spheres did not intersect, but it lost a basic feature of the Copernican system—the determination of the relative orbital distance of each planet from the sun. There had to be a better way to combine Copernicus and Ptolemy.

Sometime in the mid 1580s Tycho came up with his solution. In his new system the moon and the sun circled the Earth, and then *all* the remaining planets (not just Mercury and Venus) circled the sun. He could make this arrangement preserve the relative distances dictated in the Copernican system and still keep the Earth at rest. In fact, the new Tychonic system was observationally equivalent to the Copernican system; that is, all the lines of sight for a person on Earth were exactly the same in the two systems. This meant that, using observations alone, you could confirm both systems equally well. There was no way to distinguish one system from the other using observation alone.

There was, however, one problem. In the Copernican system the orbit of Mars around the sun was about 1.5 times that of the Earth. So when the Earth caught up

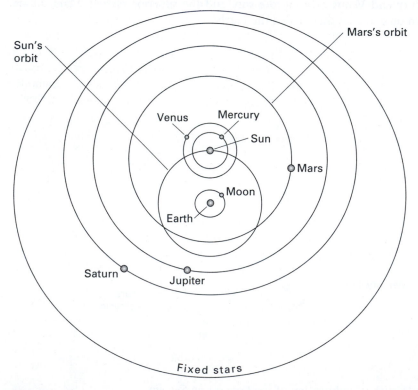

The Tychonic System

and passed Mars, it was only .5 Earth orbits from Mars. In other words, sometimes Mars was closer to the Earth than the Earth was to the sun. That caused no problem for Copernicus, but it did for Tycho. If the sun was going around the Earth, how could Mars go around the sun at the distance Copernicus required and occasionally come closer to Earth than the sun was? The only way that could happen was if Mars sometimes crossed the sun's orbital path. But that was absurd! It meant that the planetary spheres intersected.

All this was taking place during the final years in which Tycho was trying to finish his book on the comet of 1577. That was when he came across a manuscript by one Christoph Rothmann, who argued, without using measurements, that the paths of comets provided the best evidence against the existence of crystalline planetary spheres. This triggered in Tycho's mind the table in Mästlin's work on the comet of 1577. He consulted his own data on that comet and calculated its distances from the Earth, finding that they were in basic agreement with Mästlin's. He then drew the conclusion— that he later said he had been unable to entertain seriously earlier—that there were no planetary spheres.

With the problem of intersecting spheres removed, Tycho's system became viable. To accommodate the varying distances of Mars and the sun from Earth, Tycho permitted the orbits of Mars around the sun and the sun around the Earth to intersect. There were no longer any planetary spheres to worry about, so the intersection did not cause problems in that respect. And since Mars circled the sun, it could never be at the point of intersection when the sun was. That is, Mars and the sun could occupy the same position in space, but never at the same time.

Tycho had solved the basic problem that he and others had long attempted to explain: how to retain the great advantages of Copernicus's system (especially the absence of the equant) and at the same time to keep the Earth at rest. Tycho's ingenious solution, which became known as the Tychonic system, was included in the final chapter of his book on the comet of 1577, *On Very Recent Phenomena in the Aethereal Realm,* which finally appeared in 1588. Tycho considered the creation of this system to be the crowning achievement of his life's work. As we shall see in the next chapter, it was the preferred system of some Jesuit intellectuals who responded to Galileo. Further, it continued to be favored by some Dutch university scholars well into the seventeenth century.

Last years. Tycho's longtime benefactor, King Frederick II, died in 1588. His son, Christian, was only ten at the time; hence the country was ruled by four senior counselors until the boy came of age. Tycho was able to get the regents to promise that the island of Hven would revert to his heirs, but they could not bind the future king to the agreement.

Soon after the king was crowned Christian IV in August of 1596, Tycho realized that the new royal advisers did not regard him as favorably as had the regents. His most lucrative fief was recalled by the crown within a month. It became clear that the annual pension King Frederick had granted him was also in jeopardy. Tycho shut down work at Uraniborg and left the island for Copenhagen, presumably to demonstrate the drastic implications of the new policies of the crown. But it did not work. He had spent enormous sums to build what he had achieved and the crown did not regard the results as worthy of the expenditures. There was even an official request to look into a charge that Tycho had mistreated peasants on Hven. Tycho concluded that he and his family had no future in Denmark. By June of 1597 he had emigrated.

After languishing in various locations in Germany, Tycho eventually received a call in 1598 from Rudolph II, Holy Roman Emperor in Prague, to take up residence there. Rudolph appreciated scholarly achievement and he set up an estate with an annual pension, some six hours outside of Prague, where Tycho could continue his work. Arriving in the middle of 1599, Tycho began to remodel the estate so that he could do observational work. Although he did not accomplish anything here that compared to his earlier work, he was joined early in 1600 by a younger scholar named Johannes Kepler. Kepler later completed a task Tycho had undertaken for Rudolph to create new and extremely accurate astronomical tables.

Tycho died a painful death at the age of fifty-five in October of 1601. He had eaten dinner at the home of a baron, had drunk much wine, and his bladder ached. But, Kepler later related, "he had less concern for the state of his health than for etiquette" and would not excuse himself from the table. When he returned home he could not urinate and he passed subsequent days in extreme agony. Eleven days after the dinner he died.

◎   Johannes Kepler's Heliocentrism   ◎

In addition to Rheticus and Copernicus himself, Johannes Kepler (1571–1630) was the other major figure who accepted heliocentrism before the sixteenth century was out. (Although it is difficult to assess Galileo Galilei's view of heliocentrism, we shall do so in the next chapter.) It is true that the heliocentrism Kepler sketched out in 1597 was augmented and modified later in his life. But this unusual astronomer never abandoned his belief in Copernicus's system.

Becoming a Copernican

Kepler came to work with Tycho Brahe in Prague in 1600. But what kind of a person was he? Where had he come from? And above all, why had he become a Copernican? In many ways Kepler's chances of becoming an astronomer were remarkably dim. His social background was the complete opposite of Tycho's and not at all likely to produce a scholar.

Early years.   Born in late December of 1571 in the southern German state of Württemberg, Johannes Kepler was the first child of a mercenary soldier and an innkeeper's daughter. The family moved around a good deal, making any kind of sustained education for their eldest son difficult, to say the least. He attended elementary school irregularly and was not in school at all between the ages of nine and eleven. Kepler does tell us that his mother took him to a high place to see the comet of 1577 and, when he was nine, his parents called him out to see an eclipse of the moon. Kepler did end up receiving an education because the duke, who had declared for the Lutheran creed, was always on the lookout during these early years of Protestantism for precocious young talent to provide future clergymen. Once the child's unusual intellectual ability was acknowledged, he was granted support to pursue an education.

His sporadic elementary schooling meant that he was behind other students of his age. But he finally completed Latin school, then attended a monastery school at age thirteen, and two years later entered a preparatory school to get him ready for the University of Tübingen. Throughout these years his introverted and unsociable personality showed itself. He became a loner, constantly quarreling with other students and unable to establish friendships. Kepler completed his bachelor's degree at Tübingen in 1588 and his master's in 1591. He then began a three-year program to prepare himself for the clergy.

At Tübingen the most important influence on him was his mathematics teacher, Michael Mästlin, whose work on the comet of 1577 turned out to be so significant for Tycho Brahe. Mästlin, himself a product of Tübingen University, had taught mathematics at Heidelberg and then had been called back to his alma mater. While he was still a master's student at Tübingen he had purchased a copy of Copernicus's book, which he read very carefully. His annotations in the work reveal that he was something of a reluctant Copernican. He praised Copernicus highly as the prince of astronomers (after Ptolemy), but he invited astronomers to complete the goal of perfecting a geocentric system so that it agreed with the phenomena as well as Copernicus's system did. That task was beyond him, he confessed, as it appeared to be for everyone else so far. Unless the common Ptolemaic hypotheses were reformed, he wrote in the margins near the beginning of the book, "I will accept the hypotheses and opinion of Copernicus."

This was the attitude that Mästlin communicated to his young student, Johannes Kepler, who became so delighted with Copernicus that he collected together all the advantages Copernicus had over Ptolemy. One of the issues Mästlin and Kepler discussed concerned a question that Copernicus left unresolved in his book; specifically, was the sun or the center of the Earth's orbit the true fixed center of the cosmos? Copernicus had centered all the planetary orbits, including the Earth's, in a point that was offset from the sun. So, which point was the center of the fixed stars? This was not a question that could be resolved at the time, but it focused the question of the place of the sun in the cosmos. To get a truly heliocentric system, the sun should be at the center of the cosmos.

Kepler wrote that he was preoccupied with three questions: why were there the number of planets there were, why were they spaced as they were, and why did they move with the speeds they did? With questions like these swimming around in his head, the young Kepler found his preparation for the ministry cut short after his second year. Over his protest, he was sent in 1595 to fill a sudden opening created by the death of a mathematics instructor of young boys in a Lutheran school located in the Austrian town of Graz. While he was there his conversion to Copernicus's system became complete. In the midst of what he called the "agonizing labor" of teaching, he stumbled on an insight that convinced him beyond any doubt that God had created the cosmos as Copernicus had described it.

The five solid theory. The insight came as Kepler was explaining to the class why, for observers on Earth, Jupiter and Saturn came together in the sky on a periodic basis. He had drawn two orbits for the students, the orbit of Jupiter nested inside the

Inscribed and Circumscribed Triangles

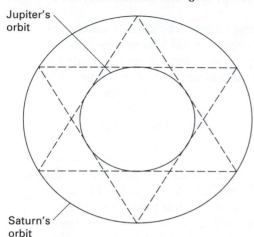

Jupiter's orbit

Saturn's orbit

orbit of Saturn, and he inserted triangles that were inscribed in Saturn's orbit at the same time they were circumscribed around Jupiter's. As he was using the properties of the triangles to explain the periodicity of the conjunctions, he was hit by a revelation. What if the Creator had set the number of planets and their distances from the center of the cosmos by nesting them using mathematical figures? He would have used perfectly formed three-dimensional figures instead of two-dimensional, and it was known already in antiquity that only five three-dimensional shapes formed perfect solids—solids whose sides were equilateral polygons. They were the tetrahedron (4 equilateral triangles), cube (6 squares), octahedron (8 equilateral triangles), dodecahedron (12 equilateral pentagons), and icosahedron (20 equilateral triangles).

If God had utilized the five regular solids, then clearly he had made six planets, because Mercury's orbit would be inscribed inside the first one and Saturn's would

Kepler's Five Solids

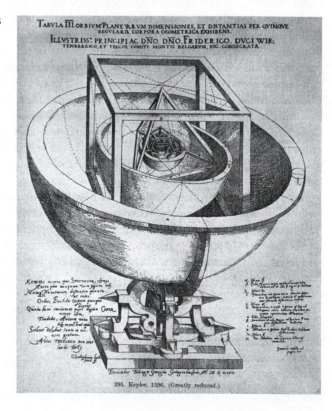

295. Kepler. 1596. (Greatly reduced.)

be circumscribed around the fifth. If there were six planets, the Earth must be one of them. The cosmos was Copernican!

Yet there were even more astonishing results to come. The shapes of the solids would determine the distances the planets were from the center, which was occupied by the sun. But in the Copernican system, unlike the Ptolemaic, the relative sizes of the planetary orbits were fixed. Was there an ordered sequence of the solids that would preserve the known relative distances of the planets from the sun? Kepler quickly found that using an octahedron, then an icosahedron, then a dodecahedron, then a tetrahedron, and finally a cube worked much too well to be accidental. "Behold," he wrote to his teacher Mästlin in 1595, "how through my effort God is being celebrated in astronomy."

The Marriage of Physics and Astronomy

Kepler wrote up his results about the planets and the five regular solids in a book entitled *The Cosmographic Mystery,* which appeared in 1597. He had answered two of the three questions that had plagued him, why a certain number of planets existed and why they were spaced as they were. Near the end of his book he turned to the third question—why the planets moved at the speeds that they did.

He did not successfully answer the third question in this work, but in taking it up he assumed that the sun somehow affected planetary motion. With this assumption he made clear that his understanding of Copernicus flew directly in the face of the interpretation Osiander had given it in his preface to *On the Revolution of the Heavenly Orbs.* Osiander had tried to assure the reader that Copernicus did not intend an actual motion of the Earth because that would insert physics into astronomy. Kepler now became the first major astronomer to demand that physical considerations in fact become part of astronomical explanations.

Kepler and Tycho.　There were numerous Protestants in Graz, but Austria itself was a Roman Catholic land. The Counter-Reformation finally caught up to the village and in the summer of 1598 the Lutheran school was closed. Near the end of September in 1598 the order came for the teachers of the school to leave. Kepler, now married to a local woman, was allowed to come back because he had powerful Catholic friends and the archduke was pleased with his discoveries. But the outlook was clearly not good for the long term.

The next summer Kepler heard that Tycho Brahe was now in Prague as the imperial mathematician to Rudolph II. He knew that Tycho had spent his life gathering the most accurate data to be had anywhere. He had sent Tycho an introductory letter in 1597, which was acknowledged the following year. But then Kepler had inadvertently been drawn into a bitter dispute between Tycho and another astronomer, and now he had to placate the Danish nobleman. Letters crossed in the mail, but the end result was that Kepler made the bold decision to present himself to Tycho in Prague. This he did at the beginning of January 1600.

Although Tycho welcomed Kepler as "a highly desired participant in our observations of the heavens," Kepler found out soon enough that he was not regarded very highly. Kepler needed Tycho's data and he was not getting access to it. For his part, Tycho needed Kepler's mathematical genius to clear up certain problems in his system. By April, Kepler's dissatisfaction with his role forced a crisis in the relationship. Because of their mutual need for each other, the two were ultimately able to establish a workable, if not always amicable, relationship.

Tycho gave Kepler the toughest problem facing all astronomers—the problem of Mars's orbit. It had proven to be the most difficult planet to fit into a circular orbit around a center. But with Tycho's accurate data Kepler made some initial progress, and with surprising results. Like other planets, Mars appeared sometimes to speed up and at other times to slow down as it traveled in its path. As noted, Copernicus refused to concede that the planets experienced actual change of speed. That violated the requirement that planets experienced only perfect uniform circular motion. He had banished the equant point, explaining the speeding up and slowing down using epicycles, so that the change of velocity was only apparent.

Kepler, however, had become convinced that the sun was somehow involved in the motion of the planets. If the sun was not exactly at the center of Mars's orbit, then there would be times when Mars was closer to the sun than at others. Any involvement of the sun with Mars would then explain why it moved quicker when nearer to the sun than when far away from it. So, breaking with both the master and those who thought that Copernicus's great achievement was to rid astronomy of the equant, Kepler accepted the nonuniform motion of Mars in its circular travels around the sun.

Alone in Prague.   After Tycho died, Kepler continued to work for another ten years as imperial mathematician to Rudolph II. His primary responsibility was to produce the astronomical tables Tycho had begun. But with greater access to Tycho's data, he relentlessly pursued the Mars problem. In his mind that task had separated itself into two parts, an accurate mathematical description of Mars's orbit and a physical explanation of what caused Mars to move as it did.

Regarding the latter part, Kepler's reading of material on magnetism encouraged him to envision a magnetic force emanating out from the sun, which, because the sun was rotating, pushed the planets around in their orbits. He assumed that such a force would get smaller as the distance from the sun increased, and if the force dropped off with distance, then he inferred that the velocity of the planet would too. Since he envisioned each possible line drawn from the off-center sun to Mars as varying in this way, then all the lines taken together constituted the area of the circle.

Kepler reasoned that if the irregular motion of Mars was governed at every point by this diminishing magnetic power, then the distance and the velocity compensated each other in such a way that what stayed constant was the area swept out in equal times as the planet traveled around the sun. This was the first inkling of what later became known as the equal areas law.

Kepler had already shown that the Earth, like the other planets, speeds up and slows down at different parts of its orbit. The equal areas law fit the earth's circular orbit well, but he found that it was off by eight minutes of arc for Mars. That divergence was very small, but Kepler trusted the accuracy of Tycho's data and refused to overlook the discrepancy. He was forced to conclude something quite unprecedented: Mars's orbit was just not perfectly circular.

If Mars did not go in a circular orbit, then what shape was it? He tried an oval orbit, but, as he wrote to a Lutheran pastor in northern Germany in the summer of 1603, he did not possess the mathematical techniques to show that an oval was consistent with his conclusion about equal areas. Finally he realized that an ellipse would fit the observations and, once he had convinced himself that an elliptical orbit was consistent with his areas law, he was able, finally, to celebrate his arrival at the end of an incredible path filled with tortuous calculations. The planets go around the sun in elliptical orbits and they do so because the sun governs them. This result has become known as Kepler's First Law, while his Second Law refers to the result concerning equal areas. Kepler's was a truly heliocentric system—the sun had to be the controlling center of the planetary orbits.

Tycho's heirs were not pleased with the conclusions Kepler had come to and they blocked the publication of his results for a while. But eventually a compromise was worked out. Tycho's son-in-law inserted a preface warning readers not to be misled by the physical claims in the book that differentiated it from Tycho. The title of the book, which appeared in 1609, was *The New Astronomy: Based on Causes, or Celestial Physics*. Kepler could not have been more clear about the new manner in which he felt astronomy should be practiced. Although he had broken new ground that would define the future of astronomy, not everyone in his time followed his lead. That included Galileo Galilei, whose relationship to Kepler we shall discuss in the next chapter.

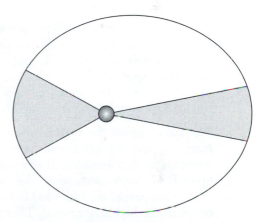

Equal Areas Law for an Ellipse

Later Years

Astronomy was not the only subject of interest to Kepler. He did fundamental work in optics, showing for the first time that the optical image is formed on the retina of the eye. Of course the emperor sought his opinion from time to time on various astrological matters. And he remained interested throughout his life in theological issues.

Up to this point in his career his choices were profoundly affected by his situation as a Protestant living in Catholic lands. That would not change soon, in spite of his departure from Prague on the death of the emperor in January of 1612. Kepler had unsuccessfully tried to obtain a position at his old university in Tübingen, but Rudolph's successor had continued his appointment as imperial mathematician and he received an invitation to pursue his work in the Austrian city of Linz.

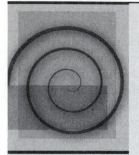

The NATURE of SCIENCE

Science and Mysticism

The motivation for studying natural science does not come from one single starting place; rather, it can spring from any number of sources. As is evident from the life and work of Johannes Kepler, that motivation includes the drive to find unity and harmony that has traditionally been associated with mysticism. What appears remarkable to us is that, as a result of his mystical convictions, Kepler was so successful in finding three laws of nature that have stood the test of time and can today be found in any physics or astronomy textbook. But, as Albert Einstein said, "The most beautiful experience we can have is the mysterious. It is the fundamental emotion that stands at the cradle of true art and true science. Whoever does not know it and can no longer wonder, no longer marvel, is as good as dead."

Just before the death of the emperor made it possible for him to leave Prague, his children had contracted smallpox, his wife had died of typhus, and the land was torn apart by religious turmoil. And even when he arrived in Linz, he found that he had not escaped all religious dissension. The local Lutheran pastor, heeding those in Tübingen who had prevented Kepler's appointment there because of his alleged friendliness with Calvinists, refused to give him communion.

The harmony of the world.   Not everything went badly for Kepler. He soon married again and had several more children, bringing the total to twelve. Then, when his mother was accused of witchcraft in the region where Kepler had grown up in 1617, Kepler successfully defended her at her trial.

A major part of his duties in Linz was the completion of the astronomical tables on which he had long worked. That was laborious and tedious work, and Kepler eased his mind by turning to a subject dear to his heart—cosmology. He had conceived of a work on this subject while still at Graz, but had not been able to pursue it. It was to be a summary of his cosmic vision, a natural philosophical and theological exposition of how everything fit together in God's universe.

Kepler is perhaps the best example of how far from the cautious view of some late medieval minds natural philosophers had come. Nicholas of Cusa in the fifteenth century had appealed to the properties of mathematics to show how inaccessible the infinite wisdom of God was to humans. Kepler did the opposite. For him, God was a geometer or, as he himself put it, "God is geometry itself." By delving into the intricacies of mathematical relationships, especially as the deity employed them in creating the world, humans could catch a direct glimpse of the mind of God. Doing astronomy was for Kepler a religious experience.

In *The Harmony of the World,* completed in 1618, Kepler explored the wondrous relationships of mathematics as they are found in geometry, music, astrology, and astronomy. Like the ancient Pythagoreans, he was impressed that musical harmonies, the relation between tones in the musical scale, could be expressed as simple numerical ratios of whole numbers. By his day seven such ratios were acknowledged (1:2, 2:3, 3:4, 4:5, 5:6, 3:5, and 5:8). Kepler found a rationale why these seven were the only ones possible in the properties of certain polygons, namely those that could be constructed with a compass and ruler.

Kepler then proceeded to seek the presence of these harmonies in human experience and in nature. Some of his efforts failed. For example, he thought that perhaps the periods of revolution of the various planets, or possibly the ratio of the perihelion (the closest point a planet comes to the sun) to the aphelion (the farthest point from the sun) might exhibit some of these ratios, but they did not. Finally, he discovered that the varying angular velocities of the planets as they go around the sun did fit into the musical ratios; that is, the ratio of the angular velocity at aphelion to that at perihelion for the planets fit various chords of the seven musical harmonies. And that wasn't all. If he compared pairs of planets he found even more harmonies. The spheres of the planets were creating music as they turned, evidence of "the delight of the divine Creator in his works."

The most well-known result from the book, however, had to do with Kepler's answer to the third question he had posed to himself many years before. Why do the planets go at the speeds that they do? He was now able to show that if he compared the periods of revolution of the planets to their mean distance from the sun, there was a ratio among whole numbers that captured the relationship. It was not an obvious ratio to be sure, but a man such as Kepler possessed the patience to seek until he found. He discovered that the squares of the periods of revolution of the planets were directly proportional to the cubes of their mean distances from the sun. This relationship, $T^2 \propto d^3$, was later culled from his work and dubbed Kepler's Third Law. Kepler himself did not list the results he came to as his three laws of nature.

Farewell to Austria. The great project of the astronomical tables undertaken initially by Tycho Brahe was finally brought to completion in 1624. Included were Tycho's catalog of one thousand fixed stars; planetary, solar, and lunar tables; and other material. Just as the printing began, the Lutherans in Linz felt the heavy hand of the Counter-Reformation descend. Kepler was permitted to leave Austria, where he had spent the majority of his life, in order to have the book printed in Germany. The Rudolphine Tables were printed in Ulm in 1627, and Kepler eventually settled his family in Sagan for his remaining days.

From this time comes a work that he had begun while a student in Tübingen, and which he had completed by 1609. *The Dream,* which concerns a trip to the moon and a description of the motions of the heavens from that vantage point, is an early work of science fiction that in its own way supported a heliocentric vision of the cosmos. It was printed after Kepler's death, which occurred in November of 1630.

◎ The Status of Heliocentrism ◎

Kepler's work was highly technical and composed in a tortuous style that did not lend itself to easy comprehension. He himself suspected that few would read the glorious results he had uncovered. At the beginning of Book V of *The Harmony of the World* he wrote that his book could wait a century for a reader since God had waited six thousand years for him, a witness who understood the subtleties of Creation.

At the beginning of the seventeenth century only Kepler unambiguously and enthusiastically embraced heliocentrism. In spite of his continuing work, geocentrism remained by far the dominant viewpoint among educated people and natural philosophers alike. Not until a champion of heliocentrism emerged, an astronomer who wrote for and in the language of the people, would the issue of heliocentrism come to a head. And when it did, it became clear that dislodging the Earth-centered view of the cosmos would not be at all easy.

Suggestions for Reading

Kitty Ferguson, *Tycho and Kepler: The Unlikely Partnership That Forever Changed Our Understanding of the Heavens* (New York: Walker and Co., 2004).

Owen Gingerich, *The Book Nobody Read: Chasing the Revolutions of Nicolaus Copernicus* (New York: Walker and Co., 2004).

Victor Thoren and John Robert Christianson (contributor), *The Lord of Uraniborg: A Biography of Tycho Brahe* (Cambridge: Cambridge University Press, 1991).

James R. Voelkel, *Johannes Kepler and the New Astronomy* (New York: Oxford University Press, 2001).

CHAPTER 6

Galileo Galilei: Heliocentrism Gains a Champion

By the end of the sixteenth century the idea that the Earth revolved around the sun was rejected by most of the people who considered it. But that would change by the time another century had passed. Two of the numerous reasons why heliocentrism gained credibility during the seventeenth century had to do with the life and work of a fascinating man from Italy, Galileo Galilei.

First, Galileo was one of the first natural philosophers to explain the Copernican system in terms that most literate people—not just astronomers—could understand. From his annotations in his copy of Copernicus's book, it is clear that Galileo's own interest had little to do with the technical details of the work. He focused on the cosmological implications. And when he wrote about the nature of the cosmos, he rarely chose the inaccessible scholarly language of Latin; rather, he wrote in the Italian vernacular. Further, Galileo often chose to frame his discussion in the form of dialogues carried on among several interlocutors. This gave the work a broad appeal because the discussants used argument, satire, humor—any tools of persuasion they could.

Second, Galileo did not shy away from controversy; on the contrary, he seemed to revel in it. Promoting Copernicus's unusual ideas was in itself enough to bring him and his work quickly to the attention of the public. But this kind of recognition was only enhanced by another skill Galileo possessed—he was good at self-promotion. This meant that he was able to associate with leading figures of Italian public life. As a result they too became involved in the controversies surrounding heliocentrism.

Galileo's role in the history of science includes more than his promotion of the Copernican system at a time when it was not widely accepted. He made important discoveries in physics and mathematics as well. But, largely because of the clash between Galileo and the Roman Catholic Church, the world knows him best as the champion of heliocentrism.

◎ Galileo's Early Career ◎

Galileo Galilei was born in Pisa in 1564. Although the Galilei name had once been more influential in Tuscany than it was at the end of the sixteenth century, it still commanded a certain respect. The family supported itself by selling valuable cloth, a respected enough calling even if Galileo's father, Vincenzio, had had to step aside from his chosen profession as a musician to take up the business.

Galileo was the oldest of the Galilei children. When he was eight, his father left Pisa and returned to his native city of Florence. He left his son and his wife in the care of a relative until just before Galileo's eleventh birthday, when the family joined the father in Florence. Galileo received some of his early education in the monastery in Vallombrosa, even becoming a novice there. His father could not afford a better education for him, but he still had higher hopes for his firstborn child than a clerical career. If Vincenzio had his way, Galileo would attend university and become a physician.

From Pisa to Padua

The university at Pisa had been reestablished under new statutes in 1543 and since then had become the best institution of higher education the grand dukes of Tuscany had to offer. While it could not compete with the venerable Italian universities in Bologna and Padua, it nevertheless attracted a sufficient number of students and faculty to become respectable.

The family stayed at the house of a relative in Pisa so that Vincenzio could afford to send his teenage son to the university. But things did not work out as the father had planned. Although he had matriculated as a medical student, Galileo just was not interested in becoming a physician. In 1585, at the age of twenty-one, Galileo left Pisa without a degree and came home. From references he made later in his life to the behavior of customers, it is likely that for a time he helped his father in the family cloth shop.

First mathematical studies.   We do not know exactly how or when Galileo became fascinated by mathematics, but his earliest biographers tell us that it was not through courses at the university. Mathematics was a minor subject at Pisa. One suggestion is that Galileo was able to make contact with a mathematician at the Tuscan court who introduced him to the works of Euclid and Archimedes and also to the study of perspective. This teacher, Ostilio Ricci, helped Galileo persuade his father to let him continue his study of mathematics with an eye to becoming a professor.

In 1587 Galileo traveled to Rome, where he met a leading Jesuit mathematician named Christoph Gau, known as Clavius. Galileo clearly was not shy about his own abilities in mathematics; by the following year he had established a brief correspondence with Clavius about mathematical issues. He also wrote to another leading figure in the field, the Archimedes scholar Guidobaldo del Monte. He impressed Guidobaldo greatly with his mathematical knowledge, enough to win his enthusiastic help in trying to land a position somewhere as a professor of mathematics. As it turned out, that happened in 1589, when he accepted a position at his former university in Pisa.

Galileo earned a very small salary at Pisa. He had hoped for a better position, but had not yet published anything that would establish his reputation sufficiently to obtain a post at one of Italy's more prominent universities. When his father died in the summer of 1591, Galileo's desire to land a better position increased. He was now the head of the Galilei household, and he had assumed the responsibility to provide the dowry for any of his sisters who should marry. Fortunately, Guidobaldo, who had access to influential people, continued to act behind the scenes on Galileo's behalf. As a result, after only three years at Pisa, Galileo was offered a higher-paying position at the University of Padua in the fall of 1592, which he was delighted to accept.

The University of Padua had been founded in 1222 and had since established a venerable reputation in law, theology, astronomy, and especially in medicine. From the beginning of the fifteenth century to the end of the eighteenth, Padua was under the jurisdiction of the Republic of Venice. The new ideas of Renaissance humanism that filled the air were much appreciated in the Venetian republic. Padua in particular was a place that valued free and independent thinking. The republic was known for its willingness to resist the authority of Rome, so the incentive Galileo had to go to Padua was not merely financial.

Considerations of Copernicus.   As a professor of mathematics at both Pisa and Padua, Galileo had to give a basic course on astronomy. In such a course he was expected to cover how the ancients had accounted for the motions observable in the heavens. Primary among the systems he would have communicated to his students were those of Aristotle and Ptolemy. While he was aware of the more recent system of Copernicus, we know that he did not publicly endorse it in his lectures.

That is not to say that he did not discuss Copernicus at all. In a manuscript intended only for pupils, Galileo noted that there were those who said that the Earth moved, but he then reviewed the reasons given by Aristotle and Ptolemy why that could not be the case. Since this anti-Copernican stance was expected, it is not possible to determine from the manuscript what Galileo's personal view was.

There are two references from 1597, however, that seem to confirm that Galileo was not only a convinced Copernican, but that he had been so for some time. The first reference comes in a letter to a professor of philosophy at his former university in Pisa. The professor had just published a book in which he came across as unalterably opposed to Copernicus. Galileo stated that he personally thought the system of Copernicus was more probably true than the systems of Aristotle and Ptolemy. He proceeded to argue that some of the professor's objections to Copernicus were not well founded.

The second reference of 1597 is where Galileo asserted that he had long been a Copernican. Johannes Kepler had sent two copies of his *Cosmographic Mystery* to Italy to be given to those who would be able to appreciate the work. By fortunate chance one ended up in Galileo's possession and he ascertained immediately from reading the preface that its author was a Copernican. In his letter to Kepler thanking him for the work, Galileo said that he rejoiced at having found someone else who also had discovered the truth. He then added, in what many scholars regard as an exaggeration, that he had accepted the heliocentric doctrine many years ago. He had not discussed Copernicus publicly, he said, because so many ridiculed his system.

When Galileo addressed the public he did not identify with any of these alleged sympathies for Copernicus. Seven years after the letter to Kepler a supernova occurred, which was seen as a sequel to the new star of 1572 that Tycho Brahe had discussed. Galileo understood clearly that the new star was beyond the orb of the moon and he mused that in the arguments surrounding the new star, the Earth's motion around the sun might be pertinent. What he likely meant by this is that perhaps this new star might display a small parallactic shift to the careful observer; if so, such a result would be consistent with an Earth that was moving around the sun.

In a work published a year after the new star appeared, a work to which Galileo did not attach his real name, he ridiculed the treatment of the new star by an Aristotelian who did not understand the basics of astronomy. The work explained in a condescending tone the significance of parallax and it contained favorable references to Copernicus's doctrine. But when, in spite of all the attention the new star received, no small parallactic shift had been observed, Galileo thought better of casting Copernicus in a favorable light. In the second edition of this work, which appeared a few months after the first, Galileo depicted the Copernican doctrine in disparaging terms. While it is hard to be certain what Galileo believed about heliocentrism in these years, it is clear that he was willing to consider it even if he had not yet uncovered any evidence to confirm it.

Early Work on Motion

We have access to several unpublished manuscripts on motion that Galileo wrote during the Pisa and Padua years. This subject was normally the province of philosophers, so Galileo's investigations were somewhat unusual for a beginning young professor of mathematics. They are an early indication that Galileo would not feel bound by the traditional division of academic subjects.

The Leaning Tower of Pisa.   Galileo's seventeenth-century biographer, Vincenzio Viviani, originated the legend of Galileo and the Leaning Tower of Pisa. The story goes that Galileo demonstrated to observers from the university that objects of the same material but different weights, when dropped from the tower, did not, as Aristotle taught, fall at rates of speed proportional to their weights. Rather, they fell at the same speed. Unfortunately, we cannot simply accept Viviani's word on this score because at other times he has proven less than reliable. Further, there is no other record of what surely would have been quite a public spectacle.

In fact, others had long before suggested that Aristotle was wrong to assert that the speeds of falling bodies varied according to their weights. What Galileo believed was not that all objects fell at the same speed; he thought that things were more complicated than that. He thought that every material would accelerate as it fell until it reached the speed characteristic of that material. It would then continue to fall at that uniform speed without accelerating further. So if Galileo did drop objects from the Leaning Tower, it would not have been to demonstrate that all objects fell at the same rate.

Galileo's rejection of Aristotle's claim about free fall was cleverly done. Imagine, he said, two stones, one twice the weight of another. According to Aristotle the heavier one will fall twice as fast as the lighter one. So tie them together with a strong string. What would Aristotle say would happen now? He might say that the joined stones would fall slower than before because the smaller one will retard the larger one's speed. Then again, he might conclude that the joined stones will fall three times as fast as the small one by itself because the combined mass is now three times greater than that of the smaller one. Clearly, Aristotle's analysis was flawed.

More conclusions about falling bodies.   Another conclusion Galileo came to occurred after he had left Pisa for Padua. It had to do with the motion of pendulums. By 1602 Galileo had been at Padua for a decade. In that year he wrote a letter to his supporter Guidobaldo in which he tried to convince him of something that runs counter to intuition. Suspend a ball on a string, draw it to one side through an arc less than or equal to 90 degrees, and release it. Its period—the time it takes to swing back and forth—will take the same time regardless of the angle it swings through. Galileo is thus credited with noting the isochronism of the pendulum, a discovery that had important implications for measuring time intervals.

In a letter of 1604 Galileo described another new discovery regarding freely falling objects. He declared that the distance traversed in equal times increased in accordance with the sequence of odd numbers. As shown in the illustration, if an object falls for four seconds, then in the first second it traverses 1 unit of distance, in the next second 3 units, in the third second 5 units, in the fourth second 7 units, and so forth (1, 3, 5, 7, . . .). Galileo then recognized that the *total* distance traversed after a given number of seconds was given by the square of the elapsed time; that is, by the end of one second the object had fallen through 1 unit of distance (1^2), by the end of the two seconds it had traversed $1 + 3 = 4$ units (2^2), and by the end of the third second $1 + 3 + 5 = 9$ units (3^2) of distance. This meant that the distance a freely falling object traversed was proportional to the square of the time, or $d \propto t^2$.

Actual and virtual experiments.   Scholars have argued about whether the results Galileo came to were the outcome of experiments that he actually conducted or whether he relied more on so-called thought experiments. It is likely that Galileo employed both approaches and that the conclusions he came to were affected by both kinds of endeavor. Consider the following examples of Galileo's reasoning.

Beginning around 1605 Galileo tried experiments of various kinds with balls on an inclined plane. For example, he rolled a ball down an inclined plane that was set at the edge of a table, putting ink on the ball so that when it hit the floor it would

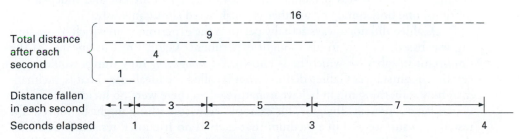

Distance–Time Relationship for Freely Falling Objects

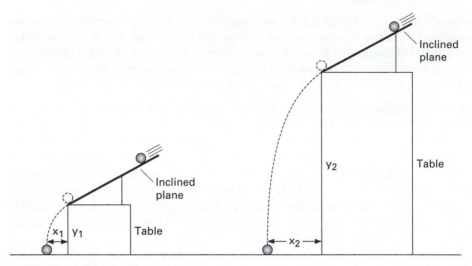

Ball Rolling Down an Inclined Plane

leave a mark. This gave him the horizontal distance the ball had moved away from the inclined plane. He also measured the vertical distance that the end of the plane was from the floor. By elevating the inclined plane apparatus to various heights above the floor, he was able to compile a set of data that correlated horizontal distances (x_1 and x_2 in the figure) and heights (y_1 and y_2).

Clearly, Galileo was depending on actual experimental results here. And from the data of these experiments Galileo was able to infer several important things. First, his measurements showed that the heights were proportional to the squares of the horizontal distance, that is, $y \propto x^2$. This correlation he recognized to be the one found in a parabola. Second, since the horizontal distance traversed during free fall was directly proportional to the time, he could substitute time for horizontal distance. That would then give $y \propto t^2$, which confirmed his earlier result about the distance fallen being proportional to the square of the time. Finally, Galileo confirmed what others had already suspected; namely, that Aristotle's followers were wrong to hold that in projectile motion the impressed force caused the object to move in a straight line until the force was expended, and that only then did the object fall straight to the ground. If the path was parabolic, then obviously two different and independent motions, one horizontal and another vertical, acted simultaneously.

But Galileo did not always actually perform the experiment on which his reasoning was based. In fact, in his thought experiments Galileo reveals another of the important insights for which he is known. By *imagining* how things would be in certain circumstances Galileo defined what is called the ideal case. That is, he imagined how something might behave in nature when there were no incidental or accidental factors present. Imagine, for example, how something might be moved if it rested on a surface and in a medium that exerted no frictional resistance at all. By doing this Galileo came to one of the most central insights in the history of science prior to that time. He concluded that under such circumstances any force, however small, would set the object into motion and that without friction to slow it down, the object would simply keep moving. He would unpack the implications of this insight later, but for now he began to understand how important it was to consider the ideal case.

Of course there is nowhere on Earth where we encounter surfaces and media that exert no frictional resistance at all. Even such slippery surfaces as ice and such nonviscous media as air exert frictional resistance. Imagining that such factors did not play a role was not something commonly done by the Aristotelian thinkers of Galileo's day. They insisted on including all of the complications they encountered in the phenomena they were trying to explain. Galileo was beginning to assume that it was instructive to establish the principles that governed the ideal case and then to explain the behavior that is actually observed by showing how the incidental factors force the object to depart from the ideal case.

Thought experiments provided other benefits than merely uncovering the ideal case. In Galileo's critique of Aristotle's position regarding the speed of freely falling objects we have already met an example of how a thought experiment could be used to analyze the merits of a received view. By merely envisioning the cases of two rocks falling separately and then tied together, Galileo uncovered results that were contradictory. Simply imagining what would happen was sufficient to show that Aristotle had been wrong. Clearly, Galileo used thought experiments as profitably as he did the actual experiments he conducted.

The relationship between nature and mathematics.   Both kinds of experiment, especially the actual ones he conducted, caused Galileo to ponder an interesting question concerning the relationship between mathematics and nature. Before discovering the parabolic shape of a projectile's path, Galileo had not assumed that the changing realm of terrestrial nature, which was filled with accidental properties, could be described using the abstract and perfectly logical relationships of mathematics. The ancients may have used geometry to describe the motions of the heavens, but the motions of things on Earth involved too many incidental characteristics to conform to the neat and trim relationships found in mathematics. In his 1602 letter to Guidobaldo, for example, Galileo noted that geometry seemed to lose its certainty when applied to things on Earth.

Now Galileo began to realize that there were contexts in which the relationships of mathematics *did* describe nature here on Earth. It was not long before he began to insist that a proper treatment of nature should include mathematical descriptions. In fact, he mentioned Aristotle's failure to do so as one of the fundamental criticisms of the ancient philosopher's explanations of terrestrial motion. Two decades later, in a work called *The Assayer,* he would identify mathematics as the language of nature.

Galileo's financial concerns.   As mentioned earlier, Galileo earned a mere pittance at Pisa, so after three years he was happy to go to Padua for triple the salary. In 1598 he was successful in obtaining a healthy salary increase at Padua, much to the annoyance of some at the university. Regardless of what others thought, Galileo never undervalued his own abilities, and he was good at marketing them.

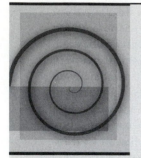

The NATURE of SCIENCE

Mathematics and Nature

In modern natural science it has become commonplace to assume that nature can be described accurately using mathematical equations. But Galileo's discovery that the motion of falling bodies follows a simple parabola should remind us that the relationship between mathematics and nature should by no means be taken for granted. After all, why *should* the precise relationships of mathematics fit the complex physical world?

In 1960 the physicist Eugene Wigner wrote an essay entitled "The Unreasonable Effectiveness of Mathematics in the Natural Sciences," which contains many references to Galileo. One of the points Wigner wanted to make was that the enormous usefulness of mathematics in the natural sciences is something bordering on the mysterious and that there is no rational explanation for it.

Of course for men like Galileo and Kepler there could be a theological explanation. God might be responsible. If God created both the world and the relationships of mathematics, then it makes sense that the two would match up. This explanation ultimately worked for Galileo, but of course not all people are religiously disposed. The problem that Galileo uncovered is one that continues to add to the allure and mystery of modern natural science.

It was understood that no matter what salary the university paid its mathematicians, they were free to engage private pupils to supplement their income. In Galileo's case he also became involved in practical projects that carried the possibility of financial reward. He was not above pursuing patents on his inventions to ensure additional income. Further, by bringing himself attention through his inventions, he publicized his value to the republic.

Still, Galileo's financial obligations continued to grow along with his salary. One of his sisters married in 1601 and he contributed substantially to the dowry. A young woman named Marina Gamba, whom Galileo had met in Venice, moved in with him and gave birth to a daughter in 1600. Another daughter came along the next year, and a son was born in 1606. Galileo and Marina would remain together for ten years. With a growing family of his own and the possibility of more dowries on the horizon, Galileo constantly felt the need to increase his income, and this in spite of another salary increase in 1606.

◎   Court Philosopher   ◎

An obvious way of alleviating the constant negotiations over salary every time Galileo's contract at the university came up for renewal was to obtain employment from a patron. Further, the steady and sure income that came with a court appointment was not the only potential benefit. He would also be much more free to carry out investigations and to write, both of which he very much wanted to pursue.

The Move to Florence

Not just any appointment would do. Galileo had, in fact, turned down an offer from the Duke of Mantua in 1604. One of the reasons he needed to find a patron of considerable power was to acquire protection should he ever need it. He was relatively safe in the Republic of Venice, where open inquiry and expression were as liberal as anywhere on the Italian peninsula. But the experiences of others suggested that even there he could become entangled in difficulties if his views were ever regarded as too extreme.

Things had been growing increasingly touchy during the preceding decades, especially concerning the control of knowledge. In 1570 the widely known natural philosopher, physician, mathematician, and astrologer Girolamo Cardano (1501–1576) managed sufficiently to antagonize officials in the Inquisition, the institution charged with the eradication of heresies, that even his willingness to stop teaching was not enough to keep him first from prison, then from house arrest. The following year the pope established the Congregation of the Index, signaling that the content of books would be coming under greater scrutiny. In some instances merely rejecting the interpretation of Aristotle's philosophy that had been crafted by Thomas Aquinas was enough to land a book on the list of prohibited writings. And then there was the example of Giordano Bruno, the Italian philosopher who was deemed a heretic and burned at the stake near the beginning of 1600. Although it was Bruno's rejection of the divinity of Christ and the notion that the Holy Spirit was the soul of the world that caused his execution, Bruno was known to defend the Copernican system, even to reject the finitude of the cosmos. Galileo would do well to be careful.

Laying the groundwork to move from Padua.   Galileo preferred, of course, to go back to his native Tuscany. The roots of the ruling Medici family went back to the twelfth century, and the current grand duke, Ferdinand, was a lover of natural philosophy.

The first breakthrough came in 1605, when Galileo was invited to use his vacations from teaching at the university to tutor the Medici prince, who would one day become the grand duke of Tuscany. Ferdinand had actually appointed Galileo to his first position at Pisa, and Galileo had made his wishes known to serve as tutor to the prince as early as 1601. Ferdinand now deemed the prince old enough to become familiar with the wonders of nature and mathematics.

When Grand Duke Ferdinand died in 1609, the nineteen-year-old prince became Grand Duke Cosimo II. Galileo made inquiries through an intermediary about the possibility of a court appointment, but he simply was not yet distinguished enough to expect that they would be successful. He concluded that he would once again have to renew his contract to teach at Padua.

What changed his prospects was the arrival of news of the invention of a new instrument—the spyglass, or telescope—which Galileo learned about in that same year of 1609. The telescope had been invented the previous year in Holland and copies were beginning to turn up in various places. Someone tried to sell one in early August of 1609 to the officials in Venice, who declined. Later that month, however, they accepted a telescope Galileo had made, which he offered to them for free. Of course, the hefty increase he then received in his salary at Padua more than compensated Galileo for his trouble. His annual salary, which the Venetian Senate now bestowed for life, was more than sixteen times what it was when he started out in Pisa.

In fact, Galileo substantially improved the telescope over others that were being produced. And while he was not the only one to turn it toward the heavens as an instrument of research, he was among the first to do so. He quickly realized that the telescope made possible Earth-shaking revelations that would astound not just the House of Medici, but the whole world. With this new instrument he undertook a new project that would land him the post in Florence he so fervently craved.

The Starry Message.   The new project was the writing of a small book. It was called *Sidereus Nuncius* in Latin. Although throughout his career he usually wrote in the Italian vernacular, he chose to write this book in the universal language of the day. The discoveries were just too profound to deliver only to Italians.

The book appeared in March of 1610 and was immediately a sensation. It described three basic discoveries Galileo made through the use of a new spyglass, which, he announced in the dedication, he had invented. Galileo meant that he had invented this particular spyglass, but many have mistakenly assumed from his words that Galileo himself was the original inventor of the telescope. The three discoveries had to do with the moon, with the stars themselves, and, most astonishing of all, with four new planets.

As for the moon, Galileo reported that its surface was different from what many philosophers believed, namely, that it was smooth, uniform, and precisely spherical. It was, in fact, very uneven, like the surface of the Earth. The telescope revealed that there were mountains and deep valleys on the moon. How could he tell this? First, with the telescope he could see that the line separating the light from the dark areas of the crescent moon was very uneven, not smooth as it should be if the surface itself were smooth. Further, there were light spots visible through the telescope within the dark region, some at considerable distance from the dividing line between the light and dark regions. These bright spots were clearly the tops of mountains, which, just as on Earth, became illuminated by the sun's rays before the actual rising of the sun.

Next came the stars. The telescope did not improve their appearance—it did not bring them anywhere near as close as it did the moon. Galileo explained this by pointing out that the telescope stripped away the fringing rays that surrounded stars, making their globes appear smaller. So its magnifying power was diminished from the start. What was astonishing to him, however, was the number of new stars that became visible through the telescope—up to five hundred within one or two degrees of arc. Finally, Galileo claimed to be able to lay to rest an old debate: was the Milky Way made up of individual stars, or was it truly a nebulous patch in the heavens? Galileo declared that it was "nothing but a congeries of innumerable stars grouped together in clusters." And not only the Milky Way—Galileo explained that the telescope resolved a nebula in the constellation of Orion and another in that of Cancer.

So far the discoveries were fascinating, although they were not truly amazing. As noted, philosophers had argued about the composition of the Milky Way for some time. That meant that many had suspected there were numerous stars in the heavens that no one had ever seen. And others prior to Galileo's observations had also suspected that the moon possessed a rough surface. The discovery Galileo saved until last, however, was a real bombshell: he had seen four new *planets*. This, he said, was the most important matter of all.

Galileo recreated for the reader his own excitement at having made this find. He narrated the discovery of these new planets as an unfolding story. He gave the dates, what he had seen, what he had first thought, and then how he had figured out that these points of light were not stars, but moons revolving around Jupiter. What was not in the narrative was that soon after making this discovery, Galileo was in contact with the Tuscan secretary of state about a work he was planning to write. What did the secretary think of the idea of naming the new planets "the Cosmic stars" for the grand duke, or perhaps "the Medicean stars" for all four Medici brothers? The secretary wrote back to suggest the latter name was better—no one could miss the allusion. When the book came out, the title page proclaimed the discovery of the Medicean stars.

Galileo provided only a few hints in the book that he harbored sympathies for the Copernican system. The reader certainly did not find an outright endorsement of the Polish cleric's heliocentric arrangement of the sun and the planets. Galileo indicated his appreciation of Copernicus in passing references that might easily be overlooked. For example, he promised a sequel to his work, to be entitled *System of the World*, in which he would prove that the Earth was a wandering body, not the center of the cosmos. This meant that he believed the Earth was in motion like the other planets. In the dedication—naturally to Grand Duke Cosimo II—he observed that the duke's new planets revolved around Jupiter, and at the same time revolved with Jupiter around the sun, the center of the cosmos. And in the text itself Galileo mentioned that the existence of Jupiter's satellites removed an objection to the Copernican system, namely, that the Earth was the only body to have a moon.

In spite of these passing references the work was more sensational than it was truly revolutionary. Nothing he had seen required anything more than an updating of the inventory of the cosmos, not of its arrangement. The reader might have to conclude that the moon had a rough surface, that there were more stars in the heavens than once thought, and that one of the planets had moons. But none of that challenged the Ptolemaic arrangement of the cosmos. It just provided updated information. The only real challenge to Ptolemy was Galileo's promise to prove that the Earth moved. The other allusions—to there being two centers of motion in the cosmos and to Jupiter's revolving around the sun—were both matched in the system of Tycho Brahe. All of this would be argued about in due time. In the spring of 1610 the dust was still swirling.

The call to Florence.   Galileo's book came out in March. He took immediate steps to implement his plan to convince the grand duke to bring him home to Tuscany. In January he had cast a birth horoscope for the grand duke. He promised to send the grand duke himself the very telescope he had used to make his discoveries. He sent a copy of his book to the Tuscan ambassador in Prague so that it would come to Kepler's attention. And then in May of 1610 he wrote again to the Tuscan secretary of state to discuss his possible appointment to the Tuscan court. By that time he was able to include the hearty endorsement Johannes Kepler had sent to Galileo. Kepler was happy to sing the praises of Galileo's work and had written back in less than a week to say so.

Galileo did not seek an increase in salary, but he did request that his appointment bestow on him the title of philosopher as well as mathematician. In fact many of the topics he addressed in *The Starry Message* concerning the existence and constitution of heavenly bodies were considered the philosopher's subject matter. As a mathematician he was supposed to confine himself to the description of the heavens, so he was technically poaching on the academic turf of others when he gave arguments for the existence of new stars, the Medicean planets, or mountains on the moon. And since philosophers occupied a higher rung on the social scale, an appointment as a court philosopher would instantly raise his status.

Of course Galileo made clear what he would do as the grand duke's philosopher. *The Starry Message* was just the beginning. He outlined the works he would be able to publish once he enjoyed the free time for research that freedom from regular teaching duties would permit. And all of this would redound to the glory of the grand duke. His petition worked. In June the secretary wrote to tell him that he had the position and, amid considerable resentment on the part of those who had just raised his salary in Padua, Galileo resigned his university post. The appointment was formally made in July and he moved to Florence in September.

Early Triumphs of the Ducal Philosopher

Life in Florence, even family life, would be very different. Although Galileo took his two daughters with him to Florence, Marina Gamba remained behind with their four-year-old son, Vincenzio. His son joined Galileo a few years later, but the separation from Marina proved to be permanent. She married another man in 1613.

The greatest difference, however, was that Galileo no longer had to teach. He continued to give limited private instruction, but that burden had also been largely lifted. He had promised the grand duke that he would make more discoveries. Before the end of the year he had made a very significant one.

A new discovery. Galileo continued to observe the heavens with the excellent telescopes he had constructed. In December of 1610 he observed that the planet Venus had phases. This sounds like the kind of observation he had made in *The Starry Message*—new information for updating the cosmic inventory. It was not. Venus could *not* have phases under the old Ptolemaic system. This discovery provided a substantial discrediting of Ptolemy's system because the only way Venus could display phases was if it were sometimes between the Earth and the sun and sometimes on the other side of the sun from the Earth. But that would mean that Venus circled the sun.

Both Galileo and the Jesuit astronomer Benedetto Castelli—who had observed Venus's phases at about the same time Galileo did—concluded that the observed phases of Venus vindicated the system of Copernicus. As can be seen in the diagram, the phases Galileo and Castelli observed are consistent with the Copernican arrangement of the planets in their trip around the sun. At position E Venus would

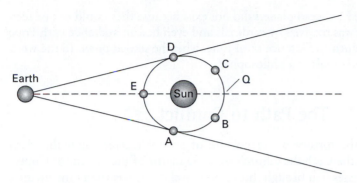

The Phases of Venus

be at new phase because the portion of Venus illuminated by the sun is opposite the side seen from Earth. It would then grow to crescent at A, then to the almost full "gibbous" phase at B. It would not be visible at Q because the sun itself blocks the view from earth, but would be waning gibbous at C. At D it would again be crescent shaped, to return to new phase at E. Further, it should be a larger crescent image than gibbous image because Venus was closer to Earth when at crescent phase than at gibbous. These were exactly the phases that Galileo and Castelli observed.

There is, of course, one flaw—a major flaw—in the inference that the phases of Venus proved the Copernican system. It is that the phases Galileo observed through the telescope were equally well accounted for by the Tychonic system, in which Venus also circles the sun. As we saw in Chapter 5, the systems of Tycho and Copernicus are observationally equivalent, so it should be no surprise at all that the telescopic observations of Venus's phases served as evidence for both the Tychonic and Copernican systems.

As historian Mario Biagioli points out, the Jesuits began to lean toward Tycho's system soon after Galileo's discoveries. Galileo, however, regarded Tycho's Earth-centered cosmos as looking backward, not forward. Tycho's geocentric system was a thorn in Galileo's side; it meant that he really could not absolutely prove that the Earth was in motion. Still, after he discovered the phases of Venus, Galileo became much more open than he had been about expressing his opinions on Copernicus. His inference that the phases of Venus meant Copernicus was correct would cause difficulties for him in the developments of the coming years.

Triumph in Rome.   Galileo's fame was increasing. As a representative of the Grand Duke Cosimo II he could not be simply dismissed, although numerous people resented his presumption to tread on ground where he did not belong. From the start there were those in Padua who downplayed his achievement. With great public success came the prospect of public enemies.

For the moment, however, Galileo was on top of the world. In March of 1611 the Tuscan ambassador in Rome invited him for a visit in order to draw attention to the grand duke's recent appointment. Of course Galileo visited Clavius, the first mathematician he had contacted when he was just starting out. He was reassured when Clavius mocked a recent attack by Francesco Sizi, author of *Dianoia Astronomica,* who declared that the Medicean planets did not exist because they could not be seen by the naked eye. He was received by cardinals and even had an audience with Pope Paul V. He did not return to Florence until June, when he settled down to the work of establishing his credentials as a philosopher.

◎ The Path to Conflict ◎

Few episodes from the history of science are of greater interest than the clash between Galileo and the Catholic Church over the merits of the system of Copernicus. The early successes that brought him public acclaim also earned him enemies who did not wish to see his celebrity continue to rise. A setback to Galileo in 1616, followed by a turn of fortune for the better in 1623, all culminated in 1632 with the publication of his famous book on the two chief world systems. This work precipitated the judgment against him that his adversaries had long hoped for.

Storm Clouds Looming

Even in Tuscany, some Aristotelian philosophers set themselves against Galileo relatively quickly. The first to publish against Galileo was Martinus Horky, who tried to discredit the reliability of the telescope. We have already mentioned Sizi's attack on the existence of the Medicean stars. These attacks focused on the observations of *The Starry Messsage.*

Not long after he had his meeting with the pope, Cardinal Robert Bellarmine, chief advisor of the Holy See, sought the view of Jesuit scholars about Galileo's observations. He was told that the telescope had definitely uncovered the presence of new stars in the heavens, including the four satellites of Jupiter; further, Venus was observed to have phases. Some doubted that Galileo had demonstrated all he said about the surface of the moon, but there was little doubt that in general the observations were real. Most Jesuit mathematicians approved of them because they were pleased with the way Galileo was raising the status of mathematicians to rival that of philosophers.

The problem of Copernicanism.   Jesuit mathematicians may have endorsed the telescope, but that did not mean that they approved of Galileo's implicit endorsement of Copernicus. This was because, as already pointed out, the observations could also be seen as evidence of the geocentric system of Tycho Brahe. There was nothing about the telescopic observations that permitted one to exclude Tycho's system in favor of Copernicus's. Approving the reliability of the observations and approving Copernicus were two entirely different matters.

Things began to change as Galileo's Copernicanism became the focus. The Florentine philosopher Lodovico delle Colombe penned a manuscript entitled "Against the Motion of the Earth." Delle Colombe's declaration that the doctrine of Copernicus was contrary to the Scriptures marked the beginning of a growing concern.

This was in 1611. Near the end of 1612 a Dominican priest, who did not even know Copernicus's correct name (he called him "Ipernicus"), mentioned to Galileo that heliocentrism did seem contrary to Scriptures. Galileo most likely realized he was going to have to deal with this question. He had already crossed over into the territory of philosophers. Now he was about to take on the theologians.

The letter to the grand duchess. One year later, in December of 1613, the mother of the grand duke raised the question anew with Galileo's friend, Benedetto Castelli, now a professor in Pisa. Castelli wrote to Galileo to tell him about the grand duchess's interest and Galileo immediately replied with his thoughts on the matter. He made it clear that this was a case when the words of the Bible could not be taken literally. In the Old Testament, for example, to prolong daylight for his army, Joshua commanded the sun to stand still (which suggested the sun, not the Earth, was moving). Galileo explained that the writer here was not taking a stand on whether it was the sun or the Earth that was moving; rather, he was portraying events in language his readers could understand. Because the matter was such a central concern, Galileo told Castelli that he could share the contents of the letter. Naturally, the letter was copied and began to circulate, sometimes among friends, sometimes enemies.

It took a year for hostile theologians—who resented Galileo's presuming to tell them how to interpret Scripture—to join forces against the grand duke's philosopher. The opening salvo came from a Dominican priest named Tommaso Caccini, who preached a sermon in Florence at the end of 1614 on the book of Joshua in which he denounced Galileo and Copernicanism as contrary to Scripture. Another Dominican, the same one who had mistaken Copernicus's name a year earlier, obtained a copy of Galileo's letter to Castelli. Early in 1615 he sent his copy of the letter to the Inquisition. Soon thereafter Caccini went to Rome himself to speak to members of the Inquisition.

When Galileo got wind of all this he became concerned that the copy of the letter being used in Rome was inaccurate, so he sent a true version to friends in Rome who would make sure it got to the right people. Against the advice of theologian friends who urged Galileo not to become involved in theological arguments about Copernicus, Galileo expanded his letter to Castelli into a treatise entitled "Letter to Madame Christina of Lorraine, Grand Duchess of Tuscany, Concerning the Use of Biblical Quotations in Matters of Science." Although not published until much later, the work represented the views Galileo held on theology and science.

In the treatise he repeated his claim that while the Bible cannot contain untruth, it must not always be taken literally. Were we to do so we would have to assign God feet, hands, and eyes, and even acknowledge that he occasionally forgets things. When the writers of the Bible used such images they were accommodating the understanding of the average person.

Galileo even included a technical argument that demonstrated why we should not take the passage about Joshua and the sun literally. To prolong the day Joshua would have to have commanded the outermost sphere of the heavens, which drove everything around the Earth once a day, to stop moving. The sun's proper motion goes against the grain of this daily motion, although very slowly. Had Joshua commanded the *sun's* motion to cease without at the same time stopping the twenty-four hour motion of the outermost sphere, the day would actually have been slightly shorter! So clearly the writer did not want us to invest a literal meaning in the words "Sun, stand thou still." The effect of this clever argument, however, might well have been simply to provoke the ire of those who did not know astronomy.

The 1616 visit to Rome.   Late in 1615 Galileo became concerned that things were moving against him in Rome, so he decided to go there himself to make his own case. He had been in correspondence with people there, including the chief advisor, Cardinal Bellarmine. He and Bellarmine agreed on some things and disagreed on others. They agreed that the Bible could not err and that true science and true religion could never conflict. Where they appeared to disagree was over the status of hypotheses. Bellarmine regarded hypotheses as assumptions of convenience, in Copernicus's case, the convenience of making calculations. He did not see them as assumptions that were likely someday to be proven true. He even made his own hypothesis about the most convenient way to handle Copernicus. Say the motion of the Earth *was* clearly demonstrated. In that case we would have to say not that the Bible was wrong, but that we did not understand it. He felt himself to be on very safe ground: the Earth's motion had not been (and would not be) clearly demonstrated.

Galileo undoubtedly saw the Copernican hypothesis as something that could be—and in his own mind had been—proven true. He had a favorite argument to demonstrate the Earth's motion, which he had first thought of while in Padua. The existence of tides, he said, resulted from the contrary motions the Earth experienced between its motion around the sun and the motion on its axis. Sometimes these two motions reinforced each other and sometimes they went against each other. The result was the sloshing of the seas against the shores. So the fact that there were tides proved the Earth was moving.

Galileo was aware that this explanation entailed just one high tide and one low tide a day, whereas two were observed to occur. But he said that other factors were also involved that were responsible for the extra tidal motions. Of course, if he were right, then Bellarmine was wrong in assuming that the hypothesis of the Earth's motion would not be proven true. Confident that he could persuade the right people, he went to Rome to vindicate himself.

Things went well for him personally. He soon established that he himself was in no danger, so he decided to push for an acceptance of Copernicus. He persuaded a friend among the cardinals to talk to the pope. The pope's response was to request that the Inquisition make a formal evaluation. Caccini had identified two propositions to the Inquisition that he deemed heretical: that the sun was at the center of the world and immobile, and that the Earth was not the center and moved with a double motion. The Inquisition determined that the first proposition was heretical because it contradicted Scripture. The second was theologically erroneous.

The pope instructed Bellarmine to communicate to Galileo the judgment that he was not to teach or defend or consider the Copernican doctrine. Bellarmine met with Galileo and apparently told him that he was neither to hold nor defend Copernicus's view. At least that is what is contained in a copy of the letter Bellarmine later sent to Galileo confirming the order. Given their discussion about hypotheses, Galileo assumed he could at least continue to use the Copernican system hypothetically in his future work in astronomy. Exactly what Bellarmine enjoined Galileo to do became the center of contention in Galileo's later trial, as we will see. The point, however, was to keep Galileo quiet so that he would not raise further difficulties.

Galileo's Famous Book

Between 1616 and 1623, when a new pope was elected, Galileo publicly acknowledged that the Copernican system was not the true system of the heavens. Of course he added that neither was the Ptolemaic system, because that had been shown to be wrong. As always, he dismissed Tycho Brahe's system. That left him able to voice the fervent hope that someday the true system would be found.

These sentiments were expressed in an exchange about comets, which Galileo became entangled in during these years. Unfortunately, as the controversy unfolded he needlessly antagonized a Jesuit mathematician in Rome named Orazio Grassi. Galileo's unnecessary attack elicited a reply in which Grassi, an adherent of Tycho's system, raised anew the issue of Copernicanism. It was not that the debate about comets entailed the question whether the cosmos was heliocentric or not, but Grassi was in a real sense baiting Galileo. He knew that Galileo could not defend his Copernican views publicly.

Another visit to Rome.   The cardinal elected to the papacy in 1623 gave Galileo renewed hope because he was a friend, Mafeo Barberini. Barberini had sided with Galileo earlier in a controversy over floating bodies. He also appreciated Galileo's devotion to astronomy, although prior to the 1616 visit to Rome he had urged Galileo not to become involved in theological debates about Copernicanism. Now he was the head of the Roman Catholic Church. Naturally Galileo's hopes were raised. Perhaps he could persuade his old acquaintance, now Pope Urban VIII, to remove the prohibition against Copernicus.

Galileo visited the pope in Rome in the spring of 1624 and had six conversations with him. They remained on friendly terms, but Galileo did not get what he wanted—permission to ignore the injunction of 1616. They understood each other well. Each had a pet argument of which the other was aware. Galileo felt that the tides proved the motion of the Earth. Urban VIII believed that no matter how things seemed to be, God could have made them that way in any number of ways. The existence of tides did not mean that God had produced them by the motions of the Earth. God could have easily caused them on a stationary Earth by some other means.

Because of their discussions, and because the pope acknowledged that the church had not condemned nor would it condemn heliocentrism as heretical, Galileo felt that he could discuss Copernicanism publicly as long as he did not defend it or appear to hold it to be true. So he set out to do just that, to write a work comparing Copernicus to Ptolemy in which he discussed the merits and demerits of each *without openly endorsing Copernicus*. Once again there would be no mention of Tycho's system, even though it was consistent with all of the telescopic observations.

Around this time Galileo began exchanging letters with his eldest daughter, Virginia, a nun who had taken the name Sister Maria Celeste to honor her father's fascination with the heavens. She was cloistered in the convent at San Matteo in Arcetri, outside the city walls on the southern hills of Florence. Through her obvious devotion and concern for his well-being, and by simply being there as a correspondent, she imparted strength to Galileo to help him cope with his struggle to be true to himself and his church.

Galileo's nephew, however, caused him nothing but grief. After Galileo arranged support for him to study music in Rome, the nephew turned out to be pure trouble.

He was antireligious and much too open about it. Fortunately for Galileo, he left Rome before any serious breach occurred; otherwise, he might have dragged his uncle into an unseemly situation at a time when he could ill afford it.

Galileo's *Dialogues of the Two Chief Systems of the World*.   Although Galileo's eyesight began to fail, he finished the work comparing Ptolemy and Copernicus by late 1629. In the spring of 1630 he went to Rome to arrange for publication. While there he had a friendly meeting with the pope. Urban VIII was not pleased that Galileo had included his old argument about the tides in his forthcoming book, although he did not demand that Galileo remove it. During the process of obtaining permission to publish, Galileo learned that the pope insisted that he portray the Copernican hypothesis merely as a system capable of accounting for what one saw in the heavens. He was not to portray it as the truth.

Galileo attempted to satisfy the concerns he knew were present by casting his work as a discussion among three speakers, two of whom were named for close friends. They were the participants versed in Copernican theory who, without declaring it to be true, were capable of answering objections to it. In this manner Galileo felt that he was meeting the requirement from 1616 that he neither hold nor defend Copernicanism as true. Galileo named the third speaker Simplicio after a Roman commentator on Aristotle. He was the defender of Ptolemy and came across as possessing less ability than the other two interlocutors. With this name Galileo in fact suggested that the character was something of a simpleton.

The book rehearsed systematically and at length all of the issues pertinent to the structure of the cosmos that Galileo had dealt with over his career. He arranged the book into four days of discussion. First he developed all of the arguments against the old Aristotelian idea that the heavens were incorruptible, that the terrestrial and celestial realms were qualitatively different places.

In the second day he took up objections raised against the alleged motion of the Earth; namely, that a rock dropped from a tower on a rotating Earth would not fall directly to the base of the tower (as it is observed to do), but, in the time it took to fall, would land "many hundreds of yards east." Galileo countered this conclusion by arguing that a rock dropped from a ship that is known to be moving also is observed to fall at the base of the mast, not somewhere behind the moving mast. Galileo devoted this section of his work to criticizing Aristotle's claim that all motion requires a mover. There is one kind of motion that does not require a mover. Motion at a uniform speed in a perfect circle will continue on forever unless it is interrupted by the action of an external force.

Galileo here was creating a new physics of motion. He was maintaining that uniform circular motion was a state of being, like rest; indeed, they were equivalent states of being. Just as we do not take it upon ourselves to explain why things remain at rest, so we should not try to explain uniform circular motion. Both are natural states—they need no further explanation. Because they are equivalent states of being, we cannot distinguish when we are in one or the other unless we can compare our frame of reference to the other. They feel exactly the same. Locked in a room, we cannot tell if we are moving or not, but once we have access to the heavens we know that either we, or the heavens, are moving. That is why we do not feel the rotation of the Earth on its axis, or the revolutionary motion of the Earth around the sun—these states of being are exactly like being at rest. In developing his argument about what is called inertial motion Galileo was answering a set of major objections to the Copernican doctrine. He was explaining how it was possible that the Earth could be moving without us feeling it.

Galileo's new understanding of motion appeared to his critics to be unnecessarily complicated. They thought that the reason why an arrow shot straight up comes down close to where it was released is because the Earth beneath it is not moving, not because it shares the Earth's motion. And even in Galileo's example of the ship, where something *is* moving, the speed is not great enough to make a difference. That is why the rock falls to the base of a moving ship.

In the third day Galileo continued to give reasons why a moving Earth made sense, and then, in the fourth, he moved to the heart of his argument: the tides. They proved, he felt, that a moving Earth made sense. The Ptolemaic cosmos had already been disproved by the phases of Venus. If he was right about the tides, then Galileo here had a means of disproving Tycho as well. Of course he was not so bold as to say that he had definitively proven the motion of the Earth—that would have disobeyed the 1616 injunction. He said merely that this tidal motion followed naturally from the supposition that the Earth moved with the double motion Copernicus had assigned it. He did, however, reproach Kepler—who had associated tidal motion with the influence of the moon—for appealing to occult causes.

It is obvious why Galileo thought the tides were so central to his work. Without them he thought he had no proof that the Earth moved. He had wanted to title his book *On the Ebb and Flow of the Sea,* but the pope, who also realized what was at stake, prohibited that. The pope was not on familiar territory—he could not show why Galileo's argument was wrong. (Others, incidentally, did show much later that Galileo's explanation of the tides was erroneous.) Urban VIII allowed Galileo to include the tides because of his own conviction that God could have easily caused them on a stationary Earth. For the pope, Galileo's argument about the tides did not definitely prove the Earth's motion.

Galileo placed the pope's favorite argument at the very end of the work. There it is given to the character of Simplicio, who declared that he learned it "from a most eminent and very learned person." Galileo apparently thought that he had satisfied the pope's concerns by ending his book with an argument "before which," Simplicio proclaims, "one must fall silent." But after spending an entire book removing arguments against Copernicus, this sop to the pope's position, put into the mouth of the simpleton, revealed that Galileo did not think much of the argument at all. The pope certainly interpreted it this way and was personally insulted. Friend or no friend, Galileo had crossed the line.

◎ Last Years ◎

Galileo's final years were fraught with tribulation. His poor health did not prevent him from being ordered to Rome to stand trial, even though his physician recommended that he not travel. Telescopic observations of the sun eventually took their toll—he could no longer see well. The ordeal of the trial itself did not go well for him and it was followed very quickly by the death of his beloved daughter Maria Celeste. Were it not for his completion of work begun long before, these years would have been bleak indeed.

The Trial

Many people, including the pope, had been aware that Galileo was working on a book that dealt with Copernicus. Galileo had the sense that as long as he obeyed the letter of the injunction of 1616 not to hold or defend the Copernican doctrine, there would be no objection to his work. That is why he had not sought permission to write the book.

But once it was written, he did need to have it licensed and obtain the required permissions to print it. Licensing was up to the pope's chief theologian, who insisted that the opening and closing of the work reinforce the hypothetical nature of the discussion. Further, he indicated that the pope did not want the work to focus on the tides; rather, it should show that, as long as one set aside the truth of revelation, the mathematical hypothesis of Copernicus could make sense of the observed motions in the heavens. Galileo got approval to use censors and printers in Florence, provided they abided by these requirements. The book appeared in February of 1632.

By August publication was suspended. The pope was outraged by the way Galileo had written the book. And he severely reprimanded his chief theologian, who had licensed the work. He turned the matter over to the Inquisition with the clear understanding that Galileo would have to answer for his misdeed. The Inquisition summoned Galileo to Rome even though, at age 70, he was not well. He arrived in February of 1633 and experienced the first interrogation in mid-April.

The trial turned on the issue of whether Galileo had abided by the injunction of 1616. Galileo understood that injunction to mean that he was not to hold or defend the Copernican hypothesis and he produced the letter Cardinal Bellarmine had sent him following the 1616 meeting in support of his understanding. The inquisitors cited passages from the *Dialogues* in which, they said, Galileo had treated Copernicanism not as a hypothesis, but as truth. They cited the *Letter to the Grand Duchess Christina* as further evidence that Galileo was a Copernican.

In addition, the inquisitors produced another document from the files of the 1616 meeting that went much farther than the one Bellarmine had given him then. It said he was not to hold or defend or *teach the doctrine "in any way whatever."* Galileo indicated that he had no recollection of such a document, which was not signed by anyone, certainly not by Galileo to show that he had received it. He might have thought that those in the church who had been aware of his wish to write a work on Copernicus should have advised him against it in light of this document. All that was to no avail. The Inquisition had found legal grounds on which to convict Galileo. In his defense, Galileo continued for a while to deny that he had held the Copernican doctrine. He was shown the instruments of torture that were used on those who did not tell the truth. Eventually Galileo decided to capitulate and concede that he had maintained a belief in heliocentrism and that he now recanted such belief. The

Inquisition condemned him for teaching Copernicanism as probable even though it went against Scripture. A year later Galileo was placed under house arrest in Arcetri, near the convent where his daughter lived. Although she died of dysentery less than four months after he arrived in Arcetri, Galileo himself lived until 1642.

Final Work and Death

Once he recovered from the experiences of the trial and then his daughter's early death, Galileo was able to return to the subjects that had fascinated him in his early career. He decided to write up the work he had done at the beginning of the century on the motion of objects here on Earth. A new book, entitled *Discourses on Two New Sciences,* appeared in 1638 even though Galileo had been prohibited from publishing further. Galileo said that he gave a copy of his papers on motion to a former pupil who had visited him. He had not wanted them to perish. That pupil, who was now an ambassador in Rome from France, saw to it that they were published in Holland.

While not as sensational as his *Dialogues,* the book summarized important work that has defined his contribution to physics. It contained a treatment of the material discussed earlier in this chapter about Galileo's early study of motion, including the work on falling bodies and projectiles, the pendulum, circular inertial motion, and even his thoughts on the relationship of mathematics and nature. While other topics were also included, here was Galileo making sure that posterity would appreciate the particulars of his work on motion. Galileo described his experiments with inclined planes, by means of which he slowed down the accelerated motion of falling bodies so that he could verify his results. Needless to say, Copernicanism was not mentioned.

Galileo died in January of 1642. The last decision to be made about this great natural philosopher was how his passing would be marked. He was a celebrated figure, to be sure. And yet he was serving a sentence for a serious crime. Naturally, the Grand Duke of Tuscany wanted to commemorate Galileo with a memorable tomb befitting of a great man. Urban VIII, however, would not hear of that. Galileo was buried privately in the church of Santa Croce in Florence. A century later his remains were moved into an elaborate tomb in the same church, where his life and work have been celebrated since.

Suggestions for Reading

Mario Biagioli, *Galileo Courtier: The Practice of Science in the Culture of Absolutism* (Chicago: University of Chicago Press, 1994).

Michael Sharratt, *Galileo: Decisive Innovator* (Cambridge: Cambridge University Press, 1996).

William R. Shea and Mariano Artigas, *Galileo in Rome: The Rise and Fall of a Troublesome Genius* (Oxford: Oxford University Press, 2003).

Dava Sobel, *Galileo's Daughter: A Historical Memoir of Science, Faith, and Love* (New York: Penguin Books, 2000).

CHAPTER 7

Natural Philosophy Transformed

During the same years that Galileo was embarking on a collision course with the Roman Catholic Church, others outside Italy developed their own alternatives to traditional natural philosophy. In this chapter we shall examine the variety of approaches that existed in the first half of the seventeenth century. By emphasizing empirical observation, experiment, and reasoning from the particular to the general (induction), and by replacing the older Aristotelian understanding of nature as organism with nature as mechanism, seventeenth-century thinkers transformed natural philosophy in several ways.

◎ British Conceptions ◎

In the first half of the seventeenth century, many in Northern Europe took up their pens in defense of new conceptions of the world in which they lived. In natural philosophy British thinkers were especially innovative in the manner in which they reacted to past approaches to understanding the natural world.

Harvey and Scholasticism

Scholasticism, the philosophical and theological systems of the Middle Ages, continued to thrive in the university curriculum, where a mastery of Aristotle's thought was still required. Indeed, fundamental work in natural philosophy leading to new knowledge was carried out in Britain, as on the Continent, from within the confines of Scholastic thought. For example, the Scholastic physician William Harvey (1578–1657), in a work of 1628 entitled *On the Motion of the Heart,* convincingly demonstrated through animal dissections that more blood passed out of the heart in an hour than the body held, suggesting that it must in some manner be reused.

Although he argued that blood moved away from the heart through the arteries and back through veins, Harvey could not demonstrate how the transfer from arteries to veins took place. But he demonstrated, again through experiment, that a transfer must occur. He tied a band tightly around the forearm, noting that the veins continued to look normal as the arteries swelled with blood. He then loosened the band to permit the flow of arterial blood down the arm, but not enough to permit venous blood to flow past the band. Now the veins became gorged with blood, suggesting that the arterial blood that had been let through had somehow gotten into the veins.

Through this and many other experiments, Harvey helped to overthrow the older view of Galen that the blood ebbed and flowed in the veins and arteries. But while Harvey's work provides an example of the successful continuation of Scholastic thought, many new currents of natural philosophy soon appeared that challenged Aristotle's worldview.

The Meaning of the Break with Aristotelianism

Almost all of the new visions of natural philosophy that made their appearance in the early decades of the seventeenth century showed themselves first through their dissatisfaction with Aristotelian Scholasticism. Galileo was therefore not the only one to express discontent with the dominance Aristotle's system still enjoyed in the university curriculum.

The difference in goals.   While there were various degrees of dissatisfaction with Aristotelian natural philosophy, a new English natural philosophy of the seventeenth century represented the most profound break. It set out to accomplish something fundamentally different from what the Scholastics were trying to achieve.

What was the difference between the goals of Aristotelian thought and those of the new English natural philosophy? As historian of science Peter Dear has explained, the intent of an Aristotelian philosopher was to understand phenomena that were *already known.* The emphasis was on logical reasoning from generalized starting points that were assumed to be true. Through their generality these premises summarized what was universally known, while the process of reasoning brought out conclusions that were implicit in the premises. Awareness of these implications supplied clarity and a fuller understanding. Gaining knowledge, then, was filling out what we already know.

The growing number of critics of Aristotle in seventeenth-century England did not set out, as Aristotle did, to unearth the implications of an *assumed* general premise; rather, they claimed that it was possible and necessary to *construct* universal statements through experiments. They believed that the major premise of a logical deduction was not self-justified, as Aristotle thought. In their view Aristotle assumed such general statements because they had been reinforced over and over again in his experience of individual events. He believed, for example, that all motion required a mover because he had seen so many things moved by movers.

As a result of this very different perspective, these natural philosophers had an approach to the observation of the natural world that was dissimilar to Aristotle's. They set out to *discover* new knowledge, not to further understand existing knowledge. Their attitude was that we must not presume we already know; on the contrary, we do not yet know and we must find out. An attitude like this meant that they were not content, as Aristotelians were, merely to observe nature's ordinary course passively. Because they assumed responsibility for discovering new truth, they were aggressive. They wished to force nature to reveal secrets by creating circumstances that did not occur naturally and seeing how nature responded to them. Nature was something to be interrogated and controlled.

The impact of craftsmen and magicians.   The new attitude of English natural philosophers did not come out of nowhere. It had precedents in the sixteenth century. In Chapter 3 we considered the stance taken in medicine by Paracelsus, who in the first half of the sixteenth century enjoyed opposing the authority of established Aristotelian natural philosophers of his day. Paracelsus was perceived as a radical, in part because he refused to abide by the established social distinctions of his day that prescribed how a physician should behave. His view was similar to that of the craftsman, who occupied a lower social position than that of university professors.

Like a craftsman, Paracelsus believed that to understand something you must master it. By constructing a finished product, the craftsman developed an intimate knowledge of it and a sense of control over it. Paracelsus felt that to understand illness and well-being he could not be content, as the Aristotelian physicians in the university were, to analyze them according to first principles. He had to learn how to produce sickness and health so he could undertake proper treatment.

Paracelsus's desire to be in command of nature also drew him to the magic tradition of his day. Natural magicians were indeed devoted to the control of nature. They undertook an aggressive program of experimentation, employing a host of means to gain power over the natural world. Theirs was, to be sure, a particular type of experimentation; they were more concerned with success than with why certain processes worked and others did not.

Paracelsus's willingness to bring the pragmatic orientations of both the craftsman and the magician to an academic subject—medicine—was an early manifestation of the desire to control nature in natural philosophy. It would grow more prominent in Britain in the early seventeenth century among those who, sympathetic to the practical concerns of craftsmen and the heritage of natural magic, incorporated the goal of controlling nature into their natural philosophy.

Two New British Visions

William Gilbert.   One of the critics of established Aristotelian learning was a physician named William Gilbert (1544–1603). Like Paracelsus, Gilbert was open to the insights of the magic tradition of the Renaissance; indeed, Gilbert was aware of Paracelsus's alchemical writings. Standing squarely in the tradition of natural magic, Gilbert shared its deep commitment to experimentation as a means of interrogating nature. This was especially true, Gilbert said, when dealing with occult forces. Here the usual Scholastic dependence on reasoning from first principles was ineffective. There was a better way. When dealing with hidden or occult forces, "stronger reasons are obtained from sure experiments and demonstrated arguments than from probable conjectures and the opinions of philosophical speculators of the common sort."

The experimental approach he preferred was particularly evident in Gilbert's interest in and treatment of magnets. His work of 1600, *De magnete (On the Magnet)*, contained a wealth of information about the magnet, which he obtained from the many experiments described in the book. At the same time Gilbert delighted to conduct experiments that dispelled legendary claims—for example, that garlic diminished the magnet's power.

But Gilbert had another motivation for writing his book on the magnet. He was a convinced Copernican and he wished to provide an explanation for why the Earth rotated on its axis. He had come to the conclusion that the Earth was a giant magnet. He also believed that magnets had the ability to turn spontaneously toward a pole. Because the Earth was a giant magnet, the Earth also had the power to turn spontaneously. But while the Earth's magnetism explained that the Earth could turn toward its pole, it did not explain why it kept turning, why it continually rotated on its axis.

Like Paracelsus and other natural magicians, Gilbert accepted that there were structural similarities that ran through the natural world at all levels. Through his work on magnets, Gilbert had become familiar with the work of the thirteenth-century physician Pierre de Maricourt, whose *Epistle on the Magnet* was first printed in 1558. In this work the author wrote that the magnet "bears in itself the similitude of the heavens." Gilbert used this similarity to draw a specific conclusion: just as the motions of the heavenly bodies showed them to possess an animate nature, so the magnetic motions of the Earth revealed it to be animate. The Earth, in other words, had a soul and that was what explained why it continued rotating every day. The point of the magnetic experiments involving the Earth was to show that the Earth had a soul. We see here in the work of William Gilbert how his commitment to experimentalism—a different approach from that of the Scholastics, who still dominated university life at the beginning of the seventeenth century—emerged from his participation in the tradition of natural magic.

The vision of Francis Bacon.   By far the most well-known natural philosopher of early-seventeenth-century England was Francis Bacon (1561–1626). Son of a highly placed courtier in service to Queen Elizabeth, Bacon was born to a life of wealth and privilege. Although he completed a degree in law, he practiced it very little. His real interest lay in a scheme he had first hit upon while still a student at Cambridge, the need for which had been reinforced during his travels in France.

His idea was to improve life in England by systematically revising the way the world was understood. As a student at the university, Bacon found himself thoroughly repelled by the Aristotelian philosophy he was taught. He failed to see how it related to the lives of English gentlemen. In France he had observed a level of refined culture that was not matched in England, but he had also observed corruption among the French. His new approach, he believed, would not only have practical relevance to English life, but it would also improve the moral well-being of the nation.

Bacon had begun to write up his grand idea soon after he was knighted. In 1605 an early version of the work appeared, called *Advancement of Learning*. The more complete account did not come out until 1620, appearing in Latin under the title *Novum organon (New Organon)*. Bacon chose that title as a way of announcing that he was replacing the *organon,* the term used at the time to refer to the corpus of Aristotle's logical writings. He had in mind nothing less than a thorough revision of Aristotelian natural philosophy; in fact, the *New Organon* was included as the second phase of a planned and uncompleted six-part work entitled *The Great Instauration.* The unusual term *instauration,* which he began using as early as 1603, but whose meaning he never specifically discussed, was intended to refer to the complete restoration or reconstruction of existing natural philosophy.

One of Bacon's criticisms of Aristotle's philosophy was that it contained no means of self-correction. He believed that the inevitable errors humankind made over time had disturbed what Bacon called the perfect "commerce between the mind of man and the nature of things" that humans once possessed. Bacon believed that Adam, the first man, had enjoyed this perfect relationship to nature, but that with the entrance of sin into the world human natural understanding had been corrupted. In the *New Organon* Bacon spelled out at length the kinds of errors—he called them idols—that had crept in.

The problem was that, left to the instruments of Aristotelian logic, these errors would go on forever. Bacon's conclusion was that there was but one course left: "To try the whole thing anew upon a better plan, and to commence a total reconstruction of sciences, arts, and all human knowledge, raised upon the proper foundations." As historian Steven Matthews explains, he saw this project in terms of Christian redemptive history. Christ's sacrifice not only provided a means of individual salvation; it also made it possible for humankind to restore a knowledge that led to God.

What were the proper foundations of knowledge? First of all, Bacon wanted to change the goal of natural philosophy from something contemplative to something active. With the entrance of sin into the world humankind had begun seeking knowledge for the wrong reasons. Natural philosophers had sometimes just wanted to satisfy their curiosity, at other times they wished merely to entertain themselves or even to build a reputation. But the real reason to seek an understanding of the world should be to benefit humankind by acquiring knowledge that was useful to everyone.

Another plank of the proper foundations of natural philosophy was the right method of procedure. Here Bacon took his cue from the inventions of the mechanical arts and crafts. History has shown us, he observed, that craftsmen learn from their experience; they improve the devices they create by building on past experience. As a result, knowledge of the mechanical arts was cumulative. It had not, as had the theoretical knowledge of nature, remained "almost in the same condition as it was, receiving no noticeable increase."

Bacon determined that an experimental approach, in which questions were put to nature that elicited a response, would permit the accumulation of practical wisdom. In this conviction he was greatly influenced by the traditions of alchemy and natural magic, with their commitment to experimentation. Like the alchemist who sought to uncover the natural sympathies and antipathies in matter, the magus strove to master nature's hidden powers and properties. In both cases the goal was practical knowledge that assisted the one who acquired it to exert control over nature.

Careful interaction with nature was the route to truth. Bacon claimed his method inverted the order of Aristotle's logic. The Scholastics jumped quickly from particulars to general premises. They then proceeded to the main concern of their analysis— teasing out specific implications of the general premises. But that would not necessarily lead back to nature. Bacon criticized those whose devotion to deductive reasoning made them adopt general premises too quickly. He claimed that his procedure emphasized the opposite direction—moving slowly and carefully from particulars to the universal (inductive reasoning). He employed induction to arrive at general conclusions about nature. By induction Bacon did not mean simply summarizing a series of individual cases—that was too simple and unreliable. He meant using individual cases to eliminate incorrect generalizations until there was but one generalization left. He proposed "to proceed regularly and gradually from one axiom to another, so that the most general are not reached until the last."

Bacon realized that an undertaking of the sort he envisioned must be done collectively. In 1626, the year Bacon died, he published a work of fiction called *The New Atlantis* that described an island where a project like the one he imagined was in place. It was a utopian portrait of what a rationally ordered society that was devoted to the acquisition of useful knowledge would be like. He described the various offices held within the society; for example, there were twelve "merchants of light" who traveled the world in disguise in search of books and experiments, three "miners" who selected and tried experiments, three "compilers" who summarized and classified the experiments, and three "interpreters of nature" who raised the discoveries from the experiments into more general axioms.

The Royal Society.   Bacon's ideas became important a generation after his death with the founding of the Royal Society. A small group of men, brought together in 1658 by a common interest in what was becoming known as "the experimental philosophy," met weekly either in the private home of one of their number or in a convenient tavern. Similar groups formed elsewhere, but the greatest activity was concentrated in the London meetings.

The group decided to include formal presentations and demonstration experiments in its meetings and to explore the founding of an organization "for the promoting of Physical-Mathematical experimental learning." By the summer of 1661 the members were trying to win the support of the crown. Charles II would not grant them funds, but on July 15, 1662, he did bestow a Charter of Incorporation on the new Royal Society of London. Reflecting its desire from the start to emphasize experimental philosophy, the charter provided for the appointment of two curators of experiments.

The members endorsed Bacon's views, especially his emphasis on the need to bring practical benefits to humankind through the study of nature. When in 1667 Thomas Sprat wrote *History of the Royal Society,* two figures flanked the bust of Charles II on the frontispiece of the book. One was the society's president, the other Francis Bacon, "Renewer of the Arts."

England was not the first country to establish a scientific society, but the Royal Society made its own distinctive mark on the early institutionalization of natural philosophy. The new curator of experiments, Robert Hooke, wrote in 1663 that the business of the society was to improve the knowledge of natural things and of useful arts and not to meddle in controversial matters like philosophy, politics, and religion. In spite of the declared intent not to discuss sensitive issues, however, the new society's loyalty to the religious and political establishment was beyond question. All was to be done "to advance the glory of God, the honor of the King, the Royal founder of the Society, the benefit of his Kingdom, and the general good of mankind."

◎ French Ideas on Matter and Motion ◎

Among Aristotelians, *organism* was the best metaphor by which to refer to nature. A major reason for this was that for Aristotle, natural processes—such as the actions of living things—occurred purposefully. In the natural world as Aristotle saw it even the four basic material substances endeavored to return to their own natural places when removed from them. They exhibited, in other words, behavior that reflected nature's larger purposeful structure.

The seventeenth century saw the appearance of a different view of matter and of the physical world. In this new conception the purposes evident in nature were not inherent in nature itself but were imposed from the outside. Here the metaphor for nature was *machine,* the workings of which accomplished the ends of its creator. To analyze nature involved acquiring knowledge of the motions of nature's moving parts. Matter in motion characterized natural process.

A New Conception of Matter

As we saw in Chapter 1, Aristotle explained the objects we apprehend through our senses as the union of form and matter. Attributes of form gave a material object its identity. The wood in a wood block supplied the matter, whereas the heaviness, square shape, hardness, and brown color were all attributes of form that gave the piece of wood its identity as a sensible object. Matter could not exist without form, nor could form exist without matter to serve as its subject.

As the seventeenth century got under way there were hints that another view of matter was emerging. In 1621 the French physician Sebastian Basso (dates unknown) published *Philosophia Naturalis (Natural Philosophy),* in which he abandoned the old Aristotelian conception of substance as the necessary union of form and matter. Basso regarded matter apart from form as something sufficient unto itself. It was permanent—fully capable on its own to establish the complete being of things that exist. Further, matter was incapable of undergoing change. It was dead, inert, and passive.

But if matter was unable to change by itself or be changed by anything else, how could there be any change at all in the cosmos? To answer this Basso and several others of his time appealed to change of place. Matter itself was wholly indifferent to change of place; that is, matter could change place without itself undergoing change. So if matter did change place, if it did move, it must be because motion was also a fundamental aspect of reality. While not required for matter to exist, motion nevertheless was always present.

A different conception of the eternality of motion from that of the ancients and even of Galileo was implied here and, as we will see, it soon emerged into natural philosophy. For the ancients and for Galileo, natural motion—that is, motion that would continue forever unless interrupted—was circular. The ancients believed that this kind of motion existed only in the heavens. Galileo suggested that it also existed below the orb of the moon. But the new conception of an ever-present motion resulted from matter's complete indifference to change of place. Matter did not care, so to speak, whether it was moving or at rest. If it was at rest, it would stay that way. If it was in motion, it would remain so. Nor did the motion in this new conception have to be circular. The next natural philosopher we consider, Descartes, argued that matter moving in a straight line would continue to do so until interrupted.

These two basic building blocks of reality—matter and motion—determined everything that existed and everything that happened in the physical world. To understand the world of nature, then, meant uncovering the particular kinds of matter and motion that characterized natural objects and their behavior. Clearly these ideas held profound implications for natural philosophy. In the first half of the seventeenth century they made their way into more than one interpretation.

Nature in Descartes's New Philosophy

The generation after Francis Bacon produced the most well-known transformation of natural philosophy based on the new ideas of matter and motion. The French natural philosopher René Descartes (1596–1650), son of a magistrate, rose from the modest beginnings of a military career to become one of the leading thinkers of Western history. As we will see, Descartes also opposed the Aristotelian Scholasticism of his day.

The influence of Isaac Beeckman.   Descartes entered law school and completed a degree in canon and civil law in 1616. He decided to enlist in the army of the newly designated Prince of Orange in the Netherlands, Maurice of Nassau. Stationed in Breda, near the Belgian border, Descartes became acquainted with Isaac Beeckman (1588–1637), who had at that time just been examined successfully for a medical degree. Beeckman was interested in many things besides medicine; for example, he became familiar with the ideas of Sebastian Basso.

Among the ideas he communicated to the young Descartes was the notion that matter was made of tiny corpuscles whose shape and size, along with their motion, provided a means for explaining natural phenomena. Of course the ancient atomists had claimed something similar. What set Beeckman apart was his belief that the relationships involved here were capable of being described mathematically. In his view, mathematics was not restricted to the eternal motions of the heavens. It also could be used to capture the motions of the unseen corpuscles. According to Beeckman, Descartes became convinced of this "physico-mathematics" where natural philosophy was concerned.

The motive for a new method.   Descartes soon left Breda, and his sojourn in the military, for several years of travel. Early on he had a dream that focused for him a task he then set for the future—to unify all knowledge into a system by creating a method.

He felt a need similar to the one that had motivated Francis Bacon—dissatisfaction with existing philosophy and the desire to create a new foundation on which to build a solid structure of knowledge. Both men saw in the Scholasticism of their day a system of knowledge that was out of touch with reality because it was erected on a foundation that lacked certainty. According to Bacon, Aristotelian thought could never produce certainty because it had no built-in capacity to correct error. Descartes came to a similar conclusion. There was much that could be doubted about Aristotle's worldview, but the Scholastics had no means of dealing with uncertainty in their understanding because the process of logical inference was regarded as above question.

Descartes received a sufficient amount of property and income from his parents to produce a satisfactory income for himself. As his thought matured he began to write down his ideas. But by the early 1630s, when he had sketched out much of his vision of natural philosophy, the condemnation of Galileo in Rome caused him concern as a fellow Roman Catholic. He withheld a work on cosmology, physics, and optics from publication, entitled *The World, a Treatise on Light,* because he suspected that its Copernican cosmology might offend. Later, especially in two works called *Discourse on Method* (1637) and *Meditations of First Philosophy* (1641) he spelled out his anti-Aristotelian ideas on the foundations of his new philosophy.

Descartes proposed to erect a firm foundation for knowledge by correcting the fatal flaw in Scholastic thought and in all other systems. He would reject everything that could be doubted, accepting for his foundation only that which could not be doubted. As optical illusions teach us, knowledge based on the senses clearly could be doubted, so his approach was clearly at odds with the inductive approach of Bacon.

René Descartes

Deductive systems were also fallible. We can deceive ourselves about the deductions of mathematics when we take as valid a set of inferences that later are shown to contain error. If both deductive and inductive reasoning could be distrusted, was there anything that was immune to doubt?

The process of doubting ended for Descartes when he tried to doubt his own existence. The very act of doubting was impossible unless he existed to do the doubting. Descartes's famous argument was summarized by the cogent conclusion, *cogito ergo sum* (I think therefore I am). Here was the basis on which to build.

Starting from this point, Descartes claimed to add only those propositions that shared the same degree of certainty. First, he knew he existed because he doubted it, so he must be imperfect as opposed to perfect (a perfect being would have no doubts). But the idea of perfection could not have been something he originated because it could not have come from something imperfect. So there must be a perfect being, God. Such a being would be less than perfect if he deceived us. When, therefore, we have ideas that we regard as clear and distinct, they must be true.

The nature of matter and spirit.   As noted earlier, one of the implications of Sebastian Basso's separation of matter and form was that matter by itself possessed the capability of establishing the complete being of things that exist. Another implication followed from that one—that mind or spirit, which in themselves had no material component, must be completely separate from matter. Basso and later Descartes accepted the fundamental reality of mind. It, too, was capable on its own of establishing being, but it was a different kind of being from material being.

Descartes further developed this idea, called metaphysical dualism, of two different basic kinds of reality. He argued that an essential difference between these two kinds of reality was that matter was "extended" being while mind was not. There were, he said, two kinds of things in the world—*res extensa* (extended things) and *res cogitans* (thinking things). Matter was the same thing as extension; it was, in other words, equivalent to space. Mind was not extended. Thoughts did not take up space. The world of material nature was constituted of extended things. God and angels were thinking things. Because humans possessed both a mind and a body, they participated in both worlds.

Natural things such as rocks, trees, and organisms (including other higher animals) were solely matter. Because there was no mind or spirit in nature, Descartes believed that he could not employ characteristics of mind when describing material nature. Nature was made of matter, which was dead, inert, and passive. That being so, nature itself and everything that happened in it must be the result of processes that were mindless. This is where the idea of a machine became helpful.

Machines, simply put, are matter in motion. The basic function of a machine is to transfer the motion of matter from one place to the next in order to accomplish the end of the machine's creator. One piece of moving matter impacts another, which presses on another, and so forth, until the last motion produced accomplishes the desired end. For example, a horse hitched to a millstone transfers the motion of its walking to the millstone, which then is used to grind wheat into flour. In such a circumstance force is communicated by contact from one place to another.

For Descartes, force is always transferred through the contact of one piece of matter with another and by no other means. By appealing to matter in motion, Descartes was able to satisfy the requirement that natural processes be mindless. A machine does not think or have purpose on its own, so the metaphor for nature in Descartes's natural philosophy became the machine. God had set the machinery of nature in motion at the Creation and it has been running ever since. All natural processes result solely from the transfer of that original motion from one place to another through material contact.

The mechanical cosmos.   Nature is full of instances where it is easy to observe a transfer of force by contact. Consider, for example, the erosive effect produced by moving water or the destruction of a house roof by a falling tree. But what about those instances where it does not appear that one piece of matter collides with or

.

presses upon another and yet force is produced or matter is moved? What about the ball that falls after rolling off a tabletop, or the effect produced by a magnet on small pieces of iron? In these cases the cause of the motion has not been the impact of one piece of matter on another. How did Descartes explain them?

First and foremost, Descartes rejected the classical explanations of Aristotelian natural philosophy because they appealed to characteristics of mind. That is, Descartes eliminated the possibility of there being forces of attraction or repulsion, because attraction and repulsion were qualities of "thinking things." Any quality of mind or spirit just did not exist for him in nature itself. Aristotle's appeal to a rock "seeking" its natural place as an explanation of why a rock fell violated this strict separation of mind and matter, spirit and nature. The same rejection applied to the so-called occult or hidden forces such as the sympathies and antipathies referred to by alchemists and the psychical influences of astrologers. Categories like these applied to minds, but not to matter as Descartes understood it.

Recall that for Descartes, matter was simply spatial extension. We should not overlook two important implications of this understanding. First, matter (extension) did not possess sensory qualities such as color or taste. Color did not belong to matter. Color arose as an idea in our minds whenever certain motions of matter impacted our sensory apparatus. The idea of color was an arbitrary sign that nature used to help us make our way, just as nature had established laughter as a sign for joy. Nature could have used tears to communicate joy, but laughter was the sign instead. While color could theoretically have been associated with a range of matter's motions, nature used it as the sign for only certain motions. The second implication of matter's equivalence to extension was that matter's motion could be subjected to mathematical analysis. Descartes had first learned this from Beeckman, but here in his developed system it emerged quite naturally. Mathematics had long been used to measure and describe changes in spatial extension. Descartes's mechanical natural philosophy lent itself naturally to mathematical expression. His would be a mathematical mechanical philosophy.

Indeed, he came upon the idea of representing position in space by choosing a reference point and designating the position through three measurements from that point. From this grew the so-called Cartesian coordinate system, whose virtue was that geometric shapes could be represented by changing sets of numbers that defined a curve.

Descartes assumed that even where it did not appear that motion was the result of contact between two pieces of matter—as in the case of a falling object—it still had to be the case that such contact existed. There could not be such a thing as a vacuum because extended space (matter) existed everywhere. This was a major reason why Descartes opposed the ancient atomists, who had said that motion of atoms was only possible if there were a void, or empty space, through which the atoms could move. For Descartes, matter could only move as the result of contact with other matter, which filled the cosmos.

In the first part of *The World*, entitled "Treatise on Light," Descartes described three different elements of matter, distinguished by their size. Large masses such as the Earth and the planets constituted what he identified as the third element. The first element was the tiny fluid particles of no specific shape that emanated from the sun and exerted pressure that we perceive as light. The second element, formed as small globules, filled in around the large masses to fill the cosmos completely and transmit motion from one point to the next. Motion in any part of this arrangement could only occur if, as matter was moved, adjacent matter moved out of the way to accommodate it. That adjacent matter then must be accommodated by the matter it displaced, and so forth throughout the plenum of the cosmos. In order to prevent motion in one part of the system from producing motion everywhere throughout the whole, Descartes asserted that motion occurred in huge circular whirlpool vortices. Our solar system, for example, was but one such vortex.

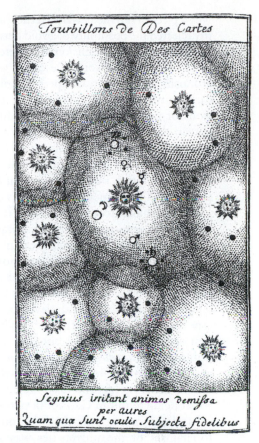

Descartes's Vortices

More than one physical arrangement might follow from the first principles he had established and Descartes was careful to acknowledge this. The matter that filled space could, through combinations of its elements, be arranged in a myriad of shapes and sizes. To see what particular physical circumstances exist in this world we have to observe the world. Then we figure out how they might be explained through the sizes, shapes, and motions of the parts. Descartes was not, as he is sometimes portrayed, a dogmatic rationalist who claimed to derive this particular view of the world out of pure ideas. More than one world could result from these motions.

Late in his life Descartes accepted an invitation from Queen Christina of Sweden, but within a few months he succumbed to an illness and died. His fame grew quickly, in part assisted by a certain notoriety he had acquired within the Catholic Church. His systematic doubt, his embrace of Copernicus, and his claim that deterministic mechanism ruled in nature all proved suspect to the authorities and his work was forbidden. But Descartes had erected a new system of natural philosophy that attracted many. His depiction of nature as a machine that could be described mathematically provided a practical means of explaining the natural world and it proved to be an extremely attractive alternative to the Scholastic Aristotelianism of the day.

The Revival of Atomism

Descartes appealed to the size, shape, and motions of the particles into which God had divided matter to explain such things as why oil was sticky, why salt tasted sharp, and why a piece of hot metal warmed the water into which it was put. In so doing he explicitly rejected the possibility of a void between particles of matter. A void could not exist, as matter was pure extension and there was no place in space that was not extended.

In rejecting the void, Descartes was voicing one of his objections to ancient atomism. As noted in Chapter 1, Epicurus, who lived from the late-fourth to the early-third century B.C., claimed that natural phenomena resulted from the collisions of pieces of matter moving through empty space. Certain aspects of Epicurean thought bore a similarity to that of Descartes. For example, both systems accepted the determinism of natural events as a result of the mechanical interaction of matter and for both systems such secondary qualities as taste and color existed only in the mind. But the absence of the void and a central role for God remained crucial, and fundamental differences existed between the two.

When, therefore, there appeared in France a revived version of Epicurean atomism by an almost exact contemporary of Descartes, it did so in opposition to Descartes's version of mechanical philosophy. Its author, the Frenchman Pierre Gassendi (1592–1655), had taken holy orders in the Roman Catholic Church and held positions as a philosopher and mathematician at various institutions of the church. What he tried to create was a Christianized interpretation of atomism.

Like Descartes, Gassendi developed an ardent opposition to Scholastic thought, especially Aristotelian natural philosophy. He had lectured on Aristotle's thought as a professor of philosophy, but grew increasingly dissatisfied with it and, in 1624, published *Paradoxical Exercises against Aristotle.* As someone gifted in mathematics and astronomy, he followed closely the results that were coming into public view during his early lifetime from Kepler and Galileo. He appreciated the critique of Aristotle he found in Galileo; in particular, he found himself drawn to the empirical and experimental approach he found there. His aversion to the dominant Aristotelianism of the universities was also bolstered by his readings of Christian humanists, including Erasmus (see Chapter 3), who appealed to ancient authorities in support of his critique of the dominant theology of his day.

Unlike Descartes, whose aversion to Scholasticism resulted in a questioning of all authority, Gassendi sought to replace Aristotle with another ancient authority. He found it in Epicurus, whose atomism he thought was well suited to the kind of empirical natural philosophy he endorsed. Emerging work with the new instrument of research, the microscope—which made its appearance around the turn of the seventeenth century—seemed to confirm the relevance of breaking objects into tiny parts for analysis. Gassendi believed, then, that natural phenomena resulted from the motions of atoms through the void of space. This was the foundation of natural phenomena—the particulars about their interaction had to be found by empirical research and experimentation.

In other words, Gassendi did not believe it was possible to learn which specific atomic motions produced given individual results in the natural world. His atomism, like his religion, was a position of faith. In fact, he distrusted the use of reason to deduce what was happening in nature. Reason could never penetrate to the knowledge of how the motion of atoms produced sensible results any more than it could uncover the truths of faith.

Not surprisingly, Gassendi believed that his vision of nature as a playground for the motions of atoms was not at all incompatible with his belief in God. Clearly, this was one aspect of the philosophy of Epicurus, for whom the gods were irrelevant, from which he dissented. Gassendi rejected rational proofs for God's existence, such as those that Descartes proposed. God was known through faith, not reason. Further, while Descartes's mechanical philosophy removed purpose from nature, Gassendi's did not. He saw final cause everywhere in nature and regarded it as evidence of God's intentions for and control of nature.

Gassendi and Descartes show us that among the new natural philosophies of the seventeenth century there could be substantial disagreement even between advocates of the same basic approach. We may regard the two as both mechanical philosophers, but they saw each other as adversaries. What was clear to all, however, was that the Aristotelianism found in the universities was encountering substantial opposition from many quarters.

◎ The Question of Materialism ◎

None of the natural philosophers of the seventeenth century that we have thus far examined questioned the existence of God. All accepted that God, who possessed the attributes assigned by traditional Christian theology, created and controlled the matter of the universe. God as spirit existed outside the physical cosmos, ruling as sovereign over it. The existence and nature of the cosmos depended directly on the will and power of the Deity.

The question arose among some, however, as to whether matter by itself could play the role that God held in traditional thought. If so, was there a function left for God as spirit to perform? As the century unfolded, those whose understanding resulted in sweeping declarations about matter's power elicited accusations of materialism—the belief that physical matter was the only reality and that everything, including thought, feeling, mind, and will, could be explained in terms of matter. This was the same charge that had been leveled against the ancient atomists. Materialism was seen as equivalent to atheism because, opponents declared, there was no role for God to play in the natural world.

Such accusations of godless materialism were not accepted by those natural philosophers who were exploring the extent of matter's scope. They felt, rather, that they were broadening the understanding of the divine. But, try as they might to explain themselves, they could not shake the charge of atheism. We will now examine the ideas of two such individuals from the seventeenth century.

The Monster from Malmsbury

When Thomas Hobbes (1588–1679) was still a boy, his father, who did not value education, left his son's schooling to his wealthy merchant brother, Thomas's uncle. From the age of eight he attended a school in Malmsbury, where his father had been a vicar. He then was sent to a private school, in which he mastered classical languages. Having demonstrated his keen intellectual abilities, he went off to Oxford at fourteen and completed his bachelor's degree in 1608.

Only in midlife did Hobbes become fascinated with mathematics and natural philosophy. Reputedly he came upon a copy of Euclid lying open in a library and on reading it became enthusiastic about the certainty present in mathematical calculation. He came to the conclusion that reason itself was nothing more than addition or subtraction or, as he put it later, "in what matter soever there is a place for addition and subtraction, there also is the place for reason; and where these have no place, there reason has nothing at all to do." While traveling to the Continent, Hobbes made the acquaintance of notable natural philosophers such as Galileo and Gassendi. He became enthusiastic about mechanical philosophy, though not about Descartes's dualistic approach that relegated it to the physical world only.

During his life Hobbes established close associations with the English aristocracy and the crown. As a result, he did not feel safe when civil war began to threaten in 1640. When revolution began in 1642, he was already in France. There he continued to associate with natural philosophers, even taking up the study of optics. He returned to England in 1651, the same year in which his most famous work, *Leviathan*, appeared. He took the title from the ancient monster of the Old Testament whose presence brought chaos in its wake.

In *Leviathan* he imagined how humankind would fare in a state of nature, without any form of government. In such a state chaos would rule; it would be a war of all against all. In order to avoid this, he explained, humans surrendered to a sovereign, who preserved order. Hobbes argued that in this arrangement the sovereign became a ruler whose authority was absolute.

As is evident from his blunt acknowledgment that humans submitted to authority in order to preserve themselves, Hobbes preferred to go straight to the bottom of things. The same was true for his understanding of nature. When he claimed that everything was either body or nothing, he was perceived to be denying that such things as spirit could exist at all. He was accused of materialism and atheism and regarded with suspicion everywhere in his homeland, despite the extensive discussion in his work of the word *spirit*, especially in connection to God. Whether he believed that God was material, or that God and spirit were simply not comprehensible, is still argued among philosophers.

In Chapter 9 of his book *On Body*, Hobbes confirmed his commitment to mechanical philosophy. He said that all change was "nothing other than the motion of the parts of the body undergoing change." Later he confirmed that the life of the mind was included among the changes brought about by matter in motion. Sensation was merely a motion of various internal parts existing inside the sentient being, while the exercise of the will was nothing more than the existence of appetite, a response to stimulus.

Like Descartes, Hobbes argued that there was no empty space in the universe. He specifically denied the possibility of a vacuum and became, as we will see, involved in a dispute with other natural philosophers as a result. Hobbes's natural philosophy, as that of the next figure we shall consider, showed that the study of nature and mathematics could produce results that confronted the very foundations of seventeenth-century Western society.

Jewish Pantheism

Just as Hobbes's understanding of nature challenged the Christianity of his day, the natural philosophy of his much younger contemporary Baruch Spinoza (1632–1677) proved to be a thorn in the side of seventeenth-century European Judaism. Although he was born some forty-four years after Hobbes, Spinoza died two years before the author of *Leviathan*. But like Hobbes, Spinoza had to deal with the accusation of materialism and atheism from those in his religious community.

Spinoza was educated in the synagogue, where he studied the Talmud and classical Jewish authors. In order to learn Latin he worked with an independent tutor who was also a lover of the natural sciences. His tutor opened up a new world to Spinoza. He read Descartes and other non-Jewish writers and became enamored of their ideas. This contact with the ideas of European philosophers led Spinoza to question his religious heritage.

Like Descartes and Hobbes, Spinoza was impressed with the clarity and certainty of mathematical reasoning. He cast his major work, *Ethics*, according to the model of Euclid's *Elements*. That is, beginning with a set of definitions and self-evident axioms, he organized each of the parts of his book as a series of propositions that unfolded through deduction from one to the next.

Spinoza's philosophy centered on his definition of substance—a difficult but crucial concept in his thought. According to Definition 3, substance is "that which is in itself, and is conceived through itself." Spinoza elaborated by adding that substance was something whose conception was not dependent on any other thing but itself. God, for instance, he defined to be a substance with infinite attributes. It did not take the reader long to find out that, in fact, there was only one substance and it was God (Proposition 14).

Spinoza's viewpoint has been called pantheism—the position that identifies God with the universe. If everything that exists is God, then whatever is—minds, matter, motions—is an aspect of the one true being. Spinoza did not shy away from the implication that God did not act by free will. Why? Because the laws of nature, which operate with logical necessity as cause and effect, were merely aspects of a divine essence that was wholly self-contained. Hence, Proposition 32 stated that "Will cannot be called a free cause, but only a necessary cause." Everything that is and everything that happens must be as it is. God could not make decisions about what to do, but God (everything) could be considered free because he was not constrained by anything other than himself.

What Spinoza presented to the seventeenth century was a determinism that reigned not only in the physical world, as in Descartes's philosophy, but in the spiritual as well. He simply refused to break reality into matter and spirit—there was but one reality, substance. Of course it is easy to see why his ideas were so threatening to Judaism and Christianity alike. This was a radically different conception of God that did not agree at all with the orthodox theology of either religion. He was dismissed as another of the materialists and atheists that arose from an overvaluation of humankind's rational capacity to comprehend the natural world.

◎ The Mechanical Philosophy in Britain ◎

We have seen thus far a proliferation of new perceptions of the natural world in the seventeenth century. The appearance of Bacon's inductive empiricism, Descartes's rational mechanism, Gassendi's atomism, Hobbes's materialism, and Spinoza's pantheism were, to some extent at least, responses to new ideas that circulated widely in the first half of the century.

Facilitating the spread of information about new discoveries and new systems of thought were a few key individuals who positioned themselves at the center of correspondence networks of interested participants in the new science. Earlier in the century the French philosopher and theologian Marin Mersenne (1588–1648) filled this role, which was later undertaken by the astronomer Ismaël Boulliau (1605–1694) and the Englishman Henry Oldenburg (1618–1677). These individuals maintained contact with a host of scholars in Britain and throughout Europe, often bringing together disparate individuals who might otherwise have remained ignorant of their common interests.

As we have seen, the participants in the discussions came from every section of society. Some had to rise through the ranks to achieve positions of greater respect than that granted by birth, while others were well placed on the basis of their heritage. Among the latter was Robert Boyle (1627–1691), son of the Earl of Cork, one of the wealthiest men in Britain. Boyle would cite the work of Mersenne, Gassendi, Descartes, and others as key sources for his development of what he was the first to call "the mechanical philosophy." This British version, as we shall see, brought its own twist to the discussion.

Alchemy Continued

Scholars have recently argued that we cannot simply accept what Robert Boyle asserted regarding his intellectual inheritance. He downplayed, for example, the role of Daniel Sennert (1572–1637), a German Scholastic scholar who wrote about the merits of atomism even before Pierre Gassendi—its most well-known exponent in the seventeenth century—revived interest in Epicurus. Boyle's debt to Sennert, while undeniable, went unacknowledged because Boyle wished to associate only with those who were critiquing Aristotelian Scholasticism—not with one who identified with it.

But Boyle's choice of whom to acknowledge and whom to ignore involved an even more intriguing matter—the debt he owed to the continuing tradition of alchemy in the seventeenth century. Boyle wrote about the mechanical philosophy from his vantage point as someone immersed in the study of chemistry. In failing to acknowledge his debt to the alchemical tradition that first captured his attention, Boyle contributed to the notion that it was unimportant, not only to him, but to the development of ideas about how material substances combined.

Historians of science have become aware of the formative role played by a persistent and lively alchemical tradition in the seventeenth century. In Boyle's case, he learned a great deal from the American alchemist George Starkey (1628–1665), who wrote under the name Eirenaeus Philalethes and who was an enthusiast of the work of the Belgian mystical natural philosopher, Joan Baptista Van Helmont (1579–1644).

Boyle observed how Starkey valued number, weight, measurement, and experiment, which are usually regarded as the later hallmarks of chemistry. These emphases had been, however, central components of the alchemist's craft for a long time.

The Christian Chemist

As a young man of privilege, Boyle followed a stay at Eton College with extensive travels on the Continent. While in Europe he had a powerful religious conversion experience as the result of witnessing a severe thunderstorm. On his return to Britain in 1644 as a youth of seventeen, he settled into an estate left him by his father and decided to devote himself to the moral betterment of his fellow gentry. He pursued this goal through writing, including the composition of his "Occasional Reflections" on ordinary events and scriptural passages that were intended to inspire.

Among the subject matter Boyle encountered was that of the chemical laboratory, which piqued his interest so much that around 1649 his attention was drawn to it in a substantial way. He set up a laboratory in his house and began to construct experiments of his own. In 1651 he met Starkey, who by then was an experienced experimenter in residence in London, and the two became collaborators and correspondents. Starkey was in effect Boyle's tutor, instructing him on chemical and alchemical experimentation techniques during the formative period of Boyle's maturation as a natural philosopher.

Shortly thereafter, most likely between 1651 and 1653, Boyle composed a fragmentary piece he titled "Of the Atomicall Philosophy," a work heavily dependent on Sennert's thought. As mentioned above, Boyle did not credit Sennert, referring in the introduction to Descartes, Gassendi, and others who, he said, had "so luckily revived and so skillfully celebrated" atomism.

In 1655 Boyle moved to Oxford, where he became associated with a group of men who were enthusiasts for what was being called "the new philosophy" or "experimental philosophy." Around this time he seriously began reading, with the help of Robert Hooke, the writings of Descartes and Gassendi. His commitment to experiment, already reinforced by his association with Starkey, was further solidified through his acquaintance with Hooke and the others in the Oxford group.

Boyle embarked on an extensive program of experimentation and writing that set the tone for many discussions among British natural philosophers. In a work of 1660 he did experiments on the "spring of air," leading to the relationship between the pressure and volume that subsequently became known as Boyle's Law ($PV = k$). He called his particular version of mechanical philosophy corpuscularianism in order to avoid the irreligious connotations of materialism and atheism that atomism carried. Here again came the denunciation of the forms and qualities of Scholastic thought in favor of explanations based on the motion of matter, in his case the corpuscles that made up larger substances.

His embrace of mechanical philosophy was not so complete that its principles could explain all of reality. Corpuscles could be endowed, for example, with chemical principles that their motion did not explain. He entertained the possibility that there were what he identified as "cosmical qualities" that transcended purely mechanical laws. Nor did he abandon his interest in alchemy; indeed, his involvement with it reached a peak in the 1670s. Boyle had no difficulty acknowledging the reality of the nonmechanical results that alchemy could produce.

In addition to writing descriptions of his experiments, Boyle reflected on the larger meaning of his approach. Through such works as *Some Considerations Touching the Usefulness of Experimental Natural Philosophy* (1663), Boyle underscored the coming of a new age of science. Additionally, he used the results of the new experimental philosophy to support his strong commitment to religion. Beginning in the 1660s and lasting to the end of his life, Boyle wrote works that repeatedly explained how the study of nature led one inexorably to the idea of a Creator. As a distinguished member of the gentry, his position as a Christian gentleman lent credence to the claims he made as a natural philosopher. This was particularly helpful to him when he clashed with none other than Thomas Hobbes over the role of experiment.

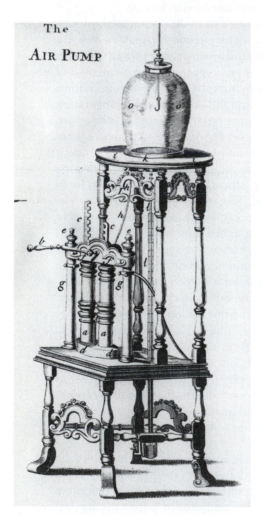

The

AIR PUMP

Boyle's Air Pump

Issues in Experimental Philosophy

One of the important factors that gave rise to the new experimental philosophy in the seventeenth century was the invention of new instruments for measuring and for magnifying. Instruments that magnified, like the telescope's improvement of our view of the surface of the moon, were not like new balances that merely improved an existing technique. Magnification intervened in nature—it gave the observer a view that was otherwise impossible to obtain through the normal use of the senses. It made possible what became known as "elaborate" experiments—testing (in a "laboratory") that carried the observer beyond the usual limits of our senses. This circumstance raised questions in the minds of some about the value of the information they provided.

In the late 1650s Boyle, with help from Robert Hooke, had an instrument built for him that produced a circumstance not normally met in nature. He called it a "pneumatical engine." It was an air pump, a device that would partially exhaust the air from a container. Using the air pump, Boyle conducted a series of experiments on the pressure of air and on the transmission of such things as light and magnetism through an allegedly evacuated space. Of course Boyle encountered all of the difficulties that accompany experimentation—the apparatus

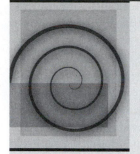

The NATURE of SCIENCE

The Vulnerability of Experiment

As the debate between Boyle and Hobbes reveals, experimentation in natural science cannot be the straightforward objective procedure it is sometimes portrayed to be. Differences in philosophical or religious outlook affect how an experimental procedure is understood. And many other factors condition the perceived meaning and significance of an experiment, not the least of which is the position in society of the persons evaluating it.

Robert Boyle was a Christian gentleman, a person of high social standing whose word and motives were not questioned by most people. However, due to the uncertainties involved in the air pump experiments, he felt it necessary to have credible witnesses confirm his results. This social conditioning enabled the witnesses to provide support for Boyle among the majority by introducing another level of credibility.

Thomas Hobbes, who was viewed as a materialist and an atheist, moved at the margins of accepted society and was excluded from the groups of natural philosophers who began gathering together around the middle of the seventeenth century. Hobbes in turn had no respect for immaterial factors such as the "spring of air" that Boyle relied on to explain his results. Such factors were dangerous deviations from the deductions about matter that geometrical reasoning inspired and that Hobbes believed formed the foundation of true philosophical knowledge. In opposing true knowledge, on which the absolute authority of the state rested, with allegedly neutral experiments, Boyle was putting the stability of society itself at risk.

The debate between Boyle and Hobbes illustrates well how philosophical, religious, social, and especially political factors can become involved in interpreting the results of experimentation. While the specific issues at stake will vary, such factors are rarely absent in any historical period, including our own.

was not perfect (in his case the pump leaked), results varied, and experimenters had to develop the ability to understand what they were seeing. There was plenty of room for objection among those who contested the process in the first place.

Thomas Hobbes was one of those who objected. When Boyle published an account of his experiments with the air pump in 1660, Hobbes responded the following year with his own treatise *against* experimentation. Hobbes opposed experimental philosophy because, he said, it was not really philosophy. Natural philosophers should explain by identifying the causes of things, not by experiment. Boyle would first have to explain what air was before he could gain any possible understanding of what was happening when he used his pneumatical engine. Because of the difficulties involved in doing the experiment, Hobbes was not at all persuaded that Boyle saw what he claimed to see. Boyle was deceiving himself. Hobbes offered alternative explanations of what was happening—the pump removed solid particles suspended in the air, but not the air itself because air, most likely, was infinitely divisible and would not be held captive by a piston.

The works of Boyle and Hobbes appeared just as Charles II was restored as English monarch after a period of revolution. Although Hobbes warned of renewed civil unrest if Boyle's new philosophy were allowed to take hold, Boyle represented the established way English society used to be and—now that the revolution was over—would be again. It was Boyle's view that prevailed.

◎ A Scientific Revolution? ◎

As historians of science just prior to the mid-twentieth century looked back to the period running roughly from 1450 to 1650, they were very impressed with the changes we have discussed in the last several chapters. What stood out clearly was the perception of various figures from those two centuries who saw themselves as engaged in something fundamentally new. Bacon, Galileo, and Kepler, for example, all used the word *new* in titles of their work. Because a number of the new attitudes would later become defining characteristics of natural science, the period was dubbed The Scientific Revolution.

More recently, however, some historians have suggested that it is misleading to refer to "The Scientific Revolution." First of all, there is no standard use of the phrase. Sometimes it is used to refer to events only in the seventeenth century while at others it means the period running all the way from Nicolas Copernicus to Isaac Newton, who will be the subject of our next chapter. But revolution usually is understood to occur in a relatively short time span, not 250 years. Further, the idea of revolution suggests that old ways were completely replaced by new ones. But, as we have seen, many of the innovations of the seventeenth century had roots running deep into the medieval period. Finally, what we mean today by the term *scientific* was a creation of the nineteenth century, so using *scientific* as if it applied to the early modern period misrepresents at least to some degree what was happening at that time.

Whether it is useful to designate a certain period of time from this era as The Scientific Revolution depends, then, on the purpose in view. There is no denying that, at least among natural philosophers, the conception of the natural world in 1650 was much different from what it had been in 1450. The change in conception can be regarded as revolutionary as long as we do not identify the period solely with the budding aspects of modern natural science that we recognize. As we have seen, there remained a rich variety of approaches to nature that did not generate a widespread consensus among the era's leading thinkers. That variety would continue for many years.

Suggestions for Reading

Peter Dear, *Revolutionizing the Sciences* (Princeton: Princeton University Press, 2001).
John Henry, *The Scientific Revolution and the Origins of Modern Science* (New York: Palgrave Macmillan, 2002).
William R. Newman and Lawrence M. Principe, *Alchemy Tried in the Fire* (Chicago: University of Chicago Press, 2002).
Steven Shapin and Simon Schaffer, *Leviathan and the Air Pump* (Princeton: Princeton University Press, 1989).

CHAPTER 8

———————◎———————

Isaac Newton: A Highpoint of Scientific Change

Among the names of famous scientists that have remained widely recognized by the public, that of Isaac Newton ranks near the top. His exploits, especially the publication of his *Mathematical Principles of Natural Philosophy*, have inspired legends, many of which began in his own day. As he passed Newton on the streets of Cambridge, a student is reputed to have observed to his companion, "There goes a man that writt a book that neither he nor anybody else understands."

Almost everyone has heard about the famous apple, whose fall sparked an idea in Newton's mind that changed science forever. The idea was that all matter attracted all other matter and it made possible a mathematical description of the laws governing the motions of matter in the heavens and here on Earth. This achievement was an early step in the process of unification of nature's forces that has dominated physics ever since. Newton also made fundamental discoveries in mathematics and in the study of light and color.

Newton himself, in a moment of presumed modesty, claimed that if he had seen farther than others it was because he had "stood on the shoulders of giants." Indeed, Newton's accomplishments were only possible because of the work of the many natural philosophers who went before him. But there is also a sense in which Newton's brilliant integration of the disparate threads of prior individual achievements into a whole represented a plateau of scientific achievement that solidified the expression of a new worldview.

◎ The Background to Newton's Achievement ◎

Because Newton was not born into a life of privilege, the impression is sometimes given that he had to triumph over poverty in order to receive a university education and achieve what he did. Such was not the case.

Newton's Early Years

Isaac Newton was born early on Christmas Day in 1642, the first child from the marriage of Isaac Newton and Hannah Ayscough. At first glance, one would have little reason to predict that one of the world's greatest scientific minds would emerge from the match because no member of the Newton family before 1642 had had enough contact with formal education to sign his or her own name. That did not mean, however, that Newton's forebears were unsuccessful people. Isaac's grandfather was so prosperous a member of the yeomanry—the class of small farm owners below the gentry—that he was able to become lord of the manor of Woolsthorpe in 1623. This improved social rank also explains why his son, Isaac's father, married a woman from the gentry class, bringing additional wealth to the union. What the estate was worth became known only too soon, for Isaac's father died seven months after he married, leaving behind a pregnant wife.

Hannah Newton became the wife of the Reverend Barnabas Smith when Isaac was three, leaving him in the care of his maternal grandmother. It is clear from Newton's own confessions that the removal of his mother as his primary caretaker left a permanent mark on his development. His exceptional intellectual abilities made him all the more sensitive to the loss of her emotional support. Aware that he was unlike others because he had no father, Newton withdrew into himself. The guilt he felt for sins such as "punching my sister" was profound. He remained distant and mysterious to others and was known to virtually everyone as a difficult person.

As a small boy Isaac attended schools in nearby villages, but far more important than what he learned in school was the return of his mother to Woolsthorpe when he was nine. The Reverend Smith had died, leaving his mother with three new children, with whom Isaac now had to compete for her attention. Within two years Isaac was sent off to grammar school in Grantham, where he lodged with an apothecary who acquainted him with the fascinations of chemical composition, especially in medicines. Late in 1659 Newton's widowed mother called her 17-year-old son home from school to learn how to manage the estate, only to discover how unsuited he was for such a responsibility. On advice from her brother and the schoolmaster in Grantham, she consented to his return to school to prepare for the university.

Cambridge University

When Newton went off to the university he began an association with Cambridge that would last for the next thirty-five years. Naturally, what he accomplished during this time was in part due to the benefits that a university education and career offered him.

Trinity College. In June of 1661, 18-year-old Isaac Newton entered Trinity College of Cambridge University. Obtaining a university education had changed in the preceding fifty years. Not that the curriculum had altered that much. The core was still Aristotle's thought, especially logic, and it, along with his physics and cosmology, were among the formal subjects Newton encountered early. But studying Aristotle hardly represented the cutting edge of European thought; in fact, students at Cambridge learned mainly through the rote mastering of texts that generated little if any intellectual passion. Apparently, the major justification for retaining the curriculum was simply that it had always been that way.

What had changed at Cambridge was the manner in which the college system operated. Whereas earlier tutors had taken their responsibilities to younger pupils seriously, by the second half of the century many fellows simply took their stipends without concerning themselves with their younger charges, who were expected to fend for themselves. Newton began to go his own way quickly, even though his tutor suggested a standard course of reading assignments. It must have become obvious to Newton that he possessed abilities in excess of those around him, including some of his professors.

The impact of self-instruction.   The new direction Newton began to follow early in 1664 resulted from his reading of works by Descartes, Gassendi, Galileo, Hobbes, and others. His procedure was to record in a special notebook the questions that these authors provoked as he read their explanations of natural phenomena, even suggesting possible tests by which his questions might be answered. Newton was drawn more to Descartes's mechanistic explanations—according to which natural phenomena were explained as the result of impacts between kinds of matter—than to the so-called qualities of matter Aristotle had designed precisely to fit the explanation sought. But Descartes's system also worried him. At first, Descartes's philosophy appeared to be friendly to religion, but Newton began to ask whether Descartes's confinement of spirit to the realm of "thinking things" meant that God had been excluded from nature.

Newton bought Descartes's book on geometry just before Christmas of 1664, although he had already read it six months earlier. Mathematics captured his attention, even though he had no real background in it and had to teach himself for the most part. Mathematics was regarded as an esoteric subject in the university. If he wished to win election as an undergraduate to one of the sixty-two scholarships the college controlled, studying mathematics was not a good way to distinguish himself. But Newton was in fact elected, some assume because of the support of someone who was well placed in the structure of Trinity College who intervened on his behalf.

◎ Newton's Central Interests ◎

Newton spent the next four years preparing for his master's degree, which, when he obtained it, made him a permanent resident of the university as a fellow of Trinity College. However much Newton depended on those who had preceded him, clearly he was one of a kind at Cambridge. He stayed mainly to himself, making few friends. One exception to this pattern of isolation was his attendance at the lectures of Isaac Barrow (1630–1677), the Lucasian professor of mathematics. Barrow had learned enough about Newton's mathematical abilities during the years when Newton was preparing for his degree to be highly impressed. When Barrow resigned his position in 1669, he recommended that the young master of arts succeed him in the Lucasian chair. In the fall of 1669 twenty-six-year-old Isaac Newton landed a professorship, his future all but assured.

Mathematics and the Theory of Color

Newton brought innovations to two subjects that early captured his attention. Even before he assumed the Lucasian chair of mathematics, he embarked on the creation of a new approach to the study of things that change continuously with respect to each other, now known as the calculus. Inventing a means of representing such change, whether the rate of change was uniform or not, opened up new possibilities for the mathematical depiction of natural processes. In the study of light, Newton combined his talent for experimentation with his acute power of reasoning to produce a new understanding of the nature of color.

Newton and the calculus. Newton came across a work by John Wallis (1616–1703), in which the Oxford geometer had used so-called infinitesimals in calculating the area under certain curves. The idea of infinitesimally small quantities, in particular an infinitesimally small piece of a line, dated back at least to the Middle Ages. Wallis used this idea to compare the area of certain curved geometrical figures to that of a square.

Newton took Wallis's work one step further. Rather than conceiving of a curve or line as being composed of infinitesimally small pieces statically joined together, Newton began to think of curves as being generated by motion. The idea of motion entails, of course, change over time, so it was natural for Newton to wonder about what he called the "moments" of change. Curves and lines express how one varying quantity (the dependent variable) changes in response to a change in the other (the independent variable). In straight lines the relationship of change is uncomplicated. Newton now employed the infinitesimal to express the moment of change in a *curved* line at a given instant of time. He did this by considering the ratio of the infinitesimally small change of the dependent variable to that of the independent variable, a ratio of what he called *fluxions*.

The "infinitely little lines" of each variable, as he called them, were both real and not real because an instant of time represents an interlude of no duration. Somewhat later Newton's fellow countryman George Berkeley criticized him by observing that his "evanescent increments" appeared both to exist and not exist, adding, "May we not call them the ghosts of departed quantities?" But Newton treated them as real, manipulating them as he did other algebraic entities. In so doing, he had invented a new and powerful means of analyzing and solving highly complex mathematical problems. Time would show that Newton's invention also would have a huge impact on the solutions to the problems of everyday life.

In October of 1666, he wrote a tract on resolving problems by motion. There is no indication that he showed it to anyone; nor did another general work on the analysis of equations from 1669 make its way into public view. A few individuals saw the second tract, but perhaps because it did not make any explicit or pointed use of the fluxional notation, no one deciphered from it the scope of Newton's abilities.

Newton did later publish his method of fluxions as an appendix to his famous book, *Mathematical Principles of Natural Philosophy*. Eventually there erupted a protracted disagreement about who invented the calculus, with bitter charges flying back and forth across the English Channel. Gottfried Wilhelm Leibniz (1646–1716), a German philosopher, mathematician, and diplomat who had seen a private copy of Newton's 1669 work on equations in 1676, assumed at the time that Newton's mention of infinitesimals contained nothing different from what others, including Wallis, had done. The year before, Leibniz had invented what amounted to an alternative form of Newton's method of fluxions. In the question of who invented the calculus, then, there were clearly two winners and no losers, since scholars agree that both men created the same mathematical tool independently.

The theory of color. For his first course of lectures as a new professor at the beginning of 1670, Newton chose a subject he had been investigating before his appointment—the nature of colored light. Newton described experiments he had performed with prisms that suggested a new understanding of the prism's effect on a beam of light. He rejected the common explanation that the prism separated white light into colored light by weakening it somehow. In that explanation the red light (and all other colored light) that emerged from the prism was really just the white light that had been forced by the prism to appear red.

Newton concluded instead that colored light constituted the white light's component parts. Colored light was more basic than white light because the latter resulted from combining all the various forms of the former. Newton came to this conclusion using what he called a crucial experiment, by which he meant an experiment that was able to settle the matter once and for all.

When he let a beam of white light enter a prism, it was broken into the expected colored beams. By rotating the prism he was able to select one of the colored beams, for example red, so that it passed through slits and entered a second prism. Here he noticed that the beam of red light was not changed by the second prism as it passed through it. Newton noted that the second prism had not weakened the red beam, as it should have under the usual explanation. What *was* the same, he observed, was the angle through which the light had been bent. The angle formed by the incident beam of white light and the emerging red light in the first prism (angle A in the figure) was the same as that between the entering red light and the existing red light of the second prism (angle B).

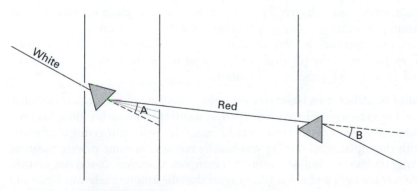

Newton's "Crucial Experiment"

Furthermore, he saw that when he selected a different beam of colored light to pass through the second prism, the size of the angle through which the light was bent was different from that of red, but the angles in the two prisms were equal— just as they had been in the case of the red light. He concluded that he had established that the beams of colored light, far from being a modification of white light, actually were the component parts of white light, and that the angle through which a particular colored light was bent was its defining feature.

As part of his studies, Newton built a reflecting telescope of which he was quite proud. When in 1671 members of the Royal Society in London asked to see it, Newton sent it to them and was promptly elected to full membership in the society. Early in 1672 he sent them a paper summarizing the several years of work he had done on color. As a result of the telescope and the impressive paper on color, which was immediately published by the Royal Society, Newton's name began to be mentioned by those living outside Cambridge.

Newton's work on color aroused opposition from Robert Hooke, a defender of the modification theory of color, and Christian Huygens, who objected that, by only appealing to the merely accidental characteristic of colored light's refrangibility, Newton had never really explained what color was. Newton's responses made clear that he was a testy, if gifted, thinker who would tolerate little criticism. His overreaction was childish, indicating, at the very least, an extremely eccentric personality. Newton simply withdrew, intending, as he put it, "to be no further solicitous about matters of philosophy." But his understanding that colored light formed the basic components out of which white light was composed became the dominant view.

Alchemy and Theology

After this brief contact with the scientific world beyond Cambridge little was heard from Newton for over ten years. He turned to work he had already begun on the motions of heavenly objects and to his serious interest in both theology and alchemy. His treatment of these latter two subjects, both of which concern themselves with the relationship between matter and spirit, indicates Newton's growing resistance to Descartes's mechanical philosophy. In Descartes's approach spirit is by definition excluded from nature (see Chapter 7). Newton was, in fact, close to rejecting the Cartesian assumption that the only way one body can exert force on another was by means of an impact between the two, as occurs in the working of a machine. If spirit were somehow present in the physical world, might not it mean that this presence would be reflected in the interactions of matter?

The centrality of alchemy in Newton's thought.   Because of his work on colored light Newton began to receive letters from people wanting to know his thoughts on a variety of subjects. Repeatedly, Newton would excuse himself from giving a substantial reply with the explanation that he was heavily engaged in some private business that was taking up his time and demanded his complete attention. It was not mathematics and it was not light and color. Many agree that the it most likely was Newton's study of alchemy.

From at least his grammar school days Newton had harbored a curiosity about chemistry. Sometime around 1666 he began to organize in his mind how one might go about studying the way in which material substances interact. One of the first authorities he consulted was Robert Boyle (see Chapter 7), in particular Boyle's book on forms and qualities. Newton learned about furnaces and their operation, an unmistakable clue to his intention of doing chemical experiments for himself. Before long it became clear that his real interest in the subject, if it had not been from the start, was alchemy.

Newton undertook the study of alchemy in the same systematic way he had investigated the theory of color. His procedure was to set down axioms to govern his investigations and to compile notes for and from experiments. He assumed that whatever changes he observed involved a chemical process rather than some kind of mystical transformation; hence he determined to take exact physical measurements, as he had in his optical experimentation. Newton disdained the appeal that alchemy held for those he saw as "ignorant vulgars," who sought how to become rich by learning how to turn lead into gold.

Newton always remained convinced that particles of matter in motion constituted reality. But never did he believe that a description of matter in motion supplied a complete description of reality. That view was too narrow and restricted, and it did not presume to explain the nobler motions of matter we humans encounter. To understand a material entity, Newton was not satisfied with hypothetical corpuscles whose only characteristic was extension. He took his cue from the human body because it also possessed a mind. Unlike Descartes, who separated mind and body, Newton saw them as united. The manner in which the human mind related to the body—a mental decision to move one's arm could result in a physical movement—was a more complete model for understanding why matter moved than the mere mechanical analysis of impact.

Newton suggested that the motions of matter controlled by the human mind provided a good means of imagining how the motions of the heavens were subject to God's control. In both cases passive matter was animated by an active agency. Newton was thus able to claim that an action did not have to rely on an intervening medium to be transmitted and at the same time avoid attributing the action to powers belonging to matter itself. This way of understanding matter and its forces was quite compatible with the view of matter in alchemy. A fundamental alchemical conviction, for example, was that material nature was infused with the active principles of the feminine and the masculine in whose union generation of some kind proceeded. Newton agreed. He felt that if we could understand which substances possessed which principles it might be possible to find out what combinations generate new substances. Newton also spoke of what he called "the principles of vegetable actions," which he contrasted with mechanical actions. These were nature's agents, "her fire, her soul, her life," and they involved the presence of a subtle kind of matter that he thought of as diffused throughout the "grosser matter." This new kind of matter, an ethereal substance, was the bearer of the active agency, for "if it were separated there would remain but a dead and inactive earth."

Animating force lay at the heart of Newton's thought. He speculated about other kinds of ethereal substance that produced activity in nature. One he suggested might be involved in the propagation of light. Other "ethereal spirits," he said, might be involved in the production of electrical and magnetic phenomena and perhaps in the gravitating principle. The idea of an animating force, then, links his interests in alchemy to his conception of nature's forces in general, including his view of gravity. He let his mind freely wonder if maybe all of nature might be nothing more than the precipitates of "certain ethereal spirits" that God initially shaped into various forms and that had been molded "ever since by the power of nature."

A theological crisis.   Among the interests seething in Newton's mind in the 1670s was theology; in fact, theology forced itself on him with an urgency that pushed alchemy into the background for a brief time. Newton had always approached theology with the same seriousness he devoted to all his studies. His careful examination of the Bible convinced him that the Scriptures had been corrupted. He believed that writers in the fourth century had in fact altered original texts in order to promote the divinity of Jesus. Newton's theology agreed with that of Arius, the fourth-century Alexandrian priest who taught that Jesus was not coequal with God the Father but was inferior to him, having been created and then elevated to his right hand. This unitarian view threatened his future at Cambridge in a very pressing manner.

As a master of arts and a fellow of Trinity College, Newton was required to be ordained to the Anglican clergy or be expelled from the college. With the deadline for his ordination approaching in 1675, Newton knew his private nontrinitarian views were wholly incompatible with ordination. He asked to be excused from the requirement, but since he did not think his request would be granted, he prepared to leave Cambridge. Then a special dispensation from the crown exempted the holder of the Lucasian chair from the requirement of ordination. No one knows for sure why the dispensation was granted, although it is unlikely that it was intended to permit Newton to retain his secret unitarian beliefs. It is more probable that Newton and all future Lucasian professors, were, as mathematicians, deemed unsuitable candidates for the Anglican ministry.

The Motions of the Heavens

In 1687 one of the most famous books in the history of science appeared in England. It was a sensation that made Newton an undisputed authority in natural philosophy. *Mathematical Principles of Natural Philosophy* (known widely since then as the *Principia*), revealed its author, still largely unknown to many of his day, to be among the world's most gifted thinkers. Readers quickly discovered that Newton was aware of all the important recent achievements of natural philosophers in Britain and on the Continent. Further, Newton had clearly thought carefully and in great detail about the nature of matter and motion and he had supplied impressive new mathematical treatments of the complex motions of the heavens that men such as Kepler and others had struggled with before him. The book may have seemed to many to burst forth out of nowhere, but Newton had in fact been studying natural philosophy and the motions of the heavens for some time.

The problem of the moon's motion.   Newton agreed with Descartes that natural motion, or motion that did not require a mover, occurred in a straight line and not in a circle as Galileo believed. But if that were so, then something must be preventing the moon from moving in a straight line by bending its motion into an orbit around the Earth. It was as if a cosmic string of some sort attached the moon to the Earth, pulling it into a circular path around the Earth much as a rock could be twirled on a string. But what was this cosmic string?

The well-known story about the fall of an apple did not come directly from Newton. An acquaintance of Newton named William Stuckley reported that on April 15, 1726, the year before Newton died, the two of them dined together and then went into the garden to drink tea under the shade of some apple trees. Newton told Stuckley that he had been in the same situation as a young man when the fall of an apple triggered an idea in his mind about how to solve a problem that had been puzzling him. The problem had to do with the moon's motion. But Newton's work with the problem of the moon extended over a much longer period than many have assumed. Only gradually did he become clear about what the complicated motion of the moon entailed, some aspects of which required almost two decades to resolve.

Falling apples and a falling moon.   When the young Isaac Newton casually saw an apple fall from a tree during his stay at home in Woolsthorpe, it apparently occurred to him to consider more carefully the reason *why* it fell. Aristotle's idea of natural place, according to which the heavy elements earth and water move toward the center of the cosmos, no longer satisfied him. He had come to regard that explanation as begging the question. He preferred to think of the apple as subject to a force that caused it to fall, a force that was somehow associated with an object's heaviness, or what was known as *gravitas*.

Part of Newton's insight was to recognize that he did not need to solve the problem of how the force was applied in order to understand what made the moon bend into an orbit around the Earth. What if the force, regardless of how it worked, affected the moon in the same way it affected apples? The biggest drawback to this line of thinking was that the fall of apples occurs at the surface of the Earth, while the moon is a very long distance away. Newton reasoned that because things like apples continue to fall even at the tops of high mountains, perhaps the force acting on them extends much farther from the center of the Earth than people normally had assumed. Maybe it even extended all the way out to the moon. If that were true, then could the moon, like apples, be considered a falling body?

Much later, after he had figured out his solution to the problem of the moon's motion, Newton published a diagram (see artist's rendition on next page) to explain why one might, in fact, regard the moon as a falling body. He imagined throwing an object like an apple from a mountaintop located at the top of the Earth. (See the figure.) If one threw the object along the tangent line VP in the diagram, then when the object was released it would undergo natural straight-line motion unless acted on by

The Moon as a Falling Body

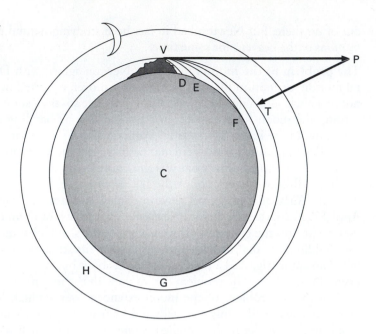

some force making it act otherwise. But *gravitas* affects objects on mountaintops, so the object would fall toward the Earth's center at the same time it experienced natural straight-line motion along the tangent line. The combination of the two motions would result in a curved path leading from the mountaintop to the Earth's surface. Newton depicted several different paths of fall to the Earth's surface (VD, VE, VF, VG), each depending on how hard the object had been thrown along the tangent line.

Newton's diagram also depicted how the object could be thrown so that it orbited the Earth and yet could be still considered on one of the paths of "fall" to the Earth (VH). In the case of a satellite, however, the object falls without ever getting closer to the Earth's surface. One can understand this phenomenon by separating the curved motion of the path the object traverses into the two simultaneous motions that make it up. If the object is thrown just hard enough along the tangent line from the mountaintop, it would travel away from the Earth far enough in any unit of time (from V to P in the figure) so that the distance it falls back toward the Earth *in that same time* (from P to T) would place it at the same distance above the Earth as when the object was thrown. The moon does in fact orbit the Earth, so could one not conclude that it "falls" toward the Earth like any other falling object? Newton had in fact grasped a way in which the moon might be like the apple he had seen fall in the garden. If he was right, then the moon, too, was subject to *gravitas*.

Learning a lesson from Hooke.   As he thought more about the motion of objects, one particular challenge emerged. As noted, Newton agreed with Descartes, who had died in 1650, that the motion objects would undergo if left to themselves was uniform motion in a straight line. But there was also a difference between the views of Descartes and Newton. Descartes held that an object undergoing such natural motion was not being acted on by a force. Newton, on the other hand, thought that natural motion resulted from the action of an active force that matter possessed "by which any being endeavors to continue in its state and opposes resistance."

Newton was not content, as was Descartes, to confine the action of force to the impact between two masses. He acknowledged that force was applied when one piece or one kind of matter struck another, but he could not agree that this was the only way in which force was exerted. Newton's understanding of matter as a passive mass that was animated by an active principle was as far from mechanical philosophy as it was close to alchemy. He was certain that God was the ultimate source of this active principle. "God who gave animals self motion beyond our understanding," he wrote in 1675, "is without doubt able to implant other principles of motion in bodies which we may understand as little."

Newton apparently did not realize that his conception of active force had produced an inconsistency in his thinking. Like Descartes he had referred to "the moon's endeavor to recede from the earth," but unlike Descartes he assumed that this tendency was due to an active force present in the moon's matter that caused uniform straight-line motion. Circular motion he saw as the balance between two equal but opposite active forces, one toward the center of motion (causing, in the case of the moon, its "fall"), and the other away from the center (due to the moon's "endeavor to recede"). In 1679 he received a letter that woke him up to what was wrong with this assumption. And worst of all, the letter was from an old critic of his theory of color, Robert Hooke.

Hooke, who was secretary of the Royal Society, tried to draw Newton into a discussion of ideas on the system of the world. Five years earlier in 1675, Hooke had claimed that the motions of the planets around the sun could be explained as a combination of their natural tangential motion with "an attractive motion toward the central body." This was clearly too close to work Newton had been considering for a long time for Newton to ignore. He had been thinking about such matters ever since he had seen the apple fall as a young man in his early twenties. Hooke's renewed contact had the effect of drawing him out again into an exchange of views. It would also force Newton to face squarely the implications of his ideas of force.

In the ensuing correspondence it became clear to Newton that Hooke had understood something Newton had not. He may have hated to admit it, but Hooke's explanation of planetary motion avoided the mistake he had made in thinking of circular motion as involving both inward and outward forces. Hooke explained the motion as the result of the planet's tangential motion, combined with an attractive motion toward a central body, *making no reference at all to a force that made the moon tend to recede from the Earth*. Newton now realized that a consistent account of the cosmic string holding the moon in its orbit needed only natural straight-line motion and the presence of a force that pulled the moon *out* of that motion into an orbit around the Earth.

Edmond Halley's famous visit.   One day in August of 1684, some five years after his exchange with Hooke, Newton received a visit from the astronomer Edmond Halley. Halley knew of Newton's mathematical gifts, and, finding himself in Cambridge, decided to consult with him about a problem on the minds of several people in London. Halley knew of Hooke's work on the system of the world and he was aware that it included a specific conjecture about the attractive force acting toward the center. Hooke had even suggested a mathematical formula for calculating how strong the attraction was at various distances from the center. Halley himself had confirmed that if one started with a circular orbit, one could show that it was governed by Hooke's formula.

The London group suspected that if the formula was correct, then it should be the foundation for the laws governing celestial motion. In fact, theoretically it should be possible to show the converse of Halley's demonstration; that is, start with Hooke's formula and derive the orbits of the planets from the force law that determined them. Going in this direction, however, was much more difficult; further, everyone knew that the orbits were not circles but ellipses.

Halley put the question straight to Newton: if the planets were drawn toward the sun according to the formula, what path would such a formula entail? In one account Newton is said to have answered immediately that the formula entailed an ellipse for the planets. Halley was astonished that he answered so quickly and confidently. "How do you know that?" he asked. "Because I have calculated it," Newton reputedly replied. When Halley requested to see the calculation, Newton claimed to have misplaced it, but he promised to send it to him.

Few Newton scholars take him at his word about the lost calculation. Some suggest he simply did not want to disclose it hastily for fear of what Hooke and others might do with it. Others wonder if Newton had in fact completed the calculation by that point. In any event, by November of 1684, he sent Halley not only the solution to the problem, but much more as well— a tract of nine pages on the motion of bodies in orbit that contained several general conclusions with broad implications. For example, Newton showed that Hooke's formula entailed an orbit that is a conic section, which is elliptical when the velocities are slow enough, as they are for planets.

Newton's proof that gravity affects the moon.   Halley's question to Newton in 1684 touched on a subject Newton had in fact thought about over many years, ever since he had first considered the problem of the moon's motion. Back in the mid-1660s, when he was at home because plague had forced the university to close, he had devised a strategy for testing whether gravity affected the moon. It involved using Galileo's figure for the diameter of the Earth, which was in fact not very accurate. The results he had gotten in 1666 were good enough to convince him that he was on the right track. But they were not close enough to what he had predicted they should be—based on his own beliefs and on his knowledge of Descartes, Kepler, and Galileo—to satisfy him that he had completely solved the problem. The proof Newton developed in the wake of Halley's visit used the same strategy, this time with more accurate data, and it became part of his famous book on natural philosophy.

The strategy for testing whether gravity affected the moon came out of a reply Newton gave to a criticism of Copernican astronomy. Like Galileo and Kepler before him, Newton was a Copernican. Opponents of Copernicus had argued that an Earth rotating on its axis would fling objects on the surface off into space. Newton showed that the heaviness of objects supplied a much greater force than that outward tendency generated by a spinning Earth. Shifting his focus from a rotating Earth to the moon rotating around the Earth, he compared the tendency of the moon to be flung out of its orbit by the force of its revolution around the Earth to the gravitas that made it a falling object.

In Book 3 of the *Principia* of 1687, Newton explained how one might prove that the force that made apples fall also acted on the moon. He established his conjecture that the apple force supplied the cosmic string he sought by using a clever line of reasoning. First he *assumed* he was right about the apple force also affecting the moon. By combining that assumption with other knowledge he had about how objects move he realized he had enough information to make a prediction about how far toward the Earth the moon would "fall" in one minute. He then could check to see if his prediction could be confirmed. If it could, then his assumption must have been correct. First, we must understand the foundation for his prediction, then the prediction itself, and finally the confirmation.

1. *The foundation for the prediction.* Before Newton could make a prediction that he could test, he had to find a formula that expressed how the apple force varied over distance. He suspected that the farther away apples were, the weaker the gravitational force he believed was pulling them toward the Earth. But he had to find out precisely how the attractive force varied. The relationship he discovered has become known as Newton's inverse square law. It is the same formula that Hooke suggested in the system of the world he proposed nearly a decade after Newton first came to it in 1666.

Without recreating the exact route to the inverse square law, suffice it to say that Newton was able to deduce it by building on earlier conclusions. He began with his claim that a body would naturally continue in uniform straight-line motion forever unless interrupted. An obvious implication of this conviction was that any motion that was not natural, such as curved motion or motion that was otherwise accelerated, was being caused by a force. Newton, in other words, had learned to associate force and acceleration. For Newton, then, $f \propto a$ and $a \propto f$.

From here Newton drew on other things, such as Kepler's third law, to conclude that the apple force (and therefore also the acceleration of a falling apple) would diminish according to the formulas $f \propto 1/r^2$ and $a \propto 1/r^2$, where r is the distance the apple is from the Earth. This is Newton's famous inverse square law and its discovery served as the foundation for a prediction he could verify.

2. *The prediction.* Newton's prediction was that if the moon was affected by the same force that makes apples fall, then the distance an apple would fall at the Earth's surface in one minute was 3,600 times greater than the distance the moon fell in the same amount of time. He was able to calculate this prediction so precisely because the moon was known to be 60 Earth radii away, or 60 times farther away from the Earth's center than falling apples were. So, if whatever made apples fall also made the moon "fall," then the rate of acceleration of the moon's fall would, by his inverse square law, be weaker by a factor of $1/60^2$. The assumption that gravity affected both apples and the moon also meant that the distance the moon "fell" in a given amount of time would be $1/60^2$ times less than the distance apples would fall in the same amount of time.

Using an argument from geometry and his knowledge about the moon's distance from the Earth, Newton calculated that the moon actually "fell" 15.083 Paris feet (approximately 16 English feet) toward the Earth in one minute. If his assumption

The NATURE
of SCIENCE

The Status of Newton's Proof

Newton's inference that gravity holds the moon in its orbit is an example of scientific proof. But exactly what kind of reasoning is involved? Consider the statements p and q below:

p: the same force that makes apples fall also makes the moon "fall"

q: apples on Earth fall 3,600 times farther than the moon in the same amount of time

Newton's argument is:

If p is true then q is true.

q is true.

_____

Therefore p is true.

As impressive as Newton's demonstration is, its logic does not always hold true. There are many examples of this form of logical argument that are untrue. For example, let p be the statement that I won the lotto and q be the statement that my taxes increase. The previous argument then runs:

If I win the lotto then my taxes will increase.

My taxes have increased.

_____

Therefore I won the lotto.

Most scientific proof uses an argument of this structure. We conjecture that something causes a certain result and then seek evidence that the prediction is true. Finding the evidence, we conclude that the conjecture has been verified. Of course the persuasiveness of the proof depends on various factors, such as how exclusive the proposed cause appears to be or how improbable or precise the prediction seems. Because other factors may be involved in the production of the predicted result, we can never be certain beyond all doubt that the identified cause is exclusively responsible for the result. In fact, even the conceptual and linguistic categories we use when forming a hypothesis can carry with them hidden assumptions that affect the meaning of the result and that only become clear to later generations or people from different cultures. So the permanent acceptance of the cause is never guaranteed.

that the acceleration of the moon's fall was 60^2 times weaker than at the Earth's surface were correct, that would mean that objects near the Earth should fall $60^2 \times 15.083$ feet in one minute, or, because distance fallen varied as the square of the time, 15.083 feet in *one second*.

3. *The confirmation.* The first time Newton had reasoned this out, back at home during the plague years, he had simplified things by assuming the orbit of the moon was circular, and he had used Galileo's faulty data. The value he predicted from his calculations then was close to the observed value, but still too far away to serve as a clear confirmation of the prediction. By the time he wrote the *Principia*, Newton had shown that elliptical orbits were implied by the inverse square law and he had replaced Galileo's erroneous measure of the diameter of the Earth with a more recent and more accurate figure. In the *Principia* he delights in citing Christian Huygens's measurement of how far objects at the surface of the Earth fall in one second: 15.083 Paris feet. On the basis of the assumption that the moon is affected by the apple force, Newton had made a corrected prediction that, after some twenty years, he was able to confirm.

The Principia *and Its Aftermath*

There are few works in the history of physics whose impact has been as great as that of Newton's famous work. And yet its immediate reception was not without criticism, especially concerning his notion of attractive force. But there is no doubt that the book quickly catapulted him to fame in England and abroad.

A system of the world. If Halley had heard stories about Newton's abilities before his visit to Cambridge, when he received Newton's promised answer to his question about orbital shapes he knew there was no question about his rare talent as a natural philosopher. Most likely it was during Halley's second trip to Cambridge in the fall of 1684 that he discovered that Newton was working up an expanded treatise on the material he had sent him. With Halley's enthusiastic encouragement the work continued to grow. Halley became in effect Newton's editor, urging him on in his work, proofreading the text, and arranging all the details for printing the final product. The Royal Society, to whom Newton had agreed to send the finished product, was unable to bear the costs of printing it; consequently, Halley took that burden on himself as well.

The first volume of the work received the imprimatur of the Royal Society in July of 1686, and the whole project appeared in Latin in the summer of 1687. It was immediately recognized as a major achievement and

Isaac Newton

brought Newton great fame. Written in the format of the ancient mathematical text of Euclid, the work began with a series of definitions and axioms, the latter spiced with many corollaries. Definition 5, for example, made clear Newton's recognition of the centrality of centripetal force, the force that impels a body toward a center.

The innocent statement of the first two axioms, also called laws of motion by Newton, disguised a change in his thinking that had occurred while he was revising and expanding the treatise he had sent to Halley. Law 1 said simply: "Every body continues in its state of rest, or of uniform motion in a right line, unless it is compelled to change that state by forces impressed upon it." Here was an unequivocal claim that rest and uniform motion in a straight line were similar states, because the presence of an unbalanced force disturbed the one just as it did the other. Newton did not think that rest was *caused* by a force of any sort—it simply existed as a natural state of being. He now accepted that uniform straight-line motion was just like that—it, too, simply existed as a natural state of being. This meant that Newton had finally abandoned the idea that uniform motion was caused by an inherent active force and he now accepted Descartes's understanding of natural motion.

The way was now clear for Newton to recognize that there was more than one way for an impressed force to change the state of a moving body's natural state of being. If rest was the only natural state of being, then the only way an impressed force could change it would be to change its speed from zero to some finite amount. But if uniform rectilinear motion was also a natural state of being, force could be used to change the direction as well as the speed of the body. From this point on, a body moving in curved motion, clearly under the influence of a force, had to be regarded as accelerating just as much as a body whose linear speed was changed by the application of a force. The *Principia*'s Law II reiterated that the change of motion (or acceleration) of a mass (m) was proportional to the force that caused it, $F = ma$.

After the introductory section, Newton moved on to Book I, "The Motions of Bodies." Here he included not only the demonstration sent to Halley in November of 1684, but a total of 210 pages of propositions that unpacked all manner of detailed conclusions (many cast in general form), that arose for bodies moving under the influence of force. In Book III he came to "The System of the World." To construct a system of the world was a classically philosophical endeavor, but Newton noted that he would continue to present the material "in the mathematical way."

It must be emphasized that Newton's removal of the active force in matter that he had once thought caused uniform rectilinear motion by no means meant that he had embraced Descartes's entire mechanical approach. Newton hardly abandoned altogether the idea of an active force animating matter. As we know from his ideas on gravity and from his alchemical work, which continued even as he worked on the *Principia*, active forces were too deeply embedded in Newton's disposition to eradicate completely.

Newton knew that his readers would not permit him to make unwarranted inferences. He knew in particular that he would be hard pressed to convince them to accept the active force pulling the moon toward the Earth and the planets toward the sun. That would be difficult enough, but while drafting the *Principia*, Newton had become convinced that the force determining the planets' motions arose, as he would later put it, "from the universal nature of matter." That was equivalent to saying that not just the planets were affected by the sun's gravity, but that *every body of matter was drawn to every other body* by a force that varied as the inverse square of the distance between them. This grand generalization has become known as *universal gravitation.* Mechanical philosophers would surely not tolerate this celebration of an inherent active force of matter, because for them force was only transmitted by impact. Assigning matter the capacity to attract other matter would amount to an appeal to occult or hidden forces. Newton knew he would have to build his case carefully.

Newton had written to astronomers for data on the planets and their satellites in order to be sure that their observed positions did indeed agree with the predictions of his system. Just because he had successfully described the Earth–moon system as the result of gravitational attraction did not mean that he could simply assume it applied to all the other celestial systems. As specific data came in, he was gratified to learn that it was consistent with his claims. He showed that the paths of comets, not always elliptical but sometimes parabolic, were anticipated by his results. He showed how the oceans should be affected by the pull of the moon and the sun on the Earth, working out a rudimentary scheme explaining tidal motions. He prepared the way, in other words, for his claim late in Book III to have proven that such forces arose "from the universal nature of matter."

Newton took pains in writing the *Principia* to treat this attraction mathematically and not to assert anything about how it was caused. He hoped that he had made a case for this claim that would stand on its own. He did not want to become engaged in a debate about the mechanism by which gravitational force was transported from one body of matter to another. That, he saw, involved speculation.

The reception of Newton's attractive force.   The *Principia* impressed its readers with its thoroughness, its mathematical depth, and the sheer scope of its subject matter. Prior to its appearance in England, few if any books there or elsewhere had been as widely acknowledged. But acknowledgment was not the same as agreement. Readers steeped in the tradition of Descartes and mechanical philosophy balked at the central place Newton had given to attractive force in his system. They insisted that his failure to identify a medium by which gravity's force was transmitted was equivalent to saying that it was transmitted without using any medium at all. And that, for a mechanical philosopher, was not only unacceptable—it was impossible. Christian Huygens, who called Newton's attractive force "absurd," said about him: "I esteem his understanding and subtlety highly, but I consider that they have been put to ill use in the greater part of this work, where the author studies things of little use or when he builds on the improbable principle of attraction."

If Newton's attractive force did not require a medium to be transmitted, then mechanical philosophers assumed it behaved like a psychical force. They understood that psychical powers of human beings, for example, were supposed to be transmitted from one being to another without reference to an intervening medium. Such forces were said to "act at a distance," meaning that the effect of a force exerted at one point was immediately felt at another point some distance away. Natural philosophers in the Middle Ages had not hesitated to appeal to this kind of force to explain natural phenomena. Newton's endorsement of a gravitational force that acted at a distance did not sound like a step forward.

The black year of 1693.   The sudden fame his book brought him marked a profound change from the relatively solitary life Newton had known. He met numerous prominent people, including the philosopher John Locke (1632–1704), with whom he shared his anti-trinitarian convictions and opened a discussion about alchemy. He also became enamored of a talented 25-year-old Swiss mathematician, one Nicolas Fatio de Duillier (1664–1753). For four years beginning in the summer of 1689, Newton and Fatio engaged in a protracted correspondence and even spent blocks of time with each other. The relationship, which has fueled debate about Newton's sexuality among historians, broke off abruptly in early 1693, for reasons that are not clear.

Some historians point to the breakup of the friendship as the reason for Newton's mental breakdown later that year. Extant letters to Locke show Newton to be in an extremely disturbed state, rumors of which circulated at the time. There were reports that Newton was at death's door as late as 1695. Although it is clear that Newton did endure some kind of mental trauma, there has been no agreement about its cause. While some point to the breakup with Fatio, others have suggested that Newton suffered from mercury poisoning because of repeated exposure to mercury during alchemical experimentation. Although a chemical analysis of a hair found in one of his books in the 1970s revealed a high mercury content, this explanation is not consistent with Newton's relatively rapid recovery to full vigor.

◎ Fame and Power ◎

The years around the *Principia*'s appearance were momentous for England. In 1685 King Charles II died, bringing his Roman Catholic brother to the throne. Ever since King Henry VIII had broken with Rome over the question of divorce 150 years earlier, Protestants and Catholics in England were engaged in a heated rivalry. The Anglican Church had been consolidated under Queen Elizabeth as the official Church of England in the sixteenth century, but suspicions were immediately raised any time a new monarch showed sympathy for Rome. At such times England was thrown into instability until the crisis was resolved.

When James II unwisely attempted to win freedom of worship for Catholics in England, this action united Whigs and Tories in defense of the Anglican Church. Newton, certainly no devout Protestant, nevertheless shared the widespread opposition to James's actions. In early 1687, as he finished up Book III of the *Principia,* he made known his objection to the king's position and emerged to rather sudden prominence within the university. The next year James was forced to flee England during the so-called Glorious Revolution that brought William and Mary to the throne. Newton, now a famous natural philosopher, was elected to Parliament at the beginning of 1689, where he served one year.

Mastering the Mint and the Royal Society

In Newton's correspondence from the years after the *Principia* there is more than one mention of a possible appointment to an official post. An offer was finally made in April 1696, and Newton accepted it. He was to be warden of the mint, a position that would bring him a handsome salary and would not require much work. Because the real work was usually done by the master of the mint, Newton could have continued to live in Cambridge had he so desired. He chose, however, to move to London, where he took in his seventeen-year-old niece, the daughter of his stepsister Hannah, who had recently been widowed. By aiding his stepsister, Newton also benefited himself. He grew very fond of his niece Catherine Barton, one of the very few women who affected him in any meaningful way during his entire life.

He took his new post very seriously, warming to the responsibility of apprehending and arraigning counterfeiters. He developed a reputation as a ruthless prosecutor among those he flushed out and brought to judgment. When the master of the mint died in December of 1699, Newton replaced him.

In London, Newton could easily attend meetings of the Royal Society; indeed, he was elected to its governing body twice in the waning years of the century. But Newton took no interest in the administrative concerns of the society and only rarely attended its general meetings. Then in March of 1703, Robert Hooke, a prominent presence in the society since its inception, died. Newton, who had allowed his name to be put forward as a candidate, was elected president at the age of sixty later that fall. He would not relinquish the title during the remainder of his life, becoming, as one historian has put it, "the autocrat of science" in England.

Although Newton was elected to this position of honor, he still had enemies. Hooke was gone, but Hooke's partisans were not. Those who had felt the sting of Newton's invective and those who simply resented Newton's tendency to exploit his fame in a high-handed fashion were suspicious of what he might do in a position of power. They were right to worry. As president, Newton became a dominating presence in the society, both in its administration and in its regular meetings. A number of younger men who had become devoted to Newton's natural philosophy were rewarded with professorships, and little if anything that was entered into debates about the Newtonian philosophy escaped the president's personal involvement and even supervision.

The Opticks

If Newton's rivalry with Robert Hooke had played a part in his delayed involvement in the Royal Society, it was the determining factor in the publication of Newton's larger work on light. Newton had promised himself that he would not publish this work, which had long been under preparation, until Hooke died. After the spring of 1703 the way was clear, and the *Opticks* appeared, in English, a year later. Those on the Continent who did not read English would have to wait for the Latin translation, which came out in 1706. Anyone who read it, however, found that it was easier going than the *Principia* had been. For this reason the impact of the work was as great as that of the *Principia*.

The first edition of the *Opticks* culminated in sixteen "queries," innocent-sounding questions apparently thrown out to titillate the reader's curiosity. Among other things, the queries amounted to a defense of the position he had taken in the *Principia* on attractive force. No one doubted that the questions were really Newton's answers, that when he asked: "Do not bodies act upon Light at a distance, and by their action bend its Rays?" he meant that he believed they did in fact behave in this manner. In the Latin edition that appeared on the heels of the first edition, Newton added to the queries until their total was twenty-three. He speculated on the presence in nature of a whole range of forces whose activity at a distance produced such phenomena as electricity, magnetism, and chemical interaction. His reinforcement of the necessity of active principles in nature made clear once again that he did not wish to be counted among the strict mechanical philosophers of his day.

In the last queries of the Latin edition, Newton tried to clarify where he stood in comparison to those who made up hypotheses in order to explain all things in terms of mechanical interaction. He still believed as he always had that God animated matter with powers that acted at a distance. His reference to these powers, however, made no direct appeal to mechanical interaction. That did not mean that Newton regarded the powers as mysterious qualities. They were simply phenomena that obeyed laws of nature; only their causes were hidden. But knowing the laws by which they acted was, he thought, "a very great step in Philosophy," even if he did deliberately leave their causes to be found out later. As for the first cause, Newton outdid himself: "Is not infinite Space the Sensorium of a Being incorporeal, living, and intelligent, who sees the things themselves intimately . . . and comprehends them wholly by their immediate presence to himself?"

God and Nature

Not surprisingly, Newton was criticized, especially by Continental thinkers, for what they took to be a philosophy (and theology) laced with problems. In 1710, for example, Leibniz went on record against the idea of action at a distance, which he saw to be equivalent to an embrace of miracles. He even suggested in a review of a Newtonian work that it seemed a return to "a certain fantastic scholastic philosophy," thereby hinting that Newton was trying to take natural philosophy backward rather than forward. It is understandable that Newton spoke out in the face of such accusations.

He tried once more to answer his critics about matter and attraction in a new edition of the *Principia*. In preparation for some time, it finally appeared in 1713 under the editorship of Roger Cotes, Professor of Astronomy and Experimental Philosophy in Cambridge. At the end of the work Newton waxed eloquent not only about gravity, but about its relation to God. Concerning gravity, he criticized those who insisted on speculating about its cause. He insisted on staying within the limits of his mathematical treatment, declaring in a famous phrase, "I feign no hypotheses." Concerning God, Newton declared that the beautiful system of the sun, planets, and comets could only proceed from an intelligent being who ruled over all. Newton declared that God was omnipresent not only in virtue, but also in substance.

Leibniz did not think much of Newton's abilities as a philosopher. He recognized that Newton and his editor had him in mind in their new edition of the *Principia,* and he was ready to reply. To do so he wrote to Princess Caroline of Ansbach, a young girl he had tutored at the court in Berlin who was now wife of the heir to the

English throne. Caroline had read Leibniz's *Theodicy* and had sought her former teacher's opinion of the theology of her new homeland.

Leibniz informed the princess that Newton made God into a corporeal being who used space as an organ by which to perceive things. He added that Newton also believed that God had to step in from time to time to wind up the watch of the clockwork cosmos to prevent it from running down. Newton's God "had not, it seems, sufficient foresight to make it a perpetual motion." This latter view Leibniz apparently inferred from a passage in the final query of the Latin edition of the *Opticks*, in which Newton observed that the irregular movement of comets would eventually disrupt the system of the planets "till this system wants a reformation." Indeed, Newton acknowledged that the repeated elliptical orbits of planets are never exactly identical, and he believed God occasionally caused comets to strike the sun as a means of refueling its power.

To Leibniz, Newton had demeaned God by suggesting that God's handiwork was in need of repair. Newton's God was, as one historian has characterized him, no better than a "cosmic plumber," fixing the occasional leaks that sprang in the universal system. Princess Caroline also found the notion distasteful that God had "to be always present to readjust the machine because he was not able to do it at the beginning." As she wrote to Leibniz in the beginning of 1716, she did not believe that any philosophy could give her confidence "if it showed us the imperfection of God." Leibniz's God, of course, did not need to intervene in nature, having perfectly anticipated every contingency from the beginning.

For Newton, God was intimately tied to and in complete control of the physical world, present in it by virtue of the active principles that animated matter. Newton's God could exercise infinite power and wisdom to anticipate the needs of sparrows and all other creatures, and to respond to the prayerful petitions of human subjects to intervene on their behalf in the normal course of events. The disagreement between Newton and Leibniz about how God related to nature would reverberate down through the centuries from that point on. Had God made nature perfect from the start, as Leibniz held, or was God's constant supervision of nature needed, as Newton believed?

Leibniz died in the fall of 1716, and the bitter controversies that had divided him from Newton began to subside. The next year saw a new edition of the *Opticks*, which was unaltered except for the section containing the queries. Among the eight new queries was what at first glance appeared to be a concession to his critics, the mechanical philosophers. Newton postulated the existence of "an aether, exceedingly more rare and subtile than the Air, and exceedingly more elastik and active," to explain gravity itself. But this "aether" could never satisfy his critics because it was composed of particles that repelled each other; in other words, here was action at a distance all over again.

During his last years Newton gave a great deal of attention to the study of religion, specifically the history of the ancient kingdoms portrayed in the Bible. As the end approached, he began to put his things in order. His health declining, he attended fewer meetings of the Royal Society, presiding for the last time on

March 2, 1727. As he lay dying later that same month, Newton affirmed the rebellious religious stance he had so long embraced by refusing the sacrament of the church. Three days after his death on March 20, the records of the Royal Society marked his passing with the terse announcement: "The Chair being Vacant by the Death of Sir Isaac Newton there was no Meeting this Day."

When Isaac Newton set off for Cambridge University in the early summer of 1661 there was not yet a consensus about the viability of the new Copernican view of the cosmos. Galileo had offered a reason why planets would continue to move forever around the sun in circular orbits, but Kepler had shown that the orbits were not circular. Why did the planets continue to move in elliptical orbits around the sun? Not only did Newton give the answer in the *Principia* through his laws of motion and universal gravitation, but his answer provided a means of analyzing the motions of all matter, whether in the heavens or here on Earth. Newton united natural philosophy into one comprehensive system that would dominate for the next two centuries.

Suggestions for Reading

Gale E. Christianson, *In the Presence of the Creator: Isaac Newton and His Times* (New York: Free Press, 1984).

Betty Jo Teeter Dobbs, *The Janus Faces of Genius* (Cambridge: Cambridge University Press, 2002).

Richard Westfall, *Never at Rest: A Biography of Isaac Newton* (Cambridge: Cambridge University Press, 1983).

CHAPTER 9

Newtonianism, the Earth, and the Universe During the Eighteenth Century

The novel ideas that came into science in the seventeenth century were incompatible in many ways with the more comfortable cosmos of former times. Copernicus had already moved the Earth off to the side, away from the center of the system of spheres that had always provided humans a home. But even in the early versions of the Copernican system, including that defended by Galileo, the cosmos at least remained finite in extent. After Descartes and especially after Newton, it was no longer possible to insist that space did not extend infinitely in all directions.

It took some time to build a consensus about the meaning of Newton's achievement. After all, there was much more about it to disagree with than just the question of whether the universe had a center or not. The linchpin on which all depended in Newton's system was his notion of an attractive force that acted at a distance. For mechanical philosophers who continued in the heritage of Descartes, this was a major stumbling block. The transmission of Newton's force appeared to make use of an intervening medium that was occult, and that was simply unacceptable to them.

◎ The Rise of Newtonianism ◎

In spite of the fame Newton enjoyed among his fellow British citizens, his system initially found few followers abroad. After 1730 Newton's system began to attract followers—particularly in France—who defended a worldview that has been called Newtonianism. But prior to 1730, the continuing influence of René Descartes in France and Gottfried Leibniz in the German states was sufficient to assure that the Cartesian and Leibnizian worldviews provided strong competition for Newton's thought. Only in Holland did Newton's system find avid defenders across the English Channel.

Competing Systems of Natural Philosophy

The basic assumptions individual natural philosophers made about how nature worked determined differences among them that carried implications throughout their systems. In the early eighteenth century these differences produced an important debate about force and action in nature and also involved the issue of God's relationship to the natural world.

Cartesians, Leibnizians, Newtonians. The most important issue separating Newton's system from those of Descartes and Leibniz remained an understanding of the nature of force. The Cartesian position was clear: force was a push or pull that acted on material objects by means of material contact. All natural effects were due to mechanical motions of matter, making the appeal of the Cartesian philosophy its intuitive clarity. Cartesians in the first half of the eighteenth century did not feel obligated to accept the specific mechanical motions Descartes had used to explain individual phenomena, but they did not doubt that things like magnetism resulted from *some* combination of such motions. Descartes exerted a strong hold on the French mind because his readers understood him to have clarified the basis for intelligibility itself in physics.

Because followers of Descartes insisted that force was transmitted only through collisions of matter, they refused to associate force with nonmaterial agencies in nature. Nature was a realm of the material. It was unacceptable to offer explanations of natural phenomena that depended on spiritual or nonmaterial occult agencies. To Cartesians, the assertion that force acted at a distance was equivalent to an appeal to a nonmaterial agency.

Leibniz's system was represented after his death by the natural philosopher Christian von Wolff, whose work was available to German readers within a year of Leibniz's death in 1715. Wolff regarded Descartes's explanations of the physical world as helpful but limited. The Cartesian approach applied to what we see, but it did not relate to the deeper reality Wolff believed lay beneath appearances. For the superficial level of appearances, Wolff was content to embrace Descartes's mechanical interactions to make the appearances intelligible. To explain how force acted, he too rejected the occult agencies of medieval Scholastic thought (and therefore also action at a distance) in favor of forces transmitted only through contact between masses. Like his mentor Leibniz, he described the physical world as a clock designed by God to work perfectly. Wolff emphasized Leibniz's appeal to the principle of sufficient reason, according to which we understand the existence of something when we find the reason for it. Because everything has a sufficient reason, we can use our reason to show that the world has been made perfectly.

The difference between the Leibnizians and the Cartesians emerged at the deeper level of reality's basic components. Leibniz had held that matter was not equivalent to extended space, as Descartes taught, but was made up of unextended points he called monads. Monads were nonmaterial metaphysical entities that resembled souls. They were the *source* of the force; indeed, they were the source of all the activity that accompanied matter. By making a distinction between the source of force and the means by which it was transmitted, Leibnizians were both critical of Newton's action at a distance and of Descartes's banishing of spirit from the natural world.

Newton's cause was taken up abroad by the Dutchman W. J. 'sGravesande (1688–1742), who published an introduction to the philosophy of Newton in 1720. 'sGravesande answered those critics of Newton who asserted that his action at a distance amounted to a return to occult causes by declaring that gravity was not the cause of anything. It was an effect. Gravity was the name we give to the movement of bodies toward one another when left to themselves. According to 'sGravesande, physics should focus its attention on the results of experiments rather than try to devise grand causal explanations. Like other Newtonians in England, he ignored Newton's own attempt to find a cause for gravitational force in the special kind of ethereal substance that Newton made public in the 1717 edition of the *Opticks*. When Newton died in 1727, many who defended his system shunned the question of the cause of gravity, understanding the system to rest simply on Newton's laws of motion and a gravitational force that acted at a distance according to the inverse square law.

The *vis viva* controversy. Over the course of the eighteenth century Cartesians, Leibnizians, and Newtonians became embroiled in a disagreement known as the *vis viva* controversy. It centered on the question of whether force in the universe could be lost—that is, whether the total amount of force in the cosmos could become diminished, in which case the cosmos, left to itself, would run down and eventually come to a standstill. To many this prospect was inconsistent with their understanding of God's creative abilities. But if force was conserved and could not be lost, how was force to be measured?

In his *Principles of Philosophy*, Descartes had asserted that because God was unchangeable, he "conserves the world in the same action with which he created it." Descartes envisioned the universe as he imagined God saw it from the outside—a realm filled with material objects in motion. All this motion, which involved many collisions of matter, constituted the world's action or activity. Descartes felt that God had invested this activity in the world at the Creation and that he held it constant. The constant exchange of motion over time among portions of matter constituted the history of nature itself. Descartes felt that the universe was a machine that would not run down because, in spite of the exchanges, God made sure that no motion was lost. The sum total of all the activity always remained the same because God had given to individual motions of matter the property, as Descartes put it, "of passing from one to the other, according to their different encounters."

But how was one to measure this "action"? Discussion of this problem continued into the eighteenth century and beyond, pitting those who preferred Descartes's measure—something he called the "quantity of motion"—against others who opted for something Leibniz called *vis viva*.

When Descartes asked himself what might be a measure of the quantity of motion, he thought about the force that a piece of matter exerted when it encountered another piece of matter. That, he reasoned, obviously depended on two factors: how big the mass was and how fast it was moving. He concluded that the force of motion could be expressed as the product of mass (m) and velocity (v), and he determined that this was a measure of the quantity of motion.

If we consider just two pieces of matter moving toward each other, we can calculate the force of motion of the first piece (m_1v_1) and also that of the second (m_2v_2). Adding these two amounts, we have the total force of motion of the two ($m_1v_1 + m_2v_2$). Descartes held that, after the collision, this total amount remained the same, although the individual velocities of the two pieces of matter might change. Whatever velocity was given up by one piece of matter was given to the other, so that the total sum of the masses times their velocities remained the same. What happened in the case of just two pieces of matter also happened in every other collision in the universe. The sum total of what Descartes identified as the force of motion remained the same, while the changes in the velocities of individual pieces of matter due to collisions constituted the activity of the universe. For Descartes, God's immutability meant that the total force of motion in the universe was conserved and the universe would run forever.

There are problems with Descartes's claim, the most obvious of which is that it does not work for what are called inelastic collisions. If two equal blobs of clay move directly toward each other at equal velocities, when they collide they do not rebound at the same velocity but stick together, and the motion stops. What happened to the total force of motion in this case? It would appear that it has not been conserved but destroyed. To incorporate situations like this into Descartes's analysis, his follower, Christian Huygens, asserted that it was necessary to specify the direction in which the masses were moving. In other words, the forces of motion of masses moving directly toward each other must be considered opposite in sign.

If in the above case the masses are equal, and if the first mass of clay is assigned a positive force of motion ($+mv$), then the second would have an equal negative force of motion ($-mv$). Adding up the total before and after the collision would give zero in both cases. Had the masses not been clay, but some perfectly elastic substance, then the total force of motion would still have been zero before and after the collision, except that the velocities of the two equal masses would have changed sign as they rebounded from each other. The contrary motions God had put into the universe at its beginning balanced each other in the end.

This improvement made by Huygens, however, still left a major problem. With every inelastic collision there would be less motion in the universe. That would mean that the actual motion in the universe was running down, a result unacceptable to Descartes. He had proposed his idea in order to guarantee that the machinery of the universe would continue to run.

In an article in 1686 entitled "A Brief Demonstration of a Notable Error in Descartes," Leibniz pointed out that Descartes's measure of the force of motion would not, in fact, prevent the universe from running down. He proposed a different measure of the force of motion, something he called *vis viva*, or "living force."

The problem of the running down of the universe was an issue as long as the force of motion was regarded as a signed quantity—one that could be positive or negative. As such one force could destroy another, diminishing the total God had originally invested in his creation. Leibniz proposed that a better measure of the force of motion was proportional to the mass times the square of the velocity (mv^2), which was always a positive quantity. He claimed that in inelastic collisions, like the one involving blobs of clay, the *vis viva* was not destroyed when the pieces of clay stopped moving after collision; rather, the motion was transferred to the particles that made up the clay. So the total motion continued at another level, the amount of *vis viva* in the universe remained the same, and the universe did not run down.

Many people did not accept *vis viva,* if for no other reason than it was too abstract a notion. Nor was Leibniz persuasive with his explanation of why *vis viva* was not lost during inelastic collisions. Among those who came out in favor of *vis viva* as a measure of the force of motion was the Dutch Newtonian, 'sGravesande. His major contribution to the discussion—which resulted from his wish to base conclusions as much as possible on experiments—was to think of measuring the *effect* a moving mass might have, rather than merely the force it might exert. Thinking of the force of a mass in motion as the *effect* (or damage) the mass produced in a collision, as opposed to the *push* exerted during a collision, proved to make a difference.

'sGravesande did a series of experiments in which he dropped masses onto clay and then measured the dents that were made. He varied the heights and the weights of the masses, measuring the various dents produced. He found that the impressions in the clay were the same if, when he used a mass with half the weight of another (although of the same size and shape), he dropped it from twice the height. Descartes, of course, would conclude that, if the dents were the same in the two cases, then the measure of the motion should be mv in both cases. But 'sGravesande showed that because the lesser mass was dropped from a greater height, it hit the clay at a greater speed ($\sqrt{2}v$). He demonstrated that the product of the lesser mass ($\frac{1}{2}m$) and the greater velocity ($\sqrt{2}v$) was not mv, but $\frac{\sqrt{2}}{2}mv$. He concluded therefore that Descartes's measure of the force of motion, mass times velocity, had to be in error.

'sGravesande said the correct measure of the force of motion was $\frac{1}{2}mv^2$. This measure covered both of the preceding cases. In the first case, when the mass was m and the velocity was v, his formula gave $\frac{1}{2}mv^2$. In the second case, when the mass was $\frac{1}{2}m$ and the velocity was $\sqrt{2}v$, the product of one-half the mass times the velocity squared also gave $\frac{1}{2}mv^2$. So for 'sGravesande the measure of the force of motion causing the dent made in the first case *did* equal that causing the dent made in the second. 'sGravesande had shown to his own satisfaction that Leibniz's *vis viva* was a better measure of the force of motion than Descartes's quantity of motion. By siding with Leibniz here, 'sGravesande not only opposed the Cartesians. In this instance he also went against Newton, who did not regard *vis viva* as anything real.

Just as Leibniz had found, 'sGravesande discovered that not everyone immediately agreed with him; in fact, the debate about conservation of quantity of motion and of *vis viva* continued throughout the eighteenth century. The discussion, recall, had been initiated in a theological context having to do with God's preservation of action in the world. With the exception of those who agreed with Newton (who felt that God would step in to correct the universe if it ran down sufficiently), it was important to the participants in the discussion to find an explanation that would prevent the universe from slowly degrading.

The Growth of Newton's Reputation

Newton's work finally came to the attention of a wider public in France through a popular account of its basic conclusions that appeared in 1733. In addition, a number of issues came to the surface after 1730 whose outcomes promoted Newton's reputation as a man ahead of his time. Not only had he seen farther than those who came before him, but in some cases he appeared to have anticipated solutions to problems that arose only after he had departed. The accumulated effect of these developments contributed to the emergence by the latter part of the century of a prominent group of French Newtonian natural philosophers.

Voltaire

The popularization of Newton in France. The introduction of Newton's ideas to many in France occurred in 1733, when François Marie Arouet, who had taken the pen name Voltaire, published his *Philosophical Letters*. The French authorities had imprisoned Voltaire earlier in his career because of satirical things he had written about the French government. When he insulted a powerful nobleman in 1726, he was given the choice of another stint in prison or a period in exile. He chose the latter, living in England for the next three years.

While in England he studied the customs of the English, their form of government, and the ideas of their philosophers, and he was especially drawn to the work of Newton. In his *Letters* he praised Newton, whom he called "this destroyer of the Cartesian system," and went on to present a comparison of Newton's system to that of his countryman Descartes. After declaring that Newton had proven by experiments that Descartes was wrong about the universe being filled everywhere with matter, Voltaire proclaimed that Newton "brings back the vacuum, which Aristotle and Descartes had banished from the world."

In the *Letters* Voltaire carefully explained the role played by gravitational force, "the great spring by which all Nature is moved," reproducing a summary of Newton's proof that the moon and planets are held in their orbit by this force. The reader quickly realized that in Voltaire's view Newton's system was far superior to any other. Along with his preference for Newton, it was clear that Voltaire also preferred English customs, laws, and society to their French counterparts. The message of the book got Voltaire into trouble once more and he again had to leave Paris. He took refuge in the independent province of Lorraine at the chateau of the marquise du Châtelet, a friend he had recently met and with whom he collaborated until her death in 1749.

Du Châtelet also contributed to the popularization of Newton's thought. She collaborated with Voltaire on the publication in 1738 of *Elements of the Philosophy of Newton,* a more complete exposition of the Newtonian system than Voltaire's earlier work. She also completed a translation into French of Newton's *Principia,* which appeared after her death. Although du Châtelet aligned herself with the Newtonian "party," as the growing number of French defenders of Newton called themselves, she was not a slavish follower of Newton. Persuaded of the merits of Leibnizian metaphysics, she also published a book on Leibniz's system in 1740.

The controversy over the shape of the Earth. The question about whether the Earth's shape resembled an egg or a pear provoked a controversy that ended up pitting the systems of Newton and Descartes against each other during the 1740s. Earlier in the century a long-standing project to map the kingdom of France had uncovered discrepancies in the terrestrial lengths of degrees of longitude. The leader of the project repeated the measurements to confirm their accuracy, and announced to the Paris Academy in 1718 that the results meant that the Earth was not spherical, as everyone had assumed, but that it had a slightly elongated shape, something like that of an egg. The problem was that both Newton and the Cartesian Christian Huygens, basing their conclusions on calculations made from their respective systems of mechanics, had much earlier predicted that the Earth should bulge slightly at the equator, like a pear. Initially, the question had been whether to believe the predictions of natural philosophers or a claim that appeared to rest on careful measurement. In the 1730s and 1740s the question became something very different.

Pierre-Louis Moreau de Maupertuis (1698–1759), son of a recently ennobled merchant, went to Paris as a teenager to study philosophy, but soon found his real interest was mathematics. In the early 1720s, while Maupertuis was learning the intricacies of higher mathematics, he became aware that the disagreement about the shape of the Earth bore on theoretical systems he had been studying. In the summer of 1728 he spent twelve weeks in London, where he immersed himself in Newton's work.

Between 1732 and 1736 Maupertuis turned his attention to the question of the shape of the Earth. When it was decided that new expeditions would be sent out to determine once and for all whether the Earth was flattened or elongated at the poles, Maupertuis led the group that traveled to the proximity of the North Pole to make measurements of the distance along a longitudinal line between two established latitudes. Another group went to the equatorial region of Peru to do the same thing. Because the distance between the equator and the North Pole is divided into equal degrees of latitude, any variation in the measured distance between two sets of latitudinal positions would indicate that the Earth was not spherical. A distance less than expected would indicate an elongation, and greater than expected would mean a flattening.

There was no reason why the issue of the Earth's shape had to be regarded as a disagreement between the systems of Descartes and Newton; there were partisans on both sides that made arguments for an Earth flattened at the poles. Nor did most of those arguing about the Earth's shape initially regard it as a test between these two rival systems. But Maupertuis had taken on the role of a crusader for the Newtonian system, on the one hand recruiting younger impressionable academicians to his side, and on the other ridiculing the Cartesians in the Paris Academy.

It was a decade before the expedition to Peru returned with its findings. By then the group that had gone to Lapland with Maupertuis had been back for eight years with measurements that proved consistent with an Earth flattened at the poles. Maupertuis exploited these results to the advantage of his defense of Newton; indeed, his duplicity in the affair earned him numerous enemies, some of whom criticized him for defending a foreign English system over the French system of Descartes. Voltaire also helped polarize the issue by portraying Maupertuis as France's Galileo in his struggle to promote Newton's system in Paris. The upshot of the matter was that the Newtonian party used the incident to make Newton's system appear superior to that of Descartes.

Questioning the inverse square law. Newton's reputation in France also grew because his system survived direct challenges. One such challenge surfaced in the late 1740s when a brilliant young French mathematician announced that Newton's famous inverse square law was incorrect. Alexis Claude Clairaut (1713–1765), son of a Parisian mathematics teacher, was among the gifted young mathematicians who joined the Newtonian party of Voltaire and Maupertuis. Clairaut's challenge to Newton grew out of his interest in another theoretical challenge—what has become known as the three-body problem.

Newton's original consideration of the problem of the moon's motion had considered the gravitational interaction of the Earth and the moon. But if the more general conclusion he had come to in the course of solving that problem was true—namely, that all matter attracts all other matter according to an inverse square law—then an object like the moon would be affected by a large body like the sun at the same time it was being attracted by its much nearer neighbor, the Earth. In fact, there were irregularities in the moon's motion that Clairaut and others hoped to explain by taking the *three* mutually attracting bodies into account. The competition for the first successful solution to this three-body problem extended beyond France into Switzerland.

Clairaut and his competitors were able to write the equations that described the interacting inverse square attractions of the three bodies, but they then determined that solving them directly was impossible. The best Clairaut or anyone else could do was to devise a means of approximating a solution. The differing methods of approximating a solution used by those engaged in the problem all showed the same unexpected result: certain positions the moon was predicted to have based on inverse square attractions of the three bodies were way off from the positions the moon was observed to have. Clairaut concluded that the discrepancy was due to the inverse square law itself—it must not be correct as Newton had stated it ($f \propto 1/r^2$); it should rather have the form $f \propto (1/r^2 + 1/r^4)$. (Because r^4 is a huge number, the correcting factor of $1/r^4$ would be tiny.) His public challenge to the authority of the great Isaac Newton, made in an announcement to the French Academy on November 15, 1747, stirred a pot already boiling about the merits and demerits of the Newtonian system.

It was not long before Clairaut realized that he had made an error in approximating a solution to the Earth-moon-sun problem. In the course of working through the complicated equations he had made a mathematical simplification that seemed harmless, but on closer inspection it proved to make a big difference in the outcome. Clairaut realized that his competitors had also employed the same simplifying assumption and that this explained why they had all come to the same result. When he corrected his mistake, his approximation of how three interacting inverse square forces affected the moon produced results that agreed with the observed positions of the moon. Less than a year and a half after his first dramatic announcement to the French Academy he made a second one: there was no need to correct Newton's inverse square law after all. To Newton's supporters it seemed that the master had known better all along.

Halley's Comet. Newton's reputation received yet another boost during the 1750s from a prediction that had been made a half century earlier by Edmund Halley. Halley had concluded that a comet that had appeared in 1682 had a path similar to comets that had been observed on four previous occasions, the earliest from 1456. He had determined from the similarity of the paths and from the time between appearances that all the observations had been of the same comet and that it would reappear next about 1758. He refused to be precise about the exact date of the next return of the comet because he could not be sure how large planets such as Jupiter and Saturn might affect the path the comet traversed.

Because Clairaut had become the leading expert on the three-body problem, he decided to apply his knowledge of Newtonian mechanics to the problem that Halley could only anticipate. With assistance from a few colleagues, he calculated that the comet would be at its closest point to the sun within thirty days of April 15, 1759. He announced this prediction in the fall of 1758 to the Paris Academy. The comet actually arrived at its closest point two days outside of this thirty-day margin of error, on March 13, but no one considered this an error on Clairaut's account. The appearance of a comet was something even people on the street were interested in. To them, Clairaut's prediction meant that he must understand the motions of heavens better than anyone before him had. Being hailed as a new Newton in the public press now brought undisputed fame to the Frenchman, Clairaut.

Perfecting celestial mechanics. Another irregularity in the moon's motion led to the solidification of support for the Newtonian system among French natural philosophers. The problem also originated in Halley's study of past astronomical events, this time in a paper he had read to the Royal Society in 1693 about the dates of ancient eclipses of the moon. If the machinery of the heavens that Newton had described were run backward, then the position of the moon would not have resulted in an eclipse at those times when eclipses had been recorded. Halley suggested that one way to reconcile the discrepancy was to assume that the moon's orbit had shrunk slightly in the intervening time. As the orbit shrank the moon would revolve at a faster pace around the Earth, thereby decreasing the length of time in a month and providing a means to eliminate the discrepancy mentioned.

The gradual shrinkage in the moon's orbit was in fact confirmed by subsequent observations. While this strengthened Halley's suggested solution to the problem of ancient eclipses, it created another problem: it implied that the Earth-moon system was unstable, that it was running down. Yet another brilliant young French Newtonian took up this problem, this time from the generation after Clairaut. Just before the outbreak of the French Revolution, 38-year-old Pierre Simon Laplace (1749–1827) showed that the planets in the solar system exert a gravitational effect that alters the shape of the Earth's orbit very slightly. As a result of the Earth's changing position with respect to the sun, a corresponding variation in the sun's effect on the moon is introduced. The presence of this set of perturbing factors is so small that it could only be detected over long periods of time.

But did that mean that Laplace had shown the system to be unstable? In fact the opposite was the case. Laplace demonstrated that after many years the factors that caused the moon's orbit to shrink would begin to move it in the opposite direction. The moon's orbit underwent an oscillation in and out, one cycle of which took thousands of years. Newton's universe was stable after all. It would not run down. From this and his other work on Newtonian celestial mechanics, Laplace imagined a determined system of the world, of which we would have perfect knowledge if we could but know "the state of all phenomena at a given instant, the laws to which matter is subjected, and their consequences at the end of any given time." Others might think it presumptuous and arrogant to speak with such boldness. To Laplace it was simply the perfecting of what Newton had begun.

◎ An Expanding Cosmos ◎

As we learned in Chapter 2, the notion that God may have created other worlds was long a theological concern. This historical reference to other worlds referred specifically to heavenly homes for living beings. With the growing consensus among natural philosophers of the seventeenth century that Copernicus had corrected an ancient error about the structure of the cosmos, interest in this specific theological issue increased. Natural philosophers weighed in on the implications for theology of life elsewhere.

Other Worlds

Over the course of the eighteenth century speculation about life elsewhere in the universe continued unabated. There were those who objected to the general enthusiasm in favor of pluralism, as historians have dubbed belief in the existence of other inhabited worlds. The philosopher David Hume based his skepticism on rational analysis. But most of those who objected did so mainly for theological reasons, the primary one of which centered on the meaning of Christ's death on the cross. If there were millions of worlds similar to the one in which we live, then why would God give his son for this one?

By far, however, writers in the eighteenth century—whether concerned with theological or philosophical issues—readily accepted the existence of life beyond Earth. They established a consensus of opinion that blurred the lines that otherwise divided religiously minded individuals from each other or that separated religious thinkers from more secular thinkers. It was a consensus that would enjoy remarkable staying power.

The rise of the new science had an impact on theological practice beyond merely stimulating interest in the specific question of extraterrestrial life. It also raised the status of natural theology, a branch of theology that had not previously enjoyed prominence. Reasoning in natural theology did not commence with the truths of a

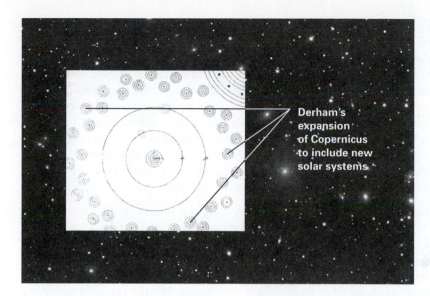

Derham's Solar Systems in *Astro-Theology*

Derham's expansion of Copernicus to include new solar systems

divine revelation, as in other branches of theology. The natural theologian began instead with the knowledge of nature. On the basis of evidence of intentional design uncovered in the natural world, natural theologians reasoned to the existence of a divine designer. The development of works of natural theology was not confined to individuals formally trained in theology. Many natural philosophers were delighted that their pursuit of the new science was not only compatible with their personal belief in God, but provided impressive new forms of the argument from design—that it was possible to infer the existence of a designer from evidence of design in nature.

Among the early works of natural theology devoted to the plurality of worlds was William Derham's *Astro-Theology*. Derham was an Anglican clergyman who became chaplain to the Prince of Wales in 1715, the year his *Astro-Theology* appeared. He wrote the book as a companion to his *Physico-Theology* of 1713, in which his natural theological argument centered on knowledge of terrestrial nature. Both of his works were enormously popular in Britain throughout the eighteenth century, running to fourteen English and six German editions by 1777. In the *Astro-Theology* he used Newton's work on astronomy not only to justify a Copernican arrangement of the planets around our sun, but also to infer what he called a new system that went beyond the Copernican. Derham argued that "there are many other Systemes of Suns and Planets, besides that in which we have our residence; namely, that every Fixt Star is a sun and encompassed with a Systeme of Planets." What made Derham confident that so many solar systems existed was that they were "worthy of an infinite Creator."

Nebular Hypotheses

Observers of the heavens, even before the invention of the telescope, had identified more than just stars and planets. Some of the lights in the heavens appeared as luminous cloudy patches, which could be mistaken for comets until the observer noticed that the patches retained their position just as stars did. Ptolemy recorded seven such objects, Tycho Brahe six. Included in the 1690 star catalog of the Polish observer Johannes Hevelius were sixteen "nebulous stars." Others compiled lists of such nebulae prior to 1750, but it was not until the second half of the century that they became the focus of attention as possible island universes of their own.

In speculations from the time, the concept of nebulae had two distinct meanings. Writers referred to nebulae as the distant luminous patches in the sky that, if seen from the proximity we have to our own Milky Way, appear as a cloudy film. Nebulae in this sense denoted systems of stars. Another meaning concerned the matter of the primitive universe, understood as having been distributed in a thin homogeneous fluid. Although different from each other, both meanings contributed to the speculations that ultimately became known as nebular hypotheses.

Kant's natural history of the heavens.   Among the most famous names in the history of Western philosophy, Immanuel Kant's ranks at or near the very top. His philosophical contributions, which are treated in Chapter 14, derive from work done primarily during the last half of his adult life. As a young man he was interested in natural science. He studied the systems of both Wolff and Newton at the university in Königsberg, where he later taught. As a young man of thirty-one, he wrote the *Universal Natural History and Theory of the Heavens,* published in 1755. It contained his ideas about cosmology, the theory of the heavens, and cosmogony, an account of the origin and development of the universe. In both enterprises Kant used Newton's principles, which he invoked in the subtitle of his work, as a starting point for his reasoning. But Kant went beyond what Newton was willing to consider. He suggested that there were systems of stars (systems of systems) that rotated around a central mass. Our Milky Way, he contended, was one such massive system whose orbital motion prevents it from collapsing into its center. According to Kant, nebulae were other "Milky Ways," each presumably containing systems of stars with their planets.

The cosmogony in the second part of the work utilized natural laws more than it did a Creator to explain how such massive systems had originated. Nebulous matter diffusely distributed in an infinite universe gradually coalesced into dense masses as a result of gravitational force, first into rings and then into spheres. Kant thought he could account for the rotational motion that commenced around the primitive centers of gravitational force by introducing repulsive forces acting between particles of mass. This same process occurred at various levels, first in planets that ended up revolving around central suns, next in suns rotating around their own massive centers, and finally in other "Milky Ways" rotating around the center of the universe itself. Although he did not explain how an infinite universe could have a center, he imagined that the formation of "worlds without number and without end" had begun near this center and spread out as the order introduced by gravitational force gradually conquered the chaos of diffuse matter. He referred to the "mountains of millions of centuries" that it would take for the formation of worlds to reach perfection. While he conceded that God was the ultimate explanation for the existence of order that conquered chaos, his interest was primarily in explaining how that order worked.

Laplace's nebular hypothesis and the solar system.   Another cosmogony of the second half of the eighteenth century appeared in 1796. It was written by Pierre Laplace barely a decade after his dramatic demonstration that the solar system was

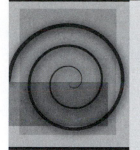

Was Newton Right About Hypotheses?

The NATURE
of SCIENCE

Newton's famous claim, "I feign no hypotheses" (see Chapter 8), served as a justification for many in the late-eighteenth century to refuse to engage in speculation, as if natural philosophy should content itself only with facts. The prize competitions of numerous scientific societies from this time, for example, specified that acceptable answers should confine themselves to matters of fact alone.

Natural science relies on careful empirical observation and experimentation, but it often also requires creative imagination to formulate theories that in turn suggest new ideas. As is evident in this section, even during a time when speculation was widely frowned on, leading natural philosophers willingly constructed hypotheses to explain how the cosmos had come about. Newton's claim may have been invoked by some in this time to justify their anti-hypothetical viewpoints, but in so doing they took his public statement out of context. As we have seen, Newton did speculate about numerous matters on many occasions.

not running down. Laplace restricted his attention to the origin of the solar system, rather than the entire universe, but its more limited context did nothing to diminish the grandiose implications of his conclusions.

By the time Laplace had formulated his hypothesis the astronomer William Herschel had already used powerful new telescopes to confirm the presence of hundreds of new nebulae in the heavens. They appeared as structureless masses of a finely distributed substance, some of which displayed apparent condensation in the center. Laplace inferred that they represented various stages in the formation of planetary systems and reasoned that our own solar system had originated from a similar process. In his book, entitled *An Exposition of the System of the World,* he postulated a rotating, primitive nebulous solar fluid that contracted as a result of gravitational force into a central mass surrounded by smaller revolving masses.

Laplace argued that the origin of our solar system from a rotating nebula explained why all the planets and known satellites revolved around the sun in the same direction and why they were all in planes only slightly inclined to each other. Newton had used this same coincidence of circumstances to argue that the solar system had originated from the direct intention of God. Laplace, too, believed in God, but he did not believe that God's presence was required to supervise the workings of the cosmos. According to an account that originated in the middle of the nineteenth century, when Napoleon asked him where God appeared in his system of the world, Laplace replied: "Sire, I have no need of that hypothesis."

◎ The Earth as a Cosmic Body ◎

It has been said that some of the natural philosophers of the eighteenth century wanted Newton's physics without Newton's God. More and more they preferred Leibniz's God, who created laws that made the universe run by itself, to Newton's repairman God. In 1692 Richard Bentley defended his friend Newton's position against what he called *deism,* a term that has come to characterize the belief that God was necessary to create the physical and moral world orders, but not to superintend them. The embrace of both Newton's physics and deism in the second half of the eighteenth century by many French natural philosophers confirmed that it was indeed possible to separate Newton's description of how the heavens worked from religious views about their origin and governance.

Causal Theories of the Earth

Buffeted about by the impersonal forces of gravitational attraction, the Earth at the midpoint of the eighteenth century no longer enjoyed anything close to the exalted position it had once held in God's Creation. The Earth was not exempt from the laws astronomers used to understand heavenly bodies. It was inevitable that the same attitude that led some natural philosophers to explain naturalistically how the heavens originated would lead others to consider how the Earth came to be as a result of the operations of natural laws.

To the average person the Bible was clear about how long God's creative activity had taken—seven days. Furthermore, the Bible provided clues about the duration of history. A seventeenth-century English scholar, Archbishop James Ussher, had used his extensive biblical knowledge of the genealogies of Adam's lineage to determine the date of Adam's creation. Ussher's calculation of 4004 B.C. as the date of the creation of the universe confirmed the impression of most that the universe and the Earth were approximately six thousand years old.

But as early as the seventeenth century natural philosophers had supplemented the biblical record with what became known as theories of the Earth—conjectures about the *causal means* God might have used. In the earliest of these theories of the Earth the physical causes and mechanisms identified did not challenge the Genesis chronology; on the contrary, the older theories of the Earth used the new science to support it. That would change in the eighteenth century.

The *Telliamed* of Benoît de Maillet.   Sometime between 1692 and 1718 France's ambassador to Egypt, Benoît de Maillet (1656–1738), composed what he called "a new system on the diminution of the waters of the sea." It was an attempt to explain what had caused the Earth and life to develop as they had. By the time the manuscript reached the public in 1748, de Maillet had been dead for ten years. He had certainly intended to see the work published during his lifetime, but unfortunate delays had frustrated his plan.

De Maillet had traveled widely in the Mediterranean, taking with him an intense curiosity about the features of the Earth's surface in the regions he visited. He did not limit his interest in the Mediterranean area to its geography. He mastered Arabic, read the histories of Arabic writers, and became familiar with historical landmarks. His travels exposed him to cultures whose understanding of history, including the history of the Earth, was very different from that of Christian France. He determined that he would incorporate this broader perspective into his new system.

De Maillet's grandfather had become convinced that the sea was diminishing, through observations he had made of the seashore near the family home. From his grandfather's observations and from knowledge he acquired on his travels, he composed

Telliamed (which was de Maillet's name spelled backward). De Maillet knew his manuscript would test the limits of acceptability, so he tried at the outset to deflect criticism by attributing the views expressed in the book to a pagan foreigner. The subtitle declared that the work consisted of conversations between a French missionary and a philosopher from India named Telliamed about the formation of the Earth being due to the diminution of the sea. De Maillet utilized mechanical interactions of vortices together with his own observations to create a specifically non-Christian cosmogony.

From the alleged Indian understanding of the Earth's past the French missionary learned that the Earth was originally covered with water, whose currents carved out the mountains beneath its surface. The depths of the primitive seas gradually decreased, exposing the highest mountains, which immediately began to wear away. Eroded material from the shore settled onto the ocean floor as sedimentary rock, which, as the sea level continued to drop, was exposed as new mountains. As the process of diminution continued, more dry land emerged and on it, life began.

Telliamed himself did not invoke the direct act of God to explain the successive appearances of animal life. He did not give details, but he maintained that various forms of aquatic animals had changed during the time the sea was gradually receding in accordance with natural process. Air above the seashore was so moist "that it must be considered an almost equal mixture of air and water," breathable, for example, by flying fish. While escaping a predator or having been thrown onto the land by the waves, such fish found their features altered. "The little wings which they had under their belly, and which like their fins helped them to walk on the sea bottom, became feet and served them to walk on land."

Clearly such processes had taken a great deal of time, far longer than six thousand years. Telliamed in fact estimated from structures in ancient Carthage that the rate the sea level had dropped from earlier times to his day was three feet every thousand years. Using this rate he concluded that over two billion years had passed since the primitive waters had begun to recede. Humans themselves were over 500,000 years old!

The public immediately saw through De Maillet's tactic of camouflaging his ideas in a pagan philosophy. The reaction was outrage. But retribution could not be exacted on de Maillet, who was long dead. Another writer who speculated publicly that same year had no such refuge.

From *Natural History* to *Epochs of Creation*.   Although Georges-Louis Leclerc (1707–1788) was born into aristocracy, the name by which he has become known to history—Buffon—was given him by King Louis XV of France in 1773 for what he had achieved during his lifetime. The king bestowed on him the title Comte de Buffon (based on the name of an estate he inherited from his mother when he was twenty-five), because of his extensive accomplishments as a natural philosopher. Buffon is remembered for his monumental *Natural History,* a multivolume work about the living world that even nonspecialists could understand. The first three volumes were published in 1749.

In the first volume Buffon included a history of the Earth because, he said, it was "the history of nature in its most ample extent." It became immediately clear that Buffon believed the Earth was extremely old; he announced that the more recent changes of the previous few thousand years were insignificant compared with those that occurred in the ages following the Creation. Because Buffon viewed the Earth as just one of the planets, its history was tied to that of our solar system.

Readers of the first volume of Buffon's *Natural History* encountered an intriguing idea of how the Earth originated. Buffon explained what caused all of the planets to circle the sun in the same direction and within the same plane: a comet had struck the sun at an oblique angle, knocking off huge pieces of mass that settled into orbits at various distances away and then began to cool. To justify his idea that a comet might have struck the sun he invoked the authority of "the great Newton," who had suggested that comets occasionally collided into the sun and refueled the sun's power. Buffon concluded that as it cooled, the Earth became covered with water from the condensing atmosphere. Tidal motions of this primitive universal sea carved out mountains and valleys beneath the surface. He was reluctant to say how dry land came about as time passed, although he did make reference to likely violent revolutions.

Some reviewers of Buffon's work immediately noted that his explanation of the origin of the Earth was incompatible with that given in the book of Genesis. In the biblical account the Earth was created *before* the sun, moon, and stars, which did not appear until the fourth day of creation. One reviewer, who regarded Buffon's work as outlandish heresy, noted that it required a world "far older than Moses made it out to be." Buffon had not said exactly how old, but the reviewer asked whether there really was any difference between Buffon's view and that of authors who believed the world was eternal.

Early in January of 1751 the faculty of theology at the Sorbonne in Paris notified Buffon of some fourteen propositions from the first three volumes of the *Natural History* that they regarded as reprehensible. Among these were Buffon's speculations on the Earth's fiery origin. In order to avoid censure, Buffon published a retraction in the fourth volume of his *Natural History*, which came out in 1753.

It is clear from his continuing work that Buffon's recantation was not genuine. He knew about recently published measurements of the heat in mines and hot springs that had been made in order to support the claim that the center of the Earth was hot. He also knew of Newton's estimation that an iron sphere the size of the Earth would take more than 50,000 years to cool from red hot to the temperature of air. Buffon set out in the coming years to conduct his own experiments on the rates of cooling for various substances that make up the Earth. He published his results in a book on minerals in 1774 in which he inferred—he thought conservatively—that it had taken almost 75,000 years for the Earth to cool to its present temperature and over 33,000 years to cool to the point when organic life could begin.

Four years later, in 1778, he brought his conclusions to widespread attention in a book that came to be regarded as a classic of French prose, the *Epochs of Creation*. By this time the so-called Age of Enlightenment, marked by the appearance of numerous ideas that challenged tradition, was in full sway (see Chapter 14). The threat of censure was no longer as immediate as it had been at mid-century, nor was Buffon the only one considering a prolonged age for the cosmos and the Earth. For all that, it was Buffon's *Epochs* that more than any other work introduced to the reading public the notion of an extended period of history, prior to human history, in which no life had existed. That is not to say that he was generally persuasive. Most people in Europe remained convinced that history coincided with human history.

Buffon repeated his theory of the comet striking the sun, splitting off matter that congealed into hot fluid masses circling the sun. He closed this first epoch of creation, which took 2,936 years, at the point when the cooling process had produced a solid Earth that had lost its incandescence. In the next epoch the cooling Earth continued to contract, producing mountains and subterranean cavities over the next 30,000 years. The cooling now condensed the water vapor of the atmosphere in a third epoch, causing torrential rains that covered all but the highest peaks with water. Over the next 20,000 years the first life, shellfish and plants, emerged and thrived in this primitive universal sea. Volcanic activity marked the fourth epoch, a relatively short time of about 7,000 years, opening routes for the water to recede into the Earth and for the appearance of dry land. Animal and plant life appeared on land near the cooler polar regions during the fifth epoch, which lasted another 5,000 years. During the sixth epoch, which lasted the same length of time as the fifth, life migrated toward the tropical regions and the continents began to separate. Some 70,000 years had passed by the dawn of the seventh and final epoch, in which humans appeared.

A Scottish theory of the Earth. Seven years after Buffon's *Epochs of Creation* appeared in France, James Hutton (1726–1797) communicated to the Royal Society of Scotland his ideas about the Earth's past. This paper appeared in the Society's *Transactions* in 1788, although a longer two-volume work appeared in 1795 under the title *Theory of the Earth, or an Investigation of the Laws Observable in the Composition, Dissolution and Restoration of Land upon the Globe*. Hutton rented out the farmland he had inherited from his father and was able to retire to Edinburgh, where he compiled his reflections about the cause of the Earth's development.

Hutton's understanding of the Earth began with two assumptions that colored his conclusions. First, he believed that the Earth had evidently been made for humankind. For example, a completely solid Earth would not be habitable because plant life requires soil, and humans depend on plant life. It was not accidental that natural forces had broken up the surface of the hard, solid Earth so that it could support life. The second assumption was that the action of nature's forces was not sudden and dramatic, but, as Hutton put it, "the operations of nature are equable and steady." To wear down rock into soil, which was then carried by moving water to the sea, required an enormous amount of time. Hutton observed that "the course of nature cannot be limited by time."

Hutton asked what agency had caused strata of rock, especially those that appeared porous, to form at the bottom of the sea. After much consideration he rejected the possibility that they had been precipitated out of the water, embracing rather the idea that they could only have been fused by the action of subterranean heat. Hutton next asked how materials that collected at the bottom of the sea were raised above its surface and transformed into continents of solid land. Once again he concluded that this had not occurred by the receding waters of the sea, but by the same action that fused the strata—a deep subterranean heat. The continuous action of heat explained how and why the Earth's surface had changed.

The final section of his paper was where Hutton introduced his most unusual claim. He believed that the development of the Earth as he had described it was just a part of a larger, more general process. He thought that, by asking about the state of the Earth *before* the present land appeared above the surface of the waters, he could acquire some knowledge of the larger system that governed the world. He asked, for example, where the materials at the bottom of the sea, fused by heat into the strata he had identified, had come from. Some of the strata were composed of the fused remains of marine organisms. But where had *they* come from?

Hutton could only conclude that there had been a phase of development prior to the one he had described. He even allowed that plant life had flourished on land during this phase; indeed, he asserted that cycles of decay and renovation constituted nature's means of sustaining plant and animal life according to a wisdom that had been in operation for indefinite successions of ages. Hutton may have been convinced that his scheme reinforced the central role life played in nature, but he convinced no more people than Buffon had that the age of the Earth went back indefinitely. Few found any comfort at all in the famous declaration that ended Hutton's treatise: "The result, therefore, of our present enquiry is, that we find no vestige of a beginning,—no prospect of an end."

Hutton differed from Buffon and de Maillet in his concern to demonstrate, through geological phenomena, the presence of a divine plan governing terrestrial processes. Other deists from his time argued that the time scale for geological change could not be constrained by traditional interpretations of Genesis. Hutton agreed, because of the immensely slow pace at which he believed the forces of heat acted. But Hutton differed in his emphasis on the purpose behind the divine plan, one that accommodated the interests of plants and animals. The reason why there were volcanoes was to raise strata so that rivers could break rocks into soil for living organisms. Hutton's work stood as an example of how deism compared with natural theology, in which the knowledge of nature supplied a basis for inferring God's control over nature. For Hutton the prolonged time scale of Earth's past revealed intelligent design.

Mineralogy and Earth History

As noted, the eighteenth-century theories of the Earth, with their emphasis on causal law, stood in a tradition that reached back into the seventeenth century. The search for the causal agency that had molded the Earth according to some grand natural law, however, was not the only means of access to an understanding of the Earth's past. Paralleling these theories of the Earth was another approach, also with roots in the early modern period, in which the starting point was the composition of the Earth's minerals. Minerals traditionally included four classes: "earths" (including rocks), metals, salts, and sulfurs. Scholars gathered information about these various forms of solid materials found on Earth and then, in light of the data assembled, suggested how such diversity might have come about. Here the emphasis was on the description of the development of the Earth from its beginnings to the present in all its complexity, without reference to a single unifying causal law.

The German mineralogical tradition. This treatment of the history of the Earth was common in the German states, where the presence of rich deposits of ore drew primary attention to metals and accounted for the long-established mining tradition in regions such as the Erz Mountains of Saxony. Mining officials wanted practical information about the location and properties of such valuable metals as lead, copper, and silver. In an earlier period, state-appointed officials drew on individuals trained in the universities to oversee the acquisition of mineralogical knowledge, but in the eighteenth century they established separate technical schools for the purpose of training the officials they required. As a result, the German approach to mineralogy expanded beyond a primary interest in metals.

German mineralogists of the eighteenth century began to subject rocks, previously regarded as mere conglomerations of individual minerals not worthy of study in their own right, to classification. They categorized rocks according to the effect heat had on them (the "dry way"), the purest rock being that whose mineral content remained unaltered even by intense heat. They began to gather more information than just the mineral content of the rocks; for example, they recorded such things as the elevation of rocks, their fossil content, their contour, and they listed impressions about the age and mode of origin of the rocks as well.

For "earths" other than rocks mineralogists preferred the "wet way," which could run in two directions. They could test the solubility in water of minerals with names like magnesia and baryte, or they could precipitate out the mineral contents of waters from hot springs and health spas. Chemists, who were also interested in earths, contributed their understanding of the interactions of earths with acids and bases. From numerous investigations experimenters differentiated a whole range of earths based on their solubility.

Where the history of the Earth was concerned there was widespread acceptance among eighteenth-century mineralogists that the original ocean referred to in Genesis had been a thick gelatinous aqueous fluid made up of minerals in solution, and that rocks and most other solid minerals formed over time by a process of consolidation. There were various explanations of exactly how the consolidation of rocks occurred, but the end result was that rocks began to form and were laid down under the primal ocean. The oldest rocks, which formed the Earth's core, were therefore almost the same age as the Earth itself. On top of these primal rocks came others, whose diverse properties reflected the variations in the contents of the primitive ocean waters at different locations. Eventually the primitive waters diminished, at least in part due to evaporation, and the rocks were exposed to air. The variation in position that rocks now displayed as exposed land was a reflection of the effect that underwater motion—sometimes chaotic and sometimes calm—had on the pattern of their consolidation.

Abraham Werner and the Freiberg School. The most influential figure in the history of geology from the late eighteenth century was Abraham Werner (1749–1817), who studied and later taught at the mining academy in Freiberg. Werner inherited the general ideas described in the preceding section from his predecessors and he openly acknowledged his debt to them. Although he published little, his powerful influence on his contemporaries and on a succeeding generation of scholars on the Continent and in Britain came from his considerable abilities as a teacher and from the new system he created. As a result, his influence extended well beyond Saxony and lasted into the third decade of the next century.

Werner's greatest contribution was to articulate that the period during which rocks were formed, rather than their mineralogy, was their most important feature. He gave to geology the historical entities that he called formations, which were rocks that had been produced in the same period. Werner focused on the variety of information mineralogists had begun to gather about rocks. Unlike his predecessors, who relied only on mineral content when classifying rocks, his goal was to develop a systematic knowledge of all the data gathered about individual regions in order to determine when and how their rocks had been laid down. He called his new approach geognosy, based on the Greek word for abstract knowledge, to emphasize the intellectual reasoning needed to put together the results of careful and widespread observation.

In Werner's account of the Earth's history, the oldest rocks from the calm waters of the primeval ocean, many of which were crystalline but also included metals, consolidated in successive individual formations to form a "primitive class." Next came a small class of formations he called transition rocks, some of which had formed in turbulent waters. The third class of formations he called stratified rocks; some of these resulted from mechanical pressure while others consolidated by chemical means. The final class of formations, called the recent class, came from eroded material deposited by moving water and from the extruded material of volcanoes.

Contrary to a widespread impression, Werner did not appeal to sudden and dramatic events to explain how the Earth had developed; rather, like Hutton, he held that the processes going on in the present were the same as those in the past. For example, he believed that the primeval ocean had gradually retreated over time and that there was evidence to indicate that the retreat had occasionally reversed itself. Werner preferred not to endorse speculations about where the retreating water had gone. He believed it was sufficiently clear that the waters *had* retreated and that speculating about the cause was relatively unimportant. However, late in his life he invoked the new knowledge that water was composed of gases to suggest that primal waters had decomposed when forming the atmosphere.

At the close of the eighteenth century Werner joined others who were willing to extend the history of the Earth far beyond the six thousand years inferred from a literal reading of the Old Testament. Once again, his preference was not to speculate about matters that did not easily lend themselves to precise determination. The most he would concede was an oblique reference to a time "when the waters, perhaps a million years ago, completely covered the earth." As the century came to a close, then, there was ample indication that natural philosophers had begun to accept the Earth as a cosmic body whose past had been shaped by natural processes that they were responsible to identify and comprehend.

Suggestions for Reading

Michael Crowe, *The Extraterrestrial Life Debate, 1750–1900* (New York: Dover Publications, 1999).

Thomas Hankins, *Science and the Enlightenment* (Cambridge: Cambridge University Press, 1985).

Rachel Laudan, *From Mineralology to Geology* (Chicago: University of Chicago Press, 1994).

Mary Terrall, *The Man Who Flattened the Earth: Maupertuis and the Sciences in the Enlightenment* (Chicago: University of Chicago Press, 2006).

CHAPTER 10

---◎---

The Emergence
of Chemical Science

Although chemical science was a product of the eighteenth century, references to "chymistrie" began to emerge early in the seventeenth century. In a 1605 translation of a Latin work devoted to the maintenance of health, for example, the author referred to "those philosophers which have written of chymistrie." This of course tells us nothing about what the term meant. It soon becomes clear that in the seventeenth century there was no clean separation of chemistry from alchemy. By the 1650s, for example, in a work with the wonderful title *Mag-astro-mancer; or the Magicall-Astrologicall Diviner Posed and Puzzled* (1652), there was no doubt that at least some people viewed chemistry with the same suspicion that often plagued alchemy. Chemistry was "a kinde of præstigious, covetous, cheating magick." Another author writing in the 1650s associated the sinful sons of Adam with "the devil's chymistry."

The existence of separate terms for chemistry and alchemy signals that the two enterprises, however much related and however often confused with each other, were not identical endeavors. "Chymistry" was the more inclusive term. That is, chemists early on shared the alchemist's search for the philosopher's stone by which they could transmute one substance into another and for a medicine that would produce immortality. But chemists also sought other more mundane knowledge about how substances combined.

◎ "Chymistry" in the Seventeenth Century ◎

The four basic elements originally identified by Empedocles and adopted by Plato and Aristotle—earth, air, fire, and water—were still accepted by many natural philosophers of the seventeenth century. In addition to the elements, however, there were other theories of matter. There was a tradition of identifying material

principles—basic characteristics of various forms of matter that natural philosophers had noticed. Medieval natural philosophers referred to two such principles.
Substances that were volatile, for instance, were said to be mercurial, or to possess
the principle of mercury. Combustible matter was sulfurous—it possessed the principle of sulfur. In the sixteenth century Paracelsus added a third principle—that of
salt, or incombustibility. In the seventeenth century, then, some natural philosophers preferred to think about matter in terms of the four elements, some in terms
of the two or three material principles, and some in terms of still other combinations of elements and principles.

The Changing Status of Chemistry

An important development of the seventeenth century was the expansion of chemistry as a field. This occurred even though chemistry did not have a regular place in
the curriculum of the universities. Chemistry in the seventeenth century still lacked
the solid intellectual and theoretical foundation required of university subjects.
Like alchemy, chemistry was associated with the practical skills of the craftsman. Just
as the alchemical task of trying to change base metals into gold demanded a hands-
on knowledge of procedures that could only be gotten through long experience with
furnaces, retorts, and other apparatus, so too did many of the interests of chemists
require practical knowledge. Chemists were involved in activities such as the development of new medicines, the removal of impurities from metals, and the processes
of brewing and distilling. Such doings were traditionally the concern of people
trying to make a livelihood, not those who were well-to-do. As a result of their service
to the craft tradition, chemists suffered a low social status.

Over the course of the seventeenth century there were more and more figures
who, like Boyle and Newton, tried to bring a theoretical dimension to the study
of both chemistry and alchemy. The challenge was greater where alchemy was
concerned because it had such a close proximity to unethical individuals who had
little or no interest in the theory of alchemy. Such people were often enough unprin-
cipled charlatans, who were solely out to exploit the subject for the profit it could
bring, even if that required them to make deceitful promises of secret knowledge
that could make their patrons rich.

The effort to improve the respectability of chemistry was more successful.
Some, including the humanist physician and school inspector Andreas Libavius
(ca. 1550–1616) from Saxony, overtly denounced secrecy and tried to bring the
discussion of chemical prescriptions into the open. In his textbook on chemistry,
the first of several to appear during the seventeenth century, he argued that the
appropriate place to conduct experiments with a furnace and chemical apparatus
was in the house where the chemist lived—an early example of the emergence of
the chemical laboratory. Libavius wished the chemist, as he said, "to bring luster to
his profession by an upright household."

Another indication of the changing status of chemistry was the establishment
of several teaching positions in the discipline. The first was at the University of
Marburg in Germany in 1609, when Count Moritz of Hesse-Kassel appointed his

personal physician, Johannes Hartmann (1568–1631), to the chair of "Chymia-trie." Hartmann was primarily interested in chemistry as it related to the prepara-tion of medicines. He began a tradition in pharmacy at Marburg of which the university is proud to this day. Over the course of the century numerous other universities in Germany, France, England, and the Netherlands established courses in chemistry.

Chemistry also acquired visibility outside the university setting. Guy de la Brosse (1586–1641), apothecary to Louis XIII of France, helped persuade the king to set up the Jardin des Plantes, a garden of medicinal plants, in 1626. In his book of 1628, *On the Nature, Virtue, and Use of Plants,* he included a lengthy discussion of chemistry. He thus helped pave the way for a professorship of chemistry to be set up in the seventeenth century at the Jardin des Plantes. Further, when the Royal Academy of Sciences was created in Paris in 1666, chemistry was a major activity from the start. In virtually all of these institutional contexts chemistry continued to be closely linked to pharmacy, from which it would not be separated until the middle of the following century.

The Influence of Joachim Becher

Although the colorful and fascinating German medical professor Johann Joachim Becher (1635–1682) has become known primarily for his involvement with alchemy, he played a much larger role than that in the seventeenth century. His work proved to be important for the future of the new natural science in general and for chemistry in particular. Becher was able to use his position as a professor to capture the attention of patrons through his carefully worded promises of wealth. He found a way to exploit the outlooks of the craftsman and the merchant as he successfully convinced those with high social status that it was worth their time to consider matters they normally would have regarded as far beneath their dignity.

In a world that was changing from the older feudal order to a more commodity-driven society, princes found themselves strapped for money. They were open to Becher's presentation of extremely creative schemes that would make them money through the production of wares. Of course, one of the commodities Becher prom-ised was gold itself, which he hoped to obtain through transmutation.

He also enticed the princes with various other wonders of the natural world, always with the lesson that nature was productive and therefore the source of great wealth. Becher argued that we need to know how to get nature to produce for us, or to teach us ways of producing profitable commodities for ourselves. Becher developed his ideas into a comprehensive theory of economy similar to what has become known as mercantilism and he attempted to convince his contemporaries of its merit. Its basic tenet was to increase wealth by producing and exporting more commodities than were imported, and therefore to amass a greater store of bullion than other countries possessed.

Becher is also known for a work called *Subterranean Physics* (1669), in which he tried to treat chemistry from the point of view of general natural science. One par-ticular idea in this work that proved to be influential in chemistry arose from

Becher's matter theory. He accepted only two of the four elements of antiquity: water and earth. He did not regard earth as one single element; there were, he said, three different kinds of elemental earth. These "earths" appear to have been based on the three Paracelsan principles of mercury, sulfur, and salt. One of them, *terra pinguis,* or "oily earth," Becher believed was the constituent present in all substances that could be burned. It was this notion that caught the eye of one of his countrymen, who subsequently built upon it to form a new theory of combustion that dominated much of eighteenth-century chemical thought.

◎ German Rational Chemistry ◎

As we have noted, there were those as early as the seventeenth century who had begun to criticize the secret pursuit of natural knowledge. With the new century came a growing appreciation of the achievements of the new science and new attitudes about the power of reason. The study of matter and its transformations experienced a mounting trend toward separating chemistry from alchemy and imparting a new status to the work of the chemists. This was done by representing chemistry as an open and rational science in opposition to the secret and questionable procedures of alchemy.

To accomplish this, chemists had to meet a two-fold challenge. First, they had to develop a theoretical foundation for the science of chemistry that would enable it to be viewed as an intellectual enterprise, worthy of the attention of educated people. Due to the work of men such as Andreas Libavius in Germany, Guy de la Brosse in France, and Robert Boyle and Isaac Newton in England, this process was well underway before the end of the seventeenth century. Chemists also had to impart a new importance to the laboratory experimentation that had always associated them with craftsmen. Thanks in part to the value that such famous men as Galileo and Newton gave to experimentation in general, it became easier for chemists to portray their laboratory work as intellectually meritorious.

Georg Stahl's Reform of Chemistry

A central figure of early eighteenth-century chemistry is the Halle University professor of medicine, Georg Stahl (1660–1734). Stahl became the court physician to the dukes of Weimar, then later received a similar appointment to the court in Berlin under Friedrich Wilhelm I. He was a devoutly religious man who was convinced that the practice of medicine must take into account the state of the soul, whose condition he believed profoundly influenced health and disease.

The critique of alchemy. Stahl's personal moral commitment turned him against the practice of alchemy and led him to write a biting critique of it. He conceded that the words *chemistry* and *alchemy* had long been used interchangeably, but that they had come to represent completely different enterprises. Chemistry, in his view, was a rational science, while alchemy was not.

Stahl identified alchemy as the mainly confused and largely vain attempt to make gold. It was not that Stahl rejected the possibility that one element could be transmuted into another or, for that matter, that a base metal could be transmuted into a more noble one. As a chemist he allowed that transmutation was among the changes substances underwent. What Stahl objected to were the temptations to immorality that plagued those who engaged in alchemical experimentation.

For the most part, Stahl declared, alchemists had blown things out of all propor-tion by focusing solely on transmutation, an emphasis that inevitably encouraged swindling. It was no wonder that so many alchemists had acquired suspicious rep-utations. Further, by enticing weak individuals to quick riches, the practice of alchemy diverted them from their obligations to God. As almost an afterthought, Stahl criticized the alchemical tradition for not producing a cadre of teachers, something that was of course incompatible with the alchemists' secrecy, another trait of the practice that Stahl could not condone.

Rational chemistry. Stahl had already developed his interest in chemistry as a youth and he did not relinquish it after he became a physician. What he recom-mended was something he called *rational* or *true* chemistry. He employed these two terms in something of a circular fashion; that is, he used one term to define the other. But while he never defined the words precisely, it was clear what his goal was in using them. Stahl did not want to dissociate himself from experimentation or even to disparage the craft tradition with which it was associated, but he did wish to impart to chemistry, including its practical side, the rapidly emerging value of rational analysis. He wanted to claim for chemical practice an intellectual and natural philosophical status.

In taking this step Stahl was also dissociating himself from those of lower social ranks who were, in his mind, less concerned with ethical standards. It was as if Stahl were saying to the society of his day that as a true chemist he was *not* one of those people whose practices were open to question. He was using social class to distin-guish himself as a chemist from the alchemists, who could rightly be viewed as less socially respectable, in his opinion.

True chemistry, Stahl said, resulted from rational enthusiasm for research. It came from a desire to obtain a true knowledge of material composition for its own sake, not because it could make the chemist rich. True chemistry was the product of rational processes that enabled chemists to accomplish useful tasks, such as improving medicines, mineral processing, distilling, glassmaking, and brewing. The chemist's relation to these practical activities was therefore part of a larger rationality.

When the chemist investigated transmutation it was to be done in the interest of useful knowledge, not because it had the potential of material wealth. Stahl's suspi-cion of the motive to personal gain appears to have overruled any suggestion he might have picked up from Becher that chemistry and natural philosophy could be used positively to improve private and public economic conditions.

Although Stahl did not elaborate on the meaning of his terms *rational* and *true* chemistry, he did provide a concrete example of rational chemical theory. From his explanation of combustion, which was originally inspired by his reading of Becher, we get a good idea of how different chemical practice was from alchemy.

The Phlogiston Theory

Through reading Becher's work Stahl was inspired to develop his own theory of combustion. It can be found in a 1715 book he called simply a book of chemical-physical medicine. In it he built on Becher's idea of oily earth as the element present in substances that burned. In Stahl's work this combustive principle became what he named *phlogiston,* a term derived from the Greek word meaning burnt or flammable. Stahl was not the first person to employ the term *phlogiston*—others had used it for almost a century before Stahl picked it up—but he was the one who made it famous.

The nature of phlogiston.   Stahl thought of phlogiston as a substance, but not as a material substance. That is, phlogiston was a thing, but it was not matter. In this respect it was analogous to (but not equivalent to) the soul, which was commonly thought of as an *immaterial* substance present in the human body. Phlogiston functioned like the material principle of sulfur of the medieval natural philosophers we met at the beginning of this chapter. Because it had substance, phlogiston could be added to, inherent in, and given off from regular material substances. But since it was not material, it did not weigh anything—it was weightless substance (again, analogous to the soul's weightless presence in the human body). Finally, phlogiston's presence could not be detected by the senses.

Stahl explained combustion as the *release* of phlogiston from a material substance. Combustible materials such as oils or charcoal were obviously rich in phlogiston and they gave it up readily. Materials that did not burn easily clearly did not possess much phlogiston and therefore had little to give up. They either never had any phlogiston or they had already released it. So the burning process consisted of the releasing of phlogiston. The process was frequently, but not always, accompanied by the presence of fire. But Stahl was clear that phlogiston was not the same as fire, because fire *could* be detected by the senses. Phlogiston, he said, was the motive power of fire particles—it made them move.

Explaining combustion.   Stahl discussed his phlogiston theory primarily in the context of the rusting, or calcination, of metals, which he regarded as an example of a substance undergoing change because it lost phlogiston. Calcination, then, was a form of combustion. When metals rusted they formed what was called a calx on their surface, Stahl said, because they lost their phlogiston (Q in the figure). This meant that he thought of a metal as a compound—it was a calx of some kind in chemical combination with phlogiston, indicated in the figure at the left as (calx + Q). Calx, the surface blemishes

Metal
(= calx + Q)   Calx (rusted metal)

The Calcination of Metal

in the figure on the right, resulted from the giving off of phlogiston and was therefore the simpler elemental substance.

Stahl paid no attention to the weights of the material substances involved in calcination. Had he done so, he might have noticed that the calx weighed *more* than the metal originally had before it rusted. In fact, one of Stahl's admirers, a man named Johann Juncker (1679–1759), did notice the weight gain that resulted from calcination. He had misunderstood Stahl's theory of phlogiston, because Juncker interpreted it as a material, not an immaterial, substance. As a result, he felt obliged to account for why rusted metals weighed more after they lost their phlogiston than they had before they began to rust. In his *History of Chemistry*, written in 1830, Juncker praised both Stahl and Becher, but suggested that phlogiston exerted a buoyant effect on metals somewhat like that exerted on objects that float in water. When the phlogiston was given off in calcination, the buoyant effect was removed and the calx assumed its real weight.

Phlogiston theory exerted a persuasive influence on natural philosophers of the early eighteenth century because it was so powerful. One indication of its strength was its capacity to make sense of other forms of combustion, in addition to calcination. For example, the theory predicted accurately what would happen if a burning candle were placed under a bell jar. In this case the confined air would become saturated with the phlogiston given off by the candle and thus prevent the release of any more. The burning, in other words, would cease and the candle would go out. Likewise, a mouse placed under the jar eventually died because the digestion of food must also entail combustion. The phlogiston in the mouse's exhalations eventually would saturate the confined air, preventing further breathing. One theory, therefore, successfully linked calcination, flame combustion, and digestion and respiration as phenomena involving a single process—combustion.

Phlogiston theory quickly became known as a helpful new idea worthy of attention. In Stahl's mind, and increasingly in the minds of a rapidly growing number of adherents, it stood as an example of rational science as opposed to the nonrational approach of alchemy. As such, phlogiston theory represented progressive natural science during the first half of the century of the Enlightenment.

Although phlogiston theory was most well known in the German states, it gained adherents in France, Sweden, and Britain as chemists discovered its usefulness in their continuing explorations of material change. The increasing needs of those in the metallurgical industry also led to an interest in German chemical texts. As we noted in the previous chapter, the German tradition in mining and metallurgy was particularly rich. As a result, many German chemical texts were translated into French and English between 1750 and 1760. By 1770, then, phlogiston theory enjoyed a wide popularity throughout Europe.

◎ British Contributors ◎

British experimenters in chemistry were just as active as their counterparts on the Continent throughout the eighteenth century. Largely due to the reputation and accomplishments of Robert Boyle, there was a rich tradition in chemistry on which to draw. British achievements in the eighteenth century varied from improvements in instrumentation to the elaboration of existing theoretical ideas and the development of important new ones. As a result, the British chemists were among the leaders in the field as the century drew to a close.

Stephen Hales

Among the early British experimenters was a remarkable cleric named Stephen Hales (1677–1761). He entered Cambridge University, where he received his bachelor's and master's degrees, and was ordained in 1709 into the Anglican Church. Hales was interested in many subjects, including medicine, botany, physiology, and chemistry, and he made contributions to each. Here we are concerned with his work in chemistry, which, as we shall see, also involved his treatment of plants.

Botanical experiments.   In the early decades of the eighteenth century most natural philosophers assumed that atmospheric air was, as Empedocles and Aristotle asserted, elemental. That is, they did not imagine that the air we breathe was made up of a variety of gaseous components. Nor were they aware of the existence of gases other than common air. Of course they occasionally encountered various foul or pleasant-smelling fumes, but these they understood to be pollutions or enhancements of atmospheric air, not generically separate gases. As a result there was limited interest in such fumes.

Hales liked to experiment with plants. In a book of 1727 called *Vegetable Staticks*—by which he meant the study of the laws of the circulation of the fluids in plants—Hales tried to find out everything he could about the constitution of plants. He conjectured, for example, that plants got part of their nourishment from the air and that light, "by freely entering the expanded surfaces of leaves and flowers, contribute much to ennobling principles of vegetables."

Hales also conducted experiments in which he burned plants. He noticed, of course, that fumes were produced when he did this. He did not think of the various fumes he produced in these experiments as qualitatively different from common air. Like others he thought of them as modifications of ordinary air. So he measured the amounts of the air produced, but he did not inquire about its specific properties.

But he did make an important assumption; namely, that the air produced when he burned a plant must have come from the plant. Hales helped to establish the idea that air was bound to or fixed in the plant and that it could be set free in the burning process. He called the vapors "fixed air."

The pneumatic trough.   In carrying out his measurements of the amounts of air he obtained in his experiments, Hales devised an ingenious means of collecting the air. He arranged the flask in which the burning occurred so that the fumes could be led away through tubing. He then found that if he led them into vessels that were filled with water and held upside down in a larger basin of water, the fumes would bubble to the top of the vessel, forcing the water level in the vessel to drop. This procedure isolated the fumes so he could measure how much fixed air had come out of the plant.

Pneumatic Trough

Plant matter

Water

Whether or not Hales realized the distinction between cases in which the fumes were soluble in water from those in which the fixed air was not, he did not assume that different plants gave him qualitatively different products. The burning generated air, although different plants might have modified the air differently. His innovative pneumatic trough was a success, especially in Britain, where those who came after Hales realized soon enough that it could be used to differentiate different kinds of air.

The Work of Joseph Black

From among the fifteen children born to John and Margaret Black of Scotland, Joseph (1728–1799) truly distinguished himself. He went to Edinburgh to study in the arts, where he came across a course on chemistry. He decided to study medicine and was able to become an assistant in the laboratory of the chemistry teacher. Eventually he was appointed a lecturer at Glasgow University, a post he assumed in 1756. A decade later he accepted the chair of chemistry and medicine in Edinburgh, where he remained for the balance of his life.

Black's most path-breaking achievements came early in his career when he was in Glasgow. He made fundamental contributions to the study of heat, including the invention of the calorimeter, an instrument for measuring heat. He also is known as the first to understand and explain the concept of latent heat—the heat needed to change the state of matter from solid to liquid or from liquid to vapor. But his work in chemistry is our focus here.

The importance of weighing. Around mid-century Black began experimenting with a substance called magnesia alba, known today as calcium carbonate ($CaCO_3$). As a student of medicine he was investigating the possible properties of the substance as an antacid. From the course of his experimentation on magnesia alba we can detect qualities of his mind that made him stand out among his contemporaries. He noticed things that his contemporaries did not and he thought about the problems he encountered in a manner wholly unlike anyone else.

Black subjected magnesia alba to two different tests. First, he examined its interaction with an acid and then he heated it. When he did so he noticed that, not surprisingly, two different residues resulted from the reactions he had caused. But Black also noticed that in both cases the materials he began with underwent a loss of weight in the reaction and that the weight losses were identical.

This observation *was* surprising, but only because Black paid so much attention to the weights involved. Such scrutiny was unusual. Careful weighing of the reagents before and after a chemical reaction was not something routinely done, but that would soon change. This practice became more and more important as the century progressed, marking, in fact, a central feature in the creation of modern chemistry. We will see it emerge as a formal principle when, later in this chapter, we examine developments in chemistry in the 1780s.

But how did Black make use of his recognition of the identical weight loss in the two reactions? Here, too, Black showed how unusual and creative his mind was. He decided, in effect, that he would treat the chemical reactions like algebraic equations. He would subtract the second equation from the first, as if the weights of the reagents somehow behaved like x's and y's! The presence of heat in the second equation did not affect the weights because it was believed to be weightless. As a result, the subtraction gave only the acid on the left side, and the difference in the residues on the right:

$$\text{Magnesia alba + acid} \rightarrow \text{residue}_1 + \text{weight loss}$$
$$\underline{-(\text{Magnesia alba + heat} \rightarrow \text{residue}_2 + \text{weight loss})}$$
$$\text{acid} = \text{residue}_1 - \text{residue}_2$$
$$\text{acid} + \text{residue}_2 = \text{residue}_1$$

Black then "added" residue$_2$ to both sides of the result. This suggested that if he were to add the acid to residue$_2$, residue$_1$ would result. When he actually did add the acid to residue$_2$, the reaction resulted in the first residue. The lesson was that quantitative analysis and paying close attention to weights before and after a reaction was important.

The existence of new airs.   Black's work with magnesia alba had one additional impact. He suspected that the weight losses in these two reactions were equal because both caused the release of air that had been fixed in the magnesia alba. This focused his attention on the fixed air. He decided to examine it further and found that, when a burning candle was immersed in this air, the candle went out immediately. One of his students showed that a mouse forced to breathe the fixed air soon died. In other words, the fixed air behaved just like ordinary air that had become saturated with phlogiston.

This result was not particularly surprising for the magnesia alba that had been heated, because a phlogiston-rich source would have to have been used as fuel to produce the heat. But it was not expected for the magnesia alba that had been exposed to the acid. Black concluded that this fixed air was not just a modification of ordinary air—it was a qualitatively different kind of "air." For one thing, this new air was soluble in water, whereas common air was not. Black had in fact discovered carbon dioxide (CO_2).

Black's conclusion opened chemistry to the realization that there were separate airs in nature—what we call gases. Once this awareness settled in, chemists everywhere began searching for new gases and developing techniques to distinguish their properties. For his new gas Black appropriated the term *fixed air,* which Hales had used originally to refer to what he believed were just the modified forms of common air released in chemical reactions. But from this point on in the eighteenth century, *fixed air* referred to the gas we know as carbon dioxide.

Joseph Priestley's Discoveries

The individual who identified more new gases than anyone else in the late-eighteenth century was a radical thinker named Joseph Priestley (1733–1804). Priestley was not a man who favored the status quo. Coming from modest social origins—his father worked as a cloth-dresser in the woolen industry—he was one of the many individuals we have met who used their intellectual gifts to bring themselves to the attention of the larger public. Priestley did this in numerous ways, through his religious beliefs, his politics, and his achievements in the sciences of electricity and chemistry.

The mind of a radical.   Raised in the house of dissenters from the official Anglican Church, Priestley received an education in more than the classics. Dissenters particularly valued the study of the sciences and mathematics and they made sure these were emphasized in their schools. Joseph was a bright student who learned Latin and Greek as a youth, but he also received instruction in physics, philosophy, algebra, and even some Near Eastern languages. He was ordained a minister in the dissenting Presbyterian sect in 1762 and subsequently taught at two dissenter academies.

Politically, Priestley supported the American and French Revolutions. The latter in particular he regarded as a sign of the end times. It represented the first stage in the end of earthly governments, which would all disappear in anticipation of the onset of the Kingdom of God. In this connection he was alleged to have called for the head of King George III in a cartoon depicting a Birmingham toast given on July 14, Bastille Day. That same night a mob attacked and burned his house and laboratory, forcing Priestley to flee. Eventually he decided to move to America. He had become close friends with Benjamin Franklin, who encouraged him in both his political convictions and his work in electricity. Priestley concluded that Pennsylvania would be a place where he and his sons could set up a model society. Although the community he envisioned never became a reality, Priestley did build a house with a laboratory in his new homeland where he could continue to study nature and its laws.

Priestley's work in gas chemistry.   What first brought Priestley to the attention of the English natural philosophers was his work in electricity. He became a member of the Royal Society in 1766 as a result of the electrical experiments he had done. He summarized these one year later in a book, which, in addition to describing his own experiments, also contained a history of electricity and an assessment of the state of the discipline at that time.

In 1772 Priestley presented a paper to the Royal Society on different kinds of air. Once again he followed his presentation with a book, this one coming out in 1774 and entitled *Experiments and Observations on Different Kinds of Air.* In the book he distinguished nine different kinds of air, explaining their properties and the means by which he had isolated them. The most interesting of these new gases was one Priestley named "dephlogisticated air," because it appeared to be bereft of phlogiston. He knew this because it so rapidly absorbed phlogiston; in other words, because it supported combustion so readily.

The story of Priestley's work with dephlogisticated air is well known. Like many of his contemporaries, he was convinced that Stahl had correctly explained combustion as the release of phlogiston. In the context of the calcination of metals, he and others had learned how to recombine phlogiston with a calx to give back the metal. This was done through a process called reducing the calx. By heating the calx, usually slowly for long periods of time, chemists were able to recover the metal they had started with. As already noted, metal was thought to be a compound that rusted or calcinated by breaking into its component parts of calx and phlogiston. But patient heating of the calx could force some phlogiston back into the calx to form the metal again. Priestley assumed that the phlogiston in this case came from the charcoal, a material rich in phlogiston, which was burned to supply the heat for the experiment.

In the summer of 1774, in the course of doing his many gas experiments, Priestley came up with a particularly interesting result. He had gotten hold of a large 12-inch burning lens, which he wanted to use to produce a more intense heat than he could with just a flame. He applied the heat from the lens (without using a flame at all) to some mercury calx and found that he was able to reduce the calx; that is, he was able to produce the metal mercury. Although it was not clear where the phlogiston that united with the calx to form the metal was coming from, Priestley assumed it had to be coming from somewhere.

In this experiment there was a gas that accompanied the process, a fact that in itself was not new. Priestley had noticed the appearance of gases in other reduction experiments that he had done. But Priestley, as mentioned, was an expert in identifying the defining characteristics of new gases. As he set out to determine the properties of the gas, he noticed how wonderfully the gas supported combustion—a candle, for example, burned brightly in it. He concluded that he had produced laughing gas, what we call N_2O, since it was one of the airs he knew about that supported combustion.

A little later, in the fall of 1774, Priestley took a trip to France. Of course he met and conferred with French chemists during his visit, informing them of the result of his experiment with the mercury calx. As it turned out, French chemists had also done the same experiment earlier that fall, in September. They had reported the results of their experiment—in which they had heated mercury calx without using a flame—to the Paris Academy of Sciences. But they had taken no interest in the gas produced in the experiment.

1 vol nitrous air

1.8 vol mixture nitrous
and common air

Addition of "Good"
Common Air to
Nitrous Air

Add 2 vols common air ◦

Testing the "goodness" of air, and the discovery of a new gas. When Priestley returned to England he did some further tests on the gas. Two years earlier, working with another of the gases he had isolated, he had developed a means of testing common air for what he called its "goodness," by which he meant respirability. The test involved combining common air with the other gas and examining the mixture for its solubility in water. This test gas he called nitrous air, which we know today by the formula NO. He collected some of the nitrous air over water (it was insoluble in water), then added common air to it by bubbling air up through the water so that it could mix with the nitrous air already in the vessel.

When the common air he bubbled was "bad" (that is, if it contained the fumes from certain chemical reactions), then two volumes of the common air mixed with the nitrous air above the water to produce three volumes of gas insoluble in water and a drop in the water level. But if the common air was "good"—normal atmospheric air free from contaminants—what resulted was curious. Red fumes were given off that were soluble in the water and the amount of gas left above the water was 1.8 volumes. Clearly, when atmospheric air was good it reacted with the nitrous air, resulting in two products, one of which was soluble in water. (What occurs here is that nitrogen dioxide is formed, a red gas soluble in water.)

Priestley had published his test for the goodness of air in 1772 and it was known in chemical circles. So both he and the French chemist Antoine Lavoisier had, in fact, used the test on the gas they had obtained from the mercury calx. But both were at first deceived by the result. What they found was that when they bubbled the gas released from the reduction of mercury calx through the water to join with the test gas, they got results similar to when they used "good" atmospheric air—red fumes that dissolved and 1.6 volumes of air above the water. This was close enough

1.6 vol mixture nitrous
and mercury calx air

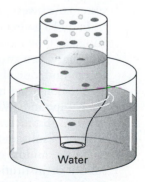

Add 2 vols mercury calx air ●

to the 1.8 volumes for good atmospheric air that they did not examine things further. At first, Priestley most likely concluded that both gases—the good atmospheric air and the mercury calx air (thought to be laughing gas)—gave similar results because they both supported combustion.

But when Priestley came home from France in 1774, he decided to do some additional tests on the gases left above the water in the two cases. What he discovered was that the 1.8 volumes that resulted from the mixture of good common air with nitrous air did not support combustion. (The combustion-supporting component of the good atmospheric air combined with the nitrous air to form nitrogen dioxide.) But the 1.6 volumes resulting from bubbling the mercury calx air into the nitrous air test gas supported combustion dramatically. (After all of the nitrogen in the nitrous air combined with the mercury calx air, there was still mercury calx air left over.)

Priestley was therefore convinced that the gas produced by the reduction of mercury calx was something new. He convinced himself that he had been wrong about it being laughing gas. It was a new, previously unknown gas, which he called dephlogisticated air for its remarkable ability to support combustion. Because of these experiments Priestley is one of the eighteenth-century chemists who have been credited with discovering what we know today as oxygen (O_2).

British chemists were obviously central to the development of chemical knowledge over the course of the eighteenth century and, as we will see in Chapter 20, they would continue to contribute in fundamental ways after the start of the nineteenth century. At the end of the 1770s and on into the 1780s, however, Europe's attention was drawn to the Continent and the claims of a young natural philosopher in France.

◎ The New French Chemistry ◎

As noted earlier, by the end of the eighteenth century chemistry had long been part of the French academic scene. It had been present as a major activity in the organization of the French Royal Academy of Sciences in 1666 and by the turn of the century there was considerable interest in France in the chemistry of salts—the systematic investigation of the products of the interactions of acids and bases.

In 1718 a chemist named Etienne Geoffroy, who worked at the Garden of the King, set down a rule about the way certain substances combined and split up. He said that when two substances that are disposed to combine are found joined in a compound, one of them can be displaced from the compound if another substance comes along that has an even greater affinity for it than the one already present in the compound. What Geoffroy was getting at was that there are degrees of affinity among substances. He even arranged materials in a table that showed the relative affinity of substances to each other.

By the middle of the eighteenth century, then, chemistry had established itself solidly in institutions and was making excellent theoretical progress in France, England, and the German states. By that time there had come on the scene in

France a talented young lawyer named Antoine Lavoisier (1743–1794), whose work over the next decades would mean a great deal to the development of the science of chemistry.

The Rise of Antoine Lavoisier

Lavoisier was the son of a wealthy lawyer who followed the dictates of family tradition to become a lawyer himself. But his heart was elsewhere—in the study of the natural sciences. While preparing for his baccalaureate degree he studied under a distinguished astronomer named Nicolas Louis de Lacaille (1713–1762). Lacaille awakened Lavoisier's passion for astronomy and mathematics and impressed on him the importance of having and using good instruments for research. During this phase of his education Lavoisier also heard lectures on chemistry.

Having cultivated all of these subjects and shown real ability in them, it was not surprising that Lavoisier began to seek admission to the Paris Academy of Sciences. If successful, he would gain the social prestige that went with membership in this dignified institution and, in addition, he would help underscore how important natural science was becoming in prerevolutionary France. By 1768, at the age of twenty-four, the academy rewarded Lavoisier's campaign to join their ranks with an appointment as an adjunct in the chemistry section.

Lavoisier brought to his work in chemistry the convictions he harbored from his exposure to experimental physics. Two years before he was elected, while still engaged in efforts to join the academy, Lavoisier wrote a letter to the secretary in which he argued that the academy had made a mistake in 1699 when it had reorganized itself. It had not given a central role to experimental physics and, as a result, progress in that science had come to a halt. When he joined the ranks of the academicians, then, Lavoisier insisted on bringing the standards of experimental physics to the task he had given himself—to reconstruct the study of chemistry. To do this he would use the same standards of proof, the same careful quantitative techniques, used by experimenters in physics.

A New Theory of Combustion

By the time Priestley came to France in the fall of 1774, Lavoisier had become familiar with the work of Joseph Black—likely through the assistance of his wife, who translated things from English for him. He liked Black's careful, quantitative approach. It spoke to Lavoisier's experimental side, which preferred exactness over imprecision.

Lavoisier was not overly impressed with Priestley's report of his experiment with the mercury calx in the fall of 1774. He had read the report of the French chemists who had done the same experiment earlier that September. True, they had not examined the air produced to see what qualities it possessed. So when he learned from Priestley that the gas supported combustion, Lavoisier decided he would do the experiment for himself.

Antoine and Madame Lavoisier

Because he liked the precision of weighing things carefully, Lavoisier had in fact been doing calcination experiments, with metals that gained weight when they rusted, for some time. He was not happy with Stahl's phlogiston theory of calcination, which he saw as seriously flawed because the properties of phlogiston seemed inconsistent. He found it hard to account for the changes in weight using Stahl's imponderable fluid. So when in 1772—two years before Priestley came to France—he was investigating why some substances gained weight when they rusted, Lavoisier began to suspect that the metals were somehow fixing air to themselves. But he could not imagine how they could be doing that and losing phlogiston at the same time.

Around this time Lavoisier learned of the work a French colleague had done with phosphorus. The colleague knew that when phosphorus was exposed to air it burned; that is, it produced a vapor. If he collected the vapor and then condensed it, he got an acid. The weight of the acid was always greater than the weight of the phosphorus that had burned away. Of course the first assumption was that the increased weight must have come from water vapor that condensed along with the phosphorus vapor.

Lavoisier, realizing the parallel between burning and calcination, repeated this experiment in October of 1772, but he added an additional step to the procedure. First he burned the phosphorus and collected the vapor. Then he condensed the vapor to obtain the acid, confirming that the acid weighed more than the phosphorus

Burning Phosphorus

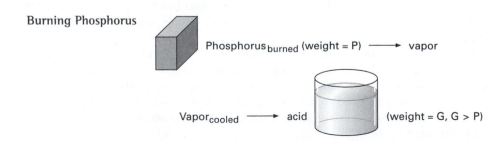

$Phosphorus_{burned}$ (weight = P) $\longrightarrow$ vapor

$Vapor_{cooled}$ $\longrightarrow$ acid   (weight = G, G > P)

that had become vapor. To check to see how much of the weight had come from water vapor that had condensed along with the phosphorus vapor, he poured out the acid and filled the beaker with water to the same level at which the acid had been. Then he weighed the water. What he found was that, as expected, the water weighed less than the acid. So he subtracted the weight of the water from that of the acid and compared the result with the weight of the phosphorus that had been lost in combustion. *The remaining acid still weighed more, considerably more than the original phosphorus.* Lavoisier concluded that the only source for the additional weight had to be the air in which the combustion took place. The phosphorus was fixing air to itself as it burned.

By the time Priestley came to France two years later, Lavoisier was convinced that combustion, including calcination, involved the fixing of air into the substances that burned. Priestley's account of his experiment with the mercury calx spurred Lavoisier to try the experiment for himself. Being familiar with the use of a burning lens, Lavoisier used it to reduce some mercury calx. But he also decided to do a second test alongside this first one. In the second experiment he reduced mercury calx using a flame for his source of heat.

With his attention now fully engaged, Lavoisier carefully examined the results of his two experiments. He noted that the gas given off when using a burning lens supported combustion, just as Priestley said. But in the other case, when he reduced mercury calx using a charcoal-burning fire, the gas that he got was quite different—it did not support combustion. Lavoisier did a systematic comparison of the two different gases. One supported combustion; the other did not. One was insoluble in water; the other was soluble. One calcinated metals; the other did not. It was not long before he identified the gas obtained in the flame reduction of mercury calx—it was Black's fixed air, known by us as carbon dioxide (CO_2).

Lavoisier reported his findings to the Academy of Sciences in the spring of 1775. His so-called Easter memoir was published that same spring. What did Lavoisier conclude from his experiments? The answer was nothing less than a reversal of Stahl's conception of combustion. That is, where Stahl associated combustion with the release of something, Lavoisier inferred that it consisted of the addition of something. Specifically, Stahl had said that the combustion process was due to the loss of phlogiston, an imponderable fluid given off when a metal rusted or a piece of wood burned. Lavoisier now argued that there was something "which combines with metals during calcination and which augments their weight" and that it was "nothing other than the purest part of the very air which surrounds us, which we breathe."

We must be careful to note here that Lavoisier was unaware that what was added was a new gas. He believed that common air was fixed to the metal in combustion, albeit uncontaminated common air. He noted that when metallic calx was reduced, he was able to isolate this common air in its pure form, adding that if a gas was obtained "in the form of fixed air in all the metallic reductions in which charcoal is used, this effect is due to the charcoal itself."

It was only later, in a revised form of the Easter memoir, that he acknowledged what Priestley had discovered—that the air produced in the reduction of mercury calx using a lens was a new gas. He also came around to Priestley's conclusion that this new gas made up about one-fifth of atmospheric air. In much of this Priestley felt slighted. In his view, it was his work that had laid the foundation for Lavoisier, and it was he who had first realized that a new gas was involved. In fact, Priestley never accepted Lavoisier's explanation of combustion. He remained a phlogistonist to his dying day.

As we have seen, however, Lavoisier was already critical of phlogiston theory and was exploring an alternative theory of combustion before he met Priestley in the fall of 1774. In 1777, when he wrote up a summary of his theoretical views on air and read it to the academy, he was clear about what he thought he had accomplished. "Today," he said, "I risk proposing to the Academy a new theory of combustion." He did not openly attack the phlogiston theory directly—that would wait until 1785, in a pamphlet entitled *Reflections on Phlogiston*.

In this new theory Lavoisier had not abandoned all thought of an imponderable substance. Admittedly, he no longer accepted the existence of phlogiston. But he did hold that heat was an imponderable element. The matter of fire, which he called caloric, existed to some degree in all substances. When lots of caloric was packed into something it became very hot, so in some sense the temperature of an object was dependent on the density of the caloric in it. But heat was weightless, as Lavoisier more than anyone else could determine by carefully measuring weights of an object at different temperatures.

In his new theory of combustion this weightless heat was also present in air. When air was fixed into a piece of wood as it burned, the air separated from the caloric, which was released. So in a very real sense for Lavoisier, it was the air that burned, if by burning we mean the release of heat.

Campaigning for the New Chemistry

If the open break with Stahl's phlogiston theory came with the *Reflections on Phlogiston* of 1785, by 1787 Lavoisier had embarked on a campaign on behalf of his new theory. This was necessary if for no other reason than the fact that a majority of his fellow French chemists in the Academy had not yet accepted his ideas. He began the campaign with an argument to reform chemical nomenclature, in a book entitled *Method of Chemical Nomenclature*.

Clearly the new names Lavoisier proposed were based on his new conception of combustion. For example, in 1777 Lavoisier had proposed the term *principe oxygine,* oxygen principle, for the substance that fixed in materials when they combusted. In the book of 1787 it had become simply oxygen. Lavoisier created this word from Greek roots to convey (as it turned out, incorrectly) the notion that it was the acidifying principle; that is, he believed the new element was present in all acids.

Oxygen became a central feature in the new scheme. Although Lavoisier declared that he was not trying to create a new list of names as much as a new method of naming, when he proposed names for metallic calxes his method betrayed how dependent the names were on his conception of combustion. There is, he said, one generic substance that causes acidity and that combines with bodies when they are calcinated or burned. This, then, was the substance from which the generic name of the metallic calxes was taken—in English the generic name would be oxide.

Capping off the campaign was a book of 1789, Lavoisier's *Elementary Treatise on Chemistry*. The work carried an authoritative tone, conveying a sense that it represented the last word on chemistry—the way the subject should be understood. For example, although he was occasionally dependent on others, Lavoisier did not see fit to cite them overtly. Here was a straightforward, rational account of chemistry that did not apologize for its debts to the methods of experimental physics.

Organized in three sections, the first reviewed his understanding of heat and his theory of combustion. In the second he drew on the work of others as he discussed acids and bases and how they combined to form neutral salts. In this section he listed some thirty-three elements, substances that could not be broken down further by chemical means. Heat was included, of course, and so was light. All these elements Lavoisier described in detail.

In the final section Lavoisier explained the instruments and operations of chemistry as he understood them. Instruments were clearly essential for him because they conveyed the importance of rigorous experimental procedure. As for the operations of chemistry, Lavoisier included here a conclusion for which he has been heralded many times—the conservation of matter. He did not claim to have originated the idea because it was already something that characterized practice in experimental physics. But he did see himself as the one who brought it into the study of chemistry.

> Nothing is created either by human action or in natural operations. It is a fundamental truth that in all operations there is the same quantity of matter before and afterwards and that the quality and quantity of the material principles are the same; there are only alterations and modifications. The entire art of making chemical experiments is founded on this principle.

On the basis of this explicit claim Lavoisier has frequently been called the father of modern chemistry.

The Premature End of a Career

Just before Lavoisier became a member of the Paris Academy of Sciences in 1768, he took the advice of a family friend and bought a share in a private organization that underwrote and managed the collection of certain taxes. Although it was an additional source of income for him, he hardly needed it. He had received a handsome sum from his mother's estate and his father had given him an even greater amount as an advance on his inheritance.

It was clear to all that he was among the privileged members of French society. Of course his position in the academy underscored his high position and brought him considerable public attention. So he was a known public figure who over the course of his career made substantial profit from his role as a tax farmer, as the members of the tax-collecting organization were known. When financial crisis emerged in France during the years leading up to the outbreak of revolution, Lavoisier's fame and his membership in the company placed him in a vulnerable position. A great deal about him marked him as one of the wealthy and privileged.

Lavoisier's fate and that of natural philosophy itself during the years of the French Revolution are the subject of Chapter 15. Suffice it to say here that Lavoisier and twenty-seven others of the thirty-two members of the tax farm company could not escape the judgment of the National Convention that they deserved to die on the guillotine. Lavoisier was executed on May 8, 1794. He was the fourth associate of the company to mount the scaffold, just after the beheading of the senior partner of the firm, whose daughter he had married many years earlier.

The Reception of the New French Chemistry

Lavoisier resented the perception that the explanation for why metals gained weight when heated in air was the theory of French chemists. In 1792 he replied to this assumption by declaring that it was not the theory of French chemists—"it is mine, and it is a property that I claim before my contemporaries and posterity."

The disorder brought on by the outbreak of revolution disrupted Lavoisier's campaign for his new theory and prevented the rapid formation of a Lavoisian school of thought. Eventually his conception of combustion, along with his declaration of a law of conservation of matter, would carry the day in France and elsewhere. But especially in Germany there was substantial opposition to his claims.

In order to understand the nature of the disagreement that some German chemists expressed about Lavoisier's claims, it is important to realize the long and proud tradition in chemistry that existed in Germany. It had been Stahl, after all, who had called for the establishment of a rational approach to chemistry. And Stahl's phlogiston theory represented a real advance over the preponderance of alchemical notions that still circulated widely at the beginning of the eighteenth century. Since that time more than one German prince had recognized that it was in his interest to build on the solid foundation already in place in German chemistry and the related endeavor of metallurgy. By doing so, as historian Karl Hufbauer has shown, German leaders sought to bring greater glory to themselves and their states.

Some German chemists were therefore not quick to abandon a perspective that was associated with their homeland. By itself, however, loyalty to the German tradition in chemistry would not have been a sufficient basis on which to resist new French ideas—there were, in fact, some German chemists who agreed with Lavoisier. But there were other reasons why many remained at first unconvinced, reasons that came from the experiments involving the alleged production of Lavoisier's oxygen. These experiments entailed complications that provided room for differences of opinion. The reduction of mercury calx, for example, was a process that could take a long time. This alone increased the opportunities for impurities to contaminate the experiment.

The first German chemist to dispute Lavoisier's findings was the Halle University professor of physics and chemistry, Friedrich Albrecht Carl Gren (1760–1798). In early 1790 he wrote to the editor of the leading German chemical journal of the day that he had discovered Lavoisier was wrong. Gren said that he had reduced the red calx of mercury and no dephlogisticated air (he did not refer to Lavoisier's name of oxygen) appeared. He did not deny that the French chemists had obtained this gas, but he explained that they had gotten it by making a mistake. Their error was to use old calx, which had absorbed moisture from the air. This moisture, Gren argued, was the source of the dephlogisticated air.

In fact, Lavoisier in France and Henry Cavendish (1731–1810) in England had both shown a decade earlier that water was not an element. It was made of two gases—"inflammable air," which Cavendish had discovered in 1766 and which Lavoisier later named hydrogen, and the new air from the mercury calx experiment. Gren was asserting that when dephlogisticated air was present in the reduction experiment, it had come from the dissociation of water. Lavoisier was therefore incorrect to say that the calx had air fixed in it and that the calx was the source of the dephlogisticated air. Gren told the editor that as a result of his discovery the mainstay of Lavoisier's system was abolished, that no fresh metal calx contained air, "that embodied air is actually a chimera." When Gren's sentiments appeared in print, the gauntlet had been thrown down.

Two years later Gren's observation was confirmed by a fellow German chemist named Johann Friedrich Westrumb (1751–1819), the Hanoverian Mining Commissioner who was to become Lavoisier's foremost critic. Westrumb informed Gren that he had used some fresh mercury calx he had been carefully preparing for a long time. In the reduction of the calx, which he did before witnesses, he had got some water vapor, but not "a single bubble of air." Gren sent the letter to a prominent German journal read widely in the German states, where it was published. As for Gren, he claimed that Westrumb's experiment was a demonstration of "the tireless striving of our German chemists to find the truth."

But, as already noted, there were German chemists who sided with Lavoisier. In response to Westrumb's claims, a professor of chemistry in Berlin declared that he had used freshly prepared mercury calx and that he had obtained the purest of vital air, a clear reference to Lavoisier's oxygen. Another German chemistry professor reported that he too had been successful.

This forced Westrumb to repeat his experiment. This time he twice got the pure air he had earlier denied was present and he wrote, dejectedly, to Gren with the bad news. But a week later he changed his view—an assistant had not dried the apparatus used to heat the calx! Residual water must have been the source of the dephlogisticated air. He tested this conjecture by sprinkling his calx with water as it was being reduced and the vital air came off in abundance. Westrumb and Gren therefore held the line. Gren granted that red mercury calx could yield dephlogisticated air when reduced, but, he insisted, "I maintain that it yields this air only insofar as it contains water and retains this water until it glows."

Others became embroiled in the dispute and the impasse persisted. It went on for a year before both Gren and Westrumb finally conceded that mercury calx did contain fixed air. This did not occur until all sides agreed on the experimental results. Gren and Westrumb had to be convinced that all of the possible sources of water had been taken into account and ruled out. The end result was that the heightened scrutiny Lavoisier's claims endured only served to add to his reputation. By the beginnning of the nineteenth century Lavoisier had largely won the day against the phlogistonists.

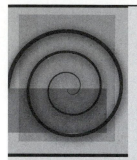

The Challenge of Objectivity

The NATURE of SCIENCE

While it is tempting to attribute the reluctance of Gren and Westrumb to accept Lavoisier's oxygen theory of combustion to bias, perhaps due solely to their devotion to the theory of a fellow German, the account here demonstrates that it was more complicated than that. Indeed, both sides in the dispute claimed to embrace the same values of openness and honesty in their search for truth. And each side blamed the other for not being objective. Gren referred to the prejudice of the antiphlogistonists that was engendered by "the fascination for novelty." One of Lavoisier's German defenders, on the other hand, criticized Gren for being a mere theoretician when "only arguments based on experience are worth anything in this dispute." Both sides insisted on conducting their experiments in the presence of witnesses.

It was Gren, whose position history has judged as incorrect, who denounced the other side for saying that what was most important for the new system was the conversion of Richard Kirwan in England and Martin Klaproth in Germany, both highly respected chemists. Against this assertion Gren proclaimed that "in the kingdom of truth, no authority rules," adding that "the names of famous men can never serve as protection against the skepticism of those who would test their doctrines." Gren declared that "truth can only be found and insured through doubt and controversy," that "freedom and equality reign in the laws of research, proof, acceptance, and rejection."

This episode illustrates that it is one thing to hold objectivity as a value and quite another to achieve it. Those on both sides thought of themselves as the objective contenders for truth who were faced with opponents blinded by adherence to dogma. The history of science contains a great deal of evidence in support of the view that pure objectivity is an impossible goal to attain in research. For all that, natural philosophers continue to embrace objectivity as a guiding value in their research, knowing that to aim any lower makes success all the more unlikely.

As the century came to a close there were those who harbored the hope that chemistry could mature into a science that resembled Newtonian mechanics. They wished to discover the forces responsible for producing chemical change, knowing that such forces could only act over the incredibly short range dictated by the interior of material corpuscles. They hoped not only to uncover the nature of these forces, but, like Newton, to unearth the mathematical formulae that accurately described them.

Others declared that such a dream was fruitless, that chemistry involved too many different elements to be accounted for in the kind of simple laws Newton had found for the motion of large pieces of matter. In this view chemistry would always remain an empirical science; that is, it would be like natural history, where classification, not mathematization, defined the task of the natural philosopher.

As happens frequently in the history of science, chemistry went in a direction after the turn of the new century that the defenders of neither of these views had

anticipated. But chemistry had made incredible strides over the course of the eighteenth century. It entered the nineteenth century with an identity much different
from the one it had possessed in 1700.

Suggestions for Reading

Arthur Donovan, *Antoine Lavoisier: Science Administration and Revolution* (Cambridge:
    Cambridge University Press, 1996).
Karl Hufbauer, *The Formation of the German Chemical Community* (Berkeley: University
    of California Press, 1982).
Robert Schofield, *The Enlightenment of Joseph Priestley* (State College: Penn State
    University Press, 2000).
Pamela Smith, *The Business of Alchemy: Science and Culture in the Holy Roman Empire*
    (Princeton, N.J.: Princeton University Press, 1994).

CHAPTER 11

The Nature of Electrical Fire

If the eighteenth century was a time when chemistry came into its own, the same can be said of the study of electricity. At the beginning of the century natural philosophers had for some time been intrigued by the mysterious properties of certain substances to attract lightweight objects when rubbed. But it wasn't until around 1700 that they began to conduct systematic experiments and to build new equipment with which to create electricity and to measure its effect. Over the course of the century they pursued two different tasks. In one task they gathered information; that is, natural philosophers explored the contexts in which electrical effects appeared and the ways these effects could be artificially produced. In the other task they erected theories to explain what was happening.

In this chapter we are concerned with the initial attempts in the eighteenth century to address both of these tasks. They were confined to the storage and discharge of what we now call static electricity. Here the electrical phenomena investigators observed consisted largely of electrical effects due to forces that were produced when certain substances were rubbed. For example, rubbing a glass tube could cause it to attract a person's hair, while shuffling across a rug wearing socks could produce a shock when a key is inserted into a metal lock. It would not be until the end of the century, in the second phase of the development of the science of electricity, that natural philosophers learned how to sustain electrical discharge into what became known as a current (see Chapter 16).

◎ The Historical Legacy of Electricity ◎ and Magnetism

While the focus of concern in this chapter is the activity of investigators in the eighteenth century, they were not operating completely in the dark. Since antiquity, individuals had taken note of basic electrostatic phenomena and some had even

THE HISTORICAL LEGACY OF ELECTRICITY AND MAGNETISM

tried to account for them. For the bulk of this time these natural philosophers regarded as similar all substances that exhibited the capacity to exert an attractive force. No distinction was made, for example, between substances such as amber, which attracted light objects (electric effect) when rubbed, and lodestone, which attracted only iron (magnetic effect). As we shall see, just prior to the eighteenth century natural philosophers began to distinguish between electrostatic and magnetic attraction.

Electricity and Magnetism in the Ancient and Medieval Worlds

The substance the Greeks called ἤλεκτρον (electron) is known to us as amber, a beautiful gemstone formed from the gradual solidification of the resin of ancient trees over millions of years. Amber possessed a property that intrigued the ancients, and its qualities are mentioned in the writings of several early Greek writers. In an ancient work we first encountered in Chapter 1, the *Timaeus,* Plato referred to amber's ability to attract lightweight objects when rubbed. In the same context he mentioned the attractive power of what he called the Heraclean stone, later known as the lodestone. References to the capacity of this naturally magnetic iron ore to attract little pieces of iron predate even those citing amber's unusual property.

Historical explanations of electrical and magnetic attraction included both appeals to the motion of matter (materialistic explanations) and reliance on hidden qualities of substances (occult explanations). Among the former, for example, were early accounts of the lodestone. Epicurus in the fourth century B.C., and his follower Lucretius three centuries later, appealed to the motion of atoms. Much later a priest of the Delphic order known to history as Plutarch (A.D. 45–125) adapted the materialistic explanation of Epicurus and Lucretius by appealing to strong exhalations from the lodestone that set up currents of air around it. The currents were formed as the air that was pushed aside by the exhalations from the lodestone were immediately replaced by other air in order to prevent the formation of a vacuum. As the air circled back it carried small pieces of iron in the vicinity with it, thus explaining how the lodestone attracted bits of iron.

The explanation of why magnetic and electrical attraction occurred changed in the medieval period with the rise of Scholastic natural philosophy, in which occult qualities explained attraction. In accordance with Aristotle's treatment of qualities, the Scholastics distinguished between the four active qualities (hot, cold, wet, and dry), which were immediately identified through the sense of touch, and hidden or occult qualities, which were not immediately revealed by touch. Prominent among the hidden qualities some bodies possessed were magnetism and heaviness. Simply touching a body that was at rest on the ground would not disclose that it was heavy or that it attracted other substances to it.

Scholastic philosophers such as Thomas Aquinas and Jean Buridan, then, routinely accounted for gravitational, magnetic, and electrical phenomena through an appeal to hidden or occult qualities. Amber attracted lightweight objects because it possessed a hidden quality that caused it to do so. This allowed Scholastics to account easily for the difference between amber and lodestone. It was in the nature of the lodestone to attract only iron bits, while the nature of amber was such that lightweight objects of several substances moved toward it when it was rubbed.

Medieval investigators also added new information to the compendium of magnetic and electrical knowledge. In Chapter 3 we learned of the important impact of the compass on navigation in the fourteenth century. The compass resulted from observations and inferences made over time about the behavior of lodestone. Clever minds had discovered that a small object like a needle could be made to behave like a lodestone—it could be magnetized. Once it was realized that a lodestone inside a floating wooden bowl always turned so that a part of it faced to the north, investigators learned that a magnetized needle placed on a wooden stick did the same thing. By the fourteenth century, captains were regularly relying on the compass to guide them at sea, especially when they went out of sight of land.

Medieval thinkers knew from antiquity that there were several gems that displayed the amber effect. They learned on their own that jet, a black gem made from fossilized coal, also possessed the property. When diamond was added to the list, scholars began to think in terms of a group of substances that exhibited the effect when rubbed and to distinguish this type of attractive power from that of lodestone.

The Early Modern Era

Among the most intriguing figures concerned with the attractive force of substances like amber and lodestone was Girolamo Cardano (1501–1576), the Italian astrologer, mathematician, and physician. Known as a difficult man, Cardano cultivated a self-acknowledged habit of deliberately antagonizing those around him, even while gaining considerable fame as a physician. As a result, controversy followed Cardano over the course of his career. In spite of the disapproval that came his way, Cardano's work contained many observations of lasting value.

In a work from 1550 entitled *De Subtilitate Rerum (On the Subtlety of Things)*, Cardano described the supposed medicinal uses of amber and then proceeded to distinguish amber from the magnet. He stated clearly that the phenomena of attraction associated with the two substances were qualitatively different—amber and the magnet did not attract in the same way. To justify his contention he gathered results from the work of predecessors, none of whom had distinguished between electrical and magnetic events as thoroughly as Cardano did. First there were the obvious differences, which had been noted by others. Amber attracted a variety of lightweight substances while the magnet only attracted iron. But Cardano went further. Amber's attraction was increased by rubbing, which did not augment magnetic attraction. Cardano also pointed out that he could negate the so-called amber effect by placing a barrier between amber and the objects it attracted, while a similar barrier did not similarly hinder the magnetic effect. In addition, magnets attracted at an end, a condition not observed with amber.

Cardano was not content with the Scholastic explanation that the attractive power of amber was due to the presence of occult force. He suggested that when amber was rubbed it emitted a moist humor that was absorbed by the chaff in the vicinity. Then, just as dry things that absorb moisture move toward the source of the moisture, the chaff moved toward the amber. Cardano preferred, in other words, to refer to a physical process he had observed elsewhere in nature to account for electrical attraction.

Cardano was not the only one to consider this subject in the sixteenth century. We have already examined the general ideas of the Englishman William Gilbert, who took up magnetism near the end of the century to demonstrate that the world had a soul (see Chapter 7). In his book of 1600 on the magnet, Gilbert permitted himself a short digression in one chapter to discuss the amber effect as well. He too emphasized the difference between amber and the magnet. But he then went on to make explicit the notion that there was a whole class of substances that behaved like amber. Drawing on the Greek word for amber, he called them "electrics," and he listed well over a dozen—diamond, sapphire, carbuncle, iris gem, opal, amethyst, beryl, rock crystal, glass, antimony glass, fluorspar, belemnites, sulfur, mastic, hard sealing wax, hard resin, orpiment, rock salt, mica, rock alum. Gilbert was the first to use the new word, electricity, to indicate the amber effect.

Electricity was not an occult phenomenon for Gilbert any more than it was for Cardano. Gilbert believed that electrical events were incompatible with an occult sympathy because there was such a diversity of electrics. They were so different that there could be no common occult quality responsible for the attractive capacity they all displayed. He appealed to the direct action of matter, referring to watery humors present in the amber and similar substances that were released on rubbing. They united with lightweight objects, and, like the action of surface tension uniting two drops close to each other, "lay hold of the bodies with which they unite, enfold them, as it were, in their arms, and bring them into union with their electrics." This type of material explanation of electrical attraction was also characteristic of the era that followed.

The Seventeenth Century

For the majority of natural philosophers who considered the subject in the 1600s, electrical phenomena continued to involve the exhalation of a material effluvium, or byproduct, of one kind or another that was given off by an electric and then circulated back. But why did the effluvium not carry small objects in the vicinity of the electric *away* from it as it was given off—why did it only carry them back toward the electric on its return? One answer was found in the thinness of the stream as it left the electric. Because it was so thin, it either did not encounter the objects, or if it did, the impact was not spread over enough of their surface to move them. During circulation, however, the effluvium expanded, so that on its return it was able to affect the bits of material that the electric then "attracted."

There were a few individuals who did not accept this materialistic approach. Among these was Otto von Guericke (1602–1686), one of the inventors of the air pump in the mid-seventeenth century. He preferred to view electricity as the result of an incorporeal virtue that spread out instantaneously through space. In this he was like Francis Bacon, whose new natural philosophy we met in Chapter 7. Bacon included electricity among the "virtues" that did not require a material means to convey it from one place to another. Both von Guericke and Bacon spoke of electricity "acting at a distance," a phenomenon regarded as impossible in materialistic explanations. Others, such as the Portuguese physician Duarte Madeira Arrais (d. 1652), included electricity among the occult forces that diffused around the electric that possessed it and awoke a potency in neighboring bodies.

A few investigators noticed that on occasion lightweight objects seemed to be repelled from the electric, but this did not mean that they recognized that electrostatic force could be repulsive as well as attractive. As historian of electricity John Heilbron has observed, for every seventeenth-century electrician but one, electricity was by definition a faculty of attraction. It was Christian Huygens (1629–1695), the disciple of René Descartes (see Chapter 9), who clearly recognized electrostatic repulsion and one of the fundamental contexts in which it appears. But, as Huygens published nothing of his studies of electricity, much of what he realized had to be investigated by others in the eighteenth century.

◎ Gathering Information: Early ◎ Eighteenth-Century Experiments

We noted at the beginning of this chapter that a major concern of early-eighteenth-century investigators of electricity was to gather information about electrical phenomena. As natural philosophers uncovered more and more electrical effects, this endeavor proved to be challenging. For example, what seemed to be identical experimental procedures might work on one day but not on the next. It would require time to realize that a standard part of good investigative technique might mean taking atmospheric humidity into account.

Advances in Instrumentation

As the list of electrics in Gilbert's book shows, it was understood that many substances could be electrified by rubbing them. There were some substances—for example, metals—that did not appear to be affected in this manner, although the name nonelectric was not given to them until the 1740s in England. Naturally, investigators were interested in conducting experiments on electricity throughout the seventeenth century. But it was not until advances in electrical instruments made possible a whole new set of discoveries that the beginnings of a science of electricity could be seen.

Hauksbee and the Royal Society. A key figure in this endeavor was Francis Hauksbee (1666–1713), demonstrator for the Royal Society. As the new eighteenth century dawned, the Royal Society was but 38 years old. But by the end of 1703 Robert Hooke was dead and his old enemy, Isaac Newton, had become the new president. Changes were in the air, including the revival of a former practice—weekly experimental demonstrations. Newton installed an obscure and not well-educated demonstrator, Francis Hauksbee, as chief experimentalist. It is likely that Newton chose him for his reputation as an established instrument maker. In the service of the Royal Society, Hauksbee was a careful experimentalist who did not jump to conclusions too quickly.

The society asked Hauksbee to investigate a well-known phenomenon—the fact that some materials glow under certain conditions. Hauksbee knew that if mercury were jostled around in the vacuum created in the space at the top of a mercury barometer, it would sometimes glow, so he set about to investigate the situation. Being familiar with the work of Robert Boyle on the air pump, he placed mercury in a tube, pumped out air, and then gradually let air back in, breaking up the mercury into droplets. The droplets rolled down the sides of the vessel and emitted light as they did so. But droplets that did not roll down the glass did not glow. It was the contact between the mercury and the glass that was the principal cause of the glow. But was it the glass or the mercury that, when rubbed, caused the glow?

Next Hauksbee tried evacuating a vessel and rubbing its *exterior*, without mercury or any other substance inside the vessel. He got an impressive light that let him read the letters of a book nearby. On letting air into the vessel the light was affected and it disappeared when the vessel was full of atmospheric air. From this Newton concluded that the light had been coming from the glass, not from the various substances put inside it. Hauksbee, however, was unsure whether the mercury

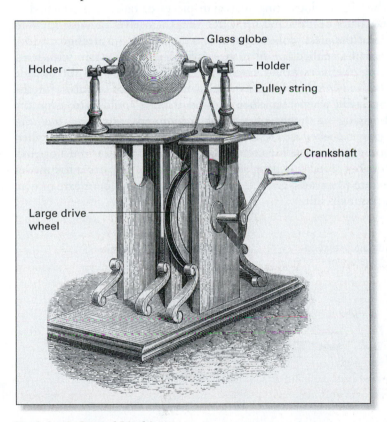

Hauksbee's Second Machine

might have contributed some of the light when it was used. The many different experimental results confronting Hauksbee made him cautious.

Next came two advances in devices that enhanced the production of the electrical effect. First, Hauksbee made a hollow tube of flint glass 30 inches long and 1 inch in diameter. It could be rubbed much more extensively than the smaller bits of electrics previously in use; hence, it produced more dramatic events, especially because Hauksbee employed thin leaves of brass instead of the bits of paper and straw that were commonly used. And although he reported seeing pieces of brass occasionally driven away from the glass violently, he still did not attribute fundamental significance to electrical repulsion.

The second machine (see the figure on page 225) was even more elaborate and made the rubbing process extremely efficient. Hauksbee mounted a 7-inch glass globe that had shafts protruding at opposite ends onto holders that allowed the shafts, and therefore the globe, to spin. One of the shafts could be connected to a pulley string that was moved by a large drive wheel that was turned by a crankshaft. The globe, in other words, could be made to spin at high speeds.

Hauksbee used his new machine to perform a number of new experiments (see the figures below). If he inserted a shaft all the way through the globe (left), on the middle of which was a loose ring to which pieces of hair were attached at equal intervals, the hairs would stand up, extending themselves radially outward toward the inside of the glass globe when it was rubbed. If he arranged a ring around the outside of a rubbed spinning glass cylinder (right), again with hairs attached to the ring, the hairs would extend radially inward toward the outside surface of the glass. These electric spider webs impressed the members of the Royal Society, especially when Hauksbee showed that he could turn aside the rigid hairs by bringing his finger near to their pointed ends, *and that this happened even if glass was interposed between his finger and the hairs* (as it was when the hairs were inside the globe). He concluded that the effluvium did not rush around in a vortex, but stood in stiff, glass-piercing chains. But while the movement of the effluvium permeated glass, it could be shown not to permeate muslin cloth, a truly perplexing result.

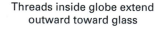

Threads inside globe extend   Threads outside cylinder extend
outward toward glass   inward toward glass

Experiments Performed with Hauksbee's Machine

The early work of Stephen Gray.   Around the time Hauksbee was conducting experiments for the Royal Society, the secretary received a communication from Stephen Gray (1666–1736), a dyer by trade, who was also very interested in the study and investigation of nature. In 1707 he was brought to Cambridge by Roger Cotes (1682–1716), a fellow of Trinity College in Cambridge who was soon to become a professor of astronomy and experimental philosophy there. Cotes planned to set up an observatory in Cambridge and needed an assistant.

Through this connection with Cotes, Gray became familiar with Hauksbee's experiments on electricity. He investigated further the mysterious movement of the electrical effluvium and reported on experiments he had done with a glass tube in a letter to the secretary of the Royal Society in early 1708. On rubbing the tube he observed that a down feather was drawn to the tube. But then it would leave the tube and go to any nearby solid body, repeating the coming and going up to ten times or more before coming to rest.

Gray included in his communication a theory to account for the complicated movements of the feather. His idea was that all objects around the tube were stimulated to themselves emit effluvia when they came into contact with the effluvia produced by rubbing the glass tube. He devised an explanation of the complex motions of the feather based on this assumption. The Royal Society did not print Gray's experiment in the pages of its journal. Instead, the secretary asked Hauksbee to conduct Gray's experiment. In a piece published in the society's transactions, Hauksbee tried to account for what Gray had observed using his own theory of stiff chains of effluvia. His effort was, however, unpersuasive and he soon abandoned experimentation in electricity.

Communicating the Electrical Effect

Gray lasted with Cotes in Cambridge for only a little more than a year. A shy man, he did not get along well with his superiors and returned to Canterbury, where he continued his astronomical observation and experimentation with electricity. The next year he sent a paper to the Royal Society in which he described a class of electrics unlike the numerous hard substances Gilbert had identified. His list included hair, silk, paper, and other nonrigid semisolid substances. It was not until the end of the decade of the 1720s, however, that his most significant discoveries were made.

Communicating and blocking the electric effect.   In 1729 Gray made a breakthrough in his treatment of electricity. It came as he was trying to produce the electrical effect on yet more substances, notably, on metals. Everything he did with metals had been unsuccessful. He tried rubbing them, heating them, and pounding them, but none of this resulted in an electrified metal. He then tried to see if perhaps he could succeed using his old familiar glass tube. Maybe the effluvia he created by rubbing the tube would stimulate the metal to produce its own effluvia, as it appeared to have done in nearby solid objects in the earlier experiment with the feather.

To test out this idea he used a flint glass tube. He had learned from Hauksbee that the tube should be free of dust, so he used corks at each end to keep out unwanted contaminants. But naturally he asked himself if using corks might affect

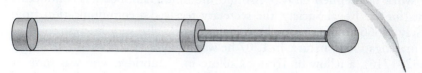

Communicating the Attractive Capacity of Rubbed Glass

the tube's production of effluvia. While checking to see if they did he stumbled on an unexpected result. The corks did not affect the tube's electrifying capability—the electrical effect was still there. But when he released a feather near the end of the tube, he noted that the feather went, not to the tube, but to the cork. The effect he produced by rubbing the glass had been communicated to the cork!

Having determined that the electrical effect could be directly communicated, Gray now proceeded to find out how far he could communicate the attractive capacity of the rubbed glass. He stuck a stick, with an ivory ball on its end, into the cork, and rubbed the glass. The feather was attracted to the ivory ball. Gray now distinguished between a line (the stick) and a receiving body (the ivory ball) and he set out to vary the substances used for each. In his mind the line was functioning more impressively than air had as the medium through which electrical effluvia passed.

Now the question was, exactly how far could the electrical effect be communicated? In one experiment Gray went up to the tallest height available to him, some 34 feet, where he held outward the tube with an 18-foot pole stuck into it and from which hung 34 feet of twine. When he rubbed the tube and observed the electrical effect at the end of the twine, he had transmitted the effect 52 feet.

Another experiment, designed to transmit the effect horizontally, foundered. He had tried to communicate the effect horizontally through twine that was hung from the ceiling by shorter lengths of twine. From his failure to observe a positive result, Gray concluded that horizontal communication was not possible. A collaborator in his experiments did not buy this idea and suggested that silk be used to hang the twine from the ceiling because silk thread was so narrow it might block the flow of effluvia and prevent its escape. This in fact solved the problem—they were able to transmit the electrical effect horizontally through twine up to a few hundred feet. So they tried suspending the twine with brass wire, which was even narrower than the silk. To their surprise, the procedure did not work. On July 3, 1729, they came to an extremely important conclusion: it was not the shape of the substance used to support the twine; it was the nature of the substance itself. Some substances led the effluvia along while other substances blocked or insulated the passage of effluvia through them.

For a couple of years Gray was the main contributor to the study of communicated electricity. He looked out for more substances that acted, like silk, to block the flow of electricity and thereby allow it to pass along the length of the twine. He could then use these substances as supports. Hair fit the bill, as did resin and glass. At the same time he increased the number of substances through which the electrical effluvia flowed and from which the attractive effect could be displayed. In addition to ivory he found that metal, vegetables, and even the human body worked well. A boy suspended in air using the proper blocking supports, when touched by a rubbed tube, could in turn attract to his fingers light objects brought near him. Electrical science was beginning to be very intriguing indeed!

Changes in terminology.   When first introduced by Gilbert, the word *electric* had meant any substance that could be made to exhibit the attractive effect. By the early 1740s so many substances fit that description that the term was losing its effectiveness. The substances Gray had discovered that blocked the communication of electricity fell under the category. Gray had even been successful in showing that metal could be used to exhibit the attractive effect, although by communication and not by rubbing. A new, more precise terminology was needed.

It began to emerge in the work of Jean Desaguliers (1683–1744), the son of an immigrant Huguenot pastor who was educated at Oxford. In 1714 he went to London, where he gained the confidence of Newton and succeeded Hauksbee as demonstrator in the Royal Society. Always interested in electricity, Desaguliers took Gray's place as England's leading contributor to the investigation of electricity in the late 1730s and early 1740s. He introduced the English term *electric per se* to refer to substances that could be electrified by rubbing or heating, and the term *nonelectric* for substances that could not. He called such nonelectrics *conductors,* because they could be used to conduct or communicate electricity from one place to another. Desaguliers also used the word *insulator* for electrics that blocked or terminated the communication of electricity.

Electrical repulsion and the two electricities of Charles Dufay.   Among those across the English Channel who found out about Gray's experiments was a wealthy member of the French Academy named Charles Dufay (1698–1739). He had started out in chemistry, but had moved across disciplines from one kind of investigation to another. He was investigating various properties of phosphorus when he came upon Gray's results in electricity.

After he began his own study of electricity he quickly concluded that all bodies, except metals and soft or fluid bodies, could be electrified by friction or heating. The power to attract small objects when rubbed he deemed to be the almost universal property of material bodies. Where communication of electricity was concerned, Dufay declared that all bodies except flame display the electrical affect once they were touched by an electrified substance. Dufay determined that the communication of electricity had to be done with the object to be electrified resting on a support of sufficient thickness; that is, it had to be sufficiently insulated so that the effect would not be drained off into the ground. This, of course, was the case when any object was hung in the air by appropriate support cords. When the electrical effect was communicated to the object, it could not jump through so much air to the ground, and it was blocked by the support cords from flowing through the ceiling and walls into the ground. This requirement of insulating the body to be electrified became known as the Rule of Dufay.

In the fall of 1733 Dufay took on a young assistant named Jean Antoine Nollet (1700–1770), who, as we shall see, eventually became equally as famous as his master. The two collaborators soon observed a phenomenon that led them to construct a new theory about electricity. The phenomenon had to do with an alleged *repulsion* that could occur after an object had been attracted to a rubbed glass tube. As noted earlier, Huygens and Gray had observed this, as had others prior to Dufay. But, once convinced of its reality, Dufay set out to provide an explanation.

In his experiment, he observed the attraction of a gold leaf to a glass tube, from which it then was repelled. Dufay reasoned that the gold leaf was attracted to the electrified glass when it was in an unelectrified state. Once it touched the glass, electricity was communicated to it and it then was repelled. In other words, the pattern he observed was attraction, contact, and then repulsion. He then electrified another gold leaf and brought it near the first leaf. He observed what he expected to see— that the two leaves would repel each other just as each leaf had been repelled by the glass. But when he then brought a different electrified rod to one of the leaves, one made not of glass but of a copal resin, he was shocked to observe that the leaf was *attracted* to it. This was a complication that was hard to fathom.

To explain what he had discovered Dufay decided that there were two kinds of electricity: vitreous, obtained by rubbing glass, and resinous, from rubbing copal resin. The two different electricities attracted each other, but each repelled its own kind. Thus, when an object such as a gold leaf was attracted to a substance electrified vitreously or resinously, it would take on that kind of electrification. That is why the leaf would be repelled after coming in contact with the other gold leaf — they had become similarly electrified. But if a leaf that had been electrified vitreously came near an object that was resinously electrified, the leaf would be attracted to it.

Dufay observed one more phenomenon of significance—electric shocks. In an experiment in which he himself took the place of the boy Gray had suspended in air, Dufay found, as Gray had described, that when an electrified tube was held to his toes small pieces of leaf-metal flew to his face and hands. The electric effect had been communicated to his body, which now attracted the small objects to it. A piece of leaf-metal had also been attracted to his body at his leg. When a bystander attempted to pick it off, both he and Dufay received a slight shock. Dufay noted that accompanying the shock was a snapping noise; further, if the experiment was done in the dark, he could see a small spark as the shock occurred. He could not explain why this only occurred when he was approached by another person after he had been touched by the tube, but not when he was touched by the tube itself. Be that as it may, shocks were now accompanied by sights and sounds!

When Gray learned about the experiments and ideas of Dufay, what impressed him was not the description of how repulsion could follow attraction and contact, nor was it Dufay's explanation of that phenomenon through two electricities. Gray was impressed by the sparks and shocks the French experimenter described. In spite of the work of Gray and Dufay, however, electricity did not arouse a great deal of attention in the 1730s. But sparks and shocks would in fact create extraordinary interest in electricity in the 1740s, especially once natural philosophers learned how to store the electrical effect.

Storing the Electrical Effect

Word of the achievements of Gray and Dufay soon reached the German states. Of course German investigators tried to duplicate the experiments about which they read. In so doing, they demonstrated a flare for the subject, arousing considerable public interest in the new subject of electricity, and winning public acclaim for themselves in the process. In addition, they introduced new modifications to the electrical experiments that led to a novel discovery whose significance was not immediately recognized—how to store the electrical effect.

Electricity on display.   One of the German experimenters who was intrigued by the subject was a young instructor at the University of Leipzig named Georg Bose (1710–1761). He had read everything he could find on the subject, including various accounts of Hauksbee's experiments with the spinning globe. He used a distiller's globe he had gotten from a glassmaker to put together a version of Hauksbee's electrical machine. Bose's capacity to entertain soon became evident as he delighted students by drawing sparks from the spinning globe. In the course of entertaining he also introduced an improvement that was to have important consequences.

In the fall of 1737 Bose obtained papers published by Dufay, and he immediately set out to repeat the experiments Dufay had described. Having become thoroughly captivated by the subject, Bose decided he would use his electrical machine to redo Dufay's experiments. Where Dufay had used a rubbed tube to electrify insulated objects, including the human body, Bose would replace the tube with his electrical machine. This modification enabled him to produce much stronger electrifications than Gray or Dufay had ever achieved with a glass tube.

In 1738 Bose took a position at the University of Wittenberg, where, over the ensuing years, he conducted numerous experiments and demonstrations. He first decided to communicate the electricity produced by the spinning globe to a piece of metal on glass caps; then later he used silk cords to suspend the metal in the air. By running a conductor in contact with the surface of the spinning globe to a sword or iron bar suspended in the air, Bose could show an amazed audience how he could draw sparks from the suspended metal—soon to be known as the prime conductor. The effect was powerful and dramatic.

Bose made the most of his newly found expertise by creating novel arrangements with which to entertain visitors, often persons of high social standing. Electricity even became a means to entertain royalty. In one case, Bose had several people, including the wife of an Austrian count, stand on cakes of wax. They joined hands, forming a chain. The person at one end of the chain grasped a gun barrel that was connected to Bose's spinning globe, while the person at the other end of the chain held his hand above a plate on which were gold leaves. Bose became the hero of the hour when the gold leaves leaped from the plate to the outstretched hand. In another demonstration Bose electrified a woman who was positioned on an insulated stand. He then proceeded to kiss her, receiving a shock that, he said, pained him to the quick.

A portable electrical machine.   One of the entertainments Bose came up with turned out to contain an important element that was to lead to unanticipated results—the discovery of a portable sparking machine. It was not accomplished by

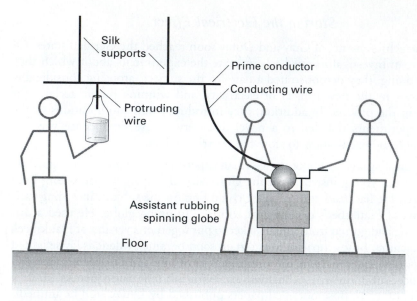

Von Kleist's Experiment

Bose, but by a clergyman named Ewald von Kleist (1700–1748) in a remote part of the northern German state of Prussia. Bose had set the stage for the discovery by showing that he could even draw sparks from a glass of water. He did not explicitly say how he had done it, but later experimenters who tried to duplicate Bose's achievement ran a lead from a suspended prime conductor to the water, which was either on an insulated table or held by someone positioned on an insulated stand. Putting the electrical machine into operation, Bose then drew sparks from the water with his finger or with the point of a sword.

Von Kleist, who had initially learned about electricity as a student in Holland during the 1720s, took up experiments for himself in the wake of all the attention created by Bose and others. In the middle of the 1740s he built an electrical machine and soon stumbled on a result whose significance he did not know how to evaluate. In the course of carrying out experiments with his machine in October of 1745, he decided to increase the mass of the prime conductor—the metal suspended in the air to which electricity was communicated from the spinning globe. He was operating on the assumption, false though it was, that the sparks would increase in proportion to the mass of the prime conductor.

Bose had demonstrated that water could be electrified, so von Kleist took a glass flask containing water, put a wire into it that protruded out of the neck, and held it up to the suspended prime conductor. For a reason he did not explain, von Kleist did not insulate himself when he brought the wire near the prime conductor. Perhaps he thought the glass itself was sufficient to insulate the flask, as Dufay's Rule required when drawing a spark.

This arrangement produced some surprising results. First of all, von Kleist found that that when he removed the flask from the prime conductor a flare appeared on the inside of the flask and continued for some time. He could walk into the next room and the flare would continue for a while. Secondly, he discovered that after removing the flask from the machine and walking around he could give himself a shock by touching the protruding wire or he could take the flask into the next room and use it to ignite turpentine. He had, in other words, stored the electrical effect in a portable sparking machine, the equivalent of what today is known as a capacitor.

At first von Kleist did not know what to make of the results, but when he communicated them to a member of the Berlin Academy of Sciences, he learned quickly that what he had stumbled upon was interesting indeed. As delighted as he became with the discovery, however, there were a few aspects of the results that continued to puzzle him. He found, for example, that he could not get his portable sparking machine to emit sparks if he set it on a table and then touched the protruding wire. In that situation there was no spark, only a violent hissing. But if he picked up the flask again and then touched the wire, he received a shock. "What really surprises me in all this," he later wrote to a friend, "is that the powerful effect occurs only in the hand."

Von Kleist's bewilderment was typical of many experimenters in this era of gathering information. He knew what he had obtained, but he had no idea why things happened as they did. Although von Kleist wrote of his experiments to a few selected acquaintances, including descriptions of how he had proceeded, they were even more bewildered than he was because none of them was even able to duplicate what he had done.

There was a major reason why other Germans could not repeat the experiment. Von Kleist had neglected to say explicitly that during the electrification of the flask through the protruding wire the experimenter had to hold the flask in the hand and stand on the floor. Apparently those who tried to duplicate von Kleist's experiment throughout the remainder of 1745 and the early months of 1746 used what had become standard procedure according to the Rule of Dufay—they made sure that the object being electrified was well insulated from the ground. Not assuming that the glass of the flask accomplished this insulation by itself, they stood on a cake of wax or in some other way guaranteed the flask was insulated. And even if they did observe the flare von Kleist claimed to have obtained, they would not have been able to discharge the spark because in all the experiments they knew about a second person always drew off the spark from the electrified person by either touching or, in Bose's famous display, kissing them. It was not until March 5, 1746, that anyone had success, and then only by accident. An assistant to one of those trying to do von Kleist's experiment happened to touch the wire in an electrified flask he himself was holding in his other hand.

The Leyden jar.   As sometimes happens in the history of science, different investigators come to the same conclusion around the same time without direct knowledge of each other's work. This occurred with the discovery of the capacitor, or, as it became known in the eighteenth century, the Leyden jar. In both the case of von Kleist and that of Dutch experimenters, the result came about unexpectedly.

The common link between the Dutch and German accomplishments was Bose's electrification of water in a glass. At the university in Leyden, the new professor of experimental physics, Pieter van Musschenbroek (1692–1761), was trying to draw sparks from water just a few months after von Kleist had begun his experiments. In the early days of 1746 van Musschenbroek set out to do what Bose had done—he placed the water to be electrified on an insulating stand and ran a wire lead into it from the prime conductor, and drew sparks from the water.

By chance an acquaintance of van Musschenbroek, who sometimes liked to observe the physicist perform experiments, became intrigued by the attempt to draw sparks from water. The friend, a lawyer named Andreas Cunaeus, decided to try the experiment at his home. Of course he did not have the equipment van Musschenbroek did with which to electrify the jar of water—presumably he had to rub a tube or other glass container. And being alone, he had to hold the vessel with the water in his hand at the same time. He did not know the Rule of Dufay, so he merely stood on the ground—that is, he did not insulate himself. Finally, because there was no one else present to whom he could present the jar, he attempted to draw the spark himself. When he received a real shock, he quickly related his experience to his friends in the laboratory.

An assistant repeated the experiment as described by Cunaeus. He then reported his results to van Musschenbroek, who set up an elaborate experiment with a more powerful electrical machine and a bigger vessel of water. After putting the machine into operation, van Musschenbroek, standing on the ground, held the flask of water up to the prime conductor so that the wire came down into the flask. While the machine continued to turn van Musschenbroek reached out with his other hand to draw sparks from the prime conductor. He was, he reported to a French colleague in the Paris Academy of Sciences, "struck with such a force that my whole body quivered just like someone hit by lightning." He advised his friend never to try the experiment himself because he had only narrowly escaped death.

As a professor of physics, van Musschenbroek knew how to report the procedure in such a way that anyone who wished to could duplicate his experiment, regardless of his warning against it. Further, he was well connected to the network of natural philosophers, so it was not long before scholars in France and England heard about the Dutch experiment. As a result, the new discovery became known as the Leyden jar, a Dutch invention that took its name from the city in which van Musschenbroek lived. Of course others did try the experiment, soon realizing not only the capacity of the Leyden jar to amplify the discharge of electricity, but also its ability to store electrical force.

But van Musschenbroek was no clearer about why things worked as they did than von Kleist had been. Gathering information about what happened under which circumstances was important, but the puzzling results, dramatic as they were, called out for an explanation. Van Musschenbroek himself gave vent to the frustration he felt: "I've found out so much about electricity," he wrote to his French colleague, "that I've reached the point where I understand nothing and can explain nothing." The big question confronting electricians was: why is it important *not* to insulate the outside of the Leyden jar? Fortunately, there were theorists waiting in the wings to provide answers to the question of what electricity was and why it behaved as it did.

◎ Erecting Theories: What Is Electricity? ◎

In the years around mid-century numerous theories about electricity appeared that proposed to make sense of the new phenomena. Of these there were two that commanded the most attention. One appeared in France in the work of Jean Nollet, whom we met earlier as Dufay's young assistant and who by the 1740s had become a lecturer in natural philosophy. In 1744 he even instructed and entertained the queen on electricity at Versailles. The other theorist was Benjamin Franklin in the American colonies. The two theorists did not agree in their attempts to account for the increasing storehouse of information about electricity that had accumulated by the mid-1740s.

Nollet's Theory of Double Flux

Nollet began lecturing on astronomy and physics in 1738, including electricity and magnetism. He recognized the value of demonstrations in his work and used them to his advantage to awaken interest in the subject matter he discussed. That meant, where electricity was concerned, bringing his audience up to date on the experiments of his former master Dufay and the Englishman Stephen Gray. In the demonstration at Versailles, for example, he is pictured conducting an experiment using the familiar glass tube to electrify a suspended boy. Metal leaves fly to the boy's hand as a woman—perhaps the queen—reaches out to draw a spark from the boy's nose.

Once he heard about the German experiments of Bose, however, Nollet reproduced the more powerful electrical machine that was in use on the other side of the Rhine River and came up with impressive demonstrations of his own. In the wake of these experiments he laid out his conjectures about electricity to the French Academy at the end of April in 1745.

In Nollet's view electricity was a combination of the elements of fire and earth, hence a very thin substance, that existed in all bodies. Rubbing and other mechanical means could cause the matter of electricity to leave bodies. In the case of metals, of course, rubbing did not work, but the electrical matter could be forced out of them by applying electrical matter itself using an electrical machine. The electrical matter that was expelled from bodies, called effluent, streamed out of tiny

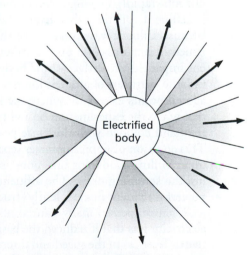

Outflowing Cones of Effluent

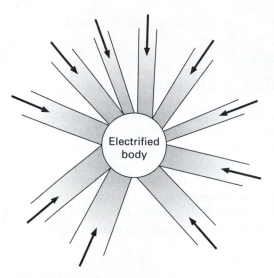

Inflowing Corridors of Affluent

narrow jets and spread out in cones as it dispersed. Nollet put powder on a prime conductor which, when it was electrified, spurted out in jets from individual points on the surface.

Once the effluent had been stimulated into existence by rubbing—that is, at the same time that electrical matter was expelled from electrified bodies—electrical matter, called affluent, also moved *toward* the bodies, replenishing what had left. Nollet noted that the electrical matter removed from the surface of spinning glass globes was never exhausted; hence, it had to be the case that electrical matter from the air and from other objects in the vicinity moved toward electrified bodies. Notice here that Nollet had given up the idea of his former mentor, Dufay, of there being two electricities. For Nollet there was only one electricity. It was only the differing directions of movement that distinguished effluent (the electrical matter that streamed out of the body) from affluent (the electricity moving toward the body).

In addition to general direction, there were also differences in the *way* effluent and affluent moved. Effluent emerged from bodies in strong streams through tiny narrow jets in the surface of the body that were spaced apart from each other. So effluent did not come out from everywhere on the surface, but only at the separated points where there were jets. And as electrical matter came out of the jet, it spread out into rapidly moving cones of moving effluent.

Affluent, on the other hand, did not move as strongly as effluent. This was because affluent was a mixture of the effluents of nearby bodies; hence it was not issued in one direction only. Further, as it came toward the electrified body, affluent impacted the surface of the body virtually everywhere. As is evident in the figure, the corridors of affluent intersected the surface of the electrified body at virtually all points except for where the jets of effluent were located. Nollet explained that when the experimenter brought a finger near an electrified body, affluent from the hand collided with the more powerful effluent jet coming out from the body. This collision of opposing fluxes separated the elements of earth and fire that made up each flux, producing luminous sparks. The collision also squeezed the air, causing the snapping noise. The affluent, being forced back to the hand by the more powerful effluent flux, violently struck the finger, producing the feeling of a shock.

What impressed many natural philosophers of the day about Nollet's theory of electricity was that it reduced the basic explanation of the electric effect to quantitative differences in the speed and direction of the flow of one universal electrical fluid. In addition to giving an account of the discharge that occurred when drawing sparks from a prime conductor, Nollet's theory accounted nicely for the attraction, contact, and repulsion that experimenters had frequently noticed. In this case, lightweight objects in the vicinity of the body, caught up in the affluent flow, moved toward the electrified body. When they made contact they were stimulated to emit their own effluent jets, which then repelled them away from the electrified body.

Between 1745 and 1752 Nollet's hypothesis about the nature of electricity enjoyed a broader acceptance than any other theory that had been put forth. The success of Nollet's conjecture, however, did not mean that it did not possess considerable difficulties. For example, it was not always the case that lightweight objects were repelled after making contact with the electrified body to which they were drawn. Most significantly, Nollet's explanations did not apply well to the Leyden jar once it came on the scene. A major drawback here was what Nollet said about the property of glass. In his explanation of the spider web of threads Hauksbee had produced inside a spinning glass globe, Nollet had made it clear that the electrical fluid easily penetrated the glass. But if that were so, then how was it that von Kleist and van Musschenbroek were able to carry a flask of electrified water around for a while, discharging it when they decided to? Nollet's theory did not appear to handle the new portable sparking machine that gave such powerful shocks. When an alternative theory of electricity emerged from across the Atlantic, it would rely on claims that revealed a fundamental disagreement with Nollet's understanding.

Benjamin Franklin's Theory of Electricity

All American schoolchildren learn of Benjamin Franklin's (1706–1790) beginning as a young apprentice in the Boston print shop of his brother and of his eventual success as a journalist on his own in Philadelphia. They hear about his achievements as a representative of the American colonies to France and his role in the Continental Congress. They also learn a little about his exploits in electricity. The story of Franklin's kite experiment in a thunderstorm is among the most well-known sagas of American history. What is generally not understood is the degree of Franklin's involvement with electricity, his contribution to its theoretical understanding, and his stature in Europe as a natural philosopher.

Franklin's early work on electricity.   By the 1730s Franklin had become established in Philadelphia as the printer of *The Pennsylvania Gazette* and the publisher of *Poor Richard's Almanack*. But it quickly became clear that his interests extended well beyond journalism. He engaged in several public works projects for the city, was instrumental in the creation of a lending library, and, in 1743, helped to found the American Philosophical Society. As a person who possessed intense natural curiosity, Franklin enjoyed learning about what was already known and investigating for himself subjects that were not yet understood.

In 1743 he was in Boston, where he attended the show of an itinerant lecturer on electricity from Scotland. Franklin was intrigued enough that he brought the man to Philadelphia in 1744 to entertain his acquaintances with the marvels produced by rubbing a glass tube. It was the standard fare developed by Gray and Dufay, even to the point of electrifying a boy suspended in the air.

The following year brought word of even more amazing electrical happenings to Franklin's attention. A British businessman with interests in the colonies had agreed to help supply materials for the lending library. In the spring of 1745 he sent over a glass tube along with an account of the work of Bose and others in Germany that had appeared in a popular English review called *The Gentleman's Magazine*. The account of the Leipzig experiments that made its way across the Atlantic exhibited an international pedigree that illustrated the widespread attention electricity was commanding. It was an English translation from the French of a review in a Dutch journal written by a Swiss natural philosopher who was a professor in a German university!

With some associates, Franklin set out to repeat the experiments described by the article. Before long he was hooked on the new subject. Within a year he had heard about the Leyden jar and was doing experiments to learn as much as he could about the wonderful bottle from Holland.

Franklin's explanation of the Leyden jar. As he worked with the phenomena produced by the Leyden jar, Franklin began to formulate a theory about why it worked as it did. While the new theory challenged some notions in circulation, others it agreed with. For example, like Nollet, Franklin thought of electricity as an effluvium that was set into motion by rubbing. It was either a form of common fire or perhaps an element unknown to Aristotle. Electricity, then, was a material substance, even if it was matter that differed qualitatively from so-called gross matter—solids, liquids, and the various vapors known at the time.

But Franklin developed a set of ideas to account for the behavior of the Leyden jar that implied much more about electricity. For one thing, he proposed that gross matter and electrical fire mutually attracted each other. As a result, the denser a body was (the more gross matter it possessed), the more electrical matter it attracted to its surface. An implication of this for Franklin was that earth attracted to itself a vast amount of electrical fire. Where receiving or giving up electrical matter was concerned, earth (or the ground) was like a good well—it could quickly receive as much electrical matter as an experimenter could give it and it could surrender equally fast as much as an experimenter could extract.

Franklin further declared that electrical matter had the interesting characteristic of repelling itself. Left to its own devices electrical fire would attempt to flee from itself, to expand to fill space. But of course electrical matter did not exist in empty space because the gross matter of solids, liquids, and vapors was always in its vicinity. This meant that an equilibrium would be set up between the attractive force that drew it to the surfaces of gross material substances and the repulsive force that drove it away from itself. The result of these two opposing tendencies was that a characteristic amount of electrical matter would end up on the surface of bodies.

One final innovation marked Franklin's understanding of the Leyden jar. Unlike Nollet and others, Franklin held that glass was absolutely impermeable to the electrical fire. This meant that electrical fluid could not get through glass at all. It could, in other words, be trapped inside the jar. But the repulsive force electrical matter exerted toward itself *could* pass through glass. This was because it acted at a

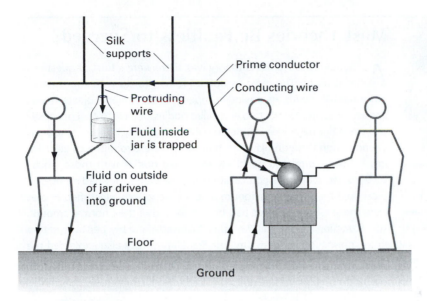

Franklin's Explanation for the Leyden Jar

distance, just like the gravitational force that Newton said all matter exerted on other matter. Franklin confessed he did not understand how a body could act where it was not, but action at a distance was part of his explanation of the Leyden jar.

With these provisions Franklin was now in a position to provide an explanation for why the Leyden jar behaved as it did. In the standard arrangement, there would be a characteristic equilibrium amount of electrical fluid on the surface of the spinning globe and on both the inside and outside surfaces of the glass jar. Franklin thought of the operation as pumping electrical fluid from the ground into the jar, where it was trapped. As the globe spun and electrical fluid was rubbed off into the conducting wire that ran to the prime conductor, it would be replaced immediately from the ground through the body of the person rubbing the globe. Fluid then traveled along the prime conductor, down the wire and into the flask, where it accumulated on the inside surfaces of the flask and on the surface of any water in the flask. It created what Franklin called an electrical atmosphere, which took the shape of the electrified surface.

Obviously the quantity of trapped electrical fluid inside the jar was much greater than the equilibrium amount initially present. As a consequence, there was much more repulsive force present than normal. According to Franklin, that force *could* be exerted through the glass even though the fluid itself could not penetrate the flask. When it was exerted through the sides of the flask, it repelled the equilibrium amount of electrical fluid present on the outside of the flask. That fluid ran through the body of the person holding the flask and into the ground.

Franklin's explanation made sense of a number of things about the Leyden jar experiments. First, it explained immediately why the person holding the flask had to be standing on the ground as the jar was being charged. If the person was

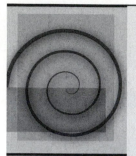

The NATURE of SCIENCE

Must Theories Be Faultless to Succeed?

As ingenious as Franklin's theory was, there were a host of questions that it raised. The most troublesome had to do with the theory's incompatibility with an obvious property of electrified objects. It was known, for example, that two electrified bodies, one electrified positively and the other negatively, attracted each other. Dufay had explained this phenomenon through his claim that there were two different electricities. Franklin correlated positively electrified bodies with those whose surfaces had acquired electrical atmospheres; that is, they had more electrical fluid than their equilibrium amount. Negatively electrified bodies were those whose surfaces had been deprived of their normal amount. The attraction of one for the other followed naturally because nature would strive to re-establish the normal equilibrium amount. Franklin's theory also explained the case in which two positively electrified bodies repelled each other. Here the excess electrical fluid on the surfaces of two bodies would cause the self-repulsive force of electrical fluid to increase and drive the bodies apart.

The problem came when Franklin tried to explain why two negatively electrified bodies also repelled each other. Franklin's theory could not account for this. Two negatively electrified bodies were both deprived of their normal equilibrium amount of electrical fluid. There was, therefore, no reason why they should repel each other. And yet they did.

In spite of this drawback, Franklin's theory underwent modifications and won widespread approval for what it *was* able to explain. When Franklin used his theory to explain and tame the action of lightning, his fame grew enormously in France and elsewhere. His theory was far from perfect, but, on the basis of explaining the preponderance of the observed data, it still has to be judged a huge success.

insulated, then the fluid could not be repelled into the ground, and if that were so, then the fluid could not accumulate inside the jar in the first place because it could only build up as the fluid on the outside surface left.

Franklin explained that if the normal amount of electrical fluid on the inside and outside surfaces of the jar was 20 units, then if 1 extra unit was trapped inside (giving 21 inside), 1 unit would be driven away from the outside (giving 19 outside). The total amount of fluid inside and outside remained the same, but as the amount inside built up and the amount outside diminished, there was a growing unevenness in the way the total was distributed. Franklin observed that when 20 extra units had been deposited inside, giving a total of 40 units inside, then there would be no more fluid on the outside surface and the process ceased. If the experimenter tried to force more fluid into the flask, there would be loud cracks that signaled nothing more could be done.

Further, Franklin's theory explained why the same person who held the flask had to be the one to discharge the jar. Discharging the stored electricity was accomplished by returning the uneven distribution of electrical fluid to its normal equilibrium condition. To do that a route had to be found that would allow the extra 20 units of electrical fluid inside to return to the outside so that there would again be 20 on the inside and 20 on the outside surfaces. That route could only be supplied by the body of the person holding the flask. When he or she touched the protruding wire at the top while holding onto the outside of the flask, the extra fluid inside could travel up through the wire, through that person's finger, down the arm, across the chest, and out the other arm to the hand holding the flask by its outside surface. Presenting the jar to a second person who was not holding the jar did not provide a direct route from the inside surface to the outside surface.

Franklin, electricity, and lightning.   Franklin was certainly not the first one to compare lightning to electricity. For one, his rival theorist and critic in France, Jean Nollet, did so a year before Franklin formally set down his reasons for the similarity. But Franklin was the first one to suggest an experiment to demonstrate it. In his famous sentry-box experiment, first proposed in 1750, Franklin suggested that an iron rod protrude 20 to 30 feet from a sentry box in which a man was to draw a spark from the rod. Franklin described ways he thought the man might insulate himself for purposes of safety. It was the French translator of Franklin's *Experiments and Observations on Electricity* of 1751 who actually first set up the experiment in a village near Paris in May of 1752. Its success brought Franklin's system to the attention of all of Europe, prompting others to try the experiment, until the following year, when a Swedish investigator was killed while trying to draw lightning down a rod.

Legend has it that Franklin himself, unaware of the French success, attempted somewhat later to use a kite to draw down lightning from the heavens. There is no direct evidence that confirms he actually did the experiment, although he appears to have given his blessing to later accounts and it was not in Franklin's character to deliberately deceive the public about science.

Franklin's great fame in Europe was based on his being the person who had tamed lightning. He described his idea for the lightning rod in the book of 1751. In accordance with his theoretical understanding of electricity and his belief that lightning was itself electricity, Franklin reasoned that buildings could be protected from lightning strikes if a conductor was attached to them. In this way the lightning could be led safely into the ground without destroying the building in the process. Although a Czech priest claimed to have had the idea independently of Franklin, scholars have argued that it was likely the news of the death of the Swedish experimenter that set the priest to thinking about a lightning rod. If so, his idea was not entirely independent of Franklin.

By the 1770s electrical science had made great strides, even if there were many phenomena that could not yet be consistently accounted for by any one theory. When compared to what was known and understood at the beginning of the century, however, things had changed dramatically. The avid interest in electricity that now existed everywhere in Europe and America would only increase as time went on. When, as the century wound down, a link between electricity and living things led to knowledge about how to prolong electrical discharge in a flowing current (see Chapter 16), the subject became more important than ever.

Suggestions for Reading

Joyce E. Chaplin, *The First Scientific American: Benjamin Franklin and the Pursuit of Genius* (New York: Basic Books, 2006).

I. Bernard Cohen, *Franklin and Newton* (Philadelphia: American Philosophical Society, 1966).

John Heilbron, *Electricity in the 17th and 18th Centuries* (Berkeley: University of California Press, 1979).

Duane Roller and Duane H. D. Roller, *The Development of the Concept of Electrical Charge* (Cambridge: Harvard University Press, 1967).

CHAPTER 12

○

The Organization and Growth
of Living Things

As in the case of chemistry and electricity, natural philosophers drew upon a rich heritage of ideas in their considerations of living things. We have already examined in Chapter 4 the interest sixteenth-century investigators had in natural history, which included animals, plants, and minerals. As part of a renaissance of natural knowledge, these scholars reworked earlier ideas they had recovered from ancient authors not only in natural history, but also in animal and human anatomy. While they expressed enormous respect for what they inherited from ancient authorities, they were not uncritical of errors they uncovered in ancient works during the course of their own investigations.

This renewed interest in exploring the world of living things was but one aspect of a growing curiosity that had been awakened about the world in general. In addition to gathering information about animals and plants from classical sources, voyages of exploration provided another source of new knowledge. Between 1500 and 1700 there was a veritable explosion in the number of plants and animals recognized.

One of the results of the proliferation of botanical and zoological knowledge was a change in the meaning of the information. Traditionally, treatments of living things regarded flora and fauna not merely as things, but also as emblems of higher meanings. In this so-called emblematic worldview, the investigator sought to use animals and plants to convey spiritual or moral lessons. The strutting peacock with its unfolded tail feathers, for example, could be used to express warnings about pride. As the sheer number of familiar plants and animals increased, natural philosophers became more and more content simply to provide a depiction of living things as they existed in themselves. The result was that during the seventeenth century the emblematic use of plants and animals was replaced by a more descriptive approach.

◎   How Living Things Are Arranged   ◎

As the eighteenth century commenced, some natural philosophers concerned themselves with the challenge of bringing order to the many descriptions of plants and animals that had accumulated. Botanical books from the past, for example the many herbals that existed, might provide a wealth of detailed description, but often they used the vernacular name from a region where the plant grew. Likewise animals might claim a number of names. Cats, for example, could be categorized under the Latin name *musio,* but could also have the names *cattus, muriceps,* or *murilegus.* There was, in other words, no accepted standard way of naming individual plants and animals. What was needed was an agreed-upon rationale for arranging the myriad of living things.

The Great Chain of Being

The most general understanding of plants and animals that had been handed down from antiquity was the notion that the living world constituted a chain of being. Beginning with Plato's assumption that the natural world had originated through a process of the gradual unpacking of the mind of God, the idea was that, in reflecting their source in the perfect divine mind, all living things that could exist did exist. This implied that plants and animals could be arranged from the simple to the complex. In his comments on the classification of animals, for example, Aristotle noted that all living creatures were arranged roughly in a scale of perfection. Later this idea was made much more systematic in the notion of the *scala naturae,* or ladder of creation. In this idea, living things existed as a great chain of being in which there were no missing links—no gaps or places for a being that theoretically could have existed but did not in actuality.

   As Greek ideas about the world were assimilated into the outlook of Western Christianity, the natural tendency was to associate the rungs in this ladder of creation with the "kinds" referred to in the biblical account of creation. The author of Genesis noted that on the fifth and sixth days of Creation, God had directed the waters and the Earth to bring forth life, always with the instruction that the creation of individual creatures was to be done "after its kind." In recognition of how pervasive the notion of a scale of perfection had become in the Western mind, a historian of the twentieth century, Arthur Lovejoy, dubbed this arrangement "the great chain of being" in his well-known book with that title.

   By the seventeenth century the philosopher John Locke gave voice to a common assumption that this great chain of being ascended upward from inorganic matter all the way to God, with humankind somewhere in the middle:

> In all the visible corporeal world we see no chasms or gaps. All quite down from us the descent is by easy steps . . . and until we come to the lowest and most unorganical parts of matter . . . we have reason to think . . . that the species of creatures should also, by gentle degrees, ascend upwards from us toward [the Maker's] infinite perfection as we see they gradually descend from us downward.

The Fixity of Species

Naturalists in the eighteenth century inherited from their predecessors the notion that the many species were fixed unalterably in place. This assumption came about as the idea of the ladder of nature or the great chain of being settled into the mental universe of the Western mind. It became natural for Christians to associate this vision of the world of creatures with God's original Creation as depicted in Genesis. That association carried with it an implicit assumption: because God's Creation was perfect, the collection of species, or kinds, called into existence at the Creation of the world represented God's final decree concerning living things. To suggest that it was otherwise, or could become otherwise, would be tantamount to second-guessing God's intent.

From our perspective the idea of what came to be known as the fixity of species entailed a number of implications. It meant, for example, that God had created the final set of creatures that would inhabit the Earth. No new creature would come into existence at some later time in human history. That would imply that they had been overlooked in the Genesis Creation, which would cast doubt on the completeness and perfection of God's original work. There could not, in other words, be what later came to be known as an origin of species, by which was meant the appearance of a new species *after* God's original creative act.

By the same token it would not have occurred to many that a species might change over time from one kind into another. After all, the Genesis story indicated that each creature was to reproduce "after its kind." If somehow over time it became a different kind through reproduction, such a process would run directly against the meaning of Scripture. Of course scholars at the beginning of the eighteenth century were aware that the cats depicted in the most ancient of records looked just like the cats they were familiar with. Viewing species as fixed in place gave no reason to suspect that species might transform or evolve over time.

Finally, the fixity of species implied that no species could go out of existence or become extinct. To do so would mar God's Creation and frustrate the intent of the original design. Of course natural philosophers and theologians were quick to acknowledge that God could cause such events to occur—if God wished to eliminate a species of animal or create a new species it was within the divine prerogative to do so. But prior to the eighteenth century there was little reason to assume that God had done so or would do so in the future. As the eighteenth century dawned the common understanding of the fixity of species prevented consideration of an origin of species, an evolution of species, or an extinction of species.

The Goals of Classification

Since antiquity, natural philosophers had attempted to bring order to the diversity of the living world. While Aristotle's *History of Animals* set the tone for much of what came after for fauna, his student Theophrastus attempted in several works to provide a rough classification of plants into wooden plants, herbaceous perennials, vegetables, and cereals.

What changed as the early modern period developed was the sheer number of new plants and animals that were known. Medieval and early modern herbalists, as we have seen (Chapter 4), attempted to reign in this explosion of knowledge into books devoted to careful description of plant anatomy. In this period some began to organize plants according to their fruits and seeds, leaf structure, or flowers and fruits, so that by the end of the seventeenth century there were various schemes of classification based on fruits and individual aspects of plant morphology.

Where animals were concerned, questions arose as to whether similarity of appearance was sufficient to merit grouping animals together. And what constituted similarity of appearance? Given that new discoveries were presenting animals so complex as to complicate any attempt to make judgments of overall similarity, should the investigator focus on similarities only in certain parts of organisms? To do that introduced a degree of arbitrariness or artificiality not present when considering all the features of the entire organism. Lurking behind the wish to bring order to the incredibly diverse living world lay the hope, not easily attained, of arriving at a *natural system of classification* as opposed to an *artificial system of classification.*

The idea of finding a natural system was to correlate *all* the resemblances between two kinds of animals or plants, just as God saw them in the plan he used when they were originally created. With enough information and enough work, the naturalist could, at least theoretically, find which animals and plants shared common characteristics except for the one or two that made them unique. The challenge here, however, was obvious. Humans, after all, are not God and they cannot be expected to recognize as God did all the similarities two organisms might have. Still, many harbored the hope that humans would one day attain a sufficient mastery of the characteristics of organisms that they could erect a reasonable approximation to a natural system.

Creating an artificial system was a more attainable goal. The natural philosopher could deliberately restrict attention to one or a few characteristics in order to simplify the task of classification. These features would have to be evaluated independently of other characteristics the organism possessed, but they might serve to bring together different kinds of organisms in a meaningful way. While admittedly more arbitrary, artificial systems of classification were much simpler to erect and consequently they were less open to disagreement. Further, as we are about to see, they could be very suggestive of new insights.

◎   The World of Carl Linnaeus   ◎

Among those who took up the question of a natural system of classification in the eighteenth century was a Swede named Carl von Linné, whom we know by his Latinized name of Carl Linnaeus (1707–1778). Because he created a system of classification that was enormously successful, he has become know as the father of classification. But his traditional family name was not Linné or Linnaeus. These names were unknown among his ancestors before his father, whose name was Nils Ingemarsson. Carl's father gave the name Linné to himself in tribute to a linden tree growing next to the family farm.

Youth and Education

Carl's parents hoped their son would go into the Swedish Lutheran ministry, just as his father had done. His mother was the daughter of a pastor, so it was all the more natural to expect that Carl too would become a pastor. But when he went off to the university in the fall of 1727 at the age of twenty, Carl chose medicine as his field of study.

Carl was not, at least in his own mind, rebelling against the religion of his parents when he went into medicine. Linnaeus would always retain the religious heritage he inherited from his parents. But taking religion seriously was not the only thing he inherited from his father. He also picked up from him a love for gardening. Carl's father was an avid gardener who deliberately encouraged the same love of plants in his son. When Carl decided to abandon any plans for the ministry that his parents had for him and to study medicine, eventually focusing on the area of botany, he did not at all see this as rebelling against his religious upbringing. That was because he regarded his later occupation with botany as a religious calling. In fact, he developed a confidence about this that could come across as arrogance.

Linnaeus first attended Lund University in 1727 and a year later went on to Uppsala. In Uppsala there was a herbarium of three thousand species, something that really attracted him. The library's holdings, however, were woefully outdated. But Linnaeus was able to get hold of the botany books in the private library of one of the professors and he made good use of them. He so impressed his professors and others with his intellectual abilities that by 1732 he was able to obtain support from the Royal Society of Sciences in Uppsala for a research trip to Lapland, during which time he studied the flora and fauna of the region and also made observations about the customs of the Sami people who lived there.

Linnaeus's trip to Lapland provides another glimpse at how he never hesitated to fashion his own image favorably, a factor that no doubt made it possible for him to dominate those around him. For example, he felt no compunction about bending facts to his advantage. He left for Lapland on May 12, 1732, and returned on

Carl Linnaeus in Costume

October 10 of the same year. Although much of the time was spent getting to and returning from his destination rather than actually being in Lapland, he did cover some 2,000 miles. But in his report to those funding the trip he said he had gone 4,500 miles and he included a fictitious map that completely misled them about where he had gone. When he wrote up his travel diary he upped the number of miles he had traveled "in one year on land" to 6,200.

It was not possible to acquire a formal medical degree in Sweden, so Linnaeus decided to follow the common practice of going abroad. In 1735 he went to Holland, where, after only a week, he defended a thesis on ague and received his medical degree. While abroad, he brashly exploited his travels in Lapland by adopting a Sami persona and extolling his accomplishments as an explorer. At parties he wore a Lapp costume, complete with a Lapp drum, to the delight of the Dutch. He stayed on the Continent for three years, traveling, corresponding with some of Europe's botanists, and refining his classification work. Although he remained centered in Holland for three years, he never learned Dutch; in fact, by his own account, he also did not learn English, German, French, or Lapp. In 1738 he returned to Sweden, where he practiced medicine for three years before finally, in 1741, he was offered a position as professor of medicine in Uppsala. Here he would remain as professor for the rest of his life.

Classification and the Sexuality of Plants

Consistent with his strong sense of self-confidence, Linnaeus decided early in his student training that the botanical work he had been reading was inadequate. Hence, he determined that he would take upon himself the task of describing all flowers accurately. What he would do, as he later said, was to bring flowers "into new classes, reform name and genera, in a completely new way."

Linnaeus made plant sexuality the key to his new system. He was certainly not the first one to notice that plants had sexual parts. In the previous century Nehemiah Grew (1641–1712) had suggested in his *Anatomy of Plants* of 1682 that the stamen and pistil of a flower corresponded to male and female sex organs. The Tübingen professor Rudolph Camerarius (1665–1721) made the conclusion even more explicit in his *Letter on the Sexuality of Plants* (1694). This work convinced the French botanist Sébastien Vaillant (1669–1722), who then wrote his own treatment in 1717 entitled *Discourse on the Structure of Flowers, Their Differences and the Uses of Their Parts.* Although he may not have grasped its full implications at the time, Linnaeus had first been introduced to the notion by a teacher he had in secondary school, even before he went off to university.

In 1729, when he was twenty-two, Linnaeus read a journal review of a lecture Vaillant had given in 1717. He was unaware of the publications of others before Vaillant that had also discussed the sexuality of plants. But he determined that he would make it the key to the new system of classification he was committed to creating. Throughout his career Linnaeus tended to downplay his dependence on others where possible and he did so in this case. He did not like acknowledging the work of Vaillant.

In the early 1730s, as a young student, Linnaeus wrote out his first thoughts on a sexual system of plants. After noting the analogies that existed between plants and animals—they both depend on nutriments, they both suffer diseases, they both receive nutriments through veins and vessels—he examined all the parts of a flower to see which ones served as sexual organs. Having considered all of the parts, he settled on the stamens, the pollen-bearing parts, as the male organ and the pistils, the parts on which the pollen falls, as the female. These organs were most usually close together in the same flower, but they could be separated in the flower, or they could even be found in separate, individual male or female flowers. When the latter was the case, Linnaeus observed, the male flowers generally stand above the females so the pollen can fall easily onto the pistils.

When he turned to a system of classification, worked out in 1730 and presented again in 1735 in a work entitled *System of Nature,* Linnaeus argued that nature itself determined sexuality as the basis for classifying plants because fruiting occurs so consistently. In his system he used the number of stamens and their relation to each other as the basis of the major divisions of plants into classes. For example, Class 14 of the twenty-four classes of flowering plants included those whose stamens were arranged in a specific way. In particular, if there were two stamens adjacent to each other that exceeded the others in size, the plants belonged to Class 14. While other authors had commented on nature's different arrangements of stamens and pistils, no one before Linnaeus had thought to use these as the basis for a systematic classification of plants.

The first edition of *System of Nature* was a slim book. Over the course of his career Linnaeus expanded it in numerous editions, which eventually grew into several volumes. The basic idea about using plant sexuality to create a system of classification, however, remained.

Linnaeus was always clear that his system of classification was an artificial scheme. It did not in his mind represent the ultimate goal of the naturalist—a natural system of classification that captured the plan God had employed when he created living things. Linnaeus conceded that his was a taxonomy based on one characteristic, sexuality, rather than a complete set of characteristics. This idea of a natural classification eluded him all his life, even though he called it the "first and last goal" of botany. Though Linnaeus was clear that he was creating an artificial system, he believed that its merit would be its ease of use.

Linnaeus's most noted critic was the Comte de Buffon (see Chapter 9), a natural philosopher who was equally celebrated in his French homeland as Linnaeus was in Sweden. Above all he did not approve of Linnaeus's apparent abandonment in his system of a natural classification. Buffon mocked Linnaeus's artificial choice of sexuality as the basis for classification. In one of his works he joked that a particular description of a certain tree was unclear because, of course, it was necessary to count its stamens to know what it really was. But in spite of such criticism, Linnaeus's system proved as useful as the Swedish naturalist hoped it would be. It quickly found favor throughout Europe, much to the consternation of Buffon and others.

Binomial Nomenclature

A major problem confronting botanists in these years resulted from the different names a plant species could have. For one thing, plants had different names in each of the many European languages. Because there was no common scheme, the number

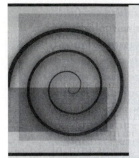

The Subtleties of Classification

When in secondary school we first encounter the challenge of mastering our modern system of classifying plants and animals, we likely make the assumption that the designation of species, genera, class, family, and kingdom correspond unproblematically to real divisions that exist in nature. When we do this we are, in our own special way, retaining a belief in the existence of a natural classification, even if we no longer think of it in relation to God's original creative activity. For us the natural classification is the one that modern scientists have found to exist in nature.

The NATURE of SCIENCE

Because our modern system of classification owes so much to Linnaeus, and because he was quite aware that his system was in the end an arbitrary system, we do well to realize that *any* system of classification cannot claim to represent the way things are unambiguously. Every system of classification, including those of the present, reflects assumptions that have helped to shape it. The noted paleontologist Stephen J. Gould observed how he once suddenly realized that his own assumptions about how life had evolved on Earth were ruling out from the beginning certain possibilities concerning how living things might be classified. When we encounter new forms of life that do not easily fit into the existing system of classification, the tendency is to make them fit rather than to question the structure of the system itself. But nature is if anything complex, always capable of presenting us with new surprises.

of possibilities for naming a species was hopelessly large. In the end, the multiple names for a plant species were due to two primary factors. First, the names were dependent on the scheme individual authors chose and second, they were meant to describe the plant as well as to distinguish it from others.

Since well-known botanists had for some time been publishing compilations of plant species, there were in circulation numerous standard works. This meant that if someone inquired about the names of plants, the first decision to be made was whose system to use. For example, one day an Uppsala professor saw Linnaeus in the botanic garden and quizzed him on the names of the plants. Linnaeus first had to decide whose names to employ. He gave the professor the names as they had been identified by the French botanist and explorer, Joseph Pitton de Tournefort (1656–1708).

The second factor, the use of names to describe plants species, produced equal confusion. To provide an adequate description of the species usually required a string of words. Indeed, many of the names in existence were long, making quick recognition of the species and easy use of the name difficult, if not impossible. In addition, not everyone chose names that described a plant's characteristics in the same way. Some might emphasize the features of the plant's growth, the geographical range in which it flourished, the climate required, or other aspects vital to the species.

Linnaeus's greatest invention, the one for which he is most famous, is the invention of what is called binomial nomenclature, the efficient use of two arbitrary names as a simpler way to identify a species. He had tried other schemes before settling on the one that would eventually bear his name. Prior to inventing binomial nomenclature he commonly used three word identifiers—a generic name, an abbreviated title of the book where he first described the species, and their number in that work. As new species were discovered, however, it became unwieldy to list them in new editions of older works because their place in the sexual classification system already had sequential numbers that would then have to be altered.

In the late 1740s and early 1750s Linnaeus began using just two arbitrary Latin names, without trying to use names to describe the species. For instance, he named butterflies only after deities and individuals of classical mythology. What we know as the Red Admiral received the name *Vanessa atalanta,* after Venus, the Roman goddess of love, and the ancient heroine Atalanta. This was easy to remember because of the story of Atalanta, who, having agreed to marry only if a man could beat her in a race, was distracted by Venus and lost to a suitor. Linnaeus did worry a bit that his highly simple scheme might seem too arbitrary to some (which it did), and that some might forget how important accurate descriptions of plant species were in their own right. He believed that the botanist must not cease describing plants, just that they should not try to make the name do the describing.

Linnaeus did not anticipate how quickly or how widespread the idea of his arbitrary approach to naming plants would catch on. When he began to use what soon became his famous binomial nomenclature he did not think of it as a crucial innovation. For example, he did not regard the particular names he had come up with as written in stone. He fully expected that others might change the names he had chosen. His introduction of the system was more a response to the haphazard way his students were abbreviating the names of species with which they were working. Over time, as he realized how popular his simplification of naming plant species had become, Linnaeus himself began to portray his contribution to nomenclature as a highly significant innovation. Toward the end of his life he observed that, whereas trivial names were unheard of before, now they were everywhere because two names were easier to remember.

Experimenting with Plants

Historian of science Lisbet Koerner has argued that Linnaeus simplified existing systems of nomenclature when he did because of a practical motivation that was tied to his powerful devotion to his Swedish homeland and his general interest in promoting its economy. Linnaeus believed strongly in a divine order of things and that divine order included the economic arrangements by which societies functioned. An integral part of the economy obviously involved the local cultivation of agricultural products, which he felt should be done by Swedes. If Swedes did not have sufficient knowledge, then agriculture would be dominated by foreigners. By mastering knowledge of the science of plants and animals, including a nomenclature that made that knowledge more efficient, Linnaeus believed that he could make Sweden more independent of other nations. He feared dependence on others. "Without science," he once said in a speech to the royal family, "our herring will still be caught by foreigners, our mines will be mined by foreigners, and our libraries will be weighted down with foreign works."

Linnaeus set out to address this situation by improving the understanding of living things as a way to benefit his homeland. He undertook a particular kind of research as an expression of his commitment to improving the Swedish economy by making it more self-sufficient. This research involved his famous endeavors to acclimatize plants that were not native to Sweden, even plants from tropical regions, to the Swedish environment.

As a famous professor in Uppsala, Linnaeus had many students. He sent them all over the world as his emissaries to gather information and to bring back products for his acclimatization experiments. His assumption was that plant species exposed to a colder climate would develop into a stronger variety. His instructions to the students indicated that he was more interested in the potential usefulness of a specimen they might bring back to him than he was in its purely scientific value. Were he successful, then Sweden would not only be the center of this kind of research, but it could become less dependent on other countries.

Clearly, Linnaeus believed that plants possessed a tolerance for variations in temperature. Over time, with careful nurturing, specimens from foreign lands could be tricked into growing in Sweden's harsher climate; that is, they would develop into a hardier variety. He never specified the mechanism by which the process of acclimatization was to occur, nor did he conduct experiments that empirically tested his adaptation hypothesis. He imagined more generally that tropical plants might be thought of like birds that migrated to Sweden in the summer.

In spite of overblown optimism and rumors of success at growing such things as tea, coffee trees, and Chinese herbs for medicine, most of these experiments had very little chance of success. What is important, however, is the reason Linnaeus undertook them: to use the divinely ordered laws of natural philosophy to support his deep devotion to his native land. The results of his plant experiments, however, would have important implications for his views on the permanence of species.

◎ New Ideas Challenging the Fixity of Species ◎

If in 1700 species were regarded by virtually everyone as fixed by God's activity at the Creation, over the course of the eighteenth century there would be those who questioned various implications of the fixity of species. A strict understanding of the fixity of species suggested, as noted earlier in this chapter, that no new species had come into or gone out of existence since the original Creation. That meant, as well, that no species had so changed over time that it had turned into another species.

We saw in Chapter 9 that the eighteenth century produced highly speculative theories of the Earth's history by Benoit DeMaillet and Georges Buffon. In these theories, the development of higher forms from lower forms of life was assumed, although no specific account of how this had occurred was provided. Here we will investigate the more specific challenges to a strict understanding of the fixity of species.

Linnaeus and the Fixity of Species

From his experiments on acclimatization it is clear that Linnaeus did not think living things were so fixed in their characteristics that they could not adapt to a new environment, even if that environment was substantially different from the one they were used to. His exhaustive study of plants over decades, by which he became familiar with many new plants with unusual features, brought him to a different understanding of God's work at the Creation. One plant, in particular, that a student showed him in 1744 had such unusual features when compared to all similar plants that it may have caused him to begin to doubt the fixity of species.

Where had these varieties and those features come from? Linnaeus began to consider the possibility that not all presently existing plants had been created as the result of God's original creative activity. Some must have originated since that time. He did not believe for a moment that these new species appeared apart from God's control—any origin of new species had to have been intended by God. But if God had not created them during the activity described in Genesis, then by what process had God caused them to originate at some later point?

Linnaeus considered the likelihood that their origin could be accounted for by a difference in the soil in which they grew, but he decided this was not the case. He began entertaining the possibility that the emergence of varieties was the result of a natural process of hybridization. By the 1760s he had come to the conclusion that hybridization occurred in nature and that it had occurred in history. Some species, he came to believe, were what he called "children of time."

Linnaeus reasoned that God originally created one species in each natural order. That would mean that in the beginning there were only a small number of species. Some of these species could and immediately did fertilize each other, thus producing a new species through hybridization. This process, then, established the original *genera,* each of which contained two original species and a new hybrid species. Permanent varieties resulted from the cross-fertilization of species within the same genus. But the hybridization among the original species was not restricted to species within the first genera; it also occurred between species in *different* genera to produce new species and this is how the complex variety of species had occurred.

Editions of Linnaeus's work, *System of Nature,* contained the widely accepted conclusion that there were "no new species." Like most everyone else, Linnaeus believed for much of his life that all of the species that existed had been directly created by God. But in the 1766 edition of his work the words "no new species" were removed. This change did not go unnoticed. After his death a German theologian named Zimmerman accused Linnaeus of atheism. Linnaeus's son defended him by insisting that his father believed that the natural order was the work of God, even if there were species that were the work of time.

We must note how profound the change was that Linnaeus had introduced into his conception of the world of living things. One way of summarizing it is to say that Linnaeus had changed goals. He was no longer trying simply to provide an *inventory* of nature; rather, he was attempting to depict a *program* of nature. The shift from a static goal of nature's inventory to the dynamic conception of a program of nature represented a fundamentally different direction. But the prevailing strong embrace of a static vision of nature in Linnaeus's day meant that this aspect of his thought was not influential and did not assume a place as part of the Linnaean legacy.

Buffon and the Mutability of Species

As noted earlier in this chapter, the Comte de Buffon did not think much of the Linnaean system of classification. He would not have been unhappy with Linnaeus's ideas about God, if he was aware of them, or about his eventual rejection of the fixity of species. Buffon was another natural philosopher in the eighteenth century who preferred to emphasize natural process over God's direct involvement in nature, and he too concluded that species were not as fixed as was commonly assumed. But his conclusion about what had happened in history was different from Linnaeus's. He agreed that species had changed over time, but not in the way Linnaeus imagined.

Buffon worked primarily on animals rather than plants. He used the fact that animals reproduce through the mating of males and females to create a new definition of species. Two animals were members of the same species, he said, if they can mate and produce fertile offspring. This definition made the decision about whether two individuals belonged to the same species much more determinative than the appeal to similarities of appearance had been. If two animals could not mate, or if when they did mate they produced an offspring that— like the mule that comes from crossing a horse and a donkey—was sterile, then they did not belong to the same species.

Where animal species were concerned, Buffon came to the conclusion that what Linnaeus would call different species were really variants of an original ancestral form. He believed that over time the ancestral form had "degenerated" because as individuals changed locations they encountered differences in external conditions. Factors such as climate caused the original ancestral forms to degenerate into the diversity we now have. Lions and tigers, for example, were degenerative forms of an ancestral cat. Buffon believed that practical reasons made it impossible for these degenerations to interbreed at present. But, theoretically, if the external conditions that caused the degeneration to occur were removed, the ancestral form would reemerge as quickly as it had degenerated.

It is important to remember that the ideas of both Linnaeus and Buffon that challenged the fixity of species did not represent the majority opinion. Most naturalists continued to accept the idea that God was responsible for creating everything that existed and that what he created had always been that way. If species had changed in either the way Linnaeus or Buffon had suggested, the first question that arose was how much time had been required? As we learned in Chapter 9, challenges to the traditional understanding of the Earth's history were often rejected for what they were—speculation. Voltaire, who was hardly one to fear radical new ideas, found it ridiculous to think that, as he put it, the seed of a millet had retained its shape while the Earth had changed its. It made more sense to most people to discount as not worthy of serious attention the notion that the Earth and the living things on it had been developing from an ancient past to the present.

◎ How Living Things Grow ◎

Considerations of species and genera focus the attention on groups of living things. If by the time of Linnaeus and Buffon natural philosophers had begun to ask about how species may have developed over time, they were also interested in questions about individuals and how they developed. The process of growth is so common a part of human experience that it is often taken for granted. Nevertheless, investigators in the eighteenth century wrestled with a challenging question about growth— especially animal development from conception to adulthood—that led to fascinating ideas about how things grow.

Regardless of the differing views of the male and female roles in sexual reproduction that came down to the eighteenth century from the past, all agreed that the sexes had to cooperate if an embryo were to develop. The knotty question had to do with how the embryo, which appeared to start out as a formless mass, grew. Clearly it took on specific forms as it developed. But what governed this process? If the embryo were truly formless at the beginning, then all embryos were similar as they started out. How did one embryo know to develop into a chicken and another into a horse? What guided this process? This question was not new to the eighteenth century, but the issue was now sharpened by a major debate.

Numerous thinkers from the past had considered the dilemma raised by the question of the embryo. The philosopher René Descartes, for example, said that in procreation male and female semen were mixed together, that the mixture underwent a process of fermentation, and that as a result the parts of the body slowly formed. While Descartes was at least trying to provide a naturalistic explanation (as opposed to saying simply that God directly caused the growth of every embryo), he hardly solved the problem. Although Descartes held that fermentation resulted from particles of matter interacting mechanically, the obvious question was *how* the fermentation guided the embryo's development. Put another way, how did the formless chicken embryo know to follow the mechanical laws that would produce a chicken? The prospect that there was one set of mechanical laws that produced a chicken, another set of laws for a horse, and another set for each of the countless adult forms that existed was not an attractive option.

The Theory of Preformation

One attempt to improve Descartes's treatment of the embryo was given in the late seventeenth century by Nicholas Malebranche (1638–1715) in what has become known as the theory of preformation. He agreed with Descartes that as the embryo developed it followed mechanical laws. But he wanted to make clear that an appeal to these laws alone could not answer the question of what directed the embryo's growth. For Malebranche, an intelligent agency had to be responsible for directing the development. Mechanical laws acting blindly by themselves could not, in his view, provide the direction needed unless a purposeful agency had set them up to do just that.

He solved the problem by suggesting that God had supplied the directive agency at the time of the original Creation. But Malebranche was careful not to undermine natural process by claiming that God continued to guide the development of every new embryo directly. God had created the original embryo with structure—for Malebranche, then, the embryo was *not* a formless mass. It had a preformed structure; in fact, the chicken embryo had the structure of a chicken and the horse embryo had the structure of a horse. Embryonic development amounted to the unfolding or expansion of this original structure into the adult form. The form present in the embryo was an adult form. This unfolding of the embryo proceeded according to mechanical laws God had designed to produce expansion. So the laws produced the expansion of the structure, but they were not responsible for creating the structure itself.

All this was fine for the original embryo of each organism, but what about the embryos of all the organisms since? If God's directive role was to be limited to his original creative work, where did subsequent embryos get their preformed structure? Malebranche explained that God had encased all future adult forms in the embryo of the first adult. The first chicken embryo, for example, contained encased inside it the forms of the embryos of the next generation, and these in turn carried within them the forms of the generation after that, and so on. In this way each embryo contained the embryos of all future individuals, encased in one another. And, as mentioned, it had been that way since the beginning. "All bodies of men and animals," wrote Malebranche, "which have been born up to the consummation of the century, have perhaps been produced as long ago as the creation of the world."

Preformation in the early eighteenth century. As the eighteenth century began, preformation theory enjoyed widespread acceptance. It solved the thorny problem of what guided embryonic development by denying that the embryo began as a formless mass. And it did so in a manner that was consistent with a divinely created world that operated according to mechanical laws.

There was some disagreement among preformationists about whether it was the egg or the sperm that carried the preformed adult forms. In the traditional position, which was based on observations of chicken eggs and small mammalian embryos, the determinative role was given to the egg of the female. But there were some, for example the prestigious Dutch physician and admirer of Newton, Hermann Boerhaave (1668–1738), who claimed that the sperm carried the adult forms. This was the minority view, however, since only one sperm of the many present in procreation was required to produce each individual. If the sperm carried the adult forms, then a host of future adults would be wasted in every act of sexual intercourse.

Preformation in the egg received new support when in 1740 the French natural philosopher Charles Bonnet (1720–1793) discovered that aphids, also known as tree lice, could reproduce themselves for several generations without fertilization by a male. Called parthenogenesis, this was evidence that the miniature forms of future adults were stored in the female egg.

Challenges to preformation theory.   Around the same time that Bonnet found support for preformation, another discovery was made that cast doubt on the theory. Abraham Trembley (1710–1784), a Swiss naturalist who was working in Holland, came across an organism, a freshwater polyp, which initially he thought was a plant. When he observed that it was capable of independent motion, however, he changed his mind and identified it as an animal. Then he found that the polyp was capable of something else—it could regenerate a complete adult form even after being cut in two. If this were so, then a new adult form was being produced from an incomplete adult form. This meant that it was not necessary, as the preformationists maintained, for the embryo to contain a complete adult form from the start in order to develop into a new adult.

Trembley's was not the only challenge to preformation. Around mid-century Georges Buffon also criticized the theory. First he noted that a close examination of the developing embryo did not confirm that a miniature adult form quickly emerged. The embryo, he said, did not show any change at all for some time, and then it only gradually developed. Buffon cited an additional criticism, which had been made by others before him, that went to the heart of the preformationist claim. If the adult form were encased in the egg, or even in the sperm, then why did offspring often resemble *both* parents? Clearly the mixing of the seminal fluids from both the male and the female was required. The challenges by both Trembley and Buffon did little to supply an alternative explanation of how the embryo developed. They were criticisms of preformation more than they were solutions to the problem of development. Buffon did attempt to supply something of an explanation. He suggested that nature must have provided what he called an internal mold that was responsible for directing the development. How this internal mold worked to produce individual structures for the developing embryo, or why attributing structure to a mold was different from locating it in a preformed embryo, was not specified. It was clearly easier to criticize preformation theory than it was to provide a persuasive alternative to it.

The Theory of Epigenesis

An alternative approach to explaining how the embryo developed was called epigenesis. In this view the embryo *was* regarded as a formless mass—it had no pre-existing structure. Epigeneticists stood in the tradition of those who appealed to the action of mechanical laws. They held that these laws operated in stages on the formless embryo to create a structure and then to make it more and more complex.

The earliest forms of epigenesis simply asserted that mechanical laws were sufficient by themselves, without elaborating further. As a result, natural philosophers such as Malebranche associated epigenesis with atheism because it seemed to say that God's presence was not necessary, that matter acting on its own could account for the development of life. Of course an epigeneticist could reject the charge of atheism by saying that God was responsible for setting up the laws that produced the structure, just as Malebranche said God had set up the structure itself. But removing God one step away from the actual structure was a dangerous precedent in the eyes of Malebranche. It introduced the possibility that someone might say the laws themselves were adequate for the job. As the eighteenth century proceeded the issue was sharpened by further developments.

Maupertuis and epigenetic theory.   We first met Pierre-Louis Moreau de Maupertuis in Chapter 9, in connection with his contribution to the development of French Newtonianism in the mid-eighteenth century. In 1745 he published, anonymously, an epigenetic explanation of embryonic development that was based on his work with the Newtonian force of attraction. He proposed that male and female semen were made up of particles. There was not just one kind of particle in the semen; rather, there were particles sent from each part of the body. As the semens mixed in procreation these individual particles were attracted to their respective counterparts. For example, particles from the heart of the male were attracted to particles from the heart of the female. In this way the various parts of the embryo were formed. Maupertuis pointed out that nonliving structures like crystals appeared to form as the result of forces of attraction; hence, it seemed reasonable to him that similar attractive forces could explain the structure that emerged in the developing embryo.

Anti-Newtonian critics soon attacked the author of the anonymous tract. They opposed the introduction of occult forces of attraction to explain the formation of the fetus just as they had fought against them in Newton's physics. Even if these forces were assumed, one critic said, he did not see how they could account for the formation of the intricately coordinated structures of the body, for example, the vessels and valves and a host of other structures. What Maupertuis had done, he continued, was simply to proliferate the number of attractive laws at will, in order to account for the myriad of complex forms in the body.

Maupertuis was stung by the criticism that he had created a new attractive force for every one of an organism's structured parts. He responded by backing away from strict epigenesis. He conceded that blindly acting attractive forces were insufficient. Perhaps an intelligent agency was present after all. He located the agency, however, not in God, but in matter itself. The particles might have a capacity to "remember" where they had come from so they would be able to arrange themselves as necessary.

The Haller-Wolff debate.   Epigenesis clashed with preformation theory again in the 1760s and 1770s in a debate between Albrecht von Haller (1708–1777), a well-known senior Swiss natural philosopher and journal editor, and a newly minted young doctor of medicine, Caspar Friedrich Wolff (1734–1794). The clash of views in this exchange between Haller, a preformationist who for a period in his life had actually been an epigeneticist, and Wolff, the confident young epigeneticist, involved the careful examination of experimental results on both sides. This illustrated how in natural philosophy a determination to base one's theoretical views on observation and experiment does not guarantee agreement.

Haller's teacher in the 1720s was Hermann Boerhaave, mentioned earlier as one of those preformationists who believed that the structured embryo was located in the sperm rather than in the egg. Haller accepted his teacher's views on preformationism as a student, but when he heard about Trembley's polyp in the early 1740s he changed his mind and became an epigeneticist. Although he now accepted that the embryo was a formless mass, that did not mean that he knew how to explain why it took on the structure it did as it grew. He asserted simply that the organization of the embryo emerged "according to laws that are unknown to us but which the eternal wisdom has rendered invariable."

Around mid-century Haller read the critique of preformation theory of Georges Buffon, described earlier in this chapter. Surprisingly, he found that he disagreed more with the reasoning of his fellow epigeneticist than he agreed with him. As a result he began to reconsider preformation theory

For three summers in the 1750s Haller conducted experiments on incubated chicken eggs. After prolonged and careful examination of the membranes visible in the yolks of the eggs, he concluded that they resembled the membranes of the intestines of the embryo. From this observation he drew the following conclusion: "The yolk itself is only an expansion of the small intestine of the chick. It is from this that one can draw a very plausible reason to give the female the true beginnings of the fetus." Haller was once again a convinced preformationist, although he now disagreed with his teacher Boerhaave's view that the preformed structure was to be found in the sperm. This was because the yolk existed before the male even became involved.

Haller announced his conversion back to preformation theory in a publication of 1758. In this work he tried to answer his own previous objection to preformation based on the regenerative ability of the water polyp. He adopted a reason given by other preformationists in response to Trembley's discovery: the water polyp was able to regenerate itself from half an adult form because it contained pre-existent germs in various parts of its body that were stimulated to develop whenever the organism was injured.

Haller's publication caught the attention of Caspar Friedrich Wolff, who had just completed a doctoral dissertation entitled "A Theory of Generation," in which he argued an epigeneticist view of embryonic development. Wolff had studied at Halle University, a fact that played a central part in the development of his views. Halle was known for much of the eighteenth century as a university in which the philosophy of Gottfried Leibniz reigned. Leibniz himself had died in 1715, but as noted in Chapter 9, where Leibniz's thought was briefly examined, his ideas lived on in the work of his major eighteenth-century interpreter, who taught at Halle. Caspar Friedrich Wolff imbibed Leibniz's philosophy at Halle, and he determined that he would be the first one to apply its principles to the study of embryology.

Leibniz's outlook, unlike that of Isaac Newton, permitted matter to possess active agency. That is, matter was made up of unextended points Leibniz called monads, which were nonmaterial metaphysical entities that resembled souls. As a result, for Leibniz it was not a contradiction to attribute active agency to matter. In fact, when Maupertuis had suggested that the particles of male and female semen "remembered" their former location, he drew on the Leibnizian view of matter he had learned while serving as president of the Berlin Academy at the request of Frederick the Great.

Caspar Wolff also interpreted Leibniz in such a way as to support epigenesis as opposed to preformation. In his view the embryo developed as the result of the secretion of fluids. Beginning with the yolk (or placenta), material foreign to it was secreted through repulsion. The secreted material then solidified and attracted similar material to itself from the surrounding nourishing fluids. This was how each new part of the developing embryo was formed. From here new material was secreted through repulsion, which also solidified into new parts, and so forth. After each new part was formed through solidification, fluids flowed into it that formed vessels that in turn defined the new structure.

Wolff insisted that, as a result of his careful observations, he had confirmed that fully formed parts did not emerge as the expansion of pre-existing structures. Similar to Buffon, Wolff asserted that new parts formed slowly. What he saw at work was the activity of nature's forces, certainly in harmony with the Creator's intent, but not directly or immediately under his control. Wolff objected to the preformationists' direct appeals to God to account for the embryo's increasingly ordered structure. He preferred to show that the finished product was, as he put it, "not something to whose production natural forces are completely insufficient."

Of course Haller responded to Wolff's claims with critiques and counterassertions. Neither convinced the other to change his mind because they were each beginning from a different philosophical outlook. Haller was, like his teacher Boerhaave, a convinced Newtonian. This meant that he could not attribute active agency to matter itself. Like Newton, he believed that the source of active agency was outside matter, which in itself was purely passive. Also like Newton, Haller feared that if matter were allowed to possess active agency by itself, as the epigeneticists seemed to demand, then, however much they proclaimed their religious beliefs, godless materialism would not be far behind.

Wolff, on the other hand, saw no threat to his religion from his belief in matter's active capacity to direct the development of the parts of the embryo. Like his mentor Leibniz, Wolff accepted that God had created the cosmos perfectly and that it was capable of running by itself. God's will could not be thwarted because everything happened in accordance with His plan. But it was also true that God exercised control remotely, through the natural forces and the laws governing their action that he had instituted. These natural laws were sufficient to account for how the embryo developed, just as they were for how the heavens moved.

The exchanges between Haller and Wolff in a real sense serve as a model of scientific debate. Each man was thoroughly convinced of his interpretation of the observations he had made, even when the same phenomena were being observed by, and differently interpreted by, his opponent. Both men spent a great deal of time observing and commenting on the formation of the blood vessels that bring nourishment to the embryo from the yolk during the development of chicks. Both men did the same with regard to the earliest visibility of the heart, which for Haller pre-existed as a heart while Wolff asserted that they were seeing the heart in stages of its formation. In their disagreement, however, they displayed the highest civility and mutual respect.

What underlay the debate was a common assumption that both men shared—a devotion to finding the truth as best they could. The two corresponded sparingly over almost two decades, from 1759 to 1777. Haller eventually published the first seven letters Wolff sent him, with the result that everyone was able to see exactly how Wolff dissented from his reading of the observations. For his part, Wolff always maintained the polite deference due his elder, but his high regard for Haller and his abilities was clearly genuine.

In 1766 Wolff acknowledged that their different reading of the observations had demonstrated the viability of both positions, that there was no definitive reason why he should choose one position over the other. If epigenesis tuned out to be true, Wolff wrote, he knew Haller would defend it because "the truth alone we both pursue." If it turned out to be false it would be an odious monster to himself as well as to Haller. If preformation were shown to be true, then Wolff would quickly submit to it, while he knew that if it turned out to be false, he would not need to speak because Haller would reject it. Wolff spoke here about the triumph of truth in a manner typical of his time. As so often happens, however, subsequent events had a way of developing on their own.

The Triumph of Epigenesis in Germany

Historian of science Shirley Roe, who has studied the debate between Haller and Wolff, notes that there was "an element of incommensurability" present in the views of the two men. She means by this that because of the philosophical assumptions each brought to the task of explaining how the embryo developed, there was no single experiment or observation that would have settled their differences in interpretation. That does not mean, however, that the view of one or the other, complete with the assumptions that lay behind it, might not become the consensus among groups of natural philosophers.

In fact in the German states, where the Haller-Wolff debate had taken place, preformation theory fell out of favor during the last decades of the eighteenth century. This development, and the subsequent rise of epigenesis among German natural philosophers, was not due to a perception that Wolff had prevailed in his discussions with Haller. It had to do with philosophical developments in Germany that flourished in the 1780s and 1790s. Given what we have seen to be the determinative role of the philosophical outlooks of both Haller and Wolff in their disagreements, it is not surprising that the rise of new intellectual options would be responsible for the development of a consensus about epigenesis.

By far the most significant figure behind the new outlook was the philosopher Immanuel Kant. More will be said about Kant's views in Chapter 14, in a discussion of the meaning of the Enlightenment. Here we are concerned primarily with what he said about the understanding of living things. His outlook set the tone for how German natural philosophers, who were to dominate the development of embryology, would approach the subject until almost the middle of the nineteenth century.

Kant's approach to the organic realm has been described as "teleomechanical," a word that combines the Greek word for purpose or goal (*telos*) with the idea of a mechanical system. Kant viewed organisms, then, as purposeful machines. What is important here is to recognize that he did not think of organisms as regular machines, which do not, *in themselves,* create the purposes for which they are used. Regular machines always receive their purpose from outside of themselves, from the builder of the machines.

Kant's point was that we cannot think of organisms as regular machines. That is because, he argued, whenever we observe organisms we cannot separate the purposeful behavior they express from the mechanisms that underlie that behavior. From the beginning of our perception of an organism, the purpose is present—it *comes with* the empirical perception and cannot be separated from it, as we can do with regular machines.

For this reason Kant vehemently asserted that the usual kind of mechanical explanation that is given for natural objects—for example, the behavior of the planets—could not hope to describe an organism completely. Regular machines, which receive their purpose from outside of themselves, would not be able to capture the purpose that does not come from outside the organism, but is essential to it.

Kant's position was that while we should use regular mechanical explanation as much as possible to explain organisms, we will never be able to give a complete explanation of an organism in this way. We will miss the purpose that is the essence of the organism. So, where the world of living things is concerned, we must *assume* the purpose from the beginning.

Kant gave many reasons for his position that need not occupy us here. Suffice it to say that his reasons were very persuasive to many German natural philosophers of his day. That being so, it was no longer necessary for the German natural philosophers concerned with the world of living things to have to resort to preformation theory to explain how the embryo developed. Purposeful behavior was part of the definition of living things; hence, there was no longer a need to explain why the embryo acted purposely. The mechanical laws that produced the changes in the embryo operated purposefully because it was the nature of organisms to behave that way. While Wolff had never defended his epigenetic view of development in these terms, it was easy for those impressed with Kant's outlook to adopt epigenesis—the purposeful development of life in accordance with natural mechanical laws—as an expression of the teleomechanical view.

By the end of the eighteenth century the image of the organic world as a great chain of being had undergone numerous changes in the minds of many natural philosophers. As the century came to a close other new ideas about life and its past emerged, and the result was that more and more new perspectives found their way into the wider public arena. When that happened many found it difficult to adjust to the numerous implications the new perceptions suggested.

Suggestions for Reading

Tore Frangsmyr, Sten Lindroth, and Gunnar Eriksson, eds., *Linnaeus, the Man and His Work* (Cambridge, Mass.: Science History Publications, 1994).

Lisbet Koerner, *Linnaeus: Nature and Nation* (Cambridge: Harvard University Press, 2001).

Timothy Lenoir, *The Strategy of Life* (Chicago: University of Chicago Press, 1989), Chapters 1 and 2.

Shirley A. Roe, *Matter, Life, and Generation* (Cambridge: Harvard University Press, 2003).

CHAPTER 13

―――――◎―――――

Understanding and Treating Illness

Human beings traditionally assign themselves a special place among living creatures. In the West that special place derived most directly from a religious outlook that identified cosmic history with humankind's fall from grace and its redemption. One person, of course, constituted a very small part in the great drama of history, but because the state of the soul was a vital question that involved every individual, humans placed themselves in a much different category from animals. Humans, after all, were made in the image of God and given domination over the beasts of the field and all living things.

However special they might be, humans were still subject to the patterns and whims of nature. In this respect they were not unlike animals. They too had to learn how to survive in a world of events that could take life from them unpredictably and suddenly. And they too were subject to sickness and disease. These contingencies only underscored the urgency and importance of caring for the soul, for the thread that tied humans to life was well understood to be very frail.

As we have seen in the preceding chapters, humans had for a long time sought to understand nature's course as much as they could. By the time of the seventeenth century it was even possible in some quarters to hear a new attitude of confidence that rejected surrendering to nature's whims as simply the will of God, something clearly beyond human ken. Of course this boldness was hardly shared by all, but more and more the idea spread that new knowledge could improve the lot of humans by placing them more in control of nature rather than being subject to its apparent caprice.

Most of the kinds of natural knowledge we have considered so far captured the attention of just a small segment of society. Alchemy and astrology found devotees from all social ranks, but detailed studies of subjects such as astronomy, motion, anatomy, physiology, chemistry, electricity, flora and fauna, and the development of the fetus failed to capture the attention of the majority of people.

The same cannot be said of medicine. The condition of the human body was a matter of direct and immediate concern for everyone. Sickness was (and remains) a great leveler; it had no respect at all for social class or any other means by which human beings distinguished themselves from one another. What people feared about sickness was that it might not pass and that it might be untreatable. For all his power, the king who suffered from an incurable disease had no advantage over a pauper in the same situation. As a result, many people, not just from the educated segment of society, became interested in whatever knowledge was available about healing.

◎ Healers in the Eighteenth Century ◎

Although there will be occasional allusions to several different countries, our discussion of healing in this chapter focuses mainly on the situation in the German states. Of course medical treatment varied from the city to the country, from one German state to another, and from one country to another. Here we are concerned with the general features of the understanding and treatment of disease in the eighteenth century. While the factors we will consider that determined who got treatment, and of what kind, were indicative of central Europe, they were not drastically different from those elsewhere. Our intent is to provide an example of the issues that people living at the time confronted.

Sanctioned Healers

One of the first distinctions that can be made among eighteenth-century healers was whether or not they had a license to practice. As we will see, however, as far as the eighteenth century is concerned, it is important not to read too much into that distinction. For example, it would be a mistake to assume that healers who had a license possessed a vastly different conception of what disease was and what should be done about it from those who operated without legal sanction.

Physicians.   Physicians were distinguished from other healers primarily because they possessed a university degree, which served as their license to practice. The medical degree identified its holder's middle-class status to other members of society, a station that permitted interaction with the classes both above and below, depending on the needs and circumstances present. Nobility tended to draw on physicians, while the poor, as we will see, often distrusted them.

In the eighteenth century, medicine remained one of the three "higher" faculties of the university, sharing this status with the faculties of law and theology. The lower faculty was philosophy, in which studies were distributed among the various arts and sciences. To complete a university training in any of these areas qualified one to assume certain established positions within society. Law students became the bureaucrats in civil administration, theology students took posts associated with the church, and medical students became physicians. In each of these cases there was the possibility of continuing academic study and remaining within the university structure as a professor. That was the best option for graduates of the philosophy faculty, who, other than becoming tutors to the children of noblemen or instructors in a lower school, had few other vocational options their university degree helped them obtain.

After receiving a degree from a faculty of medicine, a new physician could set up a practice and begin to see patients. This was easier said than done, however, because a new physician could have substantial difficulty supporting himself at the beginning of his career. (In the eighteenth century, students of medicine were overwhelmingly male. The first woman to graduate with a medical degree was in 1754, at the University of Halle.) To make the transition as easy as possible, new graduates in medicine would normally return to the area where they had grown up and where they were known. Even then they might have to agree to treat poor people for free or for a lower fee in order to establish a reputation.

In addition to normal duties, some physicians tried to supplement their income by taking on the responsibilities of overseeing the practice of medicine in a district, which usually comprised a village and its environs. These district physicians answered to the mayor or town council of a village, who were responsible for funding the position but who, as we will see, often failed to supply the support needed. As a result the district physician was very often caught in the impossible position of having to guarantee good medical practice without the financial means or the legal support to do so.

As already mentioned, a medical student might be able to move up the academic ladder within the university structure. To become a professor of medicine required the completion of publications, most importantly books, that were recognized as meritorious. Once established as an academic, a physician's

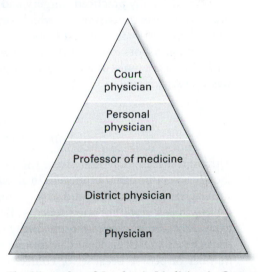

The Hierarchy of Academic Medicine in Germany

income, while not huge, was generally adequate. If the professor's reputation grew substantially, his income could become enough to support a comfortable life. A physician or professor of medicine might hope to become the personal physician to a nobleman or, at the top of the ladder, the court physician to royalty.

Other sanctioned healers.   In addition to physicians there were other medical professionals who enjoyed a sanctioned legal status, such as pharmacists, midwives, and surgeons. They were most often regulated through guilds, which in Germany possessed strict procedures governing training and apprenticeships. In addition, these professionals enjoyed a monopoly on their trade: pharmacists were understood to be the ones who made and sold drugs, midwives delivered babies and often treated other issues important to women, and surgeons operated on patients. As will become clear, there were pressures in the eighteenth century that caused some of these hard and fast lines to be crossed. Physicians, however, were not trained to do any of these activities.

In Germany, pharmacists, midwives, and surgeons required little if any formal education other than that provided through the apprenticeship. Moving up the ladder through an apprenticeship, however, could be very difficult indeed. Frequently there were costs that had to be borne by the apprentice, and often the apprenticeship could end only if there was a vacancy to be filled. With no guarantees, some found the road simply too difficult to follow.

The status of surgeons, in particular, was not the same in all parts of Europe. Unlike in Germany, surgery could be taught in the university in Italy and Spain. Indeed, in France and Britain the surgical profession made great strides, so that by the end of the eighteenth century the surgeon stood at a considerable distance from the barber and bleeder with whom he had once been compared.

As traditionally practiced, surgery had to do with the surface of the body. Thus, there were numerous ways in which one might need the services of a surgeon beyond merely performing an operation on the body: fractured bones, burns, knife and gunshot wounds, tumors, ulcers, and skin diseases. However it was handled, through a guild or a college of surgeons, the training and practice of surgery was well scrutinized.

Nonsanctioned Healers

Although increasingly there were rules demarcating who had a right to do what, the rules were not always obeyed. In all Western societies a host of healers assumed various special roles. They did so for a number of reasons, the main one being that there was a demand for their services. Because everyone in society was vulnerable to sickness and disease and occasionally had need of advice, there simply were not enough sanctioned healers. Consulting a physician was not an option for a great number of people because, of course, they could not afford to pay the fee. But equally important, there was an inherent distrust many people from the lower ranks of society felt about those above them, especially where their life or livelihood was concerned. This was the situation in France at that time. "Two centuries ago," writes historian Matthew Ramsay, "most Frenchmen and Frenchwomen saw 'healers' as familiar figures and doctors as exotic ones." The result was that the poor did not hesitate to go to a variety of healers among the many types that were available to them.

Most of these healers, but not all, specialized in one kind of ailment or another. For example, the expertise of corn doctors was clear from their title. The same was true for the oculist and dentist. Less obvious is why others, including peddlers, executioners, and wise women, prospered. It is clear from documents that many of the sick simply went back and forth across the line between these unsanctioned healers and those who enjoyed official recognition. People went to whomever they could, without regard for society's categories. The testimony concerning a man suffering from consumption in 1767, about whom an official inquiry was made, makes this clear. It indicated that the man had conferred with an executioner named Schwartze, but, "as Schwartze was unable to help, he sent to Dr. Müller for medicine; thereafter he consulted with the cowherd in [the village of] Liebenberg, and now Dr. Streuberg in Goslar is treating him."

The Administration of Healing

Often, discussions of medical regulation focused solely on physicians. In France, for example, it was the medical faculties of the universities that made sure standards were maintained and also that the numbers of physicians were controlled so as to increase income. In England, outside of London, there was little regulation, virtually guaranteeing that all sorts of healers would grace the countryside. Nor was there any uniformity to English medical education. Historian of medicine Roy Porter has observed that medicine in Britain "tacitly espoused the principles of Adam Smith, a sort of competitive individualism." In the American colonies things were no better.

In the German states, however, there was an attempt at regulation, not just for physicians, but also with regard to healers of various types. Determining which healers received official sanction, and therefore some oversight, was accomplished to varying degrees in the Germany of the eighteenth century. While it inevitably entailed the interaction of political and medical personnel, the level of political involvement depended in large measure on the size of the state involved. In a duchy, for example, the duke's privy council might coordinate the interaction of a board of appointed physicians with the town councils of villages.

The medical board.   The board of physicians, with the approval of whatever state council or legal body lay above them, established the regulations governing the activities of healers. As physicians and professors of medicine acquired and made known new medical ideas, the medical board might well attempt to establish a new policy that incorporated the latest wisdom. Or it might institute new standards of hygiene that were to obtain in public places, or recommend that the prince make certain decrees in response to the spread of a plague.

Medical boards in the smaller states were notorious for crafting special arrangements with individuals that often complicated things a great deal. Many of the nonsanctioned healers were itinerants, going from one place to another, making it difficult if not impossible to regulate their activity. But if, for example, a cowherd who permanently resided in a certain region was known to have successfully treated chronic indigestion, he might be able to persuade the medical board that it was in everyone's interest to permit him to ply his trade in the region with legal sanction.

Just how bad the situation could be is highlighted by historian of medicine Mary Lindemann, who refers to the bewildering array of healers that populated the countryside, almost all of whom, she has noted, "purported to have, and many could actually prove, a legal right to practice." Her list includes ordinary guild surgeons, privileged bathmasters, veterinary empirics, executioners, shepherds, manufacturers of medicines and their agents, dealers in patent remedies, 'emergency' apothecaries, sellers of cosmetics and secret remedies, itinerant *operateurs,* including oculists, lithotomists, dentists, and corn doctors. There were also laymen, who inoculated the cowpox, or promised to restore hunch-backs, twisted limbs and clubfeet to straightness, "experimentalists" who applied electricity, galvanic fluids, and magnetism, and those who claimed to possess the touch or to heal by sympathy.

The effect of such special arrangements was of course to undermine further any clear distinction between sanctioned and nonsanctioned healers. If an officially constituted body publicly recognized a cowherd's right to practice healing, then it became clear to all that the basis on which healers were separated into authorized and nonauthorized groups was, in the end, not so much their training as the efficacy of the treatment. Of course, as noted, society was full of all kinds of people who claimed to have effective treatments.

The district physician.   Keeping track of who was doing what in the district was the job of the district physician. It was an impossible task, not only because of the numerous healers who skirted the law by practicing outside of it, but also because the district physician had to be able to count on the support of civic authorities who balked at any measure that would draw on their budgets. If local officials originally harbored resentment against the medical boards for creating a measure they felt was either unnecessary or unfair and that they would have to fund, their actual failure to act was felt most directly by the district physician whose job it was to see that the measures were carried out. For example, a medical board in the Harz district required local authorities to pay for the medicines needed by the district physician to combat the outbreak of an infectious disease, a requirement they resisted strongly. District physicians could lodge complaint after complaint with civic authorities about their inability to carry out their duties, but it often fell on deaf ears.

As mentioned earlier, many from the lower ranks of society distrusted physicians, whose middle-class status separated them from the majority of the population. The tendency to distrust was merely accentuated where the district physician was concerned because he was perceived as someone who was out to prevent healers from the lower classes from doing their work. A report of the privy council in a small German state near the end of the century reinforced this state of affairs. "We doubt," the author observed, "that human laws can constrain a person to see a physician in whom he has no faith, or even mistrusts, and the district physician, no matter how skilled he may be, often enjoys the least confidence among the common folk."

Quackery

The word *quackery* in present-day usage is sometimes understood to refer to market-oriented healing. Quacks are those whose primary motivation to practice medicine is based on their desire to make money, whether or not they actually can provide healing. Given this meaning, the eighteenth century has been called the golden age of quackery. As can be inferred from our discussion of healing thus far, however, there is a sense in which this definition is inappropriate because, at least where the granting of permission to practice was concerned, the effectiveness of the treatment was the bottom line. As long as there was a perception that a prescribed regimen was efficacious, there was a chance that a healer could obtain an official sanction to utilize it. Such practice was certainly market driven, yet it often was done legally.

There were, of course, those whose healing claims were simply and completely fraudulent. When exposed and apprehended, such individuals were punished as swindlers. But in the 1700s determining clearly who such people were was often not a simple task. Itinerants were most suspect because their refusal to remain in one place meant that they did not have to stand behind their claims. Many people could be deceived because they were often desperate for relief from a condition that no healer—sanctioned or not—had been able to address.

Judging quackery in the eighteenth century was, surprisingly, somewhat simpler than it is today. This is not to say that the decision was completely straightforward and unambiguous or that there was never a need for recourse to the law. But quackery, at least in eighteenth-century Germany, had a precise meaning. This made the decision easier than it would have been had the definition depended simply on whether a treatment was truly effective or not. The meaning of quackery went straight to the economic implications that, while certainly present in twenty-first-century disputes, are not generally acknowledged to be the primary factor of consideration.

A quack in the German states of the eighteenth century was someone who poached on the territory of another and in so doing upset the proper economic order. Eighteenth-century Germany was dominated, as it had been for some time, by a strong sense that an ordered society depended on each person being aware of and accepting his or her place. Each individual represented an important piece of an ordained order. In that order each person had specific obligations and rights that must be protected if the greater good was to be maintained.

The need to protect rights and obligations was especially visible in the economic realm. In an era when guilds still regulated much activity, the rules were strict. A baker, for instance, was required to use the right amount of dough for a loaf of bread. Too little or too much could result in a penalty. And for that loaf of bread the baker was expected to charge a fair price that was neither too high nor too low. If a baker or any tradesman was found to be greedy in his price or if he tried to undercut the price of fellow tradesmen in order to gain advantage over them, he was subject to a penalty. Harmony in society resulted from everyone doing his or her own job for a fair price.

Quacks, then, were interlopers who stole the livelihood of others. When a cowherd practiced a healing art without permission he stole from those who had the sanctioned authority. Many of the healers confined themselves to one form of treatment, so it was relatively easy to determine if a person had the right to practice. The medical board of one German state specified in 1747 that physicians were to practice internal medicine, apothecaries were to prepare and sell medicines, first-class surgeons were responsible for major surgery, barbering and cupping (the application of a heated cup to the skin to draw blood to the surface) was the prerogative of barber surgeons, and childbirth belonged to midwives.

Whenever one of these individuals strayed into a neighboring area, or if someone unauthorized presumed to perform one of these practices, they were liable to the charge of quackery because they were stealing the livelihood of others. When medical boards granted special permission to a healer to practice, they were in effect guaranteeing that the state of the local economy would not be unduly disrupted if an exception were made.

This conception of quackery was not restricted to healing treatments regulated by guilds. Physicians too could be and were accused of quackery when they presumed to step beyond their bounds. At the end of the seventeenth century in Braunschweig the municipal government warned physicians to stop dispensing medicines in order to prevent the ruination of apothecaries. A century later, in 1795, a physician was accused of "surgical quackery" because he had set a broken leg, reduced a hematoma, and lanced a swollen gland.

Although the meaning of quackery had its origins in the world of guilds, its use where healers were concerned applied at all levels. Those engaged in healing practices regulated by guilds as well as physicians who came out of the university all understood quackery to mean an unhealthy and unacceptable disturbance of the economic order. The same understanding existed within the medical boards and within the chambers of the ducal council. The general agreement about what quackery was resulted in its condemnation in economic, social, and moral terms. Quackery could not be tolerated because it disrupted the social order.

◎ Understanding Health and Disease ◎

The focus of this chapter has not confined itself to physicians but has included the many varieties of healers available to people in the eighteenth century. The understanding of health and disease, however, has frequently been portrayed through the ideas of physicians because they, as educated and literate healers, often published works on medical theory that evaluated existing conceptions and explored new notions of their own. These works were informed by and reflected broad intellectual trends of the eighteenth century.

Popular Medical Works

Many physicians were committed to disseminating their ideas in a form that was accessible to the literate public. Especially in the second half of the century many physicians, seeing themselves as the beneficiaries of an enlightened age, determined to extend the benefits of the knowledge they had acquired to others. Among the many possible examples of this was a 1761 book by the Swiss physician Samuel Tissot (1728–1797), entitled *Advice to the People about Health*. It was translated into numerous languages and reappeared in scores of editions.

Who read such books? Tissot acknowledged that his readership would be limited. "Nineteen out of twenty will probably never know of its existence," he wrote. "Many may be unable to read it, and still more unable to understand it, plain and simple as it is. I have principally calculated it for the perusal of intelligent and charitable persons who live in the country, and who seem to have, as it were, a call from providence, to assist their less intelligent poor neighbors with their advice."

While it was not uncommon to hear the sentiment expressed among physicians that medicine needed to become, as they put it, "more philosophical," the actual application of the new ideas associated with the increase in knowledge of the seventeenth century did not produce a major change in practice. In Leyden, Hermann Boerhaave (1668–1738), the Newtonian teacher of Albrecht von Haller, whom we met in the previous chapter, insisted that medicine would benefit by taking its cue from mechanical physics. Health and sickness could be approached as questions of mechanical pressures on bodily structures in which the free flow of fluids had to be maintained. His student Haller later preferred to center on the qualities of irritability and sensibility of the nervous system. Over the course of the century various rival schools of medicine developed, each of which was marked by a particular theoretical idea.

There was an important sense, however, in which the basic understanding of health and disease had not changed a great deal from what it had been for a long time. And when it came to these basics, neither the therapies the physician advocated nor his explanations of disease differed greatly from what other healers believed and did. Thus, what distinguished the physician from other healers in the eighteenth century was not the content of his learning. Everyone basically believed the same things about health and disease.

If the physician was not distinguished from other healers because of what he knew, then on what grounds was he identified? We have already noted that the physician was perceived first and foremost as someone who had earned a university degree. This meant that a physician possessed what was called scholarliness, the formal acquaintance with historical intellectual tradition. The knowledge articulated within the tradition of scholarship to which the physician was exposed intersected with the general assumptions most people made about what gave rise to good health and what produced disease. At the most fundamental level, however, it did not challenge the popular wisdom, which had been in circulation for a long time.

Health

If all members of eighteenth-century society understood health similarly, what were the basic principles that lay behind this perception? Good health depended on the common-sense maintenance of balance among bodily fluids and among a list of factors known as the non-naturals.

Humors and balance.   The most important component of the understanding of health in this era was that it depended mainly on the notion of *balance*. This was an ancient notion that continued to endure throughout the medieval and Renaissance periods and on into the eighteenth century. One of the old ideas that expressed this was the doctrine of humors. Humoralism, as historians have named it, was still alive in the eighteenth century. Although it had changed somewhat from earlier times, in fundamental ways the understanding was the same and, at a very basic level, it conditioned how people felt about health. The body contained four humors, or fluids, each one linked to one of the four ancient elements of earth, air, fire, and water. The corresponding humors were *black bile, yellow bile, blood,* and *phlegm.* A precondition of health was that these humors be in equilibrium.

The six non-naturals.   Most everyone understood that maintaining good health was the best way to prevent disease. To accomplish this a few basic factors were generally understood to be important. Learned healers were aware that these basic factors were associated with an old tradition, known as the non-naturals. They were, however, very commonsensical, so that paying attention to them had become a customary feature of common belief.

The name *non-naturals* strikes a contemporary person as odd. It derived from an understanding of nature—constituted of the naturals—as something that was beyond human control. Natural factors might indeed affect an individual's well being or even threaten life, but the course of nature was not something that humans could control. Non-naturals, then, were factors that were theoretically within a person's capacity to command.

While everyone in society would have recognized the relationship between the non-naturals and good health, not everyone was able to exercise individual control over them to the same degree. Whether an individual could or could not depended largely, as we will observe, on social class. But, to the extent that one could take responsibility for them, balance in the body could be maintained and good health promoted. By tradition there were six non-naturals: *fresh air, food, exercise, sleep, evacuations,* and *passion.*

From Hippocratic times there had been a belief that it was important to control the quality of air. Airing out a house just made good sense. On the other hand, long-standing, foul air was not good for the health. Indeed, individual diseases were thought to originate from vapors, fogs, and various kinds of exhalations from bogs or swamps. Those with means could address the presence of bad air by moving away from it, either temporarily or permanently. The novelist Henry Fielding (1707–1754) moved from London to the country village of Ealing because, he said, it had the best air in the whole kingdom. Others made it a point to seek out good air to "recruit the lungs" in coastal areas with moderate climates such as Livorno, south of Pisa in Italy.

The second non-natural, food, was part of the dual concern to regulate "what one took in and what one put out." Once again the notion of balance emerged, for here the watchword was moderation. Do not eat or drink to excess, nor consume too much of any particular food or drink. How much of a particular food was the right amount varied, sometimes with region or country, often with social class. In high society dark bread was considered indigestible, while it was a staple of the poor, who most likely knew by instinct that it was better for them than the white bread the rich consumed.

Everyone knew as well that proper amounts of exercise and sleep, again some-thing theoretically within the control of the individual, were important aspects of good health. Exercise reinforced, after all, the social value of industry as opposed to laziness, which could be denounced as something bad for the health. As for sleep, we cannot control whether or not we sleep, but the understanding was that the individual needed to get the right amount of sleep. Here, too, whether a person could act on what might have been common knowledge depended on how much time was at one's disposal.

The fifth non-natural, evacuations, or what one put out, was the counterpart of the second non-natural, what one took in. Evacuations included the excretion of feces, urine, and perspiration. Because irregularity of the bowels and bladder was something that was noticed quickly, the importance of proper evacuations was patently clear. People from all social classes understood this equally well. Among physicians the examination of feces and urine was a valued diagnostic tool when something was awry.

The last non-natural, passion, again called for moderation. Too little passion or too much were both to be avoided if good health was the goal. Everyone understood that listlessness on the one hand and manic behavior on the other bespoke an unhealthy condition. The key once more was moderation and balance between extremes.

In the eighteenth century, the art of living a healthy life, of actively pursuing balance among factors that could be controlled, was known as dietetics. Dietetics, coming from the Greek word *diaita,* which implied way of life, was understood here in a very general sense, not the narrower one common to the twenty-first cen-tury. Dietetics did include food, but it dealt with other factors as well. In the eigh-teenth century it was understood in its traditional sense of general regimens neces-sary to living a healthy life. It involved the general rules of conduct and behavior one should follow to promote health.

Explaining and Treating Illness

Although the eighteenth century saw the emergence of new ways of explaining disease, treatment often reverted to traditional means. New ideas about the body being governed by mechanical laws of motion, for example, did little to change the common conviction that a given disease was due to the buildup of morbid humors in the body and that they must be discharged. For example, fevers, known to be an indicator of epidemic disease, were often understood to be the result of a crisis within the body due to the presence of infectious matter. With the expulsion of peccant or disease-producing humors through pores and orifices there was some hope of resolving the condition. Disease also resulted when an imbalance among the normal distribution of the humors developed. Here the task of the healer was obvious—to restore the sick person's body to normal equilibrium. But how did the imbalance arise in the first place? The most common cause of illness in the eigh-teenth century was thought to be hampered evacuations, which obviously produced imbalance in their wake. As a result, the treatment of disease most often revolved around promoting evacuations.

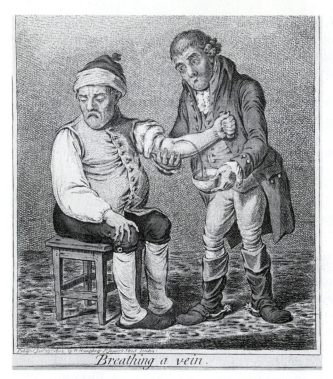

Breathing a vein.

"Breathing a Vein"

There were several ways to assist the body in its evacuation, depending on what was being hampered. For example, enemas were frequently administered. From long-established lore both authorized apothecaries and unauthorized healers of various sorts made use of herbal drugs, most of which acted either as a purgative or a laxative, or perhaps they promoted urination or sweating. The idea was to assist the body in expelling the hostile excess that had built up.

By far, however, the most common way of addressing unwanted excesses in the body was through bleeding. Of course barber surgeons made regular use of this technique in order to rid the body of noxious causes of disease; in fact, the familiar red and white barber pole, whose colors could be associated with blood and bandages (or cloth tourniquets), originally identified a place where one could be bled. But barbers were not the only ones to bleed the sick. Many common folk either bled themselves or bled each other—what they referred to as "breathing a vein"—when they became ill. In fact, there was a widespread belief that bleeding could be done preventatively in order to address an accumulation of bad humors before they became a problem. Phlebotomy, as bloodletting is known, lasted into the nineteenth century.

◎ New Directions in Medicine ◎

The treatments described in the preceding section represented the most basic and general ideas employed by healers in their attempts to alleviate sickness and disease. Bleeding, purging, and administering an emetic (to cause vomiting) constituted by far the greatest proportion of medical treatments that were utilized. But as the eighteenth century proceeded, healers from the educated classes were far from idle in proposing new treatments. Physicians in particular made use of new ideas and discoveries to come up with novel ways of understanding health and illness and new means for treating certain diseases.

Innovations in the Eighteenth Century

Historians of medicine have differed about the significance of the contributions of physicians in the eighteenth century. Some suggest that, in spite of considerable rhetoric about making science more "philosophical," by which physicians generally meant drawing on the rich heritage of the new sciences of the seventeenth century, what resulted was a proliferation of general medical systems, few of which exhibited staying power. Such historians point to the lack of a medical Newton, who could provide a synthetic theory around which medicine could forge an identity and on which it could build its future.

Others have noted the prominent place physicians held as spokesmen for Enlightenment ideas and the role medicine played in furnishing the foundation for a new vision of the eighteenth century, the so-called sciences of man. They suggest that the hopes expressed by physicians represented optimism for the future. Whichever of these generalizations one prefers, there were noteworthy individual accomplishments and trends that can be recognized.

The advent of measurement. One of the lessons learned by natural philosophers of the sixteenth and seventeenth centuries was the importance of gathering precise data. Whether from the successes of astronomy or the advancement of business through accurate methods of accounting, the idea arose that measuring was important.

Already in the early seventeenth century a medical professor at Padua named Santorio Sanctorius (1561–1636) had invented a thermometer and hygrometer with which to measure degrees of heat and moisture. He believed that a precise determination of temperature was necessary to let the physician know of small changes, which in turn would tell the physician whether the patient's condition was improving or getting worse.

The seventeenth-century British author of *Political Arithmetic,* William Petty (1623–1687), equated what was real with what could be measured. Some in the eighteenth century attempted to extend this idea to include data about humans. Taking a cue from Petty, all kinds of data were collected. From bills of mortality, not new to the eighteenth century, now came important information about life spans in cities versus the country, one region versus another. The continued publication of such data was a boon to sellers of life insurance and annuities, whose vocation enjoyed noticeable expansion.

After mid-century, physicians increasingly studied death rates from various epidemics, hoping that with such information they could get clues that would be useful in preventing or limiting the number of future casualties. Of particular importance here was the physician Johann Süssmilch (1707–1777) in Prussia. One implication of this line of approach was that these physicians were removing their attention from the patient as an individual and placing it on the environment.

We have already met Stephen Hales in our discussion of the emergence of chemical science in the eighteenth century (Chapter 10). In addition to his experiments on the production of gases from burning vegetables, Hales also experimented on animals. He was, in 1726, the first to measure blood pressure in a horse, noting that the pressure he measured in an artery was much higher than that in a vein. Within a few years Hales had published an account of his work on measuring blood pressure.

Volunteer hospitals.   Hospitals as a place where the sick were housed and treated existed long before the dawn of the eighteenth century. Through the influence of Christianity, the practice of isolating sufferers from the rest of the community changed in the Latin West during the early medieval period. The church acknowledged an obligation to care for the bodily as well as the spiritual needs of those enduring illness. As a result, monastic hospitals appeared, many associated with the order of St. Benedict, in which both kinds of care were provided, even if the emphasis lay with the care of the soul.

In the late Middle Ages and in the early modern period lay people began assuming greater responsibility for supporting places to treat the sick. The motive here was to fund small hospitals as a means of buying God's grace and favor. It was a public manner in which an individual's charity could be put on display, bringing with it in many cases an increased social status. This means of supporting hospitals became especially important in England when the English Reformation resulted in the loss of monasteries.

But it was not until trade increased with the expansion of towns in the eighteenth century that the development of hospitals became widespread. In the first half of the century, for example, five general hospitals were founded in London alone. While clergymen clearly appreciated and supported new hospitals, the established church was no longer the primary benefactor. Frequently, minority religious groups provided the wherewithal for the venture. The pattern was to first enlist the aid of a few aristocrats, who were happy to be seen as supporters of such a worthy endeavor. These individuals would then encourage those of lower social standing to contribute. Because donors had the right to admit patients, they could serve their own self-interest at the same time that they earned public favor through their support of the new hospital.

The new hospitals were set up with the understanding that they were for "the deserving poor." Thus, people with means would seek assistance elsewhere, while vagrants and the destitute were not worthy of the charity envisioned. Those who did qualify for treatment had to secure an admission ticket, not from a doctor, but from a benefactor. Once they had a ticket, they incurred no cost for treatment as long as they abided by strict rules, the breaking of which could result in being dismissed regardless of condition.

Male midwives.   One new trend, limited for the most part to larger cities in Britain and individual locations in the Netherlands and France, was the appearance of the "man-midwife." Traditionally, birthing, and even the care of gynecological issues, was left to women. With the appearance of training in obstetrics in some medical schools, for example in London under the physician William Hunter (1718–1783), males began to supplant females in deliveries of newborns.

Of course Hunter and others offered various justifications for usurping a customarily female role. Hunter, for example, prided himself on being less interventionist than the traditional midwife. Unlike time-honored midwives, *accoucheurs,* as the man-midwife was also known, used surgical instruments like forceps for difficult deliveries. Naturally, their services were restricted to the upper echelons of society, who were attracted by their frequent association with the new lying-in hospitals, where it became fashionable to give birth. Man-midwives did not hesitate to abandon older ideas such as swaddling newborns, preferring to give them freedom of movement, and they preferred breast-feeding by the mother as opposed to using the customary wet nurse.

The understanding and treatment of mental illness. In medieval and early modern times individuals suffering from mental disorders were either kept track of by members of their family or locality, or they were neglected and not infrequently mistreated. In the seventeenth century it became increasingly common for the insane to be separated from the rest of society in special "madhouses." In France, these institutions were overseen by the church or by public authorities, while in England they tended to be run under private auspices.

Madhouses continued to exist in the eighteenth century, in some countries expanding their role. What changed was the understanding of the cause of madness and mental illness. Whereas in earlier eras insanity was associated with demonic possession, those familiar with the new sciences that emphasized mechanical law began to reject evil spirits as the source of madness, especially after the witch craze of the first half of the century had played itself out.

By the eighteenth century physicians were arguing that the cause of insanity was physical, located in the body, and not due to occult invaders. Some appealed to imbalances of yellow bile and black bile to account, respectively, for manic behavior and depression, the latter known at the time as melancholia. Those who invoked mechanical principles to depict the workings of the body conjectured that nerves were tubes that carried waves of impulses and that disruption of the nervous system was the cause of mental disorders.

If mental disease was due to a disturbance of the proper functioning of the material body, it followed that to treat mental conditions the physician had to treat the body. Various approaches were taken, from those that drew on traditional bloodletting, induced evacuations, and special diets to newer attempts to right the body's disorder by shocking it with cold showers or, when it became available, with electricity. Others suggested that pacifying the body was better than shocking it. They employed drugs like opium or confinement in dark rooms. All agreed that it was important to isolate the mentally disturbed in madhouses because that prevented them from being neglected and enabled controlled treatment. In spite of what were undoubtedly good intentions, patients suffered many cruelties because of the treatments to which they were subjected.

After the mid-eighteenth century another new idea arose, namely, that the treatment of madness should focus on the mind itself rather than on the body. Madness was a psychological disorder. What was required was a better understanding of the way the mind worked. Clues were already present in the thought of such philosophers as John Locke, for whom the mind was a blank tablet at birth, after which it was imprinted with sensations that permitted the formulation of ideas. Physicians at the end of the eighteenth century and on into the nineteenth were interested not only in the patterns of insanity, but also in the unusual psychic abilities associated with movements such as Mesmerism and the claims of sleepwalkers.

This new psychological approach to mental illness exhibited a far greater sympathy toward the patient. Its advocates called for what they identified as moral therapy, urging kindness and understanding over interventions that, however unintentionally, permitted brutal means of treatment. What was not challenged, however, was the need to seclude the mentally ill in asylums, in which the number of patients grew dramatically in the new century.

The Story of Smallpox

Contagious diseases periodically visited Western villages and cities, and had done so for centuries prior to the eighteenth century. Infectious maladies such as plague, typhus, measles, meningitis, dysentery, diphtheria, scarlet fever, whooping cough, influenza, smallpox, and pneumonia were sometimes known to have killed 40 to 50 percent of Europe's children before they could reach the age of fifteen. Smallpox in particular, present from early medieval times, was a deadly form of epidemic that killed ruthlessly. In some years it could be responsible for up to 10 percent of all deaths. It could disfigure those who survived it and could also leave blindness and sterility in its wake.

By the eighteenth century the lessons of experience suggested that smallpox, like other devastating epidemic illnesses, was spread by contact. In the case of some diseases, for example syphilis, there was no question that they were communicated from one person to another. In the case of smallpox, however, there was one key factor that raised a question about how it spread. In a given household some family members might contract the disease, but others remained untouched. Further, appealing to person-to-person contact as the source of spread sounded to some among the more educated like bygone appeals to occult influences or spells, something they no longer could sanction.

Among some healers from the lower classes in Europe and surrounding areas there had been for some time prior to the eighteenth century an awareness that a small dose of smallpox could prevent the disease. But the idea that deliberately exposing someone to smallpox could make the person immune to it was not more widely accepted until the eighteenth century. By 1714 an account of artificial inoculation appeared in the official publication of the Royal Society in Britain. There was little reaction to this scholarly publication. But it was another matter when a highborn British lady endorsed inoculation as an effective technique. Lady Mary Montague (1689–1762) was the wife of the British consul in Turkey, where she learned of a Turkish peasant custom in which crusts from skin lesions of an infected individual were inserted into the skin of a healthy person in order to induce long-term immunity from the disease. Of course not every trial produced the mild case of smallpox desired, one that did not kill or disfigure the recipient of the crusts. But the success rate was sufficient enough that, in 1721, Lady Montague was convinced she should inoculate her young daughter.

Once the serious attention of British physicians focused on the possibilities of inoculation, further trials ensued. Condemned prisoners made ideal subjects of experimentation with inoculation. With the publicity surrounding the inoculation of two daughters of the Prince of Wales, soon to be King George II, the acceptability of inoculation was assured. But when British physicians latched on to the technique and devised a protocol that required extensive periods of preparation and isolated recuperation, they effectively removed inoculation as an option for the lower classes. However, others soon began introducing a small amount of inoculant into a scratch on the arm cheaply and quickly, and with good success. It eventually became clear that inoculating only part of a village could actually cause the disease to germinate in those who had not been inoculated, so the goal soon became to administer inoculations to entire local populations at the same time.

At the end of the century a new technique was discovered by Edward Jenner (1749–1823), who observed that milkmaids who contracted the milder disease of cowpox appeared to avoid contracting smallpox. He had the idea of replacing the crusts of smallpox used in inoculation with a small dose of material from someone with cowpox. This turned out to be an effective procedure, with less risk of contracting the deadly disease. The practice, known as vaccination, was first performed in 1796 and soon gained widespread acceptance in Britain.

The British experience with inoculation turned out to be somewhat exceptional when compared to the Continent. Although in France the death of Louis XV from smallpox in 1784 led to calls for greater acceptance of inoculation by leading intellectuals of the day, in German-speaking lands there was greater reluctance to recognize its merit. The cause was not helped by the failure to carry out safe inoculations in the cities, where there were always sizable numbers of people who were overlooked or missed and who were then exposed to and came down with the disease. Only with the availability of vaccination was it possible to control the disease effectively.

The Application of Animal Magnetism

As the story of smallpox illustrates, introducing new techniques into medical practice was often accompanied by controversy. The same can be said about the ideas from the new science that were so evident to the educated classes of the eighteenth century. That was because the new ideas could produce divisions even among the natural philosophers themselves. There was not yet a consensus view in Western society about what constituted a science or what it meant to "be scientific." The emergence into society of a recognized practitioner of natural science would not occur until well into the nineteenth century. As a result, there were many diverse claims that surfaced whose proponents associated themselves with the heritage of earlier natural philosophers.

This circumstance was certainly true of academic medicine, where there was no single foundation accepted by all as the basis of sound medical theory. The physician, after all, needed to know anatomy and physiology, including pathology; he had to investigate how to diagnose disease, explain what it was, and classify diseases; and finally, he had to provide therapies and treatments. The physician could only look with envy at a science like astronomy, which by the end of the eighteenth century had congealed around the vision of Isaac Newton. We turn now to a case in which a physician attempted to supply a foundation for a new medical theory from the physical sciences.

Franz Anton Mesmer.   Born in 1734, Franz Anton Mesmer was the son of a forester to the archbishop of Constance on the German side of the Bodensee (Lake of Constance). His father determined that he should have an education suited to his demonstrated abilities. Franz attended Catholic school and later Jesuit school in Constance, then went off to a Jesuit university to study for the priesthood. When he changed universities and came into contact with the Leibnizian philosophy of Christian von Wolff (see Chapter 9), he encountered criticism of Jesuit thought for the first time. He decided that he preferred a career in medicine rather than the priesthood, and went to Vienna, where his teachers were students of the celebrated Dutch physician and defender of Newton, Hermann Boerhaave (see Chapter 12). Boerhaave's defense of experiment and his reference to mechanical operations as a means of understanding the body were widely known in Europe and proved to be an important influence on Mesmer.

Franz Anton Mesmer

The circuitous route he had followed in achieving his medical degree meant that he was thirty-two when it finally was bestowed, in 1766. His dissertation investigated the possible influence that planetary forces might exert on the innermost parts of living things. Mesmer called it animal gravity, clearly borrowing on Newton's claim that planetary masses reciprocated the attractive force the collective mass of the Earth exerted on them. Mesmer's idea was that perhaps the inanimate masses of celestial bodies exerted a force or forces that interacted with animate matter and that such an interaction played a part in health and disease.

How did the interaction work? Mesmer asserted that the innermost parts of living things were made of a matter that was so fine it could not rightly be called a material at all. He suggested that light offered a better analogy for this imponderable fluid or substance that vital creatures possessed. In fact, light was a good way of thinking about the kind of matter he envisioned because light appeared to be transmitted by an imponderable substance and it clearly exerted an influence on living things. Animal gravity, the unique force that interacted with life forms, was transmitted by the special imponderable fluid found in living tissue. Mesmer's idea was that in a healthy person the imponderable fluid flowed naturally and unimpeded through the body, but in a person suffering from an ailment, the normal flow was somehow blocked. The many variables humans present, such as age, sex, and temperament, resulted in individual responses to animal gravity, but in Mesmer's mind the known correlation between health and the phases of the moon provided general evidence for his theory.

We can see here that Mesmer was attempting to draw on existing ideas from natural philosophy that were in circulation in his day. The most obvious parallel to what he was suggesting was the new science of electricity, in which an imponderable substance was also the bearer of a force that could be directed through bodies, animate and inanimate alike. After the discovery of the Leyden jar, it was commonly recognized that electrical force could be artificially blocked, so that a buildup of the fluid occurred, and that when the blockage was released, sudden and dramatic effects resulted.

In addition to similarities to electrical science, the basic structure of Mesmer's theory also reminds us of acupuncture. In spite of this resemblance, however, no one has yet suggested that Mesmer had been exposed to ideas of Chinese medicine, possibly brought back from the East by Jesuit missionaries. Whatever the source of his theory, Mesmer's dissertation was accepted by the medical faculty at Vienna.

Two years later, Mesmer's visibility in Viennese society was increased through his marriage to a wealthy Austrian widow. Their home became known for social gatherings of educated people, often those with an interest in natural philosophy. Music was a recurring theme as well. The young Wolfgang Mozart performed at the Mesmer residence, and Mesmer himself played several musical instruments, including the glass harmonica that Benjamin Franklin had invented.

Animal magnetism.   As time passed, Mesmer began to alter his medical theory and his practice as well. By 1774 he became convinced that magnetism was a better analogue than gravity for the kind of force that he envisioned affected living tissue. He procured magnets and began using them in his practice. By directing the flow of magnetic force he was able to cure a woman who suffered from convulsions, which were accompanied by pain, delirium, and vomiting. Convinced that his work with magnets had restored a normal flow of the body's imponderable fluid, he continued to explore the new field of animal magnetism.

Mesmer soon found that he could illicit trembling responses in his patients, overwhelmingly females, without using magnets directly. He could direct the magnetic flow by moving his hands. In addition, he expanded the theory behind animal magnetism, identifying key points on the body where the magnetic force could be applied when removing blockages to restore its normal flow. One of the aspects of Mesmer's technique involved elements of what would later be known as hypnotism. His claims were unusual and naturally were greeted with skepticism, so Mesmer invited colleagues to come and witness the procedure for themselves.

In 1775 Mesmer had acquired sufficient fame that he was invited to Munich by a Catholic leader there to evaluate the claims of a priest who was healing people through exorcism. When he produced the same healing effects as the faith healer through animal magnetism, Mesmer pronounced the priest's belief that the devil had caused the illness "theologically confused self-deception." Clearly Mesmer wished to dissociate himself from beliefs in evil forces or the occult by asserting that what he was doing was based on a sound understanding of the rational-mechanical forces of nature, whose laws he was trying to comprehend fully.

But two years later Mesmer was forced to leave Vienna because of his treatment of a girl of eighteen, who had become blind when she was a toddler of three. Assisted by none other than the queen, the young woman had become a celebrated piano player. Although many doctors had tried to help her, the family of the blind pianist turned to Mesmer. His magnetic techniques partially restored her sight, but had the unfortunate accompanying effect of disorienting the girl sufficiently to affect her musical talents. Knowing that she could see disrupted her ability to perform. Unhappy about this outcome, the father of the girl removed her from Mesmer's house, where she had lived while receiving treatment, accusing Mesmer of using his daughter for experimental purposes. In addition, rumors spread about Mesmer's personal relationship with the woman, making it impossible for him to remain in Austria.

Mesmer in France.   On his arrival in Paris in 1778 Mesmer hoped that he would be able to win approval for his medical theory from the Academy of Sciences. Although he was invited to outline his theory to the members, his ideas were largely ignored. That did not stop him from setting up a successful medical practice in Paris. He began to treat groups of people at a time by running leads from a wooden tub filled with bottles of magnetized water, iron filings, and powdered glass to the areas of each individual's body that required attention. It was not long before stories of sensational cures circulated and Mesmer's fame grew among all social classes. He was willing to treat anyone who could pay.

Once again Mesmer attracted critics, both within France and from established physicians in Germany. But accusations of charlatanism did little to quell the enthusiasm of those who believed in his theory of medicine. When, however, he attracted to his cause several political radicals, the authorities of prerevolutionary France became alarmed. In 1784 the general opposition had increased to such a point that a royal commission was established to evaluate Mesmer's claims. Some well-known names were among those appointed to the commission, including Benjamin Franklin, Antoine Lavoisier, and Dr. Joseph Guillotine. After conducting tests the commission announced its verdict: Mesmer's famous animal magnetic fluid did not exist.

The report of the commission and the gradual politicization of Mesmer's theory convinced him that it was time once again to move on. He left France to return to the region of his birth. But Mesmerism as a medical technique did not die just because an academic commission had disqualified it. It continued to flourish, especially outside France, until past the middle of the nineteenth century. We noted earlier that it provided one avenue in which a more compassionate study of mental illness was carried out. Many historians locate the origins of the investigations of

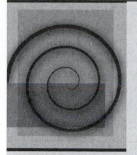

The NATURE of SCIENCE

Why Mesmerism Failed

It is tempting to conclude that Mesmerism failed simply because, as the Paris commission ruled, Mesmer's magnetic fluid did not exist. He was making false claims that had no foundation in reality. To base an explanation of his failure on such unilateral grounds, however, suggests that the differences between Mesmer's fluid and other imponderables—such as electricity and phlogiston were completely obvious to all when they clearly were not.

Explaining why Mesmer failed presents a good example of why historians often insist on multi-factored accounts. In this case it is important to repeat what has been stated in this text about the lack of a unique method of scientific inquiry, acknowledged by everyone, that could identify eighteenth-century investigators of nature as a special group. This is not to say that those interested in explaining natural phenomena did not share the Enlightenment confidence in reason. But even so, there was plenty of room for individuals hawking vastly different approaches to associate themselves with the study of nature—Mesmer being a case in point.

What must be regarded as relevant in any explanation of Mesmer's failure is his status as an outsider, not because he was a German in France, but because he disregarded the widely cherished Enlightenment value of open inquiry. He kept his methods secret, sharing them only with a chosen few. In addition, the fact that he made a considerable amount of money from his secret medical techniques made him appear to be a modern-day alchemist. As such, he could be associated with swindlers, whose main motive was to become rich. Such an individual was not socially accepted in the ranks of the educated.

the unconscious and of psychiatry in this context. Mesmerism also enjoyed particular widespread success in Britain in the 1830s and 1840s, where it was used to convey general anesthesia for certain operations.

◎ Medicine and the New Century ◎

At the close of a famous book entitled *The Birth of the Clinic*, the historian and philosopher Michel Foucault selects the turn of the nineteenth century as the time when what he calls "the dark, but firm web of our experience" was put in place. Foucault refers here to what he regards as the regrettable beginnings of a modern medical outlook in which the physician looks past the patient as an individual to his or her body alone. He cites the French physician Xavier Bichat (1771–1802), who, in his *General Anatomy* of 1803, chided physicians for prolonging confusion by continuing the ancient practice of taking notes at the bedsides of patients when, if they would but "open up a few corpses," they would make all things clear.

Foucault's judgment that the onset of modern medicine had a downside is of course highly contested. But few would disagree with his observation that medicine after the beginning of the nineteenth century began to turn in a new direction. It would take some time; in fact, it would not be until the middle of the century when medicine openly aligned itself with what was by then rapidly becoming an identifiable and socially recognized scientific community. Other countries kept pace with the direction Bichat introduced into France, each following its own course into the era of medicine as an experimental science. The German story, for example, was particularly stormy, but once the germ theory of disease became commonly accepted in the last decades of the century, so-called scientific medicine was solidly established.

Suggestions for Reading

Lawrence I. Conrad et al., *The Western Medical Tradition: 800 B.C. to A.D. 1800* (Cambridge: Cambridge University Press, 1995).
Robert Darnton, *Mesmerism and the End of the Enlightenment in France* (Cambridge, MA: Harvard University Press, 1986).
Mary Lindemann, *Health and Healing in Eighteenth-Century Germany* (Baltimore: Johns Hopkins University Press, 2001).
Andrew Wear, ed., *Medicine in Society: Historical Essays* (Cambridge: Cambridge University Press, 2003).

CHAPTER 14

⊙

The Watershed
of the Enlightenment

The Enlightenment was a cultural and intellectual movement that took place in eighteenth-century Europe and America. From the name itself it is evident that one identifying feature of this period has to do with the intellect and with human understanding. It was quite clear to writers of the Enlightenment that they were living in a privileged time due to the insights and general understanding they had acquired. They believed that this new wisdom had not been present in previous generations—they called themselves enlightened, and regarded their predecessors as having been in the dark.

A well-known historian of the Enlightenment, Peter Gay, has identified two important sources on which Enlightenment writers drew: the authors of classical antiquity and the architects of the new sciences of the seventeenth century. There is a sense, then, in which Enlightenment figures were deliberately taking stock of the collective wisdom of all Western history, from that of the ancients to that of their immediate predecessors. In their pronouncements they rendered judgment on the entire past.

Indeed, the stance that Enlightenment writers took became characteristic of an outlook that represented both a consummation of past trends and the beginning of something new. The Enlightenment, in other words, represents a watershed in Western civilization. It divides premodernity, or what historians call the early modern period, from what is known as the modern era.

The Enlightenment was a consummation of the trend in Western civilization, underway for some time, to value the rational gifts God had granted to humans. The development of the individual natural sciences prior to the eighteenth century, reviewed in earlier chapters of this textbook, is but one testimony to the increasing use of rational inquiry in human affairs. During the Enlightenment, confidence in reason's capacity to discover the truth about the cosmos and to order human society came into its own. Enlightenment thinkers wished to embrace rationalism and to submit everything to critical thinking, as done in the natural sciences, rather than to accept anything on the authority of faith alone.

At the same time that the Enlightenment represented the consummation of past developments, it also pointed in a new direction for the future. An important characteristic of what was to become the so-called modern age was a commitment to discover new truth, even if it meant abandoning the old, and a confidence in reason as the means with which to do it. These Enlightenment assumptions would dominate Western thought for the next two centuries, forming what some late-twentieth-century critics of modernity have called the Enlightenment agenda. The Enlightenment, then, is indeed a watershed in Western history, sloping backward into a time in which reason was at best a servant, and forward into an era in which reason was, at least for a time, king.

◎ The Transformation of Life and Society ◎

Not all of the changes that occurred in the eighteenth century were directly influenced by intellectual affairs or natural science. It would be a mistake, then, to overlook other forces at work that were changing the very fabric of society, including the everyday experience of the average person. In fact, it is helpful to survey briefly the historical development of the broader economic and social context in which natural philosophy developed prior to the eighteenth century, in order to gain a better understanding and appreciation of the role played by the flowering of natural science.

By undertaking such a survey we will see that the eighteenth century can be seen as a watershed period not just for new conceptions of nature and the human intellect, but for social, political, and economic innovation as well. Changes in these dimensions of human social experience, too, were the result of processes that had been underway prior to the eighteenth century, and were simultaneously the beginning of something new for the future of the West. By bringing about new attitudes toward economic, social, and political survival, these changes contributed to an openness to the future and its possibilities that was previously unknown. In other words, they acted along with the changing conceptions of the cosmos, brought about by the development of natural science, to shape the new worldview that was emerging.

Economic Pressures

From the fifteenth to the seventeenth century, Europe experienced a drastic increase in population (it almost doubled between 1460 and 1620). Such dramatic changes produced a rapid increase in the price of staples, including cereal grains, and eventually exerted considerable pressure on European agriculture. The problems intensified as some peasants abandoned the farm and moved to the towns to take jobs as day laborers. By the seventeenth century the population had outgrown the food supply, resulting in a population decline as deaths began to outpace births. To rebound from these developments Europeans had to develop new agricultural techniques.

Challenges to traditional farming.   In the early modern period the great majority of the population lived on farms or in small villages, where farming was the main occupation of peasants. The peasants who actually did the farming typically did not own the land themselves; rather, they rented it from a landlord. In exchange for a guarantee from the landlord that they could rent the land and pass that right down to their children, these peasants provided a fee or a service to the landlord, or a fixed portion of what the crops yielded. Peasants therefore usually had to struggle to produce enough to maintain themselves.

A challenge to this arrangement was the enclosure movement, which appeared in sixteenth-century England as the markets demanded more food to supply the increasing populations of the towns and cities. The traditional system of agriculture prevented large-scale farming because so much of the land was divided up among the peasants who worked it. Landlords began to use various means to take the land that the peasants farmed, which they then enclosed to form bigger farms. In some cases they changed the guarantee from the right to rent land to the right to lease it for a specified time. When the lease expired, they set the renewal price above the peasants' means, forcing peasants to become wage laborers or, in eastern Europe, little more than slaves. Prosperous farmers increased their access to the land by buying out the rights of the peasants, whose short-term gain was insufficient to keep most from becoming wage earners on the now-larger farms or in the towns.

This movement continued into the eighteenth century and was accompanied by the development of new farming techniques. For example, the older three-field system, in which each year a third of the land was allowed to lie fallow to regain lost nutriments, was slowly replaced. In the new arrangement a field would contain grain for two years, soil-enriching legumes the third year, and then pasture for several years so that manure from grazing animals could further restore the soil before grain was planted again.

Through this and numerous other new techniques agricultural production increased so impressively by the eighteenth century that historians frequently refer to the change as the agricultural revolution. The fundamental change was that larger farms producing surplus crops to sell in the market replaced the smaller, traditional plots where the peasant grew only what was needed for consumption. Once again the eighteenth century marks the consummation of a development that had been underway for some time. The agricultural revolution made possible a renewed increase in population, especially in the towns and cities. This in turn amplified the pressure to address the increasing demand for more manufactured goods.

Protoindustrialization.   A concomitant change to the commercialization of agriculture was a similar development in the production of goods and services. It is called protoindustrialization because it preceded industrialization, but it involved factors that made full industrialization possible later.

With the growth of towns and cities also came the demand for more goods and services. But traditional crafts done in towns—for example, brewing, pottery, masonry, carpentry, glassmaking, and weaving—came under the regulations of guilds, which imposed strict rules on the forms of labor, the standards of the product, the methods of sale, and the wages earned. Such rigid regulation hindered the ability of spinners and weavers, for instance, to meet the great demand for textiles to clothe the increasing population.

The market mentality that was transforming agricultural production also transformed the production of manufactured goods. This can be seen in the protoindustrialization of textile production that made its appearance in the early modern era. It broke the back of the guilds by avoiding them; the new production system took place in the rural areas, away from the guilds.

Protoindustrialization was done in the home, where family members would receive raw materials from a merchant and put out a product that the merchant then took to market. The merchant would first buy raw wool from a landlord who produced it for sale, and take it to a cottage in the countryside whose occupant had access to a spinning wheel. In the early modern period many women no longer had to rely on the medieval distaff to spin raw yarn into thread, using a spinning wheel instead. Once spun, the merchant would take the thread to a cottage with a loom for weaving into cloth, and then to a person who could dye the cloth. Finally, the merchant would pick up the finished cloth and take it to market for sale. Those who did the work in the cottages received a wage for their labor, although it was meager, because there were many laborers who had been displaced from their farms in search of work.

The beginnings of industrialization.   By the early decades of the eighteenth century the demand for finished cloth exerted great pressure on the cottage industry of protoindustrialization. The transition to a modern industrialized society, one in which inanimate power replaced human or animal power and machines replaced people, began to take shape in this century, as a natural consequence of the developments that preceded it. Continued industrialization would also be a central feature of the modern world to which the eighteenth century gave rise.

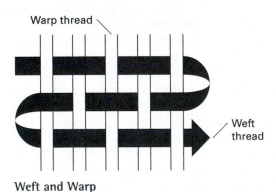

Warp thread

Weft thread

Weft and Warp

If necessity is the mother of invention, then it was the escalating demand for cloth that led to a new technology for producing it. First to show itself was the process of weaving. A loom is a machine that enables crosswise threads, called weft, to be woven through lengthwise threads, called warp. It does so by raising every other warp thread so that a shuttle, to which the crosswise thread is attached, can be passed through from one side of the warp to the other. Then the raised threads are lowered and the remaining threads are raised. The shuttle is now passed back through what is called the weft shed and the process repeats. For one operator the loom cannot be wider than the weaver's reach.

In 1733 an inventor named John Kay developed a spring-loaded box from which the shuttle could be projected through the weft shed. It could be triggered using one hand and also permitted one person to operate a large loom. Called the *flying shuttle*, Kay's invention quadrupled output in the sense that it now took four times the number of spinners than it had before to produce enough thread to keep the weaver occupied. This put enormous pressure on the technology of spinning.

Later in the century an invention called the *spinning jenny* mounted six spindles on one spinning wheel, which was still turned by human power. Originally invented by John Highs in the mid-1760s, the jenny increased the spinner's output, although at first the thread produced was weak and coarse. The next step was to power the jenny by animal or water power, further increasing the production of thread until it exceeded what weavers could handle. By the 1780s a power loom made its appearance. As the new machines were perfected, the result was a dramatic increase in production.

It was one thing to be able to produce more of a given product and yet another to get it to market. If an entrepreneur wished to utilize the water of a stream to power the new textile machines, it frequently placed the site of production distant from the market. Fortunately, Britain was blessed with so many navigable rivers that no place was more than 30 miles from one of them. This made possible the development of an elaborate canal system. Cargo could be moved much cheaper over water than over land, although many new roads were also built to supplement the canals.

The result of building new roads and canals was to make it much easier to move goods around. By building an impressive system of locks, the canals and rivers connected remote parts of the land, making it possible to sell a given product in multiple markets. This in turn further increased the demand for goods, but it also had the additional effect of making the world smaller. Now a resident of a town in one part of Britain came into contact with places that before were unknown. This improvement in communication with distant places and people would continue to mark the modern age as the process of industrialization persisted into the nineteenth century, revolutionizing first Britain and then the lands on the continent.

Social and Political Change

Where social life is concerned the eighteenth century represents a watershed of Western civilization once again. Prior to the 1700s Western culture consisted of two groups—the elites and the non-elites. Among the elites were the royal court, the feudal lords, and those with an education (often the same as the clergy). The non-elites included everybody else and were by far the great majority of the population. Over the course of the early modern period elites exhibited a growing suspicion of the masses, which would culminate in the political reshaping of society during the French Revolution at the end of the eighteenth century, and set the tone for the social and cultural divisions of the modern age.

The separation of elite and popular culture. During the Middle Ages people in the lower rank of society had little choice but to accept their lot. They lived their lives largely in public and private spaces that were separated from the courts, manor houses, and institutions of the literate elite. As laborers they frequented places like the pub and church, which were usually located close to each other in the village. But although elites and non-elites lived quite separate lives, there was a sense in which they acknowledged, at least unconsciously, the artificial nature of social distinction.

Over the course of the early modern period, however, it became evident that social distinctions were not as inevitable as everyone had once assumed. This was partly a result of the economic changes just described, which slowly altered traditional ways and made some peasants more prosperous while others were displaced from the plots of land they had always known. The elite minority, of course, had more to lose if the majority no longer simply accepted its place. By the sixteenth and seventeenth centuries elites were becoming suspicious of the lower classes, in many cases hostile to them.

Of course, society was changing in other ways too. The Reformation not only introduced a fundamental change in the understanding of Western religion, but Luther's emphasis on the priesthood of all believers meant that more people were reading the Bible and the many books being produced by the new printing presses. This made possible a broader dissemination of ideas, including, of course, the new scientific ideas we examined in earlier chapters.

All of these changes, combined with the growing poverty of non-elites, only increased the concerns of elites. They expressed their hostility toward the masses in religious terms; that is, elites began to denounce the lower classes as disorderly and their customs as pagan. The most severe expression of this development was the so-called witch craze of the sixteenth and seventeenth centuries, in which unconventional behavior, especially by women, resulted in accusations that only too often had fatal results.

Although such extreme manifestations of hostility had run their course by the dawn of the eighteenth century, the tension between elite and non-elite culture had widened and remained a fact of life during the Enlightenment. This was in part because increasing numbers of society were becoming more educated than in the past, permitting them to share the attitudes of the traditional elites. What had been outright hostility toward the masses now became a separation based on condescension. Educated members of Enlightenment society openly rejected the superstitions of the masses as phenomena incompatible with the rational explanations they preferred.

One difference from earlier times that the growing separation of elite and popular culture produced was an erosion of the simple acceptance of one's station in life. This manifested itself at both the higher and lower ends of the social spectrum. As more and more members of the lower orders of society became involved in economic gain, they began to aspire to the social privileges those above them enjoyed. At the same time many Enlightenment thinkers turned their rational gaze at human society. While most wanted simply to understand or justify why society was arranged as it was, some sought to propose ways of improving the human condition. The latter programs in particular served as an acknowledgment that what had always been need not always be.

By the eighteenth century the increasing separation of elite and popular culture had sharpened the fear of the masses felt by those in privileged positions. And with good reason. As displacement from traditional roles continued, only a relatively few from the lower ranks enjoyed a better life. For the bulk of the population poverty and dissatisfaction increased. In 1784 French elites considered it entertainment when plays like Pierre de Beaumarchais's *The Marriage of Figaro* mocked the privileges of highborn society as arbitrary. At the same time the message was unsettling, for if true, the masses might actually come to believe it. And then what?

The vicissitudes of political change. Equally interesting political changes accompanied the social and cultural trends of the early modern era, all of which reached a turning point in the Enlightenment. These political changes represented an attempt to preserve an old order that was doomed to collapse as the new trend toward enlightenment reached its culmination. It is important to understand them in order to see why they were incompatible with emerging intellectual values.

In the Middle Ages political authority rested most immediately in feudal lords who ruled over local territories. In some areas kings had begun to establish national states, but while feudal rulers might pay homage to them, the king's power typically was exercised in conjunction with various kinds of assemblies that provided advice and often acted to curb the growth of royal power and preserve the privileges of noble lords.

Beginning in the late fifteenth century some parts of Europe, notably Spain, France, and England, saw the emergence of strong monarchs with centralized authority. No similar development took place in central Europe, where German and Slavic territories remained loosely bound in the Holy Roman Empire, which had no standing army and no single powerful political leader. The power of the Spanish monarchy, however, could not keep pace with that of France and England. As a result, when Spain attempted to centralize its authority in its territories in the Netherlands at the end of the sixteenth century, it was unable to contain the resistance such action provoked. The Dutch republic that emerged was an exception to the pattern of growing autocratic rule. It was able to survive because of the central role its banks played in the flourishing economic life of Europe.

The seventeenth century is when we see the full flowering of the absolute state. While King James I of England, who occupied the throne from 1603 to 1625, declared that he ruled by divine right (meaning that he was responsible to God alone), the English Parliament differed enough from Continental models that it could still exert a counterbalance to pure autocratic rule. Although both James and his successor, Charles I (1625–1649), believed in royal absolutism, financial circumstances prevented them from implementing absolutist rule successfully. Charles, in particular, clashed with Parliament over the levying of taxes, leading to the outbreak of revolution.

Although restored to power in 1660 after the revolution had run its course, the Stuart monarchy was unable to resort to an absolutist model. When it was replaced in the Glorious Revolution of 1688, the new rulers, William and Mary, agreed to a declaration of rights that formally restricted the power of the sovereign and reestablished

Parliament's control of taxation and legislation. By 1700 there was effectively a freedom of the press both in England and in the Dutch republic, from which William and Mary had come. During this period the Royal Society was founded and the open inquiry of the new science flourished.

Things were quite different in France. There is no better representative of the absolute state than Louis XIV, who ruled from 1643 to 1715. As in England, the kings in France before Louis had already set out on a path of consolidation of power. He continued the policy of centralization so thoroughly that the state became directly involved in all aspects of the life of the nation. During Louis's reign the Academy of Sciences was established in 1666 and its structure and rules of procedure clearly reflected the old order of privilege that accompanied Bourbon royal favor.

Because Louis declared that he and the state were identical, the sun king, as he was known, amassed more personal power than any monarch before him. He commanded a vast army and supervised a huge economy. His ambitions and lavish lifestyle, however, were costly, so that when his great-grandson took over for him in 1715 the country was bankrupt in spite of taxes that burdened the poor.

Over the course of the eighteenth century Louis XV tried to rule in the same manner as his predecessor. Louis XIV had dispensed with the advice of legislative or judicial assemblies, preferring to control things by himself. The image he presented to newly emerging powers such as Prussia and Russia was that of a despot, a model they quickly adopted. But the forces of modernization had proceeded too far in France to tolerate a king who demanded allegiance to traditional patterns of life. By the end of Louis XV's rule all attempts to deal with the economic and social problems that were created when the Old Regime tried to govern in a modernizing world had failed. The dam broke for his successor, Louis XVI. The French Revolution, which began in 1789, was the logical end to a trend long underway and it was the beginning of a new phase of Western civilization.

◎   Enlightenment Intellectual Culture   ◎

One of the forces of modernization that was not to be denied by absolutist monarchs was the growth of new conceptions about humankind and the world. We have sampled in earlier chapters the great diversity of new thoughts about the natural world and religion that emerged during the early modern era. These new ideas spread especially among the rapidly increasing literate classes of the eighteenth century. Scholars and clergy were no longer the only ones with the desire to read; more and more members of the middle class, including women, were joining them.

Kings and popes might try to contain the dissemination of new ways of thinking, but they were not able to stem the tide. Although Pope Urban VIII successfully forced Galileo to retract his belief in Copernicanism, Galileo's influence continued to be felt throughout the seventeenth century. By 1700 many scholars accepted the Copernican system over the Ptolemaic and Tychonic options, due in considerable measure to the impact of Isaac Newton, but also to the continuing influence of Galileo's eloquent examination of Copernicus. In France, Louis XIV outlawed Protestantism in 1685, forcing many educated people to leave France for England or the Dutch republic. But in spite of his attempt to control what people were allowed to think and believe, France was too big to prevent the flourishing of intellectual debate.

In the realm of ideas the Enlightenment also represents a watershed moment. Several developments that occurred during this time were the natural consequence of intellectual tendencies that had already been underway, yet they represented features of the modern age to come.

The Emergence of a Public Sphere

As mentioned previously, in the early modern era elites and non-elites lived their private lives in largely separated spaces. There were, however, public spaces in which people from various levels of society might come into contact. The public life at court was of course dominated by traditional elites, but public life in the church, at least, brought members of society together in the same place.

At the dawning of the Enlightenment a new development occurred: the creation of what scholars have called a *public sphere*. The public sphere is best understood as akin to the modern notion of "the public." It was something abstract—the acknowledgment of a common context that all shared. Prior to this time there had been no sense of a widely shared common view that rulers ignored at their peril. In feudal times it was understood that authority, not truth, made the law (*auctoritas non veritas facit legem*). With the public sphere a new social factor appeared on the horizon—the existence of what was called "public opinion." But what determined this powerful new feature of Western civilization? Public opinion was not dictated by kings and queens, but was arrived at as a result of discussion and debate.

The new forum particularly appealed to the literate and educated members of the middle class. They were the ones most eager to take advantage of the increased availability of reading materials and to expand their influence in society by taking on a publicly visible role. The impact of the public sphere was primarily secular, emphasizing political issues affecting everyone while generally avoiding the promotion of one religion over another. In the new public sphere a fundamental characteristic of the modern society began to gain a foothold—an embrace of the open exchange of ideas as a value.

Coffeehouses. One public location took on considerable importance in the emerging public sphere just prior to the eighteenth century—the coffeehouse. This new establishment made its initial appearance in mid-seventeenth-century London. Before long coffeehouses had become centers of social life in London, distinguishing it from other cities on the Continent. For a penny admission, patrons could drink coffee, smoke their pipes, and, because journalism was not yet developed enough to reach everyone, find out the latest news. Of course patrons also rendered their opinions on current events, including the significance of new ideas and the latest discoveries of natural philosophy. Many coffeehouses had reading rooms where newspapers and pamphlets were available. They were places for exchanging information, including announcements of sales and auctions that businessmen posted and came to read.

It was understood that the coffeehouse was no respecter of persons; that is, the rules of behavior explicitly declared that everyone was equal—no one was expected to give up his seat to someone of higher station. Freedom of speech reigned, although patrons had to maintain civility in stating their views. Those who started a fight or used unacceptable language suffered penalties. Coffeehouses became sites for discussions about the changes that were happening all around and of the new ideas contained in the many new books that were appearing.

The public examination of ideas and issues that began in coffeehouses and pubs sometimes moved beyond these confines as adherents became organized. In England, one group in particular began to become more visible in the public arena, gaining a reputation for free thinking even though their actual meetings were held apart from public scrutiny. The Freemasons, who had their origins in stonemason guilds, expressed a special interest in the new sciences and formed lodges in which the solidarity of the guild carried over into their commitment to seeking an alternative to existing religious belief. Originally they met in pubs, where fraternal equality was reinforced. Later in the century, lodges proliferated, some becoming important centers of social and cultural activity.

With the turn of the new century the era saw a marked increase in the number of lectures, demonstrations, and meetings of societies of various kinds, including institutions that were concerned with natural philosophy, such as the Royal Society. In these contexts the important focus was the exchange and promotion of new ideas, all contributing to and attempting to influence the formulation of "public opinion."

Salons.   The public sphere emerged and prospered at different times in different forms in the various lands of the West. The development of the public sphere in France during the eighteenth century occurred in several contexts, including the flowering of many learned societies and academies. More will be said about the role of the Paris Academy of Science in the next chapter. Here we shall focus on the famous French salon.

Originally the salon was a room in the estate of a nobleman where polite society gathered for leisure activities of various sorts. In eighteenth-century France the salon took on another function. It became a place for intellectual exchange, for the open discussion of ideas, however unconventional they might be. The people who attended the salons were literate and possessed enough wealth to have some leisure time. Some aristocrats showed an interest as well, putting aside any aversion to mixing company with those without formal titles.

Individual salons, especially those hosted by outstanding female intellectuals, became well known. They were frequented by the leading thinkers of the day, some of whom published works that formed the basis for conversation. These writers were known as *philosophes,* a French term that literally meant philosopher but came to describe authors whose works examined the current state of human knowledge and wisdom. Many of the ideas considered at meetings of the salons, for example, scrutinized existing beliefs and institutions.

The Salon of Madame Geoffrin

Christianity, in particular, came in for critical examination. Naturally, the findings we have examined in earlier chapters that challenged biblical assertions about the nature of the cosmos and its history were fair game. While philosophes were willing to tackle God's role in nature and history, there were very few atheists among them. Like the natural philosophers of the time, most believed that the origin of nature, its laws, and morality could not be explained without reference to a divine power, for whose creative handiwork there was ample evidence in the natural world. Their God, however, was more abstract than personal, a deity who did not interfere with the operation of natural law.

The philosophes were dismissive of organized religion, which they considered hypocritical and entangled with superstition. And they were skeptical of the autocratic power of kings, who in their view possessed merely arbitrary, as opposed to natural, authority. The philosophes authored treatises on natural law, natural rights, and natural religion as a consequence of their desire to find the foundations for laws, rights, and religion in nature itself. In celebrated cases of religious intolerance, in which Protestants were accused of crimes they had not committed, they publicly opposed what they regarded as fanaticism.

This increased expression of intellectual opinion, made possible by the appearance of the public sphere, reinforced a characteristic attribute of the modern society that emerged after the Enlightenment. Now argument, not status, determined authentic social authority. Modern rulers and anyone aspiring to a position of leadership did well to heed public opinion. As this new arena of public discourse grew over the years of the Enlightenment, the future shape of modern society took root and began to flourish.

The expansion of print culture.   In Chapter 3 we examined the invention of movable type in the fifteenth century. Printing introduced a level of precision into written materials that was particularly beneficial to natural science. This was because the loyal reproduction of tables, charts, figures, numbers, and graphics that printing made possible was simply not obtainable in the era of scribes. On the other hand so-called polyglot editions of the Bible, in which the text appeared in parallel columns in different languages, complicated the study of Scripture. "By the end of the seventeenth century," writes historian Elizabeth Eisenstein, "God's 'works' were appearing in ever more uniform guise, His 'words' in an ever more multiform one."

The veritable explosion of the number of newspapers, journals, pamphlets, and books available both accompanied the growth of the public sphere and contributed to it. In some regions copyright laws were relaxed, making the printing of classic works less expensive to produce and hence less expensive to buy. Other factors that lowered the costs of printing enabled cheap editions of poetry and plays to appear, to say nothing of a variety of books on subjects of all sorts. Bookshops proliferated everywhere. If in 1700 the English town of Birmingham was typical in not having a bookseller, by 1740 many towns had two. The number of printing outlets in England rose from four hundred in 1740 to a thousand in 1790. Ten years later Newcastle-upon-Tyne alone had twenty printers, twelve booksellers, and three engravers.

In the German states of the latter decades of the century journal activity was close to overwhelming. Members of the many societies, of course, could obtain proceedings of meetings. And there were specialized journals, many focused on philosophy, from which to choose. But the number of general literary newspapers such as the *Jena Allgemeine Literaturzeiting*—each serving to review the latest publications in natural science, philosophy, literature, philology, aesthetics, economics, history, and to some extent even politics—was so great that competition became severe. Many publications were short-lived as a result.

The situation was not different in France. We have already mentioned the translation of Newton's *Principia* done by Madame du Châtelet in 1749 (see Chapter 9). A huge project, undertaken by two well-known philosophes, was the *Encyclopedia,* edited by Jean le Rond d'Alembert (1717–1783) and Denis Diderot (1713–1784). It was a collaborative undertaking that appeared between 1751 and 1777 and contained twenty-one volumes with more than seventy thousand articles on subjects of all sorts. The project intended to gather together for the public the latest ideas and information available, especially concerning natural philosophy, technology, and even mathematics. It aimed to illustrate how to reason critically, reflecting the Enlightenment confidence in rational analysis, for which the philosophes were famous.

The availability of written materials that described the many new ideas cropping up everywhere had a direct impact on the creation of a new worldview. As the

1700s came to a close, anyone who could read and write had a public forum for the civil expression of their views. And when despotic rulers attempted to suppress that forum by curtailing freedom of expression, public opinion did not suddenly cease to exist. It continued to be molded by writers who went underground.

The Congealing of German Cultural Identity

It was not until the end of the eighteenth and the beginning of the nineteenth century that public opinion became a factor in German cultural life. The reasons for this are several, but one was that Germans, like other peoples on the Continent, were used to deferring to the perceived supremacy of French literary culture. That began to change in the second half of the eighteenth century.

In Germany, the public had long been able to enjoy the musical and artistic work of their fellow Germans without having to rely on foreign composers and artists. The same was not the case where literary works and studies of natural science were concerned. Those writings that did exist—such as the erudite philosophy of Gottfried Wilhelm Leibniz considered in Chapter 9—were only appreciated by scholars.

In the second half of the century, however, there appeared a popular new genre of German literature known as "storm and stress." The writers who contributed to this movement, such as Johann Wolfgang von Goethe (1749–1832) were mostly middle-class young men in their twenties who had inherited Enlightenment ideals in their education. They appreciated in particular the Enlightenment acknowledgment of the role of the passions as a balance to rational analysis. They celebrated individual genius—often through psychological portraits of the dilemmas that confronted those who struggled passionately with circumstances in their lives that were dictated by moral and social convention.

At the same time that native writers were commanding the attention of the rapidly increasing German reading public, major changes were also occurring in the central institution of German higher learning, the university. Unique to Germany, these changes occurred as the result of what one scholar has called the leavening effect of the empirical sciences on other branches of learning. In effect, the approach of the natural philosopher, who aspired to seek new discoveries through independent empirical research, gained a wider foothold in other academic disciplines.

Until the middle of the eighteenth century the university was regarded as the place where acquired wisdom was preserved and passed along to the next generation. Professors were renowned for their *Gelehrtentum*, or scholarliness—the mastery of what was known. Theirs was not so much to question the knowledge they had inherited as to communicate it to their students. Their primary function was to transmit knowledge, not to create new knowledge.

The development of an expectation that university professors should engage in research as well as teach was an achievement of the second half of the eighteenth century. This occurred first in two of Germany's newer universities at the time, Halle, founded in 1694, and Göttingen, established in 1737. In both places a devotion to what was known as *Wissenschaft* characterized the approach to academic study. *Wissenschaft* is sometimes loosely translated to the English word *science,* but since theology and philosophy were considered *Wissenschaften,* it is better rendered as systematic scholarship that was intended to expand human understanding.

German historians point out that the leavening impact exerted by the growth of natural philosophy, with its emphasis on empirical investigation, was responsible for the change at Halle and Göttingen. Professors at these universities were no longer content with merely mastering what was known; they began to add to the corpus of knowledge through original research.

The place where natural philosophical research and experimentation was pursued at the time was in the academy. The earliest academy for natural philosophers originated in 1652 in Halle. Leibniz founded the first so-called academy of science (*Akademie der Wissenschaften*) in Berlin at the turn of the eighteenth century. Others followed later—Göttingen (1751), Munich (1759), and Heidelberg (1763). The merging of the roles of the academician with that of the university professor gave rise to what historian Steven Turner has called an ideology of scholarship (*Wissenschaftsideologie*).

The merging of the roles of academy researcher and university professor took place over the second half of the eighteenth century, with Halle and Göttingen taking the lead. The leading exponent of Leibniz's philosophy, Christian von Wolff, was recalled to Prussia by Frederick the Great when he took the throne in 1740. Frederick's father had banished von Wolff for his open inquiry into theological questions. He had, in the interim, advised Peter the Great regarding the establishment of an academy of science in Russia. When Frederick recalled him to Prussia, von Wolff chose to return to the university at Halle, although he could have gone to the Berlin Academy of Sciences. By so doing, he confirmed that his understanding of the university professor's role involved research and open inquiry as well as teaching. Eleven years later, the Göttingen Academy of Sciences was founded by King George II of Britain. The second British king to come from the German royal house of Hanover, George associated the academy directly with the university, thereby communicating a similar understanding of the responsibilities of university professors.

By the end of the century, scholarship based on research and open inquiry became a hallmark of the German university. Professors inherited the dual obligation to teach and to undertake original research; further, they regarded open inquiry as so essential to understanding that they passed the expectation on to students to carry on research as well. These attitudes became part of German education explicitly when the universities were reformed early in the nineteenth century. Several American universities, for example, Cornell, Johns Hopkins, and Stanford, openly adopted the German model for themselves when they were established later in the nineteenth century.

◎   The Fate of Reason   ◎

Because of the widespread appreciation of the power of rational analysis among the educated people of the Enlightenment, the eighteenth century has been called the Age of Reason. But it would be a mistake to assume that Enlightenment thinkers respected reason alone among humankind's mental capacities. For example, they appreciated the creative role of the passions, even if they believed it was necessary to allow reason to keep passions in balance. Indeed, several key eighteenth-century figures revealed that reason had its limits and that we do well to acknowledge them. As the century came to a close there were those, in fact, who believed that dependence on reason was leading humankind to undesirable conclusions. That put the fate of reason in question. At the culmination of the Enlightenment one central figure used reason itself to examine reason's reliability. The question was whether there was a way to establish trust in reason and if so, what would be the cost?

The Heritage of Reason

In Chapter 2 we examined the growing willingness of medieval thinkers to make use of philosophy, with its dependence on rational analysis, to cast new light on their faith. But we saw that not everyone welcomed the use of reason as a supplement to faith. For example, the impressive blending of Aristotelian philosophy and Christian faith led to the condemnations of 1277. Later, in Chapter 3, we noted the development in the fourteenth and fifteenth centuries of a tradition skeptical of the results of philosophy. Both William of Ockham and Nicholas of Cusa appreciated the power of reason, but neither believed that the reasoning of philosophy led to demonstrated and unambiguous truth about the world. Cusa in particular argued that reliance on reason led to contradictory conclusions, a result that in his view demonstrated its limitations. But the medieval qualification of the power of reason waned among important key creators of the new science. By the seventeenth century the achievements in astronomy in particular had provided impressive evidence of the power of reason. Copernicus's applications of mathematics to the cosmos brought a new level of rational coherence to astronomical theory, one built on by Galileo and Kepler. Galileo found, to his delight, that mathematical description applied not only to the perfect motions of the heavens, but also to complicated motions of objects on Earth (see Chapters 5 and 6).

Both Galileo and Kepler concluded that God employed geometry when creating the cosmos. Galileo suggested that, although God of course knows infinitely more than humans do, when humans figure out the mathematical laws governing the motions of the planets, they know these motions as well as God does because they know them in the same way God does. Kepler declared that geometry was God himself. For both, the pristine rationality of geometry was a means by which humans could get into the mind of God. There was no hesitation here about the use of reason. The heritage of medieval skepticism about the reliability of rational knowledge of the world, although still present in the thinking of other seventeenth-century figures, was not to be found among these natural philosophers. Even Hobbes and Spinoza, whose conceptions of God were far from orthodox, embraced rational analysis as epitomized by the deductions of mathematics as the foundation for their confidence in their conclusions (see Chapter 7).

A significant testimony to the confidence in reason characteristic of many natural philosophers in the seventeenth century was the striking growth of natural theology. In this relatively new branch of theological reasoning, natural philosophers used the new discoveries in the knowledge of the natural world to demonstrate the wisdom, and therefore the existence, of the Creator. Isaac Newton himself gave his stamp of approval to this use of reason in the service of religion and it continued to thrive throughout the Enlightenment period. One noted historian of science has remarked that natural theology was the enlightened science of the eighteenth century.

Sounding an Alarm

In the midst of the confidence in reason so characteristic of the Enlightenment, there were those whose works contained hints that reason's abilities were being overestimated. Two classic representatives of Enlightenment thought, David Hume (1711–1776) and Voltaire (see Chapter 9), each demonstrated, in his own way, that it was possible to invest unrealistic hope in rational analysis.

David Hume's critique of revealed and natural religion.   The Scottish philosopher David Hume showed that reason was better at uncovering error than it was at establishing truth. He used his penetrating rational insight to craft critiques that undermined both the classical defense of the Christian faith and its more recent justification through natural theology. The message to his readers was that rational inquiry and Christianity were apparently incompatible—not a conclusion that most people of the day would accept. If this were the case, then many would question whether the conclusions of reason were trustworthy.

In his early works Hume attacked the traditional foundation of religion—revelation. Those who defended this source as a worthy foundation for truth were fond of pointing out that it did not suffer from the objections made to human knowledge, gained as it was through experience and the use of the senses. The senses lie and deceive; hence the knowledge gleamed from them is fallible, not capable of serving as the sure foundation of faith. But, Hume inquired, if the truth of the Christian faith rested on revelation, then how can we discriminate between two different claims if both purport to be revealed truth? Which one is the real truth of Christianity? Revelation could not be challenged or forced to pass a test. It had to be simply accepted. Hume contended that to depend on revelation was tantamount to trusting in illusion. And that was not an acceptable basis for the beliefs of religion.

For Hume the only reliable foundation for knowledge was the senses. We depend on the regularity of nature's course in our everyday lives and we learn what this course is through repeated experience. This kind of knowledge is constantly being tested. If our conclusions are incompatible with our experience, then we reformulate them in line with the reality we experience.

But in *Dialogues Concerning Natural Religion,* a work that was not published until three years after his death in 1776, Hume proceeded to show that, in spite of the prevalence of natural theology, knowledge based on the senses could not serve to establish the fundamental belief in the God of Christianity any more than revelation could. For example, we observe that it takes an intelligent agent to build a machine and infer from the machinery of nature that an intelligent agent must have been required. But, Hume argued, we did not observe the fashioning of nature as we did the construction of the machine. We do not know if there are other means by which the complexities of nature might have originated. Even if we do allow that an agent was required, we do not know whether it was one or many, nor have we any right to conclude that the agent bore any resemblance to the God of Christianity. The program of natural theology simply would not work as a proof of Christianity.

Hume's conclusions were not welcome. He had negated the reasoning of both revealed and natural religion. In other writings, he went beyond the specific case of inductive reasoning in natural theology to criticize all inductive reasoning. He even criticized the notion of cause and effect as it was commonly understood. We think of causal relationships as involving agency; one thing *causes* the other. But really, said Hume, the only thing we know through sense observation is that one thing follows another. We have no grounds for imputing agency to what we call cause. Since causality and induction lay at the heart of natural philosophy, Hume appeared to be denying the truths of science. In both science and religion reason did not lead to certainty.

When Hume's work was read in the German states some concluded that it was the most dangerous kind of thinking of all. Hume had destroyed the only known sources of truth, revelation and empirical observation. One German writer declared that Hume's kind of thinking led to nihilism, a belief in nothingness. If that was where rational analysis led, then this German writer opted to accept the tenets of faith without trying to justify them through reason. Better to preserve religion than to permit reason to erode its contents.

Voltaire's sarcasm.   A very different kind of criticism of unbridled confidence in reason came from the pen of Voltaire. In a book of 1759 entitled *Candide,* Voltaire followed the exploits of a young man as he repeatedly suffered one major misfortune after another. Through it all the youth attempted to retain the philosophy his tutor had taught him—that whatever befalls him, this is the best of all possible worlds. By creating a series of events that ridiculed such a philosophy, Voltaire took aim at the lengths to which philosophy could go.

Voltaire intended to discredit the philosopher Gotffried Wilhelm Leibniz, depicted in the story as Dr. Pangloss, professor of metaphysico-theologo-cosmolonigology. Leibniz had indeed defended the notion that the arrangements God had instituted in this universe embodied the best possible solution to the unavoidable conflict between good and evil. Voltaire trivialized Leibniz's reasoned argument by representing it in Dr. Pangloss's slogan, "this is the best of all possible worlds." To ridicule Pangloss's philosophy Voltaire inserted real natural disasters into Candide's travels, such as the earthquake and tsunami that struck Lisbon on All Souls Day of 1755, killing tens of thousands of people. The message was that when humans trust abstract logical reasoning to the degree that Leibniz did in creating his complex metaphysical system of philosophy, the result could be far removed from reality.

Rescuing Reason

The German philosopher Immanuel Kant (1724–1804) said he had been awakened to the problem facing those who trusted reason implicitly by Hume's critiques of its use, especially Hume's undermining of the usual understanding of causality and the use of inductive inference. Because both causality and induction were vital components of scientific reasoning, and because natural science played a central role in Kant's worldview, Hume's devastating critiques represented what Kant referred to as a "black abyss" into which he did not want to fall.

In Kant the Enlightenment found its culmination, for his analysis of reason celebrated its power so much that he turned it on itself. He used reason to determine the boundaries of reason, carefully analyzing what he held to be the limits of our knowledge of the world. That knowledge, the knowledge of natural science, began, he said, with the data of the senses. Like Hume, Kant emphasized the need to be empirical, to begin by observing the world with our senses.

But, Kant argued, scientific knowledge of the world was also dependent on something else—the structure of the mind into which the sensations of the world come. Our minds operate a certain way. They perceive things, for example, in three dimensions and they link sensations together into causes and effects. Kant felt that the human capacity to link things in cause-and-effect relationships, and the ideas of space and number that made mathematical description possible, were built into the mind itself. They come with the equipment. Kant therefore rescued cause and effect from Hume's depiction of it.

Kant pointed out the fundamental role of mathematics in our knowledge of the world. When we employ the mind in trying to know the physical world, when we engage in natural science, we try to capture the causal relationships we employ in mathematical terms. To explain scientifically, Kant wrote, is to express causal relationships mathematically.

But this also meant that scientific knowledge of the world was restricted. The equipment of our minds forces the sensations that we get from nature to be viewed in a particular way. So we cannot assume that the impressions we obtain from our empirical investigations of nature represent nature, as Kant put it, "in itself," or as it really is. Our minds have no choice but to apprehend sense data in causal terms. Further, the limits we run into in scientific knowledge are present in any kind of knowledge we try to acquire of the real world.

There is another implication of Kant's approach: some aspects of the reality that humans experience cannot be apprehended as knowledge. Humans cannot know things that cannot be captured in causal relationships among sense data that are expressed mathematically. We can never, it appears, acquire knowledge that will provide answers to the great questions of religion and philosophy: What is the nature of reality? What is the right? What is the beautiful? These questions do not lend themselves to a causal-mathematical explanation. They therefore lie, of necessity, beyond the limits where reason operates. But they are clearly important questions for humans. So beyond these limits lie realms of reality that were, according to Kant, as important for humans to acknowledge as they were off-limits to scientific exploration.

Kant avoided the black abyss that Hume had opened up by restricting the use of reason to natural science, to our knowledge of the world. He showed why the natural philosopher could trust causality and induction to reveal reliable knowledge about how the world works. But where religion was concerned Kant largely agreed with Hume. Reason could never provide knowledge of the ultimate nature of things, it could not give us knowledge of God, and it could not give us final truth. All these things were beyond the scope of reason.

Kant's rescue of reason for natural science from Hume's devastating critiques meant that a chasm was created between knowledge of the world and the meaning of existence, or, put in different terms, between science and religion. If Kant's conclusions were accepted, science and religion no longer had anything to do with one another. Kant agreed with Hume's invalidation of revealed religion. Because science was separated from religion, he also agreed with Hume's critique of natural theology— science could not be used to tell us anything about God. On the other hand, because religion was separated from science, theologians could not restrict natural philosophers in their cognitive conclusions about how nature worked.

The radical restriction of reason to the world of sense observation meant that, on the big questions, humans were on their own. They could not appeal to revelation, nor could they expect rational examination of the world to uncover the ultimate meaning of life. As Western civilization perched on the brink of the modern age, human rational capacities, celebrated by Enlightenment thinkers as the foundation for hope in a better future, had been subjected to a rigorous and thorough examination. In one sense the cautions and restrictions against facile optimism for the future harked back to similar concerns that Nicholas of Cusa and others had expressed centuries earlier. This presented a number of difficult questions. How seriously must these cautions be taken? Must natural theology be abandoned as invalid? Must natural philosophers be free to depict nature's behavior with *any* mechanism they choose?

The Meaning of Enlightenment

Regardless of these concerns about the status of reason, virtually all educated people of the late-eighteenth century agreed that they were living in an enlightened age. There was so much new knowledge available and so much light had been shed on its significance, it now seemed that those who lived in the past had lived in darkness by comparison.

And yet in spite of frequent contemporary references to the age as an enlightened one, many remained uncertain exactly what that meant. The *Berlin Monthly*, a journal read by the educated classes, reflected this state of affairs when it invited readers to send in entries in its annual essay-writing competition. The prize for 1783 would be given to the best essay on the question, "What is Enlightenment?" One of the entries, though not chosen as the winner at the time, has subsequently been regarded by many as a perceptive description of what enlightenment involved. The author was none other than Immanuel Kant, who had published his critique of reason two years earlier. His description of enlightenment was

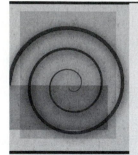

The NATURE of SCIENCE

The Fate of the Enlightenment Agenda

The Enlightenment confidence that objective rational analysis offered the best hope for the solution of problems certainly lived on into the nineteenth and twentieth centuries. That confidence, along with a belief in equality, open inquiry, religious toleration, and the reliability of the methods of natural science formed the assumptions of modernity that have been called the Enlightenment agenda. Although not universally embraced in all contexts, these assumptions by and large governed discourse in the public sphere after the eighteenth century.

In the second half of the twentieth century, however, the assumptions of modernity came under question. The problems of human society had proven so intractable that they had not yielded to modernity's best attempts at solution. While the development of Western civilization had indeed improved the lives of many, a great number of people remained marginalized, not sharing in the Enlightenment dream of a rational society.

Some began to assert that those in power manipulated knowledge in such a way as to maintain themselves in positions of privilege. It was no longer enough simply to embrace reason. Now it was also necessary to know the interests being served. The Enlightenment agenda had become politicized. In the new postmodern era even the methods of natural science did not escape censure. Critics asserted that the presence of social and cultural values affected the very formation of scientific theory, that it was an illusion to think of the development of science as an accumulation of knowledge converging toward final truth.

With the dawn of the twenty-first century, humankind faces a challenge once removed from the one it confronted as the Enlightenment drew to a close. It must first decide which abiding human values must be preserved, and then figure out how to mesh those values with the power that reason affords.

consistent with his claim that, where the big questions of life were concerned, humankind was on its own.

Kant said that to be enlightened was to be aware of something that humans in the past had not realized. Specifically, enlightened people realized that humans had created realms of reality separate from themselves on which they then had become dependent. He claimed that humans had erected transcendent religious realms—heavenly regions invested with meaning—and then had deferred to these realms because they believed these realms made claims on them. Kant declared that enlightenment involved having the courage to discern this and to act on it by getting rid of what he called self-imposed dependency. In an important sense Kant was calling humankind to assume responsibility for itself. Humans were what Kant called lawgivers to reason. Their minds, formed as they were, affected what could be known and thus helped to create the very reality they knew. It was a daunting prospect that most could not grasp.

◎   The End of the Enlightenment   ◎

The disruptions of life brought about by the French Revolution at the end of the eighteenth century made it clear to most people that Western civilization had entered a new phase. Gone was what soon became known as the Old Regime in France. But what was to replace it was unclear. What was obvious was that the confident predictions of so-called enlightened elites about the future were far from being realized. On the contrary, in many places there appeared to be a greater amount of poverty at the end of the century than there had been at the beginning.

In the midst of all this change an easy appeal to reason as the means to order society from the top down began to ring hollow. Powerful new forces had been unleashed that no one was controlling, and they were reshaping the social, political, and economic landscape from below. Western civilization was being dragged forward—where to, exactly, no one seemed to know. But the pace was almost frantic.

Enlightenment confidence gave way to a sense of uncertainty about the future, especially among those in the upper ranks of society, who had the most to lose. Where the status of reason was concerned, most ignored the cautions of Hume and Kant and assumed that rational analysis could be used unproblematically as a tool of investigation and as a means of justification and persuasion. Western civilization was plunging headlong into the modern age.

Suggestions for Reading

William Clark, Jan Golinski, and Simon Schaffer, eds., *The Sciences in Enlightened Europe* (Chicago: University of Chicago Press, 1999).

Peter Gay, *The Enlightenment: The Rise of Modern Paganism* (New York: W.W. Norton, 1995).

Peter Gay, *The Enlightenment: The Science of Freedom* (New York: W.W. Norton, 1996).

Thomas Hankins, *Science and the Enlightenment* (Cambridge: Cambridge University Press, 1985).

Dorinda Outram, *The Enlightenment* (Cambridge: Cambridge University Press, 2005).

CHAPTER 15

─────────◎─────────

Science, Revolution, and Reaction

The profound changes affecting European life in the eighteenth century included an important political dimension. France, which under Louis XIV had enjoyed a position of power in Europe, found itself increasingly hard pressed over the course of the eighteenth century to preserve its traditional way of life in light of what appeared to be ubiquitous pressures for change. It would have been difficult under these circumstances for any leader to hold things together. In Louis XV, who first came to the throne at the age of five and began to rule on his own at thirty-three, France inherited a particularly inept king. He had no interest in engaging the real problems facing his country.

The France left to Louis XVI in 1774 was confronted with a growing economic crisis that was sapping royal revenues at an alarming rate while the vast amounts of the nobility's wealth lay relatively undisturbed. A series of financial advisors to the king devised various schemes to address the problem, with the result that growing tensions between the king and the so-called second estate (the nobility) eventually broke out in angry confrontation. To settle the differences Louis XVI was forced to convene an ancient institution, the Estates General, which had not met for over two hundred years. This opened the door to developments that few had anticipated. It was not long before France was in a state of political revolution.

◎ **Weathering the Storm in France** ◎

When some Europeans looked back after the French Revolution had passed, they denounced its excesses as the logical outcome of the spirit of Enlightenment. By seeking to justify social and political authority through standards of naturalness and rationality, Enlightenment leaders had implied (so the argument went), that the traditional authority of church and state was arbitrary. The result was a destabilization of the very foundations of social and political order, due to the creation of doubt about their legitimacy. But European life was changing in more ways than merely its intellectual understanding of the world. Consequently, the clamoring for political change that broke out in France cannot be seen simply as the result of thinkers who urged humankind to trust reason to uncover the natural, as opposed to arbitrary, foundations of society.

The implications of these revolutionary events for the development of Western science were profound. An examination of the period reveals that political and social changes affected the way scientific activities were pursued and organized. None of the scientific institutions in France remained unaffected by the Revolution. Further, social and political changes even influenced the creation and reception of scientific ideas themselves. By becoming familiar with how these factors affected the scientific traditions of different countries in this period, we can begin to understand why the development of natural science must always be examined in conjunction with a study of the social context in which it occurs.

Science in France at the End of the Old Regime

The state of natural science in eighteenth-century France was directly tied to the institutions in which it was taught and in which natural philosophers conducted scientific research. Unlike the later practice of joining research and teaching together, these two activities were frequently done separately in the Old Regime.

Scientific instruction. In French universities the traditional courses of instruction did not emphasize the study of nature. The focus of the university program remained the same literary and classical study it had always been. Even when natural philosophy was covered, it was frequently taught through the historical works of past masters and not by means of demonstration and experiment.

Where, then, was natural philosophy taught? Many local academies or colleges offered lectures in scientific subjects. In Paris the Royal College of France was a venerable institution founded in the sixteenth century to counter the monopoly of education by the University of Paris. In the eighteenth century the Royal College possessed nineteen chairs, eight of which were occupied by persons teaching advanced scientific subjects. Although the professors who taught there were not known for their original contributions to scientific research, they did help to overcome the general lack of scientific instruction available.

The King's Garden was an institution originally established to shore up the scientific training of the medical students enrolled at the University of Paris. By the 1780s the King's Garden had become much more, including a botanical institute, a plant nursery, laboratory facilities, and a popular public park accessible to the population of Paris. Beyond the scientific research carried out by its associates, public lectures on anatomy, botany, and chemistry, usually comprising six-week courses, were offered by eminent figures of science.

Excellent training in science and mathematics was also part of the curriculum in the various engineering schools. First, there were the military programs, the most famous of which was the School of Military Engineering at Mezieres. Entry to Mezieres was a highly competitive process for the sons of aspiring members of French society. Entrants were supposed to be of noble lineage, but middle-class Frenchmen had figured out ways around this requirement so that the majority of the cadets in engineering were of bourgeois background. There were even special schools that offered cram courses in mathematics to help students pass the difficult entrance examinations.

Other technological institutions also provided specialized instruction. On the eve of the Revolution courses in mineralogy, assaying, mathematics, and physics were available at the School of Mines in Paris, but the most extensive technical training program might well have been that offered in the School of Bridges and Highways. Unlike the pattern elsewhere, students here were allowed to take as long as they needed to meet the high standards that had been set. Because there was no faculty, the main courses in the three-tiered curriculum were taught by the leading students in each class, while other courses were taken at the College of France or perhaps in a private lecture series. Naturally the primary intent in each of these options was to apply one's training in science and mathematics to the practical concerns of the engineer.

Scientific research.   There is general agreement that the impressive achievements of French scientific research in the latter half of the eighteenth century were a result of France's government-supported institutions. Among the institutions concerned with the teaching of science, only the King's Garden also supported considerable original scientific thought and research. Of the other state-supported institutions where scientific research was carried out, two—the Observatory of Paris and the Royal Academy of Sciences in Paris—deserve special mention.

Until 1771 the Observatory was formally the responsibility of the Royal Academy, but in spite of the intention of the Academy's founder in the seventeenth century that the Observatory serve as the center and meeting place of the new society, the two institutions gradually followed more or less separate paths. In the eighteenth century there was not much more than a technical association between the two. The most famous of the French astronomers of the eighteenth century did not use the Observatory for their astronomical observations; indeed, the major project undertaken by the Observatory in the eighteenth century was cartographical, the production of a detailed map of the whole of France.

In 1784 Jean-Dominique Cassini (1748–1845) became the director-general of the Observatory. He was the great-grandson and namesake of the first head of the Observatory and the fourth straight Cassini to serve in that capacity. In spite of poor relations with some in the Academy of Sciences, Cassini determined to instill new life into the Observatory. In conjunction with new regulations governing the Observatory issued in 1785, Cassini oversaw round-the-clock astronomical, magnetic, and meteorological observations. In the years just prior to the Revolution, Cassini tried his best to improve the Observatory's instruments, which were woefully inferior to those produced in England.

The most important scientific institution in Enlightenment France, however, was the Royal Academy of Sciences, often referred to simply as the Paris Academy.

Louis XIV had founded it in 1666 to serve the technological needs of the crown and to evaluate and adjudicate disputes about new discoveries. But it was also intended as evidence of the Sun King's cultural superiority over monarchs less generous to the cause of science than he.

Louis XIV's minister, Jean-Baptiste Colbert, excluded from participation in the Paris Academy those whose interest in natural science was superficial, as well as those who expected to be elected to a pensioned membership solely on the basis of their ability and willingness to pay for the privilege. Membership was intended for those who could discover new knowledge. It is no wonder that the most prestigious of the French scientific institutions was the Paris Academy.

Organized into divisions of mathematical and physical sciences, the technical focus of the Paris Academy clearly differentiated it from the general academy that some in the seventeenth century had originally envisioned. For most of the eighteenth century the mathematical division included individual sections of geometry, astronomy, and mechanics, while the sciences comprised sections of anatomy, botany, and chemistry.

Corresponding to each of the six sections there were three pensioned academicians who formed the core of the ruling body of the Academy. To become a *pensionnaire* one had to be recommended to the crown by the Academy, which depended first of all on a vacancy in an appropriate section and then, of course, on the scientific talent of the candidate. Below the eighteen pensioned academicians there were twelve associates, two from each section. Originally, associates could vote only on decisions involving scientific questions and not in the election of new members.

The lowest rank of membership was filled with twelve adjuncts, whose role at first was little more than that of observer. With the reform of 1785, which was initiated by the chemist Antoine-Laurent de Lavoisier, the adjunct class was absorbed into that of associates, but the number of new associates per section was restricted to three in order to keep the size of the Academy small and its membership competitive. Finally, there were twelve honorary members chosen from the nobility and several other special categories under which one could be associated with the Academy. The most coveted post, however, was without doubt that of pensioned academician.

The responsibilities of the members of the Paris Academy were varied. There was of course some expectation that academicians would continue to use their scientific skills after their election in ongoing research programs. Not all of those elected to membership did so, nor did the election process always guarantee that the best person would be chosen for a given vacancy. Nevertheless, the Academy contained an impressive assemblage of scientific talent, most of whom were actively engaged in scientific research.

The Eroding Status of Natural Philosophers

Because of the role natural philosophers played in many of the societies in France under the Old Regime, they enjoyed considerable privileges. As the political situation worsened in the years leading up to the outbreak of revolution, representatives of the established powers, such as the members of the Paris Academy, came under increasing suspicion. This was especially evident in the steps taken to protect the Academy from ideas deemed unacceptable.

Increasing tensions between official science and a changing society.   The historian Charles Gillispie has observed that the scientific institutions of eighteenth-century France exhibited in miniature the structural characteristics of the regime that sustained them—they were monarchical, hierarchical, prescriptive, and privileged. Of all the institutions, the Paris Academy became the focus of the most dissatisfaction because of its central position.

A proposal for reform four short years before the Revolution began was not the first acknowledgment that the power of privilege in the Academy should be lessened. There had been attempts in 1759 and 1769 to make the voting rights of natural philosophers in all the main classes in the Academy more equal. Both times the reforms failed, leaving the impression that the Academy represented an academic aristocracy.

Even after the reform of 1785 there were still many inequities that reflected the essentially elitist nature of the institution as a whole. Academicians looked upon the Academy as a corporate body with both the legal right and moral duty to assume an authoritarian posture in the world of natural science. Such attitudes were out of step with the growing egalitarian spirit outside the Academy in the years just prior to the Revolution.

In those years there were several encounters between the natural philosophers in the Academy and various individuals hopeful of winning the Academy's acceptance of them and of their scientific theories. The Academy was called on more than once during this time to give its approval or disapproval of those seeking academic fame. One reason for this was that it was a role of the Academy to render verdicts about the scientific merit of new discoveries, ideas, and theories. But another reason was that popular enthusiasm for science in the 1780s had been raised to a fevered pitch by spectacular balloon flights, by the sensational claims about animal magnetism of the Austrian doctor Franz Anton Mesmer (see Chapter 13) and his followers, and by a general love of the marvelous. In the encounters between the Academy and those who aspired to scientific fame a growing tension was visible between official science and the rapidly changing French society of the 1780s.

The case of Jean-Paul Marat.   Among those who inspired fear in the hearts of French citizens during the Revolution was the mouthpiece of the murderous mobs of Paris—Jean-Paul Marat (1743–1793), publisher of *The Friend of the People.*

Well before the Revolution, Marat had begun practicing medicine in Paris, although he did not acquire a medical degree until 1775, after living for ten years in England. Marat's interests were broad. While in England he authored a few pamphlets on medical topics, two philosophical booklets on the human soul, and a political book directed against Parliament and the government of Lord North, entitled *The Chains of Slavery.*

In Paris, Marat successfully treated the illness of a nobleman's wife whose condition had been declared hopeless. But in spite of his enhanced reputation as a physician resulting from this success, his interests turned away from medicine to physical science. Working with a microscope through which he directed a beam of sunlight, Marat inserted the flame of a burning candle into the light and projected the resulting pattern onto a screen. From an examination of the shadows produced by the flame and by many other objects, he concluded that although fire was not itself a material fluid, it did result from the modification of a fluid of some kind.

When he communicated his description of the 120 experiments he had conducted with his "solar microscope" to the Paris Academy, a reviewing committee was set up to evaluate Marat's claim. In its reply the committee assumed a noncommital stance on the question of the existence of a fluid. It was content to confine itself, probably at Marat's request, to certifying the precision of Marat's procedure and the accuracy of his observations. The committee even indicated that Marat's experiments contained the potential to open up "a vast field of research." Marat's manuscript was then printed along with the Academy's favorable report concerning it.

Encouraged, Marat next submitted an experimental work on light, in which he presumed to challenge the authority of Newton. Marat disagreed with Newton about the nature of colored light and even questioned the precision with which Newton had measured the angles of refraction of the various colors in his experiments with prisms. The previous committee had tolerated, though it had not approved, Marat's speculation about an igneous fluid. But to tolerate disrespect for so great an authority as Newton was a different matter. The committee ruled that Marat's account of his many experiments on light did not prove what he imagined them to. Because his claims were in general contrary to what was known in optics, the committee offered its ruling: "We think it unnecessary to enter into details to make [Marat's claims] known, and for reasons just advanced do not consider them fit for the Academy's approval or assent."

With this rebuff Marat's future as a natural philosopher turned around 180 degrees. He published his memoir on light himself and, as others had done in their disputes with the Academy around the same time, turned his appeal to the public. In spite of more essays on electricity (1782), an excellent two-volume translation of Newton's *Opticks* into French (1787), and a new collection of his discoveries about light (1788), Marat's separation from the circles of official science was complete. From his private communications there emerged Marat's firm conviction that his rejection was due to the academicians' jealousy of him as an outsider who had exposed the falsity of accepted principles of optics.

In the 1780s his friend Jacques-Pierre Brissot (1754–1793) wrote two eloquently worded attacks in which he brought to the attention of the public Marat's charge of bigotry against the academicians. Brissot reinforced the image of the Paris Academy as an institution existing in a world apart from that of most citizens. It was blinded by standards that, because they were mistakenly assumed to be objective, stood in impervious opposition to the increasingly democratic values of a changing society. Not surprisingly, an institution that was perceived in this way was not able to survive once the Revolution came. Nor was Marat, who, as a central leader of the Reign of Terror, was murdered in his bath by Charlotte Corday in July of 1793.

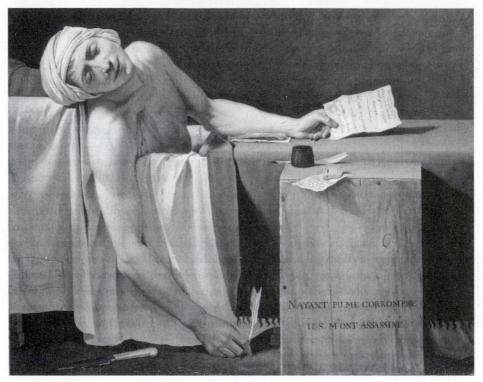

Jacques-Louis David's *The Death of Marat*

The French Revolution

Neither science nor the Academy could be isolated from the pressures that were leading inexorably to revolution. The outbreak of the first phase of the French Revolution resulted from the attempts of the monarch to address France's desperate economic situation by taxing the nobility. Events following this clash between Louis XVI and the Second Estate soon unleashed social and political forces that neither the king nor the nobles foresaw or could control. Giving rise to these forces was a widespread resentment of the gross inequality of rights among the subjects of the throne. With the model of the American Revolution before them, French citizens adopted slogans of liberty and equality as they embarked on the task of recasting their society.

In the ten and one-half years from the opening of the Estates General in May of 1789 to the creation of the Consulate in December of 1799, France experienced change unlike any in its past. But in spite of the rioting and violence in Paris and in the countryside during the summer of 1789, France remained relatively stable and peaceful for almost the first three years of the Revolution. In the early days the goal and accomplishment of the revolutionaries was to retain the monarchy, but to make clear the limits and responsibilities of power through the establishment of a constitution.

Louis XVI's early decision to throw in his lot with the aristocracy against the people, however, meant that he would never really accept the constitutional monarchy that came into existence on July 14, 1790. The king's unsuccessful attempt to flee France in June of 1791 confirmed the depth of his opposition to the constitution he had supposedly accepted. With France's declaration of war on Austria, which sought to defend the king and monarchical rule, in April of the following year, the Revolution turned much more radical, commencing what is called the Second Revolution. Soon the king was taken prisoner, the constitutional monarchy was overthrown in favor of a republic, and finally, in January of 1793, Louis XVI was executed. By the fall of 1793 the infamous Reign of Terror had begun.

Attempts to adapt scientific institutions to the revolutionary context.   During the relatively stable context of the first three years of the Revolution the scientific institutions continued to exist and scientific work even proceeded at a normal pace. In May of 1790 the National Assembly, which was the first of several successive legislative bodies of the Revolution, called on the Paris Academy to assist it in the reform of weights and measures. By accepting the request and embarking on the venture that gave the metric system to the world, the Academy acknowledged its agreement with the legislators that there were irrational aspects of the Old Regime in need of reform. Later in the same year Marie-Jean-Antoine-Nicolas Caritat de Condorcet (1743–1794), the secretary of the Academy, went beyond an implicit endorsement of the Revolution when he said publicly that science "flees from countries subjected to arbitrary rule, or it slowly prepares the revolution which must destroy them."

But there were indications that the pretentious aspect of academic life was not in harmony with the growing democratic spirit of the Revolution. When the Duc de La Rochefoucauld d'Enville (1743–1792), one of the noble honorary members of the Academy, proposed in November of 1789 that his own class of *honoraire* be eliminated from the Academy, it seemed the right course to take, especially because the nobility in the National Assembly had renounced their privileges three months earlier. But the proposal also involved erasing all social differences where voting was concerned and limiting the prerogatives of the king in new appointments, so a committee was established to study the matter and draft new statutes. After much acrimonious debate a new, carefully worded constitution for the Academy was sent to the National Assembly for approval.

While the academicians were waiting for the legislature either to accept their constitution or to issue new regulations for the Academy, the old elitist arrangement remained in force. Not only was the continuing image of the Academy out of sorts with the spirit of the times, but the freedom of the press that had come with the Revolution encouraged numerous new scientific journals. This weakened the position of the academicians as the unique spokesmen of science. In the summer of 1791 one of the Academy's functions under the Old Regime was removed with the opening of a Bureau of Patents. This eroded the Academy's prestige in a manner that was more explicit than biased anti-academic literary attacks. Over the objections of the academicians and with the strong support of the artisan community, the National Assembly abolished the judging of inventions, turning instead to a new system in which inventions would simply be registered.

Condorcet's plan for a national society.   Some scholars attribute the declining fortunes of the Academy to a growing antiscientific attitude within the Revolution. Others contend that the revolutionaries never attacked science, directing their discontent to the elitist nature of the Academy instead. It is difficult to establish whether the members of the National Convention, which succeeded the Legislative Assembly in September of 1792, thought of science as an undemocratic enterprise in principle. In any event, the more immediate occasion of the downfall of the Academy had to do with a scheme to reform France's educational system.

Because of the anticlerical fervor of the revolutionaries, responsibility for education had early been removed from the control of the Catholic Church and largely abandoned as a result. The secretary of the Paris Academy, Condorcet, put forth a proposal that called for the creation of a national society, a state-supported system of education operating in conjunction with a national institute staffed with the best minds in the country.

Condorcet made his proposal public in the spring of 1792, just as the Revolution began to turn radical. For two years the legislators had argued about possible inconsistencies between the revolutionary regime and academic practices. Condorcet's plan came at a time when political sentiment was moving more and more to the left. In light of the king's attempt to escape from France and the declaration of war against Austria, the nation was not inclined to focus on the mundane subject of educational reform.

When the National Convention finally did consider educational legislation some eight months later, it succumbed to pressures from artisan groups to remove the section calling for the creation of a national society. The artisans labeled Cordorcet's motives "a secret desire to retain citizens under the academic rod," a desire that had to be rejected by champions of liberty and equality. Once the idea of a national society had been discredited, the fate of existing learned societies became more and more tenuous. In spite of desperate attempts by Antoine Lavoisier over the next months to save the Paris Academy, it was eliminated along with France's other learned societies by an action of the Convention on August 8, 1793.

Science in the Reign of Terror.   While the closure of the academies was an indication of the growing radicalization of the Revolution, no one anticipated the Reign of Terror that began in the fall of 1793. During the Terror, which ran for almost a year, members of the scientific community felt a sense of demoralization, primarily because of the ruthless treatment experienced by some of their colleagues.

Following the declaration of war on Austria in early 1792, many academicians had assisted their country by applying their special skills to the war effort. Even earlier they had helped to assay valuable metal goods confiscated from the estates of the rich nobility who had fled France. Just prior to the closing of the Academy, a special group of investigators, including several academicians, was established to develop new techniques of defense. The closing of the Academy, then, was not intended as a declaration by the Convention of opposition to science itself, but to the manner in which scientific institutions were organized in the Old Regime. The individual investigator was viewed as a valuable and useful resource in the Revolution because of the need for technical expertise.

During the Terror, however, some well-known academicians went to the guillotine, demonstrating clearly that even highly useful scientific talent could not compensate for past political wrongs. The great chemist Lavoisier was executed because he had been a tax collector, the astronomer Jean-Sylvain Bailly (1736–1793) because, as Paris's first mayor, he had been in office at the time of an unfortunate incident in which the Paris militia had fired on the people. But the fact that Lavoisier and Bailly were executed for reasons unrelated to their association with science did little or nothing to assuage the shock felt by others left behind.

Demoralization also struck natural philosophers because of the new status of natural science in France. Instruction was often organized according to strictly egalitarian and democratic procedures that aimed to make science comprehensible to all. With the creation of "revolutionary schools" like the Normal School, for example, leading natural philosophers were expected to distill into a series of twenty-four lectures the essence of their knowledge of mathematics, physics, chemistry, and natural history.

A few of the new schools did at least divide students into classes according to intellectual ability. One of these schools was the Polytechnic School, which came into being as the worst of the Terror came to a close. This center of rigorous scientific training would become famous in later years both for its program and for its graduates.

Science after the Terror: The National Institute.   Following the execution of Maximilien Robespierre (1758–1794), the leader of the Reign of Terror, former academicians attempted to lay all blame for difficulties faced by scientific investigators on Robespierre's radical subjugation of teaching and research to his ideological needs. Forgotten was the degree to which many had collaborated with the state during the Terror. Very quickly after the fall of Robespierre the anti-intellectual, anti-Enlightenment sentiment that had characterized the mood of the Terror gave way to a desire to re-establish links with the cultural past.

A new national institute was created in 1795 as a means to maintain the renown that the French believed they had acquired among all nations through the progress of knowledge and by useful discoveries. Condorcet had died in prison in 1794, but his classic work, *Outlines of an Historical View of the Progress of the Human Mind,* written while in hiding from Robespierre, was soon widely circulated. Condorcet's idea of a national society, which had failed miserably in 1792, was now reconsidered in the new constitution of 1795 that provided for the National Institute.

The National Institute was not simply a return to the old Paris Academy under a new name. The most noticeable difference was that in the new arrangement there was no distinction based on class. But an even more significant difference was that natural philosophy, which constituted the first and the largest of its three classes, was not the sole focus of the new institute. The second class was devoted to moral and political science and the third to literature and the fine arts.

The Institute existed alongside other scientific centers where research and consultation were being done. In addition to the King's Garden (now the "republicanized" Museum of Natural History), the School of Mines, the Observatory, and several other institutions born under the Old Regime, advanced research in science could be conducted at three institutions of the Revolution's creation. These were the Bureau of Longitude (astronomy), the Polytechnic School (physical science and mathematics), and the School of Health (medicine). The Institute did not and could not dominate the prerogatives of these specialized institutions.

The Rise of Napoleon Bonaparte

Between 1795 and 1799 France was governed by the Directory, a five-man executive body chosen by elected representatives of the people. Although peace with opponents of democratic rule in Prussia and Spain was concluded early in 1795, France remained at war with Great Britain and Austria and also continued to face much social unrest at home. By 1797 it became clear that the republic was about to be voted down by a newly elected legislature. To preserve its unstable reign the Directory called on the army to support a *coup d'état*. A month later Napoleon Bonaparte (1769–1821), a general who had enjoyed earlier successes, effectively took Austria out of the war through successful military action. The stage was set for Napoleon to conduct a *coup* of his own.

In November of 1799 Napoleon's troops took over the legislature, enabling Napoleon to become first consul in a new regime known as the Consulate. The Revolution was now over. In the following years Napoleon consolidated his power, emerging in 1804 as the ruler of a militarily powerful France, known as the Empire. By means of numerous successful military campaigns Napoleon amassed enormous power, subjugating Europe to his control for the next decade. He was finally defeated at the Battle of Waterloo in June of 1815.

French science at the end of the eighteenth century.   Natural science enjoyed considerable popularity under the Directory and the Consulate. The Danish astronomer Thomas Bugge (1740–1815), who carefully recorded his observations of the scientific and cultural life of Paris from 1798 to 1799, noted that literature was declining in influence in France. He added that the sciences had obtained in the public mind a superiority resulting from the very nature of their object— utility. In the same period the astronomer Jerome Lalande (1732–1807) observed that he had never seen so many students of mathematics before.

The individuals who rose to leading positions within French natural science also assumed the authority to declare what was proper and what was not where scientific explanations were concerned. They communicated the expectation that scientific explanations should conform to the approach Isaac Newton had used in his work in astronomy. Like Newton, natural philosophers should attempt to quantify the forces of attraction and repulsion that governed the material relationships of the natural world. That is, new attempts to understand various phenomena of light, heat, chemical affinity, and capillary action should take the form of mathematical expressions of forces associated with material particles or substances. It would become clear in the new century, however, that some explanations of natural science would break free of this strictly Newtonian approach.

Napoleon Bonaparte's influence on French science. Napoleon himself liked to associate with natural philosophers and their mission. Already in 1797, fresh from concluding peace with Austria, the 28-year-old Napoleon made clear how important he believed natural science was for France. "The sciences," he wrote, "which have revealed so many secrets to us and destroyed so many prejudices, are called to render still greater services for us. New truths and new discoveries will reveal secrets even more essential to human happiness; but we must show our love for scholars and protect the sciences."

Napoleon was elected to membership in the Institute in November of 1797, soon after his successful Italian campaign. In his letter of thanks to the members of the Institute, Napoleon acknowledged that he was not their scientific equal. But he indicated how pleased he was to join them in extending human knowledge, which he called the most honorable and useful occupation of nations.

Natural philosophers were consequently among the most visible members of a new venture Napoleon undertook in the summer of 1798 to conquer Egypt and make it a new colony of France. Napoleon envisioned establishing an Institute of Egypt in Cairo, where ongoing scientific research would demonstrate France's superiority and solve practical problems in the process. During the Egyptian campaign, which eventually came to naught, Napoleon communicated to his collaborators his respect for a career in natural science when he said that there was no better way to spend life "than to work to know nature and all things of use accessible to reason in the material world."

Napoleon valued science primarily for its utility, but he did not oppose those who did research as an intellectual activity to be pursued for its own sake, unless their work threatened his authority. When the chemist Claude Berthollet (1748–1822) and Pierre Laplace wanted to establish a private scientific club in a small village three miles south of Paris, the funds that allowed the club to become the "Society of Arcueil" were in part supplied by a loan of 150,000 francs from Napoleon to Berthollet. With its laboratory facilities and its journal, the Arcueil group preserved the dedication to research that Lavoisier had symbolized and passed it on to younger men who would later be the elder statesman of French science.

Determining the nature of Napoleon's influence on French science has always been problematic. Historians debate to what extent the achievements of French researchers during these years were encouraged by the new institutional arrangements under which investigators worked and whether the manner in which they were treated by the Emperor Napoleon was good for science in the long run.

The changing status of natural philosophy. There is no doubt that French natural philosophy experienced substantial change in the period encompassing the Revolution and Napoleon's rule. While it goes too far to say that science became a profession during these years, it remains true that the social perception of investigators of nature became differentiated from the far more general image of the *savant* (scholar) or *philosophe,* which included researchers during the Old Regime. In Napoleon's Imperial University, for example, natural philosophy was intended to exist in its own faculty on a par with the faculty of letters. Previously, it had been included within the faculty of philosophy. Further, with the establishment of the Institute members received a salary in return for their teaching and research, and that implied that the government recognized these activities as a full-time occupation. It has been noted that during the last years of the Revolution and under Napoleon, investigators as a class—not just a few privileged ones as in the Old Regime—became part of the elite of officialdom.

Now, as in the Old Regime, researchers needed luck, good connections, and ability. Previously, however, an undivided career in science was not possible even for the best scientific talents. Young aspirants knew they could not live solely from their stipends as members of a learned society; even those in the Academy expected to engage in nonscientific activities to supplement their incomes.

In spite of improvements the field of science did not become fully professionalized as a result of the Revolution or Napoleon. There was no sustained and rationally planned monetary support either of the teaching of science or of clustered scientific research programs that occupied a permanent niche in French society. Bonaparte's patronage of science was selective and directed toward specific ends. It was neither extensive enough nor sufficiently independent of his paternalistic control to justify crediting Napoleon with producing a coordinated or fully professionalized scientific community.

Because the development of French science in the early years of the nineteenth century became dependent on the initiative and support of individual patrons such as Napoleon, Berthollet, and others, no permanent social base for careers in science was created that could hold its own against the vicissitudes of political change. Even the Institute, which was given back the name Academy of Sciences after Napoleon was defeated, did not concern itself with the practice of research as the old Academy had. As the nineteenth century proceeded the new Academy's chief function was to provide a platform for new ideas and the presentation of research results. Within a decade after Napoleon's defeat, French natural philosophy, dispersed and lacking coherent organization, entered a stage of decline that caused it to fall noticeably behind both Germany and England.

◎   The Reaction to Eighteenth-Century Change   ◎

What France was experiencing at the end of the eighteenth century caused shock waves to travel throughout Europe. The events in France produced two kinds of reaction, one political and one cultural. Monarchs outside France feared that revolution might spread to their countries. This concern caused them to unite politically in opposition to the French revolutionaries. In the summer of 1791 the rulers of Austria and Prussia declared that, if other powers would join them, they were prepared to intervene in France in order to restore King Louis XVI to his rightful and full authority.

Fearing the Revolution was in danger, the citizens of France responded by answering the call to arms. By April of 1792 the armies of France were engaged in war with Austria. When during the winter of 1792–1793 the revolutionary government proclaimed its willingness to assist peoples elsewhere to obtain their liberties, and then executed Louis XVI, Great Britain, Holland, and Spain joined Austria and Prussia in a coalition against France. From this point on through the eventual defeat of Napoleon in 1815, the European continent would be involved in almost continual warfare.

At the same time that the armies of European monarchs tried to resist the radical political challenges that had reared their heads in France, a different kind of resistance appeared—a cultural and intellectual resistance that took as its object the assumptions of the Enlightenment itself. Because these critics of the Enlightenment refused to give reason a privileged position, preferring instead to demand that nonrational aspects of human experience, such as intuition and emotion, were more basic than reason, they have been called romantics.

The romantic spirit flourished during the early decades of the nineteenth century, and it continued to be present and to exert a profound cultural influence in various manifestations throughout the nineteenth and twentieth centuries. In this and subsequent chapters we shall learn how romanticism periodically exerted a direct effect on the development and understanding of natural philosophy.

Germans React to Napoleon

At the end of the eighteenth century what was called Germany did not refer to a single country, but to a collection of over three hundred political units of various sizes and with widely varying notions of political sovereignty that were loosely joined into what was known as the Holy Roman Empire. Individual members ranged from the largest states of Austria and Prussia, where kings ruled, through an array of territories overseen by dukes, counts, margraves, lords, princes, knights, or even city councils. Nor was it always clear where the final authority lay. The Palatinate, for example, had 37 jurisdictions in 127 different parcels of land, and the ruling lords included both the Archduke of Austria and the King of France in addition to the local princes, church foundations, and imperial knights! All this would change with the appearance of Napoleon Bonaparte on the scene.

Napoleon reshapes central Europe.   As already mentioned, after the radical stages of the French Revolution ran their course, Napoleon assumed control of France. Through successful military action he proceeded to conquer virtually all of Europe. In the wake of conquest Napoleon brought sweeping change, especially to central Europe. In the Rhineland, for example, he eliminated the guilds, overturned monopolies, nullified privileges, emancipated the Jews, introduced religious toleration, and secularized church lands. Under Napoleon the number of states in the old Holy Roman Empire was drastically reduced, forcing new arrangements that tended to come along French lines rather than German.

The low point for these states came in 1806. Austria had been soundly beaten by Napoleon's army the previous year and in August of 1806 Napoleon forced Francis II of Austria to renounce his title as Holy Roman Emperor. With this the First

German Reich came to an end. When a Nüremberg bookseller named Johann Palm called for Prussia and Saxony to save Germany from total destruction in a pamphlet entitled *Germany in Her Deepest Humiliation,* Napoleon responded in what Germans everywhere regarded as an unjustifiably harsh manner by having him executed. Prussia declared war in October, only to suffer a crushing defeat at the Battle of Jena on October 14. The hatred that Germans felt toward the French would not be forgotten. The same Germans who were enjoying a new sense of cultural identity because of magnificent achievements in literature, philosophy, the arts, and music, were politically powerless to throw off their French conquerors.

German reforms and the new university.   As one might guess, Germans underwent a great deal of soul searching during these years. There were internal calls for change in many places, but nowhere more than in Prussia. A minority of thinkers had been urging reforms even before Napoleon began his reign. After the lesson of the defeat at Jena, the minority view prevailed. Under the leadership of Baron Heinrich vom und zum Stein and Baron Karl August von Hardenberg, Prussia moved to reshape governmental administration. Other changes were made as well, including the emancipation of the peasantry and the removal of many economic restrictions to its activity. In addition, many privileges were removed, military organization revised, and cities granted a form of self-government.

One area that felt the reforming spirit in a special fashion was higher education. It occurred in the creation of a new university structure that would have profound effects on the development of natural philosophy from this time forward. In education as in other endeavors Germans gave vent to their resentment of France by determining to avoid the French way of doing things. They preferred to focus on the unique spirit of German scholarship (*Wissenschaft*) that had been producing so many impressive achievements over the past half century.

Several German universities perished because of Napoleon, forcing the issue of how, specifically, a new vision for education would be implemented. Prussia, for example, lost the University at Halle in the settlement after Jena. But Prussia was determined to replace it, and it would do so, as the theologian Friedrich Schleiermacher put it in his *Timely Thoughts on Universities in the German Sense* of 1808, by "beginning anew." King Friedrich Wilhelm III had signaled this same sentiment the previous year when he uttered his famous remark that "the state must replace intellectually what it has lost physically."

With the founding of the University of Berlin in 1810 Prussia explicitly rejected the French model of centrally administered practical education. Before Napoleon's rise King Friedrich Wilhelm III had shown himself sympathetic to the more traditional notion that state support should be directed to useful arts and applied science. Now he permitted the new scholarly ideals of *Wissenschaft* to serve as the foundation for what Prussia was attempting to create.

In charge was Interior Minister Wilhelm von Humboldt (1767–1835), who has variously been described as linguist, government functionary, foreign diplomat, and philosopher. Von Humboldt's ideal for university education was anything but utilitarian; rather, he believed in pure scholarship and what the Germans of the day referred to as self-education (*Selbstbildung*). Students and professors formed a community of scholars in which all were learning together. Historian of science Steven Turner has noted that the Humboldtian ideal of the university largely ignored the professional functions of the upper faculties or treated them with suspicion. In von Humboldt's view the philosophy faculty, which housed many scholars interested in nature and natural science, had responsibility for evaluating the overall meaning of education. Although final appointment of professors would remain the prerogative of the state, the main duties of the state were to provide money and to ensure the freedom of professors to teach and students to learn.

The pressures of a rapidly industrializing society were too great to permit university reformers in Germany to ignore useful education completely by adopting the Humboldtian ideal purely and simply. Certain aspects of the new approach, however, turned out to have permanent staying power. Gone was the older division between the academy as the institution of research and the university as the institution that preserved and disseminated received wisdom. The new vision for education called for implementing the trend begun at Göttingen and Halle, where professors were expected to engage in both research and teaching (see Chapter 14).

Differing Visions of Science

Where natural science was concerned it is important to realize that there was not yet an established international scientific community within which there was general agreement about the nature and purpose of scientific explanation. We cannot assume that people in the past conducted their investigations of nature in the same manner that scientists do in the twenty-first century. There was not even general agreement about how nature should be understood.

The various perceptions of natural philosophy in the German states illustrate well some of the options available in the early nineteenth century. Some natural philosophers endorsed the kind of Newtonian science that had come to dominate in France, especially because Newton's mathematization of the laws of mechanics represented for the German philosopher Immanuel Kant (see Chapter 14) a genuinely scientific explanation of the phenomenal world that could be known. For them, subjects such as chemistry and biology, which could not be captured by mechanical laws, could never be explained scientifically. They remained at best what Kant called empirical sciences, in which the content of the knowledge had to be merely listed or cataloged.

Others, however, were not content with Kant's restriction of science to a Newtonian framework. Their conception of natural science differed fundamentally because of their general understanding of what the purpose of natural science was. Here we will discuss the philosophical foundations of this differing view. In later chapters we shall meet specific examples of how natural science has continued to be affected by it.

The romantic science of Friedrich Schelling. Some figures from the early nineteenth century understood the relationship between humankind and nature differently from Kant. This is not to say that they did not appreciate what Kant had achieved. They just believed that he had settled for too little with his assertion about the limits of reason and knowledge.

Friedrich Schelling

Among those who took their cue from Kant, but quickly became dissatisfied with what they regarded as a mainly negative conclusion, was a young professor at Jena University named Friedrich Schelling (1775–1854). In 1798 Schelling received the appointment at Jena at the age of twenty-three, as a result of a book he had written called *The World Soul.* In this work, as in another book from the year before entitled *Ideas for a Philosophy of Nature,* Schelling expressed fundamental dissatisfaction with the cause and effect explanations Kant had required. According to Schelling, Kant was content to observe nature from the outside when he spoke about causal explanations of the natural world. But this presumption was in Schelling's view a huge mistake.

Schelling held that the error was due to the assumption that one could regard nature as a machine whose parts interacted, as machine parts do, by passing their effects from one part to another. Machines were a perfect model of cause and effect. Kant had even conceded that while living things possess a uniqueness that differentiates them from machines, still, the only real knowledge we can have of them comes by treating them as machines.

To Schelling this was a critical error. Living things were to him more basic than machines, and nature must not be regarded as a machine, but as an organism. An important quality of an organism was the way in which it unified disparate parts into a living whole, with no aspect of reality left out. Organisms possessed complicated feedback processes that could not be understood as simple linear causes and effects. The heart pumps the blood that is needed by the heart to pump the blood.

Schelling's approach to our knowledge of nature, which soon became known among Germans as *Naturphilosophie* (nature philosophy), allowed him to break through the limits Kant had set to our knowledge of reality. We *know* living things because we *are* living things—we do not have to confine our knowledge to the laws of cause and effect that merely *describe* living things. Consequently we can know reality, which is organic, directly by drawing on our awareness of what it is to be an organism. To Schelling, if we confine scientific knowledge to cause and effect relationships, we miss what the essence of organism is. His disagreement with Kant was fundamental. Kant had insisted that natural science could not get at metaphysical "essences" because such things cannot be captured in causal and mathematical terms.

Schelling's objection to Kant did not mean, as has sometimes been claimed, that he had no respect for experimentation or the empirical data of the senses. He took care to inform himself about the most recent discoveries of his day. But his interest was to insist that nature be given its own integrity. We do not know nature because our minds are structured a certain way that makes us, in Kant's words, "law givers to nature." We know nature because we are part of nature, because we have first-hand knowledge of it.

Knowing nature was akin to knowing oneself. So it was important to Schelling that the world be regarded as organic because he saw in general organism a broader vision that healed the breach on which he believed Kant's philosophy foundered. To understand the whole of this living nature one would have to acknowledge that nature too possessed moral and aesthetic capacities. In sum, Schelling was seen to be declaring that nature was an organized whole that was understandable to human reason. The nature that was known by human souls was best comprehended as itself a world soul.

Because natural philosophers were charged with understanding nature, they must revise that task to reflect this new insight. Natural science had to include a philosophical dimension—it had to become nature philosophy. *Naturphilosophie* would affect the very problems of natural science by changing the questions the natural philosopher asked. We must not be satisfied with solving the merely practical puzzles nature throws up to the investigator. We must also include within natural science the larger meaning of any puzzles we solve or on which we choose to work. Schelling regarded his redefinition of the natural philosopher's task as an ennoblement of natural science. He was, as he put it, "giving wings" to science.

Schelling's new vision for natural science won him admirers from many quarters, including numerous scientific disciplines. Many physicians in particular found his emphasis on the organic especially appealing, perhaps because it had long been an assumption in German medicine that one could not bring about healing without seeing the body in intimate connection to the soul that inhabited it.

By the third decade of the nineteenth century, however, nature philosophers found themselves more and more on the defensive. For one thing, the followers of Kant naturally tried to defend their mentor's position from Schelling's criticisms. In addition, an increasing number of natural philosophers resisted the reformulation of their mission that Schelling called for, preferring instead to restrict their activity simply to finding out how nature worked. Finally, a number of philosophers attempted to redress the so-called Kantian breach in knowledge in a different manner from Schelling's, one that did not involve ascribing so fundamental a place to nature as Schelling had done. By 1825 there were relatively few natural philosophers who identified themselves as *Naturphilosophen* to be found in the German states. Natural science was casting its lot with more practical visions.

Other examples of romantic science.   Schelling's *Naturphilosophie* was not alone in opposing the classical vision of natural science that had been associated with Newton. The novelist, poet, and playwright Johann Wolfgang von Goethe, whom we met in Chapter 14, also regarded this vision as flawed.

Goethe was passionately interested in nature and how we should understand it. In 1775 he was invited to the court of Duke Karl August in Saxe-Weimar, where he held numerous high offices and spent most of the remainder of his life. As a result of his literary fame and his elevated court position, Goethe was revered by his contemporaries in a manner few have ever enjoyed. Although he was but one of a host of

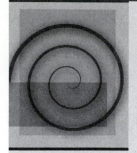

Do Investigators of Nature See What They're Looking For?

The NATURE of SCIENCE

A contribution of the German intellectual tradition of the late eighteenth and early nineteenth centuries was to oppose the notion that humans can make observations of the world in an unbiased manner. According to the classical description of the scientific method, one should be neutral in coming to nature, not prejudicing one's perceptions in any manner so that the truths of nature can shine through clearly without being forced to conform to a pre-existing idea. From Kant onward the German idealists declared that such an understanding was fundamentally flawed. It is not, as some said, that our minds are blank tablets onto which the senses imprint knowledge; rather, knowledge is a construct that results from the conformity of the data of the senses to the way our minds operate.

The interplay between what the mind contributes and what nature contributes to the creation of knowledge was a major concern of the romantics who came after Kant. Because they maintained that knowledge was constructed with the help of intuition as well as with reason, they felt they had access to more of nature than Kant did. As a result they did not elevate the mind's role above that of nature; rather, they insisted that nature's role was equal to that of the mind.

The problem depicted here is one of the thorniest in the philosophy of science: how to determine exactly what comes from nature and what comes from the mind of the scientist. Practicing scientists tend to be impressed by what nature contributes. They point to the way nature corrects their attempts to discover truth through experiment. Others insist that when we observe nature we stack the deck to a certain extent. They note that the social and cultural contexts in which the scientist works impart assumptions, sometimes unconsciously held, that influence what kind of answer will be acceptable. No one has solved this persistent problem, but Albert Einstein surely sharpened it when he declared, "The most incomprehensible thing about the universe is that it is comprehensible."

intellectual luminaries from a number of fields during these heady days of German romanticism, Goethe made it clear that he answered to no one but himself.

In the process of criticizing the view of experimental natural science associated with Newton by Laplace and others, Goethe defined what he called a *Vorstellungsart,* or "way of thinking." According to Goethe, natural philosophers utilize different ways of thinking when they make their observations. He felt that as a result of this an investigator could never be a neutral observer of nature. In 1798 Goethe wrote: "We can say that with every attentive look at the world we are already theorizing." In his view no one way of thinking could possibly suffice because the world as experienced is plural. The worst thing that could happen to natural science, then, was for one *Vorstellungsart*—be it Newton's or anyone else's—to predominate to the exclusion of all others.

Goethe was not saying that investigators of nature consciously *make up* the different ways of thinking they employ; rather, they are affected by the ways of thinking they find themselves using. His recommendation, as stated in an essay on morphology from the 1790s, was that it is a "necessity to put together all the *Vorstellungsarten,* not at all to get to the bottom of things and their essences, but to give to just some degree an account of the phenomenon and to communicate to others what one has recognized and has seen." Clearly his vision of the natural philosopher's task was different from the one in which the goal was to discover exactly how nature worked. Goethe believed that the goal should be similar to that of the artist—to give a loyal impression of the complexity and nuance one actually encountered in one's sensual interaction with nature.

During this so-called romantic era a number of other movements flourished that rejected the search for mechanism as the primary goal of science. Several of these movements explored agencies of nature whose behavior was anything but mechanical. They exhibited what one romantic, Gotthilf Heinrich Schubert, called the "dark side of natural science."

Such endeavors were especially prevalent in medicine. Franz Anton Mesmer's claim that disease resulted from the blockage of the flow of an imponderable fluid (see Chapter 13) continued to flourish in the early nineteenth century under the name of animal magnetism. It generated the psychological offshoot of somnambulism, in which the abilities of certain individuals to see without using their eyes was investigated. In this period the German physician Franz Joseph Gall (1758–1828) attempted to correlate the structure of the skull with various mental capacities in what later became known as phrenology. At the same time another physician, Samuel Hahnemann (1755–1843), founded homeopathy. Hahnemann believed that disease disturbed the body's normal ability to heal itself. The key was to stimulate the body back into action, which could be done by administering small doses of whatever would produce the illness in a well person.

Practitioners of these movements, plus those emphasizing cures based on electrotherapy and hydrotherapy, often thought of themselves as being scientific. This was because they sought to identify a material basis for the phenomena they were trying to explain, or simply because they claimed to establish systematic associations that resembled natural laws. In their own way these practitioners prolonged the reaction to eighteenth-century change by continuing to claim scientific status throughout the century in Germany and in many other counties. Once there emerged a social consensus about what "being scientific" meant, however, they would be increasingly regarded as an alternative to sound natural science.

Suggestions for Reading

Charles Gillispie, *Science and Polity in France: The End of the Old Regime* (Princeton: Princeton University Press, 2004).

Charles Gillispie, *Science and Polity in France: The Revolutionary and Napoleonic Years* (Princeton: Princeton University Press, 2004).

Robert Richards, *The Romantic Conception of Life* (Chicago: University of Chicago Press, 2004).

Dennis Sepper, *Goethe contra Newton* (Cambridge: Cambridge University Press, 2002).

CHAPTER 16

───────────○───────────

An Era of Many Forces

Napoleon Bonaparte's military successes were not the only forces of change during the first two decades of the new century. Admittedly, Napoleon profoundly disrupted the political structure of Europe. But that challenge to the old political order was just one indication of the dawning of a new era.

Change came to natural science as well. Some of it was due to new discoveries that altered old beliefs about nature. In the physical sciences, for example, new research into the forces of heat, light, electricity, magnetism, and chemistry raised a question about the nature of force in general. Other modifications had to do with the role natural science played in society. The increasing visibility science was enjoying in public life seemed more and more out of step with older institutions that prided themselves on their exclusiveness. Forces of change were shaping both the ideas and the organizations of natural science.

◎ Investigating Nature's Mysterious Forces ◎

The word *force* had long been in use by the beginning of the nineteenth century. By then it had a host of meanings. In natural philosophy, however, its meaning had narrowed, largely because of the central place force held in the work of Isaac Newton.

Newton used the word *force* to connote an influence acting on a body to produce a change, or a tendency to change, in its state either of rest or of uniform motion in a straight line. By 1800 it had become common to equate the many ways nature produced change, especially change in the motion of matter, with nature's many forces. Around the turn of the century there were individuals devoted to exploring further the forces associated with electricity, magnetism, heat, light, and chemical reactions, all of which could be used to produce motion in matter. And of course many were sure that the nature of the organic forces responsible for the kinds of changes encountered in living matter would soon be clarified.

A basic question lurked behind all these investigations of nature's forces. Were they related to each other in some way? Might it be possible that all nature's forces were individual expressions of one basic force?

Electricity

The achievements of the eighteenth-century investigators of electricity had opened up a new and exciting field of research in natural philosophy. In general these natural philosophers believed that electrical discharge was due to the sudden movement of a weightless fluid that could be associated with material bodies. Charles-Augustin de Coulomb's (1736–1806) discovery in the late-eighteenth century that the attractive and repulsive forces associated with electrical charge varied as the inverse square of distance seemed to link electricity with Newton's famous law of universal gravitation. No one could deny that electrical force itself was fascinating.

The discovery of animal electricity. On September 26, 1786, an assistant of Professor Luigi Galvani (1737–1798), most likely his wife Lucia Galeazzi, was amazed to observe that a frog's leg convulsed violently when the tip of a scalpel accidentally touched the crural nerve. Lucia, daughter of the four-time president of the Academy of Sciences in Bologna, had inherited her father's fascination with natural science and assisted her new husband in his work as professor of anatomy in that

Luigi Galvani Observing the Effect of Electricity on a Frog's Legs

city. A question immediately arose as to whether the work of another assistant, who was producing sparks with an electrical machine, played any role in bringing about this surprising result.

Galvani was quickly summoned and shown the phenomenon. It did not take long for him to demonstrate that it was indeed the nearby machine that occasioned the contraction. Galvani already knew that artificially produced electricity could contract a muscle. Physicians had for some time used electrical discharge in attempts to stimulate muscular movement in patients suffering from rheumatism and paralysis, and Galvani himself had been exploring the effects of electrical discharge on the nervous system of frogs since 1780. But in these cases the electricity was applied directly to muscles. What was going on here?

For the next five years Galvani conducted a series of experiments to find out. Because he did not want to confine himself to electricity produced from machines, he also experimented with the naturally occurring electricity of electrical storms. He ran an insulated wire from a frog, which he placed in a glass jar, to the roof of his building. When a thunderstorm passed overhead he was able to notice contractions in the frog's leg. There was no doubt that atmospheric electricity produced the same result as artificial electricity.

But then a second puzzle presented itself. Galvani noticed that frog preparations hung by copper hooks from the iron railings surrounding a balcony of his house contracted not only during thunder storms, *but occasionally even in fine weather.* Now what was happening? In his attempts to test every factor he could think of, Galvani found that he could cause the contractions outside by pressing the copper hook against the iron trellis. Could there be an additional source of the electrical discharge? He took the frog inside, out of the weather, and placed it on an iron plate. If he pressed the hook against the plate the same contractions occurred as outside. He came to the conclusion that this effect could not have been due to atmospheric electricity.

Galvani began to suspect that he had discovered a new kind of electricity, different in origin from natural atmospheric electricity and from artificially produced electricity. This new "animal electricity," he reasoned, was stored in the muscles of animals. He concluded that the internal parts of muscles contained an excess of weightless electrical fluid, while on the outside there was a corresponding deficiency. According to Galvani, this imbalance was created in the body by the brain, which, while the animal was alive, regulated the creation of an imbalance and its restoration to produce contractions when needed. It did so by permitting the nerves, which ran from the inside to the outside of the muscle, to carry what had been thought of as nervous fluid. Galvani now sided with those who claimed that nervous fluid was really electrical fluid, arguing that the outer sheath of the nerves insulated the fluid from the muscle as it flowed from inside to outside.

Without the brain's presence, as in the case of a frog's leg, an artificial means of producing a discharge was necessary. If one connected a metal contact with the inside of the nerve (which ran to the inside of the muscle) and then attached another metal lead to outside of the muscle, one could, by joining the two metal leads, create a route for the excess fluid inside to flow to the outside and restore a normal balance. When this happened the muscle contracted. This contact between two metal leads, Galvani concluded, was what effectively had occurred when he pressed the copper hook against the iron plate to produce a contraction.

Galvani's announcement of his discovery of animal electricity in a publication of 1791 was regarded by some, including Alessandro Volta (1745–1827), professor of natural philosophy at the University of Pavia, as nothing short of path breaking. At the same time that Paris was being rocked by astounding political developments, Galvani, it seemed, had uncovered a link between electricity and life itself. The era was ripe with excitement. A professor of anatomy in Mainz wrote that Galvani's discovery "supercedes by far in importance everything which has been thought and written about natural science since the time of Aristotle."

Volta and his famous pile.   As is invariably the case in the wake of an announcement of a new discovery, disagreements soon arose about the methods Galvani had employed and the conclusions he had drawn. Some agreed that his analysis was appropriate, while others suggested that the contractions resulted from an irritation caused by the metals. Volta repeated some of Galvani's experiments and at first agreed with his interpretation of the results. A professor of physics, Volta had a long history of experimentation with electrical machines and even invented new instruments for producing and detecting small electrical charges.

Perhaps because he was not an anatomist like Galvani, Volta began to focus his attention on the metal leads used in the experiments. Others had shown that one could produce a bitter taste on the tongue by joining two different metals that were both in contact with the tongue. Apparently electrical discharge could stimulate sensory nerves as well as motor nerves.

Volta soon began to think that Galvani was wrong to regard the metal leads as mere conductors of electrical discharge. He pursued the idea that different metals in contact somehow were involved in the generation of the electricity. It was not long before a heated controversy ensued between Volta and Galvani's nephew and defender Giovanni Aldini (1762–1834) about "galvanism," a name first used as a synonym for Galvani's animal electricity. In Germany, Volta's position that the electricity was produced solely from contact between two metals was criticized by Alexander von Humboldt (1769–1859), who demonstrated contraction in the frog's leg using only one metal, silver.

In 1800 Volta inserted a new factor into the debate with his announcement of a new invention. In a letter written on March 20, 1800, to Sir Joseph Banks, president of the Royal Society in London, Volta explained that his "pile" did not need to be recharged after discharging its electrical shock because it produced its discharge continuously. Volta, in other words, had invented a battery, and from it he produced a flow of electrical current whose shock could be felt continuously.

Volta came to his discovery because he was convinced that the electrical discharge detected in the contraction of the frog's leg was due to electricity produced when two different metals, both of which were touching the moist muscle, were brought into contact. The continuous bitter taste produced when two metals in contact both touched the tongue reinforced his conclusion. Perhaps contact between two metals

Alessandro Volta and His Pile

might also produce a continuous effect even if other substances replaced the tongue or muscle.

He brought together zinc and silver, both of which were in contact with brine-soaked cloth. To verify that electricity was present he had to insert himself into the circuit, so that he could feel the effects of the current. In order to magnify the current to an easily sensed level Volta piled up sets of silver and zinc discs in contact, silver on top and zinc beneath, each set separated by a paper soaked in a brine solution. This arrangement, just as in the experiment with the tongue, brought the metals into contact with each other while each metal was always in common contact with a moist carrier of the electricity produced. Replacing the moist paper at each end of the pile was a metal lead that ran from the silver (on top) and the zinc (on bottom) into cups of brine solution. To detect the magnified flow of current Volta merely had to put a finger into each cup, allowing the current to flow from one finger to the other through his body.

Volta's demonstration that two metals in contact could, under the right conditions, produce electric current was a milestone of scientific discovery. But it was not the case, as sometimes has been implied, that with Volta's work everyone abandoned the idea of animal electricity. For one thing, investigators at this time were dealing with two possible sources of the electricity that produced the contraction in the muscle tissue. One was due to contact between two different metals, as Volta argued. Another was the electricity stored in muscles, just as von Humboldt had shown in his experiment.

Not even Volta himself saw the battery as the deciding factor in the controversy. The pile was seen as an amplified form of galvanism, which occurred in both metals and animals. The battery made it much easier to produce and to study a variety of effects than was possible using the extremely weak electricity in the muscle tissue of frogs; hence, galvanism eventually did come to be seen as a phenomenon of the inorganic alone.

The flourishing of electrochemistry.   The presence of current electricity had an immediate impact. Even before Volta's letter to Joseph Banks had been published, two English chemical investigators had seen enough of it to build a pile of their own. In late April of 1800 William Nicholson (1753–1815) and Anthony Carlisle (1768–1840) noticed that a gas was forming at a drop of water on one of the terminals of their pile. They then reconfigured the apparatus so that they could pass the pile's current through platinum leads inserted through corks into each end of a tube filled with water. After permitting the current to flow for over two hours they collected the gases that had formed on the leads. Already knowing from work by Henry Cavendish (1731–1810) that water was composed of hydrogen and oxygen, they were not surprised when simple tests revealed that they had decomposed water. Electrical force had been used to produce chemical change.

The most famous electrochemist in England, however, was Humphry Davy (1778–1829), son of a woodcarver from the rural and industrial area of Cornwall. With the announcement of Volta's discovery and its application by Nicholson and Carlisle to decompose water, Davy was enticed by the new possibilities that lay ahead. With a battery of 110 double plates he quickly concluded that Volta's assertion about electricity being produced by mere contact amounted to getting something for nothing. Davy defended a different view: a *chemical reaction generated the current.*

When just after the new year of 1801 Davy received an invitation to take up a position in London's newly established Royal Institution, he moved to the city where he would make his name. There, over the next several years, he conducted electrochemical experiments on many substances. If Davy's success in the laboratory was due to his abilities as an experimenter, his fame rested also on his effectiveness as a communicator. Through public lectures at the Royal Institution he captivated the public with his authoritative command of the technical issues of the day while at the same time making sweeping claims about their significance. His conception of himself as the "Newton of chemistry" was not completely persuasive, but his imposing personality repeatedly brought natural philosophy to the attention of the public.

Nowhere was his visibility greater than when he presented Britain with his most famous practical invention, the safety lamp. Miners needed light to work underground, but using candles to enter shafts could prove disastrous if they ran into an explosive gas called firedamp (methane). In 1812, for example, ninety-two miners perished when gas exploded in a pit thought to be safe. Several individuals were trying to develop a flame lamp that would not ignite the firedamp in mines in the aftermath of this tragedy. Davy's experiments on firedamp established the limits under which it would explode. He then constructed a lamp that could burn outside these limits, thereby rendering it safe to use in mines. Although others claimed credit for similar lamps, Davy's gift as a public man of science earned him the reward of a baronetcy.

Oersted's wonderful discovery: electromagnetism. Among those who were completely intrigued by questions surrounding nature's many forces was a young Dane named Hans Christian Oersted (1777–1851). The eldest son of a pharmacist, Hans Christian and his brother Anders, who was one year younger, were sent daily from an early age to the house of a German wig maker for instruction in religion and the German language. Some Oersted scholars have argued that his exposure to things German and to religion, including much from Danish theology, disposed Oersted to adopt the unique worldview he later defended—one that drew heavily on the ideas of Immanuel Kant and on specific aspects of German romantic philosophy.

Oersted and his brother went to Copenhagen in the spring of 1794 to prepare for the university's entrance examination. The boys had been largely self-taught prior to coming to Copenhagen; nevertheless, by October of 1795 both had passed the entrance examinations with distinction. Hans Christian now continued to pursue his strong interest in poetry, but he chose chemistry as his major subject of study. In May of 1797 Oersted demonstrated on his examination that he knew much more than his examiners.

By 1799 he completed a Latin doctoral dissertation in the faculty of philosophy, not medicine. He appealed to Kant's thought in an attempt to establish a philosophical foundation for understanding nature. The central insight that he imbibed from Kant was that matter should be understood in terms of forces, not in terms of atoms, as many in France preferred. Kant argued that matter, as Newton had shown, attracted all other matter. From this fundamental fact one could explain why material bodies came together, indeed, why they congealed into the many shapes we observe them to have.

But Kant felt more was needed for a truly philosophical understanding of matter. Matter must also possess a fundamental repulsive force that accounted for why bodies cannot occupy the same space. In other words, in what is called a Kantian dynamic understanding of matter, when we feel a solid object to be hard it is really due to the existence of strong repulsive force. The existence of material bodies, then, is due to the constant interaction, often called conflict, of attractive and repulsive forces.

In 1801 Oersted made an extended trip to Germany and France that lasted until January of 1804. During this time he was able to meet and discuss natural philosophy with many notable people, especially those associated with the so-called German Romantic School in Jena. Among the philosophers he became acquainted with was Friedrich Schelling, who agreed with him about understanding matter in terms of the conflict of forces. Schelling had reformulated Kant's philosophy by extending it into the organic realm (see Chapter 15).

Oersted appreciated Schelling's insistence that all of nature must be regarded as an organized whole that could be grasped by our reason. He very much agreed with Schelling's insistence that to understand nature in its organized totality required the image of a nature depicted as a world soul. That notion melded very well with Oersted's religious vision of a unity between spirit and nature, which for him pointed to the presence of God.

Among the experimenters with whom Oersted worked was Johann Wilhelm Ritter (1776–1810), a sympathizer with Schelling who was already engaged in a series of experiments on the organic and inorganic manifestations of galvanism. Together with Ritter, Oersted did many experiments to investigate how—if matter really was due to a fundamental conflict of attractive and repulsive forces—that conflict gave rise to the specific manifestations of attraction and repulsion we observe in the phenomena of electricity, magnetism, and chemical change. An implication was that because the superficial manifestations of attraction and repulsion in these phenomena sprang from a common source in the basic forces that defined matter itself, there must be relations among these surface phenomena that can be uncovered. Oersted and Ritter were not the only ones in Germany trying to find how, in light of the successes in relating electrical and chemical forces, electrical and magnetic or magnetic and chemical forces might be related.

Oersted persisted in this endeavor after he returned to Denmark and became a professor of chemistry in 1806 in Copenhagen. Around this time he developed a theory, based on his dynamic understanding of matter as a conflict of forces, to explain specifically how electricity is propagated. The story of his eventual success in establishing a physical relationship between electricity and magnetism, which he explained in terms of his theory of "electric conflict," defines a pivotal moment in the history of physical science.

The wish to relate electricity and magnetism was regarded by many in the first two decades of the nineteenth century as a waste of time. The Frenchman André Marie Ampère (1775–1836), for example, maintained that they were two different imponderable fluids that acted independently of each other. The repeated failure to demonstrate that the forces were interrelated was seen, then, as confirmation of what many expected. Oersted, however, did not waver in his convictions because they were embedded in a philosophical and religious outlook that was unshakable.

In the spring of 1820 he gave a series of lectures on electricity, galvanism, and magnetism to advanced students at the University of Copenhagen. In preparation, he decided to rework his standard lectures on the subject and to include this time one lecture on the allegedly impossible connection between magnetism and electricity. He even thought about preparing a demonstration that he could give in public to test whether an electrical discharge, in his words, "might produce some effect on the magnetic needle placed out of a galvanic circuit."

Not having actually tried the demonstration he had imagined, Oersted determined to forego it during the lecture. But, because things were going well as he covered his subject, he decided to try to do the demonstration on the spot. There are some puzzles remaining about exactly what occurred next. As we imagine the experiment, it does not seem that much current would have been necessary to cause a magnetic needle to move. Further, Oersted was a careful examiner, so we can assume that very little would have escaped his notice. But Oersted tells us that although the magnet was disturbed, "the effect was very feeble." Elsewhere he also insists that the effect was unquestionable, but he characterizes it as "confused." In any event, it did not impress his listeners. Although at the time he probably wished he had not tried the experiment, one thing is clear. Contrary to the way some reported it later, the effect was not something Oersted happened on by accident.

Later that summer, when he had time to return to the experiment without an audience before him, Oersted repeated the attempt some sixty times and satisfied himself that current flowing through a galvanic circuit produced a clear magnetic effect. What was unexpected was the nature of the magnetic effect. Oersted showed that if current flowed through a wire in the direction of A in the accompanying figure (see next page), then a *circular* magnetic force existed around the

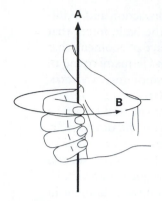

A

B

The Right-Hand Rule

wire in the direction of B, a circumstance that later gave rise to the so-called right-hand rule. This was not easy to figure out because a magnetic needle placed in front of the fingers of the right hand in the figure would point to the right, whereas it would point to the left if the needle were positioned behind the thumb. Only by trying various positions around the circle would it become clear that the magnetic force produced by the electric current was not a Newtonian, straight-line force, but a wholly new kind of action. It is possible that during Oersted's lecture, especially given the added pressure of an audience, he was confused by such unexpected effects on the magnetic needle.

Oersted's announcement of the results of his summer experiments created a sensation, as can be imagined. What was regarded as impossible, a pipe dream of overly philosophical minds, had been shown to be possible. But if Oersted's name would forever be associated with the discovery of electromagnetism, his explanation of the new effect would not. Naturally, he insisted on explaining what was happening in electromagnetism by an appeal to his old notion of an electric conflict. But he never said exactly what the electric conflict was, so his attempt to explain the effect he had uncovered was incomprehensible. No one understood him when he said that the electric conflict penetrated nonmagnetic bodies but was resisted by magnetic particles of bodies, causing them to move. After 1820 the development of electromagnetic theory passed quickly from Denmark into France and England.

Explaining what electromagnetism is.   Two very different approaches to understanding how electromagnetism was produced emerged very soon after Oersted's announcement. One, that of Ampère, assumed that any force, magnetic or otherwise, could not really act along a circular path as Oersted's description of the magnetic force around the current-carrying wire seemed to indicate. Rather, like all the forces known of at that time, Oersted's apparent circular magnetic force had to be the resultant sum of central forces, that is, forces that acted directly along a line between the centers of two masses or two charges. Ampère assumed that an explanation of Oersted's apparently circular magnetic force, then, would be found by breaking it up into straight-line component forces.

Like Oersted, Ampère was a deeply religious man. He also shared with the Danish investigator an interest in Kant's philosophy. But a nearly three-hour conversation with Oersted about his theory of electric conflict in April of 1823 did not persuade him of its merits. In its place Ampère came to the conclusion that *magnetism was electricity in motion.* Just as static electricity exerted force, so too could current electricity exert force. Within a week of hearing about Oersted's discovery he had determined that two wires situated parallel to each other with current flowing in the same direction exerted a force of attraction to each other. When Ampère wound a current-carrying wire around a bar of iron he found that he could *create* a magnet in the iron bar.

But if magnetism was electricity in motion, how to explain those bars of iron that were *permanent* magnets? They attracted iron filings without having to have current-carrying wire wrapped around them. Ampère suggested that even in this case there was electricity in motion. He postulated that there was a circular flow of electricity *around each molecule of the iron,* so that each molecule was made into a miniature magnet in the same way the iron bar becomes a magnet when wrapped with a current-carrying wire. Then, if the molecules were aligned (as they must be in a permanent magnet), their individual magnetic forces would be added, accounting for the magnetic properties of the permanent magnet. Ampère wrote the complicated mathematical equations to describe the forces that moving electricity exerted, which he assumed to be in straight lines perpendicular to the direction of the current's flow. His achievement marks the beginning of *electrodynamics*—the forces produced by electricity in motion.

The other approach to explaining what electromagnetism was came from Michael Faraday (1791–1867) in England. Faraday, who was not trained in the mathematics that Ampère's approach required, came at the challenge from a more intuitive angle. He did not rule out, as Ampère did, that there might be forces in nature that naturally followed curved lines.

Coming from a poor family, there was no possibility of formal education for young Michael, the third of four children. Of his siblings, however, he alone attended a day school where he learned how to read, write, and do basic arithmetic. Although he seemed destined to become a bookbinder, having been apprenticed in the trade at the age of fourteen, several factors combined to change that fortune. For one, Faraday became acquainted with a group of young men interested in natural science who met regularly on Wednesday evenings. On his own, he avidly read many of the books that came into the business for binding and he attended public lectures, such as those of Humphrey Davy at the Royal Institution.

As chance would have it, he was recommended to Davy to assist in writing when Davy was temporarily blinded in 1812 due to an explosion during an experiment. A few months later, when an opportunity arose to become Davy's assistant in the laboratory, Faraday abandoned plans to become a bookbinder and began work under Davy's direction. He would remain in the Royal Institution for the rest of his life, leaving a legacy that outshone that of his teacher.

The combination of Faraday's keen mind, his unusual education, and his deep religious convictions resulted in an approach to understanding nature that was more open to new possibilities than that of most of his contemporaries. Where electromagnetism was concerned, Faraday simply accepted the notion that some forces in nature may act along curved rather than straight lines. Once he had digested what Oersted had reported, he visualized a curved "line of force" acting around a current-carrying wire. To illustrate what he saw in his mind, in the fall of 1821 he ran a wire through a beaker filled with mercury and turned on a current. In the mercury he placed a small cylindrical magnet that, although it floated in the mercury, had one end connected near the base of the beaker so that it "stood" vertically in the mercury with its top protruding freely from the surface. The top of the magnet then rotated in circles around the wire as long as the current flowed, giving visual illustration to

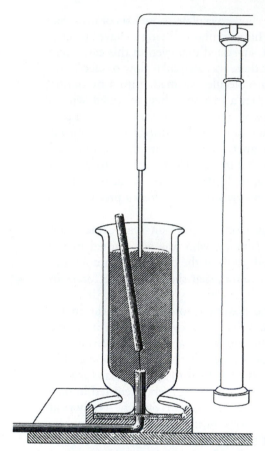

Faraday's Experiment

the circular force Oersted had discovered by literally tracing out its path. Here the continuous flow of electrical force produced continuous motion of matter, a conversion of electrical force into mechanical force.

A decade later and after years of experimenting, Faraday made another important discovery. He was not alone during these years in wondering whether magnetism could be used to produce electricity; after all, electricity could be used to produce magnetism. In America, for example, Joseph Henry (1797–1868) worked with a similar question and came to important results on his own. Faraday asked, if a current-carrying wire produced constantly acting lines of magnetic force, might another wire be able to go in the other direction? Was it not reasonable to expect that a large magnet (whose lines of force act constantly) could produce current in a nearby wire?

To test this possibility Faraday ran current through a wire to produce lines of magnetic force. He then tried to see if a second wire that was placed among the lines of magnetic force carried any current. At first he was able to induce current in the second wire only in spurts. What was clear was that, once the current in the first wire was flowing steadily, no induced current in the second wire was possible; the spurts of induced current occurred only when the current in the first wire started and again when it stopped.

The breakthrough came when Faraday realized the meaning of the starting and stopping of the current in the first wire. It was not so much the stopping and starting as it was the *changing* of the lines of force. When the current started or stopped the lines of force were forming—that was a way of making them undergo change. But there were other ways one could change the lines of force as well. For example, Faraday discovered that if he used a permanent magnet to produce the magnetic lines of force and then surrounded the magnet with a coil of wire, he could physically move the magnet in and out of the coil and produce a flow of current. As long as the lines of magnetic force were moving (changing), current flowed. He now knew how to use magnetism to produce electricity.

Faraday developed his ideas about lines of force further to explain what has become known as electromagnetic induction, or the production of electricity using magnetism. Taken together the lines of force constituted what Faraday called a *field*. He explained induction simply as the result of disturbing the lines of force in a field, which could be accomplished in several different ways. If Ampère's work gave rise to electrodynamics, Faraday's marks the origins of what has become known as field theory.

Light and Heat

All of these discoveries from the early decades of the nineteenth century by no means exhausted what natural philosophers were uncovering about the intriguing and sometimes mysterious relationships that existed among nature's many forces. In 1800, for example, the German-born British astronomer William Herschel (1738–1822) stumbled on something quite unexpected during an experiment in which he was exploring the relationship between light and heat. While measuring how hot each color of the light produced by a prism was, he noticed that if he placed his thermometer in the region just below the red end of the spectrum it registered the hottest temperature of all. Here was a region of "light" that could be felt but not seen. It would later become known as infrared light.

One year later in Germany, Johann Ritter, whose electrical views we met earlier in this chapter, was inspired by Herschel's discovery of infrared light to publish an article entitled "Chemical Polarity in Light." He had become convinced that light was the result of a chemical balance between two chemical forces, one he called a force of oxidation and the other deoxidation. In the style of German nature philosophy, he explained that in white light the two forces existed "in each other." The prism separated the forces to a state of "alongside each other" and arranged them in a descending order from the strongest oxidizing forces on the violet end to the neutral area near green to the deoxidizing forces on the red end.

Ritter asserted this based on the ability of the colored light to "reduce the muriate of silver," that is, to darken silver chloride that had been exposed to each section of the spectrum. Violet light darkened the muriate of silver most, green had no effect, and red prevented darkening even if one used other means than light to do it. Given the "polarity" evident here, Ritter asked himself if there was a polar opposite of Herschel's infrared "light." Indeed, he quickly confirmed that in the region just above the violet end there were what he called "invisible rays" that darkened the muriate of silver even more than did violet light. Ultraviolet light was for him the polar opposite of infrared. This was certainly a fertile time for ideas.

Thomas Young and the wave theory of light.   In the seventeenth century René Descartes had taught that light was a disturbance in a medium that existed between the object and the eye. The disturbance took the form of waves in the medium that were propagated by mechanical means. The waves of light moved through the medium just like impulses move through a stick that a blind person uses to feel his way forward. By the early nineteenth century, however, many natural philosophers regarded light as a stream of particles that passed from a material object to the eye as, for example, odor particles pass from an object to the nose. This was the view of Isaac Newton, who had criticized Descartes.

Newton felt that Descartes's pulse theory of light could not account for a newly discovered property that light displayed, which Descartes had not known about. How could Descartes have accounted for the polarization of light—which results in light being completely blocked by merely rotating the polarizing substance through which it is passed—if it consisted of the transmission of pulses? What about the pulses would explain why polarized light behaves in this manner? If, on the other hand, light consisted of rectangular particles, then one could associate different properties with the different sides of the particles. Polarization became for Newton a matter of the alignment of particles.

It would be safe to conclude that no one from Newton's time or in the eighteenth century felt confident that everything about light had been settled. New facts about light were still coming forth. A Danish astronomer, Ole Roemer, demonstrated in Newton's day that light from Jupiter took a finite time to reach Earth; in other words, the speed of light was not infinite as some had assumed. And even Newton knew that light had periodic properties that were hard to account for by seeing light as particles. As a result, the pulse theory was hardly overthrown simply because Newton had criticized it. When, therefore, Thomas Young (1773–1829) in England proposed in 1801 that light consisted of the propagation of waves through a medium, he was choosing an option for which the way had been well prepared.

In Young's famous double-slit experiment on light, he passed a beam of colored light from a small source through two holes and examined how the emerging light fell on a screen. What he saw was a pattern of bright and dark regions, something that did not make sense if light consisted of a ray of particles as Newton imagined. To explain it Young proposed that light consisted of waves, but not the mechanical pulses that Descartes had referred to in his example of the blind person's stick. There the compression of the wood in the stick moved in the same direction as the pulse. Young imagined that light moved through a medium between an object and the eye somewhat like waves move through water; that is, although the waves move *horizontally* across the surface of the water, the water itself only moves *up and down*. Light, he concluded, consisted of waves that moved perpendicularly to the direction of the particles of the medium through which it passes. He then explained the bright regions of the pattern he observed as the places where the crests of the waves emerging from the two slits coincided. The dark regions were then the places where the crest of one wave coincided with the trough of the other, thus canceling each other.

Within two decades Young's work on the interference of light received support in several ways. First, one could make sense of polarization using his explanation of what light was. Young had said that light consisted of waves of a medium, which Young and others called the ether. Further, particles of the medium moved perpendicularly to the direction of the wave. In general, that could occur if the particles moved along rays that emanated out from the line that described the direction of the wave. Polarized light occurs when the motion of the particles of the medium is restricted to one direction only, as in the example of water waves, where the water moves only vertically while the wave moves horizontally (see the figure).

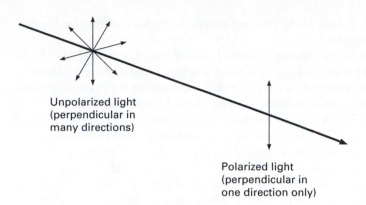

Polarized and Unpolarized
Light

Unpolarized light
(perpendicular in
many directions)

Polarized light
(perpendicular in
one direction only)

A second confirmation came from a French savant named Augustin Fresnel (1788–1827). He provided a mathematical description of how waves could be used to explain the way light bends around obstacles. A colleague, who did not accept the wave theory, then reasoned that if Fresnel's mathematical wave theory was correct, it implied that a small disk placed in the path of a beam of light would cause the light to bend around the edges and converge toward the center to produce a bright spot in the middle of the shadowed region. To his surprise that is exactly what was observed when the experiment was done. Light would be regarded as waves in the ether for the remainder of the century.

Remarkable new insights about heat and motive force. The ability to move matter by the force of heat was naturally of interest to those who had figured out how to turn steam heat into the back-and-forth motion of machines and to those who were speculating on the role of the Earth's internal heat as an agency of geological change. But a widespread appreciation of heat's ability to produce motive force did not mean that natural philosophers understood how this conversion of forces took place. This would begin to change with the work of two French natural philosophers, each of whom introduced ideas that would take some time to be fully appreciated.

During the first decade of the nineteenth century Joseph Fourier (1768–1830), a former revolutionary, member of Napoleon's army, and then Napoleon's appointed prefect of Grenoble, had devoted himself to a purely theoretical treatment of heat flow. The brilliance of the new mathematical techniques he developed to express his results was not recognized until later; consequently, his work was at first not well received and not even published. In part this was because Fourier, like Oersted, introduced a non-Newtonian element into physics that proved to be controversial. The mechanical laws Newton had formulated to describe how the machinery of nature ran were reversible; that is, they could be thought of as running backward as easily as they ran forward. In Fourier's analysis the laws formulated for the conduction of heat implied that conducted heat flow could not be reversible. If that were true, then apparently heat was an aspect of nature that defied traditional mechanical explanation. Many natural philosophers balked at accepting such a conclusion. Only later in the century would the irreversibility of conducted heat flow be fully recognized.

A younger compatriot of Fourier, Nicolas Léonard Sadi Carnot (1796–1832), fared somewhat better than did Fourier. Carnot was interested in the use of heat to move matter. While everyone knew that chemical combustion, for example, moved matter when there was an explosion, Carnot wanted to understand how heat engines worked. They used heat to produce repeated movement in the parts of machines. For some time it had been common knowledge that hot steam introduced into a chamber would produce great pressure; indeed, explosions due to mistakes in handling high pressures in steam engines had injured more than one worker. In these engines there was a piston that could move at the top of a chamber. If the piston was connected to other moving parts of the machine, then the increased pressure due to the insertion of heat into the chamber supplied the motive force of the machinery.

Carnot wanted to know the answers to some important questions. Were some substances better than others at producing a given amount of motive force? Was there was a maximal amount of motive force that could be obtained using a certain amount of heat? These were theoretical questions. People who actually used steam engines might use trial and error to determine if different engines produced different amounts of motive force from the same quantity of heat, but they had little interest in the theoretical questions Carnot posed for himself.

In the course of answering his questions Carnot came upon a very important insight whose implications would take some time to realize. Carnot saw that if heat were going to be used to produce motive force, then the only way that could happen was if heat at a high temperature fell to a lower temperature. Something about the fall of temperature was absolutely required to produce motive force by heat engines. He put down his ideas on this subject in a book of 1824, entitled *Reflections on the Motive Power of Heat*.

Carnot thought of the production of motive force from heat as nature's response to a disturbance in a normally balanced state. Historians Norton Wise and Crosbie Smith have pointed out that a typical approach to many scientific problems in the eighteenth and nineteenth centuries was to view them as disturbances of an equilibrium that was then restored. Carnot viewed the steam engine as another way of disturbing a normal state, then presenting nature with an opportunity to restore the original state. The heat engine he imagined was an ideal engine; he did not consider heat lost by conduction or by friction of the moving parts, which were viewed as weightless.

Many in Carnot's day conceived of heat as a weightless fluid called caloric, which was present in or attached to all matter. This was how readers have understood Carnot's analysis. How much caloric was present was a measure of the matter's temperature; that is, the temperature of air in the chamber of a steam engine depended on how much caloric was present in the volume of the chamber. The temperature was an index of the density of the caloric.

Carnot's analysis of his ideal heat engine ran as follows (see the figure): (1) At a normal density of caloric, that is, before the operation begins, the system is static

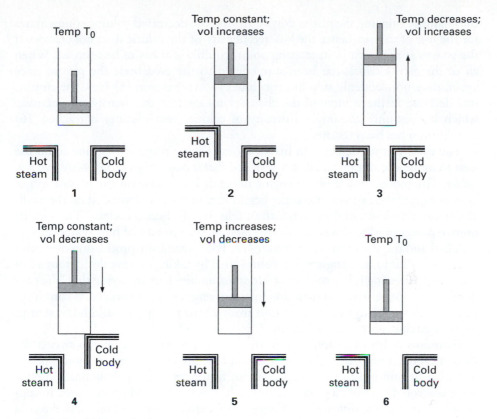

Temp T_0

Temp constant;
vol increases

Temp decreases;
vol increases

Hot steam	Cold body	Hot steam	Cold body	Hot steam	Cold body

Hot steam

1   **2**   **3**

Temp constant;
vol decreases

Temp increases;
vol decreases

Temp T_0

Cold body

Hot steam		Hot steam	Cold body	Hot steam	Cold body

4   **5**   **6**

Carnot's Equilibrium Cycle

and in equilibrium. (2) When extra caloric is introduced by briefly admitting steam into the chamber, nature retains equilibrium in the system by providing motive force—by moving a piston at the top of the chamber up so that the volume of the chamber increases. This keeps the density of the caloric, or the temperature, constant at the equilibrium amount as the extra caloric is introduced.

Carnot assumed that nature would maintain equilibrium if at all possible. (3) When the addition of heat is suddenly stopped, however, the piston does not instantly stop, but continues to move up. This means that the volume of the chamber expands more than is necessary to maintain equilibrium by keeping the density of the caloric constant; hence the density of the caloric decreases, that is, the temperature drops below that at which the process had begun. No longer is there equilibrium in the system because the normal density of the caloric has been reduced. Nature reacts to this situation by trying to re-establish equilibrium. But that cannot happen unless somehow an opportunity is made available to restore the normal density of caloric.

(4) To accomplish this the excess caloric that has been introduced has to be removed from the chamber. This becomes possible by allowing the caloric to be given to a cold body. Nature reacts to this opportunity by decreasing the volume in

the chamber (moving the piston down). At first the decreased volume compensates for the loss of caloric; hence the lowered density of the caloric does not change. If the system is to return to its starting point, equilibrium has to be restored. When all of the excess caloric has been surrendered to the cold body the piston, once again, does not suddenly stop but continues to move down. (5) Now the continued decrease in the volume of the chamber means that the density can increase, which it does until the original density of caloric (temperature) is reached. (6) Equilibrium has been restored.

The cycle Carnot depicted in his ideal heat engine revealed that one could use heat to move a piston up and down *provided that it could be given to a body that was colder*. The motive power of the engine depended of course on the production of heat to supply the extra caloric at the beginning, but it also depended on the availability of cold. Without the latter, Carnot tells us, "the heat is useless." The specific motive power produced was due to two factors, the amount of heat (extra caloric) supplied and the size of the temperature fall. For Carnot, the production of motive force from heat in heat engines is accomplished by taking excess caloric from a hot body and delivering it to a cold body. He sums up his claim by saying that "the production of motive power is then due in steam-engines not to an actual consumption of caloric, but to its transportation from a warm body to a cold body, that is, to its re-establishment of equilibrium."

By means of his novel approach to the question, Carnot was able to answer the theoretical questions that had motivated him to study heat engines. If motive power was what he said it was, then the important factor determining how much motive force one could get from a given amount of heat was not the substance used to supply the heat, but the difference in temperature between the hot body and the cold body. The maximum theoretical power obtainable from a given amount of heat from steam was the same as the maximum power that could be obtained from that same amount of heat supplied by any substance. This answered his first question.

Carnot also considered the theoretical case of running a heat engine backward; that is, instead of *obtaining* power by moving caloric from a hot body to a cold body, he wanted to *supply* power in order to move caloric from a cold body to a hot body. An engine that can be conceived of as running in either direction is called a reversible engine. (Remember, Carnot was not considering the heat flow of conduction in real engines, which, had he read Fourier, was not reversible.) Carnot's reason for considering this theoretical situation was extremely clever, for he imagined two heat engines, one of which was more efficient than the other. He then imagined using the more efficient one to drive the other one backward. But if the first engine were more efficient than the second one that was going backward, it would not take all the power it had produced to drive the second one backward. That would mean that the caloric that was moved from a hot body to a cold body by the first engine would have been put back by the engine it was driving backward, but that there would be some extra power left over from the first engine because it was more efficient. This suggests that the process could go on forever—a perpetual motion machine. Carnot regarded that as impossible, so he concluded that all ideal reversible heat engines must have the same efficiency. Both of his questions were now solved.

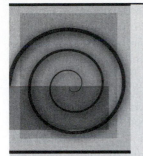

The NATURE of SCIENCE

Lasting Disagreements in Science

Occasionally one encounters the notion that there can only be one correct idea in science, especially when ideas appear to be mutually exclusive. The history of science shows, however, that it is not uncommon for disagreements to go on for a long time, even over centuries. An example of this kind of disagreement is evident in contrary views about the nature of heat.

The caloric theory of heat, which assumed that heat was an inherently light substance that permeated gross material bodies, originated with Aristotle's identification of fire as one of the four basic elements. In this conception of heat, temperature could be associated with the amount of caloric that occupied a given volume.

An alternative explanation, in which heat was regarded as the motion of the corpuscles making up a specific mass, was entertained at least as early as the seventeenth century in the context of accounting for the *creation* of heat through friction. At the turn of the nineteenth century Benjamin Thompson, also known as Count Rumford, undertook a series of experiments that involved boring canons. Rumford demonstrated that extreme amounts of heat were produced when boring metal canons; in fact, he concluded that the amount of heat that could be produced appeared to be inexhaustible. How could the caloric theory account for that if the heat were due to caloric in the metal canons that was somehow set free during the boring process? Rumford's conclusion was that the only way his results made sense was if heat were due to the motion of the particles in the metal.

Rumford's conception, however, was not able to handle as well as the caloric theory how heat was *transferred* from one body to another. How, for example, could Rumford explain the transfer of the sun's heat to the Earth on the assumption that it was a mode of motion of the corpuscles of gross matter? Neither theory had carried the day prior to the nineteenth century, nor would either theory eliminate the other for several decades to come.

◎ New Institutions of Natural Science ◎

In addition to the new centers of science that became prominent under Napoleon in France, new German universities began in the early nineteenth century to serve as a location for conducting research in natural philosophy. In England a new creation, the Royal Institution, was established in March of 1799 to provide the lay public access to the seeming explosion of scientific and technical knowledge emerging everywhere in Europe. As the continuing war with France made it increasingly difficult for the average person to obtain information coming from the Continent, the role of the Royal Institution became more and more important.

New Developments in the German States

As German students came home victorious from the defeat of Napoleon in the Wars of Liberation, they gave public voice to the increasing sentiment among members of the middle class for reform. In particular, they clamored for the consolidation of power among the German states by uniting under a single ruler. While such radical reform was not tolerated by the leaders of the states, some natural philosophers took advantage of the growing influence of popular sentiment to promote communication among educated Germans.

The founding of *Isis*. As we saw in Chapter 14, the emergence of a public sphere, and with it a new role for public opinion, gave a stronger voice to the middle classes. Although that process began in the late seventeenth century in England, it did not appear until the late eighteenth and early nineteenth centuries in the German states. One measure of the emergence of a German public sphere was the proliferation of journals of all kinds, a direct result of the flourishing of the German Enlightenment. Among these journals was *Isis,* which appeared in 1817 and concerned itself openly with the natural sciences.

The founder of the new journal was Lorenz Oken (1779–1851), a professor at the university in Jena and a devoted adherent of Friedrich Schelling's romantic nature philosophy. Oken shared the belief of the students returning to the university from the Wars of Liberation, which had resulted in Napoleon's defeat in 1815. Their victory imparted to them a powerful conviction that change was imminent and that Germany's day in the sun was in the immediate future. In many places there was general enthusiasm for doing things differently from the past; for example, the small state in which Jena was located was one of those that had granted freedom of the press in the wake of Napoleon's defeat. Oken took advantage of this freedom when he announced the establishment of his new journal.

Consistent with his philosophical convictions as a nature philosopher, Oken was thoroughly convinced that the values he held as an investigator of nature provided a model for understanding all of existence. He was a man of action who did not want to miss the chance for change and progress lying before the German states. He determined that he would establish a new journal devoted primarily to the natural sciences, as a means of instructing the public in the proper route to truth.

The new journal, which he named *Isis* after the Egyptian goddess of nature, carried a depiction of the goddess seated between her husband, Osiris, and Anubis, the god of the underworld. The presence of Anubis, whose job was to decide between good and evil, provided a hint of one role Oken saw for his journal: to use the values of research in the sciences in making possible an enlightened public opinion, which would decide the issues of the day. The journal would be a mirror of the currents of the day, looking forward or backward according to the wishes of its subscribers. Oken made it clear that no honoraria would be given for articles. He claimed to print virtually everything that was sent to him, including occasional vitriolic criticism of himself, under the assumption that the truth would prevail in the jury of public opinion.

Freedom of the press did not last long as the German states regrouped following Napoleon's defeat. Oken's open and democratic practices ran afoul of the authorities when he was linked to radical political activities. From this point on *Isis* increasingly took on a purely scientific emphasis, becoming the leading organ for the dissemination of scientific research in Germany for some thirty years. Oken, however, was not satisfied with having founded a new kind of scientific journal. He aspired to establish a new kind of scientific society as well.

The first modern scientific society.   The first modern scientific society was the Society of German Investigators and Physicians, founded in 1822. Prior to this time gatherings of those interested in the study of nature were primarily local groups, often with a narrow focus within the natural sciences. A general association of researchers, the Helvetian Research Society, convened for the first time in Bern, Switzerland, in 1816. Oken, an honorary member of the group, reported on its meetings in *Isis*. From this organization he got the idea of founding a German scientific society. The announcement of an organizational meeting of the new society for September 18, 1822, in Leipzig resulted in a meeting of thirteen participants. Approximately half of the participants were physicians and half researchers.

Several features emerged that distinguished the new society from local gatherings and from exclusive institutions like London's Royal Society or the Paris Academy of Sciences. Most important, the participants decided to meet annually in a different city of Germany, alternating between southern, northern, eastern, and western locations. They specifically rejected the idea that their society should always convene in one central place, believing that a traveling annual conference would produce a greater involvement and greater diversity of ideas.

Oken insisted that social gatherings become an essential feature of the meetings of the society. When authorities dashed all hopes for a unification of the German states following the defeat of Napoleon, they created an atmosphere in which heated debates could flare up quickly. Oken aimed to defuse this likelihood by including in the program visits to local gardens, art museums, and evenings of musical entertainment. He hoped that participants would learn to balance their sometimes strong disagreements about issues with the greater unity that moments of shared enjoyment provided.

The new society quickly became very popular and attendance at the annual meetings grew rapidly. In 1828 the meeting was held in Berlin, where the king of Prussia attended an evening social occasion of some twelve hundred persons. The inaugural address was given by one of the most well-known names of German natural science, Alexander von Humboldt, who had just been called home to Germany from a long sojourn in Paris. The address reinforced the importance of the exchange of ideas as a means for bridging intellectual differences. At this meeting von Humboldt suggested, and the participants agreed to create, seven individual sections of natural science and medicine, marking an early step in the direction of the specialization of natural scientific research. Four years later the society held its first international meeting in Vienna, with some 463 members in attendance. A new social identity had made its way undeniably into the collective life of Germany and Austria. Although not yet professionalized, those who pursued research in natural science had acquired a greater visibility than they ever had before.

British Emulation

The British had good reason to regard themselves as the leaders in industry at the beginning of the nineteenth century. British inventions were widely known and often copied by those in other countries. With improved roads and a canal system at home and trade companies taking British goods far and wide abroad, the British presence seemed to be everywhere. But in the pursuit of natural science some scholars declared that reforms were needed to keep Britain from falling rapidly behind France and Germany.

Complaints about the decline of science.   One Englishman attended the Berlin meeting of the Society of German Researchers and Physicians in 1828. Charles Babbage (1791–1871), a mathematician from London, enthusiastically reported on his Berlin experiences the following spring in the Edinburgh journal of a friend and fellow natural philosopher. A few years earlier Babbage had received a stipend from the government to begin building a calculating machine he had designed. Now out of funds, he once again had to go hat in hand to persuade either the government or the Royal Society to continue supporting the project. Babbage openly made known his dissatisfaction with the support natural science was receiving in Britain.

Nor was Babbage the only man of science at the time who complained. Babbage's close friend from undergraduate days, the astronomer John Herschel (1792–1871), shared his impatience with the older generation of natural philosophers. The son of the famous astronomer William Herschel (1738–1822), who had emigrated to England from Germany, the younger Herschel had taken over his father's work and had published a catalogue of double stars in 1824 that brought him wide acclaim from home and abroad. Now he looked across the channel and saw that the grass was much greener on the Continent. "It is idle for us to attempt competition with our continental neighbors whether French or German in matters of science," he wrote to Thomas Young in August of 1828. "We are rapidly dropping behind in the race."

In 1830 Babbage published a book in which his criticism of English natural science was forthright and pointed. His *Reflections on the Decline of Science in England* caused a great stir because of its attempt to expose English science as second class. In addition Babbage openly criticized the Royal Society of London, into which both he and John Herschel had been elected members over a decade earlier. It was, he declared, dominated by members who were far more interested in aristocratic status than scientific achievement. He did not shy away from naming those in positions of authority whom he thought unfit for their duties; indeed, he even appeared to question the integrity of some who had accepted funds for services their training prohibited them from adequately performing. Babbage's book included a series of proposed reforms that were supposed to put England back on solid footing. Needless to say, many were outraged by Babbage's attack.

Matters came to a head when later that year the Babbage forces proposed John Herschel as a candidate for the presidency of the Royal Society. The intention of the reformers was clear: to revitalize the center of English natural science through the reform of its leading institution. The younger Herschel was indeed recognized as an up-and-coming talent, a gifted astronomer whose personal credentials were impeccable. But the power of the entrenched forces of aristocracy in support of Herschel's opponent, the Duke of Sussex, combined to send Herschel down to a narrow defeat in late November of 1830. The younger generation was now more convinced than ever that something had to be done.

The British Association of Science. A few months after the defeat of Herschel, Babbage's editor friend received a report on yet another successful meeting of the German naturalists, the 1830 gathering that had been held in Hamburg. He began to circulate the idea that British men of science, as he called them, should create a similar organization. Sufficient sentiment in favor of the idea resulted in the announcement of a "General Scientific Meeting at York" in September of 1831.

Attendance at the York meeting came predominately from people in Yorkshire, seconded by the presence of a Scottish contingent. Still, many areas of Britain were at least represented and the meetings themselves proved to be, as a local York paper put it, a veritable "festival of science." In spite of the predictable wrangling over issues such as the conditions of membership and its relationship to government, what would be known as the British Association for the Advancement of Science had been born. The next two meetings were held in the venerable academic centers of Oxford and Cambridge, each year with rapidly increasing attendance. Established university professors of natural science simply could not absent themselves.

The new British and German scientific societies brought increased public visibility to the natural sciences and those devoted to them. It was in this context of a growing awareness of the presence of natural science in public life that new meanings emerged for old terms and new names were coined. During the Cambridge meeting of 1833 the poet Samuel Taylor Coleridge, long-time friend of those who sought to encounter and understand nature, was honored. He forbad members of the BAAS to call themselves philosophers, as some traditionally still referred to themselves. In response William Whewell, Master of Trinity College, coined the word "scientist" as a term that designated those who studied material nature. It would take some time for the new name to catch on, but its presence signaled a change away from natural philosophy toward a an enterprise that was more narrowly focused. Natural science was rapidly becoming a very visible part of the landscape of European culture in the nineteenth century.

Suggestions for Reading

Geoffrey Cantor, *Michael Faraday: Sandemanian and Scientist* (London: Palgrave Macmillan, 1993).

Jack Morrell and Arnold Thackray, eds., *Gentlemen of Science* (London: Royal Historical Society, 1985).

Guiliano Pancaldi, *Volta: Science and Culture in the Age of Enlightenment* (Princeton: Princeton University Press, 2005).

CHAPTER 17

New Ideas About Life and Its Past

Prior to the nineteenth century the study of living things was generally known as natural history. Those who pursued this classic endeavor catalogued differences in the external characteristics of plants or animals, arranging them in groups that constituted a classification of living things. The focus was on individual organisms, particularly on the characteristics that made them unique. The goal was to specify their place in the hierarchy of nature as clearly as possible.

Around the turn of the nineteenth century a new way of treating living things made its appearance. Natural philosophers began to ask whether all living bodies shared something in common that determined their status as *living* organisms. The focus here was not on how to classify individual organisms. For the first time the spotlight was on life, a subject that did not exist as a specific object of investigation in the eighteenth century. What resulted were new ideas about life and its past. These new ideas showed themselves in three areas.

First, some natural philosophers began to question whether living things obeyed laws that were different from those of nonliving nature. These natural philosophers insisted that living things could not be described as mere mechanisms, using the laws of Newtonian mechanics. Some began to ask if a *science of living things* was possible; that is, whether there were scientific laws that applied uniquely to living things. Several different people used the same new word, *biology*, to express what they regarded as novel insights about the study of living things. These natural philosophers were sympathetic to the romantic vision of natural science, in which nature was envisioned as an organism (see Chapter 15).

The second area in which new ideas about life and its past emerged occurred in France and centered around two individuals. As a result of his investigations of vertebrate fossils, Georges Cuvier introduced Paris to a world of extinct beasts that had roamed the Earth prior to recorded history. His colleague, Jean-Baptiste Lamarck, proposed a grand scheme of the evolution of living things that explained how present-day life had originated.

The final context in which new ideas took root occurred in Britain. In northern Britain natural philosophers responded to the traditions they inherited from eighteenth-century thinkers by trying to capture past development under a grandiose causal law. In southern Britain the claims of natural philosophy forced nothing less than a major revision of an academic discipline after geological concerns and the examination of fossil remains forced their way into the classical study of world history.

What was clear everywhere was that after the turn of the new century the old vista of natural history had expanded. New questions were being asked, and new answers were being given that challenged old assumptions about the supernatural origins of living things and about the subsequent history of life on Earth.

◎ The Romantic Understanding of the ◎ History of Living Things

The Enlightenment's emphasis on the use of reason and analysis waned near the eighteenth century's end. In the wake of the French Revolution it was displaced by a new cultural orientation known as romanticism. In this outlook the emphasis was on feeling as opposed to reason, imagination as opposed to analysis. Romanticism expressed itself openly in the arts, literature, and, as we saw in Chapter 15, in various forms of romantic natural philosophy.

German Evolution: Ideal and Actual

As the eighteenth century drew to a close, the German word *Evolution*, which in the debates over the development of the embryo (see Chapter 12) had meant "unfolding," was expanding to include references beyond individual organisms. Now the unfolding could also refer to the progressive development of *species*. This broader meaning of how living things developed opened up new possibilities for natural history, but it also led to considerable confusion and disagreement.

Recapitulation theory.   In February of 1793 a young professor named Carl Friedrich Kielmeyer (1765–1844) gave a lecture to an assembly at a small school near Stuttgart. The title of the lecture, "On the Relations of Organic Forces Among Each Other," made clear at the outset that in the realm of the living there would be no talk about mass, volume, and distance that characterized discussions of the heavens. Living things, in other words, were governed by unique organic forces of nature. He identified what he called the forces of sensibility, irritability, and reproduction, which were not present in inanimate things. He emphasized that because of the presence of these organic forces, the realm of living things was enormously complex. According to Kielmeyer, for example, the individual organic forces of sensibility, irritability, and reproduction were distributed differently in different organisms.

One of the general laws Kielmeyer identified moved the discussion to a new level. He declared that the laws that governed how the specific organic forces were distributed in an individual member of a species were the same laws that determined the distribution of the forces in the species itself. In other words, he was imagining the organic realm as a domain governed by organic forces that produced regularities that had gone undetected in times past because they occurred at different levels simultaneously.

Kielmeyer came to a general conclusion regarding the parallel levels of species and the stages of individual development: the distribution of organic forces among species in the general scale of being that ascends from primitive to complex organisms follows the same order as the distribution in the different developmental states of the individual. For example, just as an individual embryo of a complex animal begins its existence as a simple whole and, following the law governing organic development, gradually differentiates into a complex being with parts, so too does the scale of being begin with simple species and, *following the same law,* ascends to more complex species.

An implication of this conclusion was that in individuals of complex species, such as human beings, the law is expressed more fully than in individuals of simpler species that are lower on the scale of being. Kielmeyer noted that in the beginning stages of their development plants and birds are alike. Birds go on to become more complex than plants, just as bird species stand higher on the scale of being than plant species. This idea would later be expressed by saying that the laws governing the development of the species recapitulate those governing the development of the individual.

Kielmeyer's idea of recapitulation expressed a principal tenet of romanticism—that nature was more than the blind collision of matter in motion. Recapitulation implied that the animal world was ordered according to principles that express an inner purposiveness. He insisted that his view of nature required the presence of a world spirit, rejecting the idea that it was possible to depict organisms simply through factors that applied to the inanimate world, such as mass, volume, and distance. He *was* willing to acknowledge that nature was a machine—as long as it was a living machine.

Defenders of recapitulation in the early nineteenth century made clear some of its implications. An anatomist at Halle University named Johann Friedrich Meckel (1781–1833), for example, noted that in its development to maturity, the human fetus passed through the stages of lower animals. From his consideration of the parallel stages of development the anatomist and physiologist Friedrich Tiedemann (1781–1861) inferred that species had undergone an actual evolution in the past.

Ideal evolution. Tiedemann and Kielmeyer were among the few natural philosophers in the early nineteenth century to suggest that species had actually been transformed over time from simpler to more complex forms. The suggestion that species had actually evolved went too far for the great majority of German romantics. The rational patterns that linked present-day species to each other may resemble the patterns according to which the embryo developed, but for most that did not mean that the resemblance entailed the actual evolution of species.

Stages in the development of the embryo helped to illuminate the pattern according to which present-day species could be cataloged; hence the stages of embryonic development helped to make clear the categories according to which the "great chain of being" was organized. When German romantic natural philosophers spoke about present species in terms drawn from embryonic development, it sounded on occasion as if they were claiming that species evolved over time just as the embryo did. For this reason many have concluded that the German nature philosophers believed in an evolution long before Charles Darwin. A few did. But for the majority, talk of the evolution of species referred to an ideal realm, not one that had actually occurred.

G. H. Schubert's dark side of science.   The nature philosopher Gotthilf Heinrich Schubert (1780–1860) provides an example of how romantic ideas about life and its history were communicated to the larger culture in the early nineteenth century. Schubert was convinced it was possible to demonstrate the coherent interconnections of all facets of reality, including those of spirit and the natural world. Readers learned from the publication of his popular lecture series, "The Dark Side of Natural Science," which was given in Dresden in 1806, that there were many new ideas about the world of living nature, and that these new ideas could inspire fascinating conjectures about the history of life.

By alluding to its dark side Schubert referred to aspects of natural science that seemed to border on the miraculous. He wanted to show that these matters were not exceptions to the rule of universal law. What drew a large crowd of listeners, including the members of a fashionable evening ladies society, was the promise of hearing someone speak about enticing subjects like animal magnetism. But what Schubert focused on in his series was the history of life, especially its origin and development.

In the typical fashion of the nature philosophers, Schubert described the creative moment when life first appeared on Earth in idealized terms. He used metaphorical language, referring to a bolt of lightning that penetrated to the deepest crevices of Earth, igniting thousands of lamps and candles. The lightning was omnipresent but momentary, and when gone, it was not repeated. Once underway, life began to ascend the ladder of perfection. He asked about the origin of the human race, which he understood to have occurred many thousands of years ago. Did human life as it presently existed originate from a more primitive animal life? Or, more in line with the biblical story of Genesis, had present-day human life resulted from a fall from a more glorious original state? Schubert sided with the latter option.

In his secularized version of the fall of humankind, Schubert revealed the pervasive influence that gender roles played in the thinking of the time. He explained how it was that the dark, more intuitive and comprehensive understanding of nature had been sacrificed when rational natural science was born. Originally nature, the intuitive mother, nurtured the divine seed that had been planted in humans. But the seed, portrayed as a young male, took root and developed. As it did so it outgrew the need for a mother and, Schubert said, "the young boy asks about his father and about that more divine ideal through which nature and from it humans came to be." But with the wish to become godlike came a fall from the original unity humans felt with nurturing nature.

In his treatment, Schubert illustrated the worship of nature and the preference for intuition over reason that were so prevalent in romanticism. The pursuit of knowledge of nature, which favored the use of reason over intuition, disrupted the primal intuitive feeling of unity with nature. History was a playing out of the consequences of the will to power that was born with the human quest for knowledge. Great achievement and understanding had resulted, but it was always a mechanical or handicraft view of nature, with only hints of the old unity occasionally breaking through in the dark side of natural science. Schubert's message was that a broad understanding of the unfolding of life in nature mirrored the unfolding of history of mind and spirit. His vision for natural science was to cultivate its dark side and through it to restore the original higher unity that the romantics believed had been lost by the one-sided Enlightenment emphasis on reason and analysis.

The Poetic Vision of Erasmus Darwin

When Charles Darwin later came to the conclusion that life on Earth had evolved from primitive forms, he naturally was aware that his own grandfather had promoted such ideas well before him. Although Charles maintained that his grandfather had not been a major influence on the formulation of his own theory of evolution, the general notion of evolution was a part of his own literary heritage.

Charles Darwin's colorful grandfather.   Readers in England had their own stimulant to the public discussion of life and its past. The physician Erasmus Darwin (1731–1802), acquaintance of many leading industrialists, inventors, natural philosophers, and literary figures of the late eighteenth century, possessed great skill as a writer of verse. He became one of the best-known poets in the England of his day.

Erasmus Darwin

In spite of being considerably overweight and afflicted with a pronounced stammer, Darwin lived his life with abandon. Some of his children were illegitimate, as were, in the eyes of many of his contemporaries, his views about God and the history of life. He was a freethinking believer in a self-generated universe. Not all of Darwin's writings about nature took the form of poetry, although even his prose retained a poetic quality. A prose work entitled *Zoonomia,* which appeared in three parts between 1794 and 1796, and a poem entitled *The Temple of Nature,* which was published posthumously in 1803, confirmed that evolution was a dangerous subject.

Life's evolutionary past.   Although Darwin's aim in the *Zoonomia* was to gather information about animal life in order to investigate the understanding of disease, the work contained a discussion of what its subtitle announced as *The Laws of*

Organic Life. Darwin depicted the changes that living animals experience—from the remarkable transformations that individual caterpillars undergo during their lives to those wrought on an entire species by selective breeding. In addition, Darwin noted that monstrosities sometimes persisted over generations, continuing as varieties, "if not as a new species of animal." He marveled at the adaptive characteristics various species had acquired through response to the needs of reproduction, hunger, and security. The conclusion was something of a hymn to naturalistic evolution in which animal life, having once been brought into life by what he called "the Great First Cause," was ordered according to an inner purposiveness.

In *The Temple of Nature* Darwin speculated about the origins of order in the cosmos. It had emerged from a chaos that preceded time. The planets were born from exploding suns, whose light provided the stimulus to life's appearance. "Nurs'd by warm sun-beams in primeval caves, Organic Life began beneath the waves." From such beginnings the poem depicted the progression of life as the result of an enormous struggle of all against all, up to humans, who should not regard themselves as fundamentally exceptional. The wrecks of death are only a change in form; man "Should eye with tenderness all the living forms, His brother-emmets, and his sister worms."

Darwin's grand poem was not received with enthusiasm in his native country. A nature that evolved on its own, and whose meaning was not specifically defined in terms of an external God, was simply too much for most people of early-nineteenth-century Britain to swallow.

◎ Evolutionary Controversies in France ◎

We saw earlier in this chapter that the German romantic thinkers Kielmeyer and Tiedemann accepted organic evolution at the beginning of the century. Around the same time in France the first systematic exposition of evolutionary development appeared.

What first captured the attention of French *savants* during the Napoleonic years, however, was the announcement of the existence of a prehistoric world of creatures that no longer existed. The excitement produced by this announcement gave birth to the new French system of organic evolution. Ironically, as we shall see, the new French evolution was a reaction *against* the claims being made about these marvelous extinct beasts.

The Prehistoric World of Georges Cuvier

In 1795 two young men of twenty-six, unknown to the world and to each other, were both drawn to Paris following the end of the Terror and the institution of the Directory. Each was convinced that he possessed special abilities and that in this time of change there was no better place to test them than in the French capital. Although neither had been born in France proper, they seemed instinctively to know that the future prominence they would enjoy in that country required it. One of the young men was Napoleon Bonaparte, who would become Emperor of France within a decade. The other was Georges Cuvier (1769–1832), a naturalist who was no less aware than Napoleon that assertiveness and self-promotion paid off. By the end of the year the scarcely known Cuvier had engineered his election to the newly established National Institute, where he made Napoleon's acquaintance, and shortly thereafter he received an appointment as an assistant to the anatomist in the Museum of Natural History.

The advantage of an international education.   Georges Cuvier was born to struggling middle-class parents in the French-speaking, Lutheran principality of Montbéliard, a small region between eastern central France and Switzerland that was politically united to the Grand Duchy of Württemberg. Grand Duke Karl Eugen was always on the lookout for young talent for his new school near Stuttgart. When Georges came to his notice during one of the grand duke's visits to Montbéliard, he made arrangements for the 15-year-old to come to Württemberg.

The academy's main function was to train young men for positions in service to the Grand Duke; hence, the young student had to take the initiative if he was to pursue his boyhood interest in natural history. He studied on his own and also learned from other students in the school who had similar interests. In this way he was able to acquire research techniques in anatomy, zoology, and natural history. One especially important scientific influence on Cuvier was Carl Friedrich Kielmeyer, who at that time was an older student at the academy.

In general, Cuvier's mastery of German and his exposure to the social and international mix of students who had come from all over central Europe to learn from the faculty of some fifty scholars assembled by the grand duke, afforded him a more diverse education than he would have had in the French institutions of higher learning available to him at the time. Cuvier's knowledge of German scholarship would later put him at considerable advantage over his French colleagues.

Negotiating the revolution.   On completing his studies at the Karlsschule, Cuvier took a position as a tutor to the son of a Protestant French nobleman in Normandy on the eve of the French Revolution. In his new position he enjoyed considerable free time in which to pursue his study of living things. As part of his efforts to improve his knowledge he read the publications of the leading naturalists in Paris and made contact by letter with several of them.

Georges Cuvier

In 1795 Cuvier moved to the French capital and, by the end of that year, had successfully engineered entry into the world of Parisian science. Central among the

Paris contacts who promoted Cuvier was a very young professor of zoology, whose early appointment at the age of twenty-one in the Museum of Natural History was, like Cuvier's, made easier by the reorganization of scientific institutions during the Revolution. At first Etienne Geoffroy Saint-Hilaire (1772–1844) and Cuvier agreed that the approach Linnaeus had taken to the world of living things was unsatisfactory (see Chapter 12). Linnaeus had assumed that the fundamental task of the naturalist was to draw boundaries between groups of organisms on the basis of physical characteristics that would serve as the foundation for a system of classification. Both Geoffroy and Cuvier felt that such a system, when applied to animals, was arbitrary, because a simple reliance on physical characteristics grouped some animals that really did not belong together and separated others that were in fact alike.

But within a few years a fundamental difference in their approaches showed itself. Geoffroy's response to what he regarded as Linnaeus's flawed system, which in his mind could at best only produce a mosaic or patchwork quilt arrangement of living things, was to search for the common plan of organization, what he called the unity of composition, that nature had followed in producing living things. Such an endeavor, in the mind of Cuvier and many other savants of the day, required a considerable degree of speculation. Cuvier preferred to immerse himself in the study of specimens rather than to engage in philosophical issues. He captured the attention of Paris before long with new claims regarding the study of fossil bones and teeth, a subject that had been the focus of attention in Europe for some time.

The result of the differences in focus between Geoffroy and Cuvier, and of Cuvier's unusual capacity to seek out and win the support of established savants, was Cuvier's rapid rise to prominence, leaving Geoffroy in his shadow. They began to follow separate career trajectories that would intersect again many years later in a famous public clash before their peers.

Comparative anatomy and the reality of extinction.   Cuvier had an advantage over other naturalists in Europe who were interested in studying fossils, for the spoils of Revolutionary wars had brought to the museum some choice collections from conquered lands. To analyze them, Cuvier perfected the technique of comparing the anatomical features suggested by the fossils. Based on this approach, he was soon arguing for the existence of an entire prehuman world in which the Earth was populated with *organisms that no longer existed.* Such a notion may have been implied in the work of those who preceded Cuvier, but it was he who introduced the realm of prehistoric beasts to the popular imagination.

In 1796 Cuvier suggested that Buffon was incorrect in his earlier explanation of some large fossil bones that had been found in northern regions. Buffon believed that the Earth originally formed as a molten mass that slowly cooled to a point at which it could be inhabited by living things (see Chapter 9). An implication of this process was that even the Earth's northern climes had once been tropical regions. His claim that the fossil remains came from an elephant, which would have been at home in a warm environment, was consistent with his interpretation of Earth's history.

In his analysis of the bones, Cuvier drew on current knowledge of elephants, which included his own careful examination of their anatomy. On the basis of bones that had come to the museum from the Netherlands, Cuvier demonstrated how his precise description of anatomical differences in the remains made it clear that there were two quite distinct species of elephant, one from India and one from Africa.

He then proceeded to demonstrate that the fossil Buffon had identified as that of an elephant was in fact a previously unidentified species, one that was adapted to the cold of northern climes. Using the same techniques he had employed to distinguish Indian from African elephants, he showed that the anatomical features of what Cuvier referred to as a mammoth were different from those of both species of elephant. Because there was no living trace of the mammoth today, Cuvier announced that it represented an extinct species.

The role of catastrophes.   To answer the obvious question of what had become of these enormous mammoths, Cuvier appealed to sudden and violent events. "All these facts," he wrote, "seem to me to prove the existence of a world previous to ours, destroyed by some kind of catastrophe." What was this primitive Earth like that was not subject to the dominion of humans, he asked, and what kind of catastrophe wiped it out? Cuvier neatly sidestepped these questions. "It is not for us to involve ourselves in the vast field of conjecture that these questions open up. Only more daring philosophers undertake that."

The paper he wrote on this topic was the first in a series on fossils and a prehistoric world that Cuvier published during the years of Napoleon's reign. He believed that the "conditions of existence," as he called them, were so interconnected with the original appearance of organisms that the relations among anatomical parts of living things were "not at all the product of chance." It was the job of the naturalist to become familiar with the correlations among the parts of organisms (both living and fossil). He could then use what he learned to make inferences from a few remains.

Cuvier based his new approach on what he referred to as "the subordination of characters." He used this method to support his repeated claim that extinction was a reality, since no known organisms possessed the particular combination of features some fossil organisms displayed. He became bolder, even to the point of addressing the question of the nature of catastrophes he had sidestepped earlier in his career. In the "Preliminary Discourse" of his classic publication, *Investigations on Fossil Bones* (1812), Cuvier insisted that the extinction could not have been due to forces at work in the present; rather, sudden and violent catastrophic events, such as an inundation of water or a sudden elevation of land, must have wiped out the forms of life whose remains were then preserved. He pointed to the carcasses of large quadrupeds that had been encased in ice as proof of the suddenness of such events. Tremendous violence was necessary, he explained, to account for the elimination of *all* members of a species in a given region.

A new foundation for classification.   In 1817 Cuvier published a new classification of the animal kingdom. He proposed that the most general grouping of animals be based on the function of greatest importance to animals: the relationship of the nervous system to the organs of motion. Using this criterion, Cuvier concluded that there were four fundamental groupings of animals: vertebrates with spinal nerve cord and brain, mollusks with brain and scattered nerves but no central nerve cord, articulates with small brain and two ventral nerve threads, and zoophytes with nerve material arranged in a radially symmetric fashion. Each arrangement linked a nervous system to organs of locomotion.

As mentioned earlier, Cuvier had long been critical of Linnaeus's system of classification. With his new scheme he finally supplied an alternative. The Linnaean system reinforced the idea of a chain or scale of being according to which living things were arranged in an ascending order from primitive to complex. Cuvier opposed the notion that one link of the chain was less perfect than another. He called that notion "one of the most untrue notions ever introduced into natural history." He insisted that each group of organisms had to be considered in itself for the role that it played by virtue of its properties and its organization.

Opposition to transformism. Cuvier had even less patience with those who argued that the alleged scale of organic being had been produced through the transformation of inferior to superior forms over an extended period of time. He wanted to confine his attention to what organisms were in themselves. Transformism, as the evolution of species was known in France, seemed completely without solid foundation. The fossil record did not indicate a gradual transformation of species; on the contrary, its discontinuous contents were quite consistent with Cuvier's claim that past species had been rendered extinct by violent and capricious catastrophes. In his *Investigations on Fossil Bones* he discredited evolutionary ideas.

Cuvier preferred not to engage in philosophical dispute if he could avoid it. Sometimes, however, his own theories forced him into controversy. If, for example, he denied that present species had arisen from primitive life forms by transformation over extended time, then how *did* they arise, and what relation did they have to the prehistoric creatures that Cuvier had shown to be extinct? When forced to provide an alternative to transformism, Cuvier, whose religious position was more intellectual than personal, resorted to an original creation by God of all species that had ever lived or would ever live. Over time, catastrophes had caused numerous species to become extinct, while others had avoided elimination. He denied, however, that special creations were responsible for the new life that flourished following a catastrophe. These new life forms had migrated from neighboring regions that had been untouched by the catastrophes. An implication of this was that humans, whose remains were never present among the fossil bones of prehistoric beasts that Cuvier had identified, had existed at the same time as these beasts, but had not existed in the same region.

Jean-Baptiste Lamarck's Alternative Explanation of the Prehistoric World

One of Cuvier's contemporaries who accepted the idea that living things were arranged in an ascending scale of being from primitive to complex organisms was Jean-Baptiste Lamarck (1744–1829). But Lamarck and Cuvier were different in more ways than this. For example, Lamarck was Cuvier's senior by twenty-five years, having earned his stripes in pre-Revolutionary France. In addition, the two men had very different mentalities. Cuvier disliked natural philosophers who created

Jean-Baptiste Lamarck

speculative theories about the past, while Lamarck valued the role of imagination when attempting to know the natural world. During the early years of the nineteenth century the significance of this difference in outlook eventually became clear to both men.

Like most eighteenth-century savants, Lamarck was aware of arguments in the work of Linnaeus and Buffon suggesting that species might experience alterations in their form over time. He also knew that some thought of species as merely an abstraction by which one fixes nature's diverse products. But it was Lamarck who produced the first thorough systematic exposition of the evolution of species over time.

In the mid-1790s Lamarck's scholarly status was at its peak. He occupied a chair at the Museum of Natural History, he was a member of the first class of the National Institute, and he was a participant in leading French societies of natural philosophy, such as the Société Philomathique. He had made his name by becoming an authority on the flora and fauna of France, which he described in great detail. But by 1797 he resigned from the Société Philomathique because his views were being ignored. By the early 1800s his relationships with other investigators of nature had degenerated, causing a turnabout in his career. This development occurred because Lamarck was interested in more than the close empirical research by which he had established his reputation. Like his younger colleague Geoffroy, he was also interested in broad, speculative intellectual ventures.

Lamarck's spirit of system.   During the second half of the eighteenth century some French natural philosophers made clear their opposition to what they called the "spirit of system." They meant by this the erection of systems of thought about the natural world that relied on their creators' imagination more than on the facts of experience. There are scattered indications of this spirit of system in Lamarck's early work, but in his *Investigations of the Causes of the Principal Physical Facts* of 1794 it emerged into full view. This book was a grand venture into a system of physics, chemistry, and physiology and it gave rise to charges from colleagues that he was wasting time and effort on fruitless and unverifiable speculation. His colleagues did not even pretend to hide their boredom with the explanations of his system that Lamarck presented at professional meetings in the late 1790s.

Lamarck's experience provides a good example of how the community of scholars in Napoleonic France determined which kinds of questions were appropriate to pose in natural philosophy and which were not. He himself was well aware that his critics could destroy him without attacking his views openly. As he acknowledged in an unpublished manuscript from around the turn of the century, it took only a passing disparaging remark, a knowing wink, or an air of disdain to spread the opinion that his work was not worth considering.

Why Lamarck changed his mind about species.   In Lamarck's early botanical writings there is no hint that he would later challenge the assumption that a species could be transformed over time into something different. What sparked a change in this view was his disagreement with what his junior colleague Cuvier was proclaiming to crowds of listeners about extinction and catastrophes.

Lamarck initially had welcomed Cuvier's arrival in Paris. But it was not long before both realized that, in spite of mutual acknowledgment of demonstrated knowledge and achievement, they did not agree about the proper way to investigate nature. For his part Cuvier had no patience with the kind of grand synthesizing that Lamarck had displayed in his *Investigations.* Lamarck, on the other hand, found Cuvier's defense of extinction and especially his appeal to catastrophes to constitute what he thought bad reasoning in science.

Lamarck believed in a well-ordered universe, visible among other ways in the wonderful balances that functioned to keep nature in equilibrium. He marveled at what he called "the wise precautions of nature" by which everything remained in order. That a species might become extinct was to him equivalent to a violation or disruption of the natural order, something nature would not permit. If some exceptional species had become extinct, which he allowed might have occurred, it had to be because of human intervention. But he could imagine no regularly occurring mechanism by which every single member of a species would be wiped out. Rapid extinction in a well-ordered, naturally running world just was not nature's way.

Cuvier's appeal to catastrophes was also unacceptable to Lamarck. In his geological views Lamarck strongly agreed with those among his predecessors who demanded that past geological change be accounted for by means of forces operating in the present, not violent upheavals that came and went suddenly. To Lamarck, Cuvier's mechanism for extinction was so tailor-made that it was inherently suspicious. Catastrophes were, he said, "a very convenient means for those naturalists who wish to explain everything."

If the celebrated fossils Cuvier was describing to a fascinated Paris were not the remains of animals now extinct, then what were they? First of all, Lamarck did not agree with Cuvier that living counterparts to these ancient animals could not possibly exist. They might yet be discovered, perhaps in forms that had changed over time. Present species, in other words, were past species that had changed. He did not regard the past species as lost, since they had merely been modified by time. As long as the process was gradual, nature's order and balance were not violated. By 1802 the components of Lamarck's thoughts on organic development were in place, but it was not until 1809 that they were fully worked out in his work, *Zoological Philosophy.*

The components of Lamarck's theory.   Lamarck's view of evolution involved two factors that produced change, one emanating from the organism itself and another from its environment. The two factors acted in concert to alter the organism over the course of its lifetime through changes that have come to be known as acquired characteristics. Lamarck would make clear how changes that occur in an organism during the course of its lifetime might contribute to long-term evolutionary change in the species.

The power of life. First, change emanating from the organism itself was due to what he called the "power of life," a characteristic possessed by living things that made them increase in complexity over time. This was an especially important factor for the simplest forms of life and for plants, where there is no nervous system. Lamarck believed that as a consequence simply of being alive, living things became more complex. One aspect of this increased complexity was expressed in the organism's growth. Another came about because the constant movement of internal fluids would exert a continual pressure on the internal organization of living things, the effect of which would be gradually to alter the organization. A hypothesis about how these fluids could, over time, carve out new vessels and create new organs was spelled out as early as 1802: "The characteristic of the movement of fluids in the supple parts of the living bodies that contain them is to trace out routes and places for deposits and outlets; to create canals and the various organs."

To explain how this occurred, he drew upon three interacting elements: the parts of the body that contain fluids, the fluids themselves, and what he called the "exciting cause" of the motions of the fluids taking place within the organism. Like others of his day, he appealed to certain imponderable fluids to account for the exciting of the fluids' motions. Caloric, the imponderable element of heat, and electricity were specified by Lamarck as the agents responsible for having set the fluids of the simplest organisms in motion. From this description one might anticipate that the changes produced would be highly individualized and even chaotic. But Lamarck saw it differently. The increasing complexity due solely to the power of life was regular in its progression.

If the natural tendency toward increased complexity was especially applicable to the simplest forms of life a question still remained: where did these simplest forms of life come from? To explain the origin of life itself Lamarck appealed to spontaneous generation. In the *Zoological Philosophy* he wrote: "Nature, by means of heat, light, electricity and moisture, forms direct or spontaneous generations at that extremity of each kingdom of living bodies, where the simplest of these bodies are found." The creative action of spontaneous generation was applied to the "extremity of each kingdom"; that is, nature spawned the simplest plant organisms and the simplest animal organisms separately. Once present, the power of life immediately began to exert pressure to change these simplest of plants and animals. Lamarck did not believe that there were transitional forms connecting the plant and animal kingdoms. Ironically, many who adhered to the fixity of species felt that there may well be organisms within the great chain of being that linked nature's two kingdoms.

Use and disuse. In many accounts "Lamarckian" evolution is taken to refer to the development that allegedly resulted from the influence of so-called external conditions. These were accidental factors such as climate, geography, and the uses and disuses of organs that such extrinsic conditions inspire. Higher life forms in particular changed over the course of their lifetimes because of their interaction with the environment. But this for Lamarck was the second cause of evolutionary change, the first being the power of life. As with the power of life, the changes produced through use and disuse occurred during the course of the lifetime of individuals, affecting the species only as they accumulated over long periods of time.

Lamarck explained that if the environment experienced alterations, it would follow that the needs of the animals living in the environment would change. If the new needs became permanent, he wrote, then the animals would adopt new habits that lasted as long as the needs that evoked them. But if these new habits led the animal to use one of its parts in preference over another part, or to neglect the use of some organ altogether, then a part could be gradually strengthened or weakened over time. His most famous example was that of a giraffe, which had developed the permanent habit of constantly stretching its neck to reach the leaves of trees on which it fed. Over the course of its lifetime the giraffe's neck was slightly longer than it would have been had it not had to stretch constantly for foliage.

Acquired characteristics. Now if these alterations in bodily parts caused by use and disuse were passed down to the offspring of the organism, then the characteristics of the species itself would be affected. If the slightly elongated neck the giraffes of one generation had acquired were passed on to their offspring, then that generation, over the course of its life, would add more elongation as it continued to reach for the leaves of trees. Lamarck was clear that the changes induced in any individual organism during its life would be minute, and so a great amount of time would be necessary for the species to develop a new characteristic. But he was equally clear that nature had all the time that might be necessary, so that the variations that could be introduced by such means were practically inexhaustible.

Curiously, when he specified his law of the inheritance of acquired characteristics he overlooked including those changes due to the power of life and named only those changes caused by the environment through use and disuse. He made it clear, however, that in order to be inherited, the changes had to affect an entire population so that individuals of both sexes would acquire them.

Lamarck was not the first to appeal to use and disuse or the inheritance of acquired characteristics. He himself referred to these phenomena as if they were well known to all observers of nature's ways. But no one before him had put them together as part of an entire system of evolutionary development.

The reception of Lamarck's theory. Although Lamarck's achievement was indeed novel, it was largely ignored until later in the century. Cuvier opposed transformism for the same reason he rejected geological theories of the Earth—they were speculative ventures lacking substantiating factual evidence. He mocked those who claimed that "hens searching for their food at the water's edge, and striving not to get their thighs wet, succeeded so well in elongating their legs that they became herons or storks." Accompanying the public silence about Lamarck's work was private ridicule, which Lamarck knew circulated behind his back.

Not everyone rejected Lamarck's defense of an evolution of species. Because Geoffroy shared with Lamarck an appreciation for the spirit of system, it is not surprising that he came to accept much, although not all, of what Lamarck thought about the evolution of life. Cuvier provided an occasion for Geoffroy to disclose his opinion of Lamarck's theory. In 1825 Cuvier published a classification of a new fossil he had been sent, as an extinct species of gavial, a rare crocodile. Geoffroy, who considered himself an expert on crocodiles, pointed out that Cuvier had erred and that the fossil remains belonged to an as yet unknown genus of crocodiles. In the course of his correction of Cuvier, he suggested that modern crocodiles might have developed from this antediluvian animal, which he named *Teleosaurus.* Geoffroy identified the direct affect of environment as the means that produced evolutionary change, referring specifically to and endorsing Lamarck's two laws.

Needless to say, Cuvier did not take kindly to Geoffroy's open criticism of his claim. Cuvier regarded Geoffroy as he did Lamarck, as someone more interested in erecting elaborate speculative theories than in remaining within the confines of fact. Between 1825 and 1829 virtually everything either one wrote contained an attack on the other's views.

The role of religion.   Lamarck's book also found few defenders because it removed God's direct supervision of creation. Although others before him had omitted a role for God in their treatments of the inanimate physical world, Lamarck's object was the world of living things. Most people assumed that a super-natural act was required to begin life. Lamarck's account of the creation of life did not acknowledge a direct role for a divine spark; rather, the spark was one of electricity. The means employed by nature were the forces of physics and chemistry. When he did go into the details of spontaneous generation, his explanations were wholly mechanistic. Lamarck was not a vitalist; he did not believe that life was a special kind of being that was wholly different from nonliving being.

Lamarck, again like many of his predecessors in the eighteenth century, was a deist. He felt no obligation to include God directly in his explanation of organic development. That is not to say he was an atheist. He believed in a God who had created an order of things that ran on its own, producing, at first, simple life itself and then all of the wonderful diversity that later existed. His defense of this view was regarded as dangerously materialistic in the early nineteenth century.

Lamarck was among the first to claim—as Darwin would later in the century—that the organs an animal possessed did not determine the functions the animal performed so much as the animal's habits conditioned the development of the organs. This perspective was simply unacceptable to Cuvier. Although he was not a devoutly religious man, Cuvier nevertheless felt that God was much more in direct control of nature than Lamarck's remote deity allowed. As France's leading natural-ist, Cuvier eventually decided he had to speak up against what he felt were the unwarranted and merely hypothetical claims of men like Lamarck and his sym-pathizer Geoffroy. In the years after 1825 he engaged in a running battle with Geoffroy that culminated in 1830.

The heated public exchanges between Geoffroy and Cuvier that took place from late February to early April of 1830 occurred during a time of increasing tension between King Charles X and the French middle class. July would bring open revo-lution and the removal of the king. In the charged political atmosphere leading up

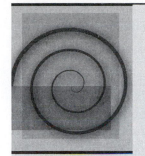

The NATURE of SCIENCE

Purpose, Mechanism, and Law in Science

Explanations of natural processes in antiquity made frequent use of what was called "final cause," the purpose or goal of the process. Aristotle explained why rocks fell, for example, by saying that they were seeking their natural place. Natural objects shared with organisms the capacity to strive toward a goal. When mechanical philosophers viewed nature as a machine as opposed to an organism, they discarded final cause as a way to explain natural processes.

Lamarck's evolution is sometimes depicted as purposeful (as opposed to mechanistic) because it is dependent on the will of the organism to introduce the changes that will be acquired. The giraffe, it is assumed, chooses to stretch for the acacia leaves by exercising its will; hence purpose is thought to be a fundamental cornerstone of Lamarckian evolution. His evolution has even been labeled unscientific because it allegedly employs final causes.

Many have misunderstood Lamarck's position. When they hear Lamarck say that the shore bird has gradually developed stilt-like legs because it did not wish to get its body wet, they forget that for him wishing is an automatic response to an external stimulus. When the shore bird or the giraffe exercised its will, no purposeful deliberation was involved. Lamarck remained true to the physical and chemical factors that he had early concluded were the determining ones.

Although Lamarck's evolutionary process is thoroughly mechanistic, that does not mean that purpose plays no role at all in his scheme. In fact, Lamarck believed that the evolution of life fulfills the purpose God imposed on nature when God created the machinery that governs the natural world. In believing this, Lamarck was like many of his contemporaries in the physical sciences. Indeed, the idea that laws have been imposed on nature and that it is our duty to uncover them has motivated many a scientist before and since Lamarck. If some drop the idea that it was God who imposed the laws, that leaves open the question of why the laws exist or where they originated. What it does not do is change the fact that we must *assume* there are laws.

to the Revolution, Cuvier came to believe that the dangerous ideas of Lamarck and Geoffroy were part of the irresponsible spirit that encouraged political radicalism. He felt motivated to speak out against those he felt were undermining public order. He wanted to destroy once and for all the unacceptable foundation on which dangerous theories like those of Lamarck and Geoffroy rested. He regarded the theories as a threat to the well-being of society.

For all his insistence that "natural history is a science of facts," and for all his bluster against speculative ideas like Geoffroy's unity of composition and Lamarck's evolution, which he thought did not belong in natural science, Cuvier conceded in these exchanges that his real reason for opposing them was religious. Historian of science Toby Appel has observed that for Cuvier the single false premise that lay at the root of all these objectionable zoological theories was the belief that nature had an autonomous existence apart from God. The deistic outlook that Geoffroy shared with Lamarck and numerous others did nothing to allay Cuvier's fears, nor did Geoffroy's charge that Cuvier had improperly mixed religion into scientific argument provoke an apology. In the end the issue that split the French savants was not scientific, but philosophical and religious.

◎ British Catastrophism ◎

Two developments produced what is called British catastrophism, the uniquely British version of the role catastrophes played in shaping the history of the Earth and its creatures. They took place in different regions of Britain, the first in the north and the second in the south. In Scotland natural philosophers engaged in a debate over what *kind* of catastrophes had been responsible, while in England the concern was to fit the world of prehistoric beasts into a classical view of history that centered only on humans. These two developments did not occur simultaneously. The debates in Edinburgh occupied the first two decades of the century, while the reshaping of world history in Oxford was a matter taken up primarily in the 1820s.

The Debate Between Vulcanism and Neptunism

As discussed in Chapter 12, treatments of the Earth's past prior to the nineteenth century had been undertaken from two differing vantage points. One occurred within an older literary genre commonly known as the "theory of the Earth," in which observational evidence was used to support grand, high-level speculative explanations of the structure and history of the Earth in terms of a few natural causes. One example of this approach discussed in Chapter 12 was James Hutton's claim that the Earth's surface had been molded over an indefinite period of time by the force of heat emanating from the Earth's interior. The other vantage point shunned speculation, emphasizing instead the detailed empirical observations of the mineral composition of local regions. Here the primary figure was a German professor at the Mining Academy in Freiberg named Abraham Werner. Werner focused his attention on the formation of minerals, especially those he believed had been formed by precipitation from a primal aqueous fluid. He called his approach geognosy to distinguish it from speculative theories of the Earth.

During the early decades of the nineteenth century, Cuvier and other writers on the Continent preferred the approach of Werner's geognosy over that of the theorists of the Earth. The group in Edinburgh transformed Werner's geognosy *into* a theory of the Earth. They then proceeded to debate its merits in comparison to the theory of the Earth of their countryman, James Hutton.

Creating a debate. The appearance of two books in 1802, *Illustrations of the Huttonian Theory of the Earth* by John Playfair (1748–1819), followed quickly by *A Comparative View of the Huttonian and Neptunian Systems of Geology* from the pen of John Murray (d. 1820), began the debate between the British followers of Werner (Neptunists) and those of Hutton (Vulcanists). Playfair made it clear that he was interested in a theory of the Earth because it openly identified causes of geological change. So he proceeded to regard the role water played in forming minerals in geognosy as an overall cause of the Earth's development in the past, and he contrasted it to the causal role heat played in Hutton's theory. Playfair was out to champion Vulcanism, the theory of the Earth that explained the historical development of the Earth's surface as the result of thermal force from the Earth's interior. In the course of defending Hutton, Playfair placed his own stamp on Hutton's work that changed the original author's emphasis. One of Hutton's main concerns was to demonstrate that geological phenomena indicated the presence of a divine plan governing terrestrial processes.

Playfair tried to remove the issue of the Earth's development as much as possible from theology and locate it within sound geological theory. Hutton, he said, explained the formation of "seas and continents, not by accident, but by the operation of regular and uniform causes." Reliance on accidental causes like floods was too easily associated with divine intervention. Playfair began the tradition of representing Hutton's system as one based on results that had been directly induced or inferred from observations.

Playfair's contemporary, Murray, was not about to permit him to claim the field of sound geological theory for Hutton. Like Playfair, Murray lived in Edinburgh, where there were others familiar with the work of Werner. His book attempted to speak for those who had been impressed by Werner's work. Murray informed his reader that Neptunist theory, as he called it, resulted from strict inductions made from close observation of minerals and how they had formed. From such observations Werner was able to organize the various geological mineral formations he identified and to infer that they had formed over a long time from a primitive aqueous fluid.

But in spite of his disclaimers, Murray was unable to resist the temptation to make Neptunism into an alternative theory of the Earth to Hutton's. He conceded that perhaps it was necessary to assert not merely that the formation had taken place, but also to show the causes that had acted to produce it. With this move to causal explanation Murray abandoned the empirical caution that surrounded Werner's own treatment. Werner had appealed to the action of water as a means to account for the consolidation of successive rock formations. In Murray's work water became the causal agent of the Earth's historical development in a new theory of the Earth that "Wernerians" felt compelled to defend. In Britain the debates of the first decade of the century would be largely about which cause was correct, heat or water, with each side asserting that its claims resulted from empirical observations.

Neptunism modified. In 1811 an Irishman named William Henry Fitton (1780–1861), who was fascinated by Earth history, acknowledged Werner's theory to be "of all others the most in vogue at the present moment." As additional information about geological strata continued to accumulate, however, it became easier in some cases to explain their origin as the result of heat and pressure than as the precipitate from a primitive aqueous solution. Both Vulcanists and Neptunists came to agree that while erosion and dislocation due to the action of water played a part in the formation of present rocks, so also did heat and chemical action. Furthermore, attention began to shift away from the formation of rocks and toward the fossils embedded in them after a new map of the geological strata of England and Wales was published in 1815. Its author, an engineer named William Smith (1769–1839), utilized the fossil remains in rocks as markers of their age. Smith's classification of strata by this means was able, as the president of the Geological Society put it later in 1831, "to disentangle the structure of a considerable part of England."

The debate between Vulcanism and Neptunism was largely a British phenomenon. When Hutton's work originally appeared in the late eighteenth century, many on the Continent had received it as but one of several competing theories of the Earth. In spite of the appearance of Playfair's defense of Hutton, Continental thinkers continued to view Hutton's ideas in this manner in the early nineteenth century. Even within Britain the replies to Playfair's elucidation of Hutton's theory were largely a regional matter, carried out by Edinburgh sympathizers of Werner. In light of the pervasive influence of Werner's geognosy in Europe well into the nineteenth century, one must be careful not to overstate the impact of Hutton's thought in the history of geology, as has been done by many later champions of his theory.

A New World History

For the majority of scholars in Britain the subject of the Earth's physical past overlapped with a long tradition of scholarship called world history, typified by that pursued at Oxford University. Scholarship in world history focused on written documents from the ancient past because British scholars assumed that humans determined history. Primary credentials of the world historian, for example, included a knowledge of the languages of antiquity, including those of Asia, and an expertise in deciphering texts.

Information bearing on the Earth's physical past was only meaningful as it fit into the reconstruction of human history. Nevertheless, historians regarded some familiarity with astronomy and the basic physical features of the Earth to be desirable. But those engaged in world history at places such as Oxford University had traditionally not paid great attention to discussions of the Earth's physical past.

Beginning in the second decade of the century a major challenge appeared to the central assumptions of British world history that the Earth existed as a home for humans and that the study of the history of the Earth coincided with the study of human history. This second development was especially important in establishing British catastrophism.

The English translation of Cuvier's "Preliminary Discourse."   The study of world history in Britain changed when Cuvier's work on fossil bones became available to English readers. When the Edinburgh Neptunist Robert Jameson (1774–1854) read Cuvier's "Preliminary Discourse" he saw it as a vindication of the historicity of the Mosaic Flood, which he identified with the last of Cuvier's catastrophes. Jameson promptly published a translation of the work into English made by Robert Kerr under the title "Essay on the Theory of the Earth," providing his own explanatory notes. The translation was an immediate success in Britain, running to three editions by 1817 and five by the time of Cuvier's death in 1832. It demonstrated that the British could appreciate an emphasis on catastrophic forces as a central feature of any explanation of geological history.

England was at war with France in 1813 when Kerr's translation appeared, so there was no possibility for Cuvier to make known in England his objection to Jameson's overt association of his work with a biblical reference. By insisting on sudden violence, however, Cuvier did explicitly reject the slow-acting, present-day forces that both Werner and Hutton had acknowledged and that Hutton and his followers preferred to emphasize. Catastrophes also provided the occasion for geological history to assert itself against the parent discipline of classical world history.

William Buckland and classical world history. No one did more to give geological evidence a more prominent role in classical world history than it had previously enjoyed than the Oxford professor William Buckland (1784–1856). A student of the classics at Oxford in the early years of the century, Buckland took holy orders and became a fellow of Corpus Christi College in Oxford in 1808. As a student he had attended lectures other than those in his major field, particularly in natural science. The result was that Buckland ended up with a position in mineralogy at Oxford in 1813. It paid so poorly, however, that a new position was created for him in 1818—a readership of geology. From this vantage point Buckland, who possessed an eccentric personality and engaging style as a lecturer, became one of the most colorful academic figures of his day.

Buckland endorsed Cuvier's idea that human history was just the last in a series of periods of Earth history and that there were long stages of history where humans were of little importance. Beginning in 1815 Buckland lectured on the remains of elephants and mastodons to students. But he began his campaign to make geology a worthy academic subject at the university in 1819, in a lecture he gave to his university colleagues in classics. The lecture had the appropriate Latin title, *"Vindiciae Geologicae" (Geological Claims).*

Buckland's defense of the Earth's catastrophic past was furthered by a surprising development in the early 1820s. In 1821 Buckland learned about some fossil remains that had been discovered by quarrymen in a cave in Yorkshire. Early the next year he visited the cave for himself and in 1823 published an account of his findings in *Reliquiae Diluvianae*, literally, relics of the deluge. A major reason for the success of the book was the manner in which Buckland fit his understanding into the tradition of classical scholarship at Oxford.

Buckland's careful description of the remains from the cave established him as the equal of Continental comparative anatomists. He had his own particular explanation of fossils; namely, he argued from the bones of hyenas and from markings on the remains of elephants, rhinoceroses, and other animals found in the cave that the hyenas had dragged parts of the other animals into the cave before the deluge had occurred. The older, traditional explanation for why different fossils ended up together was that the swirling waters of Noah's universal flood mixed together remains from different regions of the Earth. Buckland's explanation implied that all the animals had lived together in the region *before* the deluge.

Buckland even opposed the more modern notion that the flood had occurred because land had sunk, allowing the sea to overrun it and expose new land where the sea had been. In Buckland's unique view the animals whose remains were found in the cave lived in a region that was land before and after the deluge. When Cuvier himself said positive things about Buckland's theory, his rising fame was secured.

The appearance of Buckland's work had two effects. First, it called forth a spate of works opposed to the theory on the grounds that it contradicted the biblical account. Buckland took his place among those Oxford professors who rejected a strictly literal reading of the Bible in favor of a broader, classical vision of its meaning. As a result of Buckland's work, more and more Oxford dons, and scholars elsewhere in Britain, accepted the conclusion that the world of living things was far older than they had previously realized.

The second effect of Buckland's vision of the past was to provide new support for categorically rejecting the visions of Erasmus Darwin, Hutton, Schubert, Lamarck, Geoffroy, and other deists. Buckland's understanding of Noah's flood as the most recent of the Earth's geological catastrophes, which could be associated with the work of the famous Cuvier, assumed academic respectability. At the same time this so-called diluvial position minimized any potential clash with Buckland's standing as an Anglican cleric, for which a respect for the centrality of the biblical flood in Earth's history was important. By arguing that classical world history should be expanded to include geology, Buckland appeared as a progressive force within British academe.

Suggestions for Reading

Richard Burckhardt, *The Spirit of System: Lamarck and Evolutionary Biology* (Cambridge, Mass.: Harvard University Press, 1995).

Robert Richards, *The Meaning of Evolution* (Chicago: University of Chicago Press, 1993).

Martin Rudwick, ed. and trans., *Georges Cuvier, Fossil Bones, and Geological Catastrophes* (Chicago: University of Chicago Press, 1997).

Nicolaas A. Rupke, *The Great Chain of History* (New York: Oxford University Press, 1983).

CHAPTER 18

---◎---

Evolution Comes into Its Own

In the late 1820s a young man named Charles Darwin was a student at Edinburgh University, sent there by his physician father so that he, too, would become a medical doctor. Among the books Darwin read during his second year in Scotland were the evolutionary speculations of his grandfather, Erasmus Darwin, particularly the *Zoonomia*. He also was aware of the views of Jean-Baptiste Lamarck, having read the French naturalist's work on invertebrate zoology. Additionally, he had heard Lamarck's evolutionary system endorsed by Robert Grant (1793–1874), a lecturer in an anatomy school in Edinburgh. Darwin sometimes joined Grant for observational excursions into nature. Before the 1830s ended, Charles Darwin had come up with his own preliminary theory of evolution, although none of the evolutionary views he had read as a student was a major influence.

A lot was happening during those years in Britain. A major reform bill was passed in 1832 that brought greater political power to the middle class at the expense of the upper classes. Then in June of 1837 King William IV died after only seven years on the throne, and his teenage niece, Victoria, took over barely a month after she had come of age. Her reign would last almost sixty-four years and would be the longest in British history. Under Victoria, Britain escaped the political revolutions that plagued the Continent, but her rule saw the flowering of an evolutionary worldview that precipitated an intellectual revolution of major proportions.

◎ Charles Darwin's Early Life and Education ◎

Much about Darwin becomes clear simply by realizing that he came from an upstanding, upper-middle-class family. The values he embraced, the goals he set for himself, and the resistance to his achievements were consistent with the expectations of people who had themselves achieved much through hard work and, at least for the most part, through socially acceptable behavior.

The Darwins of the Midlands

At the end of the eighteenth century Erasmus Darwin's published speculations drew widespread notice well beyond the village of Lichfield, in Staffordshire, where he practiced medicine. So when Charles Darwin (1809–1882) was born, the Darwin name was recognizable to the educated classes throughout England. Charles's father, Robert, did not possess Erasmus's literary gifts, but he was a highly successful physician in the small West Midlands market town of Shrewsbury in neighboring Shropshire. Responding to widespread commercial expansion, Robert proved to be a shrewd investor, amassing a considerable fortune over the course of his career.

Darwin's grandfather on his mother's side, Josiah Wedgwood (1730–1795), became even better positioned in British society than Erasmus Darwin, with whom he was friends. Wedgwood rose from serving as an apprentice to his elder brother, a potter, to being potter to the queen. By the time of his death he had amassed a huge fortune, which, along with his thriving business, he left to his heirs. Darwin's mother alone, for example, received £25,000 in addition to a portion of the porcelain factory.

The Darwins and the Wedgwoods, then, were members of the landed gentry of Britain. These were people who could not claim an aristocratic title, but whose wealth, maintained over several generations, had given them considerable clout in British political and social circles. While Charles grew up in a context that enjoyed access to the leisure activities of English high society, he inherited from his predecessors on both sides of the family the values of hard work and frugality that had enabled them to gain entry into the upper middle class. Charles embraced these values as his own. Although he never wanted for money, he too always strove to work hard and with efficiency.

Both of Charles's grandfathers shared something else in common. Each had drifted away from an orthodox religion toward a naturalistic view of the world. Erasmus Darwin's deistic view did not even retain respect for Unitarianism, with its generalized belief in one God rather than the triune God of Christianity. Referring to Josiah Wedgwood's own gradual embrace of its secular principles, Erasmus dubbed Unitarianism a featherbed to catch a falling Christian.

If on his mother's side there was a link to Unitarianism through the local chapel meetings she attended, Darwin's father provided at best a neutral attitude toward religion. A Freemason, Robert Darwin was not a churchgoer; it was said of him that he went to church twice in his life and that he was carried both times. But if he did not attend he also was not hostile to the church. He respected the role of religion in English social life even if it was not personally important to him.

At the age of eight, Charles was sent to the Unitarian minister in Shrewsbury to be tutored. During that year his mother, who seemed always to be ill, died, leaving his sisters to assume the role she had vacated as best they could. For his part, Dr. Darwin turned his attention to his sons, Charles and his elder brother Erasmus, eventually coming to hope that they would carry on the family legacy by becoming physicians.

University Years

Darwin attended two universities before he embarked on the path that was to bring him great fame. Like students today, he struggled during these years to discover a career that would both excite him and also satisfy parental expectations. As we shall see, the career decision he came to while a student did not turn out as he originally anticipated.

Edinburgh.   After a stint in boarding school, Darwin and his brother both went to Edinburgh University in the fall of 1825. Erasmus had completed three years at Cambridge and was about to begin the final phase of his medical studies. Charles was only sixteen, younger than the normal age to begin university study. But the plan was for him to keep his brother company, attend lectures, and eventually to take up medical studies himself. Neither he nor his brother fulfilled their father's wish. Erasmus, although he eventually received a medical degree, proved happy not to pursue any real vocation at all, content to live off his inheritance as a confirmed bachelor and general man about town. Charles had much greater ambition, but it soon became clear that he too was not cut out to be a physician. His interests lay elsewhere.

Darwin was not a purely conventional student. During his second year he read a translation of Georges Cuvier's book on the revolutions of the globe and became informed about the British debates between the Wernerians and Huttonians. Although he confronted drastic ideas such as evolution and materialism, he remained unconvinced. He knew, of course, that if he became too extreme his views might be stricken from serious consideration.

Still, the freethinking atmosphere he had experienced growing up in Shrewsbury had the effect of postponing the need to decide what religious beliefs he himself should embrace. This was not a problem as long as he contemplated a career in medicine. But when it gradually became clear that medicine was out of the question, the matter of his own beliefs became more urgent because he was considering the prospect of becoming a country clergyman. There were not many other vocations available that were amenable to his talents and temperament. Did he, however, accept the dogmas of the Church of England? He decided that the creed must be accepted and, with his father's consent, left Edinburgh for Cambridge, arriving in January of 1828 to complete the bachelor's degree before going on for holy orders.

Cambridge.   At Cambridge, Darwin took the courses required for the B.A., but he spent a lot of his time pursuing other things as well. For example, he discovered beetles; that is, he realized how much he loved collecting beetles. He also made the acquaintance of one of his brother's favorite Cambridge people, John Henslow (1796–1861), professor of botany.

Henslow occupied the chair of mineralogy in 1823 and added botany in 1825. He had, however, begun to put together an herbarium of British flora in 1821, and during the time Darwin was at Cambridge he was engaged in organizing plant species with a particular goal in mind. Henslow wanted to focus on variation within a species; he wanted to show the limits within which a plant species varied continuously. The notion that the variation of a species was limited was the common assumption of the day, but Henslow was alone among British botanists in studying variation so specifically. He was looking for what he called "the precise rule for distinguishing the exact limits between which any species of plant may vary."

Charles soon became attached to Henslow, whom he respected greatly and whose anti-evolutionary views he embraced. Darwin also shared Henslow's respect for natural theology, with its assumption that the natural world contained evidence of the Creator's hand at work. For his part, Henslow saw much of himself in Darwin, and he responded to his enthusiasm. In the eyes of Henslow's other students, Darwin had become Henslow's favorite. As historian of science David Kohn has shown, Darwin learned from Henslow to be concerned about variation within a species as it compared to the differences between two species. By focusing on the question of how far a specimen might vary before its difference from the standard for the species was great enough to be considered a different species, Darwin was sensitized to an issue that would become central to his later outlook.

One other professor at Cambridge exerted a significant influence on the young Darwin. Adam Sedgwick (1785–1873), professor of geology, was the kind of rough and ready personality that loved nothing better than geological excursions into the field, sometimes in the company of the romantic poet William Wordsworth (1770–1850). Henslow persuaded Sedgwick to ask Darwin to join him during August of 1831 on his trip to Wales. Darwin had heard geology lectures in Edinburgh, but he found the professor there dull and boring. Not so with Sedgwick. He taught Darwin by showing him—how to recognize rock formations, how to record strata on a map, how to make field drawings, how to recognize the lessons vegetation held for geologists.

Like Henslow, Sedgwick used his expertise to support conventional scientific wisdom, in his case about the history of the Earth. He believed that the geologist, using the remains of organisms embedded in rock strata, could confirm the increasingly accepted view that the Earth had developed from an earlier primitive state to the one now visible. He had read a new book, just out, by Charles Lyell (1797–1875), who opposed that idea, arguing that while the Earth was incredibly old, its most general geological conditions had always been the same. Sedgwick wanted to go to Wales, where he believed he could find evidence to show that the remnants buried in the rocks would be dissimilar over time, not similar, as would be the case if Lyell were correct. Between Henslow and Sedgwick, Darwin received an excellent firsthand introduction into the burning issues of the day.

Darwin's father, however, had only so much patience for Charles's running around the countryside. He had not understood his son's delight to be out in nature when he was in Edinburgh and he still failed to see the point. Darwin had already earned the B.A. Now he needed to focus. They came to an agreement—after the summer of 1831, Charles would return to Cambridge in October to begin the special studies necessary for him to be ordained.

Voyage of the HMS Beagle

The expedition to Wales was in one sense a substitute for a much more elaborate scheme Darwin had tried to hatch earlier in 1831. He had been reading the *Personal Narrative* of Alexander von Humboldt, whose expedition to South America between 1799 and 1804 in the name of scientific research had made him one of the most widely known natural philosophers of the day. The reports von Humboldt had sent back to Europe from the wilds of the New World were devoured by avid readers. Von Humboldt's descriptions of what he saw were anything but dry, detached observations. Heavily influenced by the German romantics whom he knew personally, von Humboldt depicted the nature of the tropics in the rich, luxuriant, and evocative language of feeling. What came through to the young and impressionable Darwin was von Humboldt's passion for nature and for science. Darwin resonated with von Humboldt's emotional relation to nature.

Darwin wanted to take a month or so before returning to study in the fall to go to Tenerife, in the Canary Islands, to see for himself how exotic nature could be. In July he was still hoping to persuade Henslow to join him. "I read and reread Humboldt, do you do the same?" he wrote to Henslow. However much Henslow would have loved going, a new baby in his family made it impossible. Further, his opinion was that Darwin should learn geology before any such venture; hence the suggestion that Sedgwick take Darwin with him on the Wales geological excursion.

A voyage around the world. When Darwin returned to Shrewsbury from Wales on August 29 there was a letter waiting for him from Henslow. He had been asked to recommend someone with an interest in natural history to provide company for the captain of a projected two-year voyage around the world, scheduled to leave in four weeks. Charles and his father had opposite first reactions to the prospect. Charles, of course, was ready to sign on right away. For Dr. Darwin, however, it was one more example of Charles wasting time before settling down. Darwin initially replied to Henslow that it looked impossible, but by September 2 his father, realizing what a chance this was for his son and how much confidence the professor from Cambridge had placed in him, changed his mind.

The voyage, which lasted five, not two years, was the formative event of Darwin's life. By the time he returned in the fall of 1836 he no longer anticipated becoming a clergyman, and he hoped his father had forgotten about the earlier agreement. If anything, he saw himself emerging as one of the new generation of scientific men. Late in the voyage he got a letter indicating that Sedgwick, impressed by the specimens and letters he had sent home, had made precisely that judgment to his father.

The *Beagle* did not really get going until December of 1831, making its way to the Canary Islands, on to the eastern coast of South America, through the Straits of Magellan to the western coast, and then west to the Galapagos Islands, Tahiti, New Zealand, and Australia (see Darwin's route on the map). Next the voyagers headed north to the Keeling Islands and west to Mauritius, then to the Cape of Good Hope, across to South America by way of the Ascension Islands, north to the Azores, and finally, back home.

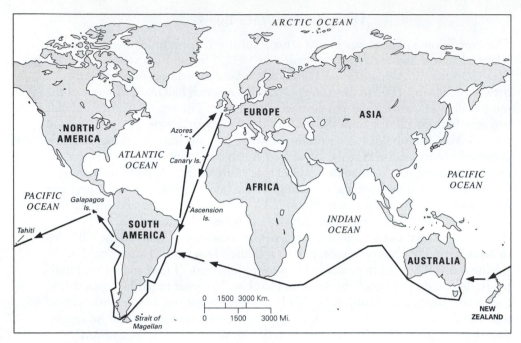

Voyage of the *Beagle*

The *Beagle,* whose primary mission was to chart the shores of South America for the burgeoning British Empire, spent just over two years on the eastern shores and another year and a half getting to, and charting, the western coast. The remaining journey around the world took the last fifteen months. During this time Darwin spent over three years on land observing geological formations, flora and fauna, and indigenous peoples. As a gentleman companion to the captain, he was technically not the ship's naturalist, a role that by tradition went to the ship's surgeon. But it soon became obvious to all, including the surgeon, who soon left the ship and returned to England, that Darwin was the much better informed and skilled naturalist. Darwin stepped into the position naturally, generously collecting specimens for shipment back to Britain.

Darwin had brought along the first volume of the book on geology by Charles Lyell, which Sedgwick disliked. He had received Volume II early in the trip, by the time he went ashore in Patagonia for a 500-mile overland excursion. He found Lyell's explanations appealing, especially because they did not try to accommodate religious ideas about past development. For example, Lyell laid out in Volume II his view of how some species had become extinct. Lyell did not appeal to catastrophes, as had Cuvier and his teacher William Buckland. Because he believed that past geological conditions had always been qualitatively the same, a view that has come to be known as uniformitarianism, he held that extinction came about as the result of gradual processes, not the dramatic upheavals of land that others claimed. When Darwin came across Patagonian fossils of a clearly extinct species in a region where there was no evidence of changes in the landscape, his respect for Lyell's views could only grow.

The Galapagos Islands.   Of the many observations Darwin recorded during the voyage, none proved more important than those made on the Galapagos Islands, near the equator in the Pacific Ocean, some 600 miles west of Ecuador. Darwin visited four of the dozen or so islands. The birds, which had no apparent fear of humans, were especially intriguing. He noticed that the mockingbirds he collected from each of the islands were different, whether varieties or separate species he did not know. On the last island he gathered several kinds of a smaller bird, organizing them according to common custom into subfamilies based on the shape and size of their beaks.

The islands were famous for giant land tortoises, which Darwin finally encountered after a day or so ashore on the first island. On the second island there was a penal colony, whose warden noted to Darwin that he could tell which specific island a given tortoise was from by looking at its shell. Darwin took no special note of this at the time, although later, when thinking about the mockingbirds, he noted that their relationships to the individual islands paralleled what he had been told about the tortoises. He had no reason to dwell on the likelihood that separate species might be indigenous to individual islands because, as he later observed, "I never dreamed that islands, about fifty or sixty miles apart, and most of them in sight of each another, formed of precisely the same rocks, placed under a quite similar climate, rising to a nearly equal height, would have been differently tenanted."

A common explanation of the geographical distribution of species at the time was known as special creation. Using divine wisdom, God had created individual species in locations to which they were particularly suited. Traveling a sufficient distance from one region to another required that the Creator populate the second region with a different species from the first if the regions were sufficiently different in climate or terrain. Or, if a geographical barrier existed between two land masses, like a mountain range or a body of water, the regions were again likely to be different enough to expect different species, each particularly adapted to the area in which it was found. Special creation accounted well for the truly marvelous adaptation individual species were known to display to their environments.

If it turned out that the individual islands of the Galapagos did contain separate species of tortoise or mockingbird, however, this would present a challenge to special creation. As noted, there was no difference in climate or environment from island to island, so why would the Creator have populated them with different species? It would certainly not have been because of God's wisdom, since no modified characteristics were called for. And attributing a simple need for variety to God was not something humans felt comfortable doing. In any event, all of these matters occurred to Darwin later, not while he was on the islands.

Geological innovations.   Of the many ideas Darwin had after leaving the Galapagos during the final year of the voyage, he was as proud of his geological speculations as any. He had begun thinking about geology much earlier—less than two months into the voyage, while on the volcanic island of St. Jago off the coast of Africa. There, Darwin had struck on the notion that the island had risen from the sea in recent geological times, bringing a layer of embedded coral, which is formed from skeletons of marine polyps, above the water, and that since then it had begun to slowly subside. Sedgwick would never have conceded Darwin's theory of subsidence, preferring to explain the exposure of the coral layer through a lowering of the water.

Later, on the western coast of South America, Darwin again used geological elevation to explain the rise of the Andes mountain range from the Pacific Ocean. But reading Lyell had convinced him that the overall geological condition of the Earth had not changed. That meant that when elevation occurred in one region, subsidence would compensate for it in another. At some later time the situation might be reversed. In this case, he conjectured that there must have been a compensating subsidence in the Pacific basin to balance out the elevation represented by the Andes.

As he sailed to the Tahitian island of Eimeo he encountered a beautiful volcanic island surrounded by a coral reef, inside of which was a lagoon. Darwin was curious about how the reef had formed. Coral polyps must have light, so they cannot grow in deep water. Drawing on his theory that the Pacific bottom was subsiding, Darwin suggested that the build-up of the reef occurred at approximately the same rate as the rate at which the ocean floor was dropping. This meant that the specific water level the live coral required would be maintained, so that the polyps at the top could continue to thrive. As they died, the polyps became part of the base of a reef that was slowing being built up as the mountain and the ocean floor subsided.

The shallow water nearer shore formed the lagoon, whose depth slowly increased as the flanks of the mountain continued to sink. If the subsidence went on long enough, the entire mountain could disappear beneath the waves, leaving the reef to form an island ring known as an atoll. It was an ingenious explanation of which Darwin was justifiably proud, especially because it was linked to a grand theory involving the Pacific Ocean floor and the Andes of South America, and because it was unlike any existing explanation of reef and atoll formation. Further, as we will see, his understanding of subsidence would prove valuable to him later in his career.

First inklings of evolution.   After leaving the waters of the South Seas, the thoughts of those on the *Beagle* inevitably began to turn homeward. Among the remaining moments of the trip one in particular stands out, because it reveals the first time that Darwin considered the possibility of evolution in conjunction with his findings. As he sorted through his notes near the end of the voyage, trying to bring order to them, he thought again about the birds and tortoises on the Galapagos. He recalled what he had been told about the association of different tortoises with specific islands and he had confirmed that the same went for the specimens of mockingbird he had collected.

He had not labeled the islands from which the other bird specimens had come. But now he wished he had. In his notes he wrote that he had to consider the various birds as varieties of a single species. Why? Because they were filling the same place in nature, so if the birds represented more than one species, the natural question was, what was going on? Darwin did not wish to dismiss such an intriguing question by saying simply that God had created more species than a perfectly produced adaptation needed. What if nature had somehow altered species over time substantially enough to make new species? If these birds were not mere varieties, then, he wrote, "such facts would undermine the stability of species."

After his return in October of 1836 Darwin's time was occupied at first by catching up with relatives and friends. But by March of 1837 he was able to talk with John Gould, a museum expert who had agreed to examine the bird specimens. Although where the museum labeling was unclear Darwin could not tell if individual species inhabited specific islands, Gould did confirm that there were many different species. So the question was, what was nature up to?

Then Darwin had the revelation that made him into an evolutionist. He thought about two patterns of differences between species. First there were the differences that existed between two species of an organism on the Galapagos. He knew, for example, how the mockingbirds differed from each other. Then there were differences he had observed, during the voyage, between the fossil remains of species and the present species. What suddenly hit him was that the differences mirrored each other. Differences between present species were similar to differences between past and present species. Whatever means nature used to produce different species at different times was the same one used to proliferate species in a given region. The present was but a snapshot of what nature had done over time. By July, Darwin opened a notebook on what he called the transmutation of species. The voyage of the *Beagle* had truly been his greatest education.

◎ A Formative Period for Evolution ◎

The England to which Darwin returned at the end of 1836 was very receptive to news about his travels. Of course natural philosophers were especially eager to learn the particulars of his experiences. Charles Lyell was enthusiastic about Darwin's use of his geological views and made it a point to meet this promising young world traveler by hosting a tea party for him. But interest in exploration was only one of the scientific subjects that captivated the attention of the British public in the 1830s and 1840s. And the nature of the other topics demonstrates that what the public understood by "science" was not always identical to what the word conveys in the twenty-first century.

The British reading public was rapidly increasing. There were more and more circulating libraries so that people from all classes could have access to books and magazines. In addition to nonfictional works on a variety of subjects, including religion and natural philosophy, novels were becoming ever more popular. Mechanics institutes and other societies for the diffusion of useful knowledge promoted literary works through regular meetings where they were the subject of lectures and discussions. They also supported the reduction in the price of books that was reflected in the rise of the cheap nonfiction publications that began appearing in the late 1820s.

Popular Science in Britain

Two topics in particular were capturing the attention of the British public just prior to the emergence of evolution as a major concern. The fascination with phrenology and Mesmerism, both imported from German sources, reveals the context in which the public evaluated natural scientific subjects.

Phrenology.   Franz Joseph Gall (1758–1828) was a German physician who was trained in Vienna. While others before him had related areas in the brain to such mental deficiencies as aphasia, the inability to speak and understand others, Gall explored the relationship in general between regions of the brain and mental capacities. He eventually identified some twenty-seven localized centers of behavior. He became convinced that the skull was molded on the brain, so that its shape registered information about the localized areas of the brain that governed an individual's mental capacities.

What was central in Gall's approach was that mental capacities were subject to material determinants. By studying the correlations he believed existed, Gall wanted to bring the workings of the mind under the laws that regulated the material world. Many, including the Austrian emperor, objected to this view on the grounds that it was materialistic, because it explained mental abilities as the result of the brain's material composition. It appeared to deny that mind and spirit were independent entities that made free will possible. In 1805 Gall and an associate left Austria for a tour of European cities, eventually settling in Paris, where his views continued to be controversial.

When Gall's associate left him and went to England, he came into contact with George Combe (1788–1858) of Scotland, a clerk in a Scottish society of lawyers. By 1815 Gall's work was being heralded as a complete system of phrenology, or mental science. Combe soon became a British advocate and in 1828 wrote a best-selling book called *The Constitution of Man.* It was one of the most popular books in the nineteenth century, selling some 350,000 copies by 1900, which represented an annual rate that outpaced the average sales per year of Darwin's later book by more than four and one-half times. Sales began taking off in 1835, when a cheap edition appeared that could be purchased for a quarter of the price of the first edition.

Combe's fundamental concern was to emphasize the rule of natural law, which in his message was all pervasive and governed not only the physical and organic realms, but also the intellectual and moral. It was in the latter areas that phrenology's usefulness shone, because an awareness of the natural laws governing human propensities, sentiments, and intellectual capacities could help individuals avoid the bad consequences of ignoring those laws. For example, Combe attributed the trade depression of 1825–1826 to an overactivity of the faculty of "acquisitiveness," whose physical center was located in the middle area of the left side of the skull. Through a rational understanding of natural law such mistakes could be avoided, human behavior could be improved, and maximum happiness achieved. Of course Combe had his critics, including natural philosophers who disputed on empirical grounds the claims made about skull shape, and religious groups convinced that phrenology's emphasis on natural law did away with the need for God. But Combe's focus on the rule of natural law, a message that the public was hearing from many quarters at the time, formed the basis for his greatest impact.

British Mesmerism.   Mesmerism involved a related aspect of mind, namely, its power over matter. Franz Anton Mesmer, whom we met in Chapter 13, argued that illness resulted when an imponderable fluid that flowed through the body became blocked. It was known in England that his claim to be able to remove the blockage and restore health had been discredited in France in the 1780s. Nevertheless, Mesmerism continued to capture the attention of some British radicals even if no one practiced it openly after the turn of the century. Various versions of animal magnetism persisted in France and in the German states in the second decade of the century and when it crossed the Channel in the 1820s to Britain, it was not the same old Mesmerism. Gone was the previous emphasis on removing blockage of a flow of fluid; it was replaced with a focus on the production of an altered state that could be of assistance to the physician.

What won new adherents among British natural philosophers was the report, after five years of investigation, of a committee of the French Academy of Medicine in 1831. After witnessing some remarkable demonstrations, including the use of Mesmerism as anesthesia during an operation to remove a woman's breast, the verdict came down: the Mesmeric effect was real. For the next three decades Mesmerism was a lively topic of discussion in Britain, gaining enthusiastic adherents among certain British physicians and surgeons, who used it in their practices, while it generated criticism from others who dismissed its effectiveness. At issue was the question of whether the results produced pointed to forces whose laws were as yet unknown or to unscrupulous collusions between patients and their physicians. The debate was carried out in the public sphere, where no one could ignore it. Science of one sort or another was very much in the air in the late 1830s.

Sketching Out "My Theory"

Once committed to the idea of transmutation, Darwin knew he was treading on dangerous ground. As a young person with hopes for recognition among England's "scientists," as natural philosophers were beginning to be called, it would be foolish to identify with an idea that was, like Mesmerism, at best contested and at worst simply discredited among the great majority of the very community whose respect he craved. So Darwin kept his conviction to himself. Besides, he had no idea how or why such alleged transmutation occurred. From everywhere he looked—including at his peers and even at a considerable faction of the public—what he required was a theory of transmutation that resulted from the operation of natural law.

The role of Malthus. According to Darwin's autobiographical account, written much later, he had a breakthrough in the fall of 1838, a few months before his marriage to his cousin Emma Wedgwood. It came from his reading of a well-known work by Thomas Malthus on population. Malthus argued that because the rate of increase of the human population outstripped the increase in food production, and because in general many more offspring in the animal world were born than could possibly be supported, nature had to check population in various ways, including early death, famine, and disease.

While nothing that Malthus said was shocking or even unknown to him, Darwin had never reflected on such circumstances as he did now. He had certainly been aware, as others were, of the struggle for existence—a competition among organisms of a population to maintain themselves in a given environment—that occurred in nature. What he saw now was that the weeding out of individuals by the various checks that caused death would most often happen to the ones least adapted to their circumstances. On the other hand, those that survived would tend to be the ones with the most useful adaptations for survival. Nature was in effect selecting the ones that would die early and those that would live longer. And the ones that lived longer would have a greater chance of reproducing offspring with *their* traits as opposed to the traits of the individuals selected against.

What all this meant was that nature was manufacturing adaptation, constantly honing individuals to fit into the environment. Should the environment undergo change, so too would the characteristics that predominated in any given species. If the process went on long enough, the changes induced might stray far enough from a given point to define a new species. That, of course, would require enormous lengths of time. But time was exactly what Lyell's geological outlook had given him in spades. He did not yet call it natural selection, but he did say that he now had a theory with which to work.

The emergence of "my theory."   The more he thought about it, the more he liked what he began calling "my theory." It was not unlike what breeders did with domesticated plants and animals, the difference being that they selected specific characteristics they wanted to breed for, while nature selected traits that promoted survival. Darwin started corresponding with horticulturalists and agricultural experts to find out what breeders could tell him about how plastic individual organisms were. The more he learned, the more convinced he became that he had struck on something big.

These postvoyage years were filled with activity for Darwin. In addition to his marriage and move to London, he was in great demand to attend society meetings and contribute articles to scientific journals. He was writing up the journal of his research and a book on the formation of coral reefs. In addition, he was ill a great deal with nausea and vomiting. It all took its toll. He dropped ten pounds during the year after his marriage, down a total of eighteen from his return home from traveling.

By 1842 he was feeling better. That summer he wrote out a sketch of his theory, in which he referred to a natural means of selection. He included in the sketch a list of the problems with his theory; for example, how could he deal with the inability of species to crossbreed and how could he account for complex organs such as the eye? Two years later he wrote out a longer sketch, some 230 pages. Although it contained the basics of his theory, he knew that it remained too speculative, without the kind of supporting evidence such a bold statement demanded. He wrote a letter to Emma in which he detailed what she was to do with the manuscript should he die.

In 1844 at least two individuals, Lyell and a young botanist named Joseph Hooker (1814–1879), were aware that Darwin was thinking about the possibility of transmutation. Hooker had just returned from an expedition to the Antarctic and was happy to receive plant specimens from Darwin's voyage that were as yet unexamined. When Darwin wrote Hooker of his belief in transmutation, he said it timidly—it was, he said, "like confessing a murder." Of course neither Hooker nor

Lyell yet knew anything about natural selection. Later in the year a book appeared that forced Darwin to abandon any idea of going public.

A Victorian Sensation

In the second week of October, 1844, the first edition of *Vestiges of the Natural History of Creation* went on sale in Britain. Its celebration of the latest natural scientific knowledge and the lessons it contained immediately captured the attention of a public sensitized to the increasing visibility of scientists and their sometimes controversial works. This particular book came on the heels of an event in Northern Britain that only made things more sensitive than ever. The year before, a sizable faction of the membership of the Church of Scotland had broken away from the mother church in what became known as the Great Disruption. The reason? The national church was being too tolerant of radical ideas and was making too many compromises with the conclusions of the modern age. Those who wished to preserve traditional interpretations of the Bible in the face of such challenges as those implied by the latest claims of geologists, for example, decided to form their own church, the Free Church of Scotland.

If in the minds of the religiously conservative, proof of the dangers of natural science were needed, the *Vestiges* certainly supplied it. Opening the book made it plain that the author endorsed the inexorable rule of natural law. "We see certain natural events proceeding in an invariable order under certain conditions and thence infer the existence of some fundamental arrangement, which, for the bringing about of these events, has a force and certainty of action." What happened in nature did so because it had to—natural law dictated it.

What kind of things did natural law dictate? Creation itself. The solar system, the Earth, and life had all come about as the result of a process identified as "creation by law." The *Vestiges* endorsed the work of Pierre Laplace, whose nebular hypothesis about the formation of the solar system as the result of the natural congealing of a nebulous fluid (see Chapter 9) capped several well-known eighteenth-century French speculations about the history of the cosmos. The book appeared to have gathered in one place all of the latest information from geology and zoology to argue that life itself had taken eons to develop and that, like the solar system and the Earth, it too had slowly evolved from primitive forms to the complex and diverse kinds presently existing in accordance with natural laws that did not require the direct involvement of God. Although there was no explanation of exactly how the laws of evolution worked, each stage of life's development was correlated with an individual geological formation.

Picking up the book, the reader had the impression that he or she had access to the myriad of scientific claims that had been circulating about in society for some time. Now here they were all in one place. The works cited and the leading experts quoted—Laplace, Buckland, Lyell, Werner, Cuvier, and others—gave the book a ring of credibility that was hard to resist.

Reading between the lines, the work imparted the message that the claims being made were facts based on the latest natural science and that it was high time everyone faced up to how science was changing humankind's views of itself and the world. It was not a godless work, however. God had clearly created the natural laws with the intention that they should operate as they had to produce the world. It was classic deism, with its absentee-landlord God. But that position was of course totally unacceptable to anyone who struggled to take the Bible as much as possible at its word.

The author of the *Vestiges* reconciled this remote but benevolent God to the rule of law by insisting that the development of the cosmos was "a stage in a great progress." In so doing, the author tapped into a strongly held conviction of the Victorian middle class—that they were living in an age of progress. British industrialization led the world and the British Empire of the day spanned the globe. Now the *Vestiges* proclaimed that the laws of progress depended on the fundamentally evolutionary nature of the cosmos itself. That could make good, upstanding middle-class citizens squirm. They wanted to identify with progress, and they liked the enterprising spirit of scientific research. But they were not necessarily comfortable with deism, which was widely regarded in polite society as a radical religious position.

Who, incidentally, was the author of this sensational work? The frustrating thing was that no one knew—it had been published anonymously. That, of course, merely hyped the interest in the book. Within a couple of years attention settled on the Scottish publisher Robert Chambers (1802–1871), who himself never confirmed publicly that he was the author. After his death, however, the twelfth edition of the book in 1884 identified him as the book's writer.

◎ The Making of Darwin's *Origin* ◎

The *Vestiges* was roundly condemned on almost all sides. Only groups perceived to be radical—those labeled by their opponents as freethinkers, atheists, infidels, and socialists—seemed to like the work. Many in the upper classes never even engaged the issue, simply dismissing the work as silly and beneath serious consideration. Upstanding members of the middle class did read the book, but found it wanting. Among scientists the highly speculative nature of its conclusions made the book suspect. Further, its identification with evolution linked it to Lamarck, whose zoological philosophy had already been harshly judged by Charles Lyell and others as not based on good science.

Among clerics the open embrace of deism was simply unacceptable. Conservatives and liberals alike were not at all ready to concede that being a Christian in the modern scientific age meant that God had become as remote as the godless French natural philosophers famously maintained. And many even among the more liberal theologians were still struggling to reconcile their respect for scripture with the enormous time spans being tossed about by astronomers and geologists.

What was clear to the young Charles Darwin was that now was not the time for him to reveal the theory he was mulling over in his mind. Not only did it force the issue of an enormously extended age for the Earth, but, if the truth be known, it also removed God from superintending the development of life in a manner far more radical than in the *Vestiges*. Darwin decided that before he could publish his theory, he would have to contemplate it more and marshal more evidence for it.

What Darwin was calling his "species book" would not appear for another fifteen years, and then only because he was forced to publish it quickly.

Family Matters

In the late 1840s several important developments in Darwin's personal life added to his reasons for not working on the species book. He continued to be sick with a great deal of nausea, vomiting, and retching. The constancy of it led, understandably, to bouts of depression. Although theories abound among scholars as to what illness Darwin suffered from, ranging from psychosomatic illness to a parasitic disease picked up during his travels, no definitive view has emerged.

As if poor health were not enough, in November of 1848 his father, who had been declining for some time, died at the age of eighty-two. Darwin had always been supported by his father, whom he respected highly. The loss was a blow that took its toll on Darwin. Among other things, his father's death triggered a pronounced outbreak of illness. But Robert Darwin continued to support his son after his death by leaving him an inheritance of over £50,000 beyond what he already had in trust. Darwin would manage it well over the course of his life. He proved to be a shrewd investor and always enjoyed financial security.

Three years later Darwin went through another life-shaping experience. In 1849 he had begun taking the water cure—a regimen of cold baths—for his symptoms. It seemed to help him. So when his oldest daughter Annie, who with her two sisters had suffered from scarlet fever in 1849, never really regained her health the following year, Darwin became anxious as she worsened. He brought her to take the water cure in the spring of 1851, intent on leaving her in the company of her sister and governess for a month of treatment. But she soon worsened and Darwin was summoned, only to go through an agonizing several days of anxiety before she finally died. She was his favorite child, "the joy," he said, "of the household."

Annie's death hit Darwin extremely hard. He had been getting by with his nominal acceptance of religion's public function, combined with his own private secular outlook on things such as miracles, heaven, and the significance of scripture. He retained his respect for those who, like his wife, could draw on their religious beliefs to find comfort. But he was denied such comfort. In fact, if anything, Annie's death marked a turning point for Darwin. According to Darwin biographer Janet Browne it was "the formal beginning of Darwin's conscious dissociation from believing in the traditional figure of God."

Amassing Support for His Theory

The trials he endured during the late 1840s understandably delayed Darwin's ability to work on the species book. In addition, he had determined that he needed to conduct a great deal more study of individual species to see if what he learned provided evidence to support the notion of evolution and his theory of natural selection as the means by which evolution occurred. He knew that before he could publish his theory he would have to address a number of objections to what he was calling transmutation and that only by gathering convincing evidence would his idea ever be regarded as more than speculation. It was in this connection that he valued the information breeders could give him and that he could learn from his own breeding experiments. The prerequisite to publication was slow and patient effort.

Barnacles. Major support for his theory came from an unsuspected source. Beginning in the fall of 1846 and continuing over eight years Darwin studied barnacles, crustaceans that glue themselves to rocks, ships, whales, and other accommodating surfaces that have contact with seawater. From inside their shells they reach out feathery legs to strain out plankton in the water. They are hermaphrodites; that is, adults possess both male and female parts. Darwin initially thought he would write a short paper on a discovery he made of a genus of barnacle that possessed two penises, but before long he grew so intrigued with barnacles that he took up an exhaustive study of them.

Early in 1848 he realized that the sex life of barnacles was absolutely fascinating. In April and May he discovered that barnacles reproduced themselves in an incredible variety of ways. First he found that there were species of barnacles that were not hermaphroditic, but had separate male and female sexes. The male was tiny, microscopically small, and lived its life inside the carapace of the females. But that was not the end of the variation. Sometimes there were two males inside the female, and even more astonishing, some *hermaphroditic* barnacles also had an extra male or two extra males living inside them. He asked himself, what was nature up to here? Why did nature need all these arrangements?

From the viewpoint of special creation, the variation the barnacles exhibited would be redundant and hard to explain. Darwin decided that the barnacles supported the idea of natural selection. According to his theory, nature would select any arrangement that proved adaptable and enhanced the survival of the individuals of a species. So what if, beginning with an original hermaphroditic species of barnacle, nature had stumbled by chance onto sexuality? Would not the hodgepodge of arrangements he observed in the barnacles be a reflection of this chance discovery?

But what was the advantage? Darwin reasoned that sexuality introduced a greater degree of variety into the hereditary material of barnacles than they would have if they all remained hermaphrodites. And, according to his theory, greater variety was always good, because nature would have a greater diversity from which to select. By stumbling onto sexuality, nature had enhanced the survivability of barnacles. The haphazard origin of sex was beautifully consistent with natural selection.

In the same year that his daughter Annie had died (1851) he completed two volumes on this amazing organism, one on fossil barnacles and the other on their living progeny. Three years later he put out second volumes to each, making him the world's authority on barnacles. But he did not take the opportunity in any of these books to use the evidence he had found in support of his idea of evolution by natural selection. In his mind those books were not the right place to reveal what he was thinking. As he recorded packing up the crates to retire his work on barnacles in September of 1854, he added a last line to the entry in his notebook: "Began sorting notes for species theory."

Supportive colleagues. By early April of 1856 Darwin was ready to be frank with Lyell. Previously, he had thought he would have to appeal to Lyell's geological notion of fluctuating land levels to explain how nature introduced the degree of variety required to have sufficient choices from which to select. But now he was convinced from his study of barnacles that variation was a natural result of reproduction; thus, with every new generation of offspring there would be variation. He did not need Lyell's cyclical elevation and subsidence of land masses to produce variation.

During a weekend visit at Darwin's home, he explained natural selection to Lyell and held nothing back. Lyell was impressed, to be sure, even if he did not like the implication of natural selection for humans. He worried about the dignity of humankind. How could humans be products of the same evolution that produced orangutans from oysters? But he knew Darwin's theory was not the same as the evolution of the *Vestiges* or the Lamarckian evolution that he himself had criticized so severely. So he wrote to Darwin and urged him to publish a sketch lest someone else beat him to it.

Darwin did not like the idea of writing a mere sketch of his theory—too many details had to be included for it to be persuasive. Late in April Darwin invited four other colleagues, including Hooker and a young marine scientist named Thomas Huxley (1825–1895), to his home for a weekend of discussion. The talk centered on the possibility of transmutation, which most conceded might have to be acknowledged even if they would draw limits around the extent to which it could transform a species.

By the middle of May, 1856, Darwin had decided he would take up Lyell's suggestion and write a sketch of his theory. But it would be a little while before he embarked on a book he intended to call *Natural Selection*. He hated the idea of writing just to establish his priority, he said, adding, "yet I certainly should be vexed if any one were to publish my doctrines before me."

Writing the Species Book

By this time in his life Darwin had moved away from any sympathy he had once had for a nature that bore witness to the larger purpose of existence. There had been a time when he had enjoyed the writings of William Paley, author of the classic work in natural theology, who argued that the complexities of nature could not have come about without the involvement of a divine designer. But the passing of the years had changed Darwin. He no longer felt obligated to try to find the larger purpose behind the innumerable observations he had made of the apparent senseless struggle for existence in nature.

There certainly was nothing in his theory of natural selection that called for a designer; indeed, the theory worked perfectly well if the changes introduced into nature occurred by chance, as Darwin sometimes appeared to imply they were. How else to understand the jumbled variations that accompanied the origins of sexuality in barnacles? He was not an atheist, to be sure. It was necessary to invoke supernatural agency to account for the existence of the material world, even for the existence of natural laws.

It was as if God had created the hardware of the universe (its material reality) and installed the operating system that governed its functioning (natural law), and then had deliberately included in the latter a random number generator that made it impossible to say in advance what change would come along next. Of course one could always say that God knew what was coming, but the theory worked just as well even if God had made the changes so genuinely random that even God did not know.

If he needed any additional reason to give up the traditional Christian conception of God's relationship to nature, Annie's death had provided it. He could not imagine a world that was ruled by divine providence if it permitted an innocent child to suffer. Mitigating the disturbing view to which he had come was the faith of his wife, which, although he could not share it, he respected. No one knew better than he did that the book he anticipated writing, by lending support to a purposeless nature, would undermine simple faith. To take up the task, then, took considerable courage and determination.

The letter from Wallace.   On June 18, 1858, Darwin's worst fears were realized. He received a letter from Alfred Russell Wallace (1823–1913), a British naturalist writing from the far-off Malay Archipelago. Darwin had met Wallace once and had read a paper Wallace had published that dealt with geographical distribution as a key for understanding closely related species. Wallace certainly was aware of Darwin's reputation and of his experience as an explorer. He wrote to Darwin now to ask for his opinion about an idea he had come to as a result of his observations in the Malay Islands.

Wallace's idea was close to Darwin's notion of natural selection with one minor difference: for Wallace the competition was among varieties whereas for Darwin it was among individuals. Still, the gist of the idea of natural selection was plainly there. After reading the letter Darwin confessed that it was as if Wallace had written an abstract of his sketch of 1842. He had to decide what to do. After consulting with Lyell and Hooker, Darwin consented to having Wallace's paper read before the Linnean Society along with two extracts from his own work, all of which were then published in the society's journal. Neither the reading nor the articles produced any particular response.

Darwin, however, knew that he would have to finish his sketch as quickly as possible if the long years of effort that had provided him with evidence for his theory were not to be lost. When the work finally came out in November of 1859 under the new title, *On the Origin of Species by Means of Natural Selection,* Darwin conceded that he had been urged to publish what he called an "abstract" because Wallace had come to almost exactly the same conclusions that he had regarding the origin of species.

The *Origin of Species.*   Hints of the idea of natural selection began to appear before Darwin's *Origin* was published, largely in the form of responses to the printed version of Darwin's and Wallace's remarks that came out in the journal of the Linnean Society. Meanwhile, Darwin worked feverishly to finish the sketch, whose length grew and grew.

Right away in the introduction to his book, Darwin made clear that he was opposing the idea that species had been independently created. Further, he declared

openly that they had descended, like varieties, from other species. With these two
claims, one negative, the other positive,
Darwin overtly positioned himself in opposition to widely received opinion. Being the
respected naturalist that he was, it was not
the kind of public declaration the British
people expected from this particular member of the Darwin family.

But Darwin also quickly signaled that his
support for evolution was different from that
of past writers. He distinguished his work
from the *Vestiges* by dismissing its presumption that some bird had suddenly given birth
to a woodpecker as we now know it to be.
That, said Darwin, was no explanation at all
because it did not take into account the way
animals adapted to each other and to environmental conditions. As he summarized in

Charles Darwin, at the Age He Wrote *Origin*

advance for the reader what he would be doing in his book, it became readily apparent that he would not ignore such matters.

Darwin devoted an entire chapter to natural selection, but in the introduction
he had already introduced the concept in succinct terms. Because species give birth
to more offspring than can survive, he explained, a struggle for existence ensues. In
this struggle, "any being, if it vary however slightly in any manner profitable to
itself . . . will have a better chance of surviving, and thus be *naturally selected*." The
selected variety would then tend to reproduce itself. Darwin acknowledged that
other factors contributed to the modification of species, but he was convinced that
natural selection was the main means. What later became known as Darwinism,
which focused on natural selection as the sole mechanism of evolution, therefore
differed from Darwin's original conception.

There was a clear logic to the development of the first four chapters. First, he
considered the variation that was well known to breeders of domesticated organisms. Here he wished to emphasize how plastic nature was under the molding hand
of the breeder. Darwin quoted a breeder to say that while a particular feather in
pigeons might take three years to produce, a head and beak took six. Furthermore,
the constant effort of dog breeders to obtain the best English pointer amounted to
an unconscious selection that, over time, had so modified it that it no longer resembled the old Spanish pointer from which it was known to have descended. The
unspoken inference was clear: if conscious and unconscious breeding of domesticated organisms was capable of altering a species into such different varieties in several generations, how much more could nature unconsciously shape a species over
the vast times at its disposal?

Darwin spent one chapter chronicling the details of variation in nature, another
documenting the struggle for existence that most everyone knew existed in the

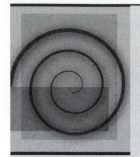

The NATURE of SCIENCE

Cultural Influence on the Formation of Theory

While it is understandable that scientific theories are not formulated in a vacuum, how much they are affected by the context into which they come is a frequent subject of debate among historians. There are those who emphasize that the significant factor behind the emergence of a lasting scientific theory is the accuracy with which it describes reality. While a culture's particular values may affect the question being addressed and while the language used to articulate the theory necessarily reflects the intellectual culture of the time, the content of the theory stands or falls on its own merits.

Others argue that the degree of cultural influence is much greater, that even the content of a theory is shaped by culture. Darwin's theory is a case in point. Darwin biographer Janet Browne has asserted, for example, that "the theory of natural selection could only have emerged out of the competitive context of Victorian England." The suggestion here is that the ruthless world of competition in the economic sphere so effectively portrayed in novels like those of Charles Dickens both suggested and reinforced Darwin's scientific depiction of the living world.

It should be apparent from the stance taken throughout this history that an overemphasis on either the context of the discovery or the discovery itself misses the most complete picture that can be given of the formulation of the contents of theories in science.

world of living things. He then came to the central concept of natural selection. He emphasized that selection acted only on "infinitesimally small inherited modifications," rejecting the idea that the changes would represent "any great and sudden modification" in the structure of organisms. While he acknowledged that natural selection might be promoted if organisms were geographically isolated, a condition he once thought necessary, now he conceded that the largeness of the area was more important.

In the next chapter, devoted to the laws of variation, it is clear that his original idea was different from what others would later make of his theory. If Darwinism came to mean the natural selection of random variations, here he said in no uncertain terms that it was incorrect to say (as he conceded he himself sometimes implied) that the individual differences important to natural selection were due to chance. He did not think of them as changes introduced randomly; rather, they came about as the result of causes whose laws were as yet unknown. The process was under the rule of law. Now the implication was that if we ever uncovered the laws we would be able to predict the individual differences in advance. But whatever causes were responsible for the slight differences that offspring bore to their parents, the important thing was that these differences accumulated as the result of natural selection in such a manner as to modify structure.

Next came the chapter candidly labeled "Difficulties on Theory." Darwin subtly established credibility with his reader by deliberately anticipating problems that his theory raised. For example, he raised the question of what would soon be called missing links. If the changes on which evolution depended were small, as he insisted, why do we see only well-defined, separate species? Where are the transitional forms?

Darwin proposed answers, not dogmatically, but persuasively. For one thing, the record of past forms was incomplete. He gave reasons why, when representative varieties inhabited two portions of a continuous area, intermediate forms *would* at first occur in the region between them, but they would not be numerous. There would theoretically be missing links, although they would be harder to find. His analysis even anticipated twenty-first-century objections that animals in a transitional state would not survive because they did not yet possess the advantageous characteristic possessed by their alleged progeny. Darwin asserted, as do his present-day defenders, that each change along the way to the final form was useful and that in this way the end result was achieved.

Continuing the defense of his theory, he argued in a separate chapter that subjecting instincts to natural selection made a great deal more of nature's complexity understandable. In another chapter he faced up to the alleged sterility of hybrids, but suggested that the line between varieties and species was often not clear. Hybrids produced by crossing species often resembled the offspring of crossed varieties. Why then should species be the result of special creation and varieties the result of natural law? In two more chapters Darwin made use of his exhaustive knowledge of geology to support his reading of the fossil record, then he further supported his theory in chapters devoted to the geographical distribution of species, which he knew well from his travels around the world, and to the morphological and embryological development of organisms.

All in all, it hardly deserved the name of an abstract. It was an impressive book of just over five hundred pages, containing careful argumentation by an author obviously in command of an enormous amount of information. Whatever the reader thought of the basic claims of the work, it was clear that it would not be a book that was easy to refute. Some British readers no doubt felt that the issue of the transmutation of species had been settled by the exhaustive criticism the *Vestiges* had received fifteen years earlier. Some French and German readers concluded that they too had heard it all before in the works of Lamarck and the German romantics. Those who greeted Darwin's book with a yawn, however, would discover that they were wrong to underestimate it.

Suggestions for Reading

Janet Browne, *Charles Darwin: Voyaging* (Princeton: Princeton University Press, 1996).

Janet Browne, *Charles Darwin: The Power of Place* (Princeton: Princeton University Press, 2003).

Adrian Desmond and James Moore, *Darwin: The Life of a Tormented Evolutionist* (New York: Norton, 1994).

James Secord, *Victorian Sensation* (Chicago: University of Chicago Press, 2003).

CHAPTER 19

The Aftermath of the *Origin*

Charles Darwin read the proofs for his book, *On the Origin of Species,* during the summer and fall of 1859. He worried about his writing style, about whether the work would be too boring, and about the possibility that it would lose money for the publisher. He even volunteered to help underwrite the cost of some of the proof corrections. The work had taken him, he calculated, thirteen months and ten days to complete.

Word of the book spread quickly. By September of 1859 the distinguished geologist Charles Lyell had given advance notice of Darwin's work to the meeting of the British Association in Aberdeen. He told the audience of scientists that Darwin's book would draw together phenomena of the affinities among organic beings and link them to issues of geographical distribution and geological succession. Once available at the end of November, Darwin sent presentation copies to a host of individuals, accompanying them with a friendly letter that addressed each person's likely reaction. By early December, Mudie's Circulating Library, which had ordered 500 of the 1,250 copies printed, advertised that the book was ready for borrowing. The *Origin* would get a widespread hearing.

◎ The Immediate Reception of the ◎ Origin of Species

The immediate reception of Darwin's work was mixed. The publisher, John Murray, sent the book out for review to almost forty journals. As newspaper notices and journal reviews began to appear, they ranged from blistering dismissals by those offended by the idea that humans were hereditarily related to lower forms of life to strongly positive endorsements carefully crafted by friends of Darwin. While the *Origin*'s defense of evolution could not claim the novelty that the anonymous

Vestiges of the Natural History of Creation enjoyed fifteen years earlier, its polarizing effect still created something of its own minor sensation. The basic reason for its popularity was the identity of the author, a respected scientist and highly upstanding member of British society.

The Emergence of Opponents and Support from Friends

Darwin expected that many in the educated class whose commitment to religious orthodoxy formed the foundation of their intellectual outlook would denounce his theory. That did not make reading reviews by such individuals any easier, particularly when they revealed in their writing that they had not understood him or when they hid behind the veil of anonymity.

What stung even more were the hostile reactions from well-established scientists such as Adam Sedgwick, with whom he had made geological expeditions as a student. On receiving his presentation copy he wrote to Darwin that it had caused him more pain than pleasure, that while there were parts he admired, others had made him laugh "until my sides were sore." Darwin, he said, had written some things that were utterly false and grievously mischievous; he had abandoned the true method of induction. What bothered Sedgwick, who saw design and purpose as self-evident in the natural world, was that Darwin appeared to ignore all rational conception of design.

Richard Owen, the superintendent of the natural history collections at the British Museum, also broke with his one-time collaborator. Darwin had entrusted fossils collected from the *Beagle* voyage to Owen for evaluation many years earlier, when Owen was an up-and-coming zoology star. Since then he had become a leading spokesman against transmutation whenever it cropped up, be it in writings intended primarily for scientists or in those that enjoyed wide public circulation. Although Darwin had held back from Owen his ideas on evolution, he had maintained polite social contact over the years.

Now Darwin paid Owen a visit in mid-December, just after the release of the *Origin,* to try to gauge his reaction. While their meeting was formal and his reception cool, Owen's opinions came out into the open with his searing attack on the *Origin* in an April review. Owen dismissed Darwin's alleged facts as nonsense, disparaged his friends, and slandered Darwin's competence and his writing style. It was the harshest review to date. Darwin now realized that his theory could turn former friends into hostile enemies.

Naturally, Darwin had allies who came to his defense. Among the early reviews was a glowing anonymous piece in the *London Times,* a widely read newspaper that guaranteed Darwin a large audience. The regular *Times* reviewer had found himself at a loss about what to say regarding the book. Instead, he let Huxley—the boisterous young marine scientist Darwin had included in the group that had come to his home to discuss transmutation in 1856 (see Chapter 18)—write the review, but submitted it himself. The result was a far stronger endorsement of a book than the *Times* normally published.

Lyell's support was put on the line by the bishop of Oxford, Samuel Wilberforce (1805–1873), who wrote a review of the *Origin* in the July issue of the *Quarterly*

Review. The review was, not unexpectedly, critical—evolution was incompatible with the Bible and with the human moral and spiritual condition—and also wittily dismissive. Referring to the well-known critique of Lamarck in Lyell's *Principles of Geology,* Wilberforce called on Lyell to denounce the basic evolutionary theme of the work because "no man has been more distinct and more logical in the denial of the transmutation of species."

The Oxford Meeting of the British Association

However much he may have harbored reservations, Lyell did not publicly desert Darwin. Nor did three other close allies—Huxley and Hooker in Britain and the American naturalist Asa Gray (1810–1888). Huxley and Hooker had been present at the annual meeting of the British Association the month before Wilberforce's review came out. Fireworks had erupted over Darwin's theory. Six months of reviews made Darwin's book a subject that hovered in the background of the opening address, in which the speaker drew attention to God's role in creation. In the initial session of the section on zoology, botany, and physiology, it did not take long for evolution to emerge into the open. Owen objected to it for want of evidence from anatomy, assuring the audience of the major differences between the brains of gorillas and humans. Huxley disputed Owen's claims about the brain, adding that even if humans were descended from apes there was little to fear.

The meeting was held in Oxford, making it convenient for the bishop to be present. Naturally he chose to attend an address on the intellectual development of Europe considered with respect to Darwin's views. After the lecture concluded, members of the audience posed a few questions. Then the chair acknowledged Wilberforce, a gifted speaker, who rose to his feet and delivered a thirty-minute harangue against Darwin's theory that no doubt drew on the review that would appear the following month. He ended by picking up on Huxley's remark of the previous day about apes as ancestors. There is no record of exactly what he asked as he turned toward Huxley, but it was apparently something close to whether it was through his paternal or maternal side that he was descended from apes.

Of course Huxley was happy to reply. He recognized the views of Richard Owen in the bishop's objections to evolution and was prepared to counter them. In addition, Huxley wanted to change the way science was done; specifically, he did not want to leave scientific research to people of privilege who pursued it in their leisure time. Huxley led the movement in mid-Victorian Britain to make science a profession in which up-and-coming men like him could make a living. He could use the relationship between science and religion to drive a wedge between scientists like himself and the Anglican men of privilege. After countering Wilberforce's position, he closed his remarks with a memorable declaration. What has come down to us is his observation that he would rather have an ape for an ancestor than a man of influence who ridiculed serious scientific discussion.

The session continued with others rising to speak. Hooker added his bit, as did Darwin's companion from the *Beagle,* Captain Robert Fitzroy. After it was over both sides claimed victory. For those present it was a truly memorable moment. In assessing the overall reaction to Darwin's work, however, it would pale somewhat in its importance. There would be other developments throughout the decade of the 1860s that would have more significance in determining how Darwin's work was to be received.

Status of Natural Selection

What soon became clear was that the concept of natural selection did not command immediate assent; in fact, sometimes it seemed not even to register with readers. The reviewer in *Fraser's*, for example, declared, to Darwin's extreme annoyance, that Darwin's view was the same as Lamarck's. Such a claim implied that all of the accepted criticisms that had long since doomed Lamarck applied also to Darwin. Readers of this review were given to think that the British public had heard it all before.

Thomas Huxley

Furthermore, although Huxley clearly came to Darwin's side, it emerged that what attracted him to the *Origin* was less the idea of natural selection itself than it was Darwin's removal of special creation from scientific discussion, and his replacement of it with natural process. Huxley enlisted Darwin's theory in a larger cause—attacking religious explanations of natural phenomena in the name of science. By nature brash and decisive, he relished creating a veritable warfare between science and religion. Huxley's bold approach did not always win friends for Darwin, who privately complained that Huxley sometimes managed to damage his book in spite of his intention to back it. It did not help Darwin's image, of course, that outspoken atheists and radicals such as Robert Grant smothered Darwin's theory with praise.

Further, it did not bother Huxley that he himself had problems with natural selection. On the contrary, in one of the several reviews he wrote of the *Origin*, Huxley exposed what he regarded as the weaknesses of natural selection. Darwin had not yet made his case, he said. He must yet show how varieties could, over time, become infertile with close relatives, a development Huxley found difficult to conceive of, given the gradual nature of the variations. If Huxley found problems with the central concept of Darwin's theory, other scientists would not be far behind.

◎ Scientific Objections to Darwin's Theory ◎

To be sure, Darwin's theory remained of interest in the early 1860s, especially among scientists. From these circles, however, serious concerns about the ability of natural selection to produce the kind of change Darwin described soon appeared. Just after the middle of the decade several pointed scientific objections were made to Darwin's theory that gave heart to anti-evolutionists and raised difficulties among its defenders. These problems continued to be controversial for the remainder of the century. During these years there was no reason at all to assume that Darwin's ideas would stand the test of time.

Critiques of Darwin's Understanding of the Past

Because of the haphazard action of natural selection, Darwin's theory required enormous spans of time to bring about evolutionary change. In the *Origin*, Darwin openly addressed the question of whether the Earth was old enough to accommodate his explanation of how evolution had occurred. In his discussion of the geological record he provided a specific estimate of how long it had taken for erosive action to wear away the great valley that stretched across southern England, called The Weald. Based on assumptions that he made clear to the reader, Darwin concluded that the erosion of rock strata in The Weald had taken some 300 million years. This figure implied that the Earth had to be much older than most readers ever would have dreamed.

The geological controversy. Darwin was convinced that Lyell's work in geology had placed vast spans of time at his disposal. In fact, Lyell's understanding of the past provided all the time Darwin might need. First, in his *Principles of Geology*, Lyell had demonstrated numerous individual examples of immensely old geological phenomena. Further, Lyell opposed the very notion of geological development, asserting that there was a uniformity of geological conditions between past and present. While local regions might have experienced uplift during certain periods in the past, they were also subjected to subsidence during others. There was no accumulated irreversible geological change. While this uniformity made any specific claim about the Earth's age impossible to determine, it was clear that our planet's indefinite age was extremely ancient. Darwin styled the case for his theory as standing or falling with Lyell's geology. Anyone who disagreed with Lyell's conclusions about how immense past periods of time had been could, he wrote, stop reading the *Origin* right then.

It soon became clear, however, that Lyell did not command everyone's allegiance and that Darwin had made a mistake to give a specific time for the occurrence of what he called the denudation of The Weald. First to question its implications for the age of the Earth was the geologist John Phillips (1800–1874), who was William Buckland's successor at Oxford and president of the Geological Society. He pointed out why Darwin's calculations had been very careless and then he proceeded to come at the problem of the Earth's age from the opposite direction. He asked how long it would take to build up geological strata rather than erode it away. His calculations, based on one of his own studies of a different location, produced an estimate of around 100 million years for the age of the Earth. Darwin was sufficiently unsettled by this criticism that he cut his estimate in half in the second edition of the *Origin* and omitted it altogether in the third.

A critique from physics. But the issue did not go away simply because Darwin retreated. At the basis of Darwin's original claim was Lyell's assertion that geological conditions in the past, including the temperature, had always been qualitatively similar to what they were now. That notion ran counter to recent results in physical science.

Leading this attack was a Scottish physicist named William Thomson (1824–1907), one of the principal architects of the new science of thermodynamics. As we will learn in the next chapter, Thomson was instrumental in formulating a conclusion about physical processes based on considerations of the nature of heat. In particular, Thomson argued that because over time energy became increasingly unavailable to do work, the universe was running down. That meant that there was an irreversibility in physical processes that was unavoidable. There was no way, in other words, that Lyell's conception of a past geological steady state, in which the temperature had remained relatively constant, could be correct.

Thompson had been engaged in the question of the age of the Earth even before Darwin's theory appeared. He had considered the implications of what he called the dissipation of energy for the age of the Earth as early as 1852. The Earth, he conjectured, had once been much hotter than it now was and it would continue to cool until it would be much colder. At both extremes of its ultimate history, then, he regarded the Earth as "unfit for the habitation of man." The irreversibility of the process meant that the geological conditions of the early Earth were very different from what they were in the present. By implication Lyell was simply wrong.

In the 1850s Thomson's attention was drawn to questions about the sun's heat, but he came back to the Earth in a paper read in 1862 and published the following year. In this paper he set out to determine how long the Earth had been cool enough to support some form of life; that is, he wanted to know how much time physics would permit for evolution to take place. To do this he attempted to calculate how long it had been since the Earth had possessed a solid crust on which living things could have existed.

Thomson began by assuming that the Earth's original hot molten form had come about when it was formed from a cosmic collision of some sort. To make his calculations he had to make certain assumptions about how the Earth solidified and about the fusion temperature of rock. His task was to establish a rate of cooling that would enable him to calculate how long ago the Earth's crust had formed. His answer was 98 million years. Because of the assumptions he had made, he felt it necessary to accept limits that varied between 20 million and 400 million years.

Thomson's main objective in his article of 1863 was to oppose Lyell's uniformitarian assumptions about geological process. But publishing in a journal of physics had little effect on the geological community, which was still heavily influenced by Lyell's position. Just before Christmas in 1865, Thomson addressed the Royal Society of Edinburgh on the doctrine of uniformity in geology. Published in 1866, the paper was an open challenge to Lyell and, by extension, to Darwin. Lyell's contention that the Earth's surface had retained its present temperature over millions of years was wrong. Thomson noted that the amount of heat known to be lost yearly, if continued over 20 million years, was sufficient to raise the temperature of a hundred Earths by 100°C!

A close friend and collaborator of Thomson, the Scottish physicist and engineer Fleeming Jenkin (1833–1885), focused Thomson's critique specifically on Darwin's theory. In a review of Darwin's book in 1867, Jenkin carefully and thoroughly criticized Darwin's calculation of 300 million years for the denudation of The Weald. He then declared that physics provided more accurate methods of computing the age of the Earth's crust than geology did. He concluded that Thomson had shown "that our world cannot have been habitable for more than an infinitely insufficient period for the executing of the Darwinian transmutation."

In the ensuing years other critics of Darwin began citing Thomson's results. Thomson took the stance that while his calculations did not disprove evolution, they were "sufficient to disprove the doctrine that transmutation has taken place through descent with modification by natural selection."

These developments set up a direct clash between Darwin's contentions and the authority of physics. To be sure, because he had no way of answering an eminent physicist, Darwin squirmed under the full impact of Thomson's critique. He conceded that perhaps evolutionary change occurred faster than he had thought, but it was still clear that he needed more time than Thomson's 100 million years. "Thomson's views of the recent age of the earth," Darwin wrote, "have been for some time one of my sorest troubles." In 1871 he referred to Thomson as "an odious specter."

The controversy continued over the remaining years of the century, making it crystal clear to observers that the scientific community was at best divided over the most recent doctrine of evolution. Thomson, who was raised to a peerage as Lord Kelvin by the British government in 1892, continued to represent a difficult challenge for advocates of Darwin's theory. The limited time that physics granted was plainly too little for natural selection, dependent as it was on chance variations, to work. As for Darwin and his followers, they were unwilling simply to abandon evolution by natural selection. They could only assume that there was something wrong with what the physicists were saying.

It was not until after the turn of the century, with the discovery of radioactivity, that more time was made available for evolution. Here was a source of heat that Thomson had not taken into account because he was unaware of it. With more heat present on Earth, it would take longer for the Earth to cool, granting more time for evolution to proceed.

Fleeming Jenkin's Review of the Origin

The review of Darwin by Thomson's friend Fleeming Jenkin, mentioned earlier, caused Darwin considerable grief for additional reasons. Jenkin took Darwin's evolutionary ideas seriously, expressing great admiration both for the ingenuity of the doctrine and for the temper in which it was presented. But Jenkin could not accept natural selection as a viable means of creating new species. His major objections had

to do with the nature of variation, and they caused Darwin
considerable difficulty.

Like Darwin himself, Jenkin
distinguished between two different kinds of variation. First
there was the common kind of
variation inevitable in every generation of offspring, variation
Darwin called "individual differences." As an example, Jenkin
cited the presence of longer or
shorter legs. The second kind of
variation, known as sports of
nature, were large changes that
appeared suddenly and occurred
rarely. Jenkin illustrated this variation by an individual born with
six fingers on each hand. He considered each kind in turn.

Jenkin freely acknowledged
that natural selection acting on
common variations could produce substantial improvements.
But he remained convinced that
these improvements were unable
to go beyond fixed limits. He
listed conditions necessary even

Fleeming Jenkin

for establishing improved varieties. First, he argued that there would have to be
enormous numbers of individuals with the same slight advantageous characteristic
to effect a change in a species. Second, he maintained that improvements had to be
in organs or parts that were *already* useful. Natural selection, he claimed, could not
produce a wholly new useful organ or part.

Darwin had sometimes written about the introduction of favorable small variations as if they were rare, not, as Jenkin said would be necessary for natural selection to work, widely represented in the population among many individuals.
Jenkin therefore took on the second kind of variation, sports of nature, which were
known to be rare, to show that they held no hope for producing species change by
natural selection. To make his case against rare variations, Jenkin drew on the
understanding of heredity common to that day, one that Darwin also assumed.
According to this understanding, called blending inheritance, characteristics of offspring were the blend, or average, of the characteristics of the parents.

If, then, a rare, favorable sport of nature made its appearance in one of the parents, its offspring would inherit this favorable trait, but not to the degree the parent
possessed it. The reason was that the other parent would *not* possess this rare trait,

so when the traits of the parents were averaged in the offspring, the favorable sport would be cut in half. In the next generation the same thing would happen again, because the mate of the offspring would also not have the rare trait. It would not take many generations before the advantage represented by the original appearance of the favorable sport would virtually disappear, having been swamped by the repeated process of cutting the advantage in two with every generation.

Jenkin supported his case using the racist assumptions common to his day. He suggested, for example, that if there were a shipwreck off Africa's coast, the obviously superior traits of a white survivor would be wiped away by those of black Africans after just a few generations, leaving little trace of whiteness. The message was clear: variations that were rare could not accumulate to produce the kind of change Darwin's theory required. The only hope was if the variation were distributed continuously and even then, according to Jenkin, the impact was confined within limits.

Jenkin's reasoning was careful, well articulated, and frequently based on arguments of mathematical probability. Many readers found themselves persuaded that he had, in fact, shown that while Darwin's theory was creative and worthy of respect, it hardly could guarantee the kind of change Darwin claimed. The impression given by Jenkin's reasoned analysis was that Darwin had overstated his case.

For his part, Darwin smarted under Jenkin's criticisms. While he continued to hold on to the belief that natural selection *could* cross the limits Jenkin claimed could not be traversed, he did abandon rare variations in favor of those more common. Individual differences were plentiful, distributed continuously on both sides of an average; they were not merely occasionally introduced into a population.

◎ Religious Considerations ◎

In the aftermath of the *Origin*'s publication two events drew the public's attention away from natural science to other matters. The first was the appearance in 1860 of a book entitled *Essays and Reviews,* written by British biblical scholars who drew on what was known as German higher criticism. During the previous decades, German theologians had published several works arguing that important insights were to be gained by viewing the Bible as first and foremost a work of ancient literature, not as a privileged repository of doctrinal truth.

In the course of making their claims, the German scholars betrayed that they rejected the historicity of miracles, which were called "Sea-Stories and Fish-Stories" by one of the more famous among them. Now British men of the cloth were also rejecting miracles and urging their countrymen to adopt a liberal reading of the Scripture. The result was an uproar on many fronts; two of the contributors were convicted of heresy in a Canterbury court, although the judgment was overturned on appeal.

The second development came from beyond Britain's shores. Pope Pius IX, distressed by what he regarded as the advance of secularism, issued the Syllabus of Errors in 1864. Here were listed some eighty errors that resulted from the advance of pantheism, naturalism, rationalism, socialism, and other evils of the modern age. Darwinism did not make the list, but natural science did. Error number nine, for example, was that "All the dogmas of the Christian religion are indiscriminately the object of natural science or philosophy, and human reason, enlightened solely in an historical way, is able, by its own natural strength and principles, to attain to the true science of even the most abstruse dogmas."

Neither of these events focused on Darwin's theory. But it was not long before objections based on religious and philosophical considerations did target Darwin's theory specifically. These protests, when joined to the disagreement evident among scientists themselves, only added to the suspicions about the merits of Darwin's achievement.

The Critique of the Duke of Argyll

George Douglas Campbell (1823–1900) became the eighth Duke of Argyll in 1847, succeeding his father in a line of Scottish nobles that went back to the early eighteenth century. The duke's interest in and writings on natural science brought him into the controversy over Darwin's theory. Because of his prominent position, his views received quick attention. In 1867 he published a work entitled *The Reign of Law,* in which his specific objections were recorded. The book was well received, appearing in nineteen editions by 1890.

Referring to a work by Darwin from 1862 on the various ways orchids were fertilized by insects, the duke praised Darwin for having traced in detail the numerous marvelous contrivances nature employed to accomplish fertilization. He objected, however, to Darwin's presumption in attributing to blindly acting natural selection the answer to how such contrivances had originated. The duke's view was that the purpose preceded the means by which it was accomplished, not, as natural selection would have it, that the purpose emerged as the contrivances were blindly produced.

The duke pointed out that Darwin himself had, contrary to his own theory, resorted to the language of pre-existing purpose to describe nature's operations throughout the work. For example, Darwin had scolded himself for having missed the reason for the strange position of the lower petal of the orchid flower, called the labellum. "I ought to have scorned the notion that the Labellum was thus placed *for no good* purpose," wrote Darwin. "I neglected this plain guide, and for a long time completely failed to understand the flower."

The duke had no complaints against the idea that natural law governed the arrangement by which nature's pre-existing purposes were accomplished. He believed in the reign of law. But the purpose was pre-existing, not produced by nature. God in fact, gave it to nature. "There is nothing in Religion," he wrote, "incompatible with the belief that all exercises of God's power, whether ordinary or extraordinary, are effected through the instrumentality of means—that is to say, by the instrumentality of natural laws brought out, as it were, and used for a Divine purpose."

One of the duke's specific objections to Darwin's theory had to do with the production of variations. Darwin had not discovered or disclosed any law according to which new forms arose. Darwin's theory, suggested the duke, was therefore not a theory about the origin of species at all; rather, it was "only a theory on the causes which lead to the relative success or failure of such new forms as may be born

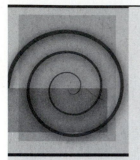

The NATURE of SCIENCE

Evolution, God, and Nature

Issues such as those raised by the Duke of Argyll have not disappeared from the scene with the passage of time. They remain very much a concern today for many people who, having accepted that evolution has occurred, want to inquire about God's relation to the process. The numerous answers that have been given run the gamut from those who claim that God directs evolution at every step to those who assert that there is no God at all. A very small minority of scientists contend that determining evidence of God's involvement is a scientific task that should be part of the science curricula of local public schools. The courts have disagreed, ruling that such an endeavor does not fall within the bounds of natural science.

Among the various possible positions are those who suggest that God causes the variations that nature then selects. They prefer a cosmos whose meaning derives, at least in part, from the purposeful direction they believe all reality, including organic evolution, possesses. Others, with a less traditional conception of God, maintain that God created the laws governing natural selection, which then acts on its own to produce evolutionary change. An interesting question for those holding this view is whether or not God knows in advance what evolution will produce so that what happens is at least in some sense compatible with God's purpose.

Some insist on natural selection so strictly that they rule out God's existence altogether. They point out that Darwin's theory works just as well if the variations are produced by pure chance as it would if the variations were supplied by an all-knowing intelligence. It is immaterial where the variations come from as long as there are variations; consequently God is not needed. They are content with the grandeur of a cosmos, which, while indifferent to life on Earth, has produced humans who create meaning wholly on their own.

into the world." As for accounting, in part at least, for the success and establishment and spread of new forms once they had arisen, the duke said that Darwin's results were more than a theory—they were "established scientific truth."

So far the duke was on solid ground because, as pointed out in the previous chapter, Darwin had conceded that variations were not due to chance but were governed by laws that were as yet unknown. The duke's position was that God intervened to produce the new variations needed for the formation of a new species in accordance with divine intent. He believed that variations introduced without regard for what was needed would not, in fact, be capable of producing a new species. He maintained that when the laws governing the appearance of variations were discovered they would be an expression of divine will; that is, the production of each new species could still be seen as a special creation. The quarrel was not over new forms arising or the existence of natural laws governing their appearance. It was over whether that lawful evolution was specifically intended by God or not.

Answering this objection was difficult and, given the persistence of the duke's view to our own day, hardly universally persuasive. Some of those close to Darwin, including Lyell and Darwin's American champion, Asa Gray (1810–1888), harbored convictions similar to the duke's.

The codiscoverer of natural selection, Alfred Russell Wallace, attempted to critique the duke's position. He said in a review of the duke's book that while he, Wallace, thought he could prove his case theoretically, he preferred to answer the duke with facts. Those facts were, he reported, that, as breeders would confirm, given a sufficient number of individuals there would always be enough variations of any required kind to permit selection toward a given end. The same, he argued, would be true in the wild. Superintending the production of variations was not necessary for the theory to work because there would always be ample variations on which natural selection could work to produce new species. Variation sufficient in amount to be accumulated in a given direction did not have to be the direct act of a creative mind. In fact, Wallace observed, to think that it was directly due to an intelligent agent attributed to an otherwise all-powerful and all-wise God actions that most considered "trivial, mean, or debasing."

The Duke of Argyll was not the only critic calling Darwin to account for using the language of purpose even while urging caution in ascribing purpose to nature. Friends and critics alike brought it to his attention. Wallace repeated to Darwin around this time a suggestion he had made earlier; namely, he urged Darwin to give up the phrase "natural selection" in favor of Herbert Spencer's phrase, "survival of the fittest." Natural selection personified nature as something purposefully seeking only the good of the species. "People will not understand that all such phrases are metaphors," Wallace wrote. He advised Darwin to replace "natural selection" with "survival of the fittest" in future editions of the *Origin,* something Wallace did in his own copy of Darwin's book. Darwin adopted the suggestion at various places in the fifth and sixth editions of the *Origin* in 1869 and 1872.

The Response of Theologians

Not surprisingly, the reaction to the *Origin* of Christian theologians, who constituted the great majority of religious thinkers of the day who responded to Darwin, was varied when it finally came. It took time for theologians to understand that there was something different about Darwin's version of evolution from that of earlier thinkers such as Lamarck and the author of the *Vestiges.* When they did realize that Darwin had identified a new (although not exclusive) means by which evolution occurred, they took solace in the numerous criticisms scientists were making of natural selection. To a large extent the response of theologians was affected by the degree to which they understood and accepted Darwin's conception of natural selection.

The orthodox response.   Among the earliest theologians to reply to Darwin was a conservative who was concerned about protecting the message of the Bible and fundamental Christian doctrine. The issue of evolution surfaced in an unscheduled floor debate during the international meeting of the Evangelical Alliance in New York in 1873. In response to the assertion that new developments implied biological evolution was not necessarily incompatible with Christian doctrine, the Princeton theologian Charles Hodge (1797–1878) rose to denounce the suggestion. He argued a case that he would make unmistakably clear in a book the following year, that the issue was whether one believed in an intellectual process guided by God or a material process guided by chance.

In his book entitled *What Is Darwinism?* Hodge revealed that he understood Darwin's theory very well, zeroing in on natural selection. As Darwin proclaimed it, said Hodge, natural selection resulted from unintelligent causes and that made it incompatible with religion. In the book he went beyond his position in New York. He granted that scientists had to use hypotheses, but he pointed out that they inevitably rested on a degree of belief. Further, no hypothesis should be tolerated if it required something that was impossible. The notion that chance could generate design was to him rationally self-contradictory and therefore impossible.

For Hodge the denial of intelligent causes made Darwin's theory the most ruthlessly naturalistic theory that could be imagined, far more so than Lamarckian evolution, which, with its divinely foreordained course, was at least deistic. "The conclusion of the whole matter," Hodge wrote, "is that the denial of design in nature is virtually the denial of God." Hodge's position was crystal clear as he replied to the question in the title of his book, *What Is Darwinism?* The answer came in one word—*atheism.* There could be no compromise.

Reconciling theologians.   Hodge's inflexible stance was not characteristic of other theologians in America and across the Atlantic. The erudition of Darwin's argument and the interest it had stirred made theologians who valued secular learning regard it as a contribution to contemporary thought that they could not summarily dismiss as Hodge had done. Further, many of them resented the conservative outcry against *Essays and Reviews,* a book they considered an honest attempt to make religion viable in the modern age. True, they did not demand that the message of the Bible be understood in any literal or even necessarily traditional fashion. But that did not, in their eyes, make them any less committed to the eternal truths of Christianity.

Of course, these theologians also had to confront the meaning of natural selection. They dealt with the problem Hodge had raised by rejecting the natural selection of chance variations as essential to evolution. They found support for this in the criticisms of natural selection that respected scientists were making and in the assurances of even some of Darwin's close friends—Lyell and Asa Gray, for example—that natural selection did not negate purpose in nature.

In other words, some theologians moved the focus off natural selection onto evolution, joining the many people who found that Darwin had made evolution fashionable. Formerly, scientists and churchmen alike had generally dismissed the biological evolution of living things from lower forms of life as the outlandish speculations of writers such as the author of the *Vestiges* or the Frenchman Lamarck. But now, as a result of Darwin's defense of evolution, evolution became a respectable topic of conversation. "It would seem at first sight," wrote an American philosopher, "that Mr. Darwin has won a victory, not for himself but for Lamarck."

Having made evolution the issue, theologians who wished to reconcile Darwin and religion proceeded to devise interpretations that incorporated the development of life into God's overall plan. Each in his own way formulated what might be called theistic evolution, meaning that, in one way or another, God superintended the past development of life on Earth. The theologians who, because they were sympathetic to Darwin, imported evolution into their theological stance appeared in at least three guises.

On the right there were those who continued to defend the fundamental tenets of orthodox Christianity while acknowledging that a strictly literal interpretation of Genesis was incompatible with the results of natural science. Typical here was the theologian and philosopher James McCosh (1811–1894), who emigrated from Scotland to take up the presidency of Princeton University in 1868. McCosh believed that the Bible was not concerned with the question of the immutability of species. He taught that evolution was "the method of God's procedure" and that "supernatural design produces natural selection," a claim that Darwin would certainly dispute. Consequently McCosh believed that evolution was not inconsistent with Scripture, although he was one of the small number of theologians who attempted to reconcile evolution with the Bible.

Liberal theologians like those who had contributed to the *Essays and Reviews* were of course not concerned about defending the Genesis record. One such was William Temple (1821–1902), the Anglican bishop of London. In 1884 he was selected to give a series of religious addresses known as the Bampton Lectures. He made clear his position on evolution and religion by taking one step back from the claim that God controlled evolution directly. Evolution, he said, resulted from the determinism of natural law that governed the universe. He objected to the notion that God intervened into this process to direct evolution. But that did not mean that evolution escaped divine superintendence. On the contrary, the purposes God accomplished through evolution resided in God's original creative decree and that left the argument for an intelligent creator and governor stronger than ever. This was the God of classic deism.

Another group of theologians who reconciled evolution and religion in the wake of Darwin's *Origin* showed once again how easy it was to avoid acceptance of what Darwin meant by natural selection. These thinkers were even more liberal than Temple. They embraced evolution and made it the cornerstone of their theological outlook. The prosperity of the 1880s in the United States made it easy for theologians caught up with the general atmosphere of progress and optimism to welcome evolution as an ally that breathed new life into stale Christian doctrine.

Representatives of this outlook included the popular minister at the Plymouth Church in Brooklyn, New York, Henry Ward Beecher (1813–1887). Beecher gave a series of sermons in the spring of 1885 in which he touched on evolution. His hero was Herbert Spencer (1820–1903), not Darwin. Spencer had interpreted evolution on a cosmic scale that Beecher found adaptable to religious purposes. His successor at the Plymouth Church, Lyman Abbott (1835–1922), made things clear in his book entitled *The Theology of an Evolutionist,* in which God was portrayed as the antithesis of natural selection but at the same time was a creative and directing force in complete control of evolution.

Radical theology.   Some theologians, especially in Germany, did not fit into the categories of liberal or conservative. They harkened back to the outlook of the philosopher Immanuel Kant, who argued that the goal of classical philosophy, to acquire metaphysical knowledge of the world, was impossible. Humans could have knowledge only of things that could be captured in causal relationships among sense data that are expressed mathematically (see Chapter 14). This was the knowledge acquired in natural science. Metaphysics carries us beyond the senses; hence natural science was not equipped to supply metaphysical truth about nature.

The German neo-Kantian theologian Wilhelm Herrmann (1846–1922) argued in the 1870s that, just as metaphysics could not be a concern of natural science, it should also not be a concern of theologians. He campaigned to remove metaphysics from theology. But what, then, was the proper purview of religion and theology? Herrmann answered that religion had a practical goal—it had to do with questions of ethics and mortality, of how to live an authentic life. To accomplish this, humans would find no help from knowledge about how nature worked.

By the same token, Herrmann argued, natural science also had a practical goal. Herrmann understood natural science as an enterprise akin to engineering. Science could not supply the ultimate truth of nature because that lay beyond the knowledge of the senses. The aim of natural science was simply to achieve mastery over nature.

Herrmann's position was that both religion and science should be restricted, each to its own practical domain. Religion was to be confined to concerns about ethics and morality, while natural science had to do with the laws governing nature. In his mind the two did not intersect; hence one did not reinforce the other nor could the two be in conflict. It was not a matter of reconciling religion and science; rather, each should show respect for the other.

As a result of this sharp separation, theologians, said Herrmann, should relinquish to the natural scientists all rights to make claims about how nature worked. Theologians should therefore grant complete freedom to scientists in their attempts to discover the laws according to which nature operated. Taking this position made Herrmann sound very liberal. When it came to addressing the central concern of religion, however, Herrmann, who came from a Christian tradition, spoke of achieving a moral and authentic life in terms of a personal encounter with Christ. This made him sound very much like a conservative.

Neo-Kantian theologians like Herrmann who called for the removal of metaphysics from both science and theology tried their best to follow their own dictates. They realized that there were some scientists who believed that because Darwin's theory provided evidence that chance events resulted in directional development, the additional conclusion that evolution did not require a superintendent followed almost irresistibly. These scientists did not hesitate to move beyond the knowledge of the senses to the metaphysical claim that nature contained no inherent purpose, that it did not bear the mark of a designer.

Herrmann's teacher, the theologian Albrecht Ritschl (1822–1889), would not condone the move to a purposeless cosmos. He made it clear that he would not accept chance as the moving force behind the ultimate causes of the world—to do so was to make a metaphysical claim. Instead, Ritschl and Herrmann took a different stance. They drew not on Darwin, but on the evidence of lived experience, which, they said, confirmed the supremacy of human moral purpose over metaphysics. Ritschl acknowledged that a purposeless cosmos was the assumption of materialistic natural science, but, because it was a metaphysical claim, it neither persuaded nor constrained him. Metaphysical claims were irrelevant to the crucial task of determining how to live an authentic life.

The radical theological response was not confined to Germany, although it proved to be most influential there. It gave rise to what became known in the twentieth century as existential theology, which was marked by the fundamental separation of science and religion and by the subordination of metaphysical claims of materialistic science to human responsibility for dictating meaning to the world. Indeed, all three theological responses to the issues sharpened by Darwin's theory—orthodox, reconciling, and radical—have continued to exist since the late nineteenth century.

◎ Implications for Social ◎
and Political Philosophy

The refined distinctions of Ritschl and Herrmann were lost on many, for whom the claims about the ultimate nature of the cosmos remained not only relevant, but important. There were those who believed that the world depicted by natural science did, in fact, contain lessons for humankind. More and more people accepted that human beings and their mental capacities were the result of evolutionary development and that therefore the story of human origins could inform the way humans organized their collective social and political lives. Darwin's work was not the sole reason why Victorians were increasingly coming to this conclusion. Anthropologists and archaeologists were coming to it on their own.

It was not at all sufficient to say that political and social models should base themselves on belief in a purposeless cosmos. Human society, especially in the late nineteenth century, was very purposeful. Those who drew on evolution as the foundation for recommendations about society also related to natural selection in much the same manner as the reconciling theologians. They invariably avoided or rejected strict natural selection in favor of a goal-directed evolution.

Human Origins

Although in 1850 most people accepted a relatively recent origin of the human race, there were few who were unaware of contrary sentiments. Lamarck in France, Schubert and others in Germany, and the anonymous author of the *Vestiges* in Britain had all authored evolutionary works during the first half of the century that implied the appearance of humans on the scene had taken place a very long time ago indeed. Although a minority view, these evolutionary accounts shared an important outlook that was compatible with the progressive spirit of the age—that evolution was a story of purposeful development toward greater and greater perfection.

Cultural evolutionists.   In 1857 two Germans announced the discovery in the Neander Valley the year before of the remains of a member of an ancient human race. Their claim did not find general acceptance at the time, but it did remind the public that some scholars took seriously the possibility that there had been forerunners of present-day humans.

In 1865 the British banker and naturalist John Lubbock (1834–1913), the first Baron Avebury, wrote *Pre-historic Times, as Illustrated by Ancient Remains, and the Manners and Customs of Modern Savages.* As the title suggests, Lubbock was convinced that humans had existed in an ancient state whose culture was similar to that of the primitive peoples known to exist in various parts of the world in the nineteenth century. He assumed that since prehistoric times, human culture had gradually evolved to the high point of Western civilization in which he lived, but that some humans had been left behind.

Those primitive tribes that still existed, according to Lubbock, had not kept pace because of environmental conditions that hindered their development. This meant that cultural evolutionists including Lubbock viewed uncivilized races to be humans of lower intelligence who possessed a primitive mentality. As such they represented a stage in evolution through which Europeans had once passed. Victorians, like Lubbock, assumed that white Europeans stood at the apex of evolutionary development and that other societies had achieved various stages of progress lower than their own.

Darwin on humans.   Although Darwin shared with his age the view that Victorian culture represented a superior level of evolutionary development, his outlook on why humans had diverged from other primates to become superior was unlike that of the cultural evolutionists. What they saw as a linear development due to a law of inevitable progress, Darwin regarded as the accidental result of a branching, non-linear evolutionary process. He attributed the development of the unique mental attributes of humans to the natural selection of individuals who adopted an upright posture. Intelligence came about because our ancestors stood upright. In other words, there was nothing inevitable about the appearance of humans.

Darwin avoided discussing human origins in his famous book of 1859, but the subject was taken up by others soon after its appearance. In 1871 Darwin made his own position clear in *The Descent of Man.* In it he drew on what is called sexual selection to help explain how the different races of humans had evolved. Sexual selection involved the preferences possessed by members of a species for certain traits present in the opposite sex, thereby affecting which individuals have the greatest chance of mating. Over time the effects of these preferences contributed, according to Darwin, to the emergence of racial features.

In another book the following year on emotions in humans and animals, he tried to show that animals possessed rudimentary intelligence and that they could exhibit behaviors that were similar to emotional responses in humans. He clearly believed that while humans possessed mental abilities that seemed to make them exceptions to evolution, their intellectual and emotional capabilities differed from those of other animals only in degree, not in kind.

Social Darwinism

As we have seen, Darwin's *Origin* was more successful in promoting the idea of evolution in general than natural selection as the means by which evolution had occurred. This meant that Darwin's work was invoked in support of evolution even by opponents of natural selection. A primary example of this association with Darwin by those whose message was not strictly "Darwinian" emerged in what has become known as social Darwinism. This term, which originated in the century after Darwin, refers to the assumption that our evolutionary past tells us how society should be arranged.

Herbert Spencer

Herbert Spencer's vision. The name most often linked to social Darwinism is that of the English writer and philosopher Herbert Spencer, who was mentioned earlier in connection with Henry Ward Beecher's theological utilization of evolution. Raised and educated in a family of religious and political dissenters, Spencer inherited an anti-authoritarian temperament.

Spencer defended *laissez faire* ideology, according to which economic activity should be left to run by itself without government interference. A small inheritance from his uncle came his way in 1853, enabling him to concentrate on writing. Spencer's literary works soon placed him in the public eye and brought him into contact with some of Britain's leading intellectuals.

In an anonymous essay published seven years before Darwin's *Origin,* Spencer publicly endorsed the idea of evolution. He set the theory of Lamarck, which he identified as "the development hypothesis," against the belief that the ten million species estimated to live on Earth arose as the result of "special creations." He defended the idea that diversity came via a natural law of development, even if "the impossibility of getting at a sufficiency of facts" made it unfeasible "to trace the many phases through which any existing species has passed in arriving at its present form." Evolution, in his view, was a far more rational notion than the idea of ten million special creations.

Later, when he wrote his autobiography, Spencer recalled being annoyed to realize that Darwin's *Origin* made it clear that parts of his own theory were wrong. Still, he seemed to feel that in the main his views were vindicated by Darwin's theory of evolution. This notion was no doubt confirmed in his mind when, in later editions of his book, Darwin adopted Spencer's phrase, "survival of the fittest," which Spencer had used in his *Principles of Biology* in 1864. The average British reader often came to the same conclusion. From the political and social implications he drew from his understanding of evolution, however, it becomes clear that Spencer remained more a Lamarckian than a Darwinian.

As early as 1851, well before Darwin had published, Spencer recorded the lesson he took from "that state of universal warfare maintained throughout the lower creation." He pointed out that natural predators removed individuals past their prime, and also weeded out "the sickly, the malformed, and the least fleet or powerful." His point was that human civilization represented a higher level of creation that, when perfected, would not be subject, in his word, to such "drawbacks."

But human civilization, now in the final stage of development, had not yet reached its consummation. To attain it, humanity would have to submit to the same severe and pitiless discipline that reigned in the adult animal world. (He noted that this discipline did not apply during the infancy and youth of individual organisms, when nature's principle of nurturing held sway.) Spencer did not shy away from what this meant: "The poverty of the incapable, the distresses that come upon the imprudent, the starvation of the idle, and those shoulderings aside of the weak by the strong . . . are the decrees of a large, far-seeing benevolence."

In his 1884 book, *Man Against the State*, Spencer cited these lines from his own work of 1851, noting that the lapse of a third of a century had brought him no reason to retreat from his earlier position. On the contrary, he named Darwin's notion of natural selection, which Spencer said was the chief but not the sole cause of evolution, as new evidence that strengthened his position. Spencer was dismayed, however, at how little an effect his views had enjoyed. He quoted the American writer Ralph Waldo Emerson's dismissal of such sentiments to illustrate how widespread the opposition was. "I care nothing for your natural-history arguments," Emerson wrote. "My conscience shows me that the feeble and the suffering must be helped; and if selfish people won't help them, they must be forced by law to help them."

To be fair to Spencer, it must be noted that he approved private philanthropy to help the poor as long as it was not done in such an indiscriminate way as to enable the inferior to multiply. What he opposed was the intervention of the state and he clearly invoked Darwin's name in support of his perception of human society and of his political recommendations.

Spencer originally formulated his understanding of the evolution of the organic world, including humans, in conjunction with his laissez faire convictions of open competition among individuals. Even though he acknowledged Darwin's achievement, he never abandoned the Lamarckian evolution he then defended. He needed the purposeful development that deistic Lamarckian evolution portended to guarantee that human civilization would achieve the consummation he promised his readers. Natural selection could offer no such guarantee.

The initial success of Darwin's book was to promote the general notion of the organic evolution of life from lower forms, not to persuade the British public of natural selection. Spencer exploited this growing social acceptance of biological evolution, even citing Darwin's work as new evidence. But he remained convinced that natural selection was not the most important cause of evolution and that enabled him to continue to regard evolution as a purposeful process in nature. Further, what was true in nature served as a model for humans. In the 1884 work, for example, he cited a distinguished professor who warned against interfering with nature. Spencer then added: "And if this is true of that subhuman order of Nature to which he referred, still more is it true of that order of Nature existing in the social arrangements produced by aggregated human beings."

Spencer's view that biological evolution justified the unbridled use of power to gain advantage was particularly influential in the United States, where it was put to use in support of the American sense of manifest destiny. Spencer's thought inspired diverse figures, from businessmen such as Andrew Carnegie (1835–1919) to academics such as the Yale professor William Grant Sumner (1840–1910). While they did not all agree completely with Spencer, their acceptance of the evolutionary justification for a laissez faire economic perspective helped create what should have been labeled social Lamarckism but instead misleadingly became known as social Darwinism.

The Social Response in Germany

The German physician and writer Ludwig Büchner offered a different take on the lesson Darwin's theory contained for society. Büchner articulated his position on the implications of science for society in conjunction with his many writings devoted to the popularization of natural science. We shall examine this wider venture in the next chapter. Here we examine what he had to say about Darwin and evolution.

Büchner came from a progressive middle-class German family. Although Ludwig became the best-known member of the family during the nineteenth century through his many writings on natural science, his brother Georg and sister Luise also came before the eye of the public. Georg was a gifted playwright and one of Germany's active communists before Karl Marx. Luise actively campaigned to promote education for German middle-class women at mid-century.

Büchner did not accept the version of laissez faire philosophy that Spencer helped make popular in Britain; in fact, he criticized its advocates because, he said, they were quick to denounce revolutionaries at the same time that they ignored the social conditions that produced revolution in the first place. The son of a physician, Büchner expressed a concern and sympathy for the poor and the sick that Spencer could not condone.

Where the two social theorists agreed was in their embrace of the principle of progress. When the *Origin* appeared in German translation Büchner wrote a review of Darwin's work. He acknowledged that the concept of natural selection removed certain teleological factors from evolution, but he criticized Darwin for overlooking external conditions that might bring about variations in species. Like Spencer, Büchner preferred Lamarckian evolution and for the same reason: the need to justify progress. Lamarck was for Büchner the real founder of evolution. In his view natural selection threatened the idea that there was progress in nature. "It is a great weakness and inconsistency in Darwin," he wrote, "that individual or random change . . . should be the forerunner of new species."

The fundamental point of disagreement between Büchner and Spencer came over the lesson that evolution held for humankind. Büchner did not believe that what was true in nature necessarily applied to human beings. For example, just because there was a struggle for existence in nature did not mean that the struggle would be the same for humans as it was for animals.

Büchner's position was that humans were unique products of evolution, the only product that possessed awareness of its own evolutionary past. Because of this awareness humans should now take over future development, ensuring that human values were preserved. "The farther [humans] remove themselves from the point of their animal origin and relationship," Büchner wrote in 1870, "and allow themselves

to assume the place of the power of nature, which power has been ruling them uncon-
ditionally, the more they become *human* in the genuine sense of the word."

What were the human values Büchner wanted to preserve? He wished to balance
individual freedom and social responsibility. To accomplish the former he argued,
like Spencer, that there were natural inequalities among individuals that had to be
respected. He resisted the calls of socialists and communists to eliminate the rights
of private property, urging instead that individuals should be free to amass as large
a fortune as they could acquire.

Unlike Spencer, however, Büchner did not endorse a competition conducted
with no restrictions. In his view society had a certain responsibility to supervise the
competition; in particular, the state should see that some individuals were not
favored over others. Büchner believed that, to the extent it was possible, the means
with which individuals engaged in the struggle for existence should be equalized. In
1890 he said that if, as natural science taught, we were to replace the power of
nature by the power of reason, then we have to "bring about the greatest possible
equalization of the means and conditions under which and with which every individual has to fight in his struggle for existence."

Büchner gave examples how society should superintend the struggle. Those natural
resources that were communally possessed should not be available for private owner-
ship. Büchner classified land along with air and sunshine in this category. As a result he
called for the elimination of ground rent. He also declared that society should insure
all its members equally against accident, sickness, old age, and death. Finally, in his
most controversial stance, Büchner called for the restriction (later he said elimination)
of rights of inheritance. Some individuals should not commence the struggle for existence with an advantage over others; rather, all should begin with means that were as
equal as possible. While a gifted individual was free to earn a large fortune, that person
could not give his offspring an unfair advantage by passing on to them an estate.

The different readings of the meaning of evolution for matters of social and
political organization underscore that there was no universal understanding of the
meaning natural science had for society. Individuals in the aftermath of Darwin's
achievement perceived the meaning of the results of natural science in accordance
with already existing opinions and philosophies. This has remained true from
Darwin's time to our own day.

Suggestions for Reading

Joe D. *Burchfield, Lord Kelvin and the Age of the Earth* (Chicago: University of Chicago
     Press, 1990).

Adrian Desmond, *Huxley: From Devil's Disciple to Evolution's High Priest* (New York: Perseus
     Books, 1999).

Frederick Gregory, *Scientific Materialism in Nineteenth Century Germany* (New York: Springer,
     1977).

James Moore, *The Post-Darwinian Controversies* (Cambridge: Cambridge University
     Press, 2003).

CHAPTER 20

○

Matter, Energy, and the Emerging Spirit of Realism

The success in France of the new approach to chemistry—which was centered around Antoine Lavoisier's work, during the last decades of the eighteenth century, on the nature of combustion—stimulated hopes that the study of matter and its transformations had entered a new era. Lavoisier, after all, had formally introduced a principle of conservation into the study of matter. And among those who saw themselves as his successors, it was clear that chemistry was no longer to concern itself with occult or hidden powers.

Some expressed the belief that bewildering chemical reactions would succumb to the kind of explanation that Newton had provided for the motions of the heavens. In what has been called the Newtonian dream, they envisioned that natural philosophers would uncover the laws of force that acted over the short range of matter's internal parts. They hoped that these short-range forces could be expressed mathematically and that they would provide an explanation of how and why matter interacted. The attempt to create a chemical mechanics, however, was unsuccessful, requiring chemistry to go in new directions.

The nineteenth century also gave rise to the new science of thermodynamics, which in turn introduced a new concept—energy. As the laws of energy took shape, the central importance of energy for the physical sciences in general soon became very evident. Energy considerations, in general, supported the fashioning of a depiction of natural processes in which nature was envisioned as an intricate machine whose parts interacted in straightforward cause-and-effect fashion. In spite of certain developments that were inconsistent with this conception, scientists in the second half of the century became more and more confident that their classical mechanical representations had caught nature "as it really is." In so doing, these scientists reinforced the emerging spirit of realism that characterized much of the era.

411

◎   New Directions in Understanding Matter   ◎

In spite of the failure of the Newtonian dream, natural philosophers in France and Germany found other ways to bring a quantitative dimension to the study of matter. For a long time, French chemists had explored the question of chemical affinity—why some substances entered into reactions while others did not. Since early in the eighteenth century, there were tables that listed the relative affinities of certain substances. Chemists established these first by noting that specific substances had mutual affinities, that is, they joined together to form a compound. They then observed that sometimes when a third substance was introduced, it united with one of the two substances in the compound, causing the other to be let go. This revealed the relative strength of the affinity of the substances, permitting the construction of a table that depicted the order in which substances replaced each other. The end of the eighteenth century saw the appearance of works in which chemists were beginning to specify *how much* of one substance combined with how much of another. Substances appeared, in other words, to combine in definite proportions by weight. This knowledge led to new inquiries in England about the composition of matter and why one kind of matter interacted with other kinds.

Atomic Theory Reborn

When the ancient Greek thinker Epicurus (341–270 B.C.) appealed to the motion of atoms to explain all natural phenomena, he specifically denied that the gods were in control. Everything was made of atoms, whose motion through space determined all. Not surprisingly, Western natural philosophers from the early Christian era onward tended to regard atomic theory with great suspicion, often equating its periodic appearance with atheism.

John Dalton's atomic theory.   The achievement of John Dalton (1766–1844) was to use the idea of atoms to raise a number of fruitful questions about matter. Although the debates he engaged in with other chemists of the early nineteenth century were not resolved at the time, the various hypotheses that came to the surface show us that the development of natural science sometimes depends as much on the exploration of contending ideas as it does on coming to a final resolution. The son of a Quaker weaver, Dalton is one example of the many religious dissenters who made their presence known in natural philosophy in the eighteenth and nineteenth centuries. His independent spirit and native curiosity inspired him to ask a diverse set of questions, covering subjects from meteorology to optics to chemistry. Here we are concerned with his *New System of Chemical Philosophy,* published in two parts, in 1808 and 1810.

One of the problems that first intrigued Dalton came from his work in meteorology. Why, if the atmospheric air was made up of different gases, did these gases not settle out into layers, with the heaviest gases at the bottom and the lighter ones on top? To answer his question Dalton appealed to the idea that gases were made up of atoms. But he made specific assumptions about gaseous atoms, namely that atoms existed within a larger particle he referred to as a globule. The atoms were

surrounded by a shell of the imponderable fluid
caloric, which many at the time thought to be
elemental heat (see Chapter 16). Caloric exerted
repulsive force, which diminished as the distance
from the particle increased.

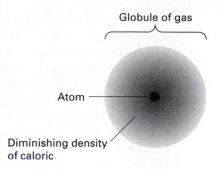

The atmosphere, which consisted of various gases,
was filled with different-sized atoms of those same
gases. Dalton reasoned that the outer caloric shells
of these different-sized particles were in contact
with each other and would tend to push each other
around in a helter-skelter fashion until some kind
of stability was reached. In other words, the globules
would not settle out in layers or clusters; rather, they would tend to remain mixed.

Dalton extended his analysis to all of what Lavoisier had defined as "elements,"
or chemically irreducible kinds of matter. That is, Dalton assumed that elements
were made of identical and unchangeable atoms that could join together to form
"compound atoms." In the process they could assume various arrangements, but
they could not be destroyed or created, just as in Lavoisier's assertion of the conservation of matter.

Because elements appeared to combine in definite proportions by weight,
Dalton inferred that they must also combine in definite proportions of numbers of
atoms. If in a given compound a certain weight of element A (which contained a
specific number of atoms of A) always combined with a particular weight of
element B (which contained a specific number of atoms of B), then there must be
a definite ratio of the number of atoms of A to that of B for the compound. Of
course he did not know how the atoms combined, whether in ratios of 1 to 1, 2 to
1, 3 to 2, or in other possible ways. The atoms of A and B were of different sizes, so
he could not know how many atoms of A or B it took to make up the amounts of
the weights that combined. He could not, in other words, determine the actual
ratio of the number of atoms of A to that of B. Faced with this difficulty, Dalton
made another assumption, one that enabled him to determine the ratio. Naturally
his answer was only as good as the assumption, but in a sense he had no other
choice if he wanted to move ahead. Dalton assumed that atoms of two elements
combined 1 to 1. If two elements, say carbon and oxygen, could combine to form
two or more *different* compounds, then Dalton assumed that one resulted from the
elements joining 1 to 1 and the others 1 to 2, 1 to 3, and so forth.

Water was the only compound of hydrogen and oxygen known at the time, so
Dalton assumed it was made up of one atom of hydrogen and one of oxygen. Given
the weights of hydrogen and oxygen that he knew combined to form water, he
determined that oxygen weighed approximately eight times the weight of hydrogen. Dalton's approach was consistent with the conclusions that others had come to
about matter combining in definite proportions; in fact, expressing it in terms of
atoms made it easier to envision.

Dalton's assumption about how atoms combine to form compounds made it
possible for him to begin establishing atomic weights. By choosing hydrogen as the

base unit with an atomic weight of 1, he could, for example, say that oxygen's atomic weight was 8. From the weights of other elements that combined, along with his assumption of how atoms joined, he determined the atomic weights of several other elements. It did occur to him that he might be oversimplifying things. He observed, for example, that he could be wrong in having just one atom of hydrogen combine with one of oxygen. It could be, after all, that two atoms of one of them combined with one of the other. If so, then the atomic weight of oxygen would either be 4 or 16, depending on whether two oxygen atoms combined with one hydrogen or two hydrogens with one oxygen. In spite of Dalton's considerable achievement, he could not make the choice with confidence.

The chemistry of gases.   Developments in the consideration of gases, first in France and then in Italy, provided a context in which chemists could extend their hypothesizing. A young man named Joseph Louis Gay-Lussac (1778–1850) was able to learn chemistry from some of France's great minds early in the nineteenth century. On the basis of his experimentation with gases, in which he measured how many volumes of one gas combined with a specific number of volumes of another, he asserted that individual gases combined in integral ratios *by volume*. His measurements gave rough approximations to exact ratios but he nevertheless believed that he was justified in his conclusion. He argued further that when the product of the combination of two gases was also a gas, its volume also bore some whole number ratio to the volumes of the combining gases. For example, one volume of nitrogen combined with three volumes of hydrogen to give two volumes of ammonia gas.

Dalton rejected Gay-Lussac's conclusions because he assumed, in his considerations of atmospheric air, that the atoms of individual elements were of different sizes and in contact with each other. When joined together, the size of the compound atom that was formed might be less than the sum of the two components, but the volume of the combined gases had to be at least greater than the volumes of either component. How could it then be that one volume of nitrogen combined with three volumes of hydrogen to give *two* volumes of ammonia vapor? Dalton distrusted Gay-Lussac's measurements, which gave whole number ratios only after being rounded off.

In 1811 the Italian physicist Amadeo Avogadro (1776–1856) depicted gases in a way that was much different from Dalton's. He did so because he based his conclusions on different assumptions. He pictured the particles of gases to be much smaller than Dalton had and, more importantly, to be widely separated from each other. This meant that the volume occupied by the gas was mostly empty space, with a minor portion of it taken up by the actual volume of the gas particles. The size of the gas particles was so insignificant that possible differences in sizes could be neglected.

Dalton's gas globules

Avogadro's conception

Dalton's and Avogadro's Depictions of Gases

1. H + O → HO

2. 2H + O → H_2O

3. H_2 + O → H_2O

4. 2H + O_2 → 2HO

5. H_2 + O_2 → 2HO

6. $2H_2$ + O_2 → $2H_2O$

Examples of Possible Combinations of Monatomic and Diatomic Gaseous Elements

Further, Avogadro conjectured that a gaseous element might be composed of one *or more* atoms of the element; that is, some gaseous elements are made of single atoms, others of two atoms joined together, others with three, and so forth. Avogadro referred to the "molecule" of gas, a term in use on the Continent that meant roughly what Dalton referred to as a compound element. But Avogadro's notion of diatomic or triatomic molecules increased the number of possible combinations of atoms of two gases that could join together to form a molecule, as is evident from the examples in the accompanying diagram for water vapor.

The obvious question was, which of the combinations shown here represented the way in which hydrogen and oxygen combined to form water vapor? Avogadro accepted Gay-Lussac's claim that gases combine by volume in whole number ratios; in particular, he agreed that two volumes of hydrogen combined with one of oxygen to give two volumes of water vapor. From the diagram it is clear that, if Gay-Lussac is to be believed, combinations 1, 3, and 5 will not work because only one volume of hydrogen is used for one of oxygen. Further, combination 2 will not work because the product is one volume of water vapor, not two, as Gay-Lussac claimed. Both 4 and 6 (and other possible combinations that are not depicted) do fulfill the requirement of two volumes of hydrogen combining with one of oxygen to give two volumes of water vapor.

Avoagadro made one more assumption, one that still bears the name "Avogadro's hypothesis." With this additional assumption he was able to draw a conclusion that would later prove to be important—that hydrogen molecules cannot be monatomic. His hypothesis was that *equal volumes of gases under the same conditions of temperature and pressure contain the same number of particles.*

If we assume that for a standard volume of gas this number of particles is x, then, because three volumes of hydrogen combined with one of nitrogen to yield two of ammonia gas, then $3x$ particles of hydrogen combine with $1x$ particles of nitrogen to give $2x$ particles of ammonia. That would mean that two particles of ammonia would contain three particles of hydrogen and one of nitrogen, or that one particle of ammonia would have one and a half particles of hydrogen and a half particle of nitrogen—an impossibility. If, however, both hydrogen and nitrogen were diatomic, then each particle of these gases would contain two atoms while those of ammonia would have four.

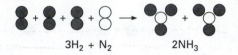

$$3H_2 + N_2 \qquad 2NH_3$$

As helpful as Avogadro's conjectures were, they were not well received when he put them forth. The most difficult notion for his contemporaries to accept was that gaseous elements, of which only a small number were known at the time, could be made up of molecules containing two or three atoms. The prevailing assumption was that similar atoms repelled each other. If this were the case, then how could two atoms exist close together in a molecule? And if, somehow, there was an as yet unknown force of attraction binding them together, why did such an attractive force not cause all the molecules of a gas to come together and cause the gas to condense?

The status of chemical atomism.   In light of these difficulties a general feeling of skepticism about atomic theory continued throughout the century. Chemists continued to extend chemical atomism by accepting some aspects of the work of Dalton, Gay-Lussac, and Avogadro while rejecting others. In particular, by 1826 the Swedish chemist Jacob Berzelius (1779–1848) had carefully coordinated the latest results in chemistry with work on the specific heat capacities of substances to construct a system of relative atomic weights that commanded attention from many.

Another achievement in chemistry, the development of a periodic table of elements, drew attention to atomic properties from a different quarter. By 1830, natural philosophers had noted the possibility of identifying patterns among elements based on their relative atomic weights. But sometimes the pattern appeared to be based as much on mysterious numerical properties as on a property of any physical significance. For example, of what value was the 1829 discovery that there were groups of elements in which the atomic weight of one element had a value equal to or close to that of the average of its two immediate neighbors?

Among later attempts to group elements was that of the Russian chemist Dmitri Mendeleev (1834–1907). In 1869 he published a book in which he arranged some sixty elements according to their increasing atomic weights. Elements that displayed resemblances in their physical and chemical properties were grouped together. As Mendeleev examined each element from the lowest atomic weight to the highest he made a new row each time an element possessed properties similar to an earlier element. This resulted in periodic columns of elements that displayed family resemblances.

As in the case with the chemical atomists early in the century, Mendeleev's results did not win universal approval. No one knew why the family resemblances occurred or whether there was any physical meaning behind them. Further, Mendeleev's data was far from perfect—there were gaps in his table where no known element existed with the atomic weight that would exhibit the expected property. And of course Mendeleev's atomic weights were based on his own system for calculating them, so his results often disagreed with the atomic weights others had assigned to individual elements.

The periodic arrangement of the elements was impressive enough, however, to encourage chemists to keep looking for family resemblances. Other results also continued to inspire confidence in atomic theory. In the latter part of the nineteenth century consistent estimates of molecular sizes emerged. These were followed by developments in the study of radioactivity and other new discoveries at the turn of the twentieth century (see Chapter 21) that established atomic theory as a generally accepted view within the scientific community.

Kinetic Theory of Gases

A development in physics around the middle of the nineteenth century also utilized the notion that gases were made up of atoms or molecules. A feature of this new approach was to envision gases as made up of molecules *in motion*. Earlier conceptions of gases for the most part saw atoms or molecules caught in a medium of caloric in which, if they moved at all, they merely vibrated. Atoms and molecules did not, that is, move freely through space. That changed with the reappearance of kinetic theory, which had first been introduced in the 1730s. Physicists began to consider the possibility that molecules might indeed move through space.

While several individuals were considering a kinetic theory of gases after 1820, the scientists whose work proved most effective in establishing it were the German physicist Rudolph Clausius (1822–1888) and the Scottish physicist James Maxwell (1831–1879).

Clausius on heat. In a paper of 1857 Clausius agreed with those who said that molecules of a gas possessed a translational motion through space. But he wanted to permit molecules to have rotational and vibrational motion as well. The pressure a gas exerted was due, he explained, to the molecules striking against and rebounding from a fixed surface, while the temperature could be correlated with the total motions of the molecules. These assertions implied certain things about the specific heats of gases, predictions that could be checked by experiment. When experiments verified that these predictions did obtain, Clausius's kinetic theory of gases became more credible.

Although there was no comparable experimental check for kinetic theory if it was extended to liquids and solids, Clausius nevertheless hypothesized that molecules in solids did not move in the solid, but possessed motion that was confined to vibration and rotation. In liquids, he said, molecules could change their position, but their motion was always affected by attractive forces from other molecules, so they did not move in straight lines. The translational motion of molecules occurred in straight lines only in gases, because they moved without being affected by other molecular forces. Molecules could, of course, collide. When they did so they bounced off each other in elastic collisions.

The statistical view of nature.   One of the results to emerge from the kinetic theory of gases was a statistical view of nature as an alternative to the strictly mechanical view of the physical world. According to the classical mechanical view, which was articulated clearly by the French physicist and philosopher Pierre Laplace early in the nineteenth century, the world is determined with rigor and precision. A mind such as God's, which at any instant could know the positions of all the matter in the universe—from the largest bodies to the lightest atoms—could calculate with certainty the past and future positions of every piece of matter. This was because God's mind was capable of comprehending all the forces of nature that act on matter.

Such a possibility is not available to humans, of course, because we do not possess such unlimited abilities. But even though Laplace was describing the ideal case, his statement brought with it an important assumption: the physical world is completely determined by the forces acting on matter. Nature is like a perfect machine whose workings govern everything that happens with absolute certainty.

In the period immediately after Laplace, natural philosophers developed a new mathematical tool—the law of errors—that did not envision an all-knowing mind and yet proved useful for analyzing experimental results. According to this law, also known as the law of normal distribution, whenever data is scattered around a mean value, it is possible to express the distribution of the data in a curve. As all students know from the practice of grading examinations on a curve, the distribution of the data resembles a bell, whose breadth represents the degree of deviation from the mean. In this way the professor can report valuable information about the performance of the class without making reference to any individual student's score.

In 1860 James Maxwell used the same general approach to analyze the speeds of the molecules in a gas. The specific curve of distribution he proposed for the molecular speeds was different from that of normal distribution, but the advantage he gained was the same: Maxwell was able to obtain valuable information about properties of gases without having to know the speeds of individual molecules. Specifically, he was able to use his approach to uncover important results about the viscosity of gases and their ability to conduct heat. Although experimental verification for Maxwell's distribution law did not come until later, his proposal soon became an accepted part of kinetic theory.

The kind of approach that was taken here marked a significant moment in the history of science. Maxwell was assuming that the apparently random motions of individual molecules nevertheless obeyed statistical regularities as a group. In other words, Maxwell claimed that important information about nature could be obtained even though he could not get at nature's inner workings in the way Laplace's all-knowing mind would. Even if those inner workings seemed to be governed by chance, the natural philosopher still had a way of investigating nature. Because Maxwell did not need to know if those inner workings actually were random or not, he did not have to entertain seriously the idea that random processes existed within the foundations of nature. The possibility that they did, however, disturbed some of his contemporaries, who envisioned nothing less than a physical world that was completely determined at all levels.

◎ Thermodynamics and the Future ◎

The 1840s was a particularly significant decade for the new science of thermo-dynamics, whose beginnings in the work of Sadi Carnot we examined in Chapter 16. The more natural philosophers considered how heat could be used to set matter into motion, the more they became convinced that heat, of all of nature's forces, was spe-cial. While heat was only one way to make matter move, for example, it seemed always to be present when any of the other forces of nature were used. Chemical explosions, electrical motors, and even mechanical impact—all of which set matter into motion—were always accompanied by the presence of heat.

At the end of the decade and on into the 1850s natural philosophers began to realize that there was something else special about heat. This second insight held implications about the future of the universe, namely, that it would one day expe-rience a "heat death." In the course of coming to this realization scientists began to make a distinction between forces, with which matter was pushed and pulled around, and a new entity—energy. The new concept would become a central fea-ture of physical science from that point forward.

Conservation of Force

The developments involved in the emergence of the idea of energy conservation are not best summarized as a story of discovery. First of all, it took some time for the concept of energy itself to be understood as something different from force. This was true even for the individuals commonly credited with introducing the idea of con-servation. Beyond that, the notion that the amount of energy in the universe always remains the same, that energy can be transformed into different forms but can neither be created nor destroyed, carried implications that took time to unravel.

It was not the case that one individual, or even several individuals separately, were able to persuade their contemporaries that energy is conserved. Of the many individuals who contributed to the subject, we shall consider only two. Historians prefer to depict this episode as a protracted struggle to understand nature that only gradually produced a consensus. It was a case of muddling through to eventual agreement, not the classic "aha!" moment of discovery.

Robert Mayer's contribution.   One of the contexts in which the idea of conser-vation arose was through a consideration of the heat in the human body. A young German physician named Julius Robert Mayer (1814–1878) began his medical career in 1840 as a doctor aboard a ship bound for the East Indies. He related that in the course of bleeding patients who were ill with a lung infection, he was sur-prised by what he called the "uncommon redness" of the venous blood. He asked himself why the blood from a vein would be lighter red—more like arterial blood—in the tropics than it was at home.

Mayer came up with the following explanation. As Lavoisier taught, animal heat resulted from the oxidation that occurred in the blood. In the hotter tropics the body produced less heat and therefore less oxidation occurred in the blood. The diminished oxidation, Mayer claimed, lessened the difference in the color of the venous and arterial blood.

Once set to thinking by this experience, Mayer began to ponder the subject of oxidation and heat further. He realized, of course, that the heat produced by oxidation in the blood performed the function of keeping the body warm. But during this voyage he also came to the conclusion that the heat produced by oxidation in the blood must also make possible the mechanical motions the body performs. Because he rejected the idea of perpetual motion, he believed that the force necessary to move the body, called motive force, could not be generated out of nothing—it had to have a source. He now came to to the insight that heat was that source, that heat must be converted into motion according to an invariable ratio. In arguing that a certain amount of heat—which Mayer and his contemporaries viewed as capable of exerting force—corresponded to a specific amount of motive force, he was asserting that heat had a mechanical equivalent.

When Mayer wrote up his ideas he cited other reasons why he thought that heat was transformed into mechanical motion. For philosophical reasons he preferred to think of forces in general as abstract causes, not as properties of matter. Because they were causes, they disappeared as the effect appeared; hence heat disappeared as mechanical motion appeared. Mayer was saying that although one force could become another force, force in general could not be destroyed.

Asserting that forces cannot be destroyed is not the same as saying that the amount of force in the universe always remains the same. Could new force be created? At first Mayer thought that God created new force as it was needed, but he later concluded that the universe ran using only the amount of force that God had originally invested in it. It should not be surprising to learn that when Mayer submitted a written exposition of his ideas they were judged to be too philosophical to merit publication as natural science.

Helmholtz's paper of 1847.   Another medical figure attempted to add to the discussion in 1847 with a paper entitled "On the Preservation of Force." Hermann von Helmholtz (1821–1894) had been part of a group of medical students in Berlin who were investigating the traditional claim that a special "vital force" was present in living things. The Berlin group was convinced that the effects caused by an allegedly vital force could be reduced to the actions of mechanical forces acting on matter.

Helmholtz considered a very general case of nature's forces. He defined two basic kinds of force at work in the cosmos: motive force and something he called tensive force. We have already met motive force, the force a mass exerts by virtue of its being in motion. The existence of matter in motion is the foundation of all change. Without it nothing happens. In one important sense, getting matter to move is the name of the game—moving matter makes possible what we know as existence itself!

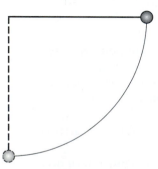

Interconversion of Motive
and Tensive Force

Tensive forces, on the other hand, were forces that were exerted but did not result in the motion of a mass. An example here would be the gravitational pull on a pendulum held in a position 90 degrees to the side. Other examples of tensive forces are a wound spring, or a heated gas exerting force on the fixed sides of a chamber. Tensive forces are important because they can become motive forces if the tension under which they exist is released—for example, if the pendulum drops, the wound spring snaps, or the heated gas causes a piston to move. And, as noted above, getting matter to move is the name of the game.

Motive forces can turn into tensive forces and vice versa. Swinging the pendulum from its vertical to horizontal position changes motive force into tensive force. If released, the tensive force becomes motive force again. When a moving a hammer collides with a nail, the nail becomes warm, turning motive force into the tensive force of heat. In a steam engine the tensive heat becomes mechanical motion.

Through a very general analysis Helmholtz concluded that the *total amount of force,* including all the motive forces and tensive forces that existed at any given moment, always remained the same. The way he expressed it was to say that the sum of the motive and tensive forces in the universe was a constant.

Two things should be observed about Helmholtz's announcement. First, he was still using the word *force,* even though he was talking about something that was different from the pushes and pulls that the word *force* usually connoted. What, then, was that something else? Helmholtz had shifted the meaning of *force* in the direction of the motion of matter on which reality rests; that is, when Helmholtz used the word *force* he did not mean just the push itself, but the ability to exert a push (or pull) *through a distance.*

Put very simply, Helmholtz was saying that in the universe there is matter that is already moving and a storehouse of tensive force that could be used to make matter move. The latter could be thought of as a capacity to produce moving matter. So what he was really saying was that there is only so much ability in the universe to make matter move through a distance. The sum total of that ability is made up of matter already moving plus the capacity that tensive forces represented to move matter though a distance.

The second observation is that once again the claim that force was conserved was regarded as too abstract to be called a scientific result. Helmholtz's paper did

Motive force ■ Tensive force

Stripes can become gray, and gray can become stripes, but the total of stripes + gray must remain the same

Motive Force + Tensive Force = Constant

not impress the editor of the scientific journal to which he sent it any more than Mayer's had. The confusion caused by using a traditional word, *force,* for this new abstract idea of force acting through a distance certainly did not help his case. Further, to what, in nature, did this sum total he wrote about correspond? The paper was judged to be too speculative and philosophical to be considered science.

The Second Law of Thermodynamics

The new ideas about thermodynamics carried implications beyond the realm of physics, challenging even some religious conceptions of the future. These implications emerged because scientists concluded that, in the long run, physical processes were not reversible—that is, they moved in a particular direction.

The challenge to Carnot's conception.   Mayer and Helmholtz agreed that heat could be *transformed into* the mechanical force exerted by mass in motion. That was different from Carnot's understanding. As emphasized in Chapter 16, Carnot did not believe that heat turned into mechanical force; rather, he thought that heat was simply a vehicle that could be used to produce motive force in a manner similar to the way water is used to turn a millwheel. Water does not become motive force— the same amount of water exists after it is used to turn the wheel as before. Just as water is conserved in this process, Carnot thought heat was conserved when used to produce motive force.

Helmholtz said that what was conserved was the total amount of force, tensive plus motive. For him, heat was only one of the forms of tensive force that could become motive force. Heat itself was not conserved.

In England another natural philosopher, James Joule (1818–1889), had also concluded, through careful experiments he conducted in the 1840s, that heat was not conserved. These experiments permitted him to calculate an actual value for the mechanical equivalent of heat. Joule had difficulty persuading his British colleagues of his view, not because he was too philosophical in presenting it to them, but because they did not believe his experiments could be precise enough to be trusted.

As midcentury approached, then, there were two opposite views in circulation concerning the use of heat to produce motive force. One (Carnot) claimed that heat was conserved in the process; the other (Mayer, Joule, Helmholtz) asserted that what was conserved was the sum total of all nature's forces and that heat itself was not conserved. In the second view heat was *transformed into* motive force in a heat engine.

Clausius's resolution.   What helped to evaluate the merits of these two views was the work of Rudolph Clausius, whose efforts on the kinetic theory of gases we met earlier. In 1850 Clausius argued that it was not a simple either/or choice between Carnot's conception and that of Mayer, Helmholtz, and Joule. He argued for aspects of both approaches. In particular, he said that those who claimed that heat was not conserved were correct. But Carnot had been right to maintain that there had to be a fall in temperature if heat were used to produce motive force.

Clausius concluded that of the total amount of heat used to produce motive force in a heat engine, some of it became the motive force and some was merely transferred from a warm body to a colder one. He was careful to point out that how much heat was turned into mechanical motion and how much was merely transferred to a colder body were strictly determined amounts. Another way of summarizing this was that not all of the total amount of heat required to operate a heat engine could become motive force.

Thomson and the dissipation of heat. Clausius's conclusion was acknowledged the following year by William Thomson in Scotland. Thomson, whose opposition to natural selection we discussed in Chapter 19, had been thinking for some time about Carnot and heat engines. But Thomson thought about real heat engines, not ideal engines. Thomson reflected on the fact that heat was lost through the sides of the chamber in a real engine. So clearly some of the heat involved in producing motive force did not get turned into motive force. It merely cooled from a higher to a lower temperature. Thomson, in other words, agreed with Clausius—only some of the heat involved actually became motive force.

Thomson focused on this heat that did not turn into motive force. He realized that if every time heat was used to produce motive force a portion of it merely cooled from a higher to a lower temperature, then Carnot had had a fundamental insight. Unless there was a drop in temperature the heat was, as Carnot had said, "useless" (no motive force could result). But what if all the heat in the universe was at the same temperature? In that case there would be no possibility of taking heat from a hot body and delivering it to a cold body, as Carnot said was required to produce motive force. If all the heat in the universe existed at one temperature, it would no longer be possible to use it to produce motive force.

As explained earlier, the presence of motive force, the force exerted by matter in motion, is necessary for change itself to occur. Without change, existence itself is impossible. Thomson began to realize that Carnot's requirement for at least one source of motive force, namely the tensive force of heat, carried ominous implications. He knew, for example, that when left to itself nature eliminates temperature differences; in fact, the unavoidable fall in temperature in heat engines was nature at work eliminating temperature differences. Thomson began to think of the long term. If nature was constantly busy eliminating temperature differences, then one day the differences would all be eliminated and all of the heat in the universe would be at one temperature. Heat, he said, was being "dissipated," by which he meant that it was gradually becoming unusable to produce motive force.

Of course, heat is not the only tensive force in the universe—there are other sources of motive force. Unfortunately, however, the other sources of motive force provide only temporary respite from the ominous scenario physicists were beginning to envision for the future of the cosmos. This is because, in transformations of one force into another, heat is a byproduct. If more and more force takes the form of heat and heat is gradually becoming unavailable to move matter, then there will ultimately come a time when all the force in the universe is in the form of tensive force of heat, and it will all be at the same temperature, unavailable to produce motive force. In Carnot's words, it will be useless. At that point nothing can happen. The universe, Helmholtz pointed out in an 1854 speech, will experience eternal death.

Energy and its laws.   In his thinking about motive force, Thomson realized what was implicit in Helmholtz's work—that he was contemplating more than just the push or pull a moving body could exert. His focus was matter in motion, so he had in mind the push being exerted *through space*. Thomson decided that a new word was needed to capture this more refined conception. He chose *energy*, a word that had been used in different contexts for some time. *Energy* came to mean the exertion of a force over a distance—that better captured the sense of matter in motion than did *force* alone.

Over the remaining decades of the century a vocabulary emerged that replaced the older language of forces. Motive force became kinetic energy, tensive force (of all kinds, including heat) became potential energy. Helmholtz's result was now summarized by saying that the total amount of kinetic plus potential energy in the universe was constant. This was dubbed the Law of the Conservation of Energy in 1853 by the Scottish physicist William Rankine (1820–1872). This result has become known as the First Law of Thermodynamics.

The insights of Thomson and Clausius, that one day all the energy in the universe will be potential heat energy that is unavailable to be transformed into kinetic energy, eventually became known as the Second Law of Thermodynamics. Clausius introduced the word *entropy* in 1865 as a measure of unavailable energy. He expressed the constant gradual increase in unavailable energy by saying that entropy change was always greater than or equal to zero. An alternative form of the Second Law has been given in terms of increasing disorder. Because it takes energy to create and maintain order, the constant increase in unavailable energy means that disorder in the universe is constantly increasing.

■ Kinetic energy   ▧ Potential energy   ■ Unavailable potential energy

As kinetic and potential energy transform into each other, the amount of unavailable potential energy increases until all the energy in the universe is the unavailable potential energy of heat

The Second Law of Thermodynamics

It took time for the implication of the Second Law to be widely accepted. For one thing, it proposed that physical processes possessed an irreversibility that ran counter to the physicists' usual conception of nature. Laplace had portrayed the universe as a stable machine that ground on eternally. Now physicists claimed that the cosmic mechanism was running down and would one day cease. They proposed a directionality to nature that seemed to be incompatible with a purely mechanical view. In the ideal setting, mechanical laws were reversible—they could be run backward as well as forward. But thermodynamics challenged mechanical reversibility by including irreversibility in the physical laws governing nature. Like the statistical view discussed earlier, here was another defection from the strictly mechanical view of nature.

◎ The Power of Classical Mechanics ◎

In spite of such challenging amendments as the Second Law and statistical laws, the classical mechanical worldview continued to exert a dominant influence over physical science. The conception of nature as a reliable machinery meshed well with the ideas of cause and effect that were the basis of explanation in natural science. As one German scientist of the time put it, "Mechanics and logic are identical." The common view was that scientific explanation consisted of identifying the material parts that made up nature's machinery and then uncovering the causal laws that governed their motion. The scientist's task was to explain the world as matter in motion.

The Success of Mechanical Models

Within the field of physics the conception of nature as a machine continued to have impressive success. In 1860 James Maxwell added to his achievement in kinetic theory by tackling a problem that bewildered many. And he did so by taking seriously the prospect of visualizing nature's inner workings by making a mechanical model of them.

The problem was to explain why electricity and magnetism were so interdependent. As we saw in Chapter 16, following the discovery of electromagnetism in 1820, French and British natural philosophers took different approaches when trying to explain why electrical and magnetic forces occurred together. André Marie Ampère concluded that magnetism was merely the force exerted by moving electricity, comparable to the force a static electrical charge was known to exert. Michael Faraday visualized curved lines of magnetic force acting around a wire. He then discovered a way to produce electrical current by cutting the lines—a changing magnetic field produced an electric field. But while both of these approaches contributed to discovering how to manipulate the connection between electricity and magnetism, a theoretical understanding of that intimate relationship was still lacking.

Maxwell suggested that just as a changing magnetic field produced an electric field, so too a changing electric field produced a magnetic field. This implied that electricity and magnetism were propagated in waves, because a changing field of one kind produced a changing field of the other, which then produced a changing

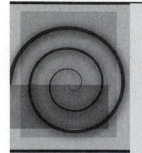

The NATURE of SCIENCE

How Seriously Should We Take Models?

James Maxwell enjoyed a great deal of success as a result of visualizing electromagnetism in a rather homespun mechanical model. Yet the question still arises as to whether he believed there really was an ether with vortices and tiny spheres that pervaded all space. Indeed, French physicists reacted negatively to the British penchant to visualize nature in mechanical models. One wrote: "We thought we were entering the tranquil and neatly ordered abode of reason, but we find ourselves in a factory." And Maxwell himself was reluctant to commit to the ontological reality of vortices and spheres.

But if such notions were only convenient fictions, then how do we explain why they so successfully captured the behavior of electromagnetism, even making possible an extension of our knowledge to include the existence of electromagnetic radiation and its relationship to light? It is not hard to understand why some wanted to believe that with Maxwell's model nature had been described realistically.

We meet here again the larger questions about whether the theories of natural science describe nature "as it really is," whether in appearing to capture one aspect of reality they must be viewed as partial truths and not to be mistaken for the whole, or whether they represent more about the way our minds work than they do about nature's truth.

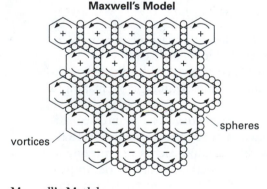

Maxwell's Model

field of the first, and so on. Electricity and magnetism, in other words, accompanied each other—they constituted waves of electromagnetism. But waves of what? Like others of his day, Maxwell imagined that space was filled with ether, an imponderable elastic medium that existed everywhere, including in the space occupied by gross matter. So there would be ether in a current-carrying wire.

Maxwell set out to create a model that would help him understand the ether waves. He imagined that there were vortices or eddies in the ether. In addition there were tiny spheres that rolled between the vortices. He let the circular-acting magnetic forces be represented by the rotating vortices, while the tiny spheres stood for the electrical charges. From his model it was literally possible to see why electricity and magnetism occurred together because the turning vortices involved turning the spheres and vice versa.

Maxwell described the motions in his model mathematically in a series of expressions, reduced by his successors to four, now known as Maxwell's equations. The equations were, not surprisingly, sinusoidal; that is, they were wave equations. This suggested that electrical current passed through a wire as waves in the ether. But because the ether was everywhere, it hinted at the possibility that electromagnetic waves could be transmitted through space, appearing as real current when they occurred in a wire or some other conducting substance. Further, because waves occur at different frequencies, there was the possibility that a variety of different kinds of electromagnetic radiation existed, each with its own characteristic wavelength. Maxwell himself never looked for such waves, but not many years passed before others demonstrated their existence.

One additional discovery reinforced the credibility of Maxwell's model even more. From quantities contained in his equations Maxwell calculated the speed electromagnetic waves would travel. It turned out to be equal to the speed a French physicist had recently determined for light! Maxwell made the deduction himself. "We can scarcely avoid the inference," he wrote, "that light consists in the transverse undulations of the same medium, which is the cause of magnetic and electric phenomena." Electricity, magnetism, and light all resulted from waves in the ether. Maxwell's model had been fruitful indeed!

The Flowering of Scientific Materialism

Successful mechanical explanations such as those of Maxwell, plus discoveries in several other realms of science, imparted considerable power and prestige to the image of the scientist in the society of the mid-nineteenth century. Even if the average person could not follow explanations about electricity and magnetism or kinetic theory, it was impossible to overlook the public affirmation that natural scientists were uncovering more and more of nature's secrets. The place of the natural scientist in society was becoming more prominent. Scientists began to replace clergymen as the recognized authorities where nature's truth was concerned.

Popularizers of natural science took advantage of the opportunity to interpret the meaning of the latest scientific developments for the public. Among these popularizers were those who wanted to exploit the successes of classical mechanical explanation by creating a philosophical outlook based on it. Known as scientific materialists, these spokesmen for science flourished in Germany during the decades after midcentury and contributed in their own way to the rise of a new secular outlook.

The basic message of the scientific materialists was that reality was *only* matter in motion. Put another way, they opposed the claim that reality could be immaterial, that it was totally separated from matter. These materialists argued, for example, that there was no such thing as an immaterial soul. Clearly, such a message raised the ire of people of faith, especially the educated representatives of institutional religion.

The first materialistic bombshell came from the pen of Karl Vogt (1817–1895), a zoologist at the University of Giessen. In his earliest writings Vogt made clear his commitment to a materialistic outlook in an outlandish declaration that immediately caught the attention of readers far and wide. To underscore that in his view, even thoughts were nothing but material secretions, he wrote in 1846 that "thoughts stand in the same relation to the brain as gall does to the liver or urine to the kidneys."

His extreme position here was matched by an equally radical political position. Vogt came from a liberal German family with a history of radicalism—his uncle and his father had run afoul of the authorities because of political activities. Vogt preached that in nature and in political relations there was "no other development than through revolution." Historian Hermann Misteli has summarized his message to be: "Doing natural science means making revolution."

Another of the scientific materialists focused more on the implications of the latest developments for the social order of the day. In 1850 Jakob Moleschott (1822–1893), a Dutch physiologist educated in Germany, wrote a book entitled *The Theory of Nutrition: For the People*. In this work, Moleschott declared that because life was nothing more than the exchange of one kind of matter for another, then diet was everything. Consistent with claims of scientific materialism, Moleschott pointed out that the kind of food taken in determined the very thought and character of individuals.

In addition to his study of natural science, Moleschott had been influenced by a famous German theologian named Ludwig Feuerbach (1804–1872). A decade earlier, Feuerbach had published a scandalous book on religion in which he had argued that the doctrines of Christianity were nothing more than projections of human needs into the heavens. Indeed, the Christian conception of God was merely a human being who was infinitely powerful, just, and loving. Like the materialists who drew much inspiration from him, Feuerbach had urged that it was time for humankind to face up to reality and admit the material basis for their idealistic conceptions.

Feuerbach reviewed Moleschott's *The Theory of Nutrition* in his now famous essay called "Natural Science and the Revolution." He endorsed both Moleschott's message about the materialistic basis for life and mind and the idea, which Moleschott had promoted, that science naturally implied revolution. In the course of his review he coined a phrase that is still used today: "You are what you eat."

Of the three natural philosophers later said to constitute an "unholy trinity" of scientific materialists, the most well known in the decades after 1850 was Ludwig Büchner, whose ideas about Darwin we encountered in Chapter 19. In 1855 Büchner wrote a book that eventually went through twenty-one editions and was translated from German into seventeen foreign languages. In English it was known under the title *Force and Matter*. The basic message of the book was captured in the slogan, "No force without matter, no matter without force." In Büchner's view the only reality there was had to be material or a property of matter.

The model for scientific explanation, according to Büchner, was mechanical interaction. He spoke of "the identity of the laws of thought with the mechanical laws of external nature," equating mechanism with causality itself. Büchner believed that because of this identity the human mind was capable of a complete explanation of nature. All that was needed was knowledge of what he called the "fineness" of matter. Büchner conveyed the impression that natural science had uncovered the bald truth that only the material world was real, that it was a machine whose movements ground on following the laws of deterministic causal relation, and that the only solace left to humankind was to become aware of itself as a tiny cog in the universal machine.

Scientific materialism prompted many responses from the ranks of those who not only categorically rejected such a deterministic view of things, but also vehemently denied that natural science implied such a world. What helped the scientific materialists to plant seeds of doubt in the minds of many were the successes of mechanical explanation, not all of which occurred in physics.

◎ Medicine Becomes Scientific ◎

While physicians had pursued knowledge of the anatomy and physiology of the human body since antiquity, it was only at the beginning of the nineteenth century that medicine began breaking away in earnest from its association with more practical arts. What medicine clearly lacked was a theoretical foundation comparable to that of other disciplines of natural philosophy. Newtonian science enjoyed great prestige in part because by the end of the eighteenth century it dominated over the older rival approaches of Descartes and Leibniz. There was simply no comparable consensus that united physicians; indeed, medicine at the end of the eighteenth century found itself ridiculed because it had no agreed focus at all.

Experimental Medicine

The situation changed after the middle of the century as medicine found a foundation in the realism of natural science. The most eloquent plea for physicians to emulate the methods of natural science came in 1865 in a highly influential work, *An Introduction to the Study of Experimental Medicine*, by a French physiologist and professor of medicine named Claude Bernard (1813–1878). Bernard vehemently opposed the idea that the study of physiology, because it dealt with living things, had to seek laws that were flexible and elastic, not certain and deterministic.

Bernard certainly acknowledged that there was something special about living beings. He is famous for having introduced the idea of an organism's "inner environment"—a part of living things that remains constant even though it is constantly interacting with the organism's external environs. The organism, in other words, possessed control mechanisms that adjusted exchanges with its surroundings to keep the physical state and chemical composition of the internal environment constant. His focus, however, remained on the physical constitution of this special context.

Many in Bernard's day insisted that living things could not be portrayed by the determinism characteristic of the laws of mechanics. As a result they demanded that physiology and medicine could not be content with using the methods of physics and chemistry. Medicine, in this view, was not a science but an art. The physician made up for the indeterminism that medicine involved by drawing on the wisdom of the artist, which could only be gained through experience.

Bernard, however, dubbed this view, which he conceded was even held by some great practicing physicians, a false opinion. He insisted that medicine could and should become a science, and that it had to give up the idea that factors governing living things were so complex that they escaped natural law. He believed that the progress of what he called the physico-chemical sciences had been so substantial that medicine was "turning toward its permanent scientific path." To do so, medicine had to acknowledge all medical conditions resulted from causes that could be found. Laws, according to Bernard, existed only in a context of determinism and "without laws there can be no science."

What Bernard particularly emphasized was the role of experiment in natural science and therefore its potential usefulness in medicine. Experimental physiology, he said, was the most scientific part of medicine, and in studying it young physicians would acquire the scientific habits they would later carry into the two fundamental aspects of medical practice—pathology, determining the nature and cause of disease, and therapeutics, the treatment of disease.

According to Bernard, physicians in the past had been content merely to observe and gather information. The time had now come when medical practitioners needed to go beyond observation by learning the rules of experimentation. That meant physicians could no longer remain passive observers. They had to take the initiative by acting on matter, analyzing its properties, and bringing about new results that nature had not brought about on its own. In so doing, the medical experimenter became "an inventor of phenomena, a real foreman of creation." Only by taking the reins could the physician be certain that medical intervention was responsible for a particular cure, rather than nature itself.

Bernard spent much of his book examining the rules and nature of proper experimentation. He gave examples from his work in physiology, always with an eye to establishing that he was doing the same thing that the physicist and chemist did in conducting experiments. And behind this claim lay a larger one: physiology and medicine depended on the same deterministic worldview of the physical scientist. "In a word," he wrote, "determinism, which insists on identity of effect bound up with identity of cause, is an axiom of science which can no more be transgressed in the sciences of life than in the sciences of inorganic matter."

The Germ Theory of Disease

A second step toward the creation of scientific medicine occurred with the rise of the germ theory of disease, the claim that sickness resulted from the presence of microorganisms living in the body. With this development physicians could point to a physical cause that made the diagnosis far more testable and precise than it had been before. Of course some physicians resisted the notion that disease and its treatment could be pinned down to a single cause. Not surprisingly, it took time for the germ theory to overcome resistance, but by the century's end its reputation had been strengthened by triumphs over several specific medical conditions.

While numerous individuals contributed to the establishment of the germ theory, Louis Pasteur (1822–1895) in France and Robert Koch (1843–1910) in Germany stood out. Pasteur, a chemist, brought his training to bear on questions about fermentation that eventually produced dramatic results when applied to the study of the diseases of anthrax and rabies. Koch followed his degree in medicine with six months of study in chemistry. He too investigated anthrax, but was most celebrated for his work on tuberculosis. We focus here on the work of Pasteur.

As a young professor of chemistry, Pasteur worked with crystals, especially those of organic origin that rotated polarized light when it was passed through them. Pasteur came to associate this ability of substances to rotate polarized light, known as the optical activity of the substance, with life. Because many of the products of fermentation were optically active, Pasteur concluded that fermentation was due to the presence of living germs from brewer's yeast.

Pasteur's position was controversial because the most famous German chemist of the day, Justus Liebig (1803–1873), ridiculed it. Liebig was a leading figure in the emerging science of organic chemistry. His work on agricultural and nutritional chemistry was widely read, especially in Germany and England, and his results added a new dimension to emerging investigations of the chemical basis of life. Liebig placed his authority behind the assertion that fermentation was not a vital process, as the young Frenchman Pasteur claimed, but a purely chemical one. By 1860 Pasteur was able to show that fermentation did involve a biological process, although after his death chemists acknowledged that chemical processes were present as well. Pasteur also went on to demonstrate in dramatic fashion that the living organisms of ferments were not, as some asserted, spontaneously generated.

Pasteur and others applied what they had learned about germs to create a theory about how vaccines worked. In Pasteur's theory, vaccinating for a disease such as smallpox involved introducing weakened germs, which produced only mild symptoms in the host, but, more importantly, consumed nutriments present in the body that were required by smallpox germs. Later, if virulent germs came into the body, there would be no nutriments for them and they would die. The body would therefore be immune to smallpox.

Using this theory, he developed vaccines for anthrax and later for rabies by learning how to weaken the germs he believed caused these conditions. In addition to being a brilliant scientist, Pasteur was an excellent publicist for science. In 1881, for example, he publicly inoculated half the sheep in a flock, then later injected all with a culture of virulent anthrax. He then announced that only the inoculated sheep would survive and that the result would be known in two days. When his prediction came true, his fame rose. When he obtained even more dramatic results in celebrated cases of rabies, his stature became legendary.

The development of germ theory by Pasteur, Koch, and others was the kind of work that came to the attention of the public quickly. It communicated the message that the understanding of medicine could be furthered by careful laboratory research, that if physicians adopted the techniques and approaches of the scientist, they could find out what really caused disease.

◎ An Age of Realism ◎

As we have seen in this chapter, scientists made remarkable strides in the nineteenth century in matter theory, in thermodynamics and the rise of energy physics, in the mechanical modeling of nature, and in the emergence of scientific medicine. The successes in each of these areas all contributed to the perception that scientists

Courbet's *The Stone Breakers*

were getting to the bottom of things, that nature's secrets were giving way to the careful, systematic, and methodical probing of natural science. They also reinforced the growing sense in some quarters that, if one were realistic about it, the assumptions and methods so successful in physical science should serve as a model for other areas of human inquiry as well.

The central feature of explanation in physical science involved the identification of physical cause and effect, captured most commonly in the notion of mechanical interaction. What came with this was the sense that nature was like a machine— regular, predictable, and determined, something whose causes were reliable and could be known. If in the past people had thought of nature as fickle, unpredictable, and filled with imaginary things, now they knew that was not how nature *really* was.

Historians have referred to the second half of the nineteenth century as an era of realism. They see in the art, literature, and politics of the time the attitude that humankind should face up to things as they really are, not as people want or imagine them to be. The realistic school in painting, seen in Gustave Courbet's 1850 portrait *The Stone Breakers,* showed life in all its dreariness and toil rather than dwelling on the romantic ideals that earlier artists had cherished. Novels such as *Madame Bovary* (1857), by Gustave Flaubert, depicted the frustration and dissatisfaction of a woman's life unfulfilled. The *Realpolitik* of leaders such as Otto von Bismarck, who engineered wars throughout the 1860s to bring about a united Germany, appealed not to the hopes and dreams of the people, but, as he put it, to "blood and iron." And following the collapse of idealistic hopes for a new European order after the failure of the revolutions of 1848, Karl Marx sat down in the British Library to discover the material basis of inevitable social change, describing his "scientific socialism" in his book of 1859, *Das Kapital.*

As we have seen in this chapter, natural science also reflected the wider cultural sense of realism. Beyond the physical sciences, the increasing acknowledgment of an evolutionary development of life contributed in its own way to the perception among some that science had arrived at what had really happened in the past, as opposed to the traditional religious accounts.

We have also noted, however, that at the heart of the physical sciences lay new alternative conceptions that did not mesh nicely with the idea of a machinelike cosmos that was self-sufficient, eternal, and completely deterministic. The implications of the Second Law of Thermodynamics and the statistical view of nature did not appear as challenges to the mechanical world picture at the time they appeared. They would, however, contribute to later developments that made clear to scientists that they had in fact not yet captured nature "as it really was."

Suggestions for Reading

Gerald Geison, *The Private Science of Louis Pasteur* (Princeton: Princeton University Press, 1996).

Frederick Gregory, *Scientific Materialism in Nineteenth Century Germany* (New York: Springer, 1977).

Crosbie Smith, *The Science of Energy* (Chicago: University of Chicago Press, 1999).

CHAPTER 21

---◎---

The Erosion of Realism

If in the latter decades of the nineteenth century there was trouble ahead for the comfortable assumptions that had led physical scientists to discoveries about kinetic theory and the conservation of energy, few were aware of it. In fact, physicists in particular were gaining increased respect because of major societal developments in the second half of the nineteenth century that were evident to everyone.

In the midst of the celebration and optimism that physicists were enjoying, they encountered some baffling new problems. These problems challenged a common assumption, one frequently responsible for their optimism—that their explanations were descriptions of nature as it really was. This did not cause undue concern among late-nineteenth-century scientists, however; rather, they provided ample and even welcome challenges to creativity. The problems had to do with the nature of the ether, which had been investigated so authoritatively by James Maxwell in his 1873 *Treatise on Electricity and Magnetism*.

As it turned out, attempts to clarify what Maxwell uncovered eventually led to consequences that shook the very foundations of physics. The path to these results took place over an extended period, running from the last decades of the nineteenth century to well into the twentieth.

◎ The Changing Structure of Order ◎

Like other human achievements, those in science reflect the character of the era in which they emerge. It is not coincidental that during this same period society at large was being subjected to other developments that would disrupt Europe's equilibrium. New economic and political realities made their appearance, as did new inventions that soon became part of the modern age.

The Challenges of Economic and Political Change

Those born in Europe in the middle of the nineteenth century certainly felt that they were living at a time when the human race was finally coming into the modern age, and doing so at a frenetic pace. "The most salient characteristic of life in this latter portion of the nineteenth century," wrote the English essayist and former businessman W. R. Greg (1809–1881) in 1875, "is its SPEED." Greg conceded that life was exciting, but he noted that there was simply no time for leisure or reflection. Brimming with newfound confidence and a strong belief in progress, people were too busy changing the world.

No doubt the outlook of realism that dominated the decades immediately after 1850 contributed to this confidence. And here, as we saw in Chapter 20, the new visibility of natural science in society, due to its impressive and sometimes even outlandish achievements, played an important role. Many assumed that scientists had finally figured out how nature worked and where humankind fit into the larger picture of the cosmos. Armed with a sense of empowerment, they focused on using it to their advantage.

Reinforcing the primacy of economic and industrial expansion that was underway in various countries of Europe was an awareness of the changing landscape. In France and Germany, for example, new railroads crisscrossed the countryside as these nations strove to open new agricultural markets. Construction of tunnels, bridges, and viaducts was taking place everywhere. Not only was the historic countryside changing, but cities felt the impact as well. Paris was rebuilt to transform its reputation as one of Europe's dirtiest capitals to one of its most modern, with broad streets and grand parks. In downtown London a new subway system was in place by the 1880s.

Progress was in the air politically as well. In Britain a new reform bill passed in Parliament in 1867 and doubled the size of the electorate, accelerating the role of the industrial and manufacturing middle class in public affairs. Of course, progress meant different things to different people. Among the working class the message of Karl Marx was beginning to take hold. Workers feared they were being left behind by the modernization happening all around them. They were still denied a role in the political arena, forcing them to gravitate more and more to new political parties calling for the end of class rule and raising the specter of revolution from below that would haunt established powers in the years to come.

By far the most visible political change, however, came with the achievement of the unification of the Italian states in 1860 and the German states in 1870. Particularly in the case of Germany, there was now a major new player in European politics, a counterweight to the traditional powers of Austria, France, and England. Germans had long been denied political power because their influence was divided among numerous small states. But Prussia, through military engagements with Austria (1866) and then France (1870), was able to unite the German states under its leadership into a new German Reich.

Having vanquished France in battle, the new German Reich was determined to flex its muscles on the international scene. Germany decided to wage a different kind of war with Britain, namely, to challenge British industrial and naval supremacy through economic production and shipbuilding. Germany also joined other European powers in their imperialistic ventures into Africa to show that it could also compete on a global stage. Efforts to maintain a balance of power in the increasingly nationalistic atmosphere of the early twentieth century proved progressively more difficult. Older structures of power were not handling the strain well and Europeans lived with a concern that something decisive was about to occur.

The general peace that had reigned in Europe for a long time was finally shattered with the outbreak of war in 1914. With it came crashing down a naive presumption made by many in turn-of-the-century Europe—that the progress of the human race, resting in part on the truth about nature and humanity's place in it that science had finally discovered, had brought humankind to a level of civilization in which differences would no longer be settled by violence.

Science and Modernization

Natural science became much more visible in Western society in the latter half of the nineteenth century than it had been in earlier times. Among the applications of physical science that made their way into the lives of citizens were those from the rapidly expanding science of electricity. These developments, however, did not automatically mean that the physicists who developed the theory behind the applications would rise to prominence more than the businessmen who brought the applications to market.

Electrical science.   The most visible confirmation of the impact of physics came in the applications that were being made of electrical science. Electrical lights produced rays of what some called a mysterious new kind of sun. Lights became a regular feature of the scientific exhibitions that were becoming increasingly popular, and they even made their way into theatrical productions. By the end of the century they were lighting streets in the cities.

Other electrical inventions continued to dazzle the imagination. At exhibitions visitors saw powerful new electromagnets—the one at the Crystal Palace Exhibition of 1851 in England could support one ton of weight. In 1879, at the Berlin International Exhibition, over 100,000 passengers took a ride on an electric locomotive around a 300-meter track.

The most impressive invention of all, however, was the telegraph. Queen Victoria summed up the feelings of many about the few seconds it took to receive a response to the message transmitted from the Crystal Palace to Manchester and other northern cities: "Truly marvelous!" By 1858, after many setbacks, a telegraph cable was laid across the Atlantic Ocean, linking Europe and the New World. It functioned only for a short time before a rupture in the line made the cable go dead, but knowing that it could be done inspired subsequent attempts, until success was achieved in the late 1860s. It was not long before inventors took the next step. In 1876 the great attraction of the Centennial Exhibition in Philadelphia was Alexander Graham Bell's new telephone, which transmitted not only electrical signals, but a human voice!

The physicists' struggle for cultural authority. The average person was duly impressed by the amazing electrical inventions in lighting and communications that were revolutionizing life. These were aspects of life that could touch nearly everyone. Normal citizens, however, knew nothing of the theoretical developments in electrical science that preceded the widespread marketing of the inventions. Their perception was fashioned by the practical devices demonstrated in exhibits, products of some enterprising businessman or entrepreneur.

In fact, it took a special kind of talent to make use of the theoretical understanding of electricity to create electrical devices that found a wide practical application in society. The interests of the physicists who through study and experimentation were uncovering new dimensions of electricity, and those of practical electricians who brought results to the broader society, were not always identi-

Cover of *Electrical Plant:* The Triumph of the Practical Man over the Theorist

cal. In fact, in the waning decades of the nineteenth century both groups laid claim to filling the most important role for society.

The division between these two groups was especially visible in England in the late nineteenth century. When one of Maxwell's followers, the English physicist Oliver Lodge (1851–1940), conducted experiments that led to a new and more complete understanding of lightning, one that ran against that of the manufacturers of lightning rods, it elicited a vehement response that was captured by the cover of a magazine called *Electrical Plant* for December 1888. The cartoon depicted a prostrate Lodge squirming beneath the boot of the triumphant practical man. Physicists realized that they were going to have to assert themselves if they were to convince the wider public that their esoteric knowledge made them not only superior to inventors, but, in the long run, more valuable to society.

By the end of the century physicists were largely successful in carving out a new cultural authority for themselves. Among the reasons for this was the further development of Maxwell's theory of electromagnetism, which led to yet another new electrical invention—the radio. Along with it came the theoretical possibility of other forms of electromagnetism. Who knew what properties they might have!

Electricity goes wireless. Maxwell himself did little to address the concerns others might have about his theory. For example, he did not try to produce ether waves. While their existence was suggested by the mathematical equations he had constructed, his interest in them was merely formal. Of course if his theory was ever to be confirmed, some kind of experimental verification that light was due to electromagnetic waves was necessary. But throughout most of the 1870s no one looked for actual electromagnetic waves or attempted to produce them with an ordinary electrical apparatus. In fact, when ways to exhibit them were found it was in connection with experiments whose primary purpose was to investigate something else.

As an adherent of Maxwell's claims, Oliver Lodge felt keenly the need to find confirmation of Maxwell's theory. In the course of his experiments he figured out how to control the surges of electrical current he had been working with, even to the point of stabilizing them into waves that traveled along a wire. This he did by reflecting them in such a manner that he created a standing wave recognizable by points on the wire that glowed. He worked up an elaborate experiment in 1888 by which to convince spectators of the existence of electromagnetic waves in a wire. Before he could do the experiment at a scientific meeting, however, an even better demonstration of electromagnetic waves was given in Germany by a young researcher with a very different motivation from Lodge.

Heinrich Hertz (1857–1894) was a student of Hermann von Helmholtz, one of the architects of the new laws of energy that had become so central to physics. Helmholtz wanted nothing to do with an ether. He thought of electrical force as something exerted at a distance, not as waves in an all-pervasive ether. To Helmholtz and other critics of Maxwell, there was nothing real about ether waves.

Hertz, then, was not out to confirm Maxwell's ideas in the work he was doing on the electrical effects of nonconducting substances such as air on conductors. He built up opposite electrical charges on two small spheres that were positioned close together until a spark jumped across the gap between the spheres. The air, normally a nonconductor of electricity, became a conductor that permitted the charges to oscillate back and forth until electrical equilibrium between the spheres was achieved.

In the course of these investigations Hertz noticed that sparks also occurred in a secondary conductor off to the side of the apparatus. As he concentrated his attention on these side effects, he discovered that they involved oscillations at the same frequency as those between the small spheres. The oscillations between the spheres, which had a frequency lower than that of visible light, *were radiating out into space* and were being received by the secondary conductor.

Now Hertz studied the radiation, devising equipment by which he could manipulate it. He figured out how to reflect it, refract it, polarize it, and display interference—all the phenomena that visible light was known to exhibit. Maxwell

Spark jumps gap between spheres

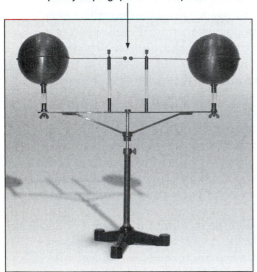

Apparatus Used in Hertz's Experiment

had been right—light is electromagnetic radiation. The only difference between light and Hertz's electromagnetic radiation was the frequency. He had demonstrated the existence of the electromagnetic waves in space that were predicted by Maxwell's theory, based as it was on the all-pervasive ether! Hertz became convinced that his work confirmed Maxwell's theory.

Lodge and others in Britain concurred with Hertz's assessment and immediately began to draw out the implications of the achievement. William Crookes (1832–1919) noted in 1892 that never before had humankind wondered if undulations in the ether whose wavelength was longer than those of light might "constantly be at work all around us." Now, he continued, we know that there is an almost infinite range of wavelengths to explore. And wavelengths other than those of visible light did not share light's limitations. Electrical waves penetrated fog and even solid walls, opening up the possibility of telegraphy without wires. Three years later Guglielmo Marconi (1874–1937) sent wireless signals over a distance of a mile and a half at his father's country estate in Italy. The radio was here to stay.

Modernizing research: the laboratory. The practice of physical science in the latter half of the nineteenth century also felt the effects of modernization. Particularly noticeable was the growth of the laboratory as the locus of research, a new phenomenon that made its appearance in the nineteenth century and culminated in the establishment of major research laboratories in Germany and in England near the end of the century.

We noted in Chapter 14 that an aspect of the reforms of the German university in the early nineteenth century involved the merging of the research function of the academy investigator with the teaching role of the university professor to create a new expectation that the professor would both create new knowledge and pass on what was known. In the physical sciences it took some time for this new expectation to produce collaborative research programs carried out in a separate space designated for that purpose. Once this trend began, however, it grew throughout Europe and North America until by the end of the century it was regarded as a necessity. "The physical laboratory system has now become quite universal," remarked William Thomson in 1885. "No university can now live unless it has a well-equipped laboratory."

The practice of involving students in experimental work appeared in Germany at Göttingen in the 1830s. Göttingen had been a leader in fostering the merging of teaching and research among German universities since the eighteenth century and now, under the physicist Wilhelm Weber (1804–1891), it took the lead once again in establishing a physics laboratory. Other German universities soon followed suit. By 1870 a textbook of laboratory procedure appeared in Germany that described measurement techniques and contained relevant tables needed in laboratory work.

By the 1880s the sentiment began to grow in some quarters that it was in the interest of a nation to establish separate institutes for scientific research where teaching was not part of the scientist's duties. Werner von Siemens (1816–1892) was a somewhat unexpected defender of scientific research because he had not been able to acquire the education he had aspired to as the fourth in a family of fourteen children in Germany. After secondary school he enlisted in the army, where, in his spare time, he studied the subjects that fascinated him—chemistry and physics. He followed his talent for inventing, first as an avocation and later full time, eventually amassing a fortune in the new electrical industry. But, having had to depend on the greater learning of others in the subjects he continued to regard as his real interest, he observed firsthand the importance of scientific research for industrial development.

Siemens echoed calls for a state institute for research that had been circulating almost since unification had been achieved in 1870. He even offered to provide the funds to establish such a venture. Eventually, in 1887, the German government agreed, and a new imperial institute for research in physics, the Physikalisch-Technische Reichsanstalt, was created in Berlin with Germany's senior scientist, the recently ennobled Hermann von Helmholtz, as its director. By then, Helmholtz had become almost an icon of German science. His appointment, and the creation of a lavishly state-supported research institute for physics, was a clear mark of the elevated status that physicists had achieved in German society by the end of the nineteenth century.

England had long possessed a celebrated institution, The Royal Institution, where research could be pursued, although its primary goal was to promote natural science through public lectures and demonstrations and to apply what was learned to practical purposes. But it had no tradition of training students. Among the first to encourage students to assist in his research experiments was William Thomson in Scotland, whose contributions to natural science we have met in several contexts in earlier chapters. As a young new professor in the late 1840s, Thomson so successfully integrated students in experimental work that within a few years his university provided him with separate laboratory space for the purpose.

Some universities were more difficult to persuade. At Cambridge, where the tradition in natural philosophy went back to Isaac Newton himself, a committee urged that developments in electricity, magnetism, and heat called for the establishment of a professorship in experimental physics, complete with a laboratory and lecture room. Because of the low state of university finances, there was major opposition to this suggestion until William Cavendish, chancellor of the university and himself a graduate, offered to fund the proposal.

The Cavendish laboratory, which opened its doors in 1874, became home to a series of brilliant leaders and outstanding achievements. First to assume the role of Cavendish professor was James Maxwell, whose early death in 1879 forced the university to find a replacement. In John William Strutt (1842–1919), a physicist better known as Lord Rayleigh, the Cavendish found a scientist who had already acquired a stellar reputation and who proved to be a worthy successor to Maxwell. Following Lord Rayleigh's relatively short stint was the thirty-four-year tenure of J. J. Thomson (1856–1940), under whose leadership the number of students increased rapidly. Because all three British physicists were at the center of developments in physics in the late nineteenth and early twentieth centuries, they assured the Cavendish a primary role as well.

◎ The Enigma of the Ether ◎

The support given to Maxwell's theory of electromagnetism by Hertz's detection of electromagnetic waves in the ether was a welcome development to its defenders. For some time physicists had been aware that the ether was a strange entity indeed, so strange that on occasion it strained credulity. Perhaps it was merely a useful hypothetical entity, not something that actually existed. Maxwell himself had noted that the wave theory of light had encountered "much opposition, directed not against its failure to explain the phenomenon, but against its assumption of a medium in which light is propagated."

There were aspects of the ether that were downright bewildering. For example, transverse waves, the kind light was supposed to consist of, could only be transmitted in a medium that offered some resistance, so that the medium would return to its original shape after it had been twisted. This was not generally true of liquids and gases, so the ether must be a solid. Further, the speed of electromagnetic waves was known to vary with the square root of the medium's elasticity divided by its density. Light was known to travel at an incredibly fast speed, which meant that the medium—the ether—had to be highly elastic and extremely rarefied. But how could the ether be such a highly elastic, extremely rarefied solid if things moving through it encountered no resistance whatever? And these were not the only conundrums involving the ether that baffled physicists in the 1880s.

In spite of the enigmatic nature of the ether and the challenges and puzzles that it produced as the century drew to a close, there was an even more basic question about the behavior of the ether that contained startling implications. Were the laws of electromagnetism like other laws of physics or were they in some sense exceptional? As we shall see, this is the question that led the young Albert Einstein to introduce his theory of special relativity in 1905. Einstein's theory was one of the factors contributing to a breakdown of the outlook of realism that had characterized the late nineteenth century.

Measuring the Ether Wind

Shortly before he died in 1879 Maxwell was in communication with a budding young American naval astronomer about the question of the motion of the Earth through the ether. It would not be possible to measure how fast the Earth traveled through the ether, Maxwell wrote, because its speed compared to the speed of light was just too small to be a noticeable factor in any set of measurements that attempted to compare light's speed in the ether to light's speed on the Earth moving through the ether.

There were reasons why Maxwell and others wanted to show that the Earth's motion affected the behavior of light, the main one being that it would provide experimental evidence for the ether's existence. But even without experimental evidence, the prospect that the Earth was at rest with respect to the ether seemed, on the face of things, ridiculous. Other celestial bodies moved with respect to the Earth, so if the Earth were at rest with respect to the ether, then all the other bodies in the heavens must be moving in relation to it. Why would the Earth alone, of all the bodies in the universe, be the only one not moving with respect to the ether? Had not Copernicus taught us that the Earth was not the center of things?

Another young navy man, Albert Michelson (1852–1931), an instructor at the U.S. Naval Academy in Annapolis, Maryland, found Maxwell's comment about the impossibility of detecting the Earth's motion through the ether interesting. For over a year he had been working on an experiment to improve earlier techniques used to measure the speed of light. He had succeeded in impressing members of the American scientific community with his new approach to the problem and had published an abstract of his experiment in the spring of 1878. In 1879 he was involved in refining the experiment to make the measurement even more precise than the improved value he had already obtained.

Michelson knew firsthand what the challenges were to measuring light's speed and did not agree with Maxwell that the Earth's velocity through the ether was too small to affect the value obtained. Michelson thought he might be able not only to determine how fast the Earth moved through the ether, but, assuming that the ether was at rest with respect to the stars, perhaps he could even find out how fast our solar system was moving through the ether. The heady prospects exhilarated him.

Michelson and the ether.   In the fall of 1880 Michelson obtained a leave of absence from the Naval Academy so that he and his young family could go to Germany, where he would work and study with Helmholtz at the University of Berlin. Michelson's idea was first to demonstrate that there was a difference between the speed of a beam of light traveling in one direction compared to the speed of a beam traveling in a perpendicular direction. If one of the directions were the same as the direction the Earth moved through the ether as it traveled around the sun, then the speed of the beam in that direction would be boosted by the Earth's speed and its travel through the ether would be at a different speed from the other beam. He envisioned the beams being reflected so they would both complete a round trip whose different durations could be measured. As he explained it later to his children, "Two beams of light, like two swimmers, race against each other, one struggling upstream and back, while the other, covering the same distance, just crosses the river and returns. The second swimmer will always win, if there is any current in the river."

To see that Michelson was correct about which beam would complete the round trip first, consider the diagram here, which depicts Michelson's two swimmers, each swimming at 5 feet/second (ft/sec). Swimmer 1 starts at A

Michelson's Swimmers

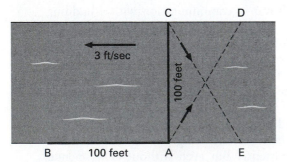

Swimmer 1: Swims 5 ft/sec from A to B and back to A
Swimmer 2: Swims 5 ft/sec from A toward D,
            back from C toward E

and swims with the stream, flowing at 3 ft/sec, to B. His speed is therefore 8 ft/sec, requiring 100/8 or 12.5 seconds for the trip. Coming back from B to A he swims against the stream, so his speed is only 2 ft/sec. This trip from B to A takes 50 seconds. The entire round trip has taken 62.5 seconds.

Because of the current, swimmer 2 must swim toward point D if she is to arrive at point C. Because ADC is a 3-4-5 right triangle, for every 5 feet she swims toward D she is carried 3 feet downstream, meaning that she has moved toward the opposite shore at the rate of 4 ft/sec. To reach point C, therefore, takes 25 seconds. On her return trip she swims toward point E, taking another 25 seconds to return to point A. The whole trip has taken her 50 seconds, 12.5 seconds faster than the trip of swimmer 1.

Michelson reasoned that if he thought of the ether as the water and the current flow as the Earth's motion, then the time taken for light to go from point A to point B and back would be longer than that taken by light going the same round trip distance in a perpendicular direction. He also reasoned that if two beams of light left point A at the same time, when their waves returned and combined at point A they would mix in what is known as an interference pattern. But with the fantastic speed at which light travels, how could he possibly be sure the light beams left at precisely the same time? Further, the experiment demanded such precision that any vibration at all, even stamping on the ground 100 feet away from the apparatus, affected the interference pattern. How would he be able to tell that a pattern was caused by the light's different transit times and not by the limitations of his equipment?

Michelson addressed both problems ingeniously. To guarantee that the light beams left at the same time he used one beam, which he then split into two directions. And to eliminate the question of what was causing the particular interference pattern he decided to look for a *change* in the pattern when the paths of the beams were switched.

A diagram of what his apparatus did is pictured here. A beam of light originates at S and is directed toward A. There it encounters a half-silvered mirror, which is a mirror that reflects some light but also lets

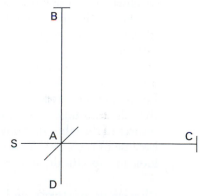

Michelson's Light Experiment

some light through. This splits the beam into two beams, one of which is reflected to B, the other of which goes through the mirror to C. At B and C there are mirrors that reflect the light back toward A. Some of the light from B passes through the half-silvered mirror at A, where it joins with light reflected from C and goes to point D. There, the interference pattern caused by the recombination of the light is observed. Now the paths are rotated 90 degrees to see if there is a change in the pattern.

Michelson completed the experiment in 1881 in Germany and announced that no shift in the interference pattern could be detected. The only conclusion he could reach was that there was no "current," that is, the Earth must be at rest with respect to the ether. He appealed to the theory of the British physicist George Stokes, who had asserted that the ether inside material objects was carried along with the objects. The Earth carried ether inside it and the ether immediately around it through space, somewhat like it drags our atmosphere with it through space. If this was so, thought Michelson, when we measure the disturbances in the ether responsible for light, it makes no difference what direction the light waves travel through the ether because it is at rest, and one direction is the equivalent of another.

Six years later, in 1887, Michelson repeated the experiment he had done in Germany. This time he had a collaborator named Edward Morley (1838–1923), a chemist from Western Reserve University in Cleveland, the same city in which Michelson had taken up an appointment at the newly founded Case School of Applied Science. The team introduced two improvements over the earlier arrangement that made the experiment more effective and impressive. By introducing fourteen additional mirrors that reflected the light back and forth several times they were able to increase the distance the light traveled, which increased the sensitivity of the experiment by a factor of ten. It was now designed to detect a speed of the Earth of as little as 2 miles/second (mi/sec), well below the Earth's orbital speed of 20 mi/sec or, if they took readings both with and against the Earth's speed, the 40 mi/sec difference. The second improvement was to mount the apparatus on a huge stone slab, which was then floated on mercury. This both stabilized the instrument and permitted it to be rotated smoothly, so that the interference pattern could be observed through diverse angles.

Once again they could detect no change in the interference pattern, no matter at which orientation they positioned the apparatus. They were now driven more forcefully than ever to the conclusion that the Earth was at rest with respect to the ether. When physicists devised means to discredit the idea that the ether was dragged along with the Earth, that seemed to leave them with the prospect that the Earth, and the Earth alone of all bodies in the universe, was at rest with respect to the ether. So unsettling was the conclusion that only the Earth was at rest with respect to the ether that physicists had to address it. It is tempting to conclude that because of these problems physicists experienced a loss of confidence in their outlook and specifically in the ether. Such, however, was not the case.

Physics at century's end.   One possible response to the Michelson-Morley experiment was simply to discount it as flawed in some way. That, however, seemed unlikely. In the 1890s two physicists independently suggested that perhaps objects contracted in the direction of their motion through the ether, making the path shorter by just the right amount to keep the time for the two trips the same. Although this so-called contraction hypothesis appeared rather extreme at first glance, it actually was based on the reasonable assumption that forces acting between the molecules of objects behaved enough like electromagnetic forces that motion through the ether affected them, too.

In the larger sphere of physics the Michelson-Morley experiment did not cause the general crisis that some historians have assumed it must have. Historian of science Jed Buchwald has pointed out that the main preoccupation of physicists in the last quarter of the century had to do with questions not closely tied to issues associated with the effects of motion through the ether. In comparison to Hertz's electromagnetic waves, for example, the Michelson-Morley experiment of 1887 was of marginal concern.

Nor did that experiment appear to cast doubt on the ether's existence. Writing two years after the second test of the ether wind in 1889, the American physicist Henry Rowland (1848–1901) said that "the luminiferous ether is, today, a much more important factor in science than the air we breathe." And Oliver Lodge in 1892 noted that people who had not kept up with physics might be surprised to learn of the intimate way physicists spoke of the ether and the assurance they had when experimenting on it. "They may be inclined to imagine," he continued, "it is still a hypothetical medium whose existence is a matter of opinion. Such is not the case."

In fact, as some physicists took stock of how far physics had come, they exhibited a general confidence not only that they were on the right track, but that they were catching glimpses of the light at the end of nature's tunnel. In 1887 a former physics professor and soon to be president of the American Association of Science, Thomas C. Mendenhall (1841–1921), declared that it was now safer than ever to say what was possible and what was impossible. Just as the next five hundred years would not add to the stock of geographical knowledge anything comparable to what had been learned since the fourteenth century, so the next hundred years was not likely to duplicate the nineteenth century where "great, original, and far-reaching discoveries" in electricity were concerned.

Michelson himself commented in 1894 that it appeared likely that most of the grand underlying principles had been firmly established and that now it was a matter of applying them. He quoted an unnamed "eminent physicist" to have said that "the future truths of physical science are to be looked for in the sixth place of decimals," as if all that was left to do was mopping-up work. The sentiments of Michelson and Mendenhall proved to be misplaced, as "great, original, and far-reaching discoveries" in physics were about to be made.

Einstein and Electrodynamics

There is no more recognizable name in the history of science than that of Albert Einstein (1879–1955). As an adolescent he had been drawn to natural science through books given him by a friend of the family. One of these sources, a series of books on popular science written with the young reader in mind, explored all kinds of scientific topics meant to captivate the imagination. In one series of essays, for example, the author took the reader on a tour into space, observing that were they to travel by horse, or even by one of the new locomotives, the trip would take forever. He suggested that they travel on a telegraphic signal.

Whether or not these essays gave the young Einstein the idea of riding on an electromagnetic signal or not, it is clear that Einstein's later famous thought experiment, in which he rode on a beam of light, proved central to his considerations of Maxwell's theory of electromagnetism. By the time he set down his ideas in a formal physics paper in 1905, he had been thinking about the problem for a long time.

Albert Einstein in 1900, at Age 21

It quickly became clear in this 1905 paper that Einstein saw something in Maxwell's theory that others did not. The ether was everywhere in space, encompassing countless astronomical systems and, through its waves, bringing light from those systems to Earth. This implied that the ether defined a single frame of reference that was spread throughout the universe, in which light traveled at speed c. That did not appear odd to most.

But Einstein thought about the result Galileo had come to more than three centuries earlier. Galileo had rejected Aristotle's claim that "all motion requires a mover" by claiming that there was *one* kind of motion that did not require a mover—uniform motion. That kind of motion, said Galileo, would, if left to itself, continue forever. Unless something caused it to change, uniform motion was like rest—it was a state of being that just persisted. In his defense of Copernicus, Galileo had declared that this was why we do not feel the motion of the Earth. Because the Earth is moving uniformly, it is as if the Earth were at rest. One way of generalizing Galileo's new insight was to say that the laws of physics are the same for all observers in uniform motion. As long as an observer is moving at a uniform speed, be that speed 0 or any other value, that observer detects the same laws of physics as any other observer moving uniformly.

Einstein realized that this had special implications for light. It implied that all observers in uniform motion should obtain c for the speed of light. Why? Because, if all observers in uniform motion should obtain the same laws of physics, then everyone, everywhere, in uniform motion—regardless of how fast that uniform motion was—should obtain the law Maxwell did that said c was the speed of light. That was the speed for electromagnetic waves that had emerged from Maxwell's examination of the ether, which was everywhere in the universe. It was a consideration of the consequences of Maxwell's theory, then, that led Einstein to this conclusion, announced in his paper of 1905. Once he had realized this, the Michelson-Morley experiment served as experimental confirmation of an expected result. In his paper, in fact, Einstein referred to "the unsuccessful attempts to discover any motion of the earth relative to the medium of light" as evidence that all of the laws of physics were the same for all observers in uniform motion.

Einstein went on to spell out what this new realization entailed. If two observers moving uniformly at different speeds both measured the speed of light to be the value required by Maxwell's equations, c, that could only be true if space and time were different for the two observers. Since $v = d/t$, velocity (v) will be constant if distance and time change simultaneously. If, for example, we wish to hold $v = 4$ ft/sec, we can do that by going through 8 feet in 2 seconds, or through 12 feet in 3 seconds, or in an infinite number of other combinations of d and t. Because d is a measure of space, and t of time, if one observer experiences different units of space and time from another, the speed of light could be the same for them both. Each observer would then obtain the same laws of physics governing the space/time relationships in their frame of reference as every other observer in uniform motion. What came to be known as the theory of special relativity was logically entailed in Maxwell's equations, provided that one accepted Galileo's claim about the laws of physics being the same for all observers in uniform motion.

Naturally, the idea that space and time were different for observers in different reference frames led to the desire to compare the experiences of the different observers. Because the speed of light tied two reference frames together, it was possible to determine what the space and time dimensions of one frame of reference would be compared to another if one knew the speed at which they moved relative to each other. In his thought experiment about riding on a beam of light, Einstein had realized that the observer riding the beam of light would see time stop in the outside world. He imagined, for example, that a beam of light was made up of an infinite number of instants and that he was riding on just one instant. Then he would see the world only with the information available to that instant—the world would look as if it were frozen in place. If that were so, then the closer his reference frame approached the speed of light, the longer time and space would stretch out to keep light's speed constant at c.

Such strange and wonderful results coming from the heart of physics could not help but capture the imagination of the age. Precisely what Mendenhall said would not happen—that there would be no more "great, original, and far-reaching discoveries" in electricity—had happened. If some scientists figured they knew what the world was really like and that it was just a matter of refining their view, Einstein's result showed that the old, naive realism was beginning to crumble. In his new scheme the vaunted ether simply vanished. It had served to define the one privileged frame of reference with respect to which light traveled at velocity c. But no longer were there privileged reference frames. Light went the speed c with respect to all reference frames. Confidence in the classical world picture would continue to erode with other developments in physics.

◎ Unrealistic Radiation ◎

Whether or not scientists realized it, Einstein's challenge to nineteenth-century physics concerning the ether contained implications that the scientific view of the world was undergoing change. But no one, least of all Einstein himself, felt that the latest theories of physics undermined nature's rationality. The new ideas were admittedly counterintuitive, giving support to those who were claiming that it no longer was obvious to assert that the theories of physical science could necessarily be understood as straightforward depictions of real entities in nature.

A development that was parallel to this story about the fate of the ether made the same point as the new century dawned. It had to do with experimental explorations of electricity that led to new knowledge about electromagnetic radiation and about the very nature of energy itself.

Strange Rays

In the second half of the nineteenth century, physicists conducted experiments that fundamentally challenged the integrity of the atom. The word *atom* was taken from a Greek word meaning indivisible and, by the nineteenth century, had come to mean the irreducible constituent of every element. Two developments having to do with the different contexts in which physicists encountered invisible rays established that the atom was not indivisible but contained subatomic parts.

The discoveries of the electron and x-rays.   As early as 1838 Faraday had experimented with electrical discharges through a tube that had been partially evacuated. He arranged electrodes at each end of a tube so that he could send current through the tube. When he did so he noticed a glow on the negative electrode, called the cathode, next to which was a dark space. Beyond the dark space a glow reappeared inside the tube and extended all the way to the anode, or positive electrode, at the other end of the tube.

Techniques for creating partial vacuums improved after midcentury, making more and more observations possible. One important discovery was that the glass of the tube glowed with fluorescence and that an object placed between the cathode and the glowing glass could block this glow. It was only natural to assume that invisible rays emanating from the cathode were causing the glow in the glass. Further, experimenters showed that a magnetic field could deflect the rays and that the properties of what were being called "cathode rays" were independent of the material of the cathode.

By the time Maxwell died in 1879 physicists had learned how to vary the shape of the cathode and to use magnetic fields to uncover two more properties of cathode rays. They could, when focused, be used to heat up thin foil and they could turn a delicate paddle wheel. Cathode rays, in other words, conveyed energy that could be transformed into heat and the motion of matter.

Two models of cathode rays emerged. In one, suggested by the English physicist William Crookes (1832–1919), the rays were what he called "a torrent of molecules" in 1879. In the other model, defended by Hertz and other German physicists who saw problems with Crookes's particle stream idea, cathode rays were thought to be an unusual form of electromagnetic waves. Hertz, for example, conducted experiments that, he thought, demonstrated that cathode rays themselves carried no charge.

The French physicist Jean Perrin (1870–1942) contended in 1895 that Hertz was incorrect in his claim that cathode rays carried no electrical charge. In experiments conducted for his doctoral dissertation he argued persuasively that cathode rays were negatively charged. This result opened the way for J. J. Thomson to postulate that cathode rays were made of subatomic particles that were constituents of all atoms.

Thomson knew about experiments showing the penetrating ability of cathode rays through up to half an inch of air. He conjectured in 1897 that if cathode rays were made of particles, they must be a great deal smaller than the molecules of air. Further, he knew that cathode rays exhibited the same properties regardless of the nature of any residual gas in the tube or the metal of the cathode. All this led him to conclude that cathode rays were made up of subatomic particles that were constituents of the atoms of all elements. Through a series of experiments Thomson was able to determine the ratio of the charge to the mass of these elementary particles, a result that was soon reached through different means by other experimenters. The particles became known as electrons, and they have remained ever since that time one of the irreducible parts of matter.

Around this same time in Germany a physicist named Wilhelm Röntgen (1845–1923), who was also working with cathode rays, noticed something odd. A piece of cardboard in his laboratory that was coated with a substance that could fluoresce was glowing. The room was darkened, although a cathode ray tube experiment was underway not far from the cardboard. With his attention drawn to this unusual phenomenon, Röntgen carried out experiments in 1895 to isolate the rays causing the fluorescent glow. Clearly they were different from those physicists had been working with so far because they obviously had penetrated much farther through air than the half inch previously known. He soon found that these rays, which he dubbed x-rays, could penetrate through a variety of materials, including human flesh (though less so through bones). An additional difference was that, try as he might, he could not deflect the rays with a magnet.

Having established that x-rays were different from cathode rays, Röntgen could only conjecture what they were. He was quite sure that they were not particles like cathode rays, but rather that they were waves. He suggested that they might be a new form of ultraviolet light, because they produced similar chemical effects, or possibly electromagnetic waves that were propagated like sound—as opposed to the normal electromagnetic waves that move like water waves. Before long, however, his assumption that x-rays were waves was shown to be correct. The new rays were electromagnetic waves with a wavelength that was even shorter than ultraviolet light.

The emergence of radioactivity.   In January of 1896 a pamphlet written by Röntgen about his discovery was the subject of discussion in the Paris Academy of Sciences. Among the listeners was a professor of physics from the Museum of Natural History, Henri Becquerel (1852–1908). He was familiar with the phenomenon of fluorescence and was intrigued by Röntgen's claim that x-rays were responsible for the fluorescing glass in the cathode ray tube. He undertook experiments to determine whether fluorescence that did not involve a cathode ray tube also produced Röntgen's x-rays.

Becquerel knew that crystals of a complicated compound that contained potassium, uranium, oxygen, and sulfur fluoresced when ultraviolet light was shined on it. But how could he determine whether x-rays accompanied the fluorescence?

Becquerel decided to produce the fluorescence by exposing the crystals to sunlight (which contains ultraviolet radiation) and at the same time to place the crystals on a photographic plate that was wrapped in heavy black paper to shield it from the sun's rays. If x-rays were present in the fluorescing compound they would penetrate through the paper and expose the plate with an outline of the crystal. The experiment worked, and Becquerel initially concluded that he had produced x-rays without using a cathode ray tube, and that they were, in fact, a part of all fluorescence.

Bad weather soon forced Becquerel to change his mind. When he tried to repeat an experiment of this type, the sky tuned cloudy and Becquerel decided to postpone things until bright sunshine returned. He placed the compound, the photographic plates, and the black paper in a drawer for a few days. For some reason, when he later took the plates out of the drawer, he developed them and, to his astonishment, noticed that they had been exposed far more completely in the darkness of the drawer than plates from the earlier experiment with the crystals in the sunlight! Apparently, the crystals did not have to fluoresce to produce rays.

Becquerel tried other compounds, some of which produced rays in darkness while others did not. He quickly determined that only those compounds containing uranium, whether or not they were fluorescent, had this unexpected effect on the photographic plates. After a few months he got hold of some uranium metal and found that its rays were more intense than any compound he had used. These rays were clearly not x-rays—they were able to penetrate substances, but they did not have the ability to reveal bones beneath the skin.

Attention soon focused on the heavy elements of the periodic table. Within two years of Becquerel's discovery, Marie Curie (1867–1934) and her husband, Pierre Curie (1859–1906), identified two new elements, polonium and radium, that produced rays similar to those of uranium. After the turn of the century even more elements were discovered to be "radioactive," as the new term characterized them. Marie Curie conducted pioneering experiments in the new subject, winning the Nobel Prize for her work in radioactivity in 1911. What she and others had opened up was a whole new field that attracted the attention of scientists everywhere. From this point, one discovery after another emerged: radioactivity involved the transmutation of one element into another, sometimes unknown, element; an element could lose its radioactivity over time; rays were of different kinds; radioactivity clearly involved a change inside an atom that also affected its chemical properties. For the next three decades scientists would devote themselves to sorting out the mysteries that were coming from the inside of the atom, which no longer could be considered the ultimate particle of matter, as it clearly possessed internal parts.

An Enigma of Electromagnetic Radiation

Although the world of classical physics was challenged around the turn of the century by the new discoveries of radioactivity, x-rays, and special relativity, it was a familiar problem having to do with electromagnetic radiation that eventually gave rise to what was potentially the most revolutionary change in perspective of all—quantum theory.

Electromagnetic radiation produced by heating.   Everyone knew that as the temperature of a body was raised it radiated heat. First it simply became warm, then the radiation appeared as a dull red glow. As the temperature continued to climb, it became brighter red and, as more colors of the spectrum became involved, eventually it might even take on a white-hot radiance. Physicists knew that increasing the temperature still higher produced radiation beyond the visible range.

A number of physicists at the end of the nineteenth century were doing experiments to determine how the amount of energy given off at various wavelengths varied with temperature. One way of doing this was to measure the amount of energy that was radiated if they held the temperature constant. They knew that, regardless of the substance, all glowing solids and liquids radiate light with the same color if they are at the same temperature. They found that for a given temperature there would be one wavelength at which the radiation would be the most intense, even though radiations at other wavelengths were present. A physicist named Wilhelm Wien (1864–1928) discovered a law that related this peak wavelength to temperature, so that by knowing the dominant color of light from a star, for example, the temperature of the star could be calculated.

Physicists wanted more. They wanted to see if they could find a more general law, one in which temperature was not held constant. They wanted to heat a substance from a low temperature to a higher one and see how the amount of energy that was radiated changed. That would tell them how much energy was produced by radiation at *any* given temperature. Here, however, the substance they heated made a difference because most substances emit radiation when heated only at certain wavelengths that are peculiar to that substance. They needed something independent of substance that would give all possible wavelengths.

When most objects receive radiation of different wavelengths, they reflect a substantial portion of it, but some—carbon, for example—absorb almost all radiation and reflect only a small percentage. By the same token carbon, when heated, emits radiation at all the wavelengths it absorbs. In their experiments physicists used substances like carbon to find how radiation fluctuated with temperature. When they tried to explain *why* the radiation pattern was as it was, however, they imagined an ideal body that would absorb radiation at all wavelengths, reflecting none (therefore being perfectly black). It was a body that also would, when heated, emit radiation at all wavelengths. They called such an ideal entity a blackbody. From their attempts to explain blackbody radiation, a revolution in physics would eventually take place.

The earliest beginnings of the quantum revolution.   No one suspected, least of all the physicist at the center of the development that would revolutionize physics, that such ominous implications were involved in the explanation of blackbody radiation. To the young German physicist Max Planck (1858–1947) it was a matter of coming to a mathematical expression that captured existing data on radiation produced by heating. He was not thinking of the physical implications of the explanation he created.

Planck was aware that two other physicists had come up with separate equations that, over a certain range of wavelengths, expressed a general relationship between radiation energy and wavelength. One equation did a pretty good job for all but long wavelengths, the other covered the long wavelengths but went awry with the short. Planck was able to figure out a way to combine the best of these two formulas into a new one that worked for every temperature. He announced the new formula in October of 1900 at a scientific meeting in Berlin. He had found the right formula, but he had not yet explained why it worked. He would not be satisfied until he derived his formula from an understanding of what caused the radiation in the first place. In attempting to do so, Planck unwittingly precipitated a new conception of energy itself.

In conjunction with his understanding of electromagnetic radiation from the work of Maxwell and Hertz, Planck assumed that an electric charge that was vibrating (a changing electric field) would generate a changing magnetic field, which in turn would generate a changing electric field, which would produce a changing magnetic field, and so forth. The result, according to classical theory, would be an electromagnetic wave.

So Planck assumed that in the walls of the blackbody there were vibrating electric charges, which he called resonators, that vibrated at different frequencies. The electron was a very new such electric charge and it may have been that he thought of it as his vibrating resonator. His idea was that as heat was added to the blackbody, it caused the resonators to vibrate at their different frequencies, thus radiating energy by emitting electromagnetic waves. Now he needed to show that the amount of energy for a given temperature and frequency that was given by his formula was consistent with this idea. He would have to calculate the amount of energy of the different resonators and see if it matched what his formula gave for the different frequencies.

To do this calculation Planck employed a technique common in mathematics and familiar to anyone who has taken calculus. To calculate the area under a curved line a common procedure is to divide up the area into small rectangles. By calculating the area in the individual rectangles and then by counting up the total, it is possible to give an approximation of the area under the curve. To get an exact measure for the area under the curve the mathematician uses a technique known as integration that increases the number of rectangles by making them thinner and thinner, then identifies what their sum would be if their width went to zero.

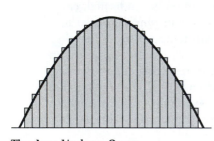

The Area Under a Curve

Planck started to do something like this for the total energy radiated by each resonator. He assumed that the total energy at a given frequency could be divided into equal pieces whose total would then give him an approximation of the radiation energy of each resonator. What he found, however, was that the results he got by breaking up the energy in this fashion and adding them up matched his formula just as they were. He did not, in other words, have to take the final step of letting the little pieces of energy shrink all the way to zero and get the sum by integration.

Planck presented these conclusions in 1901. He was gratified that he had been able to give a mathematical description of his resonator model that matched the experimental data available. The business of not taking the final step was unusual, but at least he had a mathematical solution to the problem. He did not try to think of the physical implications of this step beyond saying that in his model you had to think of the energy coming in pieces. For each frequency there was a smallest piece of energy, and the total energy of the resonator with that frequency would be some multiple number of these pieces added together. Planck called these little pieces energy quanta.

Planck included one more implication of his model that gave additional information about the pieces of energy. As noted, resonators each vibrated at their own frequency. Planck said that the size of the piece, the quantum of energy, was proportional to the frequency ($E \propto f$). That is, resonators that vibrated at high frequencies radiated energy in bigger pieces than those at lower frequencies did. Planck was even able to calculate the constant of proportionality so that the exact size of the energy pieces could be given for different frequencies. He found the number to be, not surprisingly, very small, making the pieces of energy very small. It has become known as Planck's constant and is given the symbol h. Its value (without units) is 6.626068×10^{-34} or .00000000000000000000000000000006626068. The size of energy quanta, then, is given by the equation $E = hf$.

Advantages of Planck's Model of Blackbody Radiation

There were two existing problems that Planck's approach addressed, even though he had not crafted his solution specifically to deal with them. One came from the very area in which he was working, while the other was a continuing challenge in electrical theory.

The ultraviolet catastrophe. Planck looked on his result as a mathematical solution to the problem of blackbody radiation, as did everyone else. There was, however, one conceptual advantage of looking at things the way Planck did that quickly became obvious. Planck had first found his formula by combining two existing formulas, one that worked for all but the long-wave radiation, the other only for the long-wave region. The latter formula, however, contained an unacceptable implication, namely, that the amount of radiation in the ultraviolet or short-wave region of the electromagnetic spectrum would be infinite. This was known from experiment not to be the case, so clearly the formula was only useful in the long-wave range. This implication of the formula was called the "ultraviolet catastrophe."

Planck's resonator model provided a way to explain why there was no ultraviolet catastrophe. Because $E = hf$, at very high frequencies (or very short wavelengths as in ultraviolet radiation), the size of the energy piece was large—so large, in fact, that many of the pieces would not be radiated. Most of the radiation—the wavelength peak—occurred at more moderate frequencies and wavelengths, just as the formula had predicted. So by quantizing energy Planck's model provided an explanation of a lingering puzzle.

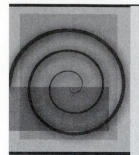

The NATURE of SCIENCE

Is Light a Particle?

Einstein's light quanta may have spoken to the mysteries of the photo-electric effect, but that did not mean that physicists, including especially Planck, were ready to accept the idea that light was a particle of energy. As we saw in Chapter 16, Newton's conception of light as a stream of particles was displaced in the early nineteenth century by the wave theory of light. That understanding of light had been confirmed in numerous ways since, not the least of which was by Maxwell's achievement. If light was a wave, as everyone knew it was, then it could not be a particle.

Einstein himself had called his use of light quanta "a heuristic viewpoint," by which he meant an assertion from which facts of observation could be produced. He had not said that light quanta existed; rather, he explained that monochromatic radiation behaved "as if it consisted of independent energy quanta of magnitude *hf.*" Much later, in the early 1920s, an experiment conducted by the American physicist Arthur Holly Compton convinced scientists of the existence of light particles, thereafter called photons. In the interim, physicists such as Einstein did what scientists occasionally have to do—they get by with language that conditions reality without conceding that it is either an accurate description of reality or that it has no real meaning whatever.

The photoelectric effect. Four years later, in 1905, another development occurred that brought renewed attention to Planck's model. This was another example of how an old problem found an explanation in Planck's idea of energy quanta. Physicists had known that it was possible to generate a current by shining light on certain metals, a phenomenon known as the photoelectric effect. Somehow, the energy in light was able to excite the electrons in the metal atoms sufficiently to enable them to escape the metal and create a current.

According to classical theory, however, there were two aspects of producing electrical current in this way that made no sense. First, because light was made of electromagnetic waves, it would take some time for them to impart sufficient energy to an electron, assuming the electron could accumulate it, to cause it to break free of the metal. This was because the energy of a light wave was spread over the entire wave, so an electron could receive only a small part of its total energy. But this was not what happened in experience. Electrons started coming off as soon as the light was shone on the metal surface.

And there was also a second problem. For some mysterious reason the color of the light was very important. Colored light near the blue end of the visible spectrum was fine, but not at the red end. If the light shone on the metal was too red, no current resulted. But both blue and red light were waves, so why should the length of the wave matter?

In 1905 Albert Einstein published a paper in which he provided answers to both questions by applying the idea of Planck's energy quanta to light. If the energy communicated by light was thought of not as being spread over waves, but as concentrated in Planck's little packets, then they could impart all their energy to an electron and the current would commence as soon as the light hit the metal. Further, the size of the packet was bigger for blue light, which had a higher frequency than red ($E = hf$). The packets of red light were not sufficiently large to eject electrons, while the blue ones were. Planck's energy quanta explained both mysteries.

As we shall see in a later chapter, it took some time before physicists realized that there was something fundamentally important about the notion that the radiation and absorption of energy occurred not continuously, but in discrete quanta. Nevertheless, Einstein's use of the idea in his treatment of the photoelectric effect added to the other unsettling developments we have examined in this chapter that were eroding the old confidence in scientific explanations as real descriptions of nature.

Suggestions for Reading

P. M. Harman, *Energy, Force, and Matter: The Conceptual Development of Nineteenth-Century Physics* (Cambridge: Cambridge University Press, 2005).

Gerald Holton and Stephen G. Brush, *Physics, the Human Adventure* (New Brunswick, NJ: Rutgers University Press, 2001).

Iwan Rhys Morus, *When Physics Became King* (Chicago: University of Chicago Press, 2005).

Robert D. Purrington, *Physics in the Nineteenth Century* (New Brunswick, NJ: Rutgers University Press, 1997).

CHAPTER 22

―――――◎―――――

The Changing Contours of Biology

During the sixty or so years of the nineteenth century in which evolution dominated much of the discussion of the science of living things, other developments in biology were also underway. As scientists sought a greater understanding of plant and animal organisms and as improved microscopes became available, new approaches emerged. Increased magnification led naturally to a focus on the material structure of organic tissue as the foundation for explanations of growth and disease in organisms, and that in turn emphasized explanations that involved physical and chemical processes.

The new trend of explaining biological processes through the interaction of material forces, however, ran counter to a traditional outlook inherited from earlier in the century. It had been assumed that the science of biology would be based on laws that were unique to living things, that biological relationships were not reducible to the laws of physics and chemistry. Living things, for example, were thought to possess a special vital force that was not present in inorganic matter. This vital force was responsible for directing the physical processes involved in the complicated stages of growth in the embryo.

The clash between traditional "vitalists" and their opponents in the nineteenth century, the "mechanists," over how biological structure and process were to be understood, appeared to run parallel to the opposition between purposeful and nonpurposeful views of evolution. As we shall see in this chapter, the issue of purpose in nature was so fundamental that it continued to be debated throughout the century as it related to the topics of evolution and other areas of biology.

◎ **The New Physiology** ◎

In the first part of the nineteenth century, physiology was not regarded as a wholly independent field of knowledge. Traditionally, it was linked with anatomy and clinical medicine. When, for example, Alexander von Humboldt, the grand old man of

German science, gave the keynote address to the Society of German Researchers and Physicians at its annual meeting in 1828, he recommended that the society be divided into scientific sections. One of them was a single section comprising anatomy, physiology, and zoology.

Things were, however, beginning to change, at least in Germany and France. The first physiological laboratory in which experiments could be done was established at the University of Freiburg in 1821. It was under the direction of an anatomist, who instituted the first course in experimental physiology. Within a few years there were courses at six German universities, but physiology still took a back seat to anatomy. Most of the early physiology laboratories were housed in small rooms in the anatomy building.

But the rise of physiology as an independent experimental science was underway. It occurred first in Germany and France in the middle decades of the century, followed at the end of the century by Britain. As it emerged the new physiology based itself on a commitment to experimentation, on an embrace of mechanism, and on a complete opposition to the idea of a special vital force. But, as we will see, opposing vitalism with mechanism did not necessarily mean a complete elimination of purpose in nature.

New Directions in German Physiology

As noted in Chapter 15, German science during the early years of the nineteenth century felt the influence of different visions of natural science. Some natural philosophers from this period viewed one of these visions, that of romantic nature philosophy, as so caught up with the philosophical interpretation of natural science that it overlooked the foundational importance of empirical observation and experimentation. They further objected to the idea that nature must be regarded as a living organism, with unique laws that were different from those of the physical world.

These critics became more and more hostile to the nature philosophers as the emphasis on experimentation gained favor. By the 1840s a number of German physiologists were united in their opposition to nature philosophy and in their conviction that physiology had to be both experimental and mechanistic.

Johannes Müller and his students. The Berlin physiologist Johannes Müller (1801–1858) is well known for his discovery of the specific energy of nerves. Müller demonstrated that when a sensory nerve is stimulated, the kind of sensation that results does not depend on the mode of stimulation, but upon the nature of the sense organ. So, for example, whether the optic nerve is stimulated by light, mechanical contact, or pressure, the response is always luminous impressions.

But Müller is also known for another reason: he inspired a group of talented students who worked with him, several of whom made major contributions to the development of physiology. During the early stages of his career, Müller embraced the nature philosophy of Friedrich Schelling and his followers. But as his career matured, his interests focused less on the meaning of natural science in philosophy than on the strictly empirical investigation of organisms.

In Berlin, Müller attracted a group of students and collaborators who appreciated his new focus on careful observation. These students went beyond Müller in their insistence that experimentation in physiology must be based on the assumption that no special vital force existed and that all explanations must be based on physical processes. Müller himself, however, never went as far as some of his students in abandoning the notion that physiology could investigate nonmaterial entities.

Of the many who worked with Müller in Berlin, two names clearly stand out as pioneers in physiology. We have already met Hermann von Helmholtz in our discussion of thermodynamics (see Chapter 20). Trained as a physiologist, Helmholtz applied the laws of physics to the study of the body while a young researcher working with Müller in Berlin. As we have seen, his study led him to the very general conclusion about the interaction of physical and biological forces that would later become known as the law of the conservation of energy. He continued to work at the interface of physiology and physics for many years, publishing important results in what he called physiological optics and acoustics. One of his memorable contributions to physiology was the invention of the ophthalmoscope, which he presented to the Berlin Physical Society in 1850. It has remained the standard instrument with which physiologists and ophthalmologists examine the retina and vitreous in the eye.

Müller encouraged another of his students, Emil Du Bois-Reymond (1818–1896), to take up the study of electrical discharge in animal tissue, a subject in which he became one of the world's experts. In the course of his investigations Du Bois-Reymond developed sensitive measuring devices to detect and compensate for the tiny amounts of electrical discharge produced in the tissue, always with an eye to providing a physical explanation for physiological processes.

Both Helmholtz and Du Bois-Reymond argued vehemently against the existence of a vital force, insisting on a rigidly mechanical understanding of all vital processes. Du Bois-Reymond once wrote to a friend that he had "sworn to expose the truth, namely that there are no other forces operating in the organism except those physico-chemical ones." That did not mean that he believed the mechanical, materialistic approach could explain everything. In a famous speech later in his career, Du Bois-Reymond conceded that scientists would never be able to know the origins and nature of consciousness. He even once admitted that the purposeful behavior of organisms challenged the mechanical approach, however much he opposed appealing to special vital factors to account for organic behavior. "Teleology is a kind of lady," he wrote, "whom no biologist is able to live without, but he is rather reluctant to be seen with her in public." Purpose in nature continued to be a challenge for mechanists.

The Ludwig school.   If anyone influenced German physiology more than Müller did, it was the physiologist Carl Ludwig (1816–1895). This was due mainly to his publication of an influential textbook in physiology and his training of students from at home and abroad.

Ludwig's publication of his two-volume *Textbook of Physiology* between 1852 and 1856 influenced many young physiologists. In it he signaled the change in

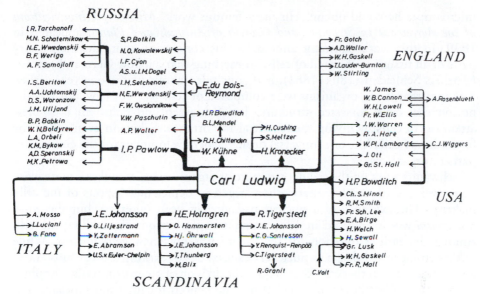

Ludwig's Students

direction physiology was taking. Physiology would be the study of physics and chemistry as applied to living organisms. His new approach, he said, "demands that any object contains within itself the causes for its actions and effects, in accordance with the law of causality, which must be upheld in order to think properly." According to Du Bois-Reymond, Ludwig was the flag bearer of the new school of physiology.

In 1869 Ludwig established a new physiological institute at the University of Leipzig that became a model for many that followed. During the course of Ludwig's directorship, the Leipzig institute attracted over two hundred students from Germany and foreign lands, giving it an international reputation. He put one of his collaborators in charge of maintaining personal contact with his many foreign students, with the result that his approach to physiology and his organization of institute research spread far beyond Germany's borders.

Cell theory.   As mentioned earlier, the field of physiology lay close to that of anatomy until the second half of the century, when physiology became a more independent area of study. Müller, for example, occupied the chair of anatomy and physiology in Berlin. Part of his influence on nineteenth-century biology extended to work carried out by students and collaborators in anatomy, particularly in the development of cell theory.

Central here was the anatomist Theodor Schwann, who studied with Müller when he was at the University of Bonn and then again at the University of Berlin, where he received his medical degree in 1834. Encouraged by Müller to pursue an academic career, Schwann took up the study of anatomy using the best microscopes he could obtain. His most famous work, *Microscopic Investigations of the Agreement in Structure and Growth of Animals and Plants,* appeared in 1839. In this work Schwann announced his conclusion that "the elementary parts of all tissues are formed of cells," something that a fellow German botanist, Matthias Schleiden (1804–1881), had concluded about plants one year earlier. The idea that living organisms were composed of cells was not new, nor was the notion that cells possessed structure. But Schleiden and Schwann drew new attention to cells by giving them central importance. Schwann even called the formation of cells "the one universal principle of development for the elementary parts of organisms."

Schwann's work on the cellular structure of organic tissue stimulated more work in its wake. Within a few years others began to depict new aspects of the cell's makeup. The existence of a nucleus had already been observed, but the word *protoplasm* was introduced in 1846 to refer to the opaque fluid filling the cell. Among the earliest questions of cell theory was how new cells formed. While Schleiden suggested that new nuclei crystallized out of existing cellular substances, it soon became clear that cells formed from the division of pre-existing cells. The physiologist Rudolf Virchow (1821–1902) became famous for his Latin proclamation, "omnis cellula e cellula" (all cells from existing cells).

Cell theory gave rise over the course of the century to further clarification and refinement. Especially after Virchow's 1858 book, *Cellular Pathology,* cells became the foci for investigating disease, which began to be attributed to changes in the cells. The science of living things had, for the moment, found its basic constituent for analysis.

Experimental Physiology and Medicine in France

As in Germany, physiology in France at the beginning of the nineteenth century was imbued with vitalism, the idea that life processes arise from causes that cannot be reduced to the laws of matter. But the French physiological tradition was more monolithic than its German counterpart. In Germany, physiologists who confined their attention to the empirical study of organisms balanced those who approached their science from the vantage point of nature philosophy, where the goal was to move beyond the formulation of empirical laws to the higher philosophical level of demonstrating the ideal laws governing the acquisition of knowledge in general. In France there was no nature philosophy to distract attention away from the acquisition of empirical information about the body and its vital processes.

The heritage of Magendie.   Although French empirical physiologists at the beginning of the century attempted not to go beyond the facts of observation, they did, as mentioned, believe that they were observing the actions of special vital forces at work in organic processes. Further, the restriction of their attention to what could be observed also meant that these physiologists conducted only simple experiments, in which no measurements were involved.

Both of these convictions changed in the work of François Magendie (1783–1855), a physician who founded the first French journal of experimental physiology in 1821. Magendie was thoroughly committed to extensive experimentation, some of which was conducted on living animals, to the great disgust and criticism of his detractors. He was also a skeptic by nature; that is, he distrusted theories, preferring to accept only what he could verify by observation and experiment. He was suspicious of even the theoretical vital force that his predecessors believed was demonstrated in their observations.

Magendie's public reputation was enhanced by numerous physiological discoveries, including foundational studies on swallowing and vomiting, cardiac functions, and the effects of new medicinal drugs on animals and humans. Much of his mature work, including his 1839 *Lessons on the Physical Phenomena of Life,* was translated into German, reinforcing the new ideas already being proposed there. Magendie also left his mark on French physiology through his influence on its most famous figure, Claude Bernard.

Claude Bernard and experimental physiology.   We have already met Claude Bernard as one of the architects of the effort to make medicine into a science (see Chapter 20). He insisted that medicine be based on deterministic laws, just as the scientific study of nature in general demanded. Bernard's role in promoting the scientific study of medicine, not surprisingly, found a parallel in his contributions to the development of physiology in the nineteenth century. Here we are concerned with his discoveries and his influence on the students who came after him.

As a young man Claude Bernard thought he wanted to become a playwright. After completing two productions, however, he decided to attend medical school in Paris. There he met Magendie, who was engaged in medical experiments at the College of France. Between 1839 and 1844 Bernard worked as Magendie's assistant, even though he was also carrying out medical duties in a Paris hospital. In 1848 Bernard was named a professor in the College of France, eventually inheriting his old mentor's position.

Bernard published an extraordinary amount of scientific research over his career, so much so that it was said he made discoveries at the rate others breathed. Among his famous discoveries were fundamental insights into the physical agents of digestion and his study of the neurological effects of poisons. Where digestion was concerned, he investigated how gastric juice broke down cane sugar and he also uncovered the role of pancreatic juice in the digestion of fats. He came to the latter insight by showing that fats were not digested if the pancreatic duct was tied off. As for his work with the action of poison on the body, Bernard demonstrated the nature of the action of curare on the endings of motor nerves, causing muscles to relax and cease working.

As with Karl Ludwig in Germany, Bernard's leading role in French medicine and physiology brought him considerable fame both inside and outside his native land. He attracted to Paris numerous students who wished to study under him and who subsequently made major contributions to the development of experimental physiology in the second half of the nineteenth century.

◎ Heredity Reconsidered ◎

The plant experiments of the Austrian monk Gregor Mendel during the latter decades of the nineteenth century marked a new approach to the study of heredity. Mendel sought to determine if there were specific laws governing inheritance, a process that up to his time was understood only in more general terms.

Earlier Ideas About Hereditary Material

The understanding of how traits were passed down from one generation to the next had intrigued natural philosophers well before the nineteenth century. Various explanations were given. One, the so-called preformation theory, solved the problem in one fell swoop. It suggested that God was responsible for determining the traits of every individual by forming every single embryo himself, and that growth was essentially the unfolding or expansion of the preformed embryo into its adult dimensions. In this theory, which originated in the seventeenth century, the embryos of all future beings were encased, preformed, in the original embryo of each kind of living thing that God had made at the original Creation (see Chapter 12).

By the beginning of the nineteenth century, preformation had fallen out of favor, having been replaced by various attempts to attribute the formation of traits to the action of matter and the forces that governed its interaction. Vitalists, of course, proposed that a special vital force present in organic matter directed the formation of the material combinations that made up the body's parts. That explained how a chicken embryo, which looked very much like that of a duck, developed into a chicken and not into a duck. Mechanists, on the other hand, rejected vital force. They were firm in their conviction that the development of the physical traits in an individual resulted solely from the action of material forces. While they were unable to say exactly how blindly acting forces could exert a directive role, they remained convinced that the answer to this mystery would someday be found.

It was possible, of course, to pursue the explanation of heredity without wrestling with the thorny problem of how the embryo developed. Many natural philosophers chose not to become embroiled in a philosophical debate about forces, simply noting that material from both parents mixed together according to laws not yet known to produce the traits displayed in the offspring. In the most commonly assumed understanding of heredity at the middle of the nineteenth century, hereditary material from two parents was thought to be averaged, or blended, in the offspring (see Chapter 19).

Mendel and the Laws of Particulate Inheritance

One individual, Gregor Mendel (1822–1884), attempted to say more about laws he believed were at work when hereditary material from two parent organisms combined. His work was little known and, for reasons that will become clear, was largely ignored even when it was read. Nevertheless, his achievement eventually served as the basis for a lasting theory of heredity.

Mendel's life. Had Johann Mendel been born twenty-seven years earlier, there would not have been an elementary school in his home town. Young Mendel did so well in school that his teacher urged his parents to give up the idea of passing the farm on to their son and to send the eleven-year-old to a middle school some thirteen miles away instead. Eventually Mendel decided, with his parents' blessing, to become a priest.

When in the fall of 1843 Mendel became a novice in the Augustinian monastery in Brno, the capital of Moravia, he took Gregor as his monastic name. Four years later, with one more year of formal theological training to undergo, he was ordained a priest. After he completed his study of theology, however, Mendel's service as a parish priest did not go well. According to a superior he completely froze when visiting the sick and people in pain, to the point of making himself dangerously ill. This same supervisor,

Gregor Mendel

noting Mendel's diligence in studying the sciences, intervened with authorities to have Mendel fill a vacated teaching post in languages and mathematics in a secondary school.

Mendel was well received at the school in the fall of 1849. The evaluation of his performance was excellent. But he had filled the position without the requisite credentials, so in the spring of 1850 the governing board of the school requested that he be admitted to the examination process for secondary school teachers in two subjects—natural history and physics. Mendel took these examinations that spring and summer, but, having to prepare for them without the benefit of university training and to rely solely on self-instruction, he failed. After successfully substituting a year later at a different school for a teacher who was ill, Mendel secured permission to attend the University of Vienna to prepare himself in the natural sciences.

Mendel attended Vienna from the fall of 1851 to the spring of 1853. In the spring of 1854 he was appointed to fill a vacated position in physics and natural history in a newly established secondary school back in Brno, still without having passed the examinations to become a permanent teacher. Once again the administrators of the school were pleased to have him and endorsed his application to take the examinations. And once again, possibly because he found the examination procedure unbearably stressful, Mendel failed to pass the exams.

Still, he remained at the school in his provisional capacity until 1868. During his teaching days he continued to live at the monastery, where he took up experiments on plant hybridization. Unfortunately, Mendel did not reveal his motivation for undertaking his experiments, prompting scholars to suggest that he was interested in contributing to the debate about evolution that had been in the air for some time. Indeed, Mendel was interested in Darwin's theory, once it came out, although he thought it was incomplete. But Mendel's interest was less theoretical than empirical. He wanted to uncover patterns displayed by the hybrids, but he did not speculate on what mechanism might be responsible for what he observed.

In 1868 Mendel was elected abbot of the monastery. The added duties that came with his new responsibility made it much more difficult for him to continue to work in his garden, putting an effective end to the productive program of experimentation he had established.

Mendel's experiments and results. Among the garden areas around the monastery, Mendel was given a strip of land 120 feet by 20 feet on which he could conduct experiments. He was interested in cross-pollinating peas, which required him to collect pollen from the anther of one pea plant with specifically identifiable traits and deposit it on the stigma of another (see the illustration). This was painstaking work that required great patience from the experimenter. Once the pollen had been deposited, Mendel had to wrap the plant with paper or cloth to keep bees from polluting his experiment with pollen from some unknown source. And then he had to keep careful records that indicated where the pollen had come from, clearly label the seeds the harvest produced, and then grow the seeds so he could see what traits resulted.

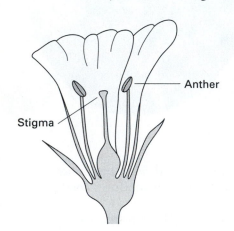

Mendel was not the first to conduct experiments on plant hybrids, but he diverged from the approach of his predecessors by simplifying things. First, he confined his work to varieties of one species, rather than trying to include representatives of diverse species. Second, he selected varieties that differed in but one or a few characteristics, so that he could isolate the effect on the traits in the offspring. Earlier experimenters, commenting on the effects of cross-pollination when numerous character traits were involved, were able to describe only general patterns in the offspring because of the complexity of traits present. Finally, Mendel summarized the relations among the hybrids he got by comparing how many showed which traits; that is, he tried to see if the number of hybrids with one trait bore a numerical ratio to the number of hybrids with a different trait. Further, he did this for more than one generation, requiring him to keep individual generations strictly separated.

Mendel identified pairs of traits in his pea plants. For example, one variety had seeds that were wrinkled, another smooth. Another variety had tall plants he could cross with a variety of dwarf plants. In all he came up with seven pairs of traits to test. He conducted experiments on hybridization in peas over a period of eight years, from 1856 through 1863, publishing his results in 1866. His paper appeared in the journal of the Brno Society for the Study of Natural Science, which had just been founded in 1862.

What did he find? What struck him right away was that crossing plants with a pair of traits produced offspring with only one of the traits of the pair. For example, if he crossed tall pea plants with the dwarf variety, all of the offspring were tall. Mendel called the tall trait the "dominant" trait of the pair. If he crossed these tall offspring to produce a second generation, he noticed that most of the resulting plants were still tall, although some were short. He was able to determine that the ratio of the tall to short in the second generation was 3:1. Because the dwarf variety had receded in the first generation of offspring and then reappeared in the second, Mendel named it a "recessive" trait.

With the concepts of dominant and recessive traits, Mendel now defined inheritance in particulate terms. He thought of the mixing of traits in cross-breeding as a combining of tall and short trait *units*. He depicted the dominant character as A, the recessive character as a, and the hybrid form in which both were joined as Aa. From this he concluded that the expression A + 2Aa + a showed the makeup of the offspring of the second generation. Here only one offspring expressed the pure recessive trait (a), while in the other three offspring the dominant trait (A) was present.

The reception of Mendel's results.   As mentioned earlier, heredity was commonly understood in Mendel's time to be a matter of the mixing or blending of hereditary material. The implications of Mendel's empirical regularities, for all his reluctance to say that heredity was a mixing of actually existing heredity units, appeared to go against that assumption. When, therefore, Mendel shared his results with a leading German botanist of the day at the University of Munich, they were not deemed significant.

Karl von Nägeli (1817–1891) was convinced that when inheritance involved material contributed from two differing sources the result was a blend. What Mendel saw as a compound made of two discrete components, with one dominant, Nägeli regarded as a continuous blend that could produce a host of possible trait variations. Further, Nägeli was very interested in evolution and did not want to believe that traits could remain as constant as Mendel's ratios implied, even though Mendel had shown that they remained true for up to seven generations. "The constant forms require to be tested further," Nägeli wrote to Mendel. "I expect that (when inbred) they would be found to vary once more."

Nägeli urged Mendel to include some hawkweed plants in his experiments and even sent him additional species for that purpose. Nägeli had worked with hawkweeds and knew that the way they passed on traits was unlike what Mendel had observed. In fact, hawkweed reproduction is very complicated, involving sexual and asexual processes. Hybrids of different species of hawkweed follow yet different patterns. Because he knew of the complicated results hawkweeds displayed, Nägeli naturally assumed he knew far more than an amateur monk, whose forays into botany had apparently led him to premature and artificially simple conclusions about nature.

Mendel's attempt to experiment on hawkweeds led him nowhere. He spent five years trying to find ratios among traits in hawkweed offspring, eventually abandoning the attempt. Nägeli's position prevented him and others from asking whether it might be that hawkweed reproduction was exceptionally complicated and not that pea plants were exceptionally simple. Mendel did not create a stir in Brno with his mixed results, so there was little hope of recognition from elsewhere.

It is not clear how much scientists were aware that there was a new Society for the Study of Natural Science in the remote and relatively isolated town of Brno or that it published a journal. While many European libraries did possess the journal, the fact remains that Mendel's work received less than a dozen citations before 1900. In 1881 a German botanist named Wilhelm Focke noted Mendel's work in his book, *Die Pflanzen-Mischlinge (Plant Hybrids),* a volume, incidentally, that Darwin owned. The pages dealing with Mendel's ratios, however, remained uncut in Darwin's copy. Existing evidence suggests that Darwin was never aware of what Mendel had said.

Scientists could have learned what Mendel had published if they received one of the forty reprints Mendel obtained to send out himself. But even then it was not likely that the reaction would be different from Nägeli's. Mendel's ratios were judged to be interesting, but of no theoretical value. As a result, his work remained largely unappreciated for over thirty years.

◎ Competing Ideas of Evolution ◎

One result of Darwin's *Origin of Species* was to make the subject of evolution fashionable. Prior to the *Origin* the idea that present species had developed from past lower forms did not enjoy widespread credibility. Neither Lamarck's *Zoological Philosophy* near the beginning of the century, nor Chambers's *Vestiges of the Natural History of Creation* in the 1840s, had been able to persuade the majority of people that evolution had actually occurred. But that changed in the decades after Darwin's famous book. As the century came to a close many people came to believe that living things had been evolving for a long time.

Acceptance of the fact of evolution did not, however, mean that people agreed with Darwin's explanation of *how* new species had developed. As noted in Chapter 19, some theologians and scientists alike were impressed by the difficulties natural selection entailed, even though they had become convinced by Darwin that evolution had in fact occurred. The problem with natural selection was that it seemed so unconcerned with an overall goal for evolution that it appeared to escape all purpose and direction. Somewhat naturally, then, they reconsidered the earlier theories of evolutionary change, for example that of Lamarck, and they came up with new theories that could preserve some form of purpose.

In the latter decades of the nineteenth century a number of different developments conditioned the ways in which scientists and nonscientists viewed evolution. These developments affected the debates between those who continued to defend natural selection as the primary agency of change and others who diminished the

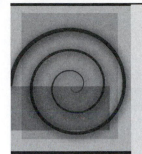

Evolution Versus Natural Selection

All too often students fail to distinguish between the theory of evolution and theories about *how* evolution has occurred. They are not the same. The theory of evolution asserts that species transform and that present species have not always existed, but have developed over time. In various forms of this theory the evolutionary development begins with one or several original forms and has taken place over differing stretches of time. Some theories of evolution include in their narrative the beginning of life, the origin of consciousness, the emergence of the soul, and even the appearance of human morality. Others restrict evolution's action, excluding one or more of these phenomena as outside what evolution can achieve.

To maintain simply that species have changed over time does not, however, reveal how the change has occurred. Lamarck attempted to clarify how evolution worked with his primary and secondary laws. As we have seen in Chapter 17, Lamarck was able to craft an evolutionary scheme that was both mechanistic and purposeful by locating the source of nature's purpose in God's fashioning of laws that predicted evolution's future direction. Darwin's natural selection, on the other hand, appealed to the production of unpredictable variations that did not permit one to know in advance precisely where evolution was going.

Of course conservative minds continued to object both to evolution and to theories of how it occurred. But as the age became more open to freer interpretations of God's role in history and nature, it became easier for many people to become comfortable with the notion that evolution had occurred, even if they rejected Darwin's explanation of how.

role of natural selection in favor of other mechanisms. In general, the differences among these versions of evolution revolved around whether, and to what degree, they emphasized or de-emphasized natural selection.

Darwinian Evolution

If we define Darwinian evolution as evolution in which natural selection is the featured mechanism of evolutionary change, then there were several different versions in circulation during the decades after the *Origin*. A related issue that distinguished evolutionary schemes during these years was the relationship of evolutionary change to the question of purpose in nature. Because the great majority of evolutionary theories accepted some degree of cosmic purpose, we need to be clear about how the various Darwinian theories differed on this question.

Darwin and purpose. Darwin himself conceded that evolution was a purposeful process, even though the way in which he understood it was not apparent to most of his readers. One reason he was misunderstood was his acceptance of a role, albeit a minor one, for the inheritance of acquired characteristics by use and disuse (see Chapter 17). Although Darwin, like Lamarck, did not regard the exercise of use and disuse as the result of consciously voluntary acts of individual organisms, many did. They could then read Darwin's acknowledgment of the inheritance of acquired characteristics as an acceptance of purpose in nature.

If the inheritance of acquired characteristics was not the real source of Darwin's acknowledgment of purpose in nature, where *did* he locate purpose? We can detect places where Darwin thought of evolutionary change in terms of progress—clearly a purposeful process. For one thing, Darwin believed that the evolution of human society had progressed impressively from a primitive state to a highly civilized one. But purpose was even present in his understanding of the evolution of organisms themselves. Near the end of the *Origin* he suggested that his evolution was progressive: "As natural selection works solely by and for the good of each being," he wrote, "all corporeal and mental endowments will tend to progress towards perfection."

How could Darwin hold this position while at the same time appearing to endorse the role of chance in natural selection? The answer lies in his belief that variations were not really due to chance, but that they appeared as the result of cause and effect. At the beginning of Chapter 5 of the *Origin,* Darwin noted that up to this point he had sometimes spoken as if variations were due to chance, adding: "This, of course, is a wholly incorrect expression, but it serves to acknowledge plainly our ignorance of the cause of each particular variation." In other words, there are laws of cause and effect that governed the production of the variations among which natural selection must choose, but we do not yet know them.

There are two important implications in Darwin's position that help us understand the way in which Darwin's evolution was progressive. First, because we are ignorant of the laws governing the production of variations, we can treat them *as if* they occurred by chance. Because we have no way of predicting them, they might as well be considered random. Second, it is not necessary to know these laws for natural selection to work. All that is necessary is that there be individual differences, whether random or not, and natural selection will go to work. So, while natural selection *could* operate on random variations, Darwin did not believe that the variations were truly random, but were subject to laws not yet discovered.

If, in fact, variations were governed by causal laws, then the newness that natural selection introduced was limited in its effect because natural selection was not free to create just anything. Darwin believed that the lawfulness governing the production of variations had to do with the conditions of life under which the evolving species had flourished. Had Darwin lived to enjoy modern science fiction, he might have explained that the conditions of life on Earth had dictated that many animal organisms tend to have a trunk, a head, and four appendages, while conditions in other worlds produced the bizarre life forms, featured in many science fiction movies, that are not possible here. If natural selection were constrained like this, then it was proceeding in a direction, one Darwin clearly felt moved toward greater perfection.

But this very general sense in which evolution was constrained was far too subtle to mean anything to most thinkers. The fact that natural selection clearly worked well, *even if the variations were actually random,* was too much for them to accept. The astronomer John Herschel, for example, regarded Darwin's natural selection as a "law of higgledy-piggledy." Many reasoned simply that the complex patterns visible in the evolution of living things just could not result from the chance productions of individual differences among organisms. For the German Ludwig Büchner, for example, such a claim was literally nonsense—"ein Unding."

Haeckel and recapitulation. We first met the idea that developmental changes on the species level are recapitulated, or repeated, on the individual level, when we considered the origins of biology as a science in Chapter 17. There, in the context of German romantic science, nature itself supplied the directing purpose as it evolved toward ever-higher forms of perfection. In this view it was to be expected that the purposeful, built-in structure of reality—realized in the worlds of both nature and mind—would be reflected at different levels.

This idea that reality itself, which was both mental and material, took the place of the traditional God as the source of transcendent purpose exerted a powerful hold on the German mind. Historian of science Timothy Lenoir has argued that many German natural philosophers adopted a "teleomechanical" outlook, in which nature was regarded as both purposeful and governed by mechanical law, and that this outlook uniquely influenced the development of German biological thought in the first half of the nineteenth century. We saw echoes of it, for example, in the outlook of the physiologist Johannes Müller, discussed earlier in this chapter.

Not surprisingly, we find further evidence of this viewpoint in a self-proclaimed German Darwinist's understanding of evolution. Ernst Haeckel (1834–1919) began his career in zoology at the University of Jena in 1861, just two years after Darwin published his *Origin of Species.* He specialized in the systematic study of marine organisms, some of which were tiny, requiring careful observation with a microscope, while others, like deep-sea jellyfish, were huge by comparison.

Haeckel was particularly interested in the differences between one-celled organisms and multi-celled organisms. He divided all animals into two groups—protozoa (single-celled organisms) and metazoa (multi-celled organisms). In his description of the earliest stages of life, in which protozoa evolved into primitive metazoa, Haeckel was one of the first in Germany to bring Darwin's theory to bear on his work. He eventually became known as Germany's most enthusiastic Darwinist, prompting Darwin himself to credit Haeckel with the success of his ideas in Germany.

Haeckel expanded his understanding of evolution into his philosophy of monism. Like German romantics before him, Haeckel contended that at the most fundamental level reality was one, but that it revealed different sides of itself as it evolved, each of which mirrored the whole. As a natural scientist, Haeckel delighted to discover how the structure of the one ideal substance, which was evolving toward greater and greater perfection, found expression in the material realm.

One example of this evolution was his statement of recapitulation theory, which held that ontogeny (the growth of the embryo) recapitulated phylogeny (the evolution of species). Haeckel held that once the embryo of a species reached its adult form, additional variation occurred that caused the evolution of a higher species.

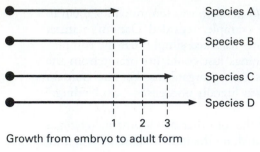

Species A
Species B
Species C
Species D

1   2   3

Growth from embryo to adult form

Recapitulation Theory

If each solid line in the accompanying diagram represents the development of an embryo to its adult form, then the difference between, for example, species A and species B lies in the additional development past dotted line 1. The embryonic development up to dotted line 1 is identical for all four species, while that to line 2 is identical for species B, C, and D, and that to line 3 for species C and D. Each species recapitulates or repeats the embryonic development of the species above it in the diagram. Haeckel's famous slogan, "ontogeny recapitulates phylogeny," became very popular in the late nineteenth century, earning even Darwin's support as evidence of evolution. Although biological scientists eventually largely rejected recapitulation theory as an idealistic claim resting more on analogy than on a real material cause, in the late nineteenth century it summarized for some what they took to be an identifying feature of Darwinian evolution.

Because Haeckel enthusiastically endorsed the action of natural selection in the course of his very public exposition of evolution, he became known as the German Darwin. He also openly acknowledged a role for the inheritance of acquired characteristics. Scholars disagree whether Haeckel believed that natural selection operated only at the level of the species or whether he allowed it to act on individual organisms as well. In either case, the selection among species always proceeded in accordance with his idealistic monism, toward greater perfection. For many, his denial that God was directing the course of evolution masked his strong belief that nature itself directed evolution to serve its built-in, higher purpose.

August Weismann and strict natural selection.   Darwinian evolution emerged in its strictest sense in the work of the cell theorist August Weismann (1834–1914) in Germany. Weismann became convinced that the inheritance of acquired characteristics did not occur and that heredity, and therefore evolutionary change, depended solely on natural selection. In opposing the inheritance of acquired characteristics, Weismann went against a notion that was commonly accepted, even by Darwin and Haeckel. Weismann's understanding thus represented a stricter version of Darwinian evolution than Darwin himself held.

On the basis of new techniques in preparing and staining preparations viewed under the microscope, which greatly enhanced cytology (the study of cells), Weismann devoted himself in the 1880s to studying heredity at the cellular level. He became convinced that hereditary material was contained in the nuclei of cells and that this material was not affected or altered by changes the body underwent over the course of its life.

Weismann reasoned that the change in the organism that had been allegedly induced by external circumstances would have to be somehow communicated to the cells. But how was that said to occur? Weismann rejected an explanation

according to which so-called nerve influences starting at the modified part produced a corresponding change in the hereditary material of the cells, especially
since no one had yet said how that change was *materially* communicated. He
rejected as well the hereditary theory of pangenesis that Darwin had suggested.
Pangenesis, which rested on the inheritance of characteristics (even those acquired),
carried by particles, also provided no means to incorporate acquired bodily changes
materially into the cellular material.

In a series of experiments Weismann induced an artificial change in a group of
mice to see if the acquired characteristic was passed on. He cut off the tails of mice
over numerous generations and observed that no shortening of the tails occurred.
Others called attention to the fact that even though over two thousand years had
passed, Jews still had to continue circumcising their male children. Those who
favored inheritance of acquired characteristics replied, however, that changes that
were humanly produced, like the severed tails, were not the same as changes caused
by external circumstances naturally.

In 1893, Weismann responded to an article, "The Inadequacy of Natural
Selection," in the journal *Contemporary Review.* He gave his reply the title "The All-
Sufficiency of Natural Selection," making clear that no role at all should be reserved
for the inheritance of acquired characteristics. While Weismann's position regarding evolution was seen as extreme in the late nineteenth century, his fundamental
work on cell theory provided the basis for future work.

Non-Darwinian Evolution in the Late Nineteenth Century

In spite of the willingness of Weismann to defend the all-sufficiency of natural
selection, most scientists were tempted to seek alternative explanations of the major
agency of evolutionary change, or, at the very minimum, to allow that means other
than natural selection played at least a subordinate role. This was due in the main
to the objections to natural selection, which we examined in Chapter 19. As the
century drew to a close, these difficulties had found no persuasive answer. Criticisms of natural selection and, as we will see, of continuous variation, two pillars of
Darwin's theory, became so widespread that some even began to talk of the death
of Darwinism.

Many sought other ways to promote evolution than those directly in Darwin's
line. These non-Darwinian schemes dispensed with natural selection as the central
feature of evolutionary change.

Neo-Lamarckism. New versions of Lamarck's theory, in which the inheritance of
acquired characteristics played a dominant role, differed from the original largely
because they did not acknowledge God's role in directing evolution. Lamarck
believed that God had designed specific natural laws that caused life to appear and
to evolve just as his specific purpose intended (see Chapter 17). No organism made
its appearance that was not anticipated and intended by God. Like many people
prior to Darwin, Lamarck assumed that God was running the agenda in the history
of nature.

While neo-Lamarckism did not embrace deism in this fashion, it resembled Lamarck's scheme in its acceptance of the law of the inheritance of acquired characteristics through use and disuse. For late-nineteenth-century neo-Lamarckians, inheritance of acquired characteristics was more important than Darwin's natural selection, which was relegated to a minor role. They did not rely solely on Lamarck's long-outdated book; rather, they cited recent research in support of their new version of Lamarckian evolution.

There were, as we saw in Chapter 19, elements of neo-Lamarckism in the writings of Herbert Spencer, who opposed natural selection alone. In 1893 he declared: "Either there has been the inheritance of acquired characteristics or there has been no evolution." Spencer wrote the article on the inadequacy of natural selection that prompted Weismann to defend its all-sufficiency. But for Spencer it was not God who supplied the overall purpose directing evolutionary change. That was guaranteed through the inevitable progress toward a better society, which he believed nature's law was producing.

Other neo-Lamarckians argued that it was less use and disuse that produced the adaptive change than the direct influence of the environment. The Anglican cleric and noted botanist George Henslow (1834–1926) asserted that plants automatically respond to altered environmental conditions as they grow. Henslow was not concerned with demonstrating that such acquired changes were inherited because, he argued, they would continue to respond in the same way as long as the unusual environmental conditions remained. However, the lack of an established demonstration that acquired characteristics could in fact be inherited remained a stumbling block to neo-Lamarckism for many.

Orthogenesis.   An interesting variant of non-Darwinian evolution in the late nineteenth century was known as orthogenesis. It was non-Darwinian because it did not regard natural selection as the primary mechanism of change. Rather, like several other theories of the time, orthogenesis shared the assumption that evolution followed a predetermined direction that was dictated by the laws of nature. It differed from other explicitly purposeful evolutionary schemes in that orthogenesis gave no guarantee of greater perfection; in fact, it did not even guarantee that newly evolved forms would be adaptive.

According to proponents of orthogenesis, there were internal forces in organisms that steered evolutionary change in a straight line. As a result, evolution did not deviate from this direction because of local conditions or changes in the environment. This meant that the preset direction of evolution might well lead to changes that were nonadaptive, causing the species to become extinct. In orthogenesis, natural selection played no positive role in producing adaptive changes; rather, when adaptation did occur, it was coincidental. Advocates of orthogenesis identified examples of nonadaptive characteristics, which they cited as evidence of internal directive forces. Most famous of these was the Irish elk, which, before it became extinct, acquired greatly oversized antlers that served no obvious function in the view of orthogeneticists.

Orthogenesis was popularized in the 1890s in the work of Theodore Eimer (1843–1898) in Germany and it continued to flourish in a few different forms over several ensuing decades in the United States and in Russia.

◎ Turn-of-the-Century Debates ◎
About Darwinism

On November 22, 1859, Thomas Huxley finished reading Darwin's *Origin of Species*. The next day he sent a letter to Darwin expressing his admiration for what Darwin had achieved. He did, however, mention two difficulties, one of which had to do withDarwin's insistence that variations were so small as to be continuous. "You have loaded yourself with an unnecessary difficulty in adopting 'Natura non facit saltum' [nature makes no jumps] so unreservedly," Huxley wrote. "I believe she does make *small* jumps."

Given the objections to Darwin's natural selection that soon arose, Huxley's concern had merit. If Darwin's contemporaries had trouble envisioning how natural selection could produce the incredible changes over time that Darwin claimed, insisting that the variations on which it worked were continuous only made things worse. In the years after 1859, then, there was motivation to recast natural selection in terms of larger, discontinuous variations.

The widespread disagreements over the means of evolution examined in the previous section meant that there were those by the end of the nineteenth century who sought evidence for larger, discrete changes that were introduced suddenly. Because such changes would then have a greater impact on the direction evolutionary change took than would continuous variations, these scientists began to entertain the idea that the selection of the changes was of less importance than the nature of the changes themselves. Two building blocks of Darwin's theory, then, were under attack at the turn of the century: continuous variations and natural selection.

The Defense of Darwinism

By the 1890s Darwin's insistence on small, continuous variations received new support from an unanticipated quarter, the emerging field of statistical analysis. The support was unanticipated because at first it appeared that the application of statistics to the study of evolution went against Darwin.

The contribution of Francis Galton.   Among the pioneers of the application of statistics to the study of animal and human characteristics was Darwin's cousin, Francis Galton (1822–1911). Like Darwin himself, Galton received a generous inheritance on the death of his father that enabled him to lead the life of a gentleman without having to concern himself about the career in medicine he had been pursuing.

By the time Darwin's *Origin* appeared in 1859, Galton had settled down from a life of travel and adventure. The *Origin* stimulated Galton's interest in a scientific approach to the study of humans. Specifically, Galton sought to compile tables and charts of information about historical figures of high reputation in order to establish his claim that genius was a matter of inheritance, with little due to education and hard work. He published a preliminary form of his work, which went against the grain of Victorian values, in *Macmillan's Magazine* in the summer of 1865.

When his book, *Hereditary Genius,* appeared in 1869, Galton was delighted to capitalize on his cousin's fame by citing Darwin's approval of his conclusions.

Galton learned how to examine the characteristics of an entire population by determining their distribution statistically. To do this he established the average value for a characteristic and then plotted the variations of the trait around that mean. For example, if he wanted to learn about how tallness of individuals varied in a population, he found the average height and then recorded the numbers of individuals at various heights at and around the mean. He found that most individuals in a population possessed average height, with those deviating from the mean diminishing in number the farther from the mean in each direction. Today we would say that the distribution could be pictured in the familiar bell curve.

Galton realized that because this range of variability remained relatively constant from generation to generation, it must be the case that the members of a population who express a trait to the extreme—in this case the tallest and shortest members—do not, on the average, produce members respectively taller and shorter than they. If they did, then the average height would change from generation to generation. What must happen is that members of average height must produce some offspring who are taller and shorter than they, while taller and shorter members must produce some offspring closer to the average. This phenomenon of preserving the range of distribution of a trait Galton called the principle of regression.

Galton's principle of regression cast doubt on natural selection because even those individuals with advantageous characteristics would, on average, produce sufficient members with average traits so as not to alter the mean value of the trait in the population. But Darwin had said that by selecting advantageous characteristics nature *could* change the mean value in a population, so much so that over time the very species changed. Galton concluded that the changes driving evolution must not be the small, continuous, individual differences his cousin had insisted on; rather, they must be large and discontinuous. Those who insisted on larger variations claimed Galton as a hero as the century came to a close.

The work of Weldon and Pearson.   Galton's book, however, caught the fancy of a young morphologist at St. John's College of Cambridge University named W. F. R. Weldon (1860–1906). Weldon claimed Galton as his inspiration, but he also defended Darwin's small variations. He was intrigued by the prospect of studying variation quantitatively. In 1893 he wrote that "the problem of animal evolution is essentially a statistical problem," by which he meant that to estimate the changes going on in a species, scientists needed to gather information about the distribution of traits in a population. For example, what percent of a population exhibited a given amount of abnormality? How abnormal were other members of that group? How abnormal were offspring in comparison to their parents?

The analysis of such data demanded mathematical abilities beyond Weldon's. But Weldon was able to enlist the collaboration of a bright Cambridge faculty member named Karl Pearson (1857–1936), who had also been drawn to the study of evolution by Galton's statistical approach. But both Weldon and Pearson were convinced that evolution proceeded by continuous changes.

Pearson's mathematical analysis of Galton's regression showed that it contained some assumptions that he and Weldon considered to be fallacious. Pearson showed how Galton's regression law could be understood to permit the mean value of a trait to change over time so that, theoretically, small and continuous changes *could* lead to species change. Weldon devoted himself to finding evidence in nature that selection of continuous variations could alter a species.

Others remained unconvinced that the sophisticated statistical analysis of Pearson and Weldon established that evolution proceeded by continuous variation. Unable to make their case mathematically, these defenders of discrete variations attempted to show cases in which large changes did exist and others in which small variations would be ineffective. What emerged was a polarization between those using statistical methods, who favored the small individual differences on which Darwin had insisted, and those avoiding mathematical analysis, who argued for large, discrete changes.

The first public exchange between these two camps occurred in 1895 in a running debate in the journal *Nature*. By 1901 Weldon and Pearson, disappointed at the trend they saw against their views in the official publication of the Royal Society, founded their own journal, *Biometrika*. Thus, the defense of Darwin's position based on statistical analysis at the turn of the century became known as biometry.

The Recovery of Mendel and the Birth of Genetics

Although Mendel's work had enjoyed relatively little success during his lifetime, it would become significant after he died. Its reassessment provided arguments against the biometricians and even gave opponents of biometry a label of their own.

Mendel rediscovered. Two scientists, Hugo de Vries (1848–1935) and Carl Correns (1864–1933) were aware of Mendel's work when they published their own studies on plant heredity in 1900. Both of these scientists had seen references to Mendel's experiments a few years prior to 1900. Correns, a student of Mendel's correspondent Karl von Nägeli, had even consulted Mendel's work at the beginning of his own experimentation in 1896. But the *meaning* of what Mendel had accomplished only became clear to these men as they published their own conclusions.

Correns had a particular reason to be interested in championing Mendel's priority in the discovery of the numerical ratios among hereditary traits and in the existence of dominant and recessive characteristics. Just before publishing his own research, Correns received an offprint of an article by de Vries that contained the essential conclusions to which Mendel had come much earlier. This was of course distressing to Correns, who was himself about to disclose how his own research confirmed many of Mendel's conclusions. In 1901 de Vries gained further attention when he drew out the implications of discontinuous variation, not in the passing down of existing traits, but in the creation of new variations, as occurred in evolution. He named these new large variations "mutations" in a book entitled *Mutation Theory*. By making Mendel into a hero and referring to "Mendelism," Correns redirected attention back to Mendel, effectively denying priority of the discovery to de Vries.

William Bateson and genetics.   Neither de Vries nor Correns, however, really exploited the work of Mendel to become the major proponent of Mendelism. That was left to the English scientist William Bateson (1861–1926), who had been the leading protagonist in the debate against the position of Weldon and Pearson in the late 1890s. Once Bateson heard of Mendel's work, he saw in the numerical ratios evidence of the discontinuous variation he believed existed. He published a translation of Mendel's 1866 paper and became the leading spokesman for Mendelism as the basis for a new science of heredity.

Bateson named the new science "genetics" in a letter to a zoologist at Cambridge University in 1905. He introduced the term to the public in a presidential address he made at the third International Conference on Hybridization and Plant Breeding the following year. The secretary of the Royal Horticultural Society, which published the proceedings of the conference, linked the new word to Mendelism when he edited the proceedings. First, he used genetics in the title—*Report of the Third International Conference on Genetics.* Then he included, in addition to Bateson's address, full-page photos of Mendel and the monastery where he experimented, plus a brief account of Mendel's life and work. The huge society of plant breeders, some ten thousand strong, could not miss the connection between genetics and Mendelism.

Within a short time other new terms made their way into the science of genetics. In 1909, *gene* was suggested as a replacement for general references to traits or characters, followed soon by *genotype* to indicate the actual genetic makeup as opposed to the *phenotype,* which indicated an organism's general appearance. Although genetics and Mendel's work would in later years become sources of support for Darwinian evolutionary theory (see Chapter 23), in the early years of the twentieth century Darwinians regarded Mendelism as hostile to their understanding of evolution because of its endorsement of large discontinuous variations and its weakening of the role of selection.

The clash between the biometricians and the Mendelians was due in large measure to personality differences among the participants and was, in retrospect, as unfortunate as it was unnecessary. Mendel himself had allowed that his ideas could be consistent with continuous variation and, at least at the outset, those who defended large changes embraced the work of the founder of the statistical analysis of heredity, Francis Galton. As we shall see in the next chapter, it would ultimately be the blending of Mendelian genetics with statistical analysis that would lead to a new synthesis of Darwinian evolution.

Suggestions for Reading

Robert C. Olby, *Origins of Mendelism* (Chicago: University of Chicago Press, 1985).

William B. Provine, *The Origins of Theoretical Populations Genetics* (Chicago: University of Chicago Press, 2001).

Karl E. Rothschuh, *History of Physiology,* trans. Guenther B. Risse (Huntington, N.Y.: Krieger Publishing, 1973).

CHAPTER 23

───────────◎───────────

The Synthesis of Biological Issues

In 1942 Julian Huxley, zoologist and grandson of Darwin's defender Thomas Huxley, wrote a work with a bold title. In *Evolution: The Modern Synthesis* he described how the disparate and often conflicting biological issues of the twentieth century had, where the subject of evolution was concerned, been successfully addressed. While the evolutionary synthesis he depicted vindicated Darwin's original insistence on natural selection and small variations, Huxley was certainly aware that both of these tenets had been under attack at the beginning of the century. In fact, he coined the phrase "the eclipse of Darwinism" to characterize how far out of favor Darwin's theory was with some scientists at the turn of the century.

Not all of the developments in biology in the new century had reference only to evolution. For example, the continued investigation of heredity, while certainly relevant to the ongoing study of evolution, was of interest for its own sake. Even more, major strides in the investigation of the constitution of the cell, eventually even at the molecular level, opened up new frontiers of research whose benefits, while initially unknown, began to have an impact on scientific knowledge in general and evolutionary theory in particular. All of these developments converged to form a synthetic approach to the science of living things.

Some scientists, alas, were unable to participate freely in the formation of this synthesis, just as they were not, in general, able to join in the exciting undertakings in the physical sciences of the time. Women and African Americans who aspired to positions in science, for example, found it extremely difficult to rise through the ranks because of continuing prejudices that excluded them. In organic chemistry, where *synthesis* refers to the construction of organic molecules using chemical processes, the African American scientist Percy Julian (1899–1975) continually faced overt discrimination in American universities. Julian finished his doctorate in Vienna, where he was able to work more freely as a member of the scientific community, before returning to America to do pioneering work in organic synthesis. His work led to many useful applications, including treatments for disease. For example, in 1935 he was able to

U.S. Postage Stamp in Honor of Percy Julian, 1993

synthesize a component of the Calabar bean that enabled him to create a drug for the treatment of glaucoma. Seven years later he extracted a soybean protein from which a fire-retardant foam was developed that immediately found merciful application in World War II. There were a number of courageous individuals who made important contributions in spite of imposing barriers, as we will see in this chapter.

◎ Genetics and the ◎ Resurgence of Darwinism

The new discipline of genetics, as understood by the person who named it, was a science of heredity. As we saw in Chapter 22, when William Bateson coined the term in 1905, he consciously linked it to Mendel's newly recovered laws of inheritance. This reinforced Bateson's defense of large, discrete variations as the source of new species, as opposed to the natural selection of continuous changes Darwin's followers supported. Genetics and Mendelism, then, originated in opposition to Darwinism.

By 1920 the situation had altered substantially. As the second decade of the century drew to a close there were many scientists who had become convinced that Mendelian heredity was compatible with the selection of small, continuous changes. With the passing of one more decade, the evolutionary consequences of Mendelian heredity had been captured in a detailed statistical analysis of how genes combine in populations of animals and plants. This provided a theoretical foundation for the genetics of populations.

The story of this intriguing development involved several twists and turns. Microscopic investigations of the cell led to new ways of envisioning the processes involved in inheritance. The discussion thus moved from the macro level of breeding experiments, where some preferred to remain, to the micro level of the inside of the cell. With this move scientists discovered a convincing context in which to demonstrate that the Darwinian factors of continuous variation and natural selection had emerged again from the darkness of an eclipse.

Exploring the Cell

In the 1840s, as we saw in the previous chapter, the cell consisted of a nucleus and protoplasm. The steady improvement in microscopes that had made August

Weismann's study of nuclei possible also contributed to advances in the understanding of the cell's makeup and of cellular processes, which in turn led to new ideas
concerning the determination of sex.

The chromosome theory of heredity.   By the middle of the 1870s Eduard
Strasburger (1844–1912) provided a description of the complex division of plant
cells. The German anatomist Walther Flemming (1843–1905) conducted detailed
studies of animal cells, observing threadlike structures in the nucleus that received
the name *chromosomes* in 1888 from the anatomist Heinrich von Waldeyer-Hartz
(1836–1921). It was Fleming, however, who named the process of cell division
mitosis and conducted an early investigation into its stages.

From here investigators learned more and more about the particulars of cell division that came to define a theory of heredity based on chromosomes. They learned
that chromosomes came in similarly structured pairs and they began to investigate
the processes undergone by the chromosomes when cells divided.

What was clear was that something unique occurred in the division of sperm and
egg cells, which Weismann called germ cells. Consistent with his claim that hereditary material was contained in the nuclei of cells (see Chapter 22), Weismann suggested in 1893 that these cells must be capable of a special division process by which
the chromosome pairs were divided in half before the sperm and egg combined. In
this way, half the chromosomes from the sperm cells and half from the egg cells
combined in the cells of the fertilized embryo to give the proper total number.
Hereditary material from the male parent and from the female parent thus became
part of the cellular structure of the new offspring. Weismann believed that scientists
would one day understand this process in terms of molecules and their motion.

Of course not everyone agreed with Weismann's explanation of heredity, let
alone his insistence on the all-sufficiency of natural selection. It would be yet a
while before there was consensus about whether it was the nucleus, with its chromosomes, or the protoplasm that controlled the development of the embryo. For
their part, many embryologists felt that the chromosomal theory of heredity was
too similar to the old theory of preformation (see Chapter 12)—in which the
adult form was thought to exist already formed in the embryo—to have lasting
merit. But in the first decade of the new century an additional issue emerged that
eventually enabled cytologists, those scientists studying the cell, to persuade embryologists about the importance of the cell and to elicit powerful new support for the
chromosomal theory of heredity. This had to do with the determination of sex,
which throughout the 1890s was generally thought to be due to environmental
factors.

Genetics and the determination of sex.   What, after all, determined the sex of
the offspring? With the rediscovery of Mendel at the turn of the century, some
argued that sex might be a Mendelian character trait. If, for example, females were
pure strains (ff) and males were hybrids in which the male trait was dominant (Mf)
over the female, then the hereditary makeup of the offspring would be Mf, ff, fM,
and ff—an equal number of males and females. Some phenomena spoke against
this suggestion, however. Male bees came from unfertilized eggs while fertilized
eggs produced females.

Nettie Stevens

New studies of the cell just as the twentieth century was getting underway revealed another method of explaining the determination of sex. At first scientists studying grasshoppers thought that a special "accessory" chromosome, present in only half of the sperm cells, might be what governed the sex of the offspring. If a sperm with the accessory chromosome fertilized the egg, it would be one sex; if the sperm lacked the accessory chromosome, it would be the other sex.

By 1905, however, the scientist Nettie M. Stevens (1861–1912), working on a postdoctoral grant at Bryn Mawr College, argued that sex was determined "not by an accessory chromosome, but by a definite difference in the character of the elements of one pair of chromosomes." In particular, sperm cells carried large and small chromosomes that paired up with the large chromosomes of egg cells. A pairing of large chromosomes produced a female, while joining a small chromosome from a sperm cell to the large female chromosome resulted in a male. Because the overall probability suggested that each sex could be expected half the time, Stevens's view appeared to be compatible with Mendelian genetics.

Selection and Continuous Variation

During the first decade of the twentieth century many leading scientists believed that natural selection was powerless to produce new species. They were convinced that evolution depended on the production of large variations. As new research uncovered ways in which small variations could be regarded as consistent with Mendelian genetics, scientists reconsidered the compatibility between selection and small variations.

De Vries and mutation theory.   We mentioned briefly in the previous chapter that Hugo de Vries introduced the term *mutation* in 1901 to describe the large discrete changes he believed were necessary for evolutionary change. De Vries had come to this conclusion in the course of his experimentation on the evening primrose, a stand of which he had found in an abandoned potato field. He noted that most all of the plants were identical. But there were a few that were different and he took them to a garden where he could breed them separately. To his surprise, the aberrant primroses bred true; that is, they produced offspring identical to their parent plants with none bearing evidence of a recessive trait. They were not, apparently, reproducing as Mendel would have predicted.

Where had these aberrant plants come from in the first place? If only a very few of these aberrant plants showed up among the great number of normal primroses, they clearly were not a cross between two species. In that case Mendel's laws would have predicted equal numbers of offspring displaying dominant and recessive traits. De Vries concluded that what he had discovered were spontaneous changes in heredity. The English translation of his book omitted the section in which he had originally called attention to Mendel's work.

Morgan and sex-linked traits.   In America there was another scientist who was also suspicious of Mendel's work. Thomas Hunt Morgan (1866–1945), an American zoologist at Columbia University, was convinced that however well Mendel's ratios might work for plants, they did not hold up to the evidence for animal inheritance. Morgan, who began his career as an embryologist, resisted the chromosomal theory of heredity as well, even though he was very familiar with the work of fellow American scientists on chromosomes.

As a result of a trip to Europe and a visit with de Vries, Morgan became interested in mutation theory. That in turn prompted him to become involved with breeding experiments. What he required was an organism that would breed quickly so he could gather information on hereditary traits, analyze them statistically, and even relate his findings to cellular structure. After trying out a research program on a number of larger organisms, he settled on the fruit fly, also known as *Drosophila melanogaster,* which could produce over twenty generations in a year. With only four pairs of chromosomes in the nucleus, it was an ideal subject for analyzing hereditary traits.

By 1910 Morgan's experiments with the fruit fly did nothing to confirm de Vries's contention that mutations could establish new species. Nor did they over-turn Morgan's suspicions of Mendel's work. But further experimentation, urged by those working in his laboratory, changed Morgan's mind about chromosomal inheritance and about Mendel.

What these new experiments uncovered was that some hereditary traits were sex-linked; that is, two hereditary factors were being carried on the same chromosome. But how did he establish that some traits were carried with sex? Assume that a female fruit fly with red eyes, the dominant color, breeds with a male with white eyes. Females are characterized by receiving the larger sperm chromosome to create the pair LL, while males receive the small sperm chromosome to create Ls. When color is considered at the same time, certain pairings result (see the illustration on the next page; the shaded boxes represent the red trait).

Morgan's analysis established that eye color was segregated by the large sex chromosome. If this were true, then important implications suggested themselves. First, if a variation such as eye color was caused by a minor alteration in the chromosomes responsible for sex, then a focus on the source of the variation revealed that small changes could give rise to traits that were important for evolution. While these small, chromosomal changes were not the individual differences Darwin had insisted on, they were at least small variations as opposed to the large, discrete changes Darwin's critics required.

Morgan and others retained the concept of mutation, not in de Vries's sense of a fully formed hybrid that appeared suddenly, but as a change in the makeup of the chromosomes. In 1916 Morgan wrote that mutations of this kind could be

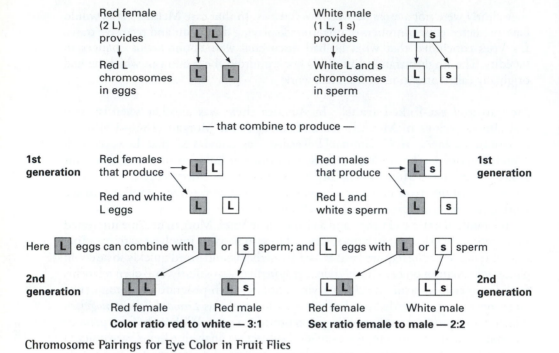

Chromosome Pairings for Eye Color in Fruit Flies

either harmful, indifferent, or beneficial. If a mutation was harmful, he said, it had "practically no chance of becoming established." If indifferent, it had only a small chance, while if beneficial to the individual, "the chance that the individual will survive is increased, not only for itself, but for all of its descendants that come to inherit this character." This increase, he speculated, might have an influence on the course of evolution. If so, then Morgan's work also provided incentive to look again at the role of selection in evolution.

Another implication was that the analysis of Morgan's mutations was consistent with Mendelian inheritance. Morgan's results resembled those of Mendel right down to the ratios he obtained, thus reinforcing the link between Mendelian genetics and the chromosome. In fact, what began to come to the fore as the unit of heredity was the *gene,* now understood as a bead on the string of chromosomes. Further, the new approach held promise for explaining earlier results from animal inheritance that had appeared to oppose Mendel. Of course, higher animals possessed chromosomal makeups that were much more complicated than the fruit fly, with its four chromosome pairs. But the theory was there to be tested.

Mendelian support of selection and continuous variation. Other developments also led some scientists to reexamine the role of selection in evolution. When the Harvard zoologist William Castle (1867–1962) turned his attention to mammalian genetics around the turn of the century, he supported the idea, accepted by many, that only discontinuous variation was compatible with Mendelian genetics and that selection had no power to call such large changes into existence. Selection, therefore, was not a factor in the *production* of new species.

But through research he conducted on the inheritance of coat color in rats, Castle and his associate found that selective breeding could, in fact, introduce slight variations that gave no indication of succumbing to Galton's famous regression back to the mean. Although these results were deemed controversial, they were sufficient to change the mind of Castle himself. Noting the Darwinian view that new species arise through the direct agency of selection, Castle concluded that his experiments supported Darwin. Extensive further experimentation lasting to 1919 and involving some fifty thousand rats solidified Castle's position as a champion of Darwin's theory of selection of small variations.

Those who resisted Castle's conclusions appealed to Mendelian genetics, arguing that Mendel's laws applied only to large changes; hence the slight modifications in Castle's rats were incompatible with Mendel. But there was a possible explanation, which Mendel himself had raised, as to why small variations might also be permanently inherited. If, for example, a trait depended on *more than one factor* simultaneously, the ratios in which the trait would be expressed would be more complicated than those for the traits of Mendel's garden peas. Further, because of the role of dominance, the number of different combinations of chromosomes expressing these traits would be even more prolific. If there were a sufficiently large number of factors, the outcomes might appear as a continuum of small changes. This might even explain why some outcomes appeared to be blended.

In 1908 the Swedish geneticist Hermann Nilsson-Ehle (1873–1949) published results of his experiments in crossing various varieties of wheat and oats. In some cases he found instances in which the traits that were involved—for example the color of the chaff—depended on two factors. He calculated the ratios expected on Mendelian principles in such a case for the first and second generations of offspring and found that, although they were more complicated than those for peas, his experimental results were very close to the theoretical calculations. He had similar success with another cross that showed dependence on three factors. He reasoned that if there were traits that depended on as many as ten factors, the number of different types would be close to sixty thousand!

Similar experimentation, independent of Nilsson-Ehle's, occurred in the United States around the same time. Of course this multifactor interpretation of continuous variation became known quickly. It took its place among the growing amount of evidence that was based on Mendelian genetics and supported Darwin's emphasis on continuous variation. Nilsson-Ehle suggested that in such crossings the possibility of recombining genes was increased and that this resulted in a great number of variations on which natural selection could operate.

The Evolutionary Synthesis

Looking back on the history of the theory of evolution after the modern evolutionary synthesis had become established, a participant in formulating the synthesis, Ernst Mayr, wrote that one of the most innovative aspects of Darwin's achievement was his introduction of "population thinking." Population thinking, however, can only be understood in contradistinction to typological thinking, the traditional way of classifying the diversity we encounter in nature. As its name implies,

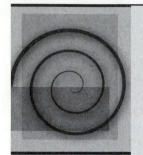

The NATURE of SCIENCE

Idea and Reality in Population Thinking

In the physical sciences typological thinking had produced phenomenal results, especially since the seventeenth century. The fixed realities (ideal types) of nature were captured in mathematical formulae or physical concepts that served as the basis for explaining why nature worked as it did. For example, Newton's law of rectilinear inertial motion, which he stated for objects not under the influence of any forces whatever, permitted him to explain why objects that *were* affected by friction or collision behaved as they did. In other words, Newton's conception of motion in the ideal enabled him to explain motion in the world we experience, which is not an ideal one.

Darwin changed this for the study of species by rejecting the traditional notion that there was such a thing as an ideal type for each species. Because Darwin believed that species were always subject to change, they did not correspond to anything real. The focus of his attention was not on how far an individual organism varied from an ideal species, but on the range of variability itself. Darwin was interested in the collective features of the population—their average, for example. But only the individuals had reality. Statistical averages were necessary and helpful abstractions, but they did not conform to anything real in the population. Darwin's new way of viewing species eventually enabled the notion of the population to come increasingly to the fore, particularly in the emerging field of population genetics.

typological thinking rests on the assumption that there are a definite number of types in nature and that variations hover around each type. In this traditional approach, the task of the scientist is to depict the idea that captures the type accurately so that the structure and behavior of nature can be grasped.

Darwin's concern was with the diversity of traits in a population and the need for it to be present for selection to work. Because diversity was a natural trait of a population, it made selection possible. By taking the focus off the ideal type of a population and placing it on the population's diversity, Darwin's perspective opened up interest in the characteristics of the population.

Assessing genetic change over time in a population involved, however, a host of factors. By 1908 two different individuals had independently expressed, mathematically, what would happen over time to the genetic makeup of an idealized population if the individuals in the population bred randomly. Given certain perfect conditions, the analyses of the German physician Wilhelm Weinberg (1862–1937) and the British mathematician G. H. Hardy (1877–1947) predicted how the frequencies of genes would be transmitted from one generation to the next. What became known as the Hardy-Weinberg Law suggested that the makeup would remain in equilibrium even if some traits occurred more frequently than others.

Of course, if the frequency of the genes in a real population remained in equilibrium from generation to generation, no evolution would occur. In fact, in their idealized mathematical analysis Hardy and Weinberg assumed that the population was free from disruptive influences that would disturb the gene frequencies of the population. As mutations came to be understood as spontaneous alterations in genes (as opposed to de Vries's sudden appearance of a hybrid species), here was a factor that might affect the frequency of genes in the population. And there were others. What if there were reasons to assume that the cross-breeding was not totally random? What about migration into a population from outside? Finally, what if natural selection operated on changes small enough to be caused by genes?

The task of taking into account factors such as mutation and natural selection required new insights and approaches, to say nothing of very sophisticated mathematical analysis. On the other hand, the architects of theoretical population genetics determined that natural selection over time could indeed affect the genetic makeup of a population. By 1932 one of these architects, J. S. B. Haldane (1892–1964), was able to write that the old criticism of Darwinian natural selection as impotent had been exploded. Darwinism was not dead—it was alive and well. "Natural selection," he wrote "is an important cause of evolution."

Still more developments in the theory of evolution were necessary before Julian Huxley could declare that a modern synthesis had been achieved. In particular, naturalists took a very different approach to the problem of speciation, or how new species actually originate. They rejected all explanations based solely on genetics, preferring to emphasize the roles of reproductive isolation and of the ecological factors of populations. The process of reconciling the concerns of naturalists with those of population geneticists began in the work of the Russian naturalist Theodosius Dobzhansky (1900–1975), who joined Morgan's laboratory in America in 1927, where he became familiar with population genetics. Others continued to integrate the results from new research in various fields, resulting in the recognition that, although mutations in genes happen all the time, left to themselves mutations act extremely slowly to introduce changes in a population. That realization in turn only heightened the appreciation of the power of natural selection.

◎ Human Evolution ◎

As noted in earlier chapters, the idea that humans possessed an ancient past, far older than implied by an easy reading of the Bible, was over one hundred years old by the time Darwin's *Origin of Species* appeared in 1859. Eighteenth-century theories of the Earth and early-nineteenth-century romantic thought contained speculations about an ancient origin for humans. Such speculation by no means represented the majority view, but it continued to exist throughout the pre-Darwinian years.

By mid-century, natural philosophers were considering whether modern humans had originated from a single pair or whether the races of humans had sprung from different individual original pairs. The defense of the latter position by the staunchly religious zoologist Louis Agassiz (1807–1873) showed that in pre-Darwinian debates the issue did not necessarily involve either evolution or a challenge to a creationist viewpoint. After Darwin, as we shall see below, evolutionists continued to dispute the question of origins from a single source as opposed to separate sources.

Human Fossil Discoveries

The popular conception that evolutionists believed humans arose from apes, although suggested by Lamarck early in the nineteenth century, really entered the public debate only after Darwin's *Origin.* It was not, for example, maintained by Robert Chambers in the *Vestiges of the Natural History of Creation* of 1844. For Chambers, the lower forms that immediately preceded modern humans were less-developed versions of the human race. When Thomas Huxley in 1863 took on the question of human origins, a subject omitted from Darwin's book, he argued that humans and apes were so similar that they must have shared common evolutionary ties. That assertion did not entail the claim that humans had descended *from* gorillas, but the pictorial comparison of skeletons he included left precisely that impression on the reader. Such a notion influenced the discussions of discoveries in this field for many years to come.

Neanderthal man and Java man.   Just prior to the *Origin,* as mentioned briefly in Chapter 19, ancient fossil primate remains, consisting of a portion of a skull and various other bones, were discovered in a cave in Germany's Neander Valley. Now, more than speculation and theory were involved, especially when several additional fossils like the Neanderthal bones were found in Belgium in 1886. As can be imagined, the Neanderthal skull precipitated a debate about its significance. The German anatomist and anthropologist Hermann Schaaffhausen (1816–1893), who wrote a description of the find, concluded that the bones had come from an ancestor of modern Germans who belonged to a brutal and savage race.

Some questioned whether the remains were human, insisting that the skull came from an abnormal creature of some sort, perhaps one that was deformed. Others

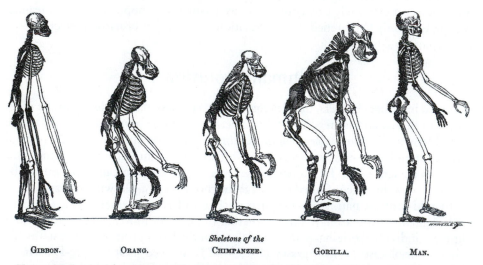

GIBBON.   ORANG.   *Sheletons of the*
CHIMPANZEE.   GORILLA.   MAN.

Photographically reduced from Diagrams of the natural size (except that of the Gibbon ,which was twice as large as nature),
drawn by Mr. Waterhouse Hawkins from specimens in the Museum of the Royal College of Surgeons.

Illustration from *Man's Place in Nature,* 1863

argued that, because its cranial capacity was comparable to that of modern humans, it had to be a primitive form of human. By the end of the century scientists frequently represented Neanderthal man as an intermediate stage between our primitive ancestors and modern humans.

The German Darwinist Ernst Haeckel, whom we met in the last chapter, held that the Indonesian orangutan was the animal most closely related to humans and that humans therefore originated in Southeast Asia. Inspired by this view and by Alfred Russell Wallace's letters on Java, the Dutch physician and anatomist Eugène Dubois (1858–1940) gave up an academic career at the University of Amsterdam to go to the East Indies in search of confirmation of Haeckel's theory. After several years of searching without success, he finally found fossil remains, including a skull (1891) and a thighbone (1892), of a human creature much older than Neanderthal man. From the skull, Dubois inferred that the brain size was much bigger than that of the largest ape, but smaller than that of humans today, and from the thigh bone he concluded that the being stood erect. To the delight of Haeckel, Dubois borrowed the German's term for his predicted hypothetical link between apes and humans—*Pithecanthropus erectus*.

Because of the location of the find, what Dubois initially insisted was "the missing link" between apes and humans came to be known to the public as Java man. Haeckel immediately declared his support, noting that the upright posture confirmed both his and Darwin's assertion that humans had stood erect well before their brains had increased to the size of modern human brains. There were those who remained suspicious of Dubois's claim, and he conceded by 1898 that perhaps Java man was not part of the direct line to contemporary humans. Still, by 1900 it was commonly assumed that human evolution had passed first through Java man and then Neanderthal man on its way to the present.

Complicating linear evolution.   This simplified linear understanding soon gave way to a more complex story. In 1907 a jawbone was unearthed near Heidelberg in Germany that raised questions. It was much bigger and more brutal looking than a human jaw, but could be dated geologically to a time when tools were known to be present. Most experts concluded that it represented a different kind of creature from the more humanlike Neanderthal man and Java man. The question that began to surface was whether human evolution consisted of many branches from an original stem, some of which had not survived, instead of being a straightforward linear process. And then there was the additional possibility, analogous to the claims of Agassiz, that there had been separate but parallel lines of development.

After examining new Neanderthal fossils between 1911 and 1913, the French paleontologist Marcellin Boule (1861–1942) asserted that Neanderthals, in spite of their brain size, shared too many features with apes to have developed into modern humans in the relatively short time span since their existence. His description of Neanderthals as brutish and apelike contributed to the view that the Neanderthals were a side branch of hominid development that did not lead to modern humans.

As yet more fossils were discovered, primate evolution was discussed among a wide array of disciplines, involving the perspectives and techniques of geologists,

archaeologists, anthropologists, paleontologists, anatomists, zoologists, and lin-
guists. Claims and counterclaims led to competing evolutionary histories, or phy-
logenies, that gave the impression of a subject in disarray, where consensus was
impossible. In addition, fossils found in 1910 and in the immediately succeeding
years, which once again led to the declaration that the "missing link" had been
found, were later determined to have been planted. Even at the time of their discovery the bones of Piltdown man were fodder for dispute.

One outlook that gained strength, complementing the other anti-Darwinian
perspectives on evolution we have already examined, was the view that hominid
evolution consisted of separate parallel lines. Darwin had argued that there had
been one common source of evolution that later developed separate branches. Anti-
Darwinian orthogenesists, on the other
hand, saw evolution as guided by a force
that could produce separate parallel lines.

In the 1940s the dominance of the anti-
Darwinian view began to change. With yet
new fossil discoveries plus the modern synthesis of Darwinian ideas about the evolutionary mechanism itself, the tide turned
against multiple sources of primate evolution. By 1950, at a symposium at the Cold
Spring Harbor Laboratory in New York
devoted to "The Origin and Evolution of
Man," the return to the Darwinian common source was evident. From here on, the
question of where to locate various ancestors of modern humans on the evolutionary
chart would still generate debate, but there
would be consensus about beginnings.

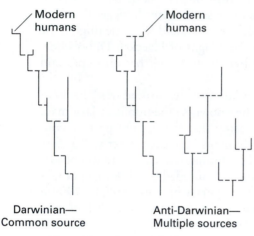

Darwinian—
Common source

Anti-Darwinian—
Multiple sources

(Actual branches not depicted)

**Darwinian and Anti-Darwinian Primate
Evolution**

The Scopes Trial

The discovery of new fossils was of interest not only to scientists. Each new sensational find naturally captured the attention of the general public as well. On the
heels of the unearthing of the Piltdown fossils a *New York Times* headline
announced, "Darwin's Theory Proved True. English Scientists Say the Skull Found
in Sussex Establishes Human Descent from Apes." But if there was a single event
that focused the public's attention on human evolution, it was the 1925 trial of
high school teacher John Scopes in Dayton, Tennessee, for violating state law by
teaching evolution in the public school.

American high schools had already included evolution in the curriculum in the
nineteenth century, although it was portrayed as a purposeful process compatible
with a belief in God. But textbooks became more openly associated with Darwin as
the new century progressed. When the American Civil Liberties Union decided to
challenge a new Tennessee law prohibiting the teaching in public schools of "any
theory that denies the story of divine creation of man as taught in the Bible,"

William Jennings Bryan, a three-time Democratic nominee for president and sec-retary of state under Woodrow Wilson, rose to oppose the attempt. Noted criminal trial lawyer Clarence Darrow offered to lead the attack on the law by representing Scopes, while Bryan became the law's defender, representing the state of Tennessee.

The trial became a national event, pitting the right of the state of Tennessee to regulate education against the question of the truth of evolution, specifically where the Genesis account of the creation of humans was concerned. The defense's case was weakened somewhat because its members, while they agreed that academic freedom was at stake, did not agree about the larger issue of evolution and religion. Some believed that there was no conflict, not even between evolution and the Genesis story. Others, like the agnostic Darrow, had both a more materialistic understanding of evolution and a lack of sympathy for religion. When on the third day of the trial, Darrow objected to beginning the proceedings with prayer, he inad-vertently began generating sympathy for the other side. Some evolutionists later saw this as a reason why the trial did not help to stem the tide of fundamentalism.

The result of the trial was that the law was upheld and John Scopes was fined $100 for breaking it. There was, of course, an appeal. Not wishing to prolong the spectacle, the state supreme court overturned Scope's conviction on the grounds that there had been improper procedures in setting the fine. By removing the con-viction the state sidestepped the possibility of further appeal.

The Scopes trial quickly took its place as a landmark in American history and in the relations between science and religion. As such, it acquired a legendary quality that reinforced among historians and others a standard portrait of science triumph-ing over irrational religion. The 1960 film, *Inherit the Wind,* which distorted details of the trial freely in the course of creating its heroic narrative, contributed to a myth that has persisted to the present. According to this portrait, in the words of the paleontologist Stephen Jay Gould in 1983, "John Scopes was persecuted, Darrow rose to Scope's defense and smote the antediluvian Bryan, and the antievolution movement then dwindled or ground to at least a temporary halt." Gould observed that "all three parts of this story are false." The flourishing creationist movement of the latter half of the twentieth century, especially in the United States, is ample evidence of the third error Gould had identified.

Eugenics

Scientific scrutiny of the human past played into more than merely religious issues. As we observed in discussing social Darwinism in Chapter 19, the altered under-standing of humankind's place in nature suggested by Darwin's *Origin* in 1859 was utilized to address existing questions about how best to organize human society. In the late nineteenth century and into the twentieth the new perspectives on human evolution gave impetus to ideological queries about what kind of human beings should make up society.

Galton and the science of eugenics.   In 1873 Francis Galton wrote a letter to the *London Times* describing his idea of colonizing East Africa with Chinese immigrants. He assumed that the Asian race was superior to the African race and would therefore displace it quickly. "The history of the world," wrote Galton, "tells a tale of the continual displacement of populations, each by a worthier successor, and humanity gains thereby." Galton was expressing his view that humankind should assist nature in producing optimal results, an endeavor on which he would bestow the term *eugenics* a decade later.

Galton believed that it was the duty of democracy to defend itself against the introduction of "degenerate stock" and to positively encourage marriages among those of good stock. He had attempted to identify, using statistical data, the qualities of the very best members of society in his book, *Hereditary Genius,* in 1869. He defined eugenics as the science that dealt with all influences that improve the inborn qualities of a race, as well as with those that developed them to the utmost advantage. As early as 1865 he was convinced it was simply a matter of breeding. In that year he wrote in *Gentleman's Magazine*:

> I hence conclude that the improvement of the breed of mankind is no insuperable difficulty. If everybody were to agree on the improvement of the race of man being a matter of the very utmost importance, and if the theory of the hereditary transmission of qualities in men was as thoroughly understood as it is in the case of our domestic animals, I see no absurdity in supposing that, in some way or other, the improvement would be carried into effect.

In the twentieth century the eugenics movement came into its own. In the United States the supporters of eugenics reinforced existing desires to pass legislation aimed at controlling reproduction. Over twenty states passed laws prohibiting the marriage of "idiots" and the insane by 1914. The eugenics movement was especially effective in bringing about new sterilization laws. In the decade after Indiana passed the first such law in 1907, fifteen more states enacted measures that permitted sterilization of a variety of so-called undesirable types, including epileptics and the mentally retarded in some regions.

The eugenics movement was never without its critics. Among the most effective was the British writer and journalist G. K. Chesterton (1874–1936), who compiled notes before the First World War opposing eugenics. It was, he later said, a time "when eugenic babies sprawled all over the illustrated papers." Chesterton published his notes after the war as *Eugenics and Other Evils* (1922). He regarded eugenics as the "scientific officialism" for which, he said, the Germans were well known. He viewed eugenics as the result of unexamined deference to German principles that could offer "nothing but the same stuffy science, the same bullying bureaucracy and the same terrorism by tenth-rate professors that have led the German Empire to its recent conspicuous triumph."

Chesterton's association of eugenics with the penchant for excess was prescient beyond his wildest imaginings. If positive eugenics sought to promote the breeding of the best biological specimens, negative eugenics wished to prevent the deficient and weak from procreating. But even Chesterton could not have anticipated the attempt of the Nazis to go yet further when they sought to *eliminate* mentally and physically handicapped persons in Hitler's "euthanasia" campaign of 1940.

Chesterton formalized his conversion to Catholicism just around the time his book was published. The Catholic Church had long been an opponent of the eugenics movement, rejecting the emphasis on the animal nature of humankind as a way to prevent degeneracy and to promote betterment through selective breeding. To the church, sin was the cause of degeneracy and virtue was the path to improvement. Although Chesterton died in 1936, he would no doubt have been proud of the German Catholic Church's outspoken and effective opposition to the Nazi "euthanasia" campaign, which was brought to an end in 1941.

The Nazi excesses went a long way toward discrediting the eugenics movement. After World War II, notes historian of science Daniel Kevles, *eugenics* virtually became a dirty word in the United States because of an association it had acquired with racism. Nevertheless, the American and British Eugenics Societies continued to pursue programs of positive eugenics, now with a focus on the use of human genetics for medical purposes. Genetics counseling clinics had already begun to appear in the United States during the war years. As the number of diseases that could be associated with specific genes increased, the number of clinics increased, especially as more and more new genetic information offered possibilities for treatment.

With the explosion of genetic information came new possibilities and new moral challenges. "Genetic engineering," a phrase coined in 1965, pointed to the deliberate manipulation of genetic material to produce new substances or to perform new functions. While somewhat less controversial in a field like agriculture, it raised prospects for humankind that were sobering. Indeed, the rapidly emerging field of medical genetics carried with it from the past both the noble aspirations and the inherent dangers of the eugenics movement.

Explaining social behavior.   If eugenics appealed to the animal constitution of humans in its attempt to improve society, other endeavors that arose in the middle of the twentieth century drew on humankind's animal nature to understand social behavior. Pioneering studies on chimpanzee behavior begun in the 1960s by primatologist Jane Goodall (b. 1934) established that chimpanzees were capable of making tools. Two other primatologists, Dian Fossey (1932–1985) and Birute Galidkas (b. 1946), devoted their lives to the study of gorillas and orangutans respectively.

Anthropologists studying aggression and defense of territory in animals in the 1960s suggested that humans were subject to the same pressures to acquire food and mates that animals displayed. While such a perspective reinforced the view that modern human society was based on competition, opponents of the suggestion rejected the idea that aggression was biologically determined. They pointed out that not all primates exhibit strong aggressive behavior. They concluded that there was no necessary evolutionary need for such aggression in humankind's development, a conclusion supported by the existence of altruistic behavior in some animals. In their view, aggressive actions in humans were better explained as the result of a poor social environment.

To explain the apparent inconsistency between the Darwinian struggle for existence and altruistic behavior the British zoologist V. C. Wynne-Edwards (1906–1997) proposed in 1962 that selection could act at the level of the group and not only of the individual. Altruistic behavior of individuals, then, promoted the survival of the group at the individual's expense. Wynne-Edwards's idea was not well received, however, not only because Darwin emphasized that selection acted on individuals, but also because there was no good explanation as to why individual selection would not favor individuals who discovered the benefits to themselves of acting selfishly.

Others restricted attention to individuals who shared many of the same genes, arguing that the instinct to survive should be keyed to genetic makeup rather than at the level of the individual organism. In other words, an individual acting altruistically does so because it helps genetic relatives to survive and reproduce. Studies showed that altruistic behavior diminished with genetic distance, suggesting that, on the human level, altruism for a sibling is quite predictable, but not for a distant cousin.

This insight of "kin selection" led the British zoologist Richard Dawkins (b. 1941) to declare that the gene was the unit of selection. As he so famously put it in his book, *The Selfish Gene* (1976), we individual organisms are nothing more than the genes' way of reproducing themselves. It has since been argued that confining attention to the gene, or even the individual, oversimplifies how selection acts. In different contexts other levels of selection can emerge.

If altruism could find an explanation in the genes, so too could other social behaviors of animals and humans. In 1975 the Harvard entomologist Edward O. Wilson (b. 1929) published a summary of research on social behavior from many areas of biology—wherever there were organisms that could be said to engage in social conduct. In *Sociobiology: The New Synthesis,* he defined the new discipline as "the systematic study of the biological basis of all social behavior." Humans were not overlooked. Wilson laid out, for example, how human social cooperation could be seen as biologically advantageous, noting that altruistic behavior occurred according to carefully regulated practices among genetically related individuals.

As might be expected, the claims of sociobiology did not sit well with some critics. The biological determination of social behavior carried with it, in the minds of some, a validation of social behaviors that some regarded as outmoded and unacceptable. For example, feminists resisted the notion that male aggression and female passivity could be explained (and therefore justified) on the basis of genes. Some sixteen people, including two of Wilson's colleagues at Harvard, signed a statement that appeared in the *New York Review of Books* on November 13, 1975, that identified sociobiology as the latest attempt to reinvigorate past theories that had "provided an important basis for the enactment of sterilization laws and . . . the eugenics policies which led to the establishment of gas chambers in Nazi Germany." Such a reaction made clear that genetics research would never be a field that would remain isolated from the public arena.

◎   The Rejection of Lamarckism   ◎

Some historians hold that a key component of the modern evolutionary synthesis was the emergence of a consensus among scientists that Lamarckism had finally been eliminated from evolutionary theory. According to this view, the so-called soft heredity permitted by Lamarckian inheritance of acquired characteristics, which depends primarily on behavior, had at last given way to hard heredity, which requires genetic change. No longer would what an organism acquired during its lifetime be of relevance for evolution; instead, only the hereditary material with which it was born would be relevant. But Lamarckism did not retreat from the stage quietly. In the same years during which the modern evolutionary synthesis was being forged, Lamarckian evolution gained ascendancy in the Soviet Union.

One other feature traditionally associated with Lamarckian evolution also disappeared from evolutionary biology—the notion that evolutionary development is purposeful. Whether evolution is purposeful or not entails matters of worldview, which are not equivalent in status to scientific statements about specific mechanisms of evolutionary change. The modern evolutionary synthesis, then, produced its own worldview.

The Lysenko Affair

The Lamarckian views of Russian agronomist Trofim Denisovich Lysenko (1898–1976), who rose to prominence in the 1930s, heavily influenced the fate of evolutionary science in the Soviet Union. Lysenko first became known for his discovery of the benefits of freezing wheat seeds to enhance their germination in the spring. He became convinced that the characteristic acquired by freezing could be inherited, something entirely consistent with Lamarckian theory.

Such convictions fit in well with the communist ideology of the Soviet Union for two reasons. First, purposeful development was much more compatible with the Marxist notion of the inevitability of communism than would be a purposeless evolution based on natural selection of random variations. Second, the inheritance of acquired characteristics depended on changes that came about during the life of the organism, theoretically including those brought about deliberately by the state. Whether or not the Soviet policy was in any way affected by such a belief, Soviet leaders were clearly more comfortable with this vision of future development than they were with an unpredictable Darwinian future.

Prior to 1929, Soviet geneticists were active collaborators with European scientists in various research endeavors. After December of that year, collaboration became increasingly difficult because of Stalin's speech to the Union Conference of Agrarian Marxists. Stalin made clear that conformity to communist policy would affect even the correctness of scientific theory. Lysenko's star rose throughout the 1930s as that of Soviet geneticists, who shared the revitalized Darwinian view of heredity, fell. Eventually the teaching of genetics was banned and several leading Soviet scientists were exiled or imprisoned. Genetics became known in the Soviet Union as a decadent bourgeois science.

Lysenko's power in Soviet biological science lasted into the 1950s, when it finally came to an end. The effect on Soviet genetics was, of course, disastrous because Western molecular scientists made amazing strides in genetics in these years. In the West, understandably, the Lysenko affair only reinforced the wish among scientists to put Lamarckism behind them.

Evolution as Worldview

Throughout this text there have been numerous examples of individuals who have exploited the results of scientific research for extrascientific purposes, be they political, ideological, philosophical, or religious. Lamarck's evolutionary view, as we saw in Chapter 17, originated in the context of a deistic worldview in which God brought about his purpose for nature through the laws of evolutionary change. While some degree of purposefulness was present in most all of the evolutionary theories examined so far, those that were explicit about purpose in nature most naturally lent themselves to the creation of a worldview based on evolutionary change. The neo-Lamarckian Herbert Spencer, for example, wrote in his book, *Social Statics,* that through use and disuse humans adapted to their environment in such a manner that their future perfection was guaranteed. "Progress, therefore, is not an accident, but a necessity. Instead of civilization being artificial, it is a part of nature; all of a piece with the development of the embryo or the unfolding of a flower." Such grandiose schemes did not disappear after the turn of the twentieth century. Hans Driesch (1867–1941), a student of Ernst Haeckel, began his career as a zoologist at the International Marine Zoology Station in Naples, where he worked for nine years. Through a series of experiments on sea urchin eggs in the 1890s, he was able to show that the embryo could form from half an egg, although it was half the size of a normal embryo. He concluded that the living cell aspired to wholeness and he formulated the view that the development of organisms was regulated by an ordering vital principle that did not contribute to or detract from the normal material or energy exchanges that occurred. Driesch later became a professor of philosophy and further developed his vitalistic views, which, because they sought to explain organic process with the help of a nonmaterial principle, met considerable opposition from many scientific quarters.

By 1930 some biologists, including some of the formulators of the modern evolutionary synthesis, were calling for the removal of metaphysics and speculation from their science. They were uncomfortable with evolutionary theories that fit into larger programs of transcendence. What these scientists urged instead was that biology should be unified around central principles, as were physics and chemistry. They were convinced that the developments in population genetics and systematics had provided the unified framework needed while at the same time purging biology of the mystical, speculative aspects they believed diverted their science into the service of religion and idealism.

It is important to note, however, that these unifiers did not achieve their aim by reducing biology to physics and chemistry. While they acknowledged and respected the regularity of physical law, in their view biology possessed distinctive characteristics that marked it off from the physical sciences. For example, in their understanding of evolution, certain unique properties of organisms *emerged* with the complexity organic molecules represented. In emphasizing the creative aspect of evolution, they avoided a straightforward materialistic determinism. By shunning determinism the makers of the evolutionary synthesis were able to reconcile their understanding of evolution with larger questions of human meaning and progress—to create, in other words, a new evolutionary worldview. In an embrace of the evolutionary synthesis, the individual could find resonance with nature's truth in a manner that helped him or her to understand humankind's place in the grand scheme. Gone was the old purposefulness of Lamarckian thought. In its place was a modern version of evolution that served as a source of meaning.

Julian Huxley spoke of "evolutionary humanism," a notion that inspired young evolutionary scientists who came after him to believe that their studies did have something to do with life's greater significance. In a 1949 book entitled *The Meaning of Evolution,* one of the architects of the modern evolutionary synthesis, the paleontologist George Gaylord Simpson (1902–1984), showed little patience for wrestling with what we have seen in this text to be the complex problem of acquiring knowledge. To him it was simple. He wrote that he assumed the existence of absolute, objective truth and that scientific results approximated that truth. "Otherwise," Simpson continued, "there is no meaning in science or in any knowledge, or in life itself, and no reason to enquire for such meaning."

◎ Molecular Biology ◎

One additional development that occurred primarily in the years after World War II was important in the synthesis of the biological issues of the twentieth century. It was the investigation of matters of heredity and evolution at the molecular level. Darwin had considered such matters on the broader level, accessible to normal observation. Evolutionists just after him focused their examination of living things on tiny organisms such as fruit flies, and on the microscopic analysis of the cell. Among the early investigators of heredity at the cellular level, August Weismann had assumed that cellular processes and the laws of inheritance would ultimately be explained in terms of molecules. His vision was realized in the quarter century after the war, called by one historian of science "the age of molecular biology."

Proteins and Nucleic Acids as Cellular Components

If molecules held the key to understanding the metabolism of the cell and the transfer of enormously complicated hereditary information, then it stood to reason that the molecules involved had to be extremely complex. But what component of the cell had molecules with the potential to account for so much variability?

In the early twentieth century there were two candidates: proteins and a substance known as nuclein. The name protein was given to organic substances present in all constituents of animal and plant bodies by the Dutch chemist G. J. Mulder (1802–1880) in 1839. Mulder was also among the first to attempt an identification of their chemical makeup. The German physiologist Johann Friedrich Miescher (1844–1895) isolated a substance in white blood cells that he called nuclein some three decades later, although initially many chemists regarded nuclein to be a contaminated mixture rather than a complex substance. By the early twentieth century, however, scientists realized that nuclein came in the form of two different nucleic acids and that they and proteins were present in the cell nucleus.

Up to the 1940s attention focused more on proteins than on nucleic acids as possible bearers of hereditary material. Most scientists viewed the latter as relatively simple and uninteresting chemicals in comparison to proteins, whose variability seemed to offer greater chance for expressing the complexity of genetic material. One approach used to study nucleic acids was x-ray diffraction, which had been developed earlier in the century. By firing x-rays at crystals, for example, the regular outline of their structure could be inferred from patterns observed in the experiment.

As techniques for analyzing x-ray diffraction patterns improved, scientists such as Max Perutz (1914–2002) at the Cavendish Laboratory in Cambridge turned them to the investigations of the large molecules of proteins beginning in the late 1930s. Perutz and his colleagues learned how to attempt to re-create the three-dimensional structure of protein molecules from the diffraction patterns. By firing x-rays at different angles they could obtain different images on the screen from which they then addressed the challenging task of creating a three-dimensional model of the molecule. In the late 1940s this work proved valuable to two researchers in London, Maurice Wilkins (1916–2004) and Rosalind Franklin (1920–1958). Working separately, Wilkins and Franklin were each focused on nucleic acids, which by then had been shown to be long-chain molecules of great molecular weight and far more interesting than previously thought.

Around the same time, nucleic acids proved particularly interesting to scientists studying bacterial viruses. A leading figure in this endeavor was the German scientist Max Delbrück (1906–1981), who studied theoretical physics at Göttingen in the 1920s. His interest in biology was triggered by the speculations of the leading quantum physicist of the day, Niels Bohr, whom we will meet again in later chapters. In his musing about the implications of the results of quantum physics for other fields, Bohr had inquired specifically about the relationship between physics and biology in an article he published in 1933. Beginning in the following year, Delbrück was part of a small group of German physicists and biologists who began to meet to discuss the subject. Delbrück came to ideas in these discussions that immediately after the war inspired another quantum physicist, Erwin Schrödinger, to write *What Is Life?* This was a small book in which Schrödinger asked whether unforeseen new laws of physics might possibly emerge from the study of biology.

Delbrück left Germany in 1937 to take a position at the California Institute of Technology, where Thomas Hunt Morgan was then located. Morgan's extensive knowledge of the gene was attractive to Delbrück, although he soon came to the conclusion that any further refinement was not likely to come from studying it as a string of fruit fly chromosomes with the methods of classical physics and chemistry. He decided not to work with a multi-celled organism like the fruit fly; rather, he would focus on a simpler organism that replicated quickly. He chose bacteriophage, viruses that attack bacteria, to carry out the investigation of which molecules carried genetic information. Soon he was joined by others in an assemblage of researchers that became known as the phage group.

The phage group workers began by studying the life cycle of viruses, how cells become infected, and the appearance of mutations in the genetic material of viruses.

While the early work focused on proteins, the group's attention turned toward nucleic acids after the appearance of a 1944 publication concerning the transformation of a benign form of bacteria into a virulent form. It had been known that if an animal was injected with both forms of bacteria, some of the harmless bacteria were transformed into the harmful type. Attempts to isolate the substance that caused this transformation showed in 1944 that the substance was not a protein, as expected, but one of the known types of nucleic acid, deoxyribonucleic acid (DNA). Delbrück was initially suspicious of this result, but by 1951 members of the phage group developed their own reasons to believe that DNA was in fact the genetic material.

Deciphering DNA

One of the young researchers who was attracted to work with DNA was James Watson (b. 1928), a graduate student at Indiana University working under one of Delbrück's associates in the phage group. Watson determined to uncover the secret of the gene after reading Schrödinger's *What Is Life?* Upon completion of his doctoral degree he went abroad on a postdoctoral fellowship, first to Denmark and then to the Perutz group in Cambridge, where he became familiar with the use of

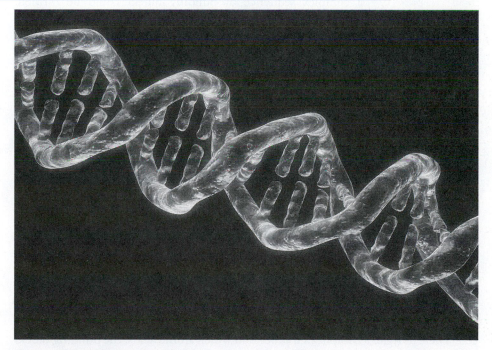

Model of the DNA Spiral

x-rays to study the structure of complex biological molecules. There, in the Cavendish Laboratory, he met Francis Crick (1916–2004) and the two quickly became collaborators in the attempt to decipher the structure of DNA.

Watson and Crick worked for two years in the early 1950s trying to put together everything known about DNA, including information from x-ray diffraction patterns. The x-ray photographs made by Rosalind Franklin, which they obtained without her permission, proved to be of critical importance. They finally came up with a three-dimensional model of the DNA molecule, a double helix whose helices are connected by pairs of nitrogen-containing bases. After many attempts, they discovered how the bases fit together in pairs in a manner that permitted hydrogen bonds to hold the helices together in place and at the same time account for various dimensions the molecule was known to have.

Knowing the architecture of the huge DNA molecule also made it possible to understand how it functioned as the genetic material, a learning process that occurred in the decade following the announcement of DNA's structure by Watson and Crick in April of 1953. First, the number of possibilities in which the base pairs might be arranged was so enormous that it could easily be imagined to account for genetic complexity. Genes, for example, could be thought of as small segments of a strand of the long DNA molecule.

Watson and Crick theorized that their model also made clear the basic process by which the DNA molecule replicated itself. The key question here was how such

a complex sequence of building blocks could be formed. Watson and Crick suggested that if the two helices were separated by rupturing the hydrogen bonds between the base pairs, then each chain could provide the information needed to synthesize a new partner. The only material that would fit onto each of the templates would be equivalent to what had been there prior to the rupturing of the double helix. As the two chains unfolded, new chains were synthesized onto their surface, forming two double helices that were identical to the original. Later it was suggested that if, by chance, new material fit onto the template that was not there before, and then became part of the replicated molecule, the sequence would be altered and thus a mutation would occur.

Having used the structure of DNA to explain replication, molecular biologists also tackled the other major challenge facing them: how to use the model to understand a cell's attributes and functions. These aspects of the cell are controlled by proteins, so a central question was how proteins could be synthesized. Scientists learned how to describe this process in great detail by utilizing a separated strand of the DNA chain as a template to synthesize a single-stranded messenger molecule, which then left the nucleus and entered the cytoplasm of the cell. There it began a complicated process in which amino acids, the building blocks of proteins, were ordered in various ways to yield the great variety of proteins known to exist.

Splitting of DNA
Molecule

The incredible advances in biochemistry and molecular biology of the middle years of the twentieth century, when taken as a complement to the modern evolutionary synthesis that had appeared around the same time, yielded a body of unified knowledge that appeared to rest on the most basic of foundations. We shall see in Chapters 25 and 26 that physical scientists were also refining their knowledge of the tiny atom and the massive universe to a similar degree of exquisite precision. But although in both fields scientists strode like gods, they were opening up new moral challenges that more than ever threatened the future of humankind itself.

Suggestions for Reading

Garland E. Allen, *Life Sciences in the Twentieth Century* (Cambridge: Cambridge University Press, 1978).

Peter Bowler, *Theories of Human Evolution: A Century of Debate, 1844–1944* (Baltimore: Johns Hopkins University Press, 1986).

Lois N. Magner, *A History of the Life Sciences* (New York: Marcel Denker, 2002).

William B. Provine, *The Origins of Theoretical Populations Genetics* (Chicago: University of Chicago Press, 2001).

CHAPTER 24

Earth in the Balance

In 1992, the year in which he was elected vice president of the United States, Senator Albert Gore of Tennessee published a book entitled *Earth in the Balance*. The vice president elect wished to use his prominence in American politics to challenge the perception held by the American public that the Earth was so large it was immune to irreversible changes that could lead to global catastrophe. He regarded the impact of global environmental change as an apocalyptic subject, equal in importance to the threat of nuclear war.

Of course the Earth had been around for a very extended time and scientists had long considered the changes the Earth had gone through and continued to undergo. As we have seen in earlier chapters, natural philosophers from the seventeenth century onward had explored different agencies in their attempts to explain alterations of the Earth's surface over time. Their efforts contributed to the birth of a new idea—that the Earth had a history. Notions of evolution in which species developed or perished in response to an environment that was constantly changing replaced the idea that the world had been divinely created by fiat exactly as it was at that time. It became at least theoretically possible to imagine that even the human species could succumb to drastic environmental change.

As estimates of the age of the Earth grew, however, the threat of danger was hard to take seriously. After the discovery of radioactive decay, scientists in the first decade of the twentieth century estimated from the amounts of uranium, thorium, and lead in rocks that the Earth had been undergoing change for over two billion years. By the time Gore wrote his book, the estimated age of the Earth had increased to over four billion years. Given this enormous span of time, he was hard pressed to persuade his reader that the changes introduced since the industrial era were significant enough to merit a doomsday scenario.

In spite of critics' objections, there were those in the scientific community who agreed that the Earth constituted a complex dynamic system whose ability to support living things could be threatened. Scientists studied various aspects of the

Earth's past stabilities and instabilities, especially those of the twentieth century, with an eye to gaining a long-term view of the planet's history and of our place in it. Those investigations, as we shall see, were prompted by a variety of questions.

◎ The Earth's Dynamic Surface ◎

Even in the nineteenth century, scientists interested in the geographical distribution of species had occasionally noted similarities of species on the African and South American sides of the Atlantic Ocean. Evidence from the past was yet more impressive. By around the turn of the twentieth century any major textbook of geology contained paleontological evidence of identical fossils on the two shores. To account for this, geologists supposed that there had once been land connecting South America and Africa that had sunk under water. The contraction of the cooling Earth had created the Atlantic, which, they argued, was a recent ocean. One young scientist, however, believed that the latest information available contradicted the idea of a sunken land bridge. His views led to the conclusion that the continents had been shifting their positions throughout the Earth's history.

Alfred Wegener and the Theory of Continental Drift

Alfred Wegener (1880–1930) enjoyed few accolades during his lifetime of research; in fact, his ideas attracted considerable criticism and even abuse. He was denounced as incompetent, dishonest, and as a plagiarist by his critics, even though he was none of those things.

The generation of Wegener's theory.   For close to three hundred years the male line of Wegeners had been Protestant clergymen. Alfred Wegener's father was a pastor in Berlin, where Alfred, the youngest of five children, was born. He and his older brother Kurt were always happy explorers around the summer home outside of the city and, when it came time to pursue studies at the university, both went into the sciences. Alfred chose astronomy, eventually completing a doctoral degree in 1905, while Kurt went into geophysics. The dreary calculations Alfred was assigned to do for his thesis did not excite him because they kept him inside, rather than in the field. He decided to go to work as an assistant to his brother, who held a post at the Prussian Aeronautical Observatory. This gave him experience in taking meteorological measurements, even from a free-floating balloon.

As a result of his academic credentials and experience, Alfred won a place on a research expedition to Greenland to study meteorological conditions over a two-year period. He earned a solid reputation as a reliable team member, surviving harrowing conditions to conduct experiments on glaciers and other factors in meteorology and geology. On his return in 1908, he took a lecturing position in astronomy and meteorology at the University of Marburg for the next three years. There he also busied himself on a publication that dealt with the thermodynamics of the atmosphere, which appeared in 1911 and brought him very positive notice as an up-and-coming meteorological authority. But something else had also captured his attention. The previous Christmas his office mate had received a world atlas as a present. Wegener wrote to his fiancée about something he noticed on his own, even though others had done so well before him—the shapes of the South American and African coasts complemented each other, as if they had once fit together.

In the fall of the next year he came upon one of the numerous existing references to the identity of fossils on the two continental shores. As he exhaustively combed through the literature of the various subjects bearing on this question, he found that the standard explanation was that the Atlantic Ocean had only recently been formed and that it had resulted from the sinking of land that had earlier connected Africa and South America. If this were true, then the congruent shapes of the African and South American coastlines was nothing more than a curiosity. But because he had been reading the very latest scientific results in preparation for his classes at Marburg, Wegener knew that the older wisdom about a one-time land connection was flawed.

Wegener relied on a recent 1909 survey of the Earth's gravitational field that confirmed something that had been debated for some time: namely, that the Earth's crust is substantially less dense than the material under it and that it, in fact, floats on the denser material. This clearly negated the claim that the crust had sunk to make the Atlantic Ocean, because a less dense material cannot sink into something of greater density. But there was more. This was right around the time when radioactivity was discovered as a process that added heat to the atmosphere and greatly slowed down the rate at which the Earth was cooling. Without substantial cooling, there was no contraction, and without contraction, no subsidence of the Atlantic Basin. The bottom line, then, was that the conventional explanation for the identical fossils in Africa and South America just would not work.

More research of the literature turned up an assessment of these developments plus the suggestion in a work of 1911 that the *continents* floated on the more dense material beneath them. From here it was not far for Wegener to imagine that floating continents may have *drifted* in the past and he set down his ideas in his first publication on continental drift in 1912. In two different journals, both very respected, Wegener suggested that the Earth was ringed with concentric shells, each more dense than the one above it. The outermost shell, the Earth's crust, was not continuous; it was broken up into segments that formed the continents, which were separated by oceans.

Although the continents floated on the layer of subcrust beneath them, Wegener imagined that they protruded into this region like the base of an iceberg does into the water in which it floats. This was possible because the roots of the continents, being composed of granite that extended kilometers down into the Earth, have a higher melting point than the basalt through which they purportedly floated. Wegener postulated that there were as yet undetermined forces that caused the continents to move or drift—perhaps the Earth's rotation. As the continents drifted, they pushed yielding material on the ocean floors between them, piling it up at the front edge of the line of movement. In this way, Wegener suggested, the mountains on the western sides of North and South America might have formed.

Wegener's theory was impressive, not only for its originality, but because of the disparate findings of the different scientific fields that he had consulted in constructing it. He incorporated evidence from geology, paleontology, geophysics, and geodesy to argue that all the continents had once been a single landmass whose continuity had been disrupted as pieces began drifting off in different directions and at different speeds.

In the same year of the publication of his continental drift theory, Wegener returned to Greenland for another two-year stint of meteorological observations, this time involving him in a perilously long crossing of a polar ice cap from which few of the participants survived. He attempted to gather information that might enable him to document that Greenland had drifted and he had plans to put all of his evidence together in a longer work, when World War I broke out. As an enlisted soldier, Wegener was wounded twice, the second time more seriously, so that during his long recovery he was able to complete a small book on the origins of the continents and the oceans, which he published in 1915.

After the war he found employment in Hamburg at the meteorological observatory and collaborated with his father-in-law, also a meteorologist, in a study of ancient climates as yet another means of supporting his theory of continental drift. He also returned briefly to his interest in astronomy, publishing a short book on the origin of the craters on the moon. Wegener held that they were not volcanoes, as many believed, but that they had resulted from the impact of bodies that had hit the moon. The moon, it turned out, provided him with a laboratory to analyze the age, physical makeup, and activity of a heavenly body, all of which he could use in his analysis of similar questions about the Earth.

Two more revised editions of his book on the origins of the continents and oceans came out in the early 1920s, the second of which was translated into five European languages. With his fame increasing, he received a call to a professorship in Graz, Austria. But he also found that his conclusions, now widely known, had become the center of controversy. Tiring of the need to answer unfounded accusations, Wegener gladly joined another expedition to Greenland that left in 1929. In an attempt to supply the base camp, Wegener, deserted by his Greenlander guides, finally made it in October of 1930. But with five men at the base and provisions for only two, it was decided that Wegener and an Eskimo companion would try to return to the coast. Wegener's body has lain entombed in the Greenland ice since that fateful attempt in November of 1930.

The controversy. Of course the major challenge Wegener faced in trying to convince his contemporaries of the merits of his theory was to overcome their allegiance to the prevailing view of subsiding land forming a recently appearing Atlantic Ocean. On the face of it, as intriguing as the idea of drifting continents might seem to the layperson, to the experts it appeared far-fetched. To persuade the experts, Wegener had appealed to recent research with which they were largely unfamiliar, sometimes because it came from cognate fields they did not know. The result was that they saw him as an outsider, who did not value the kind of evidence they respected. Because even his defenders rarely endorsed his ideas without qualification, there was no groundswell of support for his work.

Alfred Wegener (*left*) and
Greenlander Guide

Wegener's detractors were aware that others had suggested that continents floated, and Wegener freely conceded and cited their work. That did not stop the critics, who expressed outrage at the "dishonesty" and "plagiarism" of the outsider. They simply ignored Wegener's references to the arguments from radioactivity against the theory of a rapidly cooling Earth. Some downplayed the fossil similarities on the two sides of the Atlantic, postulating that there had been isthmuses across the ocean to account for the smaller number of cases they acknowledged.

The most glaring weakness of the theory was Wegener's appeal to the rotation of the Earth as the source of the force that caused continents to drift. Reputable scientists showed how such a force would not be able to accomplish the task, and Wegener really had no way of answering them. His position was somewhat like that of Darwin, who had no reply to Lord Kelvin's arguments against the amount of time available for evolution to have occurred. Darwin had to assume that there was enough time, and that the reason why would someday be found. For a scientist, that is not an enviable position. Likewise Wegener had to assume that if the rotation of the Earth were not a sufficiently strong force, one would be discovered that could accomplish the task. As a result, the American scientists were particularly hard on the theory. "If we are to believe [this] hypothesis," wrote one, "we must forget everything we have learned in the last seventy years and start all over again." Another, the president of the American Philosophical Society, was more succinct. He called it, simply, "utter damned rot."

Plate Tectonics

Not everyone discounted the notion that the substrate beneath continents might permit them to move. To avoid the objection that earthquake shocks would not be transmitted through a liquid substrate in the way we know they are transmitted, the British geologist Arthur Holmes (1890–1965) suggested in 1929 that the substrate might be glassy, that it did not need to be liquid to permit continents to move. Heat generated by radioactivity caused rising currents in the substrate that *carried* the continents along as they cooled, whereupon they sank back into the Earth's mantle again. But although Holmes's work was widely read, it would not be until after the Great Depression and World War II that new evidence overcame the strong opposition to continental drift.

During the war, P. M. S. Blackett (1897–1974), one of the former students of the physicist Ernest Rutherford in Cambridge, became involved in scientific research for the military. After the war, wishing to distance himself from the nuclear work that had led to the atomic bomb, he turned to geomagnetism. He explored for a time the question of what caused the Earth's magnetic field, before turning to the magnetism in rocks. Since early in the twentieth century it was known that cooling rocks permanently assumed their magnetic polarity at a certain temperature; that is, after a certain point in the cooling process rocks retain what is called remanent magnetism. So if over time the magnetic polarity in a region changed, then the magnetic signatures of different rocks would reveal that change.

By the mid-1950s, Blackett and his collaborators at Cambridge University had become convinced that they could show that the Earth's magnetic field had changed over the course of its geological history. Further, they asserted that the variations they observed showed that the rocks had moved relative to the Earth's magnetic field. But that raised a question as to whether the rocks had drifted away from the pole, as Blackett now maintained in support of continental drifting, or whether the pole had shifted, as many in Britain maintained.

The resolution of the issue came in the 1960s, when geophysicist Harry Hess (1906–1969) turned his attention again to the mid-oceanic ridges that formed a network within the Earth's oceans. Knowing that the ridges were volcanic, Hess suggested that the sea floor was spreading out from the ridge on either side.

Magnetic surveys of the ocean floor using sophisticated new instruments revealed a clear pattern, often in long stripes of opposite magnetic polarity. Several scientists suggested that the pattern could be used to support the spreading sea-floor theory. What was happening, Hess said, was that the lava extruded through volcanic activity cooled, preserving the magnetic polarity that existed when it reached the requisite temperature. When the Earth's polarity reversed, a new stripe was created. It was as if there were tapes slowly unrolling at each side of the ridge and recording the Earth's magnetic polarity each time the polarity reversed. And the stripes were moving toward continents on either side of the ridge.

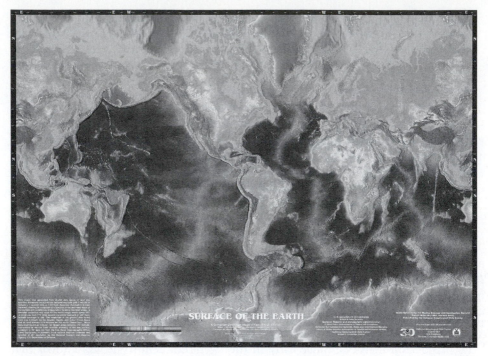

SURFACE OF THE EARTH

Mid-Oceanic Ridges

According to this explanation, the ocean floor formed something of a "conveyor belt." It was renewed by material that was extruded from the ridges and moved away in two directions. As the belt moved it either carried continents along with it, as was evident at the shallow eastern coast of North America, or it descended again to the depths, as occurred in the trench off the coast of Japan. From this theory the notion eventually emerged that just as separate continents defined the most elevated parts of the Earth's crust, so too were there separate plates beneath the crust that were in constant motion, being fueled by a circulation that emerged from below at the oceanic ridges and returned at trenches. In 1969 two different journals of science spoke of "plate tectonics" in their reference to this general idea, which became an accepted theory of geological science.

◎ Framing a Science of Ecology ◎

Around the same time that Wegener was thinking about past conditions of the Earth, others were beginning to become interested in its present state. The context for this new concern was the relationship between living things and the conditions in which they found themselves. For some time, scientists had been interested in how species fit together within the geography of a region; scientific explorers in the nineteenth century, for example, were intrigued by the geographical distribution of species. In addition, naturalists such as Darwin spoke of an "entangled bank," a complex web of relationships among plants, animals, and the inorganic world that resulted from nature's laws at work. But Darwin did not investigate the details of *how* plants and animals adjusted to their rivals. Now scientists began to focus on these details.

The word *ecology* first appeared in Ernst Haeckel's book on general morphology in 1866. Haeckel coined the term *Ökologie* from the ancient Greek terms οἶκος and λόγος to refer to the study of nature's household. He noted that the interactions among all neighboring organisms exerted an even greater influence on the change and adaptation of species than did the inorganic conditions of existence, adding that these very complicated relationships between organisms remained for the most part unknown because scientists had so far failed to attend to them. As he put it, "Ecology or the theory of the economy of nature, this being a division of physiology and one which our textbooks have totally ignored, when seen from this perspective promises to reward us with splendid and surprising discoveries."

The Context of the Emergence of Ecology

By 1893 the president of the British Association of Science could depict ecology as "by far the most attractive" of three fundamental approaches to biology, the other two being physiology and morphology. Less than a decade later, in the spring of 1902, several readers of the American journal *Science* sent letters to the editor concerning the word "ecology." One noted the origin of the word in Haeckel's work and a writer from Massachusetts commented that the subject was now prominent in all recent botanical textbooks. "Every schoolboy," he suggested, "if taught by a modern teacher, knows something of it." That same writer also provided ecology's definition as "the science of the adaptation of organisms to their surroundings," adding that botanists pursued it more than zoologists.

Ecology and the new biology.   According to some historians, the new science of ecology took its place amid a movement toward a new biology as the nineteenth century drew to a close. The older biology emphasized natural history, a traditional enterprise, pursued by gentlemen natural philosophers who accepted the complexity of nature for what it was and assumed that the scientist's task was to master nature's details as much as possible. Natural historians such as Charles Darwin, for example, were convinced that only extensive and hard-wrought experience in the field qualified one to make valid and accurate generalizations about evolution.

The new biologists sought to avoid the impression that biology could be done by amateurs doing fieldwork. They stressed the need for trained laboratory scientists who knew how to compile quantitative relationships of measurement as the foundation of their understanding of nature. Where evolution was concerned, scientists such as Thomas Huxley emphasized the laboratory study of morphology, which increasingly relied on improved instrumentation at the expense of such issues emphasized by Darwin as geographical distribution and adaptation. Reforming biology by de-emphasizing fieldwork, however, understandably strained some scientists' perception of who they were.

The new science of ecology was able to smooth over such disagreements to some degree. On the one hand it represented the new direction in biology that emphasized the need to be scientific by obtaining precise information about the impact of environmental conditions, some of which could be duplicated for study in the laboratory. It was, in other words, part of the new biology. But it also clearly recognized the requirement of fieldwork to accomplish its goal. The essential tension between laboratory and field studies did not disappear; it remained visible in the emphasis individual ecologists placed on one feature or the other. What resulted was not a single discipline of ecology, but different versions of ecological science operating from diverse institutional settings.

Progress and conservation.   Ecology also confronted another tension within late nineteenth-century society about how to pursue economic progress. As we observed in Chapter 22, purposeful evolution remained alive and well as the century came to a close. Many evolutionists came to the conclusion that the laws of natural science provided support for the strong belief in progress indicative of the age. This meant that, unlike the tendency of twenty-first-century ecologists to be suspicious of unregulated economic development, some pursued their new science as a means of promoting empire building and greater progress.

But the era also saw the growth of concern about overdevelopment and the possible alteration of the balance of nature through unchecked human intervention. The goal here was not to criticize economic progress, but to place checks on human greed before it either depleted needed resources or despoiled the beauty and appeal of the household of nature. The writings of Henry David Thoreau (1817–1862) in America not only celebrated such pristine locations as Walden Pond in Massachusetts, but delivered a warning about the impact of human attempts to tame nature. His famous line, "In wildness is the preservation of the world," appeared first in a lecture, then in an *Atlantic Monthly* essay of 1862. The previous year, Thoreau had written in his journal, "Thank God, men cannot as yet fly, and lay waste the sky as well as the earth!"

In the United States individuals successfully worked to set aside tracts of land so they could be protected from development. Both the Yosemite Valley in California and the region of the Yellowstone River near the Rocky Mountains in Wyoming became national parks by 1890. In 1864 a New England diplomat and amateur scientist, reacting to his observation of the damaging effects that clearing had on the Vermont landscape, wrote *Man and Nature*. George Perkins Marsh's (1801–1882) original title had been *Man the Disturber of Nature's Harmonies*, but he softened it because he realized that humans could not help but disturb the balance of nature. Nevertheless, he called on humankind to become good stewards of natural resources. His work was one of the factors that later helped persuade the national government to assume a part in the supervision of American forestland. In 1891 the Forest Reserve Act empowered presidents to establish national forests, and in 1905 the United States created the Forest Service as an agency of the Department of Agriculture.

Early Ecologists

The countries of Denmark, Great Britain, and the United States provided the foci for several important early ecologists, most of whom traveled considerably in pursuit of their new undertaking.

The impact of Eugenius Warming.   Among the earliest names associated with the birth of the science of plant ecology is Eugenius Warming (1841–1924), a Danish professor of botany and director of the botanical institute at the University of Copenhagen from 1886 to 1911. Warming had done extensive botanical fieldwork in the very different climates of Brazil, Greenland, and Norway prior to his appointment in Copenhagen, and in Venezuela and the West Indies while he was a professor there. The culmination of his experience appeared in a Danish book of 1895 on the fundamentals of ecological plant geography. This work, which became more accessible to scientists when it came out in German translation the following year, has been called by historian of science William Coleman the most influential publication of the early years of ecology.

Warming observed that plant species were not distributed evenly over the areas they occupied; rather, they grouped themselves into communities. He wanted to ask why they did that and why the communities displayed a variety of appearances. These questions led to a much more difficult matter, what he called the "economy of plants," that is, the demands plants made on their environments. "How do plants make use of surrounding conditions," he asked, "and how are the internal and external structure and the physiognomy of plants adapted to these conditions?" Here Warming was bringing adaptation, previously a topic coveted particularly by the evolutionist, also into the purview of the ecologist.

Eugenius Warming

In his overview of the ecological factors he believed important in the life of plants, Warming wrote of the influence of light, temperature, humidity, the movement of air, the condition of the soil and its impact on whether it was covered or not covered, and the activities of any animals or plants living in the soil. In all of this Warming stressed that acquiring and retaining water was a central concern of analysis. Of course he also included in this overview the manner in which plants of the same species competed with each other, how plant communities interacted, and how plants and animals interacted. Although Warming did want to know about the evolutionary history of plants, he held that natural selection played a minor role.

Organizing British ecology.   One young British botanist who knew German and worked through the translation of Warming's book in 1898 was Arthur Tansley (1871–1955). He immediately went out into the English countryside to see if he could find the communities Warming had described for Denmark and he also made Warming's work the basis for a course of lectures he delivered the following year at University College in London.

In 1900 Tansley left for Ceylon, the Malay Penninsula, and Egypt, where he further tested Warming's ideas in the field. On his return to England, Tansley became an effective advocate for ecology. He spelled out an agenda for the science in a lecture to the British Association of Science in 1904 that included, first, the description and enumeration of plant associations and, second, an explanation of what had been uncovered. He called for the erection of field laboratories to do the observational and experimental work that would enable ecologists to ascertain why plants came together in distinct surroundings, why they exhibited certain morphological and physiological characteristics, and what the relationship was to each other and to their inorganic environment.

Prior to World War I Tansley became known not so much for his own research, but for his efforts to promote ecology. For example, with others he implemented one of the recommendations he made in his 1904 lecture to set up a committee that would systematically survey and map the vegetation of the British Isles. After participating in a tour to observe the plant geography of Switzerland in 1908, he organized a similar expedition for the British Isles in 1911, a venture that not only resulted in the publication of his *Types of British Vegetation* in 1912, but fostered close relationships between the British and American ecologists who participated. And 1913 saw the establishment of the first formal institution of ecology, the British Ecological Society, with Tansley as its president. He became editor of the society's *Journal of Ecology* in 1917 and retained that post for twenty-one years.

American ecological pioneers. Among the Americans who joined Tansley's tour in 1911 was Frederic Clements (1874–1945), a professor of botany from the University of Minnesota. Clements was by then well known in ecological circles. Born in Nebraska, he studied botany at the university in Lincoln as an undergraduate, remaining to complete his doctoral degree in 1898. As a young student he became involved with a project being conducted by the head of the botany department and a graduate student, who were engaged in a survey of the state's vegetation. Because settlers were rapidly plowing the land, the hope was to record existing vegetation before it disappeared. The undertaking gave Clements, now a graduate student himself, and Roscoe Pound (1870–1964), valuable experience in methods of field surveying and the material for a joint doctoral thesis, which appeared in print as *Phytogeography of Nebraska* in 1898.

Clements and Pound devised a new method of gathering information, which they first described in 1898 and which, within a decade, became one of the most significant techniques in plant ecology. Rather than depending on impressionistic descriptions of large representative areas, Pound and Clements marked off a square meter of a typical situation and carefully recorded the number of plant species it contained. They also could use what soon became known as the quadrat as a control region for experiments. With their new method—described again in Clements's book of 1905 on *Research Methods in Ecology*—they brought to ecology a level of precision it had not possessed earlier.

One aspect of Clements's book that was less well received was his view that plant communities were themselves organisms. Pound, who left ecology to study law, recalled much later how as graduate students he and Clements had closely studied Herbert Spencer's *Principles of Biology,* in which human society was regarded as a superorganism. As part of his description of the effects of evolution, Spencer had observed that, in addition to individual organisms, "we may recognize something like a growing of the entire aggregate of organisms."

This attempt to merge ecology with the physiology of organisms did not please one potential British reviewer of the work, who withdrew from the task once he had read Clements's entire book. Tansley stepped into the breach, praising its general comprehensiveness while cautioning against ready assent to its more hypothetical aspects. But such criticism and hesitation did not deter Clements. In a 1916 book he developed the idea of the *climax formation* of vegetation, which as "the fully developed community, of which all initial and medial stages are but stages of development," he likened to an adult organism. This climax stage of a natural landscape was the stable end point toward which it had been driven, primarily by climate. Once attained, it existed in relatively permanent equilibrium with surrounding conditions. This idea, as we shall see, bore implications for how humans viewed environmental conservation.

Ecology Between the Wars

World War I interrupted the development of the field of ecology just as it did the pursuit of all the natural sciences. The year before war broke out, however, Clements and a colleague at the University of Chicago organized a second international tour, in which ten European ecologists participated. Tansley, reporting on the event for a British journal, noted that "in the vast field of ecology America has secured a commanding position." From the energy and number of American ecologists, he continued, there could be little doubt that America's pre-eminence in this branch of biology would be maintained.

By this time different schools of ecology existed in the United States, in Britain, and on the European Continent. Whereas the Americans wanted to record what communities of plants succeeded each other, the British concentrated more on the causal mechanisms of succession, while the Europeans focused on statistical data concerning composition and structure of vegetation. What was also clear to the interested observer was that up to the 1920s botanists had dominated ecology. After the war, however, zoologists began to increase their involvement.

The growth of animal ecology. Two universities figured prominently in the emergence of animal ecology, the University of Chicago in the United States and Oxford University in Britain. In both cases key individuals from the departments of zoology placed their mark on the study of animals in their environments.

Already in 1908 Chicago offered a course on animal ecology and within two years a sequence of studies on animal behavior and ecology. This was mainly due to the efforts of Victor Shelford (1877–1968), who gave the field a particular physiological orientation. Shelford rejected the emphases on evolution and morphology that had dominated the study of animal distribution in favor of an approach that focused on the behavioral and physiological characteristics of a group of organisms. Where vegetation was concerned, changes in the plant's structure were used to give indication of its response to environmental conditions. Shelford asserted that the corresponding indicator in animals was less the structural adaptations evolution produced than an animal's activity or behavior. His studies of animal ecology classified diverse groups based on their similar habits and used these habits to determine important environmental factors that governed how they were distributed.

One of Shelford's students at Chicago, Ward Clyde Allee (1885–1955), set up experiments to study how animals were distributed by finding out how they responded to environmental stimuli. He chose isopods, small crustaceans, one species of which live in ponds and streams. Because he dealt with the same species in the different environments of ponds and streams, he could attribute differences in behavior to the different environments. Under the traditional approach, which utilized classification based on heredity, no indication of environmental differences emerged; hence Allee argued that the traditional approach was not equipped to provide an understanding of ecological relationships.

Allee, who as a Quaker was opposed to violence and war, rejected as well the foundation on which he believed the emphasis on evolutionary study of animal behavior rested. As noted in G. K. Chesterson's critique of eugenics in Chapter 23, some in the postwar period traced the exclusive reliance on natural selection to a German understanding of evolution. Allee associated this view of evolution with the work of August Weismann (see Chapter 22) and he rejected it in favor of more "peaceful" interpretations that recognized cooperation among animals. Allee's study of animals rested on an understanding of biology in which the same natural laws governed both animal and human communities. He preferred to invoke animal ecology in support of a moral vision that did not run directly against the goals of democracy.

Oxford was the other university setting in which animal ecology emerged. In June of 1921 Oxford sponsored an expedition to Bear Island and Spitsbergen in the arctic region north of Norway. The group comprised a twenty-member team of scientists from a variety of fields. Included in the expedition was an aspiring young ecology student named Charles Elton (1900–1991) and one of his mentors at Oxford, Julian Huxley, whom we met in Chapter 23. Paying attention to local climatic conditions, Elton created zones into which he plotted his own findings as well as those of the ornithologists, geologists, paleobotanists, and glaciologists who were part of the expedition. The result was ecological maps that gave an overview of the expedition. On his return to Oxford, Elton wrote Huxley that he wanted to use his notes to "do some ecology propaganda."

There would be two more expeditions to Spitsbergen by 1924, with Elton on both of them. The last one made use of the airplane as a research instrument, providing the aerial overview that would be crucial to Elton's approach. He had climbed a mountain on the 1921 expedition to obtain an aerial view that facilitated his determination of the ecological zones between species as they related to environment and climate. Now he could see nature from above, his preferred vantage point for writing about the relations between animals and their environment. This aerial view, in the words of one historian of ecology, "was at the very core of British ecological reasoning." Before 1924 was out Elton published an article on the periodic fluctuations in animal populations. Elton was convinced that climate was a determining factor in the dynamics of animal populations and he hoped to use his findings about populations as a possible indicator of future climate patterns.

In 1928 Elton published a volume in Huxley's popular science series entitled *Animal Ecology*. In it he discussed the standard environmental zones of climate, topography, and temperature, explaining how these affected animal communities. He then moved on to apply ideas to ecology that he had gleaned from one of his teachers at Oxford. The teacher, Alexander Morris Carr-Saunders (1886–1966), had studied biometry and was vitally interested in eugenics and the need to use biology to improve society. From Carr-Saunders's discussion of economic cycles and class conflicts in England, Elton borrowed the notion of the food chain, which could be used to connect species from various places in the so-called chain of being. In nature's economic order, food was an essential commodity. A single food source might link hundreds of species in a complex web of interaction.

Like Allee, Elton linked humans to animals in the context of animal ecology. He noted that previously, human ecology and animal ecology had developed in contrast to one another, with the former being concerned only with the effects that humans had had on humans, ignoring the animals among which humans lived. Elton maintained that human and animal communities had much in common and that ecology had much to learn by realizing that. This perspective of Elton and Allee—that humans took their place in the larger world of the ecology of animals—meant that humankind's fate became linked more obviously to that of the Earth's other creatures.

Experiencing the dust bowl. One development that caught the attention of Americans and brought home the lesson that human behavior could have a dangerously disruptive impact on ecological relationships was the dust bowl on the Great Plains of the 1930s. While the people of Kansas and Oklahoma had experienced dust storms before, no one was prepared for the number and severity of the storms that began in 1934 and lasted for several years.

It was not long before an explanation was found—the destruction of the native sod over a fifty-year period by settlers growing wheat crops. By eliminating the diversity of vegetation with a single cash crop and by plowing furrows often parallel to the wind, these "sodbusters" had removed nature's buffers against wind and drought.

What enabled the settlers prior to the 1930s to overlook the periodic droughts that began already in the nineteenth century was not only the eventual return of the rains, but the pioneering spirit that assumed America's resources were unending. The song "America the Beautiful" proclaimed in 1904 that beneath America's spacious skies lay amber waves of grain, that purple mountain majesties rose above the fruited plain, and that it was all the result of God's shedding his grace on the United States. More and more Midwestern land was plowed under until, in the 1930s, the severity of the drought and dust convinced everyone that something was seriously wrong.

One constructive result of the dust bowl was the congealing of a conservation movement from loosely connected individual ventures into a more consciously ecological outlook that was more coordinated. The scientist leaders of this movement appealed to Clements's idea of climax formation in their assessment of what had gone wrong. Clements had warned against destroying the Nebraska sod in his work of 1898. Now he and his followers in the 1930s asserted that the dust bowl problem came about because the pioneers had not understood the implications of the climax formation of the Great Plains, which did not include unstable human crops.

Clements argued that the climax formation was an ecologically stable environment, which, when disrupted by climate change, led to periods of instability. But because the climax formation was like an organism, he believed that it was capable of absorbing periodic drought. His recommendation was therefore to adapt human ends to the natural cycles of drought. While ideally the plains would be conserved by refraining from intrusions into nature, Clements suggested that humans could learn how to work with nature's organic ability to respond to human intrusions so that the normal equilibrium of the climax formation was not unduly disturbed. Too great an intrusion, however, could upset the balance. The climax formation school in general opposed the unrestrictive intrusion of technology into the environment in pursuit of human interests.

While opposition to the conservation ideal associated with climax formation arose in the 1930s and reasserted itself periodically thereafter, Clements's notion enjoyed wide support and has continued to do so ever since. The assumption that humankind can learn how to establish and maintain a balance between nature's interests and those of humans, while no longer necessarily based on the idea that plant communities are superorganisms, nevertheless assumes that humans assert their rights over nature only at great risk to themselves.

Ecosystem ecology.   In the same decade that the dust bowl plagued midwestern Americans, the British ecological pioneer Arthur Tansley capped his growing criticism of Clements's ecology with a new vision that removed reference to vegetation as superorganism. Tansley became convinced that even the term *community* invested nature with unacceptable anthropomorphic implications. He did not want to regard plants and animals as possessing a psychic bond between them; rather, they were parts that together simply made up a larger whole. In his view the whole was not greater than its parts, as appeared to be the case with organisms; rather, the wholes were "in analysis nothing but the synthesized actions of the components in association." He proposed the name *ecosystem* as a term that did not separate living and nonliving components of the environment in the way that the notion of ecological community did.

By including both physical and biological aspects of the environment, Tansley's ecosystem idea brought ecology within the purview of physical science. From this perspective ecology reinforced the trend, already underway, to concern itself with the structure of energy systems. Energy, a broader category than food, enabled ecologists to survey the entire system with respect to the energy relations present. Raymond Lindeman (1915–1942) argued in the early 1940s that energy became less available

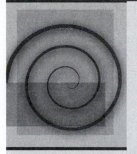

The NATURE of SCIENCE

Are Humans the Problem and the Solution?

The different ecological outlooks of Clements and Tansley raise the question about what the ultimate role of humankind regarding the environment should be. On the one hand are those who believe that because the application of technology in the pursuit of human progress has created environmental problems and has even led to a crisis, the proper response is to minimize and, where possible, to remove such distortions in the delicate balance of nature by returning to simpler lifestyles. In this view, technology is the enemy because it has allowed humankind to assume a disproportionate place in the world of living things and to exert an unnatural intervention into the natural course of things. The proper human attitude vis-à-vis the environment should be one of humility.

Others believe that although technology has been a participating cause in producing environmental problems, it nevertheless represents the best hope of correcting those problems. In this outlook, it is unreasonable to expect that the human species will forsake its pursuit of progress; hence the responsible action is to undertake human activities that permit the environment to sustain itself. Humans must therefore be confident that they have acquired an adequate understanding of ecological requirements and that they can manage collective human activity sufficiently to assure that they will not initiate irreversible damage to the environment.

Although presenting merely these two outlooks oversimplifies the complex challenge facing human society, these extremes do uncover fundamental dimensions of the problem that should not be forgotten in the ongoing debate.

as one moved up the food chain. He claimed further that ecological succession could be analyzed in terms of the energy flow through the ecosystem. Lindeman's work was at first controversial, but it soon became a central pillar of ecosystem ecology.

Tansley's concept of the ecosystem was mechanistic, analyzing the interaction of plants and animals with their physical environment in terms reminiscent of physics. His approach supported rather than questioned the perception that nature was a repository of resources to be managed. With this new ecology came the sense that humankind not only could, but should, take responsibility for the environment by controlling it in such a manner that the circulation of matter and energy became as efficient as possible.

◎ Environmental Science Comes of Age ◎

Among the tumultuous events of the war-torn 1940s, none had a greater impact on shaping the global future than the development of the atomic bomb, which was used twice on the Japanese during World War II. In the years immediately after the war the United States set out to conduct further nuclear testing of fission bombs in the Marshall Islands in the Pacific, which the Americans had captured from the Japanese in 1944. By the early 1950s the United States was also ready to test the hydrogen bomb, which it did first on a tiny island that was one of the many islands of the Enewetak Atoll, in the fall of 1952 (see Chapter 26). A year and a half later another test was held on the northwest corner of the Bikini Atoll, some two hundred miles to the east, this time yielding an even greater explosion.

As part of the testing program, the government deployed scientists to take an initial survey of the region's atolls in 1946. Later, the Atomic Energy Commission enlisted two brothers, both ecologists, to undertake an ecological study of the Enewetak Atoll in order to determine the effects of the testing on the geology and biology of the region. The brothers were embarking on careers that would shape the field of ecosystem ecology.

The Contribution of the Odum Brothers

The work of Eugene Odum (1913–2002) and his younger brother Howard (1924–2002) on the Enewetak Atoll in 1954 represented the first time that anyone had attempted to investigate a complete ecosystem with the specific intent of measuring its overall metabolism. What they achieved helped set the tone for what Eugene dubbed "the new ecology" over the next decades.

Born over ten years apart, Eugene and Howard Odum spent their youth in an academic family. Their father, Howard W. Odum, was a professor of sociology at the University of North Carolina in Chapel Hill, where both sons attended as undergraduates. Eugene stayed at Chapel Hill to earn his master's degree before attending graduate school in zoology in 1936 at the University of Illinois, where the ecologist Victor Shelford was then teaching. After earning his doctoral degree in zoology, Eugene took a position in zoology at the University of Georgia in 1940 and remained there for the balance of his career.

At Georgia, Eugene began his collaboration with the Atomic Energy Commission by undertaking an ecological survey of the proposed site for a nuclear weapons facility on the Savannah River near Augusta, Georgia. With funds received from the United States government he enlisted graduate students in long-term research in radiation ecology, eventually establishing the Institute of Ecology at the University of Georgia. His interest in ecosystems derived from this work.

As an undergraduate Howard T. Odum earned a degree in zoology in 1947. His father, who had been a visiting professor at Yale after the war, introduced him to Yale's limnologist G. Evelyn Hutchinson (1903–1991), who was taking a novel approach to the ecology of lakes. Hutchinson was convinced that ecologists were making a mistake to view the inorganic world mainly as causal factors of biological effects. He believed that the relationship between the inorganic and organic realms was mutually interactive; for example, the presence of several gases—oxygen, nitrogen, and carbon dioxide—was due to *organic* activity. As a result, Hutchinson urged that ecologists adopt a *biogeochemical* approach.

The younger Odum found Hutchinson's work stimulating, even to the point of sending articles by him to his older brother, who himself soon began corresponding with the Yale scientist. At Hutchinson's recommendation, Howard read widely in a new area called physical biology, the application of physical principles to complex biological systems. He delved especially into the study of thermodynamics, learning how and to what extent such notions as equilibrium and entropy could be related to living systems. The result was that Howard learned how to approach ecosystems as a physical scientist, a valuable complement to the viewpoint of his brother. After receiving his doctoral degree from Yale in 1951, he contributed the chapter on energy to a new textbook project that Eugene had undertaken.

Fundamentals of Ecology appeared in 1953, the first and for some time the only textbook in ecology. Translated eventually into twelve languages, it exerted an enormous influence on the field of ecology and on the broader academic world by bringing into common parlance the concept of the ecosystem as a basic unit of nature. It was not until the second edition of 1959 that Eugene Odum incorporated into the text a central insight that solidified from the work he and his brother did in the Marshall Islands, which they had taken up the year after the text's initial edition.

What their study of the Enewetak Atoll reinforced was that the reef as a whole was self-sustaining. While this result in itself might not appear at first glance as particularly profound, what was both impressive and crucial for further ecological investigation was why and how this was so. The Odums established an energy budget for the reef as a whole. It showed that the reef did not depend on nutrients entering it from the ocean; rather, the ecosystem of the atoll recycled necessary nutrients within itself—it was self-sufficient and self-regulating.

In the second edition of his textbook, Eugene Odum made use of the concept of homeostasis, originally used by an author he had read as a graduate student to refer to an organism's ability to maintain an internal stability in the midst of an environment that changed around it. Odum made homeostasis into a general principle that applied to all levels of biological organization, including ecosystems. In so doing he was carrying ecosystem ecology in a different direction from the one Tansley had initially envisioned when he went against Clements's idea of superorganism. Unlike Tansley, Odum clearly believed that the whole was greater than the sum of its parts, a conclusion he explicitly drew. In 1964, as president of the Ecological Society of America, he announced that in "the new ecology" reductionistic methods could not explain living systems adequately. Although some ecologists continued to resist a holistic outlook, the work of the Odum brothers went a long way toward establishing its association with the new ecology.

The Emergence of Ecological Consciousness

By mid-century a central lesson of the science of ecology began to spread beyond the scientific community to the general public: nature comprised a carefully balanced, complex set of relationships that could be upset. In 1949 a book by the Wisconsin conservationist Aldo Leopold (1886–1948), *Sand County Almanac*, warned about the incompatibility between what he called the "Abrahamic concept of land," in which land was regarded as a commodity, and efforts to preserve the

Howard Odum (*left*) and Eugene Odum

balance of nature. He worried that conservation was going nowhere and that the land could not survive the onslaught of mechanization.

As their reputations grew, both of the Odum brothers also became active in the conservation movement. Against developers of the coastal regions of Georgia, Eugene Odum educated citizens about the value of wetlands and was instrumental in persuading the state legislature to pass the Coastal Marshlands Protection Act of 1970. That same year, when Americans observed the first Earth Day, Odum was featured in the popular newsmagazines *Time* and *Newsweek* as a leading ecologist. Brother Howard Odum also worked to preserve wetlands. He established the Center for Wetlands at the University of Florida in 1973 both for ecological research and to develop sustainable ways of utilizing wetlands.

The background to *Silent Spring*. By far, however, the greatest stimulus to developing an ecological consciousness in the public mind was the publication in 1962 of *Silent Spring* by Rachel Carson (1907–1964). Carson's work represents an example, not the first we have encountered in this text, of the use of science to support an ideological cause, in this case humankind's responsibility to control nature.

Carson studied zoology as an undergraduate, then earned a master's degree in genetics from Johns Hopkins University in 1932. The Great Depression hit her hard, eventually making the prospect of obtaining a doctoral degree impossible. Eager to find work in a male-dominated field, Carson took the civil service examination in zoology in 1935 with the hope that a position in some governmental agency might open up. She did extremely well on the examination and finally, in August of 1936, she obtained a position at the Bureau of Fisheries, where she was able to use her considerable skills as a writer in editing various brochures meant for a general audience about fish conservation.

Carson devoted nights and weekends to writing, a pastime she had cultivated since her undergraduate days. Although her submissions prior to 1937 had been rejected, the editors of *The Atlantic Monthly* finally recognized her ability to fire the imagination of the layperson about the findings of science. In the fall of that year they published her essay depicting undersea life from the viewpoint of the creatures who lived there. This began a successful publishing career in science writing. Her serialized essays in leading magazines earned her a devoted following, and in 1951 her book, *The Sea Around Us*, won the national book award.

Now an author with considerable fame, she made use of the opportunity she had to urge the nation to conserve nature's beauty rather than despoil it. A 1958 essay entitled "Our Ever Changing Shore" appeared in a special edition of *Holiday* magazine devoted to "Nature's America." In it Carson reminded her readers of the millions and millions of years the shores had existed, noting that the shore might seem beyond the power of humankind to change or corrupt. But, she wrote, this was not so. "Unhappily, some of the places of which I have written no longer remain wild and unspoiled."

Carson and others had long been concerned about the negative effects the widely used pesticide DDT was having on the environment. Because its lethal effectiveness on insects was demonstrated, both chemical companies and the government touted it highly for use in agriculture.

While efforts were made to exhibit its safety, Carson was not alone in worrying about possible long-term effects. In January of 1958 a woman from Massachusetts wrote a letter to a Boston newspaper chronicling the deaths of the birds in her backyard, which, she asserted, resulted from spraying for mosquitoes with DDT. The woman had become acquainted with Carson seven years earlier, and wrote to her about the problem. For this and other reasons, Carson decided in the late 1950s to write a short book detailing the problem, but as she learned more about pesticides, she realized that their significance was even more disastrous than she suspected.

The impact of Carson's book.　　Other events magnified the force of *Silent Spring* when it appeared in 1962. In 1959 the Food and Drug Administration banned cranberries sprayed with the herbicide aminotriazole after studies of the previous year determined that it caused thyroid cancer in rats. Then in 1962, just before Carson's book was published, a controversy broke out about the prospective manufacture in the United States of the drug thalidomide, which elsewhere had been shown to cause birth defects when taken by pregnant women.

The book first came to light in a condensed version of three installments in *The New Yorker* beginning in June of 1962. Its chapters had provocative titles such as "Elixirs of Death," "And No Birds Sing," and "Needless Havoc," the latter of which charged that there had been a "direct killing of birds, mammals, fishes, and indeed, practically every form of wildlife by chemical insecticides indiscriminately sprayed on the land." Later chapters examined the potential effects of pesticides on human health, including the suggestion that they could be linked to cancer. She began her final chapter with an allusion to the poem by Robert Frost that spoke of two paths diverging in a wood. Carson declared that Americans had been traveling the easy road. "The other fork of the road—the one 'less traveled by'—offers our last, our only chance to reach a destination that assures the preservation of our earth."

The New Yorker received more mail from the installments of *Silent Spring* than it ever had for any article. Many praised the work for calling attention to a crucial problem facing humankind, while others severely criticized it. This would set the tone for the reaction to *Silent Spring* when it appeared as a book. The work had its devoted defenders and its harsh critics.

Leading the way for the opposition to Carson was, not surprisingly, the chemical industry, which saw its profits from pesticides threatened. One company declared that the condensed installments that had appeared were full of inaccuracies, threatening the publisher of the book, Houghton Mifflin, with a lawsuit if it went ahead with its publication, and suggesting that the work was a communist plot to destroy American agriculture and the country's economy. Former secretary of agriculture Ezra Taft Benson joined in, charging Carson with being a communist. Other political leaders pointed out that Carson had conducted no original scientific research and asked Americans, in the words of a Mississippi congressman, to "move it over from the non-science fiction section of the library to the science-fiction section, while we review the facts—in order that we may continue to enjoy the abundant life."

Such criticism merely raised the public's awareness of Carson's book and generated ardent defenders. It was soon compared with such American literary classics as *Uncle Tom's Cabin* and brought numerous awards her way. The National Wildlife Federation named her the Conservationist of the Year, while the National Audubon Society selected her as the first woman to receive the Audubon Medal. After Carson testified before the President's Science Advisory Committee in January of 1963, the committee's report on the use of pesticides, released four months later, included a section on the hazards of pesticides and supported her assertions that DDT and other pesticides had negatively impacted the environment, including the tissues of humans and wildlife. Rachel Carson had contributed in a major way to raising the country's ecological and environmental consciousness.

◎ Ecology and Evolution ◎

Although by the mid-1960s ecosystem ecology had become well established as the heart of the new ecology proclaimed by the Odum brothers, their understanding of ecology contained nuances that ran counter to the evolutionary synthesis described in Chapter 23. In particular, the notion of homeostasis introduced by the Odums to refer to the maintenance of the stability of the ecosystem as a whole clearly did not focus or depend on individual organisms. But the understanding of evolution by natural selection as it was understood at mid-century did.

For the Odums and other ecologists, the ecosystem was sensitive to various levels of organization in nature that functioned to keep it stable. From this perspective, as historian Joel Hagen has explained, the integrity of the ecosystem depended on factors whose function appeared to be geared to that purpose. For example, bacteria decompose nutrients so that they are not removed from the biogeochemical cycling necessary for maintaining the ecosystem, as they would be if dead organic material did not decompose. When ecosystem ecologists regarded bacteria to have evolved for this purpose, they were assuming that nature could use selection to promote the survival of the most stabile ecosystem.

In 1962 the marine biologist Maxwell Dunbar (1914–1995) wrote an article in which he maintained that the ecosystem could be a unit of natural selection. Having studied both tropical and polar ecosystems, Dunbar asserted that there were differences that were consistent with selection operating at the level of the ecosystem. The fluctuating environment in the polar regions, for example, produced ecosystems that experienced destabilizing oscillations, whereas in the constant tropical environment the ecosystems had evolved to a very stable state.

In the period following World War II, however, evolutionary biologists tended to disagree with the idea that selection operated at a higher level than that of the individual organism. As noted in Chapter 23, they criticized the notion of group selection proposed by V. C. Wynne-Edwards, who happened to be Dunbar's mentor. Dunbar's arguments were susceptible to the same objections, ultimately discrediting his understanding of evolutionary ecology. In the neo-Darwinian synthesis, all life forms, including bacteria, were the result of a nonpurposeful process that resulted from the natural selection of changes in individual organisms. Selection did not proceed at levels of organization larger than that of the individual organism, such as the ecosystem.

By 1970 the fields of ecosystem ecology and evolutionary ecology had begun to drift apart as the latter group was influenced by the modern evolutionary synthesis. Because phenomena such as energy flow and nutrient cycling, which were of major concern to ecosystem ecologists, were not important to evolutionary biologists, the two groups tended to go their own ways. What was clear from the disagreement was that no grand theory of ecology that could incorporate both ecosystems and evolution was on the horizon.

In 2006 former Vice President Albert Gore once again issued an urgent appeal to the general public concerning the potential disruption of the balance of ecological factors as a result of human activity. While not everyone agreed with the conclusions about global warming outlined in Gore's movie, *An Inconvenient Truth,* its appearance reinforced the central importance of the science of ecology for the future of humankind.

Suggestions for Reading

Joel B. Hagen, *An Entangled Bank: The Origins of Ecosystem Ecology* (New Brunswick, N.J.: Rutgers University Press, 1992).

Gregg Mitman, *The State of Nature: Ecology, Community, and American Social Thought, 1900–1950* (Chicago: University of Chicago Press, 1992).

John Sheail, *Seventy-Five Years in Ecology: The British Ecological Society* (Boston: Blackwell Scientific Publications, 1987).

Donald Worster, *Nature's Economy: A History of Ecological Ideas* (Cambridge: Cambridge University Press, 1994).

CHAPTER 25

The Changing Worlds
of the Large and Small

In 1905 Albert Einstein published three seminal papers. As we saw in Chapter 21, one paper introduced his theory of relativity and another utilized the idea of energy quanta to describe light as a stream of particles. The third paper, which was not discussed, provided evidence for the existence of atoms. In yet a fourth paper of that year, Einstein teased out an implication of relativity; namely, that as elementary particles moved faster they increased mass, that in fact mass and energy could be related by the formula $E = mc^2$.

Einstein's star rose after 1905 and by 1909 he had left his position as a clerk in the Patent Office in Bern, Switzerland, to assume a position at the University of Zürich. By then physicists were speaking of "the relativity theory," although for a while Einstein himself insisted that relativity was simply a principle by which he had extended Maxwell's electrodynamics. What became clear to scientists was that something new and important had been introduced into physics. Their conception of nature, especially nature writ large in time and space, was being altered in a dramatic way.

In these same years developments of another sort were accumulating that threatened to undo the comfortable and sometimes smug confidence Europeans now had in the level of civilization they felt they had achieved. The great European countries had not experienced colossal wars with each other since Napoleon, and many were beginning to think that humankind had risen above such a barbaric means of settling differences.

In the years just prior to the outbreak of World War I physicists might have known that there were some new ideas in the air, but they had no idea of the astounding developments in physics that were in store for them. These developments commenced just prior to the outbreak of hostilities in August of 1914 and would continue for the next two decades. They began with the world of the large and ended in the tiny world of the inside of the atom.

522

◎   A Changing Universe   ◎

Scientists at the beginning of the twentieth century turned their attention to the largest possible entity imaginable—the universe. In so doing they came to new insights about space and time and about how the universe itself might be changing.

General Relativity

Not long after his 1905 paper on relativity Einstein realized that his results were much too limited in scope. His reasoning had assumed that different reference frames were in uniform motion. This restriction on the motion of reference frames is why the 1905 results later came to be known as special relativity.

If the laws of physics were the same only for observers in uniform motion, that would mean that they remained invariant only in a very restricted context. Most reference frames in the real world, of course, do not move uniformly. If an observer was in a car that was accelerating as opposed to one that was either at rest or moving at a constant speed, would that observer discover different laws of physics from those obtained in uniformly moving reference frames? Einstein wanted the laws of physics to be the same for *all* observers, whether they were accelerating or not.

To show that the same laws would obtain regardless of how the reference frame was moving involved far more than Einstein anticipated and took almost a decade to accomplish. The implications of what is called general relativity are much more complex and astounding than those stemming from the results of 1905. Here we consider only the most basic premise of Einstein's new approach and indicate a fundamental inference made from it.

In physics, a reference frame that is not at rest or moving at a constant velocity is accelerating. One result of Einstein's generalization concerning reference frames was that gravity and acceleration were linked in a fundamental way. Einstein had already begun reconsidering relativity in light of the implications for gravity in 1907. Between then and 1913, when a preliminary draft of his general theory of relativity appeared, he discussed it several times and had attracted severe criticism from colleagues. Early in 1914 he noted that his colleagues were for the moment only interested in his theory "with the intention of killing it dead." By October of that year Einstein thought he had solved all the problems and he continued to feel that way until he uncovered a mistake in early November of 1915. Only toward the end of November had he finally worked out the entire theory in its final form.

To understand why Einstein was concerned with gravity, imagine an elevator deep in intergalactic space, far from any large object like the Earth that would exert gravitational force on it. If a passenger in such an elevator let go of an object in her hand, the object would just hover in space where it was released. If, however, an alien spaceship were to attach a tractor beam to the elevator and accelerate it upward at 9.8 meters per second into its bay, the passenger would cease feeling weightless and the object would fall to the floor of the elevator, just as would normally occur in an elevator that was at rest on Earth. Where reference frames are concerned, accelerated motion in the absence of gravity (the tractor beam situation) is identical to unaccelerated motion in the presence of gravity. This suggests that the laws of physics we discover while under gravity's influence on Earth are identical to those we would discover in the accelerating elevator.

Consider a different case, one in which an elevator is accelerating under the influence not of a tractor beam but of gravity. If the elevator is in free fall toward a large body like the Earth, an object released by the passenger would also hover in the air because it already shares the free fall of the elevator. There is, then, no way to tell the difference between this situation and that of the elevator at rest in deep intergalactic space before the alien spaceship shows up. Here again it is clear that it is not necessary to think of objects in reference frames as under the influence of a mutually attractive force—the effects of gravity can be explained without referring to an attractive gravitational force.

Einstein wanted to get behind gravity to something more fundamental. He found it in the properties of a four-dimensional entity called spacetime. Matter and energy, he said, distort spacetime in their vicinity. Objects in this vicinity follow the curves of spacetime, thereby giving rise to the motions we perceive as the influence of gravity. Gravity, in other words, is the same thing as the *curvature of spacetime.*

One of Einstein's hopes as he developed his new ideas was that he might be able to use them to explain the small changes in the orbit of the planet Mercury that had not been explained using Newton's law of universal gravitation. Not only was he eventually successful in using his theory to account for these changes, he also used it to make a prediction that light from a distant star passing in the vicinity of the sun would be bent in accordance with the distortion in spacetime caused by the sun's large mass. That prediction was confirmed in 1919, when a solar eclipse allowed observers to detect the bending of light as it passed the sun. This much-publicized test rocketed Einstein to fame, which he continued to enjoy for the remainder of his life.

An Expanding Universe?

Several developments in the twentieth century led to the conclusion that the universe itself had a history. This idea, however, only gradually came to be the consensus view.

Einstein's cosmological term.   Newton considered space to be infinite and absolute, whereas Einstein's general theory stated that space and time were relative. Early in 1916 Einstein drew out the implications of this difference. It was impossible, he said, to reconcile the general theory of relativity with an infinite Newtonian universe. Einstein offered a different conception of the universe. The presence of matter ensured a curvature to space that made it finite, even though it could not be said to be bounded. Although difficult to grasp, all the dimensions of Einstein's spacetime were unbounded in the same sense that we say the surface of a sphere is unbounded.

The equations of general relativity provided solutions only for a contracting universe or an expanding universe. At the time, the known universe consisted of our Milky Way galaxy, which Einstein preferred to think of as static, or not subject to changes over time. He did not conceive of the universe as having either a beginning or end, nor did he think of it as something that could shrink or expand. The equations of his theory called for an expanding or contracting universe, so Einstein introduced what he called a "cosmological term," which, he conceded, was "not justified by what we actually know about gravitation." This term provided an adjustment to the equations to make their solutions compatible with his vision of the universe.

Variable stars and red shift.   Two developments just prior to the announcement of general relativity eventually made it possible for astronomers to conclude that Einstein's assumption of a static universe might be flawed. These developments involved, first, the discovery of a means to measure how far from Earth certain stars were and, second, a way to infer information about the motion of stars in relation to the Earth.

The first discovery occurred in 1908 when Henrietta Leavitt (1868–1921), an astronomer working at the Harvard College Observatory, made a discovery that helped astronomers determine how far away a certain kind of star was. Just knowing how bright a star appeared did not, of course, tell the astronomer whether it was a small star that was close or a big star that was far away. Leavitt figured out a way to eliminate this dilemma for stars that were known as variable stars because their light varied over time in a regular fashion.

Henrietta Leavitt (*right*) with Star Spectra Theorist Annie Jump Cannon

Leavitt was engaged in cataloging information about variable stars in a region of space in the southern skies known as the Magellanic Clouds. Astronomers knew how far away the Magellanic Clouds were and they assumed that all the stars in this region were approximately this same distance from Earth. Leavitt had the tedious task of comparing the changing images of the variable stars that were obtained on photographic plates at different times in their cycles.

Not content merely to record the data on how long it took for a given star to go from faint to bright to faint again, Leavitt noticed something else—the brighter the star appeared at its maximum, the longer was the cycle of variability. Assuming that whatever caused the stars to vary in brightness was the same for all variable stars, she determined the mathematical relation that expressed the correlation between the period of variability and the brightness for variable stars.

Armed with this information, Leavitt realized that she could use it profitably for variable stars elsewhere in the heavens. It was known that the brightness of light decreased like Newton's law of universal gravitation; that is, brightness diminished as the inverse square law of the distance. If, for example, two stars were equally bright but one was twice as far away as the other, then the first one would appear one quarter as bright as the other.

Leavitt used this law in reverse, so to speak. She reasoned that if a variable star was one quarter as bright as another, then it must be twice as far away *provided that the two stars were known to have the same true brightness.* But now she had a means of telling when two variable stars in different regions of the sky had the same true luminosity. Because she knew the correlation between brightness and periodicity, two variable stars with the same periodicity would be equally bright. When she came across a variable star, all she had to do was compare its brightness with a variable star in the Magellanic Clouds that had the same periodicity. She could then use the inverse square in reverse to find out how much farther away or closer the variable star was than the Magellanic Clouds were. The distance to the Magellanic Clouds was known; therefore, she had uncovered for the first time a means of measuring the distance from Earth of variable stars.

Everyone did not immediately accept Leavitt's discovery, but its usefulness soon proved irresistible to astronomers grappling with two issues of concern. The first had to do with the size of our galaxy and the position of our solar system within it. The American astronomer Harlow Shapley (1885–1972) used Leavitt's result along with other information to argue in 1918 that our galaxy was ten times bigger than previously thought—some 300,000 light years across. He also asserted that the sun was not at the center of the galaxy, as many assumed, but many thousands of light years away from the center. Twelve years later Shapley's estimate was discovered to be too big because he had not realized that some of the light from stars is absorbed before astronomers on Earth observe it, making the star appear farther away than it really is. Once the correction was made, however, Shapley's expanded galaxy, now 100,000 light years in diameter, and his claim about the position of our solar system in the galaxy, both found acceptance.

Leavitt's discovery also provided help for astronomers debating the location of nebulae, the fuzzy luminous patches visible in the sky. Were they, as some astronomers had been claiming, "island universes" outside our galaxy, or did our galaxy contain all the stars in the universe?

Those who argued that there were galaxies outside our own relied on the so-called Doppler shift to make their case. The sound of an approaching automobile rises in pitch as the car approaches an observer and drops as it recedes. This occurs because the sound waves from the source are perceived as compressed when they approach the observer and stretched out as they come to the observer from the receding vehicle. The wavelength of the sound first gets shorter, then longer. The same effect occurs with light waves from sources coming toward or moving away from an observer; that is, the perceived wavelength is shortened for light coming from a source moving toward an observer and lengthened for a source moving away. As we know from Newton's prism experiments (see Chapter 8), visible light consists of waves that range from longer red to shorter blue and violet, and so a change in wavelength is indicated by a change of light color.

For light from distant sources that are moving toward or away from us, this means that their spectral lines would shift toward the shorter waves (blue) if the source were moving toward us and to the longer waves (red) for sources moving away from us. The amount of the shift can give us a measure of how fast the source is either approaching us or receding from us. In 1913 an American astronomer named Vesto Slipher (1875–1969) had found, using Doppler shift analysis, that the Andromeda nebula was moving toward us at 300 km/sec, a speed much faster than that known for stars in our galaxy. He soon found two other nebulae that were moving away from us at an even faster rate of 1100 km/sec. These results gave comfort to those who claimed that these nebulae were outside the boundaries of our own galaxy.

What eventually settled the matter was the discovery in 1923 by American astronomer Edwin P. Hubble that there was a variable star in the Andromeda nebula. He used Leavitt's period-luminosity relation to estimate its distance and found it to be 800,000 light years from Earth—clearly outside the reaches of our galaxy. Only those who still questioned Leavitt's result hesitated to draw this conclusion, but it was not long before the notion of island universes outside our galaxy gained greater credibility than the notion that our galaxy contained all the stars in the universe.

In 1929 Hubble proposed a further result, namely, that there was a directly proportional relationship between the speed at which a receding galaxy was moving away (v) and the distance (d). He identified the constant of proportionality, H (subsequently known as the Hubble constant), and gave the relationship as $v = Hd$. This implied that the farther away a galaxy was, the faster it was receding from us—thus, the universe was expanding. Of course there were additional implications. If distant galaxies are accelerating away from us, then they had to have been closer to us in the past. In the distant past, galaxies must have been very close together; in fact, Hubble's equation suggested a finite beginning of things.

Hubble did not think that he could use his formula to help him determine when the universe had begun because to do so involved a number of unproven assumptions. Furthermore, there were other data about stars that were not consistent with an expanding universe. For example, simply using Hubble's new law and using the best information available as late as 1950 gave an age of the universe of about two billion years. But that was somewhere around half as old as sound geological estimates provided for the earth! As a result, no consensus was yet possible regarding earlier states of the universe.

The composition and energy of the sun.   There was another reason why conclusions about the universe's past remained contentious around the middle of the twentieth century. It had to do with conjectures about how and when the basic elements of matter formed. That issue could be addressed only after another puzzle was solved: how were the elements distributed throughout the universe? The solution to this puzzle emerged in considerations of the material composition of stars.

By the 1930s astronomers confirmed a new idea about the composition of the sun. In 1925 a young British graduate student at Harvard named Cecilia Payne (1910–1979) submitted a dissertation on the spectra of stars that has been called "the most brilliant Ph.D. thesis ever written in astronomy." When elements are heated, as they are in stars, they become gaseous and glow with light. In the nineteenth century an instrument called a spectroscope was invented that separated the light from a glowing gaseous element into its component colors. For each element there is a spectrum of colors that correspond to a set of frequencies that are unique to the element. By sending the light from stars through a spectroscope, scientists could analyze the resulting sets of frequencies and identify which elements were present in the star.

Stars display a variety of spectra, leading scientists to infer the relative amounts of various elements present in the stars. But Payne used new quantum considerations to show that this variety in the spectra was misleading because it resulted from physical conditions, not from the actual presence of the amounts of elements the spectra suggested. Payne's results certainly challenged conventional wisdom. Although she had explained why the presence of iron in the spectra of our sun's light could not be trusted, still there were good reasons to accept what spectral analysis showed. For example, the amounts of elements the spectra revealed were comparable to what existed in the Earth, exactly what was to be expected if the Earth had originated from the sun, as many believed it had.

Payne's analysis contained another implication at odds with normal expectations. Her results suggested that the amount of hydrogen and helium present in stars was so abundant in comparison to other elements—for hydrogen up to a million times greater—that it was frankly unbelievable. Bowing to the incredulity of the readers of

Cecilia Payne-Gaposchkin

her thesis, Payne, who became known following her marriage as Cecilia Payne-Gaposchkin, omitted the data on the overwhelming abundance of hydrogen and helium in stars from her dissertation.

By the 1930s, however, Payne-Gaposchkin's surprising results on stellar composition were confirmed and even extended to the conclusion that hydrogen was the most abundant element in the universe. With a wholly new perspective on the composition of the sun, physicists began determining how it generated such enormous amounts of energy. In 1939 the German-American physicist Hans Bethe (1906–2005) identified a cycle of reactions—in which carbon atoms served as catalysts—that involved the fusion of protons to form helium nuclei.

Bethe explained that it was the enormous heat of the sun that made possible the fusion of protons, something never observed on Earth. In the course of the process of nuclear fusion, as we shall see later in this chapter, mass is converted to energy in the huge amount called for in Einstein's formula, $E = mc^2$. Thus, while a huge supply of energy was needed to force the protons together, the fusion of the protons itself supplied even more energy as a result. Bethe was able to show that the energy output of the cycle he identified matched the energy output of the sun.

Bethe's explanation of the process of stellar fusion did not explain how the carbon atoms he needed as catalysts had come about. He assumed they had been made somehow at an earlier time and were already present in the sun. In 1953 the British astrophysicist Fred Hoyle (1915–2001) figured out how carbon atoms might have been synthesized from lighter elements. That discovery was soon followed by schemes in which most of the other heavy elements could have formed from hydrogen and helium by reactions taking place in stars.

Big bang versus steady state theories of the universe.   By this time a rival theory had emerged that did not require the presence of stars to explain the origin of elements. George Gamow (1904–1968) had been among the first Soviet scientists to flee Stalinist Russia and come to the United States in the early 1930s. He conjectured in the late 1940s that conditions at the beginning of the universe as suggested by Hubble's law were extremely hot. Specifically, he postulated that originally there were no elements, just a very hot and dense gas made up of neutrons. As this explosive gas cooled, neutrons broke down into protons and electrons. First hydrogen (1 proton and 1 electron) resulted, then hydrogen absorbed neutrons into the nucleus, some of which separated into protons and electrons. This process formed helium, because the number of protons in the nucleus had increased to two. Elements higher in the periodic table were allegedly formed in a similar fashion, always by absorbing neutrons, which separated into protons and electrons and thereby raised the number of protons in the nucleus.

While this theory satisfactorily accounted for hydrogen and helium, the production of heavier elements by absorbing neutrons was unconvincing to many. For example, the formation of new elements would occur only as long as there was a supply of neutrons to be absorbed by the nuclei of atoms. Once that supply was used up as the universe expanded and began to cool, new elements would no longer form. This meant that all the elements would have to have formed within the first half hour of the universe's existence.

The aspect of Gamow's theory that had the universe begin in a fiery hot combination of mass and energy bore a certain structural resemblance to an earlier hypothesis of the Belgian Jesuit priest and astronomer, Georges Lemaître (1894–1966), who in 1927 had proposed that the universe began as a single superquantum of mass-energy. What was attractive about Gamow's idea was that it predicted the distribution of helium in the universe reasonably close to its observed value. A huge drawback, however, was that it shared the embarrassment of attempts to use Hubble's law to date the origin of things—the universe turned out to be younger than the Earth!

Hoyle did not like these musings about the origin of the universe at all. With two colleagues he proposed an alternative to what he mockingly referred to as big bang theories. (Although Hoyle used the term *big bang* as a criticism, he inadvertently provided the label by which Gamow's theory would thereafter be known.) In the alternative view, which came to be known as the steady state theory, the universe had no beginning; rather, the expansion of the universe is compensated for by the continuous creation of hydrogen atoms. These atoms then give rise to heavier elements in processes of nucleosynthesis that take place in stars, such as the one Hoyle himself had discovered for carbon. Eventually, matter congeals to form galaxies, whose continual recession from each other resembles what we observe in present galaxies.

The discovery of cosmic microwave background radiation.   When it was published in 1948 the original big bang of Gamow and his collaborators contained a prediction that offered the possibility of empirical confirmation. According to the theory, in the early stages of the universe, when the temperature was incredibly high, an enormous amount of radiation would be present. Most of the energy in the universe would, in fact, be in the form of radiation. As the universe cooled and the elements formed, the amount of matter would increase and radiation would decrease.

As this radiation continued to expand into space it would do work against the gravitational forces associated with matter, causing it to lose energy. According to Max Planck, $E = hf$, so the decrease in energy of the radiation would show itself as a decrease in the frequency of the radiation. As noted in the discussion of the work of Planck in Chapter 21, the distribution of radiation energy varies with temperature. The original radiation of the super-hot early universe would have existed at all possible frequencies. But over time the range of these frequencies would diminish as the temperature of the expanding universe decreased. At the present average temperature of the universe (about 3 K), the range of frequencies ought to be contained in the microwave portion of the electromagnetic spectrum. This microwave radiation, then, would be a remnant of the original big bang and should exist all around us.

The fact that no one looked for this background radiation was due to several factors. It was extremely long-wave radiation, making it difficult for equipment existing at the time to detect. Beyond that, the big bang theory did not enjoy as much credibility as its competitor because it could not satisfactorily explain the genesis of heavy elements in comparison to the processes of nucleosynthesis promoted by the advocates of the steady state theory.

Therefore, when cosmic microwave background radiation was discovered in 1965 by accident, it was a major support for the idea of big bang cosmology and, in turn, a major blow to the steady state theory. Two scientists at the Bell Telephone Laboratories, Arno Penzias and Robert Wilson, began using an antenna that had been developed to minimize "noise" in microwave transmissions from weather balloons in their work in radio astronomy. They found that they could not eliminate an annoying static noise no matter what they did. Through a series of fortunate developments, they came into contact with scientists at Princeton University who were able to confirm that the noise was due to background microwave radiation.

Although it took several years to answer all the questions raised by the discovery of the background microwave radiation, by 1980 the victory for big bang cosmology seemed assured. That is not to say that the widespread attention the theory received did not lead to modifications based on new ideas and discoveries. In fact, a central feature of the steady state theory, the production of the heavy elements in the periodic table through nucleosynthesis in stars, has replaced the original explanation of the origin of heavy elements in the new version of big bang cosmology.

◎ The Quantum Mechanical ◎ Explanation of the Atom

At the same time that scientists were investigating the largest thing that could be conceived, the universe itself, they were also plumbing the depths of the world of the very small. As noted in Chapter 21, by the beginning of the twentieth century the atom was no longer the ultimate constituent of matter. J. J. Thomson's particle of negative electricity, the electron, to say nothing of the elementary particles that accompanied radioactive decay, meant that there was a whole new realm inside the atom to be explored. The more physicists entered this inner world of the atom, the more exciting and mysterious nature appeared.

Explaining the Atom's Interior

If the atom had parts, how did physicists visualize them? In the first decade of the century, J. J. Thomson imagined the atom as a positively charged fluid shaped into a sphere. Embedded in the fluid was a sufficient number of negatively charged electrons to balance the fluid's positive charge, making the atom electrically neutral. Because the electrons resembled the raisins in plum pudding, Thomson's conception has become known as the plum pudding model of the atom. It did not last long, however.

One of Thomson's students, Ernest Rutherford (1871–1937), had come to Cambridge from New Zealand as a young man in 1894. He had enjoyed a

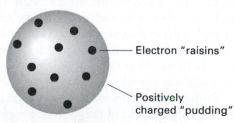

Electron "raisins"

Positively charged "pudding"

Plum Pudding Model of the Atom

stint as professor of physics at McGill University in Canada in 1898, returning to England in 1907 as the Langworthy Professor of Physics in the University of Manchester. By 1910 Rutherford had become quite successful on his own, especially in the study of radioactivity.

Rutherford's scattering experiments.   Rutherford knew how to isolate a particular particle that was given off in certain processes of radioactive decay. This particle, called an alpha particle, had an atomic mass of 4 and a charge of +2. Rutherford learned how to direct beams of alpha particles so that they collided with the atoms of various elements. The goal of this experimentation was to measure the degree to which atoms scattered the beams of alpha particles passing through them. In this way Rutherford hoped to use the high-energy alpha particles as probes to see if he could learn something new about the nature of the atom. The results of this approach paid big dividends.

Rutherford assumed that any deviation from the alpha particle's path would be caused by close encounters with electrons in the atomic fluid. He had worked out the probabilities of such encounters and they suggested that the alpha particles would be scattered through small angles of deviation, and possibly, on extremely rare occasions, through an angle as high as 45°. He set his assistant, Ernest Marsden (1889–1970), to work on the tedious task of recording the angles of scatter when alpha particles were shot at gold foil.

Marsden found, as expected, that many alpha particles passed through the gold foil, exhibiting scatter through small angles. That is, the alpha particles came out of the gold foil and hit a screen behind it at small angles of deviation from their entrance trajectory. But what was not expected was that some were in fact scattered through wider angles, a few even greater than 90°! This was shocking—Rutherford likened an alpha particle bouncing off gold foil to a mortar shell bouncing off tissue paper. The only way it could have happened was if the positively charged alpha particle had encountered a powerfully repulsive positive electric field. But how?

The Rutherford model of the atom.   Rutherford concluded that Thomson must have been wrong in his conception of the atom as a sphere of positive electrical fluid in which electrons were embedded. He reasoned that the positive charge of the gold atom was contained in a highly concentrated nucleus, making it a powerful positive charge. In this way the positively charged alpha particles that came into the vicinity of the nucleus would deviate from their paths by the repulsive positive force of the nucleus. On rare occasions the trajectory of the alpha particle would come straight enough at a nucleus that the mutually repelling positive forces would cause the alpha particle to rebound in such a large angle that it did not even enter the gold foil at all. Rutherford located the electrons as satellites circling around the nucleus, held in orbit by the mutually attractive force between the positive nucleus and the negative electrons. If the orbits of the electrons defined the size of the atom, the nucleus occupied one ten-thousandth of this size. Most of the atom was empty space!

Rutherford's model of the atom, which he announced in May of 1911, beautifully explained the results of the scattering experiments. But it suffered from a fatal flaw. An electron moving in an orbit as the model suggested would constitute a changing electric field. That, as Maxwell had shown, would produce a changing magnetic field, which in turn would produce a changing electric field, and so on. The orbiting electron, in other words, would produce a wave of electromagnetic radiation. As the electron radiated energy away it would be losing energy. That meant that it would not be able to maintain its orbit around the nucleus. Rutherford's beautiful model had the major drawback of being inherently unstable.

Rutherford's Atom

Rescuing Rutherford's model with Planck's energy quanta.   Not long after Rutherford's announcement, a talented young Danish physicist named Niels Bohr (1885–1962) used what remained of a Danish fellowship to spend a brief time with Rutherford's Manchester group. While there, he of course became very familiar with Rutherford's model and its problems. He wondered whether Planck's idea of quantized energy might be of help, but he was unable to make any progress before he had to return to Denmark.

Early in 1913 Bohr was talking to a colleague who worked with the spectral lines associated with elements, a subject we encountered earlier in connection with the work of Cecilia Payne-Gaposchkin. Bohr did not know much about this field, but he learned that the three spectral lines displayed by glowing hydrogen gas had given rise to something of a mystery: the frequency of the first spectral line of hydrogen was equal to 32,903,640,000,000,000 $(1/4 - 1/3^2)$. To get the frequencies of the other two lines, the physicist had merely to replace the 3 in the formula's parentheses by 4 and 5 respectively. No one had any idea why this empirical formula worked, only that it did.

Bohr realized that the formula for hydrogen could be written in an equivalent but slightly different form that involved Planck's constant, h. The presence of h in the formula that gave the frequencies of the hydrogen spectral lines suggested to Bohr that Planck's idea of quantizing energy *was* somehow involved in determining the frequencies permitted to hydrogen spectral lines. In fact, he made a brilliant suggestion about how Planck's technique could be used to address the fatal flaw in Rutherford's atomic model.

Bohr conjectured that the electron was restricted to certain energy levels (orbital distances) in its movement around the Rutherford nucleus. The electrons, he said, could change from one orbital distance to another, but that would mean that they either had absorbed energy (to move from a lower level to a higher one) or radiated energy (when moving from a higher level to a lower one). When, for example, hydrogen was heated, the electrons would move to a high energy level. As the gas then cooled and radiated energy, the electrons jumped from the higher energy levels to lower ones.

Bohr's ingenious idea was that the frequency of the radiation that occurred when the gas cooled was subject to Planck's formula, $E = hf$. The amount of energy, E, that was radiated when moving, say, from level 3 to level 2, would be the difference between the two energy levels ($E_3 - E_2$). Because Planck's formula, solved for f, gives $f = E/h$, the frequency of the radiation could be calculated. The frequency of the lines in the hydrogen spectrum, then, correlated with the frequency obtained by the jump from one quantum level to a lower one.

Because Bohr linked the spectral frequencies to the quantum conception, he demystified to some degree why the formula worked. But his explanation also required him to make clear the incompatibility of Planck's quantum idea with classical physics. Bohr simply had to deny the classical understanding that the electron emitted radiation because, as Maxwell said, it would represent a changing electrical field if it revolved around a central nucleus. Relying on Planck, Bohr asserted that radiation could only occur in certain specified and discrete amounts; radiation corresponded to a jump from a higher to a lower energy level. Hence the electron could not exist at just any distance from the nucleus; rather, it could only occupy orbits that were determined by the formula. It could not, for example, be in between the levels nor could it come closer to the nucleus than the lowest level.

But if Bohr demystified why the mysterious formula for the spectral frequencies worked, he also created some mysteries of his own. Strictly speaking, when an electron jumped from a higher to a lower level, it disappeared at the higher level and reappeared at the lower level, because it was not permitted to occupy an orbit in between. Further, if the electron in the highest energy level of a hydrogen atom jumped to a lower level, it would radiate at different frequencies depending on whether it jumped, say, to level 2 or to level 1. But what determined at which frequency the electron would vibrate? It was as if the electron had somehow *decided* beforehand to which level it was going to jump.

Bohr sent his paper to Rutherford, whose tentative response prompted Bohr to go back to England to confer with Rutherford. In spite of numerous questions Rutherford had about Bohr's explanation of the hydrogen spectrum, he recommended that Bohr publish his results. Bohr's paper appeared in 1913. It took a while for physicists to realize the potential of this application of energy quanta, but Bohr had made clear that he was a force to be reckoned with and he would receive the Nobel Prize for this work in 1922.

Here was another application, in addition to Einstein's treatment of the photoelectric effect, of Planck's notion of restricting the radiation and absorption of energy to discrete amounts, as opposed to the continuous flow classical physicists had always assumed. Bohr had used Planck's idea to rescue Rutherford's conception of the solar system atom from its fatal flaw. The electron in Bohr's explanation would not spiral into the nucleus.

The Creation of Quantum Mechanics

Bohr's achievement might have been impressive, but it was clearly very limited in its applicability. For example, his treatment of the Rutherford atom was based on the simple case of hydrogen. When it came to atoms with more than one electron, he was, alas, unable to duplicate the success he had enjoyed in deriving the frequencies of their spectral lines. The best he could do was to obtain solutions by patching together his new idea with older classical conceptions that did not resort to Planck's idea of quantizing energy.

But if a patching together of classical ideas with new quantum ideas was the only way to achieve results, then the idea of the electron orbits and the notion of jumping from one level to another became mere practical add-ons to traditional assumptions, much as Planck's original idea of quantizing energy had been in his description of blackbody radiation. The demystification gained in the case of hydrogen had evaporated and was replaced by the new mystery of why the patchwork system worked at all. The hybrid approach was much too ad hoc, a merely practical solution that in the end was neither old physics nor new physics. Further, it did not really impart any new understanding of the inside of the atom. Bohr himself conceded that he was "by no means trying to give what might ordinarily be described as an explanation." What was needed was a way to replace Bohr's patchwork approach with a precise system.

Wave and particles.   The ten years following Bohr's postulation of electron orbits and his use of energy quanta were filled with attempts to adjust the theory and to account for a host of new phenomena. The main reason why physicists could not simply reject Bohr's approach was because it did at least rescue the Rutherford model of the atom. That model was so clearly consistent with the empirical results of the scattering experiments that it seemed to be the only reasonable depiction of the atom. And yet, by classical theory, it was inherently unstable. Bohr's interpretation of radiated energy as jumps between electron orbits was a way around the instability.

Bohr's approach also forced into consideration a problem that had been lurking beneath the surface ever since Planck's original introduction of the quantum idea— the nature of electromagnetic radiation. In both Planck's case and in Einstein's use of energy quanta to explain the behavior of light in the photoelectric effect, there had been no claim that energy quanta represented anything more than a stopgap measure, what Einstein called a *heuristic* viewpoint. Energy quanta were not, in other words, considered a challenge to the established idea that electromagnetic radiation should be thought of as a wave.

But now Bohr was showing once again, and in a wholly different context from Einstein's, that there were advantages to thinking of the radiation of light as energy quanta. Further, there were other reasons to suggest that the established view of light as a wave was not immune to question. For example, with the acceptance of relativity theory, which banished the ether from existence, the question could be asked, "If light is a wave, what is waving?" It seemed as if there were good reasons to think of electromagnetic radiation as a wave and others that suggested it was particulate.

By 1920 there had been a sufficient number of new developments to convince physicists that quantized energy *was* somehow bound up with processes inside the atom, even though they had no better solutions to atomic theory than the patchwork approach of Bohr. This meant that physicists had become at least temporarily resigned to the idea that electromagnetic radiation in general, and light in particular, behaved like both particles and waves, depending on the situation.

Then in 1924 a French physicist named Louis de Broglie (1892–1987), who was descended from French royalty and held the title of prince, proposed that electrons themselves could behave like waves as well as the particles they were normally

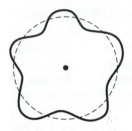

Electron Wave with
Five Wavelengths

thought to be. This amounted to saying that matter could be thought of as having a wave nature; in fact, de Broglie gave a formula for wavelength λ of mass m. No one was shocked that the formula, $\lambda = h/mv$, contained Planck's constant. Where the electron was concerned, de Broglie required that the wave representing it had to have an integral number of wavelengths over the length of the orbit around the nucleus. De Broglie's claim was made for theoretical reasons; however, when others soon experimentally demonstrated that electrons could in fact be diffracted, the wave nature of electrons was confirmed.

The solutions of Heisenberg and Schrödinger.   In 1925 two young physicists, working independently, each met the challenge of replacing Bohr's patchwork approach with a precise system that coherently gave the spectral frequencies of atoms. While their solutions were not mathematically identical, they were soon shown to be equivalent. Each solution involved the notion of quantized energy, but they did so in different ways.

The first solution that appeared was that of Werner Heisenberg (1901–1976), a brilliant young German physicist who had completed his formal requirements for becoming a German professor in 1924 at the age of twenty-two. Before exercising his right to give lectures at Göttingen University, he chose to spend some time in Copenhagen with Niels Bohr. Bohr was, of course, a key figure in the early development of quantum theory. By 1924 he had established a center of research in theoretical physics in Copenhagen that attracted many of the best minds of the day. Heisenberg spent the fall and spring with Bohr, plunging himself into the latest musings of the master on the puzzles confronting atomic physicists. He returned to Göttingen to give lectures during the summer term of 1925.

In July, suffering from hay fever, Heisenberg escaped to a small island off the coast of northern Germany to recuperate. There he came up with a new mathematical means by which he could transform Bohr's patchwork system into a consistent representation

$$\begin{bmatrix} a & b \\ c & d \end{bmatrix} * \begin{bmatrix} e & f \\ g & h \end{bmatrix} = \begin{bmatrix} ae + bg & af + bh \\ ce + dg & cf + dh \end{bmatrix}$$

Matrix Multiplication

of the processes inside the atom. Without his knowing it, Heisenberg's solution re-created a form of mathematics little known at the time called matrix algebra, in which arrays of numbers are manipulated according to rules that lead to the solution of certain kinds of problems. It allowed him to express the continuous aspects of the older physics through the discrete elements of matrices, while at the same time preserving the existence of Bohr's famous quantum jumps in the radiation of light quanta. But, *on the level of the mathematical representation,* there was no longer a patchwork between the old physics and the new—there was just one quantum mechanical system.

In the first months of 1926 the Austrian physicist Erwin Schrödinger (1887–1961) published a series of papers in which he introduced a mathematical depiction of the behavior of the electron inside the atom that was different from Heisenberg's. It preserved the now-accepted notion that energy was quantized and was, like Heisenberg's system, able to account for observed atomic spectral lines in a single quantum mechanical system. Schrödinger also did not have to supplement the quantum approach of the new physics with the classical conception of energy in the old.

Schrödinger's approach was based on de Broglie's depiction of the electron as a wave. He argued that using de Broglie's conception imparted definite advantages over Heisenberg's matrix depiction. For one thing, the mathematics needed to erect Schrödinger's system was very familiar to physicists—it was the mathematics of wave equations. For another, Schrödinger did not have to resort to quantum jumps between stationary orbits, as Bohr and Heisenberg did, to explain the quantum nature of radiation in atomic spectra.

Schrödinger accounted for the discrete nature of radiation in a different way. The electron, he said, radiated energy at the frequency suggested by the wavelength of the electron wave. The different frequencies came about because of de Broglie's requirement that electron waves must have an integral number of wavelengths over the length of the electron orbit. De Broglie had already shown that the frequencies of the hydrogen spectrum were in fact given by waves that met this requirement. Schrödinger showed that this approach could be extended to account for the frequencies of other spectra. Although, as already noted, the two mathematical representations of Heisenberg and Schrödinger were soon shown to be equivalent, Schrödinger's wave mechanics was much easier to use.

The uncertainty principle and the Copenhagen interpretation of quantum mechanics. The new quantum mechanical systems of both Heisenberg and Schrödinger were first and foremost *mathematical representations* of the puzzling behavior of atoms. Nevertheless, it was virtually impossible not to invest in each certain claims of physical significance. Heisenberg at first preferred to hold that it was misleading to try to visualize atomic processes and he rejected the notion that seeing the electron as a wave adequately accounted for the discrete radiation of quantum jumps he believed existed. Others, however, had never been happy with electrons jumping from one stationary orbital state to another and found a certain relief in the familiar idea of a wave.

In the last half of 1926 Heisenberg was back in Copenhagen working as Bohr's assistant. There he came to a startling realization. Thinking of the electron as a particle located in a specific position in its orbit, he recognized that if he were to use light of very short wavelength to measure exactly where an electron was, he would be faced with a dilemma. To get more precise measurements of the electron's position would require him to use light of shorter and shorter wavelengths (greater and greater frequencies). But, according to Planck's $E = hf$, that meant that he would be using light quanta of greater and greater energy. When the light quanta encountered the electrons they would cause it to recoil away, and the velocity of the recoil would be greater as the wavelength got shorter. So, to get more precision about *where* the electron was located meant that he would make it harder to tell how fast

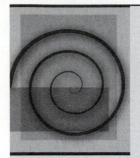

The NATURE of SCIENCE

Quantum Mechanics and the Nature of Knowledge

The development of quantum mechanics provides an example of how fundamentally natural science can impact the conception of the nature of knowledge itself. According to Heisenberg's uncertainty principle, it is impossible to know both the present position and the present velocity of an electron, so the best that can be done regarding the electron's location and velocity at any future time would be a *range of possibilities*. This circumstance means that the laws and predictions of quantum mechanics, in Heisenberg's words, "are in general only of a statistical type." Having at best only probabilistic knowledge of the present state of the electron means that the principle of causality, a bedrock of classical physics, becomes invalid because it is no longer possible to reason to an effect from a known cause.

Many scientists and philosophers have accepted the idea that our knowledge of the world of the very small will never fulfill Pierre Laplace's eighteenth-century dream of a determined system of the world of which God has perfect knowledge. As a result, not even God could get rid of the principle of uncertainty without simultaneously destroying quantum mechanics.

Others, however, have refused to admit these implications of quantum mechanics. Einstein, for example, refused to abandon his belief in causality. He expressed admiration for quantum mechanics, but said that an inner voice told him it did not "bring us closer to the Old Man's secret." Einstein added that for his part, he was convinced that the so-called Old Man "does not throw dice."

Whether or not this difference is ever resolved, new insights in natural science will likely continue to affect our conception of what knowledge is.

and in what direction it was moving away. "The more precisely we determine the position," he said, "the more imprecise is the determination of velocity in this instant, and *vice versa*."

Heisenberg's conclusion, which has become known as the Heisenberg uncertainty principle, formally captured the limitations of precision that existed in a world where quantized energy reigned. Where the electron itself was concerned, it suggested that regarding it as a particle paid unforeseen dividends.

Heisenberg's announcement of the uncertainty principle served only to sharpen the differences between his view and that of Schrödinger, for whom the electron was best thought of as a wave. Although Bohr urged him not to become one-sided, Heisenberg cast the uncertainty result as evidence in favor of seeing the electron as a particle over Schrödinger's wave conception. Indeed, intuition suggested that the electron had to be one or the other, either a wave or a particle. Many physicists anticipated that it would only be a matter of time before some kind of third conception emerged that would fuse these two notions of the electron.

Meanwhile, Bohr was coming to a different view, one that would become known as the *Copenhagen interpretation of quantum mechanics*. He slowly became convinced that wave physics and particle physics were not, as they were being treated, opposed to each other. He concluded that, as strange as it might seem, the two conceptions complemented each other and both were essential to a complete description of nature.

Bohr reinterpreted how the uncertainty Heisenberg had uncovered arose. In his view it came about because in *measuring nature,* the interrogator is forced to choose only one side of the wave–particle duality. If we ask nature to show itself as a particle, nature obliges, but the puzzles that accompany that depiction, for example, quantum jumps, betray that nature has not disclosed itself fully. Likewise, nature also obliges if we ask it to show itself as a wave, but then we are saddled with other puzzles. Therefore, if we insist on asking whether the electron is a wave or a particle, the answer must be that it is both. In the spring of 1927 at a scientific meeting in Italy, Bohr made clear that in his view the complementarity was permanent— there would be no resolution.

◎   Toward a More Dangerous World   ◎

As we have seen, the 1920s proved to be an especially exciting decade in the exploration of the world of the very small. It took place against the background of enormous political instability, precipitated by Europe's attempt to put things back together again after the devastating disruption of World War I. This was nowhere more obvious than in Germany. Along with the other defeated power, Austria, Germany was formally required by the Versailles Treaty to accept the blame for the war and to assume huge debt in the form of reparations payments to the victors. What resulted was a destruction of Germany's economy through massive inflation. This profoundly affected the daily life of the populace.

German and Austrian citizens were hardly convinced that they alone bore responsibility for the war. Their resentment toward the countries that were victorious in the war grew steadily as the decade proceeded. As average citizens tried to make sense of the chaotic circumstances of their situation, they became more and more open to the voices of a new political party, the National Socialists, or Nazis. The Nazis laid the blame for the plight of Germany on anyone whose true loyalty was perceived to lie outside Germany. Two principal scapegoats emerged: communists, whose loyalty was to the international workers movement, and Jews, who were identified as a racial group that could never be regarded as truly German.

By December of 1933, when Heisenberg accepted the 1932 Nobel Prize for physics in Stockholm, Adolf Hitler had been chancellor in Germany for almost a year. He had so successfully consolidated his power that any effective political opposition had disappeared. Over the next several years he would attempt to put in place his plan to create the thousand-year-reich, which he envisioned as an embodiment of a superior German civilization.

As unusual and foreboding as these political developments were, they were matched by events in physics and chemistry in the 1930s that made the situation dangerous to an unprecedented degree. When scientists found the key to unlocking the astonishing power latent in the nucleus of atoms, they did so at a time when the unstable world around them could not be trusted to understand the consequences of the unimaginable power that was placed at its disposal.

Going Inside the Nucleus: The Neutron

The Rutherford atom, with electrons orbiting a center of concentrated positive charge, made it possible for physicists to focus attention on specific parts of the atom. We have seen how thoroughly the behavior of electrons was scrutinized in the development of quantum mechanics. Physicists were less successful in the 1920s in their investigation of the nucleus of the Rutherford atom. They continued to explore it by bombarding nuclei of various atoms with alpha particles, as they had in the original scattering experiment. They noticed that hydrogen nuclei frequently were ejected from these collisions. Rutherford himself proposed the word *proton* for the hydrogen nucleus, which seemed to be a building block of nuclei.

Not surprisingly, the nucleus presented challenges and problems. It was natural to conclude that the increased charge of nuclei that were heavier than hydrogen resulted from the presence of a commensurately increased number of protons. But the nuclei of heavier atoms increased in mass at a faster rate than than that of charge, and the rate did not appear to be regular. For example, the helium nucleus had double the charge of hydrogen, but its mass was four times that of a proton; further, the barium nucleus increased in charge by a factor of 56, but its mass was 137 times that of a hydrogen nucleus.

Rutherford suggested that the excess mass might come from the presence of a neutral particle. He even suggested the name neutron for such a particle as early as 1920. But no one uncovered evidence for the existence of such a particle until 1932, when Rutherford's assistant, James Chadwick (1891–1974), realized that some French chemists had misinterpreted the results of their experiments.

Chadwick and the French were both pursuing the recent discovery of a strange effect that alpha radiation, which Rutherford had used in his scattering experiments, had on the element beryllium. Bombarding beryllium with alpha particles appeared to result in an uncharged form of radiation that had been discovered at the turn of the century and that Rutherford later named gamma rays. It was known that gamma radiation, which penetrated like high-energy x-rays, was not deflected in a magnetic field; in other words, it carried no charge. While alpha particles produced gamma radiation with several elements, the mystery was that in the case of beryllium the gamma rays had almost ten times the energy as in other cases, even more than that of the bombarding alpha particles!

The French experiments were conducted by Marie Curie's daughter Irène Curie (1897–1956) and Irène's husband Frédéric Joliot (1900–1958). They decided to see if such high-energy gamma radiation could be used to knock protons out of matter as alpha radiation did. Directing the gamma radiation to paraffin wax, they reported in a paper in January of 1932 that indeed protons were ejected from the collision.

When Chadwick read the paper he immediately reported the result to Rutherford, who expressed disbelief because previously collisions with gamma rays had only been shown to deflect electrons. Protons were over 1,800 times heavier than electrons, so ejecting them with the observed speed by collisions with gamma rays would be like dislodging a wrecking ball with a pool ball. Chadwick confirmed that the French were correct that protons had in fact been knocked out, but he concluded that he must "either relinquish the application of the conservation of energy and momentum in these collisions or adopt another hypothesis about the nature of the radiation."

Chadwick chose to question whether it was indeed gamma radiation that had been produced by bombarding beryllium with alpha particles. To preserve the conservation of momentum he proposed that the uncharged "radiation" was not gamma radiation at all; rather, the alpha particles striking beryllium had dislodged from its nucleus uncharged particles of mass very nearly equal to that of protons. In February of 1932 he sent a letter to the editor of the journal *Nature,* entitled "Possible Existence of a Neutron," in which he concluded: "We may suppose it [is] the 'neutron' discussed by Rutherford in his Bakerian Lecture of 1920." If neutrons were present in atomic nuclei, then the irregular pattern in atomic weights mentioned above could be explained.

The Discovery of Atomic Fission

With a new uncharged particle at their disposal, physicists suddenly had in their arsenal of bullets a much more effective projectile with which to bombard atomic nuclei. Unlike the positively charged alpha particle, the neutron had no charge; hence it would not be repelled as it approached the positively charged nucleus. A whole new realm of possibilities opened up to atomic physicists and they set to work immediately, systematically bombarding the nuclei of the elements in the periodic table with neutrons.

Among the most interesting of the many new responses obtained in these experiments were those associated with the heaviest known element, uranium, which by 1937 was known to have 92 protons and 146 neutrons in its nucleus to give it an atomic weight of 238. Once again Irène Curie's laboratory produced apparently impossible results that provoked others to look closer. In this case, Curie and a colleague reported that bombarding uranium nuclei with neutrons produced a radioactive change whose end product was difficult to identify. One reason for the difficulty was that chemists were entertaining the prospect that the uranium nucleus had absorbed neutrons to create a new element not found in nature. The Curie team concluded, however, that their experiment had produced thorium, which had 90 protons in its nucleus.

This time it was researchers in Germany who found the Curie results improbable. Lise Meitner (1878–1968), a physicist, and Otto Hahn (1879–1968), a chemist, had been collaborating on research in radioactivity for thirty years. Early in 1938 Meitner was able to show that the result of bombarding uranium with neutrons did not produce thorium. Hahn suspected that what the French had found was due to a contaminant of some kind (which he creatively dubbed "curiosum")— especially after Curie and her colleague attempted to show that the product was actinium (with 91 protons), only to find that it was not.

By the summer of 1938 political circumstances in Berlin forced Meitner, who was Jewish, to escape to Sweden. Prior to that time Meitner had been sheltered from some of the anti-Semitic laws passed by the Nazis because she was Austrian and therefore not subject to laws affecting German citizens. By the fall of 1938, however, it proved impossible for her to stay any longer. She remained in correspondence with Hahn concerning the continued experiments in radioactivity, including those on uranium.

Hahn eventually became convinced that the mystery product of bombarding uranium with neutrons was not due to a contaminant. He and a colleague carefully performed the experiment themselves in the late fall of 1938. Because they suspected that the product was radium or one of its isotopes, they utilized a technique Marie Curie had employed when she had discovered radium some three decades earlier. At that time she had used a salt of barium, which, being in the same group as radium in the periodic table, shared some chemical behavior with it. This technique allowed her to use barium's similar properties to help isolate the radium.

What Hahn found, however, was that in this case the technique did not help him to isolate the radium he suspected was present. The only element that appeared to be present was barium. And yet Hahn was convinced that the interaction of the neutrons with the uranium had produced its own product. If so, then his use of the barium salt was only confusing things. Greatly frustrated, he wrote to Meitner in December of 1938 saying that the radium isotopes acted like barium and asking for her help. "We understand that it really *can't* break up into barium. . . . So try to think of some other possibility."

Hahn dismissed the possibility of barium itself being the product because barium had only 56 protons in its nucleus. If neutrons hitting uranium, with 92 protons, resulted in barium with 56, it would mean that the neutrons had chipped off many particles at one blow, a clear impossibility in Hahn's mind. All known radioactive reactions involved small changes from one heavy element into another one that was close to it in atomic number. Further, splitting the atom must require enormous energies, far in excess of that possessed by neutrons. Still, in her reply, Meitner did not dismiss this out of hand. "We have experienced so many surprises in nuclear physics that one cannot say without hesitation about anything that it's impossible."

Hahn would have liked it if Meitner had provided an alternative explanation for the results, but not wishing to delay publication, he sent off a paper, with a copy to Meitner, describing the situation to a German scientific journal. He was careful to say that *as chemists* he and his colleague concluded that the product was not radium but barium. The insertion of "as chemists" was meant to cover himself from physicists, who were sure to say that it was physically impossible.

Meitner was spending the Christmas break with her physicist nephew Otto Frisch (1904–1979), who was visiting from Copenhagen, where he was working with Bohr. She soon realized that there might be a way in which a splitting of the nucleus

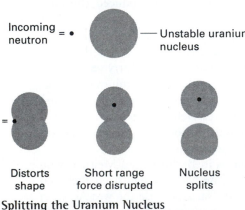

Incoming neutron = •   —— Unstable uranium nucleus

= •

Distorts shape   Short range force disrupted   Nucleus splits

Splitting the Uranium Nucleus

was possible. Because the uranium nucleus was known to be very unstable, its penetration by neutrons might be able to distort its shape sufficiently to disrupt the extremely short range over which the forces binding protons together acted. If the distortion caused the range to be exceeded, the force would not be able to bind the separated parts and the nucleus would split.

Meitner recognized that if this did in fact occur, the nuclei of the two elements resulting, being much more stable than uranium, would be packed together in a manner different from that of the original uranium nucleus. She knew, in particular, that the masses of the two parts would be less than that of uranium, and she realized that the missing mass would be converted into energy according to Einstein's $E = mc^2$. A quick calculation revealed that the energy release, per atomic event, would be incomparably greater than that of any known nuclear interaction.

All this took place as the year 1938 drew to a close. Otto Frisch returned to Copenhagen, where he saw Bohr and brought him up to date. The paper Hahn had submitted appeared on January 6 of the new year. One week later Frisch was able to confirm in the laboratory that the amount of energy released in the reaction caused by neutrons hitting the uranium nucleus was in fact what Meitner had predicted. He prepared a paper for publication on his experiment and sent it off along with another one, jointly written with Meitner, on what they titled "a new kind of nuclear reaction." In the meantime Bohr, who had set sail for America, brought the news to the other side of the Atlantic by the middle of the month. The genie was out of the bottle.

Suggestions for Reading

David C. Cassidy, *Uncertainty: The Life and Science of Werner Heisenberg* (New York: W. H. Freeman, 1992).
Albrecht Fölsing, *Albert Einstein,* trans. Ewald Osers (New York: Penguin, 1997).
Gerald Holton and Stephen G. Brush, *Physics, the Human Adventure* (New Brunswick, N.J.: Rutgers University Press, 2001).
Ruth Lewin Sime, *Lise Meitner: A Life in Science* (Berkeley: University of California Press, 1997).

CHAPTER 26

———⊚———

The Nuclear Age

The ancient Greek god Zeus warned Prometheus not to give humans divine gifts because, he said, it would only bring about misery. But Prometheus disobeyed Zeus. He bestowed many things on mortals; he even stole fire from Zeus for them. If there was any doubt about the truth of Zeus's warning of impending misery, that doubt evaporated in 1945, when the gift of fire unleashed horrendous misery on humankind.

The advent of the nuclear age came at a time of great instability in Europe. Since his installment as chancellor of Germany at the beginning of 1933, Adolf Hitler (1889–1945) had gradually implemented the initial stages of his plan to take over Europe. His totalitarian rule under the guise of patriotism enabled him to rally many in the population to his cause. Unemployment went down and the economy improved. As he became bolder, Hitler's actions became more rash.

In 1936 Hitler deliberately violated the terms of the Versailles Treaty that ended World War I by sending troops into an area bordering on France that had been officially declared a demilitarized zone. The Allied nations, beset with their own internal problems, chose not to take up arms once again to remove the German army. Then in the spring of 1938, when it appeared that a popular referendum in Austria would defeat a proposition to join with the German Reich, Hitler's troops marched across the border before the vote could be taken. Much to the delight of the Austrian Nazi party, Hitler simply annexed Austria to Germany. Next, the German dictator broke an agreement in March of 1939 with the British, who were trying to appease Hitler in order to avoid outright war. Hitler occupied Czechoslovakia, bringing that country under German control. Britain finally began to realize that the German Führer was determined to dominate Europe at any cost. It was in the midst of all this political chaos that scientists learned how to split the atom.

◎   The Path to the Atomic Bomb   ◎

Excitement among nuclear scientists about atomic fission grew during 1939 at a rate that rivaled the German escalation of the political situation in that year. Scientists soon figured out that it was not the dominant atom present in uranium ore (uranium atoms with 92 protons plus 146 neutrons in the nucleus, or $_{92}U^{238}$) that underwent fission. U^{238} tended to absorb the incoming neutrons. Rather, it was an isotope, $_{92}U^{235}$, that the neutrons split. But U^{235} made up only about .7 percent of the ore, a tiny portion indeed. In April of 1939 scientists confirmed that a byproduct of the neutron-uranium fission interaction was the release of more neutrons. These neutrons could strike other uranium nuclei present, meaning that, once started, the uranium might *continue* to fission. As each atom of uranium split, some mass would be converted to energy. Assuming there was the right amount of uranium present (called a critical mass) that could sustain a continuing reaction, the fission process, if not controlled, could produce a massive explosion.

By the summer of 1939 the international situation was extremely tense. When Hitler announced that he had concluded a nonaggression pact with Joseph Stalin of the Soviet Union, war appeared to be near. Hitler's invasion of Poland on September 1, 1939, was the final straw for Britain and France. Two days later they declared war on Germany.

For scientists on both sides the question was, what should they do with the new knowledge about atomic fission? What quickly became clear was that scientists would not be able to consider only the question of their moral responsibilities where nuclear science was concerned. They would have to weigh their political obligations to their country as well. A little over a month before the outbreak of the war, Werner Heisenberg was in the United States for a conference at the University of Michigan. In a conversation with the Italian physicist Enrico Fermi (1901–1954), he conceded that, once the war came, scientists on both sides would be expected to use their abilities to build new weapons for their governments.

German Scientists and the Prospect of a Bomb

In spite of the fame brilliant scientists had brought to Germany through their achievements and their Nobel Prizes, their value to the Third Reich was measured first and foremost by their perceived loyalty to their country. German scientists' therefore found themselves facing profound choices in the years leading up to and during World War II.

Science under Hitler.   When Max Planck once tried to intervene on behalf of a Jewish scientist, Hitler was reported to have said that national policies would not be revoked for scientists, adding: "If the dismissal of Jewish scientists means the annihilation of contemporary German science, then we shall have to do without science for a few years." That was true even for a physicist as famous as Albert Einstein.

As an outspoken pacifist Jew who had not even supported Germany's entry into World War I, Einstein was a persona non grata to the Nazis well before they officially came to power. He was in California when Hitler became chancellor and he quickly made the decision not to return to Germany. Despite his resignation from membership in the Prussian Academy of Sciences, where he had been the leading figure for over a decade, the Nazis pressured the academy to undertake disciplinary proceedings against him. While his property and bank accounts in Germany were confiscated, he soon found permanent employment in the United States, at the Institute for Advanced Study at Princeton University.

Some went further than simply denouncing Einstein himself. A few Nazi physicists even attacked his theory of relativity, which, they said, was typical of a kind of deficient science they associated with the Semitic mentality. They argued that science, like everything else, was determined by race or blood. The presence of Jews in physics, they said, had led to an emphasis on theory as the source of nature's truth rather than experiment. "Jewish physics" began with ideas born of the mind's fancy and only then asked experimenters to dutifully confirm them. Relativity, for example, was not experimentally based science; rather, it was more philosophy than natural science.

The leaders of the antirelativity campaign were two Nobel Prize–winning physicists, Philip Lenard (1862–1947) and Johannes Stark (1874–1957). Each had revealed his sympathies for the Nazi Party well before Hitler came to power in 1933. Building on the claim that race affected science, Lenard and Stark undertook a campaign to defend what they called German or Aryan physics. Aryan physics was marked by its strong experimental foundation and its rejection of materialistic mechanism. In place of the latter, Stark and Lenard declared that the great German physicists had always supported organic mechanism, that is, an outlook that envisioned nature as a living machine as opposed to a dead one. Lenard attempted to make the case for Aryan science in a four-volume work of 1936 with the title *German Science.*

Even scientists who were not Jewish experienced difficulties if their loyalty was questioned. Werner Heisenberg, for example, found himself the target of a smear campaign led by members of the German physics movement. Heisenberg, who never joined the Nazi Party, had been a central contributor to theoretical physics since he burst on the scene as a young twenty-year-old student. His close association with leading Jewish scientists such as Einstein, Max Born, and others, plus his devotion to the theory-based approach to science that quantum theory shared with relativity, marked him as a "white Jew" in the eyes of men like Stark and Lenard. Any hesitation they might have had to oppose him evaporated when Heisenberg refused to agree to a request by Stark that Nobel laureates publicly support Hitler in 1934.

Matters came to a head in 1936 when Heisenberg was nominated to succeed his mentor, Arnold Sommerfeld (1868–1951), as professor of theoretical physics in Munich. Stark attacked Heisenberg in public, missing no opportunity to associate him with the spirit of the now absent Albert Einstein. At first it appeared that Stark's efforts were in vain. Heisenberg, newly married, traveled to Munich in the summer of 1937 to take up the duties of the appointment he had been told was his. But in July, in a journal of the Nazi Party security organization known as the SS, Stark published what has been called "one of the most vicious attacks on science in general and on Heisenberg in particular to appear during the Third Reich."

With the SS now involved, Heisenberg's appointment was put on hold pending an investigation of Stark's charges of Heisenberg's disloyalty to the Third Reich. It soon became clear that Heisenberg was in grave personal danger. A charge emerged that he was in violation of an article of the criminal code that made male homosexuality a crime. Heisenberg's late and relatively quick marriage, it was suggested, was intended to cover up his real sexual preference. In 1937 this meant immediate sentence to a concentration camp.

Heisenberg was able to involve the SS leader, Heinrich Himmler (1900–1945), in the affair because of a friendship between his mother and Himmler's mother. But Himmler merely asked for a thorough investigation, which dragged on for a year before Heisenberg was exonerated of all charges in the summer of 1938, just a few months prior to the discovery of atomic fission by Hahn and Meitner.

Although Heisenberg was formally cleared, his opponents did succeed in frustrating his appointment to the chair of theoretical physics in Munich. Further, Heisenberg had to agree to certain conditions as part of the settlement of the affair. For instance, he had to separate scientific results from any Jewish physicists responsible for them. While the results themselves could be taught, no mention could be made of Jewish scientists who had contributed to them. Further, as is evident from the comment (cited earlier in the chapter) that Heisenberg made to Fermi over six months after the discovery of fission, he also clearly understood that he was expected to use his talents as a physicist on behalf of the Nazi cause. Heisenberg's acquiescence placed him in an extremely delicate and difficult position that tied him dangerously close to the Nazi regime in the years to come.

The Uranium Club.   Less than two weeks after Britain and France declared war on Germany, at the beginning of September of 1939, a number of German physicists were ordered to Berlin by the German army to explore the prospects of exploiting atomic fission. By late September the membership of this Uranium Club, as it became known, was expanded to include the leading lights of nuclear science, such as Otto Hahn and Werner Heisenberg. At this early stage Germany stood alone as the only country pursuing a military project on atomic fission.

Publications on nuclear fission in Britain and the United States remained open until the early summer of 1940, so Heisenberg had access to the latest information available as he began work. Within three months Heisenberg submitted a secret report that confirmed the technical feasibility of a controlled fission process that might be able to fuel German tanks and submarines, and acknowledged the prospect that the uranium isotope U^{235} might serve as an explosive with a power several factors of ten greater than the most powerful known.

Heisenberg soon learned what others were discovering, namely, that slower neutrons were more effective at initiating fission reactions than fast neutrons and that a new human-made element, plutonium, was also fissionable. The German team set to work to learn all it could about nuclear fission. As a result of its conquests, the German army provided the Uranium Club with resources its members would not have been able to acquire as university professors. Uranium ore came from occupied Czechoslovakia, heavy water (for slowing neutrons) from conquered Norway, a cyclotron (for separating out U^{235}) from occupied Denmark.

When by September of 1941 sufficient progress had been made that the road to the atomic bomb appeared certain, Heisenberg decided to consult with his mentor and friend, Niels Bohr, in Copenhagen. Heisenberg went to Copenhagen in October to attend a scientific meeting. Although Bohr routinely refused to attend such official meetings as a way of protesting the German occupation and to avoid any semblance of collaboration with the Nazis, he did agree to invite Heisenberg to his home. It is impossible to be certain what exactly was said at this famous get-together. Whether things transpired as Heisenberg recalled them or as Bohr later depicted, what was clear was that they could no longer remain friends.

As mentioned in Chapter 25, Bohr traveled to the United States shortly after learning from Lise Meitner about the discovery of fission. He had returned from America with a good sense of what the Americans were up to and was convinced that although a bomb was theoretically possible, it was practically unattainable. Heisenberg and Bohr went for a private walk so that their conversation would not be overheard. When Heisenberg asked Bohr about the moral responsibilities of working on uranium when it might lead to ominous military consequences, Bohr's reaction, according to Heisenberg, was one of alarm. Heisenberg wondered if Bohr had been working for the Americans and felt guilty about the question. When Bohr then asked if a bomb was really possible, Heisenberg confirmed it. He showed Bohr a sketch of a nuclear reactor he was planning to build, but noted that a bomb would require an incredible technical effort. Heisenberg then realized that Bohr inferred from his statement that the Germans had made progress on a bomb. In spite of several attempts, he was unable to dissuade Bohr that he had not intended to convey such a conclusion.

Bohr understood Heisenberg to be asking him for advice on how to deal with his involvement in nuclear research. To give it, in Bohr's mind, would amount to assisting the Nazis. While he was willing to overlook Heisenberg's personal connection to the Nazis by receiving Heisenberg for a visit, he was now angered that his former colleague would think that he would collaborate in any way, least of all where nuclear science was concerned. Perhaps, thought Bohr, Heisenberg had asked the question in order to try to gauge from his response something about American progress on the bomb. Their old friendship was shattered that September evening.

The middle of 1942 proved to be a crucial juncture for both the Allied and German bomb projects. As we will see, this was when the American project really began to congeal. For the German effort, however, it was a turning point in the opposite direction. Early in June the head of arms production, Albert Speer, who was well aware that German scientists were exploring nuclear power and the prospect of nuclear explosions, attended a meeting in which he asked Heisenberg directly how nuclear physics could be used to produce a bomb. Heisenberg replied that it could be done, but that the technical problems involved would require a minimum of two years, even if the scientists received full funding. Speer later recalled that the impression he received at the time was that the scientists' efforts were not at all likely to play a role in the war at hand. As a result, he continued to support the project, but only at modest levels.

Near the end of the war the German team believed they were close to being able to make their uranium "go critical." That is, they were on the verge of having their nuclear pile undergo a controlled and sustained fission reaction. Knowledge of how to control a fission reaction was a necessary step before either nuclear reactors for energy supply or nuclear explosions for military application could be realized. With Allied armies pressing on Berlin from both west and east, German leaders moved the nuclear project to the south of Germany and stepped up their support of the endeavor. Heisenberg and his cohorts worked feverishly. The motive for this eleventh-hour effort appears to have been to achieve a sustained nuclear reaction before the Americans did, so that the Nazi leaders would have secret information with which to bargain in negotiations with the Allies. Little did the German leaders realize that the Americans had already left them far behind in the race to build an atomic weapon.

The American Bomb Project

By the summer of 1939 some scientists outside Germany became alarmed that their German counterparts might be able to supply a bomb to Hitler. They became convinced that if Germany alone possessed an atomic bomb Hitler would be able to enslave the world. The only recourse was to make sure that the forces of freedom were able to counter any such threat with a similar threat of their own. The problem was to convince the people in power, specifically President Franklin Roosevelt (1882–1945) and Prime Minister Winston Churchill (1874–1965) of the menace facing the world. But that would not be easy. Earlier in March some had tried unsuccessfully to explain things to an American naval official, who wanted to know if the mass involved could fit into a gun. To military men and politicians who knew little about science and had other things on their minds, atomic fission smacked of science fiction and was not worth their time.

Initial period of indecision. In order to convince leaders at the highest levels of the threat that nuclear fission represented, a few scientists persuaded Albert Einstein to sign a letter, which they would ensure was delivered directly to President Franklin Roosevelt, explaining how serious the situation was. Roosevelt received Einstein's letter six weeks after war had been declared in the fall of 1939. He created the Advisory Committee on Uranium, consisting of a government scientist who headed the Bureau of Standards and representatives of the army and navy. This committee met a week later with several key nuclear scientists to hear what they had to say. In spite of major skepticism, a small sum of money was allocated to purchase the materials needed to begin work on a controlled, sustained nuclear reaction. The committee reported back to the president, agreeing that the idea was worth pursuing and recommending "adequate support for a thorough investigation." Satisfied that things were under control, Roosevelt promptly filed the report.

Scientists and political leaders each went their own ways. As scientists went about work to learn more about enriching uranium (separating out the fissionable U^{235}) and slowing down neutrons to enhance the fission process, American political leaders were preoccupied with pressures to remain neutral and stay out of the war in Europe. There were, however, two men who bridged the gap between the worlds of science and politics. They were Vannevar Bush (1890–1974), an engineer who headed the Carnegie Institution, and James Conant (1893–1978), a chemist who was president of Harvard University.

Convinced of the increasingly vital role technical knowledge was playing in public life, Bush and Conant gathered a small group of leading administrators of science and technology to form an organization, the National Defense Research Council (NDRC), which reported directly to the president. By the middle of 1940 this group administered the work of the Advisory Committee on Uranium, which now reported to the NDRC. The primary interest of Bush and Conant, however, was to confirm that, as Niels Bohr suspected, an atomic bomb was *not* feasible. The result was that government-sponsored research on uranium was not fully funded and could only proceed slowly alongside the separate lines of investigation in nuclear physics that were being carried out in university laboratories throughout the country.

Events in Britain appeared at first glance to follow a similar pattern. Around the same time the NDRC was formed, a British committee came into being with a similar purpose of determining what was and was not possible regarding military uses of nuclear fission. But Hitler's air attacks on British cities in 1940 gave the British group a greater sense of urgency than their American counterparts, who were an ocean away from the war. The British were focused on building a bomb, a fact that Conant learned to his surprise when he visited Britain early in 1941 to coordinate American and British efforts. However, Conant learned nothing specific to dissuade him from the view that a bomb was not possible.

By July of 1941 a formal British report was sent to Conant's American committee containing specific conclusions about costs and a timetable of just over two years for producing a bomb. Conant sat on it—his attitude was that the British talk was cheap because Britain was not in a position to undertake such a project by itself. When a month later a British physicist came to the United States to learn about American efforts, his remarks about plans for a bomb shocked members of the Advisory Committee on Uranium, who had no conception of a bomb project. They had the impression that their efforts were being directed toward perfecting nuclear energy for submarines.

After meeting with several American nuclear scientists, the British physicist persuaded them not only of the urgency of a bomb project, but also of the necessity for the United States to initiate it. They in turn eventually persuaded Conant to undertake a new study to confirm the British optimism about producing a bomb. The result was that on October 9, 1941, Conant decided to take the British report to President Roosevelt. Without consulting Congress or the courts, Roosevelt committed the United States to determine whether or not a bomb could be built. Scientists everywhere soon found that there were new opportunities for nuclear research. Roosevelt also decided to remove all authority over the future of nuclear research from scientists, reserving nuclear weapons policy to himself, with advice from a small secret group of trusted individuals that included only the vice president, the secretary of war, the Army chief of staff, Bush, and Conant.

By the end of November Roosevelt received the final report of the newly commissioned study. Ten days later the Japanese attacked Pearl Harbor, followed on December 11 by Hitler's declaration of war on the United States. It was clear to most of the scientists involved that there was increased interest in a bomb project, but with the major distractions of impending war before him, Roosevelt did not get around to returning the report until January 19, 1942, when, with a deceptively innocuous handwritten note to Bush, he left behind written evidence of the opening of the age of nuclear weapons with the words, "OK—returned—I think you had best keep this in your own safe. FDR."

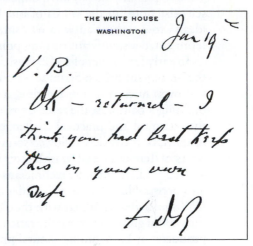

Note from President Roosevelt to Vannevar Bush, January 19, 1942

The Manhattan Project. Even before receiving the written go-ahead, Conant had decided to keep the key existing research endeavors where they were, at four American universities, for the time being. It was one thing to anticipate building an atomic bomb, but quite another to organize and assemble the massive undertaking that would be required to actually do it. Add to that challenge the fact that the project would have to be carried out at the very highest level of secrecy and the prospect boggled the mind.

By spring of 1942 enough had been learned to persuade Vannevar Bush that the new bomb would be more powerful than he had realized. When he reported this to Roosevelt in March, adding that the United States might be engaged in a race with the Germans, Roosevelt responded by directing him to push the effort. The undertaking was reorganized in a fundamental fashion—it was changed from a government-sponsored civilian program to a military weapons project under the military command of the Army Corps of Engineers. Its office in Manhattan gave rise to the creation of the Manhattan Engineering District, and Colonel Leslie Groves (1896–1970), an engineer recently in charge of building the Pentagon, was promoted to general and assigned as military director in mid-September of 1942.

Groves selected Robert Oppenheimer (1904–1967), a Berkeley physicist who had been working on the practical aspects of building a bomb, to be the scientific director of the project. Classically educated with a great appreciation for the humanities as well as physics, Oppenheimer soon found that his notion of the scientist as the independent and objective investigator of nature in search of truth for its own sake clashed with the conception of the scientist held by his military superiors. In their minds, scientists were merely employees working under orders who solved technical problems; theirs was not to question the military or political policies put in place by their superiors. This shift in the social conception of the scientist from, in the words of one historian, "the enlightened keeper of cultural ideals" to a technician who was subject to superiors with clearly vested interests, represented a significant turning point in the history of science.

In early December of 1942 physicists at the University of Chicago working under the immigrant Enrico Fermi successfully established a sustained and controlled critical mass nuclear fission reaction, a key step in the learning process necessary to building a bomb. At the same time, construction of the primary facility for solving the technical and practical challenges of exploding an atomic bomb began in Los Alamos, New Mexico, followed soon by the acquisition of land and buildings in the states of Tennessee and Washington for the production of the fissile materials U^{235} and Pu^{239}. In Tennessee, technicians forced gaseous uranium hexafluoride through semipermeable membranes in order to separate the uranium with the faster-moving U^{235} molecules from that with the slower U^{238} molecules. By repeating this process they could greatly improve the ratio of U^{235} to U^{238}. In Washington, plutonium was produced by bombarding natural uranium with neutrons that were then absorbed by U^{238} nuclei to yield Pu^{239} nuclei ($n + U^{238} \longrightarrow Pu^{239}$). In April of 1943 personnel arrived in New Mexico, met by Oppenheimer, who would direct them in the crash program ahead.

Over the next two years the scientists at Los Alamos solved innumerable theoretical, technical, and practical problems on their way to testing what they had come to call "the gadget." Three months prior to the test President Roosevelt died, leaving decisions about the bomb to an uninformed vice president, Harry Truman (1884–1972). And there were many decisions to make. In the previous November the Allies had captured scientific papers in Europe that made clear how far behind the Germans were in their nuclear research. With the threat of a German bomb eliminated, many scientists assumed that the United States would certainly not use the terrible weapon they had agreed to build as a deterrent to Hitler. When it became clear that the military was not about to let its investment in time, effort, and money go to waste, these scientists openly opposed the use of the bomb. They argued that at most there should be a public demonstration of the bomb's destructive power to persuade the Japanese to surrender. It was left to the new president to decide the issue.

May saw the final defeat of Germany, leaving only the war with Japan. In July, President Truman traveled to Potsdam in Germany to meet with his British and Soviet allies to discuss details of the settlement in Europe. While in Potsdam he received word of the successful testing of the atomic bomb, which took place early in the morning in the New Mexico desert many miles south of Los Alamos on July 16, 1945. On his return, Truman made his decision, convinced that dropping the bomb on the Japanese would hasten the end of the war. Two cities felt the impact of an atomic explosion in August of 1945, Hiroshima on August 6, and Nagasaki on August 9. The Japanese emperor made the decision to surrender on August 14, formally signing its terms on September 2.

Oppenheimer later conceded that scientists had built the bomb "because it was an organic necessity." Scientists, he said, wanted to find out how the world worked in order to control the world. Being caught up in the drive to accomplish what was obviously an incredible feat, most scientists and fewer political or military figures gave any serious thought to the future implications of what they were doing.

An exception was Niels Bohr, who was profoundly concerned that the existence of a bomb endangered civilization itself. Bohr's position, voiced directly to President Roosevelt early in 1944, was that the only hope for the future was if all potential nuclear powers collaborated from the beginning in order to establish a foundation on which to base an international nuclear policy. Bohr appeared to have persuaded Roosevelt of this course, but he failed miserably when he met with Churchill. The British prime minister soon overrode any thought Roosevelt had along these lines where Allied policy was concerned, even to the point of recommending, without success, that Bohr be arrested.

◎ The Politics of High Energy ◎

In the aftermath of World War II the question of what to do with the reality of the nuclear age forced itself to the fore when scientists discovered that legislation had been introduced in the U.S. Senate that would give the military effective control over the future of American nuclear research. The ensuing objections of scientists led to the passing of a replacement bill in the summer of 1946 that created the United States Atomic Energy Commission, a five-member civilian board that was assisted by an advisory committee and a military liaison committee. Military leaders were now fully aware that the future of warfare had changed forever and that they would have to learn how to cooperate closely with scientists.

If domestic nuclear policy proved to be solvable, the same could not be said for the development of an international policy. The United States was the only country with nuclear capability, but everyone knew that such a monopoly could not last forever. Efforts to work through the United Nations to establish an agreement among nations about the future development of nuclear energy for both peaceful and military purposes came to naught in the years immediately following 1945. They did not bear fruit until some twelve years later, with the establishment of the International Atomic Energy Agency (IAEA). Churchill's famous speech in March of 1946, in which he spoke of an "iron curtain" that divided Eastern from Western Europe, marked the beginning of the cold war.

From Fission to Fusion: The Hydrogen Bomb

There was an unresolved question left over from the Manhattan Project that reopened old issues about nuclear weapons. As indicated in Chapter 25, scientists in the 1930s had become aware of the process of nuclear fusion that took place in stars. In our sun, for example, fusing two hydrogen nuclei together to form a helium nucleus required an enormous amount of energy, but the fusion process itself precipitated the conversion of mass into energy, thus releasing even greater quantities of energy in the form of heat and light.

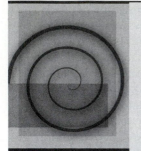

Science and Morality

The NATURE of SCIENCE

Many have the impression that the pursuit of science is a morally neutral enterprise. Morality, being something of concern to humans, is a separate matter from questions about how nature works. What humans *do* with the scientific knowledge they seek involves moral issues, but the acquisition of knowledge itself is neither good nor bad.

There have been those who have questioned this clean break between science and morality. German nature philosophers, for example, argued in the early years of the nineteenth century that both moral and aesthetic concerns are inextricably involved in the very construction of knowledge itself. Some in our own day point to issues raised in the development of science during the twentieth century to highlight the entanglement of morality and science.

Humans have always aspired to the knowledge of the gods. The question of whether the exploration of certain areas will so alter our humanity or even threaten its existence that these areas should be placed off limits will continue to be contentious. Once that exploration has occurred there is no turning back from the new moral dilemmas that are created within the larger society. Scientists who take responsibility for their part in the creation of such knowledge can offer valuable insights in the ongoing discussions and debates.

In the early stages of the Manhattan Project scientists discussed the prospect of creating a fusion bomb, which they called the Super because it would be far more powerful than a fission bomb. They had decided, however, to shelve working on the Super for a very obvious reason. The concentrated energy required to fuse two special hydrogen nuclei into a helium nucleus was simply not available on Earth. No known terrestrial source could provide the levels of energy present in solar furnaces. If, however, a fission bomb were available to act as a matchstick, then scientists would have sufficient heat energy to start the fusion process. So the fission bomb was a necessary first step to a fusion device, also known as a thermonuclear or hydrogen bomb. Oppenheimer decided that the pressing needs of the war dictated that efforts be focused on the atomic, or fission, bomb.

With the war over, one of the Los Alamos scientists, Edward Teller (1908–2003) urged that work should continue on the hydrogen bomb. But many scientists, including Robert Oppenheimer, opposed developing thermonuclear weapons. Oppenheimer believed that the potential destructive power was simply too horrific; further, he argued that an arsenal of atomic bombs was more than sufficient to meet any conceivable military need. While the issue was being debated, the Soviet Union detonated a test atomic bomb in September of 1949. Now there were two nations in a position to take the next step to a hydrogen bomb. President Truman made the decision in January of 1950 to go ahead with the development of the H-bomb.

The scientists working on the H-bomb encountered numerous technical problems, which, by early 1951, made it appear that a thermonuclear bomb was theoretically impossible. They employed what at the time was a newly developed calculating machine, one of the earliest digital computers, to help them with the incredibly complicated mathematical computations involved in simulating the blooming of a thermonuclear reaction from a fission matchstick. The model showed that the fission matchstick bomb would blow the fusible material apart before fusion could begin. Then they realized that if they physically separated the fusible material from the fission matchstick, something their design had not done, the x-ray energy from the fission explosion would ignite the fusion process before the shock wave from the fission blew it apart.

The first secret H-bomb test occurred in the fall of 1952 in the Marshall Islands in the Pacific Ocean. The building in which it was housed was on the small island of Elugelab, one of many islands making up the Enewetak Atoll. The explosive power of the test bomb, known as Ivy Mike, was equivalent to over ten megatons of TNT, almost a thousand times more powerful than the bomb dropped on Hiroshima. After the detonation Elugelab no longer existed. Three years later, in late November of 1955, the Soviets exploded their own thermonuclear bomb. The arms race was on, just as Bohr and others had feared would happen without international cooperation.

Ivy Mike

Big Science

During the First World War, President Woodrow Wilson heeded the advice of leading academic and industrial scientists and engineers when he created a special committee within the National Academy of Sciences to promote scientific research in the interests of national security and welfare. After the war, members of this committee took note of the major successes German physicists were enjoying in areas such as relativity and quantum mechanics. They decided to bolster the field of theoretical physics, which in the United States barely existed in 1918 because physics was dominated by experimental work. Their approach was to identify a small group of elite American universities that were positioned to undertake research and to supply them with funds raised from private philanthropists and industrialists, avoiding both the government and the military sources.

By 1930 American theoretical physics had risen to a place of international recognition, and the entire discipline of physics had also benefited. At the outbreak of World War II the strategy of using private funding to improve the physical sciences at America's best universities had expanded, so that 75 percent of America's physicists were employed in the top twenty universities, which produced 90 percent of the markedly increased number of doctorates in physics. Work in American theoretical and experimental physics was now comparable to the best in the world.

As World War II loomed on the horizon, however, things changed dramatically. When President Franklin Roosevelt agreed to form the NDRC in the spring of 1940, it was the first step in the direction of major governmental support of scientific work. Up to this time public funds had been used to support only agricultural projects and medical studies. In June of 1941 there was another reorganization of scientific research when the Office of Scientific Research and Development (OSRD) was created under the direction of Vannevar Bush. The OSRD was to be an umbrella organization that oversaw research on all scientific and medical issues relating to the national defense. With this move Bush introduced a system in which the government administered scientific research by contracting for services from scientists at universities and in private industry.

After World War II a number of new individual governmental agencies emerged to oversee research in nuclear science and technology. While the National Science Foundation (NSF) was created in 1950 as the government's only agency dedicated to the support of education and fundamental research in *all* scientific and engineering disciplines, the Atomic Energy Commission (mentioned earlier in this chapter) was to oversee research in nuclear and particle physics. Much later, in 1974, the AEC was replaced by the Nuclear Regulatory Commission (NRC) as part of the Energy Reorganization Act, whereupon it assumed responsibility for administering nuclear weapons and nuclear power.

As it assumed a much greater prominence in the eyes of the federal government, scientific research increased substantially in scale. One indication of this increase was the national laboratory system that grew out of the Manhattan Project. This was a network of the laboratories, not all of which we have named, in which work on the atomic bomb had been done and in which now both classified and basic research in the physical sciences could be conducted. What marked the projects undertaken in these national laboratories was the size of the enterprises. They required huge staffs, large budgets, and big machinery and equipment. In 1961 the director of research at the Oak Ridge National Laboratory used the term "big science" to underscore this new scale of research in nuclear physics and elementary particle physics.

Since World War II, research not only in nuclear science, but in genetics and other branches of science has acquired the trappings of big science. With sometimes hundreds of coauthors on new reports, new problems have grown along with the size of research teams and budgets. How, for example, is the allocation of scarce resources and an equitable distribution of funding to be handled when competing laboratories in different regions of the country have varying interests and individuals? Research in contemporary science continues to struggle with such challenges to this day.

◎ Nuclear Fears ◎

It took no time at all after the dropping of the atomic bombs on Japan for an ominous aura to settle over all things nuclear. As the news of the devastation at Hiroshima and Nagasaki became known in the West, people began to sense that humankind had unleashed a monster. They knew that if the Allies had been able to create such a horrible weapon of mass destruction it was entirely possible an enemy might some day use the same weapon on them. A young mother in New York State, who had just given birth to her second son when she learned about the bomb, wrote six days later that she had constantly been in tears or near tears, haunted by "fleeting but torturing regrets that I have brought children into the world to face such a dreadful thing as this."

Such fears merely intensified with the onset of the cold war with the Soviet Union. Worries about what the Soviets might do with nuclear weapons fed into a general and widespread fear of communism during the 1950s. Anyone suspected of having ties to the Communist Party ran the risk of being brought before a subcommittee chaired by the junior senator from Wisconsin, Joseph McCarthy, who, in the name of patriotism, denounced numerous public figures for their past associations. Questions of loyalty even haunted the former director of the Manhattan Project, Robert Oppenheimer, whose earlier links to the Communist Party and whose opposition to the development of the hydrogen bomb resulted in a formal hearing before the AEC that resulted in public humiliation and the loss of his security clearance.

The threat of nuclear weapons was not, however, the only thing that frightened people about nuclear energy. Well before World War II controversy had seeped into the public arena about the effects of radioactivity on human health. Radium, once thought to be a boon to health, became an object of fear in the late 1920s as the result of lawsuits brought against the makers of radium dial wristwatches. When female dial painters who had slowly become deathly sick finally sued their employers, articles with titles such as "Woman Awaiting Death Tells How Radium Poison Slowly, Painfully Kills" caught the public's eye. Once it became clear that nuclear bombs produced massive amounts of radioactive fallout, the public had even greater reason to become alarmed.

The Prospect of Nuclear Holocaust

On August 7, 1945, the day after Hiroshima, the *St. Louis Dispatch* warned that science might just have "signed the mammalian world's death warrant, and deeded an earth in ruins to the ants." Little did the public know that the prospect of nuclear annihilation would become far more real in the years ahead as the cold war encouraged new developments in delivery systems for nuclear weapons. In the 1950s the public learned about military testing of rockets and missiles, which had been going on since the end of the war. While the development of rockets in part served the cause of science in an effort to gather information about the upper atmosphere, the military's main interest lay with their use as long-range weapons.

Then in 1957 the Soviet Union surprised everyone with its announcement of the launching of *Sputnik,* the first Earth-orbiting satellite. Now that humans possessed the capability of escaping into space, it took only a moment's reflection to realize that there was nowhere on Earth that was safe any longer from missiles. If the Soviets could launch a satellite, they clearly could launch an intercontinental ballistic missile (ICBM). Future American wars would not necessarily be fought on enemy territory as they had in the past, because the devastation of battle could now be brought to America's great cities.

The literature of nuclear devastation.   Writers of fiction and plays had been depicting nuclear catastrophes well before the world learned about the atomic bomb in 1945. The first of these, written early in the century, often dealt with the dangerous effects of mysterious new atomic rays. But authors after 1905 who were aware of Einstein's equation, $E = mc^2$, could make the inference that only a little matter could be the source of incredible amounts of energy. In 1932, for example, British diplomat Harold Nicholson published a novel entitled *Public Faces,* in which the British, in sole possession of an atomic bomb, forced other nations to disarm. Nicholson's fictional bomb was powerful enough to cause a tsunami off the Florida coast that ended up killing 80,000 people and permanently changed the climate by altering the course of the Gulf Stream.

The announcement of the discovery of fission in 1939 resulted in a number of news items speculating on the vast energy contained in the atom. Once war had broken out, however, a general censorship prevented further news articles on atomic theory. Fiction was another matter—at least for a while. Many stories about nuclear bombs appeared in the pages of the magazine *Astounding Science Fiction* throughout the 1930s and early 1940s. In the March issue of 1944, a story named "Deadline" described a bomb that was enough like the one under construction in Los Alamos that the editor of the magazine received a visit from the Army Counter-Intelligence Corps. In January of the same year author Phillip Wylie sold a story about a Nazi attempt to rule the world with atomic bombs to the fiction magazine *Blue Book.* On objections from the War Department the magazine cancelled the sale. A note in the files of Wylie's agent, written in the very month of the supposedly top-secret Trinity Test (July 1945), indicated the reason for the cancellation: "President Conant of Harvard is working on something similar." Once the bomb had been dropped, *Blue Book* immediately repurchased the story.

Illustration Used
on the Cover of
*Astounding
Science Fiction*
(1941)

After August of 1945, when atomic bombs ceased being science fiction, the holocaust novel took on a different aura. This was especially true following the onset of the cold war and the development of hydrogen bombs. Now the explosive violence of nuclear detonations and the worldwide impact of the unstoppable massive radioactive fallout imparted a realistic tone to the unthinkable annihilation of all human life, which up to then had only occurred in science fiction. Nuclear wars, unlike wars of the past, would be sudden and short. Humankind was now actually capable of making an irreversible mistake that could end history.

No author portrayed the end of human civilization more vividly or with a greater sense of tragedy than the British writer Neville Schute, whose *On the Beach* carried the famous words of T. S. Elliot on its title page: "This is the way the world ends/Not with a bang but a whimper." Written in 1957, the same year *Sputnik* was launched, *On the Beach* came out as a film in 1959. It told the story of Australians who were the last survivors of a nuclear war that had taken place two years earlier in the Northern Hemisphere. As the lethal radioactive fallout from the war slowly made its way south, individuals faced the end in varying ways. An American submarine captain who had escaped the war voyaged north to Seattle to track down a mysterious message, only to confirm that indeed civilization had ended. Some simply took a suicide pill, while others tried bravely to continue on with their lives. One young couple insisted on planting a garden they would never see bloom. A racecar-driving scientist, who supplied the scientific explanations of the situation for the reader, participated in the last Grand Prix that would ever be run.

If Schute's work portrayed the tragic inevitability of final destruction, *Alas Babylon,* written in 1959 by Pat Frank, grappled with the prospect of surviving nuclear holocaust. Set in the small town of Fort Repose, Florida, civilization simply evaporates as those who have not been killed by nuclear blasts find that they are isolated from the outside world. The easy life of civilized society gives way to a scarcity of food, the spread of disease, and the breakdown of social order. At the same time Frank's work depresses the reader, however, the indomitable human spirit of his central characters impart hope for individual renewal. The story came into American homes in April of 1960 as an episode in the CBS television drama series *Playhouse 90.*

Among the many other early artistic attempts to wrestle with nuclear holocaust were two popular films from 1964, both of which had an enormous impact. *Fail-Safe* presented a scenario in which the best-laid safeguards of military planners to avoid accidental thermonuclear war came to naught. When an unknown plane approaches the United States, fighter bombers armed with nuclear weapons are scrambled, according to protocol. The plane is identified and recall orders are issued, but the attack code is sent by mistake to the bombers, which have gathered at the fail-safe point. Having received orders to bomb Moscow, the pilots and their crews ignore all pleas to return, assuming they are Russian tricks. The American president, ignoring the advice of a political science expert to seize the opportunity and eliminate communism once and for all in a first strike, repeatedly attempts to find a way to avoid the impending disaster. Even though the Americans assist the Russians in attacking the U.S. bombers, one plane makes it through and delivers the bomb that obliterates Moscow. The film ends as an American plane circles over New York City, ordered by the American president to drop its nuclear bomb on an American city as the sole means of convincing the Russians that the incident was an accident, thereby avoiding World War III.

Perhaps the most popular nuclear holocaust film was the black comedy *Dr. Strangelove, Or: How I Learned to Stop Worrying and Love the Bomb,* also in theaters in 1964. Through the exploitation of satirical fantasy, extreme caricature, and sexual imagery, director Stanley Kubrick used the theme of inadvertent, preemptive nuclear attack to mock the absurdity of the nuclear arms race in a cynically persuasive antiwar movie. The overall impact of the picture is captured in the film's most unforgettable scene, when actor Slim Pickens, in trying to unstick the mechanism that is preventing release of the bomb from the plane, ends up enthusiastically riding the bomb like a bronco to its final target.

The ensuing years would see the production of hundreds more stories, novels, plays, and movies dealing with the fear of nuclear annihilation, including twenty-first-century television remakes of *On the Beach* and *Fail-Safe.* They indicated the growing sense of ambiguity that many felt about natural science in the 1960s and beyond.

The Cuban Missile Crisis. A nonfictional vision of nuclear war occurred in the fall of 1962, when the United States and the Soviet Union came close to

Promotional Still for
Dr. Strangelove

thermonuclear blows over the presence of Soviet nuclear missiles in Cuba. The newly elected president, John F. Kennedy, had suffered humiliation three months into his presidency when an American-supported invasion of Cuba by Cuban exiles failed miserably in April of 1961. Not wanting to allow Russia to take advantage of his weakened position, Kennedy warned the Soviets of the nuclear confrontation that could occur if Cuba became a base for Soviet missiles.

For several days the two powers exchanged terse warnings, while behind the scenes efforts were made to work out a peaceful solution. Kennedy resisted military advice to conduct a surgical strike against the Cuban missile sites, knowing that the Soviet premier, Nikita Khrushchev, had placed missiles in Cuba to balance American intermediate-range missiles already stationed in Turkey. A strike against Cuban missiles would mean a retaliatory strike against the missiles in Turkey.

But Kennedy decided that the Russian missiles could not in any circumstances remain in Cuba. After informing the nation of the situation on the evening of October 22, the president held a meeting with advisors the next evening in which he attempted to assess realistically the prospects of evacuating cities likely to be targets of a nuclear strike. Being told that there was more protection from fallout in cities than in the rural areas, Kennedy continued to worry about doing everything possible to protect the population from the aftereffects of nuclear detonations.

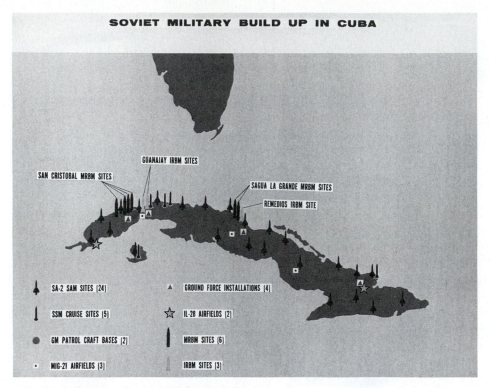

SOVIET MILITARY BUILD UP IN CUBA

GUANAJAY IRBM SITES

SAN CRISTOBAL MRBM SITES

SAGUA LA GRANDE MRBM SITES

REMEDIOS IRBM SITE

SA-2 SAM SITES (24)

SSM CRUISE SITES (5)

GM PATROL CRAFT BASES (2)

MIG-21 AIRFIELDS (3)

GROUND FORCE INSTALLATIONS (4)

IL-28 AIRFIELDS (2)

MRBM SITES (6)

IRBM SITES (3)

1961 Map Showing Soviet Missiles in Cuba

On October 24, the president declared a quarantine around Cuba to prevent any more Soviet ships from entering Cuban ports. Khrushchev called the quarantine an act of aggression and refused to accept it, setting up an impending confrontation between the nuclear powers as Russian ships approached the American line. But when Soviet ships carrying suspicious cargo stopped at the quarantine point, awaiting further instructions, the standoff afforded additional time for much-needed negotiations to find a way out of the dilemma.

In the end a solution was found that satisfied both sides. Kennedy agreed to remove American intermediate-range missiles from Turkey, although this agreement was not made public to avoid the impression he had been forced into this decision. In return, the Russians removed their weapons from Cuba. Both Kennedy and Khrushchev acted prudently in the crisis, Kennedy in refusing to conduct a strike against the Cuban weapons and Khrushchev in observing the American quarantine and in removing Russian missiles. Well after the crisis it was learned that Khrushchev also had rejected advice from the Cuban leader, Fidel Castro, to conduct a first nuclear strike against the United States in the event of an American invasion.

Diplomatic efforts.   The fear of nuclear holocaust affected politicians as well as the general public. Although the use of the atomic bomb in 1945 was an abandonment of the policy of deterrence, which had been the motivation of many Los Alamos scientists, after the war the Americans and Soviets found themselves falling back onto deterrence as the only feasible approach to the reality of nuclear weapons. But in order to be deterred, each nation had to be persuaded that it had a nuclear capacity equal to that of the adversary and that the adversary was capable of actually using its weapons. If either side perceived that the other was in a position to successfully carry out a first strike, eliminating the enemy's weapons before they could be used, then deterrence would not work. The result of this situation was a massive arms race, fueled by the determination on each side not to become vulnerable by falling behind in the race.

Thoughts of a winnable nuclear war—as contemplated, for example, in a book by Herman Kahn in 1960 entitled *On Thermonuclear War*—all but vanished in the mid-1960s when submarine-launched ballistic missiles (SLBMs) came online on both sides. Gone was all prospect of taking out the enemy's missiles in a first strike because they could be so widely dispersed that a complete retaliation was guaranteed. To use nuclear weapons first was now an act of suicide. The West had entered the era of mutually assured destruction (MAD).

Especially following the crisis of 1962, politicians envisioned the horrific consequences that would occur if the policies they had adopted to deal with the nuclear age did not prove adequate to the task. The following year saw passage of the Nuclear Test Ban Treaty, by which the United States, the Soviet Union, and the United Kingdom agreed to prohibit atmospheric testing of nuclear weapons. Although the buildup of nuclear arms continued unabated, the United States and the Soviet Union did consider formally renouncing all attempts to create a defense against nuclear weapons beginning in the late 1960s. If, they reasoned, one side possessed a defensive system (an antiballistic missile system—ABM), deterrence would no longer apply and a successful first strike would become feasible. An agreement to ban all ABM systems except one around each country's capital (neither of which was ever built) constituted the content of the first Strategic Arms Limitation Treaty (SALT I), which was signed in 1972.

The development of new weapons technology continued, in spite of periodic attempts to curb it, until the number of weapons amassed on both sides of the East-West divide numbered in the tens of thousands, enough to obliterate all life from the face of the Earth many times over. In the midst of this massive buildup, the United States under President Ronald Reagan considered the possibility of abandoning its commitment to SALT I by pursuing construction of an ABM system under a program called the Strategic Defense Initiative (SDI). Some have suggested that Reagan was responding primarily to domestic concerns rather than undertaking an initiative directed at international issues. But Reagan's motive in doing so at least in part stemmed from his idealism—he wanted to get out from under the tension of deterrence by making nuclear weapons obsolete. In the fall of 1986 he even made an offer to Soviet premier Mikhail Gorbachev to share the "star wars" program, as it was dubbed by Massachusetts Senator Edward Kennedy, among others. Realizing that Reagan had shocked his own advisors by his proposal, Gorbachev did not take the offer as a serious gesture. Following the collapse of the Soviet Union the initiative was abandoned.

A number of treaties in the 1980s and 1990s resulted in vast reductions in the numbers of strategic nuclear warheads on ICBMs, SLBMs, and bombers; in the elimination of intermediate and short-range missiles; and in a comprehensive test ban on nuclear testing above and below the Earth's surface. This reduction did not, of course, eliminate the fear of nuclear holocaust altogether because not all countries were signatories to or ratified the treaties. The catastrophic scenarios of the cold war era have been replaced by threats of a different kind, from so-called rogue nations that have acquired a nuclear capacity. While the use of nuclear weapons by such nations would be a suicidal act, the existence of nuclear weapons continues to inspire nuclear fear.

The Peaceful Use of Nuclear Power

In December of 1953 President Dwight Eisenhower addressed the United Nations General Assembly on the peaceful use of atomic energy. Acknowledging that there was a new language in the world, the language of atomic warfare, Eisenhower turned his attention away from war toward peace. He called for the establishment of an international atomic energy commission under the auspices of the United Nations that would "devise methods whereby this fissionable material would be allocated to serve the peaceful pursuits of mankind." Under the proposal, all nuclear nations would make contributions of fissionable materials to the cause. While the suggestion of sharing fissionable materials never saw fruit, Eisenhower's "Atoms for Peace" proposal, as it became known, did spark the formation of an International Atomic Energy Agency (IAEA) in 1957, which has continued since then to seek peaceful applications of nuclear energy and to inhibit its military use.

Early nuclear reactors and their reception.   The year following Eisenhower's speech the U.S. Congress passed the Atomic Energy Act, which, in ending the government monopoly on technical information concerning nuclear technology, permitted for the first time the private development of atomic energy for peaceful purposes. Soon thereafter the AEC granted the Duquesne Light Company a contract to operate a nuclear power plant, which was to be built and owned by the government, and by September of 1954 ground was broken for the first commercial nuclear power plant, located in Shippingport, Pennsylvania. By 1960 the AEC had received proposals for three more plants in locations near Chicago, New York, and Detroit. As the industry began to grow, the AEC conducted extensive research to establish regulations for licensing that included a set of site requirements, safety procedures, and shutdown protocols in case of accident.

Early antinuclear protests focused not on the peaceful use of nuclear power, but on the proliferation of weapons of mass destruction. Noted British mathematician and philosopher Bertrand Russell, known for his antinuclear sentiments, joined with Einstein and nine other scientists to create the Russell-Einstein Manifesto, which was issued in London on July 9, 1955. They called for the abolition of war, declaring that if many hydrogen bombs were used in a war, "there will be universal death, sudden only for a minority, but for the majority a slow torture of disease and disintegration."

Bertrand Russell Issuing Manifesto

Shortly after the release of the manifesto, Russell received a letter from a wealthy industrialist in the United States offering to finance a conference of scientists as a step toward realizing the goals the manifesto had articulated. From this was born the Pugwash Conferences, which became an annual event that brought together scientists from many lands and political persuasions and served as a symbol of antinuclear sentiment.

With the signing of the Nuclear Test Ban Treaty, antinuclear protests steadily diminished after 1963. Although, as mentioned, the major powers continued to expand their nuclear arsenals in this period, there grew a misguided perception of reduced danger. As the memory of Hiroshima faded and the war in Vietnam focused the ire of protesters, nuclear issues became the prerogative of technical experts. In the mid-1970s, with SALT I signed, the war over, and the Soviet Union pursuing a policy of détente, it would take an unexpected event to consolidate protesters against the peaceful use of nuclear power.

Three Mile Island.   At 4:00 a.m. on the morning of March 28, 1979, an alarm went off in the control room of one of the nuclear reactors at the Three Mile Island nuclear plant thirteen miles southeast of Harrisburg, the state capital of Pennsylvania. A pump in the secondary loop had turned off. In and of itself, this was a minor problem. Things would, however, become much worse.

A nuclear reactor uses a controlled chain reaction to generate heat, which is used to drive turbines, whose motion can be converted into electricity. The chain reaction takes place in the core of the reactor, into which control rods can be inserted to regulate the speed of the reaction. The water circulating in the primary loop is heated, then removed by way of its contact with a secondary loop that supplies new water for heating (see the diagram on the next page).

The Reactor at
Three Mile Island

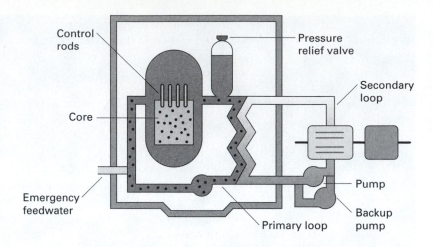

A number of problems can occur that can interrupt the normal operation of the reactor. The most feared accident is a nuclear meltdown. This would happen if for some reason the temperature of the core became so high that the cladding, the metal tubes that hold the nuclear pellets, ruptured and the pellets began to melt. In a worst-case scenario the meltdown would breach containment structures built around the reactor, not in a nuclear explosion (although if water is encountered a steam explosion could result), but in major radioactive contamination of the surrounding area. At Three Mile Island a partial meltdown occurred, but, except for a minor amount of radiation that was vented to the atmosphere, the containment facilities functioned to prevent contamination and injury.

The accident involved a sequence of events that included mechanical failure and human error. When the pump in the secondary loop shut down, heated water in the primary loop stopped being removed, causing the temperature and pressure to rise. Within a few seconds the valve at the top of the reactor opened to relieve pressure and the backup pumps in the secondary loop turned on. So far the system responded as it should to the initial event of the pump shutdown.

From here on a series of complications occurred. A cutoff valve to the backup pump was closed, unbeknownst to the operators, so the secondary loop remained disconnected from the primary loop. The pressure relief valve remained stuck in the open position even after the indicator light in the control room said it was closed, releasing coolant to a holding tank. When emergency feedwater was added automatically to the core, operators eventually turned it off, assuming the water level had returned to normal even though it had not.

A little after 6:00 a.m. the core began to be exposed and hydrogen and radioactive gases were produced along with superheated steam. Operators disagreed about whether the instruments indicating an extremely high temperature of the core could be trusted. Not until 7:00 p.m. was the system brought back under control. Meanwhile a massive amount of radioactive coolant had been discharged into the containment facilities, a small amount of which had been vented to the atmosphere. In addition, hydrogen gas had accumulated above the core in a dangerous bubble.

Handling a potential explosion from the hydrogen bubble and the leakage of radiation from the containment facilities proved to be ongoing problems that took days to resolve. The Pennsylvania governor advised pregnant women and preschool-aged children within five miles of the plant to evacuate the area, an announcement that obviously raised public anxiety. It did not help that twelve days before the accident, the film *China Syndrome,* involving a reactor accident not unlike that at Three Mile Island, had opened in theaters.

No one was injured and no health effects have been documented from the accident. Nevertheless, the image of nuclear power suffered severely, especially after the much more serious accident at the Chernobyl nuclear reactor in the Soviet Union in April of 1986. That nuclear accident did involve both deaths and health problems due to radiation. Whereas prior to 1979 antinuclear protests were mainly directed against nuclear weapons, with the peaceful use of nuclear power playing a secondary role, after these accidents public distrust and criticism of the nuclear industry grew substantially in the United States. The nuclear industry in many European countries, however, grew in spite of public distrust.

As the world's energy sources dwindle, nations have had to reconsider the role of nuclear power for the future. While not free from negative impacts on the environment, nuclear power does less ecological damage than other energy sources, such as coal, that are currently in use. Humankind therefore continues to weigh the benefits and risks of the nuclear age against the backdrop of Zeus's concern that imparting the knowledge of fire to mortals would lead only to misery.

Suggestions for Reading

Thomas Powers, *Heisenberg's War: The Secret History of the German Bomb* (Cambridge, Mass.: DaCapo Press, 2000).

S. S. Schweber, *In the Shadow of the Bomb: Oppenheimer, Bethe, and the Moral Responsibility of the Scientist* (Princeton, N.J.: Princeton University Press, 2000).

Jessica Wang, *American Science in an Age of Anxiety: Scientists, Anticommunism, and the Cold War* (Chapel Hill: University of North Carolina Press, 1999).

Spencer Weart, *Nuclear Fear* (Cambridge, Mass.: Harvard University Press, 1989).

CHAPTER 27

Ongoing Issues

There is a natural human tendency to make critical judgments about the outlook and specific views of people who, like those from the past, hold opinions that are very different from our own. This is certainly the case where knowledge of the natural world is concerned and in many instances such a judgment is well justified. But when it becomes clear, for example, that meteorites have indeed fallen to Earth from space, then it no longer is acceptable to assert, as did some natural philosophers of the eighteenth century, that peasant reports of rocks falling from the sky were preposterous claims of the uneducated.

As we evaluate the science of the past we do well to realize that our outlook in the present is not so privileged by the current state of knowledge that it represents final truth. Some textbooks of science (though by no means all), wishing to underscore the solidity of a modern theory, contrast it with a past theory that has been rejected. When such a text introduces the current view, students often read that, in contrast to the discarded idea of the past, "we now know" what the real explanation is. While there is no explicit claim that the modern theory will never change, it frequently does not occur to textbook authors to mention that prospect. Science is therefore presented merely as a body of knowledge acquired through the hard work of methodological research and analysis, not as a constantly changing articulation of our best attempts at understanding in light of factors that are dominant in a given time.

A broader perspective that is not completely focused on the present helps bring understanding to the issues of contemporary science because history is an important factor shaping current questions in the physical and biological sciences. Fundamental issues that have characterized the development of Western natural science over time continue to exert their influence in the present. For example, like the ancient Ionians, many modern physicists believe that scientific explanation of the physical world should not consist of patchwork accounts of individual aspects of nature; rather, separate facets should be brought together into a unified explanation. And in modern biological science the historical challenges about how to use

568

scientific knowledge of living things without running roughshod over moral and ethical concerns are, if anything, more pointed today than they have ever been. These and other enduring themes from the past continue to persist in the ongoing issues of the natural sciences.

◎ The Physical Sciences ◎

Among the broad issues from the history of the physical sciences that continue today are those dealing with our theoretical understanding of matter and force, others concerned with our understanding of the universe in which we find ourselves, and still others that arise from our need to utilize our knowledge for the benefit of humankind. While these three topics do not represent the only ongoing questions of physical science of interest today, they do provide an opportunity to consider questions about science itself and about its interaction with contemporary culture.

Dreams of a Final Theory

Writing in 1986, the physicist and historian of science Gerald Holton described an age-old outlook that, he said, continues to characterize the deepest aim of modern fundamental research. A decade later Holton attached to this stance the label by which it has since become identified—"the Ionian enchantment." It is "to achieve one logically unified and parsimoniously constructed system of thought that provides the conceptual comprehension, as complete as humanly possible, of the scientifically accessible sense experiences in their full diversity." Such an ambition, he noted, "embodies a telos of scientific work itself, and it has done so since the rise of science in the Western world."

Early examples of the drive for unification.   One of the ways in which the Ionian enchantment has shown itself in the history of the physical sciences is the drive for unification evident in the theories of force that have emerged. We have observed the various stages of the drive to unify nature's forces in earlier chapters. When Isaac Newton declared that the same force that caused apples to fall affected the moon in its orbit, he introduced the idea of *universal* gravitation—that every body in the universe exerts a force on every other body. By uniting together the regions of the heavens and the Earth, Newton underscored the rejection of Aristotle's understanding, already suggested by Newton's predecessors, that they constituted totally separate realms, with different laws and even different kinds of matter.

As other forces—electrical, magnetic, chemical, thermal, and optical—caught the attention of natural philosophers in the eighteenth and nineteenth centuries, the wish to unite them showed itself quickly. We observed in Chapter 16 how German romantic nature philosophers, convinced of the unity of nature, were inspired to search for the relationship among forces. With the invention of the battery at the turn of the nineteenth century the relationship between electrical and chemical forces was uncovered. In 1820 Hans Christian Oersted succeeded in showing that electricity and magnetism occurred together. Later in the century

James Maxwell revealed that light, too, was electromagnetic in nature (see Chapter 21). By the end of the nineteenth century, nature's fundamental forces had been reduced to two: gravitational and electromagnetic.

Albert Einstein was convinced that, just as Oersted had shown that electricity and magnetism were manifestations of a more basic force, electromagnetism and gravity could also be united into a single force. He gave a hint of his wish to achieve what later became known as Einstein's unified field theory as early as 1923, when he gave his Nobel lecture on relativity. "The intellect seeking after an integrated theory," he said, "cannot rest content with the assumption that there exist two distinct fields totally independent of each other by their nature." The search for a solution eluded Einstein for the rest of his life, even though he committed himself to it passionately. His failure has elicited the comment from one of his biographers that the progress of physics during roughly the last three decades of Einstein's life would not have suffered unduly had he abandoned his pursuit and spent the time sailing instead.

Two new fundamental forces.   Meanwhile, however, the new knowledge of the atom and nucleus that was emerging from the development of quantum mechanics in these years increased the number of nature's fundamental forces. If the nucleus was made up of protons and neutrons, then how could positively charged protons remain in such close proximity to each other if the repulsive force between positively charged particles increases as they come nearer? Further, what holds the neutrons in the nucleus? Physicists realized that there must be a very strong force responsible for holding the particles in all nuclei together. They posited that it must be an extremely short-range force; that is, it only acted over distances roughly comparable to the size of the nucleus. The force became known as the strong nuclear force.

But how to explain this force? A hint came from the explanation of how two hydrogen atoms combine to form a molecule of hydrogen gas that had been given in 1927 by two German physicists. To explain how two neutrally charged atoms might be held together, these scientists suggested that they *shared* electrons. In the hydrogen gas molecule the two electrons no longer belonged to one atom and the other individually; rather, it was as if they shuttled back and forth from one proton to the other and that this sharing constituted the force holding the molecule together as one unit.

A hydrogen atom has no neutrons, but all other elements (and isotopes of hydrogen itself) do. Werner Heisenberg imagined that the neutron could be thought of as a compound particle, consisting of a proton and an electron. If so, he reasoned, then perhaps the short-range force between two protons in, say, a helium nucleus resembles what happens in a hydrogen molecule. Heisenberg speculated that electrons from the two neutrons could be shared with the two protons, shuttling back and forth so that the nucleons were constantly changing their state. That is, as the two neutrons became two protons, the two protons became two neutrons, and so forth. This exchanging of electrons might then constitute the force holding the nucleons together.

Heisenberg's musing, being very general, opened the door for others to take into account the specific constraints that occur in the nucleus. A Japanese physicist, Hideki Yukawa (1907–1981), took the idea of force as particle sharing and proposed a theory of nuclear forces in 1935. When he took into account the conditions applying to the physics of the nucleus, he found that the force holding nucleons together required the exchange of a new hypothetical particle, never observed, whose mass was about 200 times greater than that of an electron. Eventually this particle, called the π-meson, was observed in 1947.

Another nuclear force grew out of research done in radioactivity. Earlier in the century, physicists and chemists experimenting with radioactive decay had noticed that the radioactive particles emitted were not always the same. Some were relatively massive and bore a positive charge, some were negative with much less mass, and some seemed to have no mass and showed no charge (see Chapters 21 and 25). Using the first three letters of the Greek alphabet, the researchers named the different kinds of radiation alpha, beta, and gamma.

Hideki Yukawa

The negatively charged radiation, beta radiation, was eventually identified with the emission of electrons and was found to raise the atomic number of the so-called mother element. To explain this, physicists concluded that a neutron in the nucleus had separated into a proton plus an electron, so that when the electron was emitted, the remaining proton increased the total number in the nucleus by one. The nuclear force responsible for this "beta decay of the neutron" was dubbed the weak nuclear force, bringing the total number of fundamental forces in the universe to four: gravity, electromagnetic force, strong nuclear force, and weak nuclear force.

Unifying the fundamental forces.   In 1968 three physicists, Sheldon Glashow (b. 1932), Abdus Salem (1926–1996), and Steven Weinberg (b. 1933), were able to show that electromagnetic force and the weak nuclear force were each aspects of a single force, now known as the electroweak interaction. This achievement reduced nature's fundamental forces to three. The three physicists regarded the new force as the sharing of two new particles, W and Z bosons, not yet discovered. In 1983 these particles were in fact discovered using the powerful accelerator at CERN (originally Conseil Européen pour la Recherche Nucléaire), billed as the world's largest particle physics laboratory.

Should physicists be successful some day in showing that the strong nuclear force and the electroweak force are aspects of a single underlying force, then all three of the forces having to do with the world of elementary particles will have been unified into one grand unification theory (GUT), so named in 1978. That would leave but one step: to merge this unified force active in the world of the very small with the gravitational force evident in the world of the large. If successful, this achievement would be known as the theory of everything (TOE), and it would depict the state of the universe at its earliest stages, when nature's fundamental forces had not yet shown themselves individually. But that has proven to be an enormous challenge, if for no other reason than the discontinuity of the quantum world of elementary particles appears to be incompatible with the continuous realm of general relativity, in which gravity is explained as a manifestation of geometry in curved spacetime.

One attempt to bridge the gap between quantum theory and relativity is called string theory, which first made its appearance in the 1970s. In this approach the basic makeup of reality is not due to fundamental elementary particles, but to tiny vibrating strings. Elementary particles, whose sharing constitutes nature's fundamental forces, are in fact identified with different vibrations of the strings. In order to incorporate gravitational force, the strings would have to be so tiny that there would be no conflict with continuous spacetime. To accomplish this, the strings would have the size in centimeters somewhere in the vicinity of Planck's constant, the level of measure of discontinuity evident in quantum theory (see Chapter 21). Early string theories accounted only for certain types of particles. This limitation was answered by so-called superstring theory, which was developed in two phases, the first around 1985 and the second around 1995.

Some physicists criticize string theory because it appears impossible to test it empirically. It has been pointed out that because the strings are as small compared to a proton as a proton is compared to the solar system, it would take a particle accelerator one thousand light years around to probe the realm of the strings! So far, string theorists have not made a prediction that can be tested, prompting one critic to say that it is "not even wrong." If, after all, a theory offers no possibility of empirical testing, then does it qualify as science? Some treat it virtually as a branch of pure mathematics. Or is it comparable to theological or philosophical speculation? Whether viable alternative theories will replace string theory in the quest to find a theory of everything remains to be seen.

The Future of the Universe

In Chapter 25 we examined the emergence of big bang cosmology and its dominance in the latter half of the twentieth century. On the assumption that the universe— that is, space, time, and matter—had a beginning, it has been natural to ask how long ago it took place, what the early universe was like, how it has changed over time, and what the future holds.

The unbelievably large amounts of energy present in the cosmic explosion of the big bang suggests that matter as we encounter it today on Earth could not have been present. Only quarks (the most basic constituents of protons and neutrons) and electrons could have existed, not in any combination, but only as a teeming broth of isolated components that has been characterized as "quark soup." The incredible expansion of knowledge about elementary particles has made it possible to speculate intelligently on the state and development of the early universe. For example, as the universe expanded and cooled, the energy required to keep quarks from combining was no longer present; hence protons and neutrons began to form approximately ten microseconds after the big bang.

By the end of three minutes helium nuclei had formed, although it would take a half million years before electrons could move into orbit around protons and helium nuclei to make atoms of hydrogen and helium. At one hundred million to several billion years the universe had cooled to a point where matter began to associate into galaxies, whose stars harbored fusion reactions that produced heavier elements such as carbon and oxygen (see Chapter 25). With supernova explosions of these stars, heavy elements were thrust outward into space, where new planets were formed. On Earth, and likely on many other sites containing these heavy elements, life emerged and evolved. Scientists estimate that this process has gone on for somewhere between twelve and fifteen billion years.

But what will characterize the future of the universe? How will it develop? According to general relativity, the universe must be expanding or contracting. Either it will expand forever or gravitational forces will cause it one day to collapse back, in what some have called a "big crunch." In the course of addressing this situation two cosmologists in the 1980s, Alan Guth (b. 1947) and Andrei Linde (b. 1948), contributed to the creation of a theory that, like string theory, is also intriguing but untestable. In this case it was the idea that extremely early in the big bang (at 10^{-34} seconds), gravity was for a very brief period (10^{-32} seconds) a repulsive as opposed to an attractive force. As a result the universe experienced a colossally rapid inflation, increasing in scale about 10^{50} times.

Why would scientists propose such an unusual idea? The answer is that an inflationary universe would produce a universe with a relatively homogeneous distribution of matter, and so the universe would look about the same in all directions. That is what we do see, but it is not something we would expect from considering the development of the universe only by examining the formation of matter from elementary particles. Further, aspects of the process of inflation can be used to explain why matter clumped together to form galaxies.

This theory once again lands us in an area that sounds as philosophical as it does scientific. And it is not without problems. For one, it suggests a density of matter in the universe that is not observed. Cosmologists have known from analyzing the motions of galaxies and from other sources that there must be much more mass in the universe than we can see. But even the positing of so-called dark matter does not produce the density called for by the inflationary universe. There may come a resolution of these problems, but where the future of the universe is concerned we do not have the option of waiting to see which scenario actually takes place.

The Nuclear Future

Developments in physical science have left us not only with ongoing theoretical issues. There are also very practical concerns that citizens of today's world must face. In the previous chapter we examined the nuclear fear that arose in the second half of the twentieth century due to the cold war threat of an exchange of thermonuclear missiles and to the prospect of a nuclear accident. Both of these sources of concern have been altered by events as the century came to a close.

The threat of nuclear weapons.   Although the end of the cold war removed the nuclear rivalry between the United States and the former Soviet Union and permitted the disarming of a large number of nuclear missiles, the threat of a hostile use of nuclear weapons has not disappeared. In place of the central control that previously existed under a union of republics, individual states of the former Soviet Union now assume responsibility for the security of nuclear weapons that exist within their borders. Such diluted supervision of even the diminished former Soviet arsenal of nuclear weapons decreases their security and increases the probability that they will find their way to any number of willing buyers, including those who would use such weapons as implements of terrorism.

In addition, more and more nations wish to become members of the world's exclusive club of countries with nuclear weapons. Iran sees no reason why it should not develop nuclear reactors to supply its growing energy need. External powers conclude, however, that Iran's refusal to permit other nations to provide the reactor technology it needs can only mean that it wishes to retain the option of developing weapons capability as well as a new source of energy. And North Korea, seeing itself isolated and surrounded by more powerful countries, regards the development of nuclear capacity as its only guarantee that it will not someday be taken over. Finally, there are those in the United States who urge development of low-yield nuclear weapons, which, they contend, can be used in conventional wars without necessary escalation to full-scale nuclear confrontation.

Once human civilization crossed the nuclear frontier by building a nuclear weapon, it became impossible to "put the genie back into the bottle." On the positive side, there has been no further use of nuclear weapons in war since the initial use of atomic bombs at Hiroshima and Nagasaki in 1945. Nuclear weapons represent an ongoing issue that will force humankind to learn how to live together or, if we give in to the temptation of using them in war, to suffer the consequences of possible annihilation. In that sense they permit us to hold out the hope, voiced by both American and German scientists during World War II, that their existence will lead to the end of war.

The future of nuclear energy.   The worldwide demand for energy not only continues to increase, but, especially given economic development in large Eastern nations such as China and India, does so at an accelerating pace. Where is this energy to come from? While it is true that we must begin with efforts at conservation, they will at best only slow the increase in the rate of demand. Alternative sources of energy such as the wind, the sun, ocean waves, hydrogen, and the Earth's internal heat, while very important to utilize, can affect only a fraction of the total need. Fossil fuels such as oil and coal have a limited future because they will someday be depleted.

Unless we are content as a species to voluntarily undergo a drastic change in the way we live our lives, we will increasingly, even in the immediate future, have to rely on nuclear reactors to power modern society. In the United States production of new nuclear reactors is already underway. Many European countries have for some time produced the majority of their energy supplies from fission reactors and have compiled a remarkable safety record in the process. All this does not mean that the lessons of Three Mile Island and Chernobyl can be forgotten; rather, it calls for a commitment to perfecting, to the greatest degree possible, the safety, efficiency, and security of modern nuclear power plants while at the same time minimizing their effect on the environment.

Looming on the horizon is also the prospect of tapping nuclear fusion in a controlled reaction to produce energy. Here special hydrogen nuclei called deuterons that have one proton and one neutron are fused together with others that have one proton and two neutrons (tritons) to create a helium nucleus, a process that involves the conversion of mass to energy. The challenge here is that it takes a great deal of energy to fuse hydrogen nuclei; to get energy, a considerable amount of energy has to be expended. To date, scientists have not been able to make fusion cost beneficial. It costs more to produce the fusion than the value of the energy that is obtained. But if a cost-beneficial way of generating a controlled thermonuclear reaction is found, society's energy needs will be more than met because of the abundant supply of hydrogen all around us. Further, fusion reactors will be relatively safe. Should something go awry, the reaction does not create a meltdown; it simply stops.

Clearly the same commitment to protecting the environment pertains to fusion reactors as to fission power plants. A major pollutant they both produce is excess heat, which has to be dispensed somewhere. Fission reactors, of course, also produce spent fuel that contaminates the environment and is harmful to plant and animal life if not disposed of properly. Meeting the world's energy needs while protecting the environment is an ongoing issue that humankind cannot avoid. The question is, how will we accomplish it?

Global Warming

Of particular concern is a problem first discovered as a theoretical possibility in 1896 by Swedish scientist Svante Arrhenius (1859–1927). He came to the conclusion that burning coal and adding carbon dioxide to the atmosphere could eventually raise the average temperature of the planet, although such an effect would take tens of thousands of years. By the 1930s some had noticed that the average temperature of the North Atlantic region had increased, but only the British engineer Guy Stuart Callendar (1898–1964) argued that it was a permanent trend and not part of some long-term cycle. In the 1950s Callendar's claim caused some scientists, with the help of government funding for weather research, to confirm that carbon dioxide could in fact accumulate in the atmosphere and would bring a temperature increase if it did. By 1961 there were careful measurements showing that carbon dioxide in the atmosphere was indeed increasing year by year.

In the 1960s scientists developed techniques for recovering past temperatures from the study of ancient fossils and pollens. This told them that climate change had occurred in the past; in fact, substantial changes had on occasion occurred within a few centuries. One calculation in 1967 suggested that the average temperature might change a few degrees over the course of the next hundred years, but no one was confident enough in the projection to urge a call to any particular action.

The environmental movement of the 1970s brought a different message to public awareness. People began to worry that the increasing pollution in the atmosphere might, by blocking sunlight, have a cooling effect and bring on a new ice age. When weather statistics appeared to confirm a cooling trend over the previous thirty years, any warning about global warming appeared to indicate that scientists were as confused as the general public. As scientists continued to learn more about climate change, disagreements continued. Scientists did develop a general agreement that climate depended on a host of interacting factors, not on one, and that in fact the delicate balance among these factors could be rather easily upset. But they did not agree about the significance of the role human activity might play.

Many in the general public found plausible the claim that other gases, hydrofluorocarbons in particular, were adding to global warming and also eroding the ozone layer that protects living organisms from harmful radiation. New measurements of increasing atmospheric temperatures over the course of the 1980s gained plausibility when in 1988 the summer turned out to be the hottest one ever recorded. Continued disagreements, however, prevented the development of an accord that was sufficient to result in governmental action.

As the issue of global warming became an international concern, stimulating research the world over, a consensus did in fact emerge. By 2001 an international government panel report declared that, although climate study was so complex that complete certainty would never be achieved, scientific analysis of climate change could reasonably conclude that severe global warming was more likely than not a grave threat to modern civilization. The question before the human race now is, what steps are we willing to take to address this looming challenge to our future?

◎ The Biological Sciences ◎

As in the physical sciences, there are ongoing issues in the sciences of life that are never far from being philosophical and even theological questions. One of them has to do with the nature of evolution itself. Put simply, is evolution a cosmic phenomenon, or must we confine our estimation of it to what we have observed here on Earth? Closely tied to this question is the long-standing issue of whether natural selection operating blindly is sufficient to characterize evolution, or must we concede that nature may contain built-in directives that affect how evolution proceeds?

On the practical level, how will we handle the ethical choices forced on us by the impressive achievements in the science of genetics, especially where the human genome is concerned? And will we be able to master what we have learned about the life and spread of viruses to stave off future pandemics? Just as with the physical sciences, our very future as a species may depend on how we face such challenges.

The Nature of Evolution

We observed in Chapter 24 the disagreement between some ecosystem ecologists and evolutionary ecologists about the unit of selection in evolutionary development. Ecologists such as the Odum brothers were convinced that ecosystems could in some sense regulate themselves, without having to draw on outside environments for nutriments. Such thinking led others to declare that the ecosystem could be regarded as a unit of natural selection. However, as a result of their association with the neo-Darwinian synthesis forged earlier in the century, evolutionary ecologists insisted that there was no higher unit of selection than the individual organism.

Reductionistic Darwinism. The modern evolutionary synthesis is usually regarded as a vindication of Darwin's original insistence, often challenged, that evolution proceeds by the natural selection of small variations in individuals. If some of its originators were able to reconcile their understanding of evolution with larger questions of human meaning and progress by proposing an evolutionary worldview that avoided determinism (see Chapter 23), others have more recently become outspoken advocates of reductionism.

The British zoologist Richard Dawkins, one of the most visible public advocates for reductionistic Darwinism, insists that Darwin's insight is central and irreplaceable. Dawkins's position has been called ultrareductionistic because he has suggested that not even individual organisms, but genes, are the real units on which natural selection operates. Genes exist, he says, to make copies of themselves. And in pursuing this agenda blindly all forms of life, and also all purpose, have arisen. Dawkins adamantly opposes the notion that God is responsible for the design and purpose encountered in living forms. All purpose comes from natural selection. While our existence once represented the greatest of all mysteries, Dawkins asserts that since Darwin that mystery at least has been solved and what is left for scientists to do is to add footnotes to this solution. That, of course, does not prohibit Dawkins from experiencing beauty and wonder from his interpretation of Darwin's theory.

A role for symbiosis. Dawkins's strong defense of Darwinism has appeared dogmatic to some, even to the point of preventing him from considering new possibilities. For example, on the question of how cells that have nuclei might have evolved from those that did not, the American biologist Lynn Margulis (b. 1938) suggested that the competition so celebrated by Darwin might not have been the driving force. What if it was not a matter of competition, but of one of the cells without a nucleus absorbing another one? If in that case the absorbed cell became the nucleus of the other, the evolution would have resulted from what is known as symbiosis—an association between two organisms that benefits each one.

Lynn Margulis

Margulis is by no means an anti-Darwinian; she insists that evolution by natural selection occurs. She merely wishes to maintain that it is not the exclusive means through which we should understand evolution. As a result, she is willing to consider wider implications of symbiosis in evolution. For example, might symbiotic relationships be a method by which genetic variation is introduced?

When the idea of symbiosis is extended to higher evolutionary levels, however, far more radical notions emerge. One of them is that living things on the Earth continually synthesize and remove the gases of the atmosphere that are necessary for its own survival. It is as if the sum of all biota on Earth constitutes one gigantic ecosystem that exhibits homeostasis. Called the Gaia hypothesis, this idea is, understandably, controversial.

Antichaos. There is another controversial challenge to strict reductionistic Darwinism, called antichaos by its originator. It challenges the notion that life and the forms its takes are the result of pure accident. Taking a clue from the dramatic change that water undergoes when it freezes, the American biochemist Stuart Kauffman (b. 1939) has tried to show, based on computer simulations, that a comparable dramatic transformation is triggered when an abstract mathematical unit reaches a certain level of complexity. In other words, when the computer-depicted agent becomes complex enough, it can suddenly exhibit *the capacity to spontaneously combine to form even larger agents,* with new properties. If complex organic molecules are like this, then we must, according to Kauffman, rethink our understanding of the appearance of life in the universe.

Like Kielmeyer and others who suspected that the laws of living things followed an order of their own (see Chapter 17), Kauffman suspects that the complex molecules that must have formed for life to begin, or the complex molecules involved in genetic mutation, follow, at least to some degree, a pre-existing law, built into the process, that guides this dramatic development. If this is correct, then the production of mutations on which natural selection operates, and even the first appearance of life, are not the purely accidental events they are said to be by strict Darwinians such as Richard Dawkins.

Critics point out that there is no necessary link between computer-generated abstractions and organic molecules. But, as we have seen from the thought of Galileo and Kepler to the string theorists of our own time, the notion that elegant mathematical theory has more than an accidental relationship to the structure of reality has been a powerful force in the history of science. Further, in this particular case, Kauffman maintains that his models, unlike those so far in string theory, *are* able to generate predictions that can be tested in the future.

Genes and People

The impressive strides in genetics and molecular biology in the twentieth century imparted confidence that scientists had uncovered the basic structures of living things (see Chapter 23). With knowledge of the molecular structure of DNA, the main component of chromosomes, and the identification of the gene as a linear sequence of nucleotides along a segment of DNA, it became possible to consider creating maps of the specific sequences that constitute the hereditary material of an organism. The entire set of chromosomes, containing the full DNA, complete with the order of its gene sequences, is called the genome. It contains the inheritable traits of an organism. Mapping an organism's genome, while it might require an enormous effort, would put at scientists' disposal an incredibly valuable set of data that could be utilized in any number of ways.

The human genome project.   Mapping the human genome, with its set of twenty-three chromosome pairs, would involve ordering approximately three billion chemical base pairs, whose sequence encodes the genetic information of DNA. The project of undertaking a map of the human genome was formally begun in 1990 as a joint venture of the U.S. Department of Energy (DOE) and the National Institutes of Health (NIH). The NIH sought to reap benefits from the project for the understanding and cure of disease. The participation of the DOE stemmed from the charge Congress had given to its predecessor agencies, the Atomic Energy Commission and the Energy Research and Development Administration, to analyze genetic structure and how it is replicated in order to learn the effects caused by radiation and the chemical byproducts of energy production.

The stated goals of the undertaking included identifying the genes in human DNA, determining the sequences of the chemical base pairs that make up human DNA, storing this information in databases, improving tools for data analysis, transferring related technologies to the private sector, and addressing the ethical, legal, and social issues that might arise from the project.

The project has marked several stages of completion. In 2000 a draft sequence of the genome was issued that contained data fragments whose size was approximately ten thousand base pairs and whose chromosomal locations were only approximately known. In 2003 scientists announced the completion of a high-quality reference sequence in which the error tolerance was reduced to the agreed-upon standard of one mistake in ten thousand bases. The DNA sequences here were still only rough drafts for each human chromosome. Finally, in the spring of 2006, researchers disclosed the sequences for all the human chromosomes. Papers analyzing the completed chromosomes in depth will continue to appear.

While a number of general fascinating conclusions have already emerged, there is much that the completion of the human genome has not revealed. For example, we do not know the exact number, location, or function of genes. Nor can we predict the susceptibility of disease based on variations in gene sequences. On the other hand, we have learned that the order of 99.9 percent of nucleotide bases is exactly the same in all people. And we now realize that so-called junk DNA—repetitive sequences that do not code for proteins—make up at least 50 percent of the human genome.

Ethical, legal, and social issues.   The Human Genome Project is the first large-scale scientific project that incorporated into its program the exploration of the ethical, legal, and social implications that emerged from the collection of data. Between 3 to 5 percent of the annual budget for each year, totaling more than $100 million over the life of the project, has been devoted to this endeavor, which has become the world's largest bioethics investigation.

Well before the project was completed, scientists and others voiced concerns. Some objected to the biological determinism suggested by media accounts, as if the prospect of possessing the power to determine hereditary characteristics was at hand. They pointed to reasons why the science of genetics itself makes such biological determinism unachievable. For example, work on the coloration patterns in maize seeds by the American botanist Barbara McClintock (1902–1992) showed that identical genomes could have cells with different functions, challenging already at mid-century the idea that the genome is a fixed set of instructions that always produce the same results. Further, American geneticist Ruth Sager (1918–1997) determined in the 1960s that not all inheritance results from nuclear DNA. Some inherited characteristics are controlled by genes located in organelles in the cytoplasm. Others later established non-DNA inheritance, that is, the transmission of heritable changes without changing DNA. All of these developments forestall a simplistic reductionistic perspective.

There is no doubt that specific genetic information can be used to advantage by groups or individuals at the expense of others. If, for example, a specific lethal disease is known to occur in people carrying a certain gene, knowledge of whether an individual possesses that gene could be the grounds on which a person is dismissed from employment or refused medical insurance. Should a young person find out whether or not he or she carries such a gene before deciding to become a parent? What right does society have for insisting that its interests are best served by legally preventing individuals with "defective" genes from reproducing?

In light of issues such as these, participants in the Human Genome Project have set forth a series of questions to be explored. In response to a general concern about acquisition and storage of personal genetic information and how it might be used, researchers asked to what extent employers, insurers, schools, courts, police, the military, and others should have access. Lurking behind this question are others that are closely related. Who owns genetic information? Should it be possible for a biotech corporation to patent genetic information?

Investigators are also asking how the individual and social perception of groups, especially minorities, might be affected by public knowledge of genetic information. Beyond that is the question of the link between genetic makeup and behavior. Do people's genes make them behave in a particular way and can people always control their behavior? If studies of genes and behavior require analysis of families and populations in order to compare those who have a specific trait with those who do not, how does one define the population? Even pursuing such issues raises questions. How, for example, can the public be prepared to make informed choices and who is to do the preparing?

The technology of cloning has opened up a number of issues, only one of which has to do with the prospect of producing a genetic twin of an existing organism. In DNA or gene cloning a DNA fragment is transferred from one organism to a bacterial plasmid, by which it is then propagated in a foreign host cell. This process enables scientists to make multiple copies of a gene for purposes of study. While this practice has not generated a great deal of opposition, embryo cloning has. Here, human embryos are produced in order to extract from them a certain kind of cell, called a stem cell, that can be used to generate specialized cells in the human body. While this capability holds great promise for the understanding of human development and the treatment of disease, it is controversial, because extracting the stem cells from the cloned human embryos destroys the embryos and with them, in the minds of some, potential human lives. Should scientists learn to produce stem cells from skin cells or other non-embryonic cells, much of the moral issue will removed.

We cannot assume that genetic testing always produces reliable results. This introduces an additional responsibility for the scientific community to evaluate the accuracy, reliability, and usefulness of the tests they develop and for health care workers to assess and communicate to patients the degrees of reliability of the information they impart. On occasion we acquire information about the existence of a link between genetic makeup and disease when no treatment exists for the disease. Should testing even be done in this instance?

Finally, we must consider the potential long-term impact of genetic information. Genetically altered foods may bring social benefits to the population at large and profits to commercial enterprises. Are they safe for individuals and for the environment? Are they marketed only among certain populations? And what of the possible evolutionary implications of human manipulation of genetic information? To what extent are our actions irreversible? All of these questions remain ongoing issues bequeathed to humankind by increasing scientific knowledge.

◎ Understanding the Nature of Science ◎

It is a common mistake to assume that understanding the nature of science can be achieved from but one avenue of approach. Historians of science sometimes portray themselves as the true spokespeople for science because they have examined its theories and the contexts in which science has been practiced over the long haul. This, they think, has resulted in an accurate and balanced view of all aspects of science, not just those that have emerged at one particular time.

Scientists understandably believe that *they* are the ones who truly understand what science is. After all, they are the ones who actually engage in scientific investigation. They know what it really means to do science. They are the ones whose passion for research sustains them through the drudgery of daily work and the frustration of experimental failure in order to be rewarded occasionally with the thrill of scientific discovery.

But philosophers, anthropologists, and sociologists of science, plus science writers and even the politicians who must decide what scientific projects are funded, are also convinced that they possess a perspective crucial to the larger understanding of science. To give a thorough representation of the nature of science, then, requires input from a variety of perspectives that would carry us well beyond the scope of this textbook.

Here we have made use of history to shed light on the nature of science. While the historical perspective is important and even vital, we do not claim that the contribution to the understanding of science that emerges from this textbook is in any sense sufficient by itself. On the contrary, along the way we have pointed out the limitations under which historical analysis operates.

The Changing Role of the History of Science

Just as scientific theories and the practice of science have not remained unaltered over the years, so too has the writing of the history of science changed over time. Especially near the end of the twentieth century, historians of science turned their attention to the various characteristics that have marked their discipline at different points in the past. This investigation has made it clear that historians have always brought assumptions to their work. From this realization has come a concern with historiography, which among other things refers to the methods of historical research. In recent years disagreements about how the history of science should be approached have even contributed to larger controversies about how we are to understand the nature of science.

Early histories of science. Already in the eighteenth century natural philosophers began writing about the history of science. Joseph Priestley (see Chapter 10), for example, composed a history of electricity and another of vision, light, and color, both before 1775. In the nineteenth century some writers moved beyond the histories of individual sciences to more general vistas. The Cambridge professor William Whewell (1794–1866) wrote two volumes on *The History of the Inductive Sciences: From the Earliest to the Present Time* in 1837, and followed them with two more volumes on the philosophy of the inductive sciences "founded on their history" in 1840.

What characterized Whewell's and other early general histories of science was the presence of an overt agenda. Whewell wished to use history to convey what he saw as the essential component of natural science—its use of inductive reasoning from particular facts to general theories. Others trumpeted different agendas. John William Draper (1811–1882) and Andrew Dickson White (1832–1918) wrote separate histories of science in 1874 and 1896, respectively, whose purpose was to illustrate, as White's title eloquently declared, the *History of the Warfare of Science with Theology in Christendom.* A more philosophical examination of the meaning of natural science pervaded the four-volume *History of European Thought in the Nineteenth Century* by John Theodore Merz (1840–1922), which appeared between 1904 and 1912. The first two volumes were devoted specifically to scientific thought. Merz wanted to underscore what he saw as an erosion in science of a sense of contact with reality at its most basic level. He believed that this erosion had been brought about by the gradual shift to investigating the purely mechanical order of things.

After World War I, histories of science were more frequent, many written by scientists about their own fields. Perhaps the best-known general history was the multivolume *Introduction to the History of Science,* which began appearing in 1927 from the pen of the Belgian immigrant to America, George Sarton (1884–1956). Before leaving Europe during the occupation of his homeland by German troops, Sarton had begun editing a journal, *Isis,* devoted to the history of science. The war years interrupted its continuation, but he resumed publication in 1919 and remained editor until 1952. Sarton's goal in his publications was to use the historical investigation of science to illustrate the progress of humankind. He was also committed to creating a new discipline in the United States—the history of science. The success of this venture became evident in 1924, when the History of Science Society, which adopted *Isis* as its official journal, was established.

New directions in the history of science. Study of the history of science, and with it claims regarding the nature of science itself, underwent substantial change in the 1930s as historians turned their attention to the forces they regarded as responsible for shaping science. For these scholars science did not develop in a vacuum; rather, more basic external factors directed how science unfolded. There were, however, disagreements about what these outside influences were.

A generation of Marxist scholars emphasized the material basis of human social experience, with its emphasis on economic factors, as the source of scientific ideas. For example, at the second International Congress of the History of Science in London in 1931, one delegate presented a paper on "The Socio-Economic Roots of Newton's Principia." The Marxist contributions to the congress later inspired a young British scientist, J. D. Bernal (1901–1971), to write a broader work in 1954, entitled *Science in History,* which attempted to examine the significance of science through its social and material context.

Others preferred to focus on human intellectual needs as the shaping force of science. In 1924, E. A. Burtt (1892–1989) published *The Metaphysical Foundations of Modern Science,* in which he claimed that the philosophical distinction between primary and secondary qualities made by the principal architects of the scientific revolution of the seventeenth century was ultimately responsible for the emergence of an understanding of nature as a vast system of mechanical motions. From this conception it followed that mathematical depictions of these mechanical motions constituted scientific explanation. The French thinker Alexandre Koyré (1892–1964) reinforced the priority of intellectual concerns. Because the intellect was the highest faculty in human beings, intellectual history was for Koyré the highest type of history. His *Galilean Studies* of 1939 examined not only Galileo's scientific writings, but also the philosophical implications of Galileo's conceptual innovations and the intellectual background against which they were introduced. For Burtt and Koyré the history of science was a special branch of philosophy.

Yet other directions began to appear as the 1950s neared and more appeared in the 1960s. In 1949 the British historian Herbert Butterfield (1900–1979), building on an earlier work in which he had objected to distorting the historical record by forcing it to reveal a story of progress, attempted to depict the history of science between 1300 and 1800 on its own terms. He opposed using history to narrate a story of success; hence he represented Copernicus as a conservative, the last representative of the Ptolemaic astronomers, not the revolutionary father of modern astronomy.

Early in the 1950s a young Princeton historian of science named Charles Gillispie (b. 1918), writing on the testy subject of *Genesis and Geology,* deliberately refused to worry about whether his subjects were making valid or invalid claims. He did not, he said, wish to "fret about epistemology;" rather, Gillispie wanted to understand why the individuals in his study of science and religion thought as they did. He had become convinced that scientific beliefs were conditioned by social and religious opinion, that every scientist was a creature of his or her social milieu. Gillispie was by no means arguing that scientific ideas were *caused* by social factors, but he did maintain that they played a key role in how scientific theories were received.

The impact of Thomas Kuhn.   No single work has influenced the historiography of science as much as *The Structure of Scientific Revolutions,* by Thomas Kuhn (1922–1996). Published in 1962, it quickly became known as a work that purported to reveal something fundamental about the nature of scientific development from an examination of the history of science. The book exerted an influence well beyond Kuhn's own discipline; in fact, one of its central metaphors, the paradigm shift, made its way into American popular culture and was even borrowed by television advertisers in their quest to sell products.

Trained as a physicist, Kuhn changed disciplines from physics to the history of science after receiving his doctorate in 1948. The decision was made in part because of an experience he had had the previous summer. He had begun to immerse himself in the works of the past, but found himself frustrated as a modern scientist in his attempt to bring his critical skills to bear on Aristotle's physics. Then he suddenly realized that what seemed to be wrong and even absurd in Aristotle's ideas made complete sense if he adopted Aristotle's system and purposes. Aristotle was not writing bad physics; he was writing good Greek philosophy. From this epiphany came the conviction that the historian must be committed to the sympathetic reading of texts.

Using this new insight Kuhn completed a study in 1957 of the Copernican revolution in which he attempted to treat incongruities with present-day scientific

Thomas Kuhn

views not as errors, but as clues to understanding figures from the past. When he found a passage that made no sense to him, even on repeated readings, Kuhn assumed that it was *his* problem, not that of the author from the past. He had to so immerse himself in the outlook of his subject that the passage *would* make sense.

What all this suggested to Kuhn became clear in his famous book of 1962. There Kuhn introduced the idea of a paradigm, by which he meant an outlook or framework, which is constructed from both open and unspoken assumptions. What the historian must do is identify, as much as possible, the paradigms operating in historical periods and for historical figures and try to see things from within that paradigm. Critics later pointed out that Kuhn used the concept of a paradigm in many different ways, from the very general level of worldview to more specific theoretical viewpoints. But the notion that the historian must be sympathetic to the past remained clear.

Armed with his new tool, Kuhn set out to examine what happens when there is a scientific revolution—what Kuhn called extraordinary science. He asserted that what occurred in extraordinary science was a shift from one paradigm to another. Such a shift contrasted with the "normal science" that usually characterized the work of natural philosophers or scientists. Normal science was the solving of puzzles using the assumptions and outlook of the paradigm. It was a matter of drawing out all the possibilities entailed in a certain outlook, or what Kuhn called "articulating the paradigm."

Something different happens in extraordinary science, according to Kuhn. There, someone realizes that a piece of a puzzle that has proven problematic to everyone will never fit because it belongs to a *different* puzzle. By seeing things from the vantage point of a new puzzle—a new paradigm—the extraordinary scientist can make sense of it and of other pieces of the old puzzle. By seeing the Earth as a moving body, for example, Copernicus was able to construct a new paradigm that answered his need for internal harmony, something he did not find in the older Ptolemaic system.

Kuhn emphasized that scientific revolutions take time to develop because they require the appearance of anomalies and the development of a sense of crisis within the old paradigm. In addition to identifying the structural sequence they follow, Kuhn insisted that the shift from one paradigm to the next was not the result of a logical process. Paradigms, he said, were incommensurable with each other; that is, the assumptions characteristic of one are different enough from those of another that the move from one to the other is much more like a conversion experience or a gestalt switch than an inference or deduction.

Kuhn's conclusions about how science developed in the past, although no doubt influenced by his training as a scientist, came primarily from his immersion in the history of science. He maintained that his was not an idealized picture of how science ought to be viewed, but one based on a historian's best analysis of how it actually has unfolded. But the results of his analysis ran counter to the understanding of science present in many quarters, both at the time his book appeared and since.

Central to the objection to Kuhn's analysis, articulated frequently by scientists themselves, is the claim that science is not carrying humankind closer to nature's truth. In 1992 Kuhn noted in a lecture that if there is no external standard by which we can judge a paradigm shift (because in his view we are all in one paradigm or another and cannot simply shift back and forth between them), then it is hard to imagine what could be meant by the phrase that a scientific theory takes us "closer to the truth." In reply to Kuhn's position, physicist Steven Weinberg once asked: "If one scientific theory is only better than another in its ability to solve problems . . . then why not save ourselves a lot of trouble by putting those problems out of our minds?" What drives scientists, Weinberg continued, "is precisely the sense that there are truths out there to be discovered."

In fairness to Kuhn it must be noted that he never wished to abandon the idea of truth or to suggest that our focus should be solely on the context (paradigm) in which a scientific discovery is made to the neglect of the discovery itself. Kuhn did believe that the presence of paradigms prevents us from ever reaching final scientific truth. But, as the American intellectual historian David Hollinger has pointed out, Kuhn's work meant that historians and scientists have had to learn to bear the tension between not knowing truth and having to aim at it anyway.

Ongoing Debates in the Historiography of Science

In spite of Kuhn's own caution regarding the need to retain truth at least as the goal toward which we strive in both history and science, others have been less convinced. As a result of a number of developments in several disciplines, numerous scholars questioned the standards of traditional scholarship to a much more radical degree than did Kuhn. Some took the position that the social context of a scientific discovery was so important that all other considerations, including the content of the discovery itself, paled in light of it. As a result, the history of science expanded to include scholars who did not come to the field from the sciences themselves, but were drawn by an interest in scientific institutions or science in its relationships to politics, religion, literature, the arts, or public policy.

In the 1970s the growing number of historians of science engaged in a debate between so-called internal versus external history, as if it were a matter of choosing between the content of a scientific theory or the social context in which it emerged. Externalists pointed out that the noble dream of attaining objective reality in history or in science was so problematic that it should be discarded. Internalists insisted that the truth or falsity of a historical claim or scientific theory was not only germane but central to its historical significance.

This debate faded as even more radical positions emerged within the field of history in general, precipitating a rift among historians of science. In what has come to be known as the postmodern perspective, even the externalists came in for criticism on the grounds that their idea of a "social context" was just as problematic as that of "objective reality." The social structures externalists identified were, so the criticism went, arbitrary and subjective. History was not about finding causal explanations according to some structured grand narrative. In place of trying to tie together a particular scientific development with the social context in which it occurred, postmodern historians argued that history should depict the interests and the power relationships

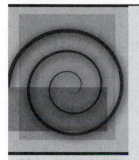

The Science Wars

The NATURE of SCIENCE

Natural scientists themselves generally have expressed little sympathy for postmodern interpreters of science and its history. In 1994 a biting criticism of this trend by two authors, a scientist and a mathematician, appeared under the title *Higher Superstition*. It was followed three years later by a large collection of critiques by scientists, historians, and others opposed to the postmodern approach, entitled *The Flight from Science and Reason*. And in 1996 a professor of physics at New York University submitted a paper to a postmodern journal on what he called the "transformative hermeneutics of quantum gravity." When it was published in the journal, its author declared that it was a hoax, that he had filled it with nothing more than fawning references, grandiose quotations, and outright nonsense. All these developments, which were picked up by the press, became known as the "science wars" and brought to the attention of the public the fundamental disagreements over the nature of science that divided academics, including many historians of science.

The rift that divided scholars at the end of the twentieth century ran deep, so much so that each side regarded the other as dogmatic. Those who wished to defend the relevance of structure, to insist on a set of standards of scholarship, and to preserve a cognitive element in the historian's work were labeled by their postmodern opponents as "self-designated guardians of orthodoxy." Those who insisted that historical texts must be liberated of all constraints, including even those of the author's intent, were portrayed by the critics of postmodernism as intellectual anarchists.

The science wars exposed positions that were holy to each side. For one group it was crucial that a proper understanding of science, past and present, included ideas that truth existed and that it should be the goal of scientific research. The other side was equally convinced that there was no such thing as scientific truth because of the constantly changing subjective criteria employed by human beings in their acquisition and construction of knowledge. We are still struggling to incorporate the positive aspects from each perspective.

among peoples linked together in a culture. An obvious gain in this "cultural studies" approach was the desire to include in historical work individuals at the margins of society who have previously tended to be overlooked, especially as they illustrate the relationships of power present in the society. And yet, as Thomas Kuhn had said earlier about extreme interpretations of science, they seemed to leave historians with no "useful notions of how science works and of what scientific progress is."

◎ The Challenge Ahead ◎

While no resolution to the disagreements among historians of science has emerged, the deep polarization and sharp divisions that marked the closing years of the previous century have dulled somewhat in the new millennium. Cultural critics of science, in their intense focus on how the historian or scientist shapes the very world we know, rightly continue to remind us that knowledge of the world or of the past is not something that simply comes to us directly from nature or the historical record unmediated by the scientist or the historian. At the same time, empirical scientists and historians who insist on the centrality of historical evidence correctly emphasize that we are not free to overlook or even deemphasize the realities that limit our interpretations.

Neither scientists nor historians have yet learned how to represent with precision the interaction between the constraints imposed by reality and the interventions of those who would know it. Until there is consensus on this knotty problem, all those who strive to understand how science has developed in the past and how it continues to operate in the present must retain open minds. In the situation where embracing one intellectual position automatically excludes the other, our only recourse is to make toleration an act of will. In so doing we display the modicum of humility that acknowledges that our position, while based firmly on our own convictions, is in the end not more than our own convictions.

Suggestions for Reading

David Cahan, ed., *From Natural Philosophy to the Sciences* (Chicago: University of Chicago Press, 2003).

John Horgan, *The End of Science: Facing the Limits of Knowledge in the Twilight of the Scientific Age* (Reading, Mass.: Addison-Wesley, 1996).

Thomas Kuhn, *The Structure of Scientific Revolutions* (Chicago: University of Chicago Press, 1996).

Spencer Weart, *The Discovery of Global Warming* (Cambridge, Mass.: Harvard University Press, 2003).

Photo Credits

CHAPTER 1
2 Mary Evans Picture Library/The Image Works.

CHAPTER 2
31 © Musée Condé, Chantilly, France/The Bridgeman Art Library; **32** From *Que hoc volumine contine (n) (tur:) Liber de intellect; Liber de sensu; Liber de nichilo; Ars oppositorum . . . insup (er) mathematicu (m) opus quadripartite (m): De numeris perfecti.* Parisiis: Ex officina Henrici Stephani, impsesis eiusdem et Ioannis Parui, 1510, primo cal. (1) Februari. Call number 798206. Image, leaf 63. By Courtesy of the Department of Special Collections, Memorial Library, University of Wisconsin–Madison.

CHAPTER 3
55 Bibliothèque Nationale, Paris, France/Giraudon/Art Resource, New York; **59** Time Life Pictures/Getty Images; **63** Mary Evans Picture Library/The Image Works.

CHAPTER 4
72 © Bibliothèque de la Faculté de Médecine, Paris, France/ Archives, Charmet/The Bridgeman Art Library; **74** Marine satyr from *Historiae Animalium,* © Academy of Natural Sciences of Philadelphia/Corbis; **79** From *A Book on fossil objects, chiefly Stones and Gems, their Shapes and Appearances,* by Conrad Gesner, 1565.

CHAPTER 5
100 © Bettmann/Corbis; **106** © Bettmann/Corbis.

CHAPTER 7
142 © Bettmann/Corbis; **145** From *Philosophe Naturalis Principia Mathematica,* by Isaac Newton, 1666; **152** Hulton Archive/Getty Images.

CHAPTER 8
169 *Portrait of Sir Isaac Newton* by Godfrey Kneller, 1689/© Bettmann/Corbis.

CHAPTER 9
182 © Bettmann/Corbis; **187** Stocktrek Images/Royalty-Free/ Getty Images.

CHAPTER 10
212 © Bettmann/Corbis.

CHAPTER 11
225 © Mary Evans Picture Library/The Image Works; **226** From *Phys.-Mech. Exp.,* by Francis Hauksbee, 1709.

CHAPTER 12
247 Photo: © Michael Nicholson/Corbis.

CHAPTER 13
274 Color engraving, *Breathing a Vein,* by James Gillray, published by Hannah Humphrey, 1804/© Courtesy of the

Warden and Scholars of New College, Oxford, England/The Bridgeman Art Library; **280** 19th-century engraving by Leopold Mar/Private Collection/Ken Welsh/The Bridgeman Art Library.

CHAPTER 14
295 Photo: © Roger-Viollet/The Image Works.

CHAPTER 15
312 *The Death of Marat,* by Jacques-Louis David, 1793. Photo: G. Blot/C. Jean. Réunion des Musées Nationaux/Art Resource, New York; **322** Pastel portrait by Christian Friedrich Tieck, ca. 1801, Schiller-Nationalmuseum, Marbach. Photo: akg-images.

CHAPTER 16
327 Photo: © Mary Evans Picture Library/The Image Works; **330** From *Les Merveilles de la Science,* by Louis Figuier, 1870, Paris. Oxford Science Archive, Oxford, England/© British Library/HIP/Art Resource, New York; **336** *Quarterly Journal of Science* 12 (1821), 186–187.

CHAPTER 17
352 Hulton Archive/Getty Images; **354** Hulton Archive/Getty Images; **358** Photo: © Mary Evans Picture Library/The Image Works.

CHAPTER 18
387 1854 photo by Mansell/Time Life Pictures/Getty Images.

CHAPTER 19
393 Photo, ca. 1860/Hulton Archive/Getty Images; **397** Photo: © Mary Evans Picture Library/The Image Works; **407** Photo: © Michael Nicholson/Corbis.

CHAPTER 20
432 *The Stone Breakers,* by Gustave Courbet, 1849/Foto Marburg/Art Resource, New York.

CHAPTER 21
437 Cover from *Electrical Plant Magazine,* December 1888; **438** John Jenkins/www.sparksmuseum.com; **446** © Topham/The Image Works.

CHAPTER 22
463 akg-images.

CHAPTER 23
478 Percy Lavon Julian Stamp Design © 1993 United States Postal Service. All Rights Reserved. Used with Permission; **480** Scan #0413, N. M. Stevens, 1909, used with permission of the University Archives, Columbia University in the City of New York; **486** © The British Library/HIP/The Image Works; **497** 3D4Medical.com/Getty Images.

CHAPTER 24
504 Foto Marburg/Art Resource, New York; **506** ETOP02/ National Oceanic and Atmospheric Administration (NOAA)/ National Geophysical Data Center (NGDC); **518** Borg Thuresson/AP Images.

CHAPTER 25
525 © Topham/The Image Works; **528** Patricia Watwood, *Cecilia Payne-Gaposchkin* (1900–1979), 2001. Oil on canvas, 119.7 × 96.88 cm (47 1/8 × 38 1/16 in.). Harvard University Art Museums, Fogg Art Museum, Gift of Dudley and Georgene

Herschbach, H743. © Patricia Watwood/Patricia Watwood. Photo: Katya Kallsen, © President and Fellows of Harvard College.

CHAPTER 26
555 © Corbis; **559** Cover art by Hubert Rogers, copyright Hubert Rogers Estate; **561** Photographer: Bob Penn/© Columbia Pictures/Photofest; **562** © Corbis; **565** Douglas Miller/Keystone/ Getty Images.

CHAPTER 27
571: © Bettmann/Corbis; **577** © Jerry Bauer; **584** © Stanley Rowin/Stanley Rowin Photography.

Index